D1525686

Books by Thomas Mann

FICTION

The Beloved Returns (Lotte in Weimar)

Buddenbrooks

Joseph and His Brothers
  I. *Joseph and His Brothers*
  II. *Young Joseph*
  III. *Joseph in Egypt* (two volumes)
  IV. *Joseph the Provider*

The Magic Mountain

Royal Highness

Stories of Three Decades

The Tables of the Law

The Transposed Heads

NONFICTION

An Exchange of Letters

Listen, Germany!

Order of the Day, Political Essays and Speeches of Two Decades

These are Borzoi Books
published in New York by Alfred A. Knopf

Also by Thomas Mann

FICTION

The Beloved Returns (*Lotte in Weimar*)

Buddenbrooks

Joseph and His Brothers
- I. *Joseph and His Brothers*
- II. *Young Joseph*
- III. *Joseph in Egypt* (two volumes)
- IV. *Joseph the Provider*

The Magic Mountain

Royal Highness

Stories of Three Decades

The Tables of the Law

The Transposed Heads

◇◇

NON-FICTION

An Exchange of Letters

Listen, Germany!

Order of the Day, Political Essays and Speeches of Two Decades

◇◇

These are BORZOI BOOKS,

published in New York, by ALFRED A. KNOPF

ESSAYS OF THREE DECADES

THOMAS MANN

[*Photo by George Platt Lynes – from* VOGUE]

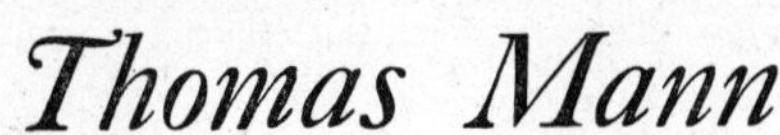

Thomas Mann

ESSAYS

OF THREE DECADES

Translated from the German by

H. T. LOWE-PORTER

ALFRED A. KNOPF *NEW YORK*

1948

THIS IS A BORZOI BOOK,
PUBLISHED BY ALFRED A. KNOPF, INC.

PUBLISHED JUNE 6, 1947
SECOND PRINTING, JULY, 1947
THIRD PRINTING, MAY, 1948

PUBLISHER'S NOTE

THE earlier history of the essays included in this volume, in German and in English, has been as follows:

"Goethe's *Faust*" was delivered in English as a public lecture at Princeton University on two evenings in 1938. The English version is here first published. The German text appeared in 1939 in *Mass und Wert.*

"Goethe's Career as a Man of Letters" ("*Goethes Laufbahn als Schriftsteller*") was delivered as an address in the Stadthalle at Weimar on March 21, 1932, and was subsequently published in the volume of essays entitled *Leiden und Grösse der Meister* (Berlin: S. Fischer Verlag; 1935). It was delivered in somewhat abridged form, in English, as a lecture at the New School for Social Research in New York City on April 22, 1937; and published in English translation by Rita Matthias-Reil (New York: Alfred A. Knopf; 1937) in *Freud, Goethe, Wagner.*

"Goethe as Representative of the Bourgeois Age" was first delivered as a lecture at the Berlin Academy of Arts in 1932 on the occasion of the hundredth anniversary of Goethe's death, and subsequently published as a pamphlet as *Goethe als Repräsentant des bürgerlichen Zeitalters* (Berlin: S. Fischer Verlag; 1932). Later the original text was given as an address at Yale University, and published, in an English translation by Professor Hermann Weigand, in the Summer 1932 issue of the *Yale Review* under the title "Goethe."

"Goethe and Tolstoy" ("*Goethe und Tolstoi*") was first published in *Bemühungen* (Berlin: S. Fischer Verlag; 1922), and in the present English translation in *Three Essays* (New York: Alfred A. Knopf; 1929. London: Martin Secker; 1932).

"*Anna Karenina*" was written as a preface to the edition of the novel published by Random House, New York, 1939, in which it appeared in a translation by Mrs. M. H. Welsh. It was published in German in the same year in *Mass und Wert.*

"Lessing" is a speech delivered at the Lessing celebration of the Prussian Academy of Art, Berlin, January 22, 1929. It was published in German in *Die Forderung des Tages* (Berlin: S. Fischer Verlag; 1930) and in English translation in *Past Masters and Other Papers* (London: Martin Secker & Warburg; 1933. New York: Alfred A. Knopf; 1933).

"Kleist's *Amphitryon*" was written in 1926 and first published in the same year in the *Neue Rundschau.* It was later included in the volume *Die Forderung des Tages* (Berlin: S. Fischer Verlag; 1930).

"Chamisso" (1911) was first published in the volume *Rede und Antwort* (Berlin: S. Fischer Verlag; 1922).

"Platen" (1930) was written as a lecture for a meeting of the Platen Society at Platen's birthplace, Ansbach in Franconia, and was published in the *Neue Rundschau* in 1930.

"Theodor Storm" (1930) was written as a preface to a German edition of Storm's collected works.

"The Old Fontane" (1910) was first published in the weekly *Die Zukunft,* founded and edited by Maximilian Harden.

"Sufferings and Greatness of Richard Wagner" was written for the fiftieth anniversary of Wagner's death, and was delivered as an address at the University of Munich, February 10, 1933, and later in the same year in Amsterdam, Brussels, and Paris. As "*Leiden und Grösse Richard Wagners*" it was published in the April 1933 number of *Neue Rundschau;* it was included in the volume *Leiden und Grösse der Meister* (Berlin: S. Fischer Verlag; 1935), and, in English translation, in *Past Masters and Other Papers* (London: Martin Secker & Warburg; 1933. New York: Alfred A. Knopf; 1933), and *Freud, Goethe, Wagner* (New York: Alfred A. Knopf; 1937). In somewhat abridged form it was delivered as a lecture, in German, at the New School for Social Research, New York City, April 19, 1937.

"Richard Wagner and the *Ring*" (1937) was given as a lecture at the University of Zürich on the occasion of a performance of the entire *Ring des Nibelungs* cycle at the Zürich Stadttheater.

"Schopenhauer" (1938) was written as an introduction to *Living Thoughts of Schopenhauer,* in the "Living Thoughts Library," originally published by Longmans, Green & Company, New York, 1939.

"Freud and the Future," delivered at a celebration in honour of the eightieth birthday of Freud, in Vienna, on May 8, 1936, was published separately as *Freud und die Zukunft* (Vienna: Bermann-Fischer Verlag; 1936). It was delivered in somewhat abridged form, in German, as a lecture at the New School for Social Research in New York City on April 19, 1937, and published in English translation in *Freud, Goethe, Wagner* (New York: Alfred A. Knopf; 1937).

"Voyage with Don Quixote" ("*Meerfahrt mit Don Quixote*") was written immediately after the Manns' return from their first trip to America, in June 1934, and was first published in the summer of 1934 in *Neue Zürcher Zeitung*. Later it was included in the volume *Leiden und Grösse der Meister* (Berlin: S. Fischer Verlag; 1935).

TRANSLATOR'S NOTE

THE TREATMENT of the verse and poetry quoted in this volume must seem to the reader somewhat capricious; a word of explanation may be in place. Some of the essays here presented have already appeared with the German quotations and an English version of them side by side in the text. This plan has been followed as far as possible in the remaining essays, but in a few cases it has seemed better to give the original German in the text and a literal English version in an appendix. This is notably true, though for not quite the same reasons, of the verse quoted in the essays on August von Platen and Theodor Storm. In Storm's case the simple, highly evocative charm does not – so to speak – stand export well. Like certain fine wines its aroma evaporates. On the other hand the inclusion of the originals enables the reader of the verses with very little German to evoke their peculiar music by reading them aloud; the prose version at the back will give him their content. As for Platen, it seemed forced to embark upon a technical imitation of a technical imitation; so the same plan was followed as with Storm.

CONTENTS

ESSAYS OF THREE DECADES

[3]

GOETHE'S *FAUST*

1938

[Delivered in English as a public lecture at Princeton University in 1938]

IN the notes and drafts for his autobiography, *Dichtung und Wahrheit*, Goethe recalls to mind a "secret archive of strange productions" which he had begun to accumulate when he was twenty-five years old. It was the period in his life when he was thinking of breaking his engagement with Lili Schönemann; the time of his first acquaintance with Baron Stolberg, who would later be the means of his going to Weimar; the time of his first journey to Switzerland.

We need not be surprised by the mention of this archive – which was, in fact, nothing more than a bundle of various scribblings. Goethe had a tendency to make mysteries; and one of his traits, on the personal as well as the artist side of his character, was a cautious reserve on the subject of his creative activities. It had more than one ground. In the first place, he held on principle that a writer should talk to no one about what he purposed to write; this because the confidant would quite likely not grasp his idea, and would be prone to discourage it. The artist himself, and only he, knew the charms of the material and the effects he could produce with it. – In the second place, Goethe's conception of art and of the intellectual life in general was somewhat esoteric in its nature. It was a conception that became only more rigid and explicit with the years; and it led him, shrewdly enough, to make a clear distinction between the social and the intellectual sphere. All lofty themes, even to the loftiest, even truth and absolute sincerity, were, he held, for the very few. The average man must be spared the knowledge of them. The conviction sprang less from aristocratic feeling than from benevolence. He reasoned something like this: if art could always be perfectly sincere it would be a great good fortune for the artist; he could speak regardless and give free vent to the boldness innate in his creative gift. But he had to keep in mind that his works would fall into the hands of a very mixed audience; he must take care lest by lack of restraint he confuse the minds of what Goethe called "the majority of good men." The phrase was characteristic.

We should do wrong to read into such utterances any spirit of temporizing or any attitude of "the middle of the road." To temporize suggests slyness; whereas what we have here is a deep and radical benevolence. It is the expression of a complex humanity: dæmonic yet urbane, positive yet polite, informed both by genius and by a sense of propriety, and on the whole a vastly pleasing, broad-minded, and unique combination. No one could feel less pleasure than Goethe in giving offence — to any human being, and how much less to his own countrymen! He said that a superior man made enough enemies even when he kept still, for how should they not hate you,

> *denen das Wesen, das du bist*
> *Im Grunde ein ewiger Vorwurf ist.*
>
> to whom the nature that you are
> Is the worst reproach by far.

The natural consequence of such an attitude as this was a tendency to be secretive. Even in his old age Goethe had literary "secrets." He kept, for instance, what he called a *Walpurgissack*, containing, among other naïve audacities, the poem in rhymed lines called "The Diary," a mixture of eroticism and moralizing, whose southern abandon made him judge it unfit for publication in his lifetime. Then there were various epigrams and diatribes, his private revenge upon the follies and vices of the time, in literary, artistic, political, and religious fields. If these were ever to be published, it could be only after his death. One is reminded of Tolstoy's remark to Gorky: "The truth about women I will speak when I have one leg in the coffin; then I will quickly pull the other one in and clap down the lid."

But to return to the secret archive of the young author of *Werther*. It contained some strange and daring compositions, ingenious, spirited, and fantastic in their kind, diatribes and "documentations of inward strife," as it pleased him to call them; and certain crude performances that could at most be shown to very intimate and trustworthy friends. All these had common characteristics: they were partly comic, partly high-flown, partly a mixture of the two, with a thread of the all-embracingly human running through the whole. Matters of the most personal nature were dealt with in the most lively, free-and-easy way, along with the cosmic and divine. Among the rest were some longer pieces, fragments of ambitious compositions in epic and dramatic form. They were "*Hans Wursts Hochzeit*" ("Hans Wurst's Wedding"), "The Wandering Jew," and *Faust.*

And *Faust.* Strange indeed it is to think of this poem, destined as it was to become a national, nay, a world possession; to absorb into itself the whole content of a long life of successful striving; and to be finished in the fullness of time by the eighty-year-old man, finished perforce, because of its own nature it might have gone on forever: to think of it, as it were in its cocoon, in a pasteboard cover, tied round with a string, and lying among other chrysalises to which no such happy metamorphosis was to be vouchsafed. No, they would remain in the chrysalis stage, and only as curiosities occupy the after-attention of a learned world, while their luckier fellow would enjoy the fabulous popularity of *Don Quixote* and the *Divina Commedia.* And yet these intellectual stepchildren of fortune were welcomed at birth by Goethe with quite as much ambitious and extravagant enthusiasm as their famous fellow occupant of the pasteboard cover. The first fragment of "The Wandering Jew," the first rags and tags of him, as the irreverent young author calls it, begins with the lines:

Um Mitternacht wohl fang ich an,
Spring aus dem Bette wie ein Toller:
Nie war mein Busen seelenvoller,
Zu singen den gereisten Mann.

I first begin at dead of night,
Leap like a madman out of bed,
Never so thrilled my heart and head
To sing of that much-travelled wight.

That much-travelled wight was of course the cobbler of Jerusalem, whose story the young would-be singer of it had read in the chapbooks. He had rebuffed — albeit not too ill-naturedly — the Saviour as He staggered under the weight of the Cross; and for that he was condemned to wander through the ages. Goethe thought to treat the legend epically and "to deal, by means of this connecting thread, with the salient points of church and religious history." Certainly quite a big enough idea to make a man jump out of bed at midnight! The vast material offered infinite possibilities of imagery and symbolism; while aside from that, it gave scope for the treatment of a religious problem which, more than any other, lay at that moment close to our poet's heart. I mean the problem of original sin: the theological and more than theological controversy as to whether the human heart is given over to utter and hopeless corruption and must address itself to grace as its only means of salvation; or whether, as the Pelagian sect would have it, so much virtue still abides in man that by good deeds and honest effort he can at least labour forwards towards grace, if not finally make it dispensable. Young Goethe, in fact, inclined to this second view, so much more honourable to human kind and particularly to himself. The late-written lines (*Faust*, Part II, Scene vi):

> *Wer immer strebend sich bemüht,*
> *Den können wir erlösen,*

> The man who labours, strives, and seeks
> Will ever find salvation,

embody the same idea which, much earlier, he put into the mouth of the Lord God Himself (Part I, Prologue in Heaven):

> *Ein guter Mensch in seinem dunklen Drange*
> *Ist sich des rechten Weges wohl bewusst.*

> The good man, howsoever dark his striving,
> Is ever mindful of the better way.

It takes some boldness, some confidence in one's own relation to the everlasting goodness, to put God into a play and utter one's views through His mouth! And not only in *Faust* but in the Wandering Jew fragment Goethe makes God appear in person and converse with the Son in the starry fields of heaven. An ingenuous humour heightens and gives point to the piece on its earthly side – in short, the whole thing has about it something distinctly Faustian; it leaves no doubt that the same brain conceived both poems. But a man writes only one *Faust*. In his autobiography the poet says that he lacked time and composure to make the necessary studies for the treatment he had designed. The "Wandering Jew" remained a few disconnected segments of verse.

Lack of time and composure can scarcely have been the grounds on which Goethe abandoned the second fragment in the archive, the farce called "Hans Wurst's Wedding." Certainly no great study was needed for this singular extravaganza. It was based on the model of the old German puppet-play; and if it also did not get beyond its beginnings, we must assume that its crude though popular attractions did not hold the poet long enough to compel him to carry it through. "A crazy piece of business": that was how Goethe later referred to it; and we may recall that the creator of Helena used the same words or something very near them to describe the first part of the Faust tragedy, to which they are certainly far less applicable. For the farce is, truly, a crazy piece of business, an enterprise risky in the extreme, and like "The Wandering Jew" containing passages only fit for private circulation. Who is Hans Wurst? He is, of course, the Jack Pudding of the old German comedy. But who is he here? The fragment contains allusions which justify the question; or rather they actually answer it. Ostensibly, Hans Wurst is a well-to-do orphaned peasant lad. Having attained his majority, he straightway decides to marry the damsel Ursel Blandine. His guardian, Kilian Brustfleck, is satisfied with the match; so is the girl's mother, also called Ursel. There is no obstacle out of which a plot might grow, save that the preparations and arrangements for the wedding laughably linger out the suspense of the young couple, who are all on fire to possess each other. The actual dramatic motive is thus simply the bridegroom's impatience, which he expresses in round, unvarnished terms. Again, who is Hans Wurst? He calls himself "a youth from Salz to Petersburg renowned, of parts so grand, what sort of bride should he demand?" In short, this Hans Wurst talks as though he were the author of *Werther*, and incensed because society is troubling itself about the kind of bride he may worthily espouse. His guardian tells him: "The world hangs on thy lips; then be not coarse, as genius often is!" It is news to us that the stout Hans Wurst of the county fair was ever a genius. But in the farce he is, and he takes up an attitude both refractory and indecorous in the extreme. He will hear nothing of the preparations for the celebration of the nuptials; nor of the guests, among whom are "all the great names of the German world." No, what he wants is just to be off with his Ursel to the hayloft. But what sort of "great names" are these? They are simply a list of the vulgarest folk-epithets in the language, with which Goethe displays an astonishing, well-nigh exhaustive conversance. I will not attempt to translate these for you. The list includes not only such common terms as Vetter Schuft, Herr Schurk, and Hans Hasenfuss, but other such gems as Schnuckfözgen, Peter Sauschwanz, Scheismaz, Schweinpelz, Lauszippel, Rotzlöffel, Jungfer Rabenas, Herren Hosenscheiser and Heularsch – and so on and on, in endless number. Such is the society that admires Hans Wurst's genius and expects so much of him. He loses very much, they tell him, by his coarseness. "To how much greatness thou wast born, to how much more thou yet shalt come!" And they warn him to behave with a little ordinary decency, because the world will stand no light improper word, though caring no whit when one in private does the basest things. But Hans Wurst has no ears for the advice, whatever fine things the world expects of him. "I do not care, just let me go my way." In short, this singular production is governed by a sort of farcical titanism, which is only another and loutish phase and expression of the endless dissatisfaction that feeds the genius of the *Faust*.

I have given you a brief account of these almost unknown literary curiosities, in order to display their family likeness with the poetic composition so highly favoured by fate, which grew up between them, in the same soil and possessing originally the same traits. They share the same origin, that of the chapbook and the puppet-play; they have the same fundamental quality, a sort of folk-simplicity which, historically speaking, was a literary fashion of the day, though at the same time it was profoundly and personally characteristic of our young author. There are qualities which, in the lower stages of their development, do not betray that with increased power they will mount to greatness, to genius. Simplicity (*Treuherzigkeit*) – that is elevated to greatness: that may be the best definition we shall find for Goethe's peculiar greatness. No wonder that he early knew how to speak its language with more conviction and melody than his contemporaries! In the earliest version of *Faust* occur the lines:

Doch werdet ihr nie Herz zu Herzen schaffen
Wenn es euch nicht von Herzen geht. . . .
Was Vortrag! Das ist gut fürs Puppenspiel.
Mein Herr Magister, hab er Kraft!
Sey er kein Schellenlauter Thor!
Und Freundschaft, Liebe, Brüderschafft,
Trägt die sich nicht von selber vor?
Und wenn's euch Ernst ist, was zu sagen,
Ist's nöthig, Worten nachzujagen?

But you will never reach the people's hearts
Unless you speak to them straight from your own.
Diction! That's rubbish, fit for puppet-plays.
My good Magister, force is what we need!
Don't be a cymbal-tinkling ass!
Won't friendship, love, and brotherhood

Express themselves without a rhetoric class?
And when you've something real to say,
Do you have to hunt for words all day?

That was spoken straight from the heart, to a whole breed of young poets. "Having early and repeatedly addressed ourselves to nature," says Goethe, "we would thus let naught avail save truth and sincerity of feeling and the swift, stark expression of the same." It was Hans Sachs, then, who served as the honoured model for these young folk: his simple mastery, his didactic realism, his easy rhyme. Goethe was never untrue to that love and allegiance. A part of his nature was in permanent contact with the Nuremberger's spirit and form – not the classic-minded, European part, but all that was solidly German, protestant and of the people. The Proverbs in rhyme still bear witness to it. Its infectious cadence dwelt in the blood and bones of the twenty-five-year-old Goethe, betraying itself in many an almost childishly close resemblance in the pages of *Faust* and the two contemporaneous poems. Take for instance Frau Marthe's little soliloquy: "*Gott verzeih's meinem lieben Mann – Er hat an mir nicht wohlgethan!*" ("God forgive my husband dear – he did not well by me, I fear") and compare it with the words of the "Pewrin" (peasant woman) in the "*Fahrendt Schüler im Paradeiss*" by Hans Sachs: "*Ach, wie manchen seuffzer ich senk, Wenn ich vergangener Zeit gedenk, da noch lebet mein erster Mann, den ich je lenger lieb gewann*" ("Many a sigh I do let fall, When the past I do recall, Ere my first man passed away, That more I loved every day").

But the stylistic critics in my audience will enjoy even more another soliloquy: that spoken by Kilian Brustfleck as prelude to "Hans Wurst's Wedding." It begins:

Hab ich endlich mit vielem Fleiss,
Manchem moralisch-politischen Schweiss,
Meinen Mündel Hans Wurst erzogen –

Now at last by toil and fret,
Moral-political trouble and sweat,
I've made my Hans Wurst into a man –

that is the beginning of *Faust*:

Habe nun ach die Philosophey,
Medizin und Juristerey,
Und leider auch die Theologie
Durchaus studiert mit heisser Müh –

Ah, I have studied philosophy,
Medicine, jurisprudence too,
And for my sins theology,
Over and over, through and through –

How strange, to hear the early-abandoned piece of horseplay beginning in the well-remembered accents of the world-renowned poem! In "The Wandering Jew" are the lines:

Es waren die den Vater auch gekannt –
Wo sind denn die? "Eh man sie hat verbrannt."

And some there were that did my father know –
Where are they all? "They burnt them long ago."

Those who know their *Faust* think at once of:

Die wenigen, die was davon erkannt,
Die thöricht gnug ihr volles Herz nicht wahrten,
Dem Pöbel ihr Gefühl, ihr Schauen offenbarten,
Hat man von je gekreuzigt und verbrannt

The few who knew, and did not hold their peace,
But to the crowd their thoughts and feelings cried,
These ever have been burnt and crucified.

The first sounds like a practice effort for the second. Or take these lines from "The Wandering Jew":

Genug, er war ein Original,
Und aus Originalität
Er anderen Narren gleichen tät.

Enough, that he was an original –
And being one,
Did just as other fools have done.

The epigram might well come from *Faust*. And in passing, it displays the independence and satirical spirit of the young writer. His *Götz* and *Werther* had placed him in the forefront of the "genius movement"; and here he makes as much fun of the boasted originality of the school as, in the figure of Wagner, he makes fun of the Enlightenment.

I might give many more examples of verbal affinities. But of course the higher destiny of the *Faust*, as against his less favoured companions in the archive, reveals itself most of all in its language. What remained pen trials and practice work in the other two fragments experienced in the *Faust* a marvellous clarification, evolution, and fulfilment, which made of it, when at last it saw the light, as a whole in two parts, the greatest and most many-sided piece of writing in the German language. The verse is often dependent, like doggerel, on the rhythm; often it moves in more even rhythms, iambics, of various lengths, three to six feet, with varying rhyme. It is unforced but telling, easy yet elegant, witty and sensitive; it is indescribably happy, fluid, clear; it shapes itself easily on the lips. To hear it is to recall Goethe's own words: "The final effect of true art is the feeling of charm." With its melodious, lyrical periods, so easily and ardently, so humanly expressive, with the stamp of finality upon all that it coins — this Faustian verse itself played a great part in the vast popularity of the piece wherever the German language was spoken. Before long our German bourgeoisie knew *Faust* by heart. Scenes and images stamped themselves on the imagination of the people — one might almost say on the imagination of mankind; native and foreign artists were at once spurred on to illustrate the poem. The text, for German ears, seems to consist of quotations. I myself once heard, from a benighted soul in a theatre, the words: "He makes it easy for himself; he just strings quotations together."

The *Faust* is a conception dating from Goethe's Strassburg period. Under Herder's influence, he had freed himself from the Anacreontic style, from French influence and the dry, pedantic spirit of the Enlightenment; he emerged as first and foremost a lyric poet, singing in accents never before heard the glorious, youthful "*Willkomm und Abschied*":

Es schlug mein Herz; geschwind zu Pferde,
Und fort, wild wie ein Held zur Schlacht!
Der Abend wiegte schon die Erde,
Und an den Bergen hing die Nacht.

My heart beat high; to horse, away,
Wild as a hero to the fight!
The eve was cradling earth to sleep,
And on the mountains hung the night.

We can hardly realize today the enormous sensation, the mental exhilaration evoked by these revolutionary rhythms in the breasts of an audience thirsting for nature and the release of feeling. The *Faust* had the like reception when, a little later, about the year 1775, Goethe began gradually to show it to intimate friends.

Merck wrote to Nicolai: "I am amazed, when I get to see a new piece of the *Faust*, to see how the fellow grows in strength, and accomplishes things that would be sheer impossibility without his great belief in himself, and the high spirits that go along with it." That was well and rightly seen and said. The self-confidence and the high spirits were natural results of the fame that the *Werther* reaped overnight for its author when still so young. But both were purely artistic reactions. On the human side, the youth's breast was full of confusion; he was guilty, depressed, weighed down with self-accusations. There was a festering wound in his conscience, inflicted by the unforgettable unfaithfulness to Friederike Brion, the Alsatian pastor's daughter; and the *Faust* is the product of a boldly burgeoning talent and the knowledge of his own very bad behaviour.

Weislingen in *Götz von Berlichingen*, Clavigo, and Faust are the three characters through whom Goethe does poetic penance for his betrayal of love. At the same time he uses the dramatic form to defend himself. Remember the masterly and in their way incontrovertible speeches in which Carlos convinces Clavigo of the necessity of deserting Marie Beaumarchais. Clavigo and Carlos are one and the same person in a division of roles for the purposes of the play. So likewise are Tasso and Antonio, Faust and Mephistopheles: a dialectic separation into two parts of the poet's personality. And always it is the same picture: feeling submits to be disciplined by ripe understanding, and genius bows to worldly common sense. On the other hand this sober and worldly sense is represented as the friend who lovingly protects genius from itself, for the sake of its ambitions; as the shrewd mentor who takes care that mere loyalty shall not lead the genius to make a disastrous marriage. It is a telling fact that Friederike's unfaithful lover was first attracted to the Faust material by the stipulation in the fable that marriage was forbidden to Faust by his pact with the Devil. Goethe's mind, searching at once for self-flagellation and self-glorification, seized on this point; he took the superficial motive of the legend and created out of it the titanism of his "fugitive and homeless one," the "hated of God," the "monster without repose or rest," whose dæmonic power can only destroy as it rages towards the abyss.

Sie, ihren Frieden musst ich untergraben,
Du, Hölle, wolltest dieses Opfer haben!

Alas, her peace I had to undermine,
Thou, Hell, wouldst have this sacrifice!

Ecce poeta! Goethe was never either a destroyer or hated of God; that is certainly a pretty strong stylization of his own character, which his own bad conscience makes him put forward here. Clavigo represents much more sincerely than Faust Goethe's character as a lover and his own sentence upon it. But indeed the relation of self-deception to truth is far less opposed in the poet's mind than in an ordinary human being's. What a poet can give himself, what he can make of himself, that is his, that is himself; and in the Homeric "poets ever were liars," the last word has a different and stronger sense than it has in common life.

In the sixteenth century, after the coming of the printing-press, there was a great need for matter to feed the presses and exploit the popular possibilities of the new invention. Almost any sort of material would do; and the printer, in order to be able to keep on turning it out, often became his own author. Thus the oldest Faust-book, of the year 1587, was probably compiled in Frankfurt by the printer, Spies. It was a collection of popular legends of the black art, up to then circulated by word of mouth; they grouped themselves round the figure of a Dr. Johannes Faustus, a charlatan who had lived some fifty years before and now embodied in the popular fancy the conception of the invoker of evil spirits. His name, it seems, was Georg Helmstetter, but he assumed the high-sounding cognomen of Sabellicus, and later, for a definite reason, the name of Faustus. On the Easter Sunday walk, Goethe makes Faust discourse to Wagner in brilliant verse, disclosing various characteristic and probable-sounding things about his antecedents and origins and about his father, the alchemist and quack physician, that "*dunkler Ehrenmann.*"

I mention this old book because it has a chapter, copied down by the printer from some source or other, in which Helena appears. Dr. Faustus summons up the most beautiful woman in the world before the eyes of his fortunate students; but then he falls in love with her himself and demands her as bedfellow from the devil who serves him, whose name is already Mephistopheles. The description of Helena's famous or infamous person is amorous, though somewhat conventional. It has elements from the Trojan tales of various literatures; and all the epithets used by Byzantine, mediæval and troubadour poets to characterize the European ideal of female beauty are lavished with somewhat mechanical enthusiasm upon it.

The idea of a love-affair between the sixteenth-century charlatan and the regal hetæra of classical antiquity is in itself rather striking. But the combination was not new, its roots strike deep down in time. The Faust-Helena combination is one of those pregnant inventions which can make a period of two thousand years seem like a single span of human life. The end of the classic age, the period of struggle between the classic and the Christian world, must have had elements of similarity with the age of the Reformation. Both were times of fanaticism and mental confusion, and in the earlier as in the later there flourished a host of charlatans, religious impostors, illusionists and self-delusionists. One of these, called Simon, came from Samaria and figures in apostolic history as having scandalously offered money to Peter to buy himself the gift of the Holy Ghost. This Simon was in fact altogether a scandal: he was held in abhorrence by the Fathers of the church because he founded a heretical sect, the Simonians, and shamelessly gave himself out as divine. Also because he took about with him a female, a former prostitute, now acclaimed by her master and his accomplices as the second highest godhead in the universe, the female deity for whom the world had been waiting. He called her Helena.

All that was true mythological hocus-pocus. The adventurer Simon confused the name of Helena with that of Selene, the moon- and mother-goddess and paramour, Astarte. It was an intentional conflation of the erotic and the idea of redemption – today, when we are entering upon another epoch of legend-building quackery, we can gauge its popular appeal better than could some of our ancestors who lived in intervening centuries more firmly anchored to the rational. Well, then, Simon and his Helena were one of those pairs of impostors such as early Christianity knew all too well. We learn from Suetonius that Simon gave an exhibition of flying before the Emperor Nero – the first in history – and crashed. Here, in the flight motif, we have a theme beloved of all the legends of necromancy and witchcraft. Flying is one of man's earliest wish-dreams; and since its fullfilment in actuality lay in the dim future, he transferred it to the realm of magic. The magnificent passage from the Easter Sunday walk, where Faust talks to Wagner about the joys of flying, bears witness to the inward marriage of the poet with his supernatural material.

Ach, zu des Geistes Flügel wird so leicht
Kein körperlicher Flügel sich gesellen.
Doch ist es jedem eingeboren,
Dass sein Gefühl hinauf und vorwärts drängt,
Wenn über uns, im blauen Raum verloren,
Ihr schmetternd Lied die Lerche singt;

Wenn über schroffen Fichtenhöhen
Der Adler ausgebreitet schwebt,
Und über Flächen, über Seen
Der Kranich nach der Heimat strebt.

Alas, our bodies have no wings to vie
With the swift pinions of the lofty spirit!
And yet 'tis nature to aspire
Upward to heights of our desire,
Whenas above, in the blue ether soaring,
We hear the lark her warbling song outpouring,
Above the rugged fir-clad steep
The outspread eagle floats and sways,
And high above o'er plains and lakes
The crane his swift way homeward takes.

The dream has been fulfilled. As the dreams of men usually are. The whirring plane has made it a disillusioning reality. Flying is a neutral, mechanical experience; you read the paper as you soar godlike in the air. And when the incendiary bombs fall from immense heights upon cities and towns, then we sympathize with Wagner, the timid pedant, who disclaims any sympathy with Faust's ideas, saying:

Wie anders tragen uns die Geistesfreuden
Von Buch zu Buch, von Blatt zu Blatt!

'Tis otherwise when intellectual pleasures
Bear us from book to book, from page to page!

To return to Simon, the Samaritan: he survived in a novel of the early Christian age. It was called *Recognitiones* (*Recognitions*), and in it, under the name of Magus, he and his disreputable companion play a thrilling role, performing all the conjuring tricks (including flying) which have become the permanent stock-in-trade in the literature of magic and diabolism. However, it says in this novel that Simon, when he and Helena made their flight, took the name of Faust.

Fifty generations later it was Georg Helmstätter's turn to practise humbuggery upon this earth. He came to Basel, and left his quack visiting-cards upon humanists and theologians. It was the year 1526, and the old *Recognitiones* was in a new edition. The taste of the time is sufficiently revealed by the fact that the antiquated trash became the fashion and went through many impressions. Helmstätter read it and straightway gave himself out as the successor to Magus, calling himself Magus II and Faustus Junior on his visiting-cards. Also, he conformed with the pattern by getting himself a travelling-companion named Helena. Obviously it was an age of great sympathetic understanding of the myth, even though the myth had long since become a species of charlatanry. Helmstätter was not merely the successor of Faustus; there was something else in play, and that was the principle of identification, the abrogation of the individual in the type. Helmstätter-Faustus continued for eleven years to practise his sense-deluding mystery. Then he died; and fifty years later, in Frankfurt, the popular Faust-book was compiled in memory of him.

Thus it came about that the name of Helena, the legendary queen of antiquity, remained bound up with that of the sixteenth-century witch-doctor. Nor had Goethe, in the beginning, any other intention than to bring his Helena at once on the stage with his Faustus. But the autobiographical triumphed temporarily over the legend. In Frankfurt there had been an early-loved Gretchen, in Alsace there was a Friederike, basely left; and these two flesh-and-blood memories put the classic shade so far in the background that the sweet and sorrowful Gretchen dominates the whole first part of *Faust*. Gretchen put Helena in the shade – yet not quite, and not even altogether in the *Faust Erster Teil*. Thanks to the folk-character of Goethe's genius, Faust and Gretchen rank among the famous lovers of literature. They are as secure a possession of our imagination as are Romeo and Juliet, Hero and Leander, Petrarch and Laura, Paolo and Francesca, Abélard and Héloïse – or Goethe's own Werther and Lotte. But in Goethe's masterpiece the pair of lovers has an interchangeable female half. Faust-Gretchen, Faust-Helena – there is an extraordinary combination indeed! Not alone because the magnificent Helena episode in the second part is, in its highly developed, highly literary way, as full of genius as are the priceless Gretchen scenes in the first part. No; I mean that in the first part itself there are dreamlike transferences. In the scene in the witches' kitchen, written in Rome, Faust, before he drinks the magic draught, beholds in the magic mirror Woman in all the splendour of her supreme loveliness, and enraptured sees in that recumbent form the summary and brief abstract of heaven itself. Whom does he there see? Obviously no individual woman, rather a wish-picture of sensual loveliness – the pattern of the female kind, as Mephistopheles says, while promising Faust that he shall soon see that pattern before him in the flesh. But she whom he will actually see – that is not Helena, it is sweet Gretchen, for whom "the pattern of the female kind" is certainly rather a high-flown description. If Faust finds her that, then the only explanation is that given in Mephisto's words:

Du siehst mit diesem Trank im Leibe
Bald Helenen in jedem Weibe

With this drink inside you, presently
Helen in every female you will see.

There, for the first time in the play, the name of Helena appears; in anticipation, and as a symbol of all that feminine beauty and delight which the sweet, simple German burgher-maid is shortly to embody. Yet it is strange to see that Goethe, in that rapturous outburst of Faust after the first meeting with Gretchen, remains faithful to the description of Helena in the old Faust-book:

Beim Himmel, dieses Kind ist schön!
So etwas hab ich nie gesehn!

Heavens, but that child was fair!
Her like I've not seen anywhere!

cries the Faust of the poem.

Der Lippe rot, der Wange Licht,
Die Tage der Welt vergesse ich's nicht!

So red her lips, her cheek so bright,
Ne'er shall I forget the sight!

And in the Faust-book it says of Helena: "*Ihre Leffzen rot wie Kirschen, rote Bäcklein wie ein Rösslin*" ("Her lips as cherries red, her cheeks like rosebuds"). And her face is described as "*überaus schön gleissend*" ("so shining fair"), of which there is a clear reminiscence in the striking phrase of Goethe: "*der Wange Licht.*" And "*etwas schnippisch doch zugleich*" ("rather tart withal") is the demure Gretchen:

Wie sie kurz angebunden war
Das ist nun zum Entzücken gar!

Her pretty, shrewish speech –
It was enchanting!

That, I would wager, is a memory, in a more charmingly turned phrase, of the "pert and roguish face" given to Helena in the Faust-book.

In short, Gretchen betrays traits, half-obliterated, of Helena. She was originally Helena, and Helena, in some small degree, she is still. Yet what an infinitely more lifelike figure the young poet created when he turned the luxurious beauty of the legend into the sweet and hapless little daughter of the pawnbroker! Infinitely more lifelike than if he had followed the old legend, instead of drawing on his own. "*Bewundert viel und viel gescholten*," "much admired and censured much," Helena will duly appear in the second part. But her phantasmagorical figure is far from having the vivid emotional appeal of Gretchen's. She remains an episode. When Faust has dreamed to the end his enchanted dream with her — laden as that is with all the weight of Goethe's mind and art — when that is over she disappears, she vanishes from Faust's sight and memory. Gretchen it is, *una pœnitentium*, who in the fullness of time becomes the instrument by which the end of Faust's story and of his life are linked to their beginning:

Neige, neige,
Du Ohnegleiche,
Du Strahlenreiche,
Dein Antlitz gnädig meinem Glück!
Der Frühgeliebte,
Nicht mehr getrübte,
Er kommt zurück.

Bend down, bend down,
Incomp'rable one,
Thy radiant face
Upon my bliss, in grace!
My early lover,
No more in sorrow,
Comes back to me.

The lines, with their parallelism to those of his early years:

Neige, neige,
Du Schmerzensreiche,

Bend down, bend down,
Thou suffering one,

round out the great circle of the poet's life. A life so abundant and manifold that there was ever present danger of its being squandered, here asserts, by the power of memory, its essential unity. *Faust* is the representative achievement, the symbol of Goethe's whole life. He himself said of it:

Des Menschen Leben ist ein ähnliches Gedicht;
Es hat wohl einen Anfang, hat ein Ende,
Allein ein Ganzes ist es nicht.

Man's life's a poem similar to this;
It has, of course, beginning, has an end too –
But yet a whole it does not come to.

It is touching to see how his mind, in the later, elder time, reaches back to give to the fragmentary and illimitable work the unity that in his deepest heart he craved. "He is," he said, "the most fortunate man who can bring the end of his life round to its beginning again."

It is always a pleasure to speak to the young, to beginning students of Goethe's great poem. For it belongs to their age, it is the conception of one like-minded to them. Originally it was nothing more than the work of a highly gifted student, wherein the author calls faculties and professors over the coals and amuses himself enormously with playing the clever mentor, in diabolic disguise, to the timid freshman newly come up. A contemporary critic — the man's name was Pustkuchen, as one might say Popover — remarked peevishly: "Faust's attack on all human knowledge is not precisely that of an Alexander standing at the known limits of the world and sighing for more to conquer. It is more like that of a student making fun of his professors — however, it was enough for the needs of the majority of his readers." And the hard-pushed critic continues: "But as it goes on, it follows the course of all the Goethian poetry. The great sinner, the titanic figure who outbids the powers of the Devil himself . . . he becomes in the writer's hands a hero like all his other heroes. A love-story unfolds, like a thousand others . . . there is a good-hearted, limited middle-class girl, like Clärchen in *Egmont*. . . ."

Yes, really, the man, in his good-hearted, limited way, is quite right in inveighing against a poetic realism which must have seemed to him like a derogation into intimate personalities of material in itself very lofty. The critic is always on the side of the material, against the poet who irreverently deals with it as an instrument, a pretext for his own personal ends. But what such critics fail to see is the remarkable phenomenon displayed in *Faust:* the genius of student youth here usurps the role of humanity itself, and the whole Western world has accepted this valuation and recognized in the symbolism of the Faust-figure its own deepest essence. Much honour is done to youth by this poem and the greatness it achieved. Its uncompromisingness, its spirit of untamed revolt, its scorn of limitations, of peace and quiet, its yearning and heaven-storming soul, are precisely the expression of what age likes to call "youthful immaturity." But, thanks to the power of genius, this immaturity becomes the representative of humanity; youth stands for the human being at large; what was youthful storm and stress becomes ageless and typical.

Of course, in the play it is not a youth but a reverend and learned doctor whom we see at his desk in the dark vault. The filthy brewage of the witches' kitchen is to take thirty years from his age, and he must be a man some thirty years old when he first addresses Gretchen; so at the beginning of the play he would be not less than sixty years old, and as such he is represented on the stage. Yet of this sixty-year-old man Mephistopheles says to God:

Fürwahr, er dient euch auf besonderer Weise.
Nicht irdisch ist des Thoren Trank und Speise.
Ihn treibt die Gährung in die Ferne,
Er ist sich seiner Tollheit halb bewusst;
Von Himmel fordert er die schönsten Sterne
Und von der Erde jede höchste Lust,
Und alle Näh und alle Fern
Befriedigt nicht die tiefbewegte Brust.

Indeed, he serves you in the strangest fashion!
Not earthly food or drink do feed his passion.
His inner ferment drives him far,
Of his own frenzy he is half aware;
From heaven he demands the fairest star,
From earth all bliss supremely rare —
And yet not near nor far
Can he find easement for his anguished breast.

Those are not words that fit a man on the threshold of old age. The poet transplants his youthful urgency into the breast of a man at the same time of life as Goethe's own when he wrote the *Elec-*

tive Affinities. His Faust is humanity itself, object at once of the divine solicitude and of the lust for conquest of the powers of darkness. But the young poet who so facilely sketched this cosmic figure gave it his own traits, his own nature; and thus the youth became a man, the man a youth.

But this particular youth strives for, and achieves, critical detachment even from his own youngness, from his unbounded urge for freedom and the Absolute. Detachment implies irony; and his need of irony just as strongly demands poetic expression as do his other cravings. Irony is his "second soul"; and Goethe makes Faust speak with a sigh of the two souls within his breast: the one the lusty hunger for love, the clinging sensuality; the other his longing for the pure and spiritual. The sigh he breathes is half-hypocritical: as well might he lament the duality of irony and enthusiasm, for well he knows that dualism is the soil and the mystery of creative fruitfulness. Enthusiasm — that is fullness with God; and what then is irony? The author of *Faust* is youth enough to see in that urge for the Absolute the divine in man; and in irony the diabolic. But this diabolism of his does not stand on such a bad footing with the divine. The Lord God says of it:

Ich habe deinesgleichen nie gehasst.
Von allen Geistern die verneinen
Ist mir der Schalk am wenigsten zur Last.

Hatred for your sort I have never felt.
Of all the spirits that deny
I find the thorough rascal least offensive.

The diabolism is of an amusing, witty kind, and God has tolerant understanding of it. It is acidulous, unprejudiced worldly sense, unapt for the emotions of the angels but not without sympathy for ordinary human need: "I feel a pity for the pains of men," says Mephisto. It makes superior mock of youthful enthusiasm; it is creative inventiveness and conscious anticipation of maturity and experience, fanaticism and worldly good sense; these are the contradiction, the "two souls" that Goethe likes to project into the dramatic form. Later he will divide himself into Tasso and Antonio; here, on a grander scale, he divides himself into Faust and Mephistopheles. Mephistopheles is the ironic self-corrective to Goethe's youthful titanism.

Mephistopheles is the most vital figure of a devil in all literature; the clearest-cut, the most animated by creative genius. He has not the emotional appeal of Klopstock's and Milton's devils; yet the characterization is so fresh and amusing, so sharply outlined and yet so various, that despite its spirit of ironic self-abrogation it made a permanent conquest of the human imagination for all time. The name Mephistopheles comes from the old Faust-book and the literature of demonology. Has it to do with mephitic? Does it signify sulphurous, pestilential? At any rate, it has the right sound, for the fellow is foul, foul in the grand style, with a sense of humour about his own foulness. He is the presiding genius of all vermin—rats, mice, frogs, bugs, lice and so on. But his protection of the more repulsive manifestations of creation is really an expression of his nihilism, his denial of creation and of life altogether.

He says so straight out, and his words have become proverbial:

Ich bin der Geist der stets verneint!
Und das mit Recht; denn alles was entsteht
Ist wert, dass es zu Grunde geht;
Drum besser wär's, dass nichts entstünde.

I am the spirit that ever denies!
And rightly so; for all that's born on earth
Merits destruction from its birth
And better 'twere it had not seen the light.

And much later on, in the second part of the tragedy, when Faust dies, he shrugs his shoulders at the angel's word: "Over!" and mocks at life's lament over its own transitoriness:

Vorbei! Ein dummes Wort.
Warum vorbei?
Vorbei und reines Nichts, vollkommenes Einerlei!
Was soll uns denn das ew'ge Schaffen?
Geschaffenes zu Nichts hinwegzuraffen!
Da ist's vorbei! Was ist daran zu lesen?
Es ist so gut, als wär' es nicht gewesen,
Und treibt sich doch im Kreis, als wenn es wäre.
Ich liebte mir dafür das Ewig-leere.

Over! A silly word.
Why over?
Over, and sheerest nothing, quite the same!
Then what's the use, eternally to strive,

When all that's made at nothing does arrive?
Over it is! What shall we learn from that?
It is as good as though it never were,
Runs round and round, the same old end to see—
The eternal void is good enough for me.

The grey-haired poet makes his devil speak just as the audacious youth had made him do, in the selfsame accents. And we must not think that the devil's nihilism, his critique of life as it is and just because it is, was remote from the poet and foreign to his soul. Through the mouth of Faust he stands up for life, "the healing, creative force," to which Mephisto opposes the "cold devil's fist." But what Mephisto says springs just as much from Goethe's own nature and feelings as does his apologia for life. Goethe, like Mephisto, is no angelic flatterer of creation; and he invents a devil in order to have a mouthpiece for all the rebellion, denial, and critical bitterness he feels in himself.

But Mephistopheles is not only the presiding genius of all the vermin. Above all he is the genius of *fire*, he has reserved to himself that destructive, sterilizing, annihilating element. The red waistcoat and the cock's feather are the outward signs of his infernal nature. It is true that the witch misses in him the other classic attributes, the cloven hoof, the two ravens, which the Christian Devil inherited from the pagan Wotan. But in Mephisto the devil of the myth is tamed down in accordance with the cosmopolitan pose which he humorously finds more appropriate to the times. The cloven hoof is replaced by a slight limp. Wotan's ravens do indeed appear in the second part ("I see my raven pair, what message do they bear?"); but they are as a rule invisible. Mephisto regards himself as a cultural product, and seeks to dissociate himself from the legendary "northern phantom." He lays aside horns, claws, and tail; as for the cloven hoof, that, he feels, would do him harm in society. He refuses to be addressed as Squire Satan, and prefers the title of Herr Baron, as a gentleman among other gentlemen. Satan, he feels, has become a fable; he accepts the man-of-the-world version of him; though at the same time he asserts that mankind has not gained very much by doing away with the Devil. "They are rid of the Evil One, the evils remain." He completely departs from the role, turns his scepticism upon himself, and quite in the spirit of the Enlightenment regards his own existence as a superstition, or at most as so moderated by enlightenment as to fit the new age. The drollest implications arise, as for instance that scene, in only four verses, wherein Faust and Mephistopheles pass by a crucifix. "Mephisto, why so fast?" says Faust. "And why cast down your eyes before the Cross?" His companion replies:

Ich weiss es wohl, es ist ein Vorurteil,
Allein genug, mir ist's einmal zuwider.

I realize it is a prejudice –
Anyhow, there it is: I do not like it.

The fear of the crucifix was a mark of the mediæval Devil. But when Mephisto speaks of prejudice, that is good eighteenth-century, and a proper modernized Satan to match. His enlightenment is not religious, it is not the crucifix that he speaks of as a prejudice, it is his own mediæval, traditional fear to which he refers, and he excuses it as a weakness and caprice which, despite all his modern culture, he has been unable to overcome.

We see how the poet plays with his conception of the Evil One, limiting at moments its reality, making it display at times a satiric abrogation of its own identity. But after all it is actually there, actually a devil, who comes when called, and is subject to the laws of demonology. "I make my homage to the learned man: you certainly have made me sweat quite soundly," he acknowledges to Faust. Sometimes one might suspect that he is only playing his part in the game; in the witches' kitchen he behaves with good-humoured, sceptical condescension towards the magic claptrap and objectionable humbug which so offend Faust's humanistic feeling.

Ei Possen, das ist nur zum Lachen.
Seid nur nicht ein so strenger Mann!
Sie muss als Arzt ein Hokuspokus machen.

Oh, suchlike little games – one laughs
At them! My good sir, don't be such an ass!
She is the doctor, she must do her stuff.

He defends the nonsensical *Einmaleins* (one times one) incantation by an attack on the pious absurdity of the Holy Trinity, in a sarcastic line or so. Yet Mephisto seems to be caught by the pentagram and subject to it; also the signature in blood, to Faust a meaningless gesture, he appears actually to need in order to execute the pact in good mediæval demonological style.

Thus we see the artist playing with the traditional figure; making it hover in changeful light or even avaunt and void the sight of its own identity. It is even uncertain, for instance, and is deliberately left uncertain, whether this is actually *the* Devil or only *a* devil; only a representative of the infernal powers (*ein Teil von jener Kraft*) or the Evil One himself in person. In the Prologue in Heaven he is plainly the Satan of the Book of Job; for why should a lesser one than he ask permission of God to try a human soul? And at the very end, when Faust's immortal soul is in question, he cannot well be other than Satan himself, the thwarted Devil of legend. But in between he functions, so to speak, as a limited liability company; refers to "us" and "folk like us"; says: "Bethink thee well, for we shall not forget," and "Did we force ourselves on you, or you on us?" Goethe even wrote for the Walpurgisnacht a scene in which Satanas himself, Herr Urian, sits on the peak of the Brocken and holds his horrid court. But this was to introduce confusion: to include the scene would have condemned Mephisto to second place in the hierarchy, and Goethe left it out, so that the Prince of Hell, the Whole, might not derogate from the importance of the part.

Mephisto's language is sharply contrasted with the earnest, emotional, passionate key in which Faust speaks. The devil's line is brisk and worldly; it has a careless wit; is eminently critical and contemptuous, spiced with foreign words, altogether diverting. He speaks as it were *en passant;* the result is happy, casual, and most effective:

Mein guter Herr, ihr seht die Sachen
Wie man die Sachen eben sieht;
Wir müssen das gescheiter machen –

Yes, my good sir, you look at things
Precisely as in fact one does;
From now on we must manage better –

and so on. That is the tone. It is the superiority of the man of the world (and Mephisto is at bottom nothing but a worldling) who shrugs his shoulders over the man with the deep and troubled emotional nature. Faust, in worldly matters, is Mephisto's pupil; he lets himself be led; and in despair over his own striving for the highest things, even strikes a bargain with the devil. Mephisto's relation to Faust is that of the experienced travelling-companion and tutor who knows his way about; he is courier, *maître des plaisirs;* again he is simply the resourceful servant who Lothario-like makes opportunities for his master. He is all these things by turns, with versatility and wit. In the Paralipomenon, one of the numerous rejected drafts, the devil pictures himself as the corrupt tutor of a young eighteenth-century nobleman:

Der junge Herr ist freilich schwer zu führen,
Doch als erfahrener Gouverneur
Weiss ich den Wildfang zu regieren,
Und afficiert mich auch nichts mehr.
Und lass ihn so in seinen Lüsten wandeln,
Mag ich doch auch nach meinen Lüsten handeln,
Ich rede viel und lass ihn immer gehn;
Ist ja ein allzudummer Streich geschehen
Dann muss ich meine Weisheit zeigen,
Dann wird er bei den Haarn herausgeführt,
Doch gibt man gleich, indem man's repariert,
Gelegenheit zu neuen dummen Streichen.

True, my young master is a trifle wilful,
But birds like that aren't hard to tame.
A tutor's job has made me skilful,
Naught he can do puts me to shame.
Go where he will, I follow with due meekness,
Since for my own ways I still have a weakness,
I preach a lot – and let him have his way.
And when some extra-stupid prank he'll play,
Then my good sense it is my turn to show,
And drag him out of harm's way by the hair:
Leaving him, while the damage we repair,
Always an opening for some new folly.

Goethe continually rhymes *zeigen* and *streichen*, *neigen* and *reichen*, as though his Frankfurt pronunciation *zeichen* and *neichen* were the universal one. It is certainly a hard pill to swallow, from the greatest lyric poet of Germany. It shows a naïve persistence in local tradition – we have simply to put up with it, and console ourselves with the thought that it is nice to hear how Goethe spoke. The rejected verses just quoted are a good illustration of the wit and variety in Goethe's portrayal of the devil: how it makes itself large and then small, expanding from the satirical human being into the magnificently diabolic and back again at will.

But in the end Mephistopheles is the personification of the hatred of light and life; he is primal night and Chaos' son, the emissary of the void — after his own kind he is on a very grand scale. "Thou vile abortion, born of filth and fire!" — thus Faust once rails at him, and it is a splendid description. Something about it, we realize, corresponds to the human intellectual elements which both impress and offend us. The filth, that is the cynicism, the obscene wit, launched by the fires of his infernal will to destruction. The essence of his nature is the profoundest lovelessness. Hatred fairly scintillates in the creature's slanting yellow tiger-eyes. "The bottomless rage that leads thee to destroy," Faust says to him: "thy tig'rish glare, thy all-compelling face. . . ." Here the humorous side fades out, and the devil emerges in all his specific majesty; not without a certain admiration the poet sees and feels it.

Goethe's own attitude towards evil is not uniform; it hovers between recognition and contempt. He says, in one of the Proverbs:

Ich kann mich nicht bereden lassen:
Macht mir den Teufel nur nicht klein!
Ein Kerl, den alle Menschen hassen,
Der muss was sein.

I still remain quite unconvinced
That it's good sense to paint the devil small:
There must be something in a chap
Who's hated so by all.

But in portraying Mephistopheles as the embodiment of evil, Goethe sometimes injects into the character a trace of self-contempt, a hang-dog note: Mephistopheles will sometimes betray his suspicion that the devil is no great shakes when all is said and done:

Mich darf niemand aufs Gewissen fragen,
Ich schäme mich oft meines Geschlechts;
Sie meinen, wenn Sie Teufel sagen,
So sagen Sie was Rechts.

Let nobody ask me on my oath
Whether I shame me for my kind;
But you, when you speak the words "the devil" —
You've something big in mind.

When you say "the devil," you really are not saying much; in other words, evil is a poor thing after all. The poet could scarcely make the idea more impressive than by putting it in the Evil One's own mouth! And in the Prologue, Mephisto feels flattered by the fact that God condescends to converse with him, the old nihilist:

Es ist gar hübsch von einem grossen Herrn
So menschlich mit dem Teufel selbst zu sprechen!

It's very handsome of so great a lord
To talk with the devil as man to man!

Not for nothing have these two light-hearted lines become so famous. Their humour is complex and subtle. Here is the Divine Absolute, in the role of the Grand Seigneur who is human enough to discuss with the Opposition; and here is the Opposition, flattered by the complaisance and recognizing its own inferiority—truly a cosmic jest, a regular poet's joke, and very characteristic of this particular poet; for when in the presence of opposition and negation, Goethe always thought of himself as the grand seigneur and representative of the government. "If I had had the *misfortune* to be in the Opposition," he once said in conversation. And yet it was precisely Goethe who created, and invested with lyric meaning, the figure of the arch-nihilist, Mephistopheles.

And further: what character in this play—racked, it is true, by disillusionment, bitterness, yearning, and despair—utters the most crushing, nihilistic words in the whole poem: the great malediction upon life, its joys and its seductions; the great curse upon spirit and sense, fame and possessions, love, hope, faith, endurance—so that the chorus of spirits must lament:

Weh! Weh!
Du hast sie zerstört,
Die schöne Welt,
Mit mächtiger Faust;
Sie stürzt, sie zerfällt!
Ein Halbgott hat sie zerschlagen!
Wir tragen
Die Trümmer ins Nichts hinüber
Und klagen
Über die verlorne Schöne!

Woe! Woe!
Thou hast laid low
With violent blow

The beautiful world –
It totters, it falls,
A demigod hath struck it.
We have borne
Its ruins into the void
And we mourn
For the beauty destroyed!

Which character is it? Mephisto? He could never have summoned the pity or pain for such an anathema against life and joy. No, it is the anguished human being, it is Goethe-Faust who utters the frightful words. Here the roles are reversed, and the nihilistic devil becomes the practical and worldly advocate for life against the desperate and rebellious human spirit.

Hör auf, mit deinem Gram zu spielen,
Der, wie ein Geier, Dir am Leben frisst,
Die schlechteste Gesellschaft lässt Dich fühlen,
Dass Du ein Mensch mit Menschen bist.

Do stop playing with your sorrows,
That like vultures feed upon your breast!
Even from the lowest company one borrows
A sense that one's a man like all the rest.

The character of Faust in the poem is no simpler, no more uniform, than that of his diabolic mentor. It varies in the same way. Or rather the whole poem in which they play their parts possesses this variability of the Time-Spirit; since the scene, ostensibly, is laid in the sixteenth century, but continually plays over into the eighteenth, the poet's own. Wagner, the famulus, speaks the language of the age of Enlightenment, praises the periods of Gottsched, and feels that science and mankind have made glorious progress. Faust-Goethe, on the contrary, stands for Herder's ideas about the "age of genius." The nature-mysticism of his soliloquies, and the religious feeling he shows to Gretchen – all that is inspired by Swedenborg, Ossian, and Lavater, in particular by the northern mystic, who died in 1772, and whose name Goethe replaced by that of Nostradamus in order to preserve the historical perspective. I spoke of Faust's humanism, the intellectual attitude that makes him fundamentally despise magic as despicable rigmarole, although he surrenders to it, that "through the spirit's mouth and might, mysteries might see the light." As a matter of fact, he remained, as Mephisto's patron, addicted to it up to his old age and made use of it in all his adventures, first with Gretchen, and then in the world, at the Kaiser's court, in battle, in the affair with Helena, whom he wins only by enchantment and illusion. Not till very late does there stir in him the desire "magic from out his path to put away." Yet even so, his attitude towards it from the beginning is highly fastidious — or at least towards its practicants and technicians and their obscene trafficking. He inveighs against the witches' kitchen as a "*Wust von Raserei*" (crazy rubbish). "Why just that old hag?" he asks in disgust. He finds the whole thing as unappetizing as anything he ever saw. Bad taste, offensive — that is his humanistic judgment on the whole of magic art: "frantic stuff, wild goings-on, disgusting humbug" — he knows and despises it already. The blood-pact — vital to Mephisto because after all, in God's name, he really *is* the devil — Faust knows about that too, it is as familiar as repulsive to him; he refers to the pact with contempt, as a piece of tomfoolery. Why must they have such a superstitious flourish as the signature in blood, when after all, in the eternal flux of things, there can be no such thing as a binding promise, however much a high-minded man would wish to cling to the delusion of truth? Mephisto duly utters his mediæval patter, just as it stands in the legend:

Ich will mich hier zu deinem Dienst verbinden
Auf deinen Wink nicht rasten und nicht ruhn:
Wenn wir uns drüben wiederfinden,
Dann sollst Du mir das Gleiche tun.

Here I bind myself unto your service,
Ever at your beck and call to be;
When we find ourselves in the hereafter,
Then you shall do the same for me.

He speaks of the hereafter as an actuality in the popular mind and his own — in the Prologue, indeed, he stands before God among the heavenly host. But Faust answers him as a humanist and earthbound human spirit, who does not believe in a hereafter, or at least is not interested in one:

Aus dieser Erde quillen meine Freuden,
Und diese Sonne scheinet meinen Leiden;
Kann ich mich erst von ihnen scheiden,
Dann mag was will und kann geschehn.
Davon will ich nichts weiter hören. . . .

My joys all spring from earthly sources,
My griefs are shined on by this very sun;
When I can sever me from earthly courses,
Let come what can and will; my race is run.
I'll hear no more of it.

Neither understands the other—either temporally or morally. The bargain is struck on the basis of two different conceptions: one primitive and diabolic, the other more evolved and with some knowledge of human dignity. "*Was willst du, armer Teufel, geben?*" asks Faust ("And what, poor devil, can you give, at best?")

Ward eines Menschen Geist, in seinem hohen Streben,
Von deinesgleichen je gefasst?

When was the human spirit's striving
E'er understanded of a thing like thee?

He makes his pact with the devil out of the same high and human aspiration that mind, science, knowledge had been unable to satisfy; with the same absolute and insatiable passion that made him despair of thought he gives himself to pleasure. And all the while he knows but too well that it will be as impotent as knowledge to still his craving for infinity.

Werd ich beruhigt je mich auf ein Faulbett legen,
So sei es gleich um mich getan!
Kannst du mich schmeichelnd je belügen,
Dass ich mir selbst gefallen mag,
Kannst du mich mit Genuss betrügen,
Das sei für mich der letzte Tag!

If ever on bed of idleness I lay me,
May I that moment die!
When thou by flattery canst wile me
In self-complacency to rest,
Or e'er with pleasant lusts beguile me—
Then may that moment be my last!

"Beguile with pleasant lusts." Thus no voluptuary speaks. Rather he who takes up with pleasure as earlier he did with things of the mind, and recognizes but one kind of slavery: inertia and ease.

Des Denkens Faden ist zerrissen,
Mir ekelt lange vor allem Wissen.
Lass in den Tiefen der Sinnlichkeit
Uns glühende Leidenschaften stillen. . . .
Stürzen wir uns in das Rauschen der Zeit,
Ins Rollen der Begebenheit!
Da mag denn Schmerz und Genuss,
Gelingen und Verdruss,
Miteinander wechseln wie es kann;
Nur rastlos betätigt sich der Mann.

All threads of thought I sever.
Knowledge abjure forever,
And in the senses deep
My glowing passions steep. . . .
Plunged in time's whirling surge,
Rolled round in life's unending urge,
Let success or failure come,
Alternates of joy and woe
Mingle together how they can;
But let man only striving know.

Thus no voluptuary speaks. Thus speaks an activist, who seeks not pleasure but life, and binds himself to the devil only so far as a man of intellect does who gives himself to life. The formal bond he despises as pedantic and futile, there being no reason to doubt his complete surrender.

Nur keine Furcht, dass ich dies Bündnis breche!
Das Streben meiner ganzen Kraft
Ist gerade das was ich verspreche.

There needs no fear this promise shall be broken:
The uttermost of all my powers
Is bent to keep what I have spoken.

One asks oneself, indeed, what does actually come of that plumbing of the depths of sense, of the intoxications of life and time, of that furious masculine activity of Faust during his companionship with Mephistopheles. I will not extend the question to the second part of the poem. There it is only after a multitude of involved adventures in magic that Faust engages in any kind of activity that could be called unresting or masculine. As for the first part, we must admit that Goethe has not gone very far towards poetic realization of the depths of sensuality or the life of action, fluctuating between success and failure, to which his hero would devote himself. What does Mephisto do for his hopeful pupil? He takes him to Auerbach's cellar, where the two perform conjuring tricks before bawling philistines just as in the chapbook. Well, at least that is by way of illustration to the lines:

Die schlechteste Gesellschaft lässt dich fühlen
Dass du ein Mensch mit Menschen bist –

Even from the lowest company one borrows
A sense that one's a man like all the rest –

though it is hardly even that, for Faust does not succeed in being hail fellow well met with his brother topers in the cellar. He and the devil behave more like high-born travelling foreigners, very spoilt and capricious at that, and with a smack of the charlatan that would make them suspect to middle-class minds. We hear that they have just got back from Spain; if that is true, what have they been doing there? We do not learn. We are equally puzzled by Faust's remark at the beginning of the Gretchen episode, when he demands that Mephisto deliver the little one straight into his arms:

Hätt ich nur sieben Stunden Ruh,
Brauchte den Teufel nicht dazu
So ein Geschöpfchen zu verführen.

If I had only seven hours free,
I should not need to call the Devil in
To teach that little creature how to sin.

If that is only said in order to excuse him for not being able to seduce the poor child by his own efforts, but needing the powers of hell to help him to do it, then we must deduce that he is occupied indeed — and with what, and how? We remain in the dark. None of the deceased charlatan's famous deeds or misdeeds come into the first part; the Gretchen story stands alone, for nothing stronger had the young poet to give! He magnified it into his own tragedy, he reduced all the rest of the Faustian program to this one exploration of the life of passion. And who would regret the fact? For the result was the loveliest, sincerest, saddest love-story in the German language, perhaps in any language, told in the simplest, most natural, convincing, and moving accents in the world.

We must repeat what has so often been said already: this little Gretchen, the pawnbroker's daughter, as we see her move before our mind's eye, in her grief, her humanness and femininity, her childlike purity, her love and devotion, her vicarious, pitiful fate, is a figure of immortal beauty. We see her in the little German imperial city, a small, idyllic setting, with spinning-wheel and fountain, christening feast and gossiping neighbours. But how the young creature, so simple, yet so warm with life, is lifted out of her lowliness and transfigured by the masculine guilt and remorse! At the end she is nothing less than the spirit of love itself, watching from above over the struggles of the erring one and preparing his welcome and redemption. Like Mignon in Goethe's great novel, she has two of her creator's most marvellous lyrics put in her mouth: "*Meine Ruh ist hin,*" and "*Es war ein König in Thule.*" But she is herself a "*Lied,*" a folk-song refined by the most personal art. At the end, in desolation and madness, in her prison cell, her soul and her song slip away into the most wondrous, awesome sphere of all folk-poesy:

Meine Mutter die Hur,
Die mich umgebracht hat!
Mein Vater der Schelm,
Der mich gessen hat!
Mein Schwesterlein klein
Hub auf die Bein,
An einem kühlen Ort;
Da ward ich ein schönes Waldvögelein,
Fliege fort, fliege fort!

My mother the whore,
She did me to death!
My father the knave,
My flesh eaten hath!
My sister so small
My bones gathered all
And laid them to cool.
And then I was turned to a sweet wood bird —
Fly away, fly away!

Such simple, native accents of uncanny fantasy are unknown to Clärchen in *Egmont*. Yet the two are sisters, Clärchen and Gretchen, unmistakably visualized and created by their author to like though varying tragic destinies. One becomes the heroine, the other the martyr of her sex. And just as they are sisters, so their lovers, Faust and Egmont, are brothers, true sons of Goethe both, representing the characteristic Goethian eroticism, a little narcissistic; which finds its peculiar ecstasy in the beguilement of simple innocence, of the little maid of the people by a lordly masculinity stooping down from loftier spheres, and in her utter surrender to her blissful fate. Egmont shows himself to the virtuous Clärchen in Spanish court dress; nothing could be more characteristic of Goethe's own wish-dream world than this scene. In *Faust*, the court dress and the golden fleece are of a metaphysical kind. An elegant, fastidious traveller, from an intellectual sphere unknown to Gretchen's bourgeois simplicity and most impressive; half nobleman, half scholar, Faust appears as from another world, and dreaming of him she says:

Ich gäb was drum, wenn ich nur wüsst'
Wer heut der Herr gewesen ist!
Er sah gewiss recht wacker aus
Und ist aus einem edlen Haus:
Das konnt' ich ihm an der Stirne lesen –
Er wär' auch sonst nicht so keck gewesen.

How much I'd give if I could say
Who that gallant was today!
He looked so very fine and proud,
And I could tell, from some high family:
A nobleman, 'twas plain to see,
So forward else he had not been with me.

Delightful lines. Gretchen betrays in them her profound curiosity and emotion after the first meeting. She is flattered that he approached her, yet feels her modesty offended and, having given no occasion for his boldness, explains it by his high rank. The childlike words betray the specific charm which lay for the poet in such a situation – as does also the later dialogue:

MARGARETE:
Ich fühl es wohl, dass mich der Herr nur schont,
Herab sich lässt, mich zu beschämen;

Ein Reisender ist so gewohnt
Aus Gütigkeit fürlieb zu nehmen;
Ich weiss zu gut, dass solch erfahrnen Mann
Mein arm Gespräch nicht unterhalten kann.

FAUST:
Ein Blick von dir, ein Wort mehr unterhält
Als alle Weisheit dieser Welt.

MARGARETE:
I realize, the gentleman is kind,
And lowers himself, it puts me quite to shame;
For travellers are not to blame
For simply taking up with what they find.
I know too well, my simple chatter,
To such a man as you are, could not matter.

FAUST:
One look from thee, one word is more to me
Than all the wisdom of this world can be.

In this everyday fragment of talk there lies great richness of feeling. It is so typical of student life; it is so typically the love-story of the university man, the academic, the Herr Doctor, and the little girl of the people, who cannot think what the clever gentleman sees in her. *In abstracto*, it is beauty, poor in spirit, blushing before the wooing of the intellect. Beauty, and "wisdom"; and the sensual abrogation of the one before the other, with all the dangers of seduction and ruin which lie for innocence and beauty in this appeal of intellect and sensuality combined. Thus intellect becomes guilty before beauty, and thus Faust became guilty before Gretchen. Certainly the Gretchen story is the tragedy of intellect becoming mortally guilty to beauty, with the cynical connivance of the devil. And here, more than anywhere else, does Goethe betray himself a revolutionary, in that he would stir our emotions against the cruelty of human society, which punishes the beauty that falls victim to the beguilement of the superior mind. This once, and never again, Goethe, owing to his own tragic sense of guilt, becomes an accuser and rebel against society. In the prose scene: "Grey day, a field," taken bodily out of the *Urfaust* and put unchanged into the fragment as well as the finished poem, Faust, after the repulsive distractions of the Blocksburg and the Walpurgisnacht dream, learns that Gretchen is in prison and has been handed over to the justice of cruel, unthinking men. Mephistopheles flings at him his cynical "She is not the first."

"Not the first! Oh, horror, horror! How can any human being understand that the writhing death-agony of the first was not enough to atone for the guilt of the rest, in the eyes of the All-Merciful! The agony of this single one pierces me to the heart—and you can stand there and grin at the fate of thousands!"

The scene is written in rough, savage, almost clumsy prose, devoid of irony; it scarcely seems to belong to a poem that otherwise, in all its inward significance, its profound human symbolism, moves with such light-footed creative objectivity. Shall we call it uncharacteristic? Certainly Goethe seems to have found it so. When the *Faust* was performed at Weimar, he left this scene out. And it is said that as a member of the government he gave society its due by signing the death-sentence upon a young girl accused of child-murder, although the Duke himself would have shown her mercy.

If this story be true, it bears witness to a stern self-disciplining of his own kindliness and pity, and their suppression in favour of established order. For order the mature Goethe held in such honour that he openly declared it to be better to commit injustice than to tolerate disorder. That too has its fine side; but more youthfully beautiful, certainly, is the rebellion against order, grounded on the remorseful feelings of Friederike Brion's unfaithful lover, and mounting in the Faust poem almost to destructive heights. Gretchen's destruction is almost the ruin of Faust as well. Nowhere else does he, the human being, fall so foul of his companion as here; nowhere does he fling the scorn of his anguished heart so furiously in the grinning face of the demon who mocks at man's double nature: "*Hund! Abscheuliches Untier!*" ("Dog! Detestable monster!")

"*Hab' ich doch meine Freude dran!*" ("I get my fun out of it too.")

Goethe, in *Faust*, has depicted love as a regular devil's holiday: the "high intuition" whose concluson and consummation Mephisto indicates with an obscene gesture. It begins so tenderly, with such extravagant soulfulness, and reaches its end in guilty despair. "*Doch, alles was mich dazu trieb, Gott! war so gut, ach! war so lieb!*" ("And all that drove me thereunto, God! was so dear, ah! was so true!") So poor Gretchen sighs; and her seducer will not have it at any price that he is betraying her when he whispers her eternal loyalty and love. Faust replies to the mockery of his companion:

. . . *wenn ich* empfinde,
Für das Gefühl, für das Gewühl
Nach Namen suche, keinen finde,
Dann durch die Welt mit allen Sinnen schweife,
Nach allen höchsten Worten greife,
Und diese Glut, von der ich brenne,
Unendlich, ewig, ewig nenne,
Ist das ein teuflisch Lügenspiel?

. . . when for my feeling,
When for the tumult in my breast,
I seek a name, and find no healing,
When through the world I range and try
With all my senses to express
This ecstasy with which I burn,
And call eternal, infinite—
Is that a devilish lie?

And the Evil One replies: "And yet I'm right!" For youthful love, the most human thing in the world, wherein the spirit and the body, the natural and the divine, mingle in a way so symbolic and so exemplary for all humanity, is truly the devil's playground, the theatre of his most prized triumphs. There he most easily performs his traditional task of betraying the highest in man to the basest. There truly is his immemorial striving: to seize on that higher part of man, so mingled with his baser self, and in the baser swallow up the higher. And he would triumph, were it not that the Eternal Goodness, with whom in the Prologue the devil is so cringingly conversable, and who sees the highest in the lowest, not, as the devil does, the lowest in the highest, opposes his will to destruction.

The whole Faust-poem is based on the Prologue in Heaven. Or rather the Prologue was afterwards shoved underneath the youthful, light-heartedly conceived composition, to prop it up. For it is in the Prologue that the figure of Faust becomes the protagonist and symbol of man, in whom the Eternal Goodness had a share, as he in it. Faust's human trait, which makes him strive after the universally human, is his noble side, the goodness which is at the same time godliness in him. So it comes about that he and the devil, who has no understanding of the painstaking spirit of man, misunderstand each other when they make their pact. When Faust says: "Let us still our glowing passions in the depth of sense," he means something quite different from what the devil thinks; he means even the sensuality with a difference: as something nobler, deeper, more serious and fervent. Despairing of thought, he turns to the world and to life. But of joy, he says, there can be no thought.

Dem Taumel weih' ich mich, dem schmerzlichen Ge-
nuss. . . .
Mein Busen, der von Wissensdrang geheilt ist,
Soll keinen Schmerzen künftig sich verschliessen,
Und was der ganzen Menschheit zugeteilt ist,
Will ich mit meinem inneren Selbst geniessen,
Mit meinem Geist das Höchst und Tiefste greifen,
Ihr Wohl und Weh auf meinen Busen häufen,
Und so mein eigen Selbst zu ihrem Selbst erweitern. . . .

To tumult I am vowed, and ecstasy of pain. . . .
My bosom, now of wisdom's craving healed,
Shall to no sorrows from this day be sealed,
But all the pangs that human lot befall,
In my own heart henceforth I'll know them all,
And with my spirit grasp their depth and height.
Their weal and woe my breast shall know,
And so my own self to their self shall grow.

The Mephistophelian "world" (the devil is only a worldling) becomes for Faust life, with its tortures and desires; but surrender to it takes on at once a human character; he wishes to live, in the fullest, most human sense, he would be a son of man, would take upon himself and exhaust, as representative and sacrifice, all the joys and sorrows of mankind. And we recall those words, spoken as in a dream, which Goethe murmured to himself on a moonlight night in his youth, mounting out of the Ilm:

Alles geben die Götter, die Unendlichen,
Ihren Lieblingen ganz:
Alle Freuden, die Unendlichen,
Alle Schmerzen, die Unendlichen,
Ganz.

All do the gods give, the eternal,
To their favourites, wholly:

All the joys, the eternal,
All the pangs, the eternal,
Wholly.

To take the joys and sufferings of mankind upon himself, in giving himself to life—nothing else is it that Faust promises the devil. But this "striving to attain man's utmost height," infinite as it always is, and sinful in the sense that it is presumptuous titanism, is after all more allied to God than to the devil; it is generous, upright, and good, and despite all the perils it entails, it never from the first holds out any great hopes to the devil.

In a poem written at the time of his betrothal to Lili Schönemann, we hear Goethe call himself "*ein guter Junge*" ("a good lad"). "Why," he asks:

Warum ziehst du mich unwiderstehlich,
Ach, in jene Pracht?
War ich guter Junge, *nicht so selig*
In der öden Nacht?

Ah, why dost thou so resistless draw me
To thy splendour bright?
Was I not, *good lad*, so happy,
In the lonely night?

"*Ich guter Junge.*" It is touching to hear Goethe so address himself; and whatever the intellectual heights he reached, however reverend he became to himself, it remained to the end a good description. We know how mild he was, how tolerant, what universal benevolence he possessed. We know his lifelong wish, "to do good to men," "to teach them to live"; we know his confession, that after every flight into solitude he needed but to see a human face "to love again." And the man of the Faustian strivings and efforts, he too is "a good boy." Just as he means well by himself, and feels that he can be saved, so also he means well by humanity: he wants its good, would have it assisted, positively, lovingly, reasonably; would not have it bewildered, would have it satisfied. In a Paralipomenon Faust says to Mephistopheles:

So höre denn, wenn du es niemals hörtest:
Die Menschheit hat ein fein Gehör,
Ein reines Wort erreget schöne Taten.
Der Mensch fühlt sein Bedürfnis nur zu sehr
Und lässt sich gern im Ernste raten.

So hearken now, if thou hast never heard:
The human hearing's very keen,
And glorious deeds can follow one clear word.
Man knows only too sore his human need,
And gladly counsel he will heed.

And again:

Von allem ist dir nichts gewährt.
Was weisst du, was der Mensch begehrt?
Dein widrig Wesen, bitter, scharf,
Was weiss es was der Mensch bedarf?

Nothing of all is granted thee.
Then how canst thou men's longing read?
Thy warped nature, bitter, curst,
What can it know of human need?

Nothing could be more Goethian, nothing more Faustian. Its conception of man, its attitude towards the human being, are a part of the Everlasting Goodness; and no differently speaks the Eternal Goodness itself, God the Lord, in the Prologue, whose characterization of man is young Goethe's characterization of himself: in it self-love grows till it embraces humanity:

Wenn er mir jetzt auch nur verworren dient,
So werd ich ihn bald in die Klarheit führen.
Weiss doch der Gärtner, wenn das Bäumchen grünt,
Dass Blüt' und Frucht die künftigen Jahre zieren.

Though still he serve me with a darkened mind,
Soon to the light of truth I'll lead his feet.
Knows not the gardener when the tree is green
That flower and fruit the coming year shall greet?

And then that primal word of the Eternal Goodness:

Es irrt der Mensch so lang er strebt.

For man must err, so long as man must strive.

And that final pronouncement of God, which in its lofty and trusting mildness has become proverbial for all mankind:

Und steh' beschämt, wenn du erkennen musst,
Ein guter Mensch, in seinem dunklen Drange,
Ist sich des rechten Weges wohl bewusst.

And stand abashed, when you at last must say,
The good man, howsoever dark his striving,
Is ever mindful of the better way.

A good man, a good boy. For our time, which seems to have fallen a helpless prey to evil and cynicism, how welcome were some kindly greatness, which should know what man needs and instead of offering him mocking sophisms, could give him serious advice in his necessities! A "clear word" and a benevolent, pointing out the better course, seems powerless today; world events pass all such over with brutal disregard. But let us hold fast to the anti-diabolic faith, that mankind has after all a "keen hearing," and that words born of one's own striving may do it good and not perish from its heart.

GOETHE'S CAREER AS A MAN OF LETTERS

1932

[A speech occasioned by the hundredth anniversary of Goethe's death, delivered at the Goethe Festival, Weimar, March 1932]

THE 22nd of March 1832 had come. In his armchair, a coverlet upon his knees, the green shade over his eyes, Goethe died. The dread and anxiety that often precede death by some time were over and done; he suffered no more, he had suffered himself out. And when he asked what day of the month it was, and was told the 22nd, he replied that, now spring had come, it would be all the easier to get well. After that he raised his arm and traced signs in the air. His hand kept moving outward, then downward to the left; he was actually writing, line under line, and his arm sank lower not only because there would be no more room above for the shadow-writing, but also because he was weak. At last the hand rested upon the coverlet, but still he continued writing. The dying man seemed to be repeatedly setting down the same thing in these invisible lines. He was seen to punctuate with care; here and there letters could be descried. Then his fingers turned blue, they ceased to move, and when the green shade was lifted, his eyes were already sightless.

Goethe died writing. In the last blurred dreams of his conscious life he did what he had always done, either in his own clear, neat hand, or by dictation: he wrote, noted, practised an activity which resolves hard fact into spirit, or which preserves as hard fact the manifestations of the spirit. The moment of death found him fixing in symbols of script his ultimate experiences in the life of the mind, which may have seemed to him a final perception most worthy of expression, though very likely it was no more than a fantasy born of his great weakness. Thus to the very end he sought to uplift what was in his heart and give it plastic form in the intellectual sphere. To the very end he was a man of letters, just as he had been in the beginning, when in an early epistle his joy at the strong creative impulse of his inmost soul made him break out in the cry: "Truly I was born to be a writer! When I have put my thoughts on paper well, I feel a purer happiness than at any other time." Just so he had been in the evening of his days, when, after the brief sleep of old age, he would struggle at dawn with the reverend weakness of his brain and wrest from it like music from the spheres the last notes of *Faust*, one short paragraph daily or even less; so linking the close of his life to its beginning with the lines:

Neige, neige
Du Ohnegleiche

Incline, incline
To us, Thou Incomparable.

A writer. It is a fruitless and futile mania of the critics to insist on a distinction between the poet and the man of letters – an impossible distinction, for the boundary between the two does not lie in the product of either, but rather in the personality of the artist himself; and even here is so fluid as to be indistinguishable. Poetical invasions into the field of pure letters, "literary" invasions into the field of poetry, are so frequent that to affirm a distinction between them is mere wilfulness, born of the wish to disparage the fruits of reason in favour of the unconscious, prereasonable – in short, of what is commonly regarded as the product of sheer genius. Goethe's prodigious mind, to which Emerson paid homage in his comment on the Helena episode in the second part of *Faust*, is really sufficient to put such quibbling to shame. "The wonder of the book," he says, "is its superior intelligence. In the menstruum of this man's wit, the past and the present ages, and their religions, politics and modes of thinking, are dissolved into archetypes and ideas."

A completely unintelligent poet is the dream of a certain romantic idolatry of nature. It does not exist. The very conception of poetry, uniting as it does nature and spirit, contradicts it. No unintelligent creative power could ever succeed in surviving into a time of life where nature no longer – or at least not to the degree it does in opulent youth – comes to the help of production; or, to speak with Goethe, a time of life where principle and character have to take the place of nature. When it comes to naïveté or directness, that is a different matter; for it is an indispensable condition of all creation. But it is hardly necessary to state – and

Goethe himself is a wonderful instance of the fact – that the purest naïveté and the most mighty understanding can go hand in hand.

Emerson called Shakespeare the greatest of poets, but Goethe, in whom the entire poetical fame of the German people reaches its apex, the greatest writer. When he was sixty-six years old, Goethe wrote: "Whoever has truly grasped the meaning of history will realize in a thousand examples that the materialization of the spirit or the spiritualization of matter never rests, but always breaks out, among prophets, believers, poets, orators, artists, and lovers of art. One or the other is always supreme at different periods of life; often both simultaneously." Often both simultaneously: here we have the confirmation of the essential unity of poetry and mind: this interlacing of form and content, of criticism and plasticity.

Nothing, then, could be further from my intention than to separate the young Goethe, out of the rhythm of whose blood immortal love-songs sprang, from him who in his old age spoke basic truths in orphic words; or to separate either of these from the masterly analyst and psychologist: the novelist who wrote the *Lehr-* and *Wanderjahre*, as well as the most daring and trenchant novel about adultery that the moral culture of the Occident ever produced: the *Wahlverwandtschaften.* When I speak of Goethe the man of letters, I use the term simply as the common designation for the life on earth of the poet; preferring the everyday, moderate, and objective phrase to the more high-flown one with all its implications. Goethe lived in the flesh, he was a human being, a citizen – and he was a man of letters. This was his lot; he not only accepted but loved and asserted it, admitting it with all its difficulties.

A strange destiny, a perplexing lot, there is no denying it. A lot that must often have seemed to him who bore it an abnormality and a curse. "To be a man of letters is an incurable disease," wrote Goethe in 1820, already an old man, "and so the best one can do is to come to terms with it." And he reminded himself and others that a human being is really only called upon to exercise influence in the present. "Writing," he declares in an anti-literary moment, "is an abuse of language, and reading to oneself a sorry substitute for speech. A man can have no effect on mankind save through his actual personality alone." But is this not also true in the intellectual sphere? Goethe knew and said that it was only through the character and personality of the author that a work actually had influence and became a monument of culture. "One must *be* something in order to *do* anything." That was his incisive formula for the organic mystery of creative production, so that, after all, the use of written language is no sorry substitute, but this very same effect of personality on a higher level. As for reading, he expressly refers Schiller's astonishingly rapid development to his urgent receptivity, his passion for reading. Moreover, there exists a fat volume consisting exclusively of the titles of books that Goethe took out of the Weimar Library to read and study. His productivity is closely bound up with his capacity, his positive genius for admiration, as we see from his conversation with Eckermann about the great Italian, Manzoni. This admiration is one of the main supports to his power of artistic creation. It was this quality that, when he studied the *Elegies* of Propertius, prompted the desire to produce something similar. He admits that he could not read without feeling such compulsion; and he brings home to all artists the fact that it is necessary for them to keep in constant touch with masterpieces, so that the creative spirit may be maintained at its height and prevented from relapsing ("*Zurückschwanken*"). The words express a sense of peril with which even he, the greatest, is familiar. It displays the modesty, the constant striving, learning, adaptation, imitation, even, which does not dread losing its particular identity, but proceeds on its way with blithe confidence in the powers of assimilation to which he refers in the lines:

Nur wer von Allah begünstiget ist,
Der nährt sich, erzieht sich, lebendig und reich.

Only he who is favoured of Allah
Feeds, learns and waxes, living and rich.

Goethe treats literary life with humour when he says: "The whole literary and critical carryings-on can be compared only with the battle of the slain in the legend, where disembodied heroes fight for their own pleasure amongst themselves; and then, as good as new, sit down at table again with Father Odin." But this same literary world, whose comic side he well knew, is praised by him in another place, with far happier words. He says: "It has the quality that nothing in it can be destroyed unless something new emerges from it. And more: it must be something new of the same kind. Here we have life eternal; this world is always simultaneously advanced in age, in manhood's prime, in youth, and in childhood. And in such cases, when despite the destruction the greater part of a work is preserved, this world is above all other estates. The result is that all who live therein enjoy a sort of beatitude and self-sufficiency of which outsiders have no conception."

Few authors in the midst of their work, in the pauses of their productivity, have paid tribute in warmer terms than Goethe to the very joy of the profession they practise. At thirty-three he cried: "How priceless it is when a glorious human brain can reproduce what is mirrored in it!" Even more saturated with the same feeling is the confession which the youth of twenty-four dashes off in a letter, at once a confession that creative writing is a destiny, and a presage of his own *furor et ingenium* as a writer: "What, after all, is the beginning and end of writing, this reproduction of the outer world by the inner, this seizing upon everything, combining, re-creating, kneading, remoulding after its own form and in its own way? — this, God be praised, is and remains a perennial mystery; I will not be the one to reveal it to chatterers and busybodies."

But this business of reproducing the outer world through the inner, which it re-creates after its own form and in its own way, never does, however much charm and fascination may emanate from it, quite satisfy or please the outer world. The reason is that the author's real attitude always has something of opposition in it, which is quite inseparable from his character. It is the attitude of the man of intellect towards the ponderous, stubborn, evil-minded human race, which always places the poet and writer in this particular position, moulding his character and temperament and so conditioning his destiny. "Viewed from the heights of reason," Goethe wrote, "all life looks like some malignant disease and the world like a madhouse." This is a characteristic utterance of the kind of man who writes: the expression of his smarting impatience with mankind. More of the same thing than one would suppose is to be found in Goethe's works: phrases about the "human pack" in general and his "dear Germans" in particular, typical of the specific irritability and aloofness I mean. For what are the factors that condition the life of the writer? They are twofold: perception and a feeling for form; both of these simultaneously. The strange thing is that for the poet they are one organic unity, in which the one implies, challenges, and draws out the other. This unity is, for him, mind, beauty, freedom — everything. Where it is not, there is vulgar human stupidity, expressing itself in lack of perception and imperviousness to beauty of form — nor can he tell you which of the two he finds the more irritating.

Übers Niederträchtige
Niemand sich beklage;
Denn es ist das Mächtige,
Was man Dir auch sage.

Over the base
Grieve not your heart away;
For baseness is stronger,
Whatever men may say.

I repeat: there is in his works more evidence than we should expect or wish of the torments that the base or stupid could inflict upon Goethe. More, indeed, than we are ready to admit or than should, in fairness, be quoted. For we are aware, especially in Goethe's case, of the powerful correctives, the compromises and assuagements produced in him by sheer courtesy and kindliness. In place of "kindliness," let me use a stronger and a warmer word — I mean "love." Goethe knew that mind and art are not much without love; indeed, that they are nothing without it; that mind cannot live with the world, nor the world with it, where love is not. It manifests itself as consideration, as delicacy, as kindness, as a truly Goethian reluctance to give pain. We have at hand that conversation with Eckermann where he says: "If only mind and real education could become common property, the poet would be well off; he could always be entirely truthful and never shrink from uttering the best he has. But things being as they are, he must always remain upon a certain level: he is forced to remember that his works fall into the hands of diverse readers and that he has every reason to be careful not to speak too openly and so give offence to the majority of decent men." Thus speaks the compliant spirit of love, which is ready to make allowance for the lowly if not for the evil. It is this kind-heartedness that we observe in the closing words of the *Wahlverwandtschaften:* the words of comfort at the death of the united lovers: "What a happy moment it will be when, at some future day, they awake together!" This is strangely compliant, truly courteous, and uttered with a flourish which commits him to nothing. For the disciple of Aristotle, with his faith in the persistence of sheer entelechy, could hardly have believed in the resurrection of the body. The whole is a sort of poetical licence, a polite turn of speech, conciliatory, simple, but by no means fundamentally dishonest; for as an old man Goethe finds it in him to say, with moist eyes, in all sincerity: "We shall all meet again above."

I should like here to enlarge upon a thought, a trend, an idea which is the main expression of that love which the intellect feels for life. I mean, of course, the idea of education. Goethe was a born educator. His two great life-works, *Faust* and *Wilhelm Meister*, are conclusive evidence of the fact. *Wilhelm Meister* in particular shows how the tendency to autobiography, to confession and self-portrayal, becomes impersonal, turns outward and becomes socialized, even statesmanly, and finds pedagogic expression. But a trend or vocation towards educating others does not spring from inner harmony, but rather from inner uncertainties, disharmony, difficulty — from the difficulty of knowing one's own self. The urge to educate in the poet-man-of-letters can be defined as a recognition of insecurity, an admission that he deviates from the norm, while he none the less feels his responsibility towards all mankind and himself as a representative of it. "True symbolism," says Goethe, "lies where the particular represents the general." This is precisely the symbolism of the poetic ego, which needs only to express itself fully to loosen the tongue of the multitude — not that it does this with intention, or with any sort of claim, or as if expecting it to be universally accepted, but simply as a person, with all the charm and qualities of a personality as such, who happens to have the quality of especial importance. The goodwill which is a part of the work of art is essentially important in this sense of being representative, of unwillingly and unwittingly standing for the many — and this though the personal destiny, the inner life, may be far from that of the many, far from average or normal. It may, perhaps must, be full of suffering and abnormality. Think, for instance, of the abnormalness of Rousseau's life, how perfect an example of his epoch he was; how his artistic production gave voice to its deepest yearnings, and how he moved his entire world simply by making his own confessions. He, who surely was no favoured darling of the gods, had a definite influence on that godlike youth Goethe. Goethe derives his entire idea of education from Rousseau. Ottilie's words in the *Wahlverwandtschaften* are at once Goethe- and Rousseau-like: "I do not deny it: I think it a happy destiny to educate others in the ordinary way, if we ourselves have been most strangely educated." One may define a man of letters as an educator who has himself been strangely educated; and in his own case education always goes hand in hand with his own inner battle; here we have an interweaving of the inner and the outer self, a simultaneous wrestling with the ego and with the outer world. Merely educating others, on the assumption of the perfectness of one's own ego, is sheer pedantry. But in this other form it is a wrestling with an extended ego — I mean the nation — an insistence upon self-discipline and self-control, a pedagogic identification with the outside world, which may, of course, look like aloofness and the coldly critical attitude observable in all great Germans, especially in Goethe and Nietzsche. And yet how responsible such an attitude is, compared with the bawling of loud-mouthed patriots, asserting their own importance and that of the "folk"!

Goethe's urge to educate and moralize is shown particularly in his tendency towards sententiousness: the moral and psychological *aperçu* which occurs in his prose and even, in antique stylization, in the classicistic dramas. The maxim, the moral and social comment, is in itself one of those excursions into the realm of the poetical which make impossible all didactic differentiation between the poet and the man of letters. For here we have a human task performed which really belongs to the poet in his quality of man of letters. This particular type of remark seldom gives utterance to anything new or startling. "New discoveries," says Goethe, "can and will be made, but nothing new can be thought out which has reference to man as a moral being. Everything has already been thought and said; we can at best reproduce it in another form." The task, then, consists in the definitive formulation of human knowledge. Humanity gives its experiences in charge to the poet to be expressed and so preserved forever. Perhaps nowhere does beauty as a sheerly human phenomenon become so easy to recognize or so worthy of respect as in a poetical *aperçu*. "We have," writes Goethe, "the daily struggle, inescapable and deadly serious, to seize upon the word and bring it into the directest possible contact with all that is felt, seen, thought, experienced, imagined." We have perhaps no utterance in which the passion that makes the man of letters, the compulsion to exquisite precision, is so well put; and here, too, we come close to a distinction between critical and plastic exactitude. The latter was Goethe's, as it is always that of the poetic man of letters. For him, even abstraction is plastic. There is another sort of exactitude which has to do with incisiveness and sharpness; but this is not his sort. His has rather to do with the precise essence of things — it is plastic.

It is not beauty's task to serve abstract perception; the abstract, pure thought, is not bound up with form, nor does it strive to be. The artist as poet and man of letters is connected through the senses with the idea of human dignity; he represents the necessity of clothing experience in its worthiest, purest, most enchanting form. His very being is based upon a union — which is not without its perils — between dignity and sensuality. The human office he performs gives him some stamp of the priest, which does not always sit well with the libertinage of the sensual man in him. Two forces are above the average strong in him: his sex life and his intellectual life; the two together inevitably make him a revolutionary, a disturbing, upsetting, even an undermining force, urging futurewards. "In every artist," says Goethe, "there is a strain of audacity without which no talent is conceivable." This audacity springs from his peculiar relation to the two forces I have mentioned, which, for the species we call artist, are the greatest incentives to life. They were that for Goethe. "For life is love, and spirit the life of life" ("*Denn das Leben ist die Liebe und des Lebens Leben Geist*"). Moral boldness in matters of sex, a revolutionary attitude in the realm of the senses, never ceased to express themselves in Goethe's works, up to the last and highest. But it finds expression most naturally and powerfully in his youth — most simply perhaps in his *Stella*. The words of the two women at its close: "We are thine!" addressed to the loving husband, have often enough been called too grotesque and absurd for any actual presentation, when the painful and impossible nature of the situation is clear at once. Yet we must accept this human liberating boldness for its own sake. If, however, we admit it here because it is Goethe we are speaking of, then we must take the consequences and admit the same audacity in any and every poet, however dangerous or morally subversive it may seem. It is, as a matter of fact, right and necessary. Why should poets be praised and sung, unless to the advantage of the poetic altogether, to the end that its peculiar value be suffered and understood?

The rebellious, pitiful lament for Gretchen's fate — which is an accusation too — has rung through the centuries; but it is not aimed at human institutions. That it was never his way to oppose institutions, that he preferred "to take hold only of the far end of the stick, and that gently" does not invalidate his lines:

Ihr könnt mir immer ungescheut,
Wie Blüchern, Denkmal setzen;
Von Franzen hat er euch befreit,
Ich von Philister-Netzen.

To Blücher monuments you raise,
You might as well to me;
He from the French, I from the snares
Of Philistines have set you free.

But he was a liberator, as is every poet and man of letters: he liberates by arousing the emotions and extending by analysis our knowledge of man. This he did even against his own conservative intent. The effect of the *Wahlverwandtschaften* made and still makes an impression quite contrary to its real social and ethical tendency. Goethe often had to defend himself against the reproach that his books had an immoral influence. "I let Gretchen be condemned and Ottilie starve to death," he cried; "what more do they want?" But it is of no use. The poet's austerity is not to be taken too literally, his relentlessness is not really to be believed in. After all, he does arouse sympathy for the human, he is akin to the power of love, which does not refuse its presence even to the greatest of sinners, and so has a disintegrating effect upon Philistia, even where in his conscious mind he is conservative — as was Goethe when he tried, in the *Wahlverwandtschaften*, to preserve the institution of marriage.

Byron's ribald jeer is well known: he speaks of the "old fox" who "would not leave his lair, but who from there uttered most proper sermons." Byron calls the *Wahlverwandtschaften* and *Werthers Leiden* a mockery of marriage, and says that Mephisto himself could not have written better. He maintains that the endings of both of these novels are the height of irony. But this is the sweeping statement of a man who, in a far greater degree than Goethe, found pleasure in shocking the world. In fact, this was not what Goethe cared for at all. But he expressly objected to being called a conservative, since the word might mean that he desired to uphold everything that was — even social evils. And he was furthest of all from belonging to that type of renegade of which Sainte-Beuve wrote that they had "nothing of a writer but the talent." He was remote from the hysterical snobbishness of the anti-intellectuals, from that "*trahison des clercs*" of which a knowledgeable Frenchman has written. "Let us cling to life and the future!" "The main thing, after all, is to go forward!" They are simple and straightforward words, not twisted or depraved; and they are his.

Goethe's career as a man of letters — and now I mean his outward career as a writer — displays characteristics so singular that its like is scarcely to be found in the history of intellectual life. It began with two great, even sensational successes, one in drama and one in fiction; one comfortingly national and the other morbid and cosmopolitan: *Götz* and *Werther*. The word "comforting" in this sense is not mine, but Goethe's, who himself, in *Dich-*

tung und Wahrheit, explains the nature of the success *Götz* scored. "There is a peculiarly comforting feeling," he says, "experienced by a whole nation when somebody succeeds in calling up its history in a telling and sympathetic manner. It rejoices in the ancestral virtues, and smiles at the ancestral failings, as at things of the past. A work of this kind is bound to reap sympathetic applause, and so I was able to rejoice in a considerable success." No more modest and at the same time apt description can be imagined. As for *Werther*, all the richness of the young man's gift was apparent in the deviation from the norm revealed by the effect of this early work. The extreme, nerve-shattering sensitivity of the little book, which made it the horror and detestation of the moralists, evoked a storm of applause which went beyond all bounds and fairly intoxicated the world with an ecstasy for death. It ran like a fever and frenzy over the inhabited earth, acting like a spark in a powder magazine, setting free a dangerous amount of pent-up force. We realize that an audience already existed for the book before its appearance. It was as though the public in every country had been privately and unconsciously waiting for this very work, produced by some unknown young citizen of some German city, to release for them, as though by a revolution, the suppressed yearning of their entire world. It hit the bull's-eye; it was salvation. There is a story told of a young Englishman who came to Weimar in later years, saw Goethe walk past, and fainted in the street, overcome by the sight of the author of *Werther* in the flesh. The tumultuous success must have been bewildering and burdensome to the young hero. It is dangerous to have the world take you to its bosom at so early an age. But Goethe proved equal to his exposed situation: he meditated upon the experience, observed it, and drew his conclusions. He cites a French writer: "When a good mind, by producing a meritorious work, has drawn upon itself the attention of the public, the public does all it can to prevent it from repeating the performance." "It is so true," he adds, "something good, full of talent and vigour, is produced in the peace and quiet of a man's youth; it gets him applause, but loses him his independence. People fret away his concentration, they worry and distract him, thinking they can pinch off a bit of his personality and adapt it to their own use." He makes the acquaintance of the inconsiderate and importunate world, with its criticism. His remarks on the subject are of an exhilarating pithiness unsurpassed by any other pen. "I early noticed a characteristic of readers," he says in *Dichtung und Wahrheit*, "especially comic in those among them who express themselves in print. They seem to harbour the illusion that if a man accomplishes something he is in their debt; that is, that he is always a little in arrears with delivering what they really wanted and needed – even though they had no idea, before they saw his work, that such a thing existed or was even possible." No more apt or witty words have ever been found for the relation between the artist, aware of the freshness and originality of his offering, and the critic limping along behind. And who was more justified in this taunt than a man whose every work, as it appeared, had a sensational effect on receptive minds, affecting them like a marvellous surprise, like something unimaginable, of which, until its sudden and vitalizing appearance, nobody could have dreamed?

"Every morning," sighs Émile Zola, "each of us has to swallow his toad." Goethe, too, had his toads to swallow – not only when he was young, but on into his old age. The contemptible things that people permitted themselves to say about this venerable old man whose intellect commanded the world are hardly to be believed, were it not that they can be quoted. He took it without flinching, but he heard it all. Composed and convinced of the inevitable necessity of what he was and what he did, he says in a letter written when he was forty-four: "We can do nothing but what we do. Applause is a gift of the gods." Such is the fatalism of a man who lives his life and knows he has to stand what the world makes of it. At bottom it is modesty that determines his attitude towards his work – I mean now each single work, each stage and creative phase of his life. "For who produces nothing but masterpieces?" he asks; and such an improvisation as *Clavigo* he abandons to its fate with the fling: "Everything cannot be just beyond words!" He calls the attention of the public to the fact that he in particular has the highest right and the highest reason to maintain that an artist is not to be judged by a single performance and that it is not fair to nail an artist down to his last work, as though that and no more were all of him. Even as a maturer man he still says: "In a progressive activity and productivity the point is hardly what particular work is worthy of praise or blame, is of importance; but rather what direction has been taken as a whole and what has resulted therefrom, not only for the individual artist himself, but for his contemporaries, and what may be hoped for the future." He is, then, perfectly willing to admit adverse criticism for this or that single product, all the more as he comes to regard each finished work in turn as a dead issue.

"Die Feinde, sie bedrohen dich,
Das mehrt von Tag zu Tage sich;
Wie dir doch gar nicht graut!"
Das seh' ich alles unbewegt:
Sie zerren an der Schlangenhaut,
Die jüngst ich abgelegt.
Und ist die nächste reif genung,
Ab streif' ich die sogleich
Und wandle neubelebt und jung
Im frischen Götterreich.

"Thy enemies all threaten thee,
More of them every day we see;
And yet thou dost not care!"
I see it all, and am not moved,
They only at the snake-skin tear
Which I long since had sloughed.
And when the latest one is ripe,
I'll do the same to it, and sport
Renewed and young and full of life
In realms where gods resort.

Just the same, he has his tender spots. He is artist enough to need praise and to drink in applause like a thirsty man. He was only twenty-five when critical observers found him "not manly enough against praise or blame." And people close to him later on, like Karoline von Wolzogen, commented on his susceptibility to praise and said that his weakness was actually increasing at an age when he should have overcome it. Goethe is a very great man; but he is like the rest of us. In spite of his great gift of admiration, jealousy is not unknown to him. There is a characteristic question in his *Westöstlicher Diwan:* "Does a man live when others also live?" And Boisserée, speaking of Goethe at sixty-six, says: "And then, regrettably, a weak side appeared, consisting of the mingled envy and pride of fearful old age." In a talk about the romanticists Novalis and Schlegel he shows this weak side; he is sensitive and childishly cross at Novalis's criticism of his prose, at Schlegel's ignoring the *Natürliche Tochter*, and so forth. This *Natürliche Tochter* is a particularly sore spot; Herder's crude joke: "I prefer your natural son," was enough to break the neck of old friendship. It would be hard to say whether the real grounds of the quarrel were the incorrect family relations at the Frauenplan or the problematic work of art. One lady of the circle relates that Goethe thought little enough of the *Wahlverwandtschaften* at the time when he finished the novel, but that the applause which the book aroused soon persuaded him to the belief or knowledge that he had produced an epoch-making masterpiece. "The world does all it can to make us indifferent to praise or blame; but it never quite succeeds, for when its verdict agrees somewhat with our own convictions, we gladly resign out of our resignation and return to them." His faith in the instinct of the public is on the whole greater than that in professional criticism, where the personal element always plays too great a part, and upon whose face there sits, nearly always, the mask of partisanship. "What would become of an author," he cries, "if he could not have faith in a few men of good sense here and there?" And again he adds that certainly this public, so flattered and so despised, is almost always wrong as regards the achievement as a whole. His apt and full-blooded judgment on public and critics is as good today as it ever was. He has sayings in prose and verse, pithy and consoling, for every artist. The artist is convinced that what he is offering is a self which despite all faults and flaws weighs heavier than the nullity that judges it; and never has the conviction been more powerfully or strikingly expressed than in the lines:

Ihr schmähet meine Dichtung;
Was habt ihr *denn getan?*
Wahrhaftig, die Vernichtung,
Verneinend fängt sie an;
Doch ihren scharfen Besen
Strengt sie vergebens an:
Ihr seid gar nicht gewesen!
Wo träfe sie euch an?

You scorn my compositions;
Yourself, what have you done?
Your very condemnation
With negatives is begun;
In vain you push your besom
To sweep me from your view –
But you yourself have never been –
Where could it get at you?

And the final calm, proud resignation of the man whose name is in every mouth, who is shrieked at, insulted, judged, he compresses into two lines:

Sollen Dich die Dohlen nicht umschreien
Musst nicht Knopf auf dem Kirchturm sein.

If you would not have the daws shriek round you,
Be not the very summit of the tower.

The striking feature, then, in Goethe's career, the unique feature, is that after these two extraordinary successes the figure of the young artist fades, retreats, and disappears. We now come to the decade following his entry into the service of the Duchy of Weimar – those ten years of his life which he "sacrificed to serious business." This fading from sight and memory of an author only lately so belauded is strange indeed. It afforded much gratification to the enemies of *Werther*. A literary historian of the time rejoices to know that the phenomenon called Goethe seemed a thing of the past. People had seen the meteor flash and had said "Ah!" and that was all. Moreover, Goethe never entirely regained the lost ground; possibly something like the hearty popular success of *Götz* was repeated briefly in *Hermann und Dorothea*, but never again. At heart he was not bent on popular success – "*popularisch*," he calls it – or on catering to the public. This is not to his taste. I have especially noted one little anecdote: in the year 1828 Tyrolese folk-singers came to his house in Weimar and filled the rooms with their songs and yodelling. The young people present were much pleased. Ulrike and Eckermann especially were charmed by "*Du, Du, liegst mir im Herzen.*" But the same source notes that Goethe himself was by no means so enchanted. He shrugged his shoulders and said:

Wie Kirschen und Beeren behagen,
Muss man Kinder und Sperlinge fragen.

How cherries and berries agree
Ask the birds and the children, not me.

That was not just a fit of bad humour, but a definite, aristocratic, humanistic rejection. We recall too how pained the good Eckermann was when Goethe told him his writings would never become popular. He says it despite the first part of *Faust*, whose popularity is not at all "*popularisch*" but elevated, ideal, inevitable in kind, yet not so real as that of more than one of Schiller's plays. The paradoxical truth is that Goethe's Germanness, his strong, substantial, and – if I may say so – his Lutheran Germanness, was not nearly so calculated to catch the public as the half-Gallic art of his friend. Goethe, indeed, declares that Schiller was far more of an aristocrat than himself. That may be true; but even so, the aristocracy of Goethe, based as it was most intimately and inwardly upon the personal aims and problems of his artistic temperament, was much more decisive for his personal destiny. He was ironic about popular success in a way quite foreign to the great demagogue Schiller. Goethe knew how the public is led by the nose. "The cruder minds," he says, "are taken in by variety and exaggeration, the more educated by a sort of gentility." And there is some of this in *Hermann und Dorothea*, that inspired poem of the German bourgeoisie, with which he once more captured the public ear and evoked the same feeling of national satisfaction he had awakened in *Götz*, over which, strange to say, he himself sometimes laughs a bit. In an unguarded letter to Schiller he writes that he feels like a successful conjurer who has shuffled his cards well. And in this high-spirited mood, out of ironic amusement at the idea of agreeing with the public, he suggests that it might be possible to write a play which would be acted on every stage and which every spectator must regard as excellent, while the author himself holds the contrary opinion – a fantasy that was surely understood by the speculative mind of Schiller. But, seriously speaking, the humane German, the bourgeois, in *Hermann und Dorothea*, elevated and refined, is his one avenue to popular success, his approach to the essentially German – which as an ethnic and cultural tendency he is against, consciously, deliberately, pedagogically. But his own mighty nature embraces both: the German and the Mediterranean, the European and the national. And this combination is, in essence, the same as that other combination of genius and intellectualism; of mystery and clarity; of the deep chord and the polished word; of the lyrical and the psychological. He is the greatest of them all because he so happily unites the dæmonic and the urbane, in a way that is probably unique; and it is precisely this combination that has made him the darling of mankind.

But let me repeat: his conscious desire to teach the people is directed against the purely folkish. Like Nietzsche, who here follows him entirely, he looks upon the barbaric and ethnic as an exotic phenomenon that can arouse curiosity but can never satisfy. A good illustration is his dislike of the whole atmosphere of the *Eddas*. He tells Eckermann: "There is as little for us in the gloomy old-German epic as we could get out of Serbian folk-songs or other barbaric folk-poetry. One reads it, of course, and for a while is interested, but only to cast it aside. Mankind is already too much shadowed by its own passions and dooms to need still more darkening by contemplating the gloom of primitive and barbaric times. Mankind needs clarity and cheer, it needs to turn to those epochs of art and literature in which superior human beings achieved a finished culture and then, serene within themselves, were able to pour out the blessings of that culture upon others." He seeks to disclaim the familiar characteristics that are supposed to distinguish the archaic stage of German art. "The uninspired naïveté," he says, "the rigid honesty, the anxious uprightness, and whatever other epithets one may use to characterize our German art: surely all of them are equally characteristic of any other archaic period. The old Venetians, Florentines, and so on possess them. And we Germans consider ourselves original because we do not rise above our beginnings!"

It is worth while to look at this statement not merely from a political or cultural point of view but as a matter of language and style. The school through which Nietzsche passed is clearly recognizable in his psychological terminology, and his prose derives directly from that of Goethe (and especially the young Goethe) – who, in his turn, derives from Luther. Let me give an instance. "It remains eternally true," Goethe writes in a letter of 1776, "to limit oneself rightly to want a subject, a few subjects, so rightly to love them, to hang on them, to turn them over and over, to become one with them – that makes the poet, the artist – the man." "Rightly to want, so rightly to love" – that is the real Luther cadence, a plain symptom of Goethe's intensive youthful reading of the Bible; it is Luther's style, mixed with the crudity of the "*Sturm und Drang*" period; a crudity that gets ennobled and elevated, cleansed, if I may say so, of its undergraduate elements by contact with the Lutheran and Biblical. Goethe's interest, as a man of letters, in Luther's Bible persisted into his old age; that is a matter of common knowledge. He compared his own prose with it and declared that at most he might possibly have succeeded in doing the more subtle passages better. Language undergoes at Goethe's hands a refinement due to his poetic genius, by contrast with the folkish quality of Luther's style, and that fact bulks large in our intellectual history. Yet Luther's bluntness is preserved by Goethe to a considerable degree.

Ohne Wein und ohne Weiber
Hol' der Teufel unsere Leiber!

The line is continued by Nietzsche, who is anything but blunt and bourgeois, and who is repelled by the all too robust Luther; none the less, in his *Zarathustra* Nietzsche imitates the style of the Luther Bible with great virtuosity. The position of pupil to teacher is as clear between Goethe and Nietzsche as it is between Luther and Goethe. "*Cantilena: die Fülle der Liebe und jedes leidenschaftlichen Glücks verewigend.*" Surely that is Nietzsche? No, it is Goethe. Frequent echoes of Goethe's habitual turns of phrase are heard in Nietzsche – for a small instance take the characteristic interpolation of "*wie billig*" in the sense of "no more than right and proper." On the whole: we may envisage Nietzsche's, nay, even Heine's relation to Goethe as psychologist and stylist, in the same light as that of Goethe to Luther. And we may rejoice over the progressive refinement of the German essence, or lament over it as decay – whichever we like.

But to resume: it was a long time before Goethe again stood out as a figure in the intellectual life of the period; very long before he became a commanding one. The conscious hope of his youth that "these dry stalks may yet give fruit and shade" took a long time before it was realized. Goethe needed time for everything. His native slowness, his inherently hesitating nature, has, curiously enough, been recognized only in our own epoch. His life was based on time – on duration. It was ruled by an instinct to leave himself plenty of time, it even shows traces of indolence and irresolute time-wasting. His prodigious achievement, growing like a tree, the mighty record of his life, was never again, as at first, to be greeted by the applause of the crowd. The response to his classical period, in *Tasso* and *Iphigenie*, was cool. There was no general perception of the enchanting, almost piquant contrast between the classical form and the poetic intimacy and boldness of the subject-matter. In no other poet in the world, perhaps, can we so well and rewardingly study the personal mystery of conception, the inward spur compelling production. There is a beautiful, disturbing saying of Degas, the French painter: "A picture must be painted with the same feeling as that with which a criminal commits his crime." This is the priceless and guilty secret I mean. "It went against my grain," Goethe confesses, "to talk of any of my projects. I carried them about with me in silence; as a rule nobody knew anything about them until they were finished." Of the wonderful story that finally bore the simple title *Novelle* ("Short Story"), which he carried about with him for thirty years, he relates that Schiller and Humboldt advised against it, because they simply did not grasp what he was aiming at. "Only the author," he concludes, "is in a position to know the interest that he will be able to impart to a subject, and therefore when an author has something in his mind to be written, he should ask nobody." In cases where the projected work has remained a fragment, as for instance the *Achilleis*, the inward spur never becomes manifest, and nobody could come on it. Looking at the Renaissance relief that the poem represents, one would never guess what impelled Goethe to this venture into Homeric archaism. One day he betrayed the secret. The point of the conception was this: Achilles knows that he must die, but he falls in love with Polyxena and forgets, in his native recklessness, his inexorable doom. Here we have the spur that drove Goethe to attack this somewhat remote material. As we can see, it was a psychological spur, for it was always the personal and the intimate that made Goethe produce—in contrast to Schiller's magnificently speculative manner of grappling with his matter from without. It is truly characteristic of Goethe that, for a time, he considered making a novel of the *Achilleis* and using psychological prose instead of hexameters. And he planned yet another novel. It is an everlasting loss for this form of literature that it was never written. It was to be called "The Egoist": a work of art, a dream, of which nothing has come down to us but one aphorism. Riemer tells us that the theme was to be that "pre-eminence is often mistaken for egoism." Here again we have an example of the intimate personal nature of the urge to production. That he was an egoist was a reproach that a man like Goethe was always running into and he knew only too well that it would always be raised against him. The two conceptions: mastery in some field and the human quality of egoism, had never before been united, seen as possibly inseparable, and we feel all the smarting curiosity of which we are capable when we try to imagine what a novel Goethe would have developed from this deeply personal experience.

"How the Germans did take on, to protect themselves from what I accomplished anyhow!" This we read in the *Sprüche*. But we should remember that all artists are more sensitive to blame than to praise, and that Goethe did actually receive devotion in his lifetime, even though he could not be described as "popular." *Wilhelm Meister* had as a work of fiction what was for those times a significant success, even extraordinary in its intensity. From the highest sphere of German culture, the romantic movement, there issued the dictum: the French Revolution, Fichte's *Wissenschafts-*

lehre (*Theory of Science*), and *Wilhelm Meister* – these three were the outstanding events of the epoch.

Amid hostilities from high and low, cultured and crude, covert and overt, accompanied too by the steadfast veneration of lofty minds, his authority grows with his years, by virtue of his length of life and the ever increasing weight of his personality. The hatred he had to endure was essentially political, it had to do with his coldly obstinate and repellent attitude towards the two main tendencies of his century, the nationalistic and the democratic. All the reproaches, all the embittered complaints that were levelled against his egoism, his lack of sympathy with the people, his "enormous power of obstruction," as Börne puts it, were chargeable to this account. They were the more violent the more strongly there prevailed in them the conviction of the man's greatness. But Goethe's conception of the German people, as an unpolitical, intellectual nation, centred upon human values, receiving from all and teaching all, will it not always have its profound justification, even in times of violent over-compensation and national self-correction?

In any case it redounds to the honour of the German intellect and culture that at a time when Germany was stirred to its depth by national feeling, patriotic men were found ready to defend this phenomenon, born out of its time, against the charge of anti-Germanism. It was Father Jahn, the great patriot, who in 1810 declared *motu proprio* that Goethe was the most German of writers, careless of the fact that the poet had so violently turned aside from "*teutsche Brüderschaften.*" And when, in 1813, he had all but succeeded in getting in bad odour as an expatriate, Varnhagen von Ense exclaimed: "Goethe not a German patriot? All the freedom of Germania was early assembled in his breast and there, to our never sufficiently acknowledged gain, it became the model for our education, the source and pattern of our culture."

Freiherr von Stein and Ernst Moritz Arndt thought and said the same. Despite certain shortcomings in the matter of national feeling, Goethe was a national writer and spoke to the nation as a whole; in his own later years the consciousness of this stood unshakably as the very foundation of his self-knowledge. And upon this principle he had to order the economy of his life, which in many ways was more suited to privacy than to greatness, and to temper his human kindliness with regard for higher claims. "About answering letters," he says, "one has willy-nilly to declare bankruptcy and only satisfy one or two creditors privately. My maxim is: if I see that people write for their own sakes and their own purposes, I pay no attention. But if they write on my account, and send me something stimulating or pertinent, then I have to reply. You young folk don't realize how precious time is, or you would pay more attention to it." The harshness with which he encountered young poets who approached him, to speak with Kleist, "on the very knees of their hearts," bringing him their verses, is tragicomic. I mention only one of them, and not the worst, the unfortunate Pfizer, who in the year 1830 sent Goethe his poems with a fervent letter. Goethe replied: "I have glanced through your little book. Since, however, in an epidemic of cholera one must protect oneself against weakening influences, I have laid it aside." One cannot help wondering whether Goethe was aware of the catastrophic effect of such an answer upon the recipient. But he had much to ward off, and we can understand his anger when people who declared themselves his disciples sent him rubbish to read.

Deine Werke zu höchster Belehrung
Studier' ich bei Tag und Nacht;
Drum hab' ich in tiefster Verehrung
Dir ganz was Absurdes gebracht.

Your works to my edification
I've studied by day and by night;
And so with profound admiration
This rubbish to you I indite.

Goethe knew very well that this matter of being a genius is to a great extent a question of luck: that it is important to be at the right place in the right moment. "When I was eighteen," he says, "Germany was just eighteen too—a man could do something. I am glad I began then and not today, when the demands are so much greater." But he is right when he tries to make the young understand that the world is served only by what is out of the ordinary; also that it is no service to reap in a field where others have sowed. "The whole trouble lies in the fact," he says, "that poetical culture is so widespread in Germany that no one ever writes bad verse. The youthful poets who send me their work are no worse than their forerunners; and since these are praised so highly, they cannot understand why they should not also be praised. And yet one must do nothing to encourage them, simply because there are today hundreds of such talents, and no one should promote the superfluous."

No doubt Goethe found it congenial to be ruthless with the young Germany of his time on the ground of his wholesale disapproval of its attitude to life. Indeed, he had never, at bottom, lost his kindness and the sweetness of his nature; and we have his own word for it that he loved the young, and himself when young, better than he loved himself now. But the words occur among others which make no secret of his impatience with the new stock, his deep-seated lack of confidence in it. "When one sees," he writes in 1812, "not only how the world altogether, and especially the youthful world, is given to its lusts and passions, but how all that is higher and better in it is crippled and cramped by the solemn follies of our time, so that what might lead to salvation ends in damnation instead — not to mention the frightful pressure of the time — then it is no wonder that men rage against one another and commit crimes." Again: "The incredible arrogance in which the young are growing up will show its results in a few years in the greatest follies." "The young will not listen any more. In fact, listening takes a special training," he says a year before his death, and it all comes out in the hopeless words applied not to youth alone, but to the time as a whole: "For this tragic generation there is no help!" Is that really, then, his last word? No, the sympathy of that old friend of life never quite died out, nor his optimism. "The old is gone," he says, "and the new not yet come. Yet much is stirring that may, in after years, be cause for rejoicing."

The loneliness and rigidity of his last years are not less affecting because they happen in obedience to natural law.

Ich bin euch sämtlichen zur Last,
Einigen auch sogar verhasst,

On all of you I am a weight,
To some the object of your hate,

as he well knows, even repeating it in his *Diwan:*

Sie lassen mich alle grüssen
Und hassen mich bis in Tod.

They are polite to me
And hate me mortally.

It seems that he reckoned with the possibility of being assassinated. Was that just the expression of his Tasso-like hypochondria, a confessional impulse characteristic of his early hero? Or was it inconceivable that some overwrought student, seeing in Goethe's stiff-necked authoritarianism an obstacle to the political rebirth of Germany, should take this frightful idea into his head?

– Goethe gives the mildest possible expression to his remoteness from his age and his world when he says: "Why should I not confess to myself that I belong more and more to the people *in* whom one may gladly live, but *with* whom, not so gladly?" Not that he led his life undisturbed; curiosity and admiration flowed in from all quarters of the globe. But genuine loyalty he gets only from the few devoted friends who surround him every day; otherwise he lives afar in the wide world and draws his satisfaction chiefly from abroad.

But in his own country he is rather like a famous fossil: an honour, yet something of a burden to have within its walls. Survivors who had known him earlier very likely told their children that he was a "wicked old man." Wicked because old and powerful at the same time – a great old man must always be an oppressive thing. There was a great relief at the death of Frederick the Great. And one is reminded of Napoleon's question to one of his marshals as to what the world would say of him after his death. The man launched into a solemn lament which he said humanity would raise, but Napoleon cut him short with the words: "Nonsense! They'll say 'Ouf!' "

Goethe knew that, loud or low, people would be saying "Ouf!" when he died. He felt himself a manifestation of that greatness which oppresses as much as it blesses the earth. He embodied this greatness in the mildest, most peaceable form which greatness can assume: that of a great poet. But even in such guise it is none too comfortable for contemporaries. Bewilderment and revulsion as well as love and amaze are its portion.

But I had not meant to speak here of his greatness, nor of his immortal growth above and beyond the mass of average mortals, so that schoolboys learn his love-affairs by heart, like Jove's. Our theme was something more sober and solid: the life of the man of letters, in which we moderns, who are but heat-conductors between that greatness and our own times, can recognize the most essential part of ourselves, for it tolerates the scrutiny of friendly and enlightened eyes. And I need have recourse only once more to the great world of his own works to strike the chord that resolves the theme. In a letter full of comfort to everyone who is fighting the fight of a life called to expression in the face of the world: "It is worth the trouble to live a long life and suffer the various kinds of pain that an inscrutable ruling providence mingles in our days, if only, at the last, through others, we see ourselves clearly and the problem of our striving and erring resolves itself in the clear light of the influence we have had."

[66]

GOETHE AS REPRESENTATIVE OF THE BOURGEOIS AGE

1932

[*A speech occasioned by the hundredth anniversary of Goethe's death, delivered at the Berlin Academy of Arts, March 1932*]

CHARGED with the task of speaking to you about Goethe, I take refuge in a memory, an experience, which will stimulate me and give my understanding the legitimacy which is the best and the decisive factor in all things. Let me invoke the feelings that overcame me when, years ago, I went for the first time through Goethe's family house, in the Hirschgraben in Frankfurt.

These stairs, these rooms, were familiar to me of yore: their style, their atmosphere. Here were the origins, the "sources," just as they are in the books – and in the book of my own life. And at the same time they were the first beginnings of the prodigy. I was "at home," and at the same time I was a timid and tardy guest on this native heath of genius. Home and fame here meet. The bourgeois and the patrician have become the resort of the Muses, where the foot falls with reverence, as at the cradle of a hero; here reign dignity and respectability, preserved and held sacred for the sake of the son who left them behind – how far behind! – in the lists of universality. I looked at it, I breathed it in, and the conflict between familiarity and awe was resolved in my heart in a feeling wherein humility and self-assertion are one: in smiling love.

I cannot speak of Goethe otherwise than with love: in other words, with an intimacy the offensiveness of which may be qualified by a most lively sense of the incommensurable. To speak of his heights – that in all modesty I leave to historians, commentators, and those cultivated spirits who feel equal to objective appreciation of the highest. That is something quite different from sharing in his substance; and only here, not in the intellectual, but in the human and natural to find a kind of right, a kind of possibility, of speaking a word. Only out of the same substance and being, out of a certain familiar, childish, boastful sense as of "*anch'io sono pittore*," can the likes of me speak of Goethe – and why deny a recognition, a right to confidence that goes far beyond the personal and reaches into the national! In these days, in this year, the world is honouring its great citizen; but only we Germans can do it with that familiarity of which I speak out of our very substance, which was his. The respectable, the bourgeois, as the home of the universally human; world fame as son of the bourgeoisie; this combination of the beginnings with the most surprising development is nowhere so much at home as with us. And all German substance that rose out of the bourgeois into the intellectual – all that is smilingly at home in the family house in Frankfurt.

One can apply to the figure of this great man and poet – or better put, this great man in poet's form – a variety of measures according to one's historic angle of vision. For instance – this the most modest perspective – Goethe as lord and master of a German cultural epoch, the classic epoch, to which the Germans owe their title as a race of poets and thinkers; the epoch of an idealistic individualism which did actually lay the foundations of the German conception of culture, and whose humane enchantment, in Goethe in particular, consists in a peculiar psychological combination of autobiographical self-education and self-fulfilment, with the idea of training, "upbringing," in such a way that this idea forms a bridge and transition from the world of the inner self to society and the social concept. This, then, is the narrowest view of Goethe: to see his figure as representative of the classic-humanistic period.

Another view is much broader, yet close to the first. It is that which one of his first non-German admirers, Thomas Carlyle, took of Goethe directly after the death of the great German. He pointed out that there have been men on this earth whose influence did not reach its height for fifteen hundred years, and even after two thousand years was still at work with all its individual force. Applying this dictum to Goethe's epoch, it can be said not only of centuries but of millennia; in actual fact there lies in this miracle of personality called Goethe, to whose contemporaries, even, the words "a godlike man" seemed freely applicable, myth-forming powers such as are only found in the greatest human manifestations that have walked this earth, and nobody can say to what extent his figure may yet in time expand.

But between these two possibilities of regarding him, the comparatively intimate and the vastest possible, there lies a third and intermediate one. For us who are witnessing the end of an epoch, the bourgeois, whose fate it is to search, in the midst of the great stress of the transition, for the path into new worlds, new orientations within and without, for us this third angle of vision is the most immediate and natural: to see him, that is, as representative of the five hundred years which we call the bourgeois epoch, from the fifteenth to the turn of the nineteenth century. Born just before the middle of the eighteenth, his vital energy carried him a generation into the nineteenth century, and though the roots of his culture lie in the eighteenth, he had an intellectual and spiritual grasp of much of the nineteenth, and that not only as seer and prophet, as in the epic work of his old age, *Wilhelm Meisters Wanderjahre,* where, an educator in advance of his time, he foresees the whole economic and social development of the new century; but also more immediately as poet, in the *Elective Affinities.* The novel has, to be sure, rococo costumes and rococo setting, but its intrinsic humanity belongs no longer to the eighteenth century and its sober rationalism; it leads the way into new mental states, darker and deeper worlds of thought and feeling.

A son of the eighteenth and of the nineteenth centuries. But just as much a son of the sixteenth, the age of the Reformation, brother to Luther and Erasmus both. Traits of striking resemblance and sympathy pointed out by himself connect his figure with both the other two; one might say that he combines the two characters in his own: as an outburst of Germanic quality, as an *ingenium* fed from the sources that nourished the people, he is close as a brother to Luther, and he himself did not fail to make the comparison. The play of thought is characteristic, wherein he imagines himself as a translator of the Bible and declares that he would only trust himself to improve the more subtle passages in it. He is a Protestant, says Riemer, expressing the view that he protests against the "priest-ridden, pope-ridden" world and will always do so; that is to say, according to his express declaration, to "press forwards." For everything that held back the continued development of humanity he called being priest-ridden, whether in church or state, science or art. "The Protestant suits nobody better than the German, yes, the German would be nothing without Protestantism." But there are also sayings that bring him closer to Erasmus than to Luther, the man of the people.

Franztum drängt in diesen verworrenen Tagen, wie einstmals
Luthertum ist getan, ruhige Bildung zurück.

> Driven by the spirit of France in our troublous days, as aforetime
> By the spirit of Luther oppressed, quiet culture retreats.

The couplet shows clearly how he would have borne himself if he had come into the world in the sixteenth instead of in the eighteenth century. In the name of the lofty conceptions of "*Bildung*," which united the two ideas *nature* and *culture*, he would have been for Rome and against the activity of the clerics, or at least would have taken up a position as equivocal and irresponsible as did Erasmus, of whom Luther said that repose was dearer to him than the Cross. He himself had declared with unconcealed sympathy that he belonged to those who rejoice that they are shrewd and feel no call to make others the same — for which one can hardly blame him either. There we have the intellectual aristocracy of the humanist, the sympathy with the refined, the uncommon, a trait present in Goethe's character as well, all-inclusive as that character was. All the same:

> *Freiheit erwacht in jeder Brust,*
> *Wir protestieren all mit Lust.*

> Freedom awakes in every breast,
> And heartily we all protest.

And however much Goethe on both intellectual and bourgeois grounds detested the Revolution, he took just as positive a position, fundamentally, towards its earlier stages, the German Reformation, the epoch of awakening individualism, the Italian Renaissance, the fifteenth century, and in that position he is utterly of his own soil. He is quite the great, yes, the supreme individual, the famous man of that epoch, and common traits connect him not only with Luther but with Leonardo as well, whose personal scope, his double-souled nature as artist and scientist, he reproduces. If further evidence were needed: he translated Benvenuto Cellini; in *Tasso* he transferred the Weimar court into that of Ferrara; and more convincing still, his verse epics *Hermann und Dorothea* and the *Achilleis* are characteristic of the period in structure and composition; they are antiquarian in effect, like the high-relief statuary of the time. He himself confessed that he preferred to read *Hermann und Dorothea* in a Latin version, which lifted it still more effectually out of the German-bourgeois sphere and into that of the Renaissance. But above and beyond everything else, that poem (next to Schiller's *Glocke*) is to me in its poetic forthrightness, its steadfast humanity, the purest and most conscious glorification and transfiguration of that human mean which we Germans call the bourgeois sphere.

The scion of the bourgeois Frankfurt house expressed himself in conversation about the difficulties encountered by a gift like Byron's, due to his inherited station, birth, and wealth. A certain middle position, said he, was much more conducive — we find, indeed, all our great artists and poets come from the middle class. This praise of the middle classes as the seed-ground of talent occurs in more than one place in his work. It is frequent in the *Conversations*, where he ascribes to them just that which in the case of *Hermann und Dorothea* we called steadfast humanity, "quiet culture" ("*ruhige Bildung*"), to use his own words, which in war and peace alike makes this order to endure.

Goethe relates: "In Karlsbad somebody said about me that I was a steady-going poet. He meant that with all my writing I remain a reasonable citizen. Some folk took it for praise and some for blame; I cannot judge, it is my ego, let others judge it." Well, I take it for neither praise nor blame, but simply the critical comment of an observer, who cannot have been a stupid man. It may be an almost comic speculation, not much more than a joke, to attribute to a man of such stature traits that can be called middle-class in a rough and ready everyday sense. But, after all, there is possible an ascent from the small and external into the greater and more spiritual, which shows the humanly characteristic in these little traits as well. Consider his outward bearing: the careful dressing, the feeling for elegance, the cleanliness and neatness borne witness to by his friends, in all that came from his hands. They are the simplest, most natural habits of people who have been "well brought up." His manner, as a contemporary put it, "was not characterized by eccentricities such as are often found in men of genius, his nature was courteous and simple." It lacked every trace of unction, pompousness, or affectation, there was nothing sacerdotal about it. He could laugh at himself; he was capable, when his intellectual labours permitted, of childlike and paternal good nature. His heart's real desire is to do good to men, to benefit the world. The notion of "ease and comfort" plays a special role in the benevolent advice he gives to people, and in an intellectual sense it is already genuinely bourgeois, when in *Dichtung und Wahrheit* all the pleasure we have in life is referred to the "regular occurrence" of outward things, the succession of day and night, the seasons, blossom and fruit, and whatever else recurs from time to time. Getting tired of this regular rhythm of manifestation in nature and in life is true insanity and a danger to life, it is the principal motive for suicide.

The stress he laid on good eating and drinking, his annoyance and depression when he found himself neglected in this particular, belong to this amusing side of middle-class traits; for instance the fact that Zelter regularly provided him with the celebrated Tiltower carrots probably was to the advantage of their friendship. That His Excellence set a very good table there is abundant evidence, and I always think of that little story which strangely enough brings him nearer to me than many more important bits of information: the Iceland traveller and writer Martin Friedrich Arendt was stopping in Weimar, a Bohemian scholar with an odd exterior and not too refined manners. He was invited to dine with Goethe, and entertained the master of the house and his more intimate friends with tales of his adventures and antiquarian researches, and ate and drank with a good appetite. Roast mutton and cucumber salad were served. After several helpings, Arendt could not bring himself to leave in his plate the mixture of gravy and salad dressing. He took his plate in both hands and lifted it to his mouth, but then in consternation looked up at the master of the house for permission. That well-brought-up gentleman displayed perfect understanding of his guest's voracity; with hearty good feeling he begged him to go on, and as he watched the guest gulp down the juice he allowed no embarrassing pause in the conversation. He set forth with great conviction the merits of a mixture of gravy and cucumber juice; and by so doing gave Arendt a chance to enjoy himself in peace. We may imagine him in that setting, in appearance somewhat like the portrait by George Dawe, dated 1819. I have always found it particularly lifelike, the eyes full of shrewd kindliness, profound experience, wisdom, and benevolence. Looking at the portrait we can see the whole lively scene and make its charm live before our eyes.

A good business man and economic administrator, in affairs he was always watchful, suspicious, a stout bargainer. He considered it no derogation of his character as poet to have an eye on his own advantage and to make as much as possible from his works. *Hermann und Dorothea* was first brought out at Michaelmas in calendar form, by Vieweg in Berlin, expressly because this popular form of publication ensured him a double royalty, a compensation which according to contemporary accounts was very large for the conditions of that time, although he himself professed to find nothing extraordinary about it. In forwarding a new literary enterprise — for instance, a periodical — he never, on principle, renounced his rights to a royalty. Schiller complains in a letter to his friend Körner that Goethe "gives nothing away." The occasion of the complaint was the *Mercury*, whose success was endangered by the burden of authors' fees it had to carry — which did not prevent Goethe from insisting on his share.

He had a middle-class love of order, which, as in general his serious conduct of life (*des Lebens ernstes Führen*), he got from his father. In age it degenerated, as it had in the elder, into downright pedantry and collectors' whimsies. In *Dichtung und Wahrheit* he speaks of a principle of the Imperial Councillor, carried to the point of fussiness, to follow through to the end what had once been begun. If they had begun to read a book together, it must be finished, however boring; in all things he obstinately insisted on the finishing of the once begun, even when it had turned out not only inconvenient but futile. He did not allow Wolfgang to leave unfinished sketches, but with his own hands drew marginal lines round the project to constrain the young man to finish it. The effectiveness for life of such pedagogic discipline is not to be underestimated. The ethics of production which demand a completed job were certainly a necessary corrective for Goethe's easily tired, restless, and exigent nature. In a sense beyond the practical or the social, it does not matter at bottom whether an artist possesses the bourgeois virtue of patience, industry, and endurance in order to bring to a conclusion a piece of work once undertaken. Pressures of a social — if you like, a bourgeois — sympathy and readiness must oppose the egoism of dreamy self-gratification, in order that the completed work be produced; and who knows whether the *Faust* would have reached even the formal completeness of which the inwardly infinite work was capable if the bourgeois father had not planted this pedagogic imperative of "finish, carry through," in the childish mind. "It is the fashion," Goethe tells Eckermann, "always to want to finish, to take no great pleasure in performance. But the real, geuninely great talent gets its greatest pleasure from the doing. One should never think of getting done — just as one does not travel to arrive, but just to travel." "There are excellent men," he remarks another time, "who can do nothing impromptu, nothing superficial; their nature demands that they penetrate each subject deeply in tranquillity. Such talents often make us impatient, because we seldom get from them what we want at the moment. But it is only in this way that the heights are won." He speaks objectively and refers to "excellent men"; but it is plain that he does to a considerable extent belong among them, and that precisely "in this way" he "won the heights." Caution and slowness, a maternal patience in production, are inseparable from his genius. As a creative artist he is more a slow than an impetuous and improvising nature. The wonderful work that to the end had no other title than "Story" he carried about with him for thirty years. *Egmont* took, from the first draft to completion, twelve years, *Iphigenie* eight, *Tasso* nine. Work on the first *Wilhelm Meister* went on for more than sixteen years; on *Faust* more than four decades. As a writer he lived on his youth, he was not a man of continual new inventions and plans; his production was essentially a working-up and working-out of ideas going back into his young days, which he carried about through the decades and filled with all the riches of his life so that they accumulated breadth and universality. *Faust*, in its inception, was a brilliant student-piece, a satire on faculties and professors, dealing in doggerel verse with the sweet pathetic tale of a humble little maid's seduction. But the potentiality of this germ was such, the secret devotion and labour upon it so continual, that in time it grew to an all-overshadowing tree, a classic poem of Germanism and humanity, which one opens as one does the Bible, to find therein the human, consolingly and mightily expressed. Thus *Wilhelm Meister*, in the beginning a novel about a young theatre enthusiast, with no purpose but to portray as it had not been done before the world of gypsies, bohemians, and Dionysiac dwellers in the wings, proved in the end to be only the prologue to an educational and cultural epic so far-reaching, so all-embracing, that a shrewd romantic critic could say that the French Revolution, Fichte's *Wissenschaftslehre* (*Theory of Science*), and the novel *Wilhelm Meister* were the three great events of the period. This unforced, unambitious, quiet, almost vegetative growth from modest beginnings to the universally significant is the most personally lovable thing about Goethe's mighty life-work.

There have been expressions of animosity and contempt about all great men, polemic, malicious utterances made clear-sighted by ill will, from which one can glean more about their subject than from the most lofty panegyrics. I am thinking of the letter written in 1775 by some Herr Brettschneider or other, to Friedrich Nicolai in Berlin; wherein the writer, with an antipathy not devoid of psychological penetration, expresses himself about the young author of the *Sorrows of Werther*, about his unreliable understanding and unsteady temperament. He grants him the following parts: "There is in Goethe," he says, "a certain grain of capacity, or rather he has a poetic genius which is effective when after carrying a thing around for some time and playing with it and gathering all the matter that can serve his purpose, he sits down at his table. He is not the sort for 'occasional' writing. For he can do nothing outside of his regular order. When he thinks of something, everything he comes across sticks in his mind and feelings, he tries to knead it into the bit of clay he is working on, thinking about nothing else but that." There is some contempt in the words; yet beneath the outward appearance of it a good deal of truth is expressed in the psychological and constitutional appraisal, which still holds good for Goethe's great creative style. There are only two ways, so Goethe was once heard to say, of reaching an important goal: force and persistence. The way of this great man was not force, he was a man of peace. His was the way of persistence, consistency, quiet endurance. He sometimes carried it to absurd lengths, showing signs of an alarming readiness to favour even stupidity, in the line of duty. "If it were my job," he says, "to keep emptying this sandbox here on my desk and filling it up again time after time, I would do it with the greatest care and tireless patience."

We can see in him a carefulness and caution which might seem to belong to his middle-class morality. "He who foresees," he said, "is master of the day." He sang the praises of the early morning, when our minds are at their best and also their most painstaking, "for painstaking," he says, "is the part of wisdom, even if only passive; stupidity knows no pains." And his praise of the morning hours as the true daytime of creative activity takes on solemnity when he cries:

Tag vor dem Tage, göttlich werde du verehrt!
Denn aller Fleiss, der männlich schätzenswerte,
Ist morgendlich.

Day before day, receive divinest honour;
For industry that's worth a man's esteem
Is always morning's gift.

It is this trait of carefulness, connected with the cult of time, the healing of time, the economy of time, that exhausts every minute and makes his life one of the most varied industry on record. He glorified the minute in the verses he wrote in his grandson's album, the maxim in which he answered a sentimental and pessimistic saying of Jean Paul's — for whom he had no great regard:

Ihrer sechzig hat die Stunde,
Über tausend hat der Tag,
Söhnchen, werde dir die Kunde,
Was man alles leisten mag.

Sixty of them has the hour,
Over thousand has the day,
All the work that's in their power,
Little son, then let them say.

Time was his acre. At bottom he knew no rest. He said of himself that those hours which others devoted to recreation he had to use for his manifold activities. They had to wait for the seventy-nine-year-old man at a gathering in his house where Tieck was one of the guests. At last they thought of sending a pretty young girl to his study, where the old man in his house-jacket is standing at his desk before a mass of writing. She asks him to gratify the guests by his presence, but it makes the old man angry. Do they think he is going to run when somebody is waiting for him? he growls. "What would become of all that?" – he gestures at the mass of papers. "When I'm dead, nobody will do it. Tell them that down there." The girl turns away disappointed; but he relents and calls her back. "An old man still anxious to work," he says mildly, "can't always turn round at other people's beck and call. If he did, posterity would not like it." A touching little episode, and one can pay no higher tribute to middle-class morality than by ascribing to it this trait of faithful industry. One may do so, I suppose; for the love of labour and effort, the ascetic faith in it, belong to a sociology that supplies a religious, a Protestant basis for the bourgeois attitude to life; it has been defined as the spiritual pendant to the bourgeois state. "Such *pain* hath God given to man," was the Scripture verse which Goethe probably oftenest quoted, dwelling on the diphthong with half-despairing, half-humorous emphasis.

This great man of peace, to whom even so to be human meant to struggle, declared that he was profoundly hostile to the titanic, heaven-storming idea. He had, he said, not given any matter to his method of composition; "rather I liked to depict that peaceable, plastic, ever tolerant resistance which recognizes the upper powers but would like to be equal with them." The far-seeing contemplative principle of his nature, which penetrates into all phenomena, knows how to speak out of all of them, and accepts life as a whole, excludes the tragic, which he acknowledges he fears, and of which he says that it would destroy him. There is in it a certain neutrality and reasonableness, which enthusiastic and seraphic souls, for instance Novalis, might find antipoetic. It is a bewildering paradox, that Novalis could describe *Wilhelm Meister* – not without adducing good evidence – as a *Candide* directed against poetry. The criticism which this hectic mystic levelled against Germany's greatest novel is in fact a brilliant specimen of the kind of polemic which I find more informative, in its negative way, than many panegyrics. Novalis dared to call the *Meister* "in the highest degree unpoetic," however poetic the presentation; a satire on poetry, religion, and so on; an appetizing dish put together out of straw and shavings; a godlike image, but behind it everything is farce. "Economic nature is the true surviving thing. . . . In it the romantic perishes, the poetry of nature, the miraculous. It deals with ordinary human affairs, nature and mysticism forgotten. It it a bourgeois, family tale, somewhat poetized. The first book shows how agreeable even ordinary everyday concerns can sound if they are dressed in simple, cultured, flowing language and move at a measured pace. It is the kind of pleasure afforded by an afternoon passed in the bosom of a family which, without having extraordinary people in it, and without markedly attractive surroundings, by the agreeableness and orderliness of the domestic scene, the working in common of their moderate talents and opinions, and the considered utilization of their sphere and their time, leaves behind it a memory gladly recalled." Does it not remind us of the man from Karlsbad and the "steady-going poet"? "Goethe is all the *practical poet*," Novalis says in another place. "He is in his works what the Englishman is in his wares: very simple, neat, comfortable, and durable. He has done, in German literature, what Wedgwood did in the English art world; he has, like the English, a fine and economical taste, both by nature and by intellectual acquisition . . . he is more inclined to round out something not very significant, to give it the greatest ease and polish, than to open up a new world and initiate something of which one knows beforehand that one cannot entirely complete it."

The ill nature of this description must not prevent us from recognizing its aptness and accuracy. The word "bourgeois" is not absent from it; indeed, Novalis like anybody else was open to the magic of the bourgeois atmosphere, as he himself betrays in a passage where he declares that, strange as it may seem, there is nothing truer than that it is only the treatment, the external, the rhythm of the style that leads us on to read and makes this or that work irresistible to us. "*Wilhelm Meisters Apprenticeship*," he says, "is a powerful instance of this magic of presentation, this insidious flattery of a shrewd, pleasing, simple, and yet varied style. He who possesses linguistic charm can relate the most unimportant things, and we shall find ourselves attracted and entertained; this intellectual unity is the soul of a book, by means of which it achieves its effect upon us."

The reasonable magic, the childlike-godlike charm of Goethe's way of writing, cannot be more precisely, if also not less sympathetically characterized than in these words of Novalis. For it is certainly true that every sort of high-flownness, every poetic extravagance, is foreign to this style, which even so always goes to extremes and keeps on the middle path with a quiet, masterly boldness, an unfailing sureness of touch; expert, precise, up to the somewhat official dictated prose of his old age. It has a rhythmic enchantment which forms the purest mixture of Eros and Logos and leads us gladly and unresistingly on. The word is not overstrained, elevated, solemn, or pontifical: if one belong to Goethe's school, and has founded one's taste upon it, that kind of style is intolerable to the ear, and hopelessly boring. No, with Goethe everything is in a middle key and volume, it is *said* in prose, even in the lyrical performance; but with an extraordinary verve, gaiety, and boldness even in the prose. The word is new-minted, not used up; fresh, unique, as though it had been for the first time lifted out of the womb of language with its meaning just now married to its form, with the result, indeed, that it goes beyond the usual accepted significance and something unearthly comes to birth: something "*goldig*," as they say in western Germany ("as good as gold"); sublime, civilized, and yet daring. The last word is used in the special sense given it by Goethe himself when he said that in every artist lies a "grain of daring," without which no talent is conceivable. It appears in *Faust* no less than in the *Diwan* and in the prose works; and if the daring is an artist quality, then the moderate, the temperate component may be called bourgeois.

And is his realism not bourgeois too? I mean the realism which he consciously opposed to the poetic attitude of Schiller, that being a product of the idea; very much as Tolstoy's Homeric plasticity opposed Dostoyevsky's spectral revelations. "Your foreordained line," friend Merck told Goethe in his youth (who always remembered and in a way kept it as his motto): "Your foreordained line is to give poetic form to reality. The rest of them try to realize poetry, and the result is nothing but stupidity." "The spirit of the actual," says Goethe, "is the true ideal" — an anti-ideal form of idealism directed against Schiller, which conditioned his whole attitude towards humanity and the human and persisted especially in the political sphere. He it was uttered the blunt words that the burning down of a farmstead was a real misfortune and catastrophe, but "the decline of the Fatherland" was just a phrase. That is a highly radical expression of his unpolitical and anti-political views, and — it is the same thing — of his anti-democratic ones, which had nothing to do with the aristocratic. He himself insisted that Schiller was fundamentally far more aristocratic than himself. It is from the more critically conscious of the two, from Schiller, that we hear the best and most apposite things about the differences in their intellectual positions, differences which had occupied Schiller so often and earnestly and to which we owe most of his essays. In his essay on naïve and sentimental poetry he speaks of the realist who proves himself to be a friend of man, without having such a very high opinion of men and humanity; and, on the other hand, of the idealist who thinks so highly of mankind that he is almost in danger of looking down on men; here the analysis quite clearly refers to himself and Goethe. And nothing can be more interesting psychologically than to see how Schiller, formulating the attitude of the idealist towards mankind, turns outward the French side of his own nature. It is characteristic of the French literary mind, described in few words, this peculiar interweaving of the humanitarian and revolutionary strain, of generous faith in mankind, together with the deepest, bitterest, yes, most mocking pessimism, concerning individual man. He defines abstract, political-humanitarian passion, contrasting it with the sense-born realism of individual sympathy. He is the patriot of humanity, with the humanitarian, revolutionary spirit. If we may speak of the author of *Götz* and *Faust*, of the *Sprüche in Reimen* and *Hermann und Dorothea* as fundamentally German and fundamentally unpatriotic; then, on the other hand, the creator of *Tell* and the *Jungfrau* must be characterized as an international patriot. He represents the bourgeois ideal in the political and democratic sense; Goethe, on the other hand, in the intellectual and cultural one. We know, of course, that it was this that made him regard the French Revolution as something so horribly inimical to him that in his own words it consumed him like an illness and came close to destroying his productivity; it is hard to say how far the intrinsically human, cultural, anti-political character of the German bourgeoisie was stamped upon it by Goethe and how far Goethe in his own person was by that token an expression of the German bourgeois character. Probably the thing worked both ways; for one cannot help feeling that Goethe, despite all his world citizenship, was a German bourgeois intellectual. True, he did equate humanity and combat in the words: "For I have been a human being, and that means to be a fighter," but for him there is no *human race* in the conflict over political and revolutionary ideas. The political and humanitarian factors that formed the emotional motivation of the War of Liberation were foreign to him. He found it necessary to insist that he was a fighter, and indeed a fighter for human freedom.

Ihr könnt mir immer ungescheut,
Wie Blüchern, Denkmal setzen;
Von Franzen hat er euch befreit,
Ich von Philister-Netzen.

To Blücher monuments you raise,
You might as well to me;
He from the French, I from the snares
Of Philistines have set you free.

On the other hand there is the confession of his old age: "It was never my way to attack institutions. That always seemed presumptuous to me, and it may be that I became courteous too early. Anyhow, it was not my way, and so I have never done anything but touch the very end of the stick." He was a fighter and a liberator, in things of culture and the mind, especially in the matter of sex; but not in civic or state affairs. In Gretchen's tragic fate, in the guilt of Faust, not a paragraph, not a social attitude, not an institution is attacked; here a poet merely discourses with the Eternal upon man's tragic lot. And so this same poet, as member of the Weimar Council of State, could sign the death-warrant of a young girl guilty of child-murder. He signed his name under the names of the other unpitying ministers, though the Duke himself would have shown her mercy. "*Ich auch,*" he wrote. I am not the first to find the fact almost as shattering as the whole of *Faust.*

The Frenchman Maurice Barrès thought the *Iphigenie* a civilizing work, which defended the rights of society against the arrogance of intellect. The words fit even better that other work of self-discipline or self-castigation, yes, of flagellation, the much-derided *Tasso* – derided on account of its primness and priggishness. With that frightful "*ich auch*" Goethe drove himself to use against the spirit his secular jurisdiction over the rights of society, the same spirit to whose liberation he had contributed so much as a poet by rousing the emotions, as a writer by the analytic broadening and deepening of man's knowledge. He defended society in the conservative sense, which is inherent in the conception of defence. One cannot be unpolitical, one can only be anti-political, and that means conservative, while the spirit of politics is in itself humanitarian and revolutionary. Richard Wagner meant the same thing when he declared: "The German is conservative." Only, as it happened with Wagner and his spiritual foster-children, the German and the conservative can only become political as far as nationalism; and against nationalism — even that which was as justifiable as the nationalism of 1813 — Goethe, the German citizen of the world, took up a position that was cold even to contempt. His dread of revolution was dread of becoming political; in other words, dread of the democratization of Europe, which brought nationalism in its train as an intellectual accompaniment. It is remarkable enough to see, and displays the persistence of German character traits, that this same horror of the coming "politicization" could recur with such violence in our time, in the years 1916 to 1919, and had to be fought through again with an immediacy which was surely not aware of the typical in it.

As for Goethe, I may make an observation here having to do with certain human and personal effects and symptoms of the anti-ideal constitution; an observation which, indeed, leads me so far into intimate and individual psychology that only indications are possible. There can be no doubt that ideal faith, although it must be prepared for martyrdom, makes one happier in spirit than belief in a lofty and completely ironic sense of poetic achievement without values and opinions, entirely objective, mirroring everything with the same love and the same indifference. There are in Goethe, on closer examination, as soon as the innocence of the youthful period is past, signs of profound maladjustment and ill humour, a hampering depression, which must certainly have a deep-lying uncanny connection with his mistrust of ideas, his child-of-nature indifference, with what he calls his amateurishness, his moral dilettantism. There is a peculiar coldness, ill will, *médisance*, a devil-may-care mood, an inhuman, elfish irresponsibility — which one cannot indulge enough, but must love along with him if one loves him. If one peers into this region of his character one understands that happiness and harmony are much more the affair of the children of spirit than of the children of nature. Clarity, harmony within oneself, strength of purpose, a positive believing and decided aim — in short, peace in the soul — all this is much more easily achieved by these than by the children of nature. Nature does not confer peace of mind, simplicity, single-mindedness; she is a questionable element, she is a contradiction, denial, thoroughgoing doubt. She endows with no benevolence, not being benevolent herself. She permits no decided judgments, for she is neutral. She endows her children with indifference; with a complex of problems, which have more to do with torment and ill will than with joy and mirth.

"Goethe's tendency to deny, his incredible neutrality, came out again very strikingly," writes Chancellor von Müller. And many contemporaries bear witness to the elemental, obscure, spiteful, confusing, yes, Satanic traits they discovered in him. The bitter and sarcastic moods, the sophistical spirit of contradiction, were noted a hundred times. "Out of one of his eyes," writes a travel acquaintance, "looks an angel, out of the other a devil; and his talk is all deeply ironical upon all mortal concerns." The most terrifying thing that has been said about him is: "He is tolerant without being kindly."

In the wonderfully agreeable impression his person must always have made, something else was always mixed, something uncanny, that made one nervous; it is quite clear that the feeling which his friend Schiller had, of distress and strangeness, came from this side of his character. "It is too bad," Schiller writes in 1803, "that Goethe lets himself go, the way he does, and does not concentrate on anything. . . . For three months, and that not because he is ill, he has not been out of his house, scarcely out of his room. . . . If Goethe only had a belief in the possibility of something good, of some result from his activities, a good deal could be realized here in Weimar, there would things be done, and this unhappy stagnation would give way." "Belief in the possibility of something good"!

"It should not be thought," was another verdict, "that he has always been firm and decided in his opinions. Not at all. But just this has secured him his freedom to survey the field; thus he has always reserved to himself the broader view and kept looking at everything in this or that light." The description is pale and euphemistic by comparison with the real truth that comes out in the words of near and affectionate friends; it always amounts to the same disquieting impression made by this protean nature, more ironic and bizarre than good-natured, more negative than positive, more whimsical than really cheery, which could take any form, play with anything, conceive and make good the most fantastic contradictions. "He talked," wrote Charlotte von Schiller, "in nothing but sentences that had a contradiction in every one, one could interpret as one liked, but one had a painful feeling that the master was saying to himself that he cared not a jot for any of them." He did not care. That would be nihilism – and in serious earnest, what did he believe in? Not in humanity – I mean in the possibility of its revolutionary purification and liberation: "It will forever sway this way and that, one side will suffer and the other profit, egoism and envy will always like evil spirits ply their trade, the struggle of parties will be unending." But did he even believe in art? Was it, as good men say, sacred to him? Certain of his retorts would seem to deny it. Never shall I forget the impression it made on me when I first read the reply he made to a young man who had enthusiastically declared that he would live for art, labour and suffer for her sake. Goethe frigidly responded: "One cannot speak of suffering in art." For enthusiasts, poetic rhapsodists of all sorts, he always had a cold douche on tap. One day, to the consternation of his companion, he said that a poem was really nothing: "Every poem is a sort of kiss given to the world. But kisses do not make any children." There he breaks off and will not continue the conversation.

I cannot help connecting with this trait a phenomenon that has often been observed to the discomfort of the observer: his lifelong and unconquerable embarrassment and confusion in contact with people; which, not being able to hide its true nature, took refuge in stiffness and ceremony. In a courtier and man of the world it was particularly striking. An Englishman writes: "Although he has probably seen more high society than any other poet in Europe he seems rather embarrassed when you are first introduced to him. I should have put it down to his not feeling well, for he was somewhat indisposed when I was there, but one of his most intimate friends told me that he had never been able to overcome the feeling!" And once when Goethe's stately official bearing toward the curious visitor or enthusiast was the subject of conversation, Ottilie von Goethe declared quite positively that, incredible as it was in so representative a man, so familiar with the best social forms, Goethe behaved as he did out of sheer embarrassment, and tried to hide it behind a haughty front. She added in explanation that Goethe was in reality modest and in his heart humble. I do not doubt it. The greater, the more comprehensive the mind, the further from it is the conceit which is always a sign of limitation. On the other hand, it was Goethe who said: "*Nur die Lumpe sind bescheiden*" (only good-for-nothings are modest) and certainly he did not lack a feeling of his own greatness, his immeasurable superiority to all those who came before him. His shyness must have had a deeper root: it must have been a sign of that ironic nihilism I spoke of, that profound naturalistic inhuman lack of conviction which is characteristic of the artist, that lack of faith, of enthusiasm for the ideal, such as possessed the ailing Schiller, to whom that human fluctuation we call embarrassment was certainly foreign.

There is no doubt that all the hatred Goethe had to bear, all the reproaches and complaints about his egoism, his arrogance, his immorality and "enormous power to hamper," really refer to this coldness towards the idea, towards political enthusiasm, whether in its national and militaristic or its human and revolutionary variety. It is true too that he lived in obstinate opposition to the main trend of his culture, the democratic and national idea. In their anger and their complaints, people forgot that Goethe's indifference to the political animal did not in the least mean lack of love: neither love of men — did he not once say that the mere sight of a human being's face could cure him of melancholy, and is he not the source of those highly humanistic words: the proper study of mankind is man? — nor love of the future. For man, love, future, that is all one, it is one and the same emotional complex of sympathy and benevolence, which despite all his unpoliticalness was the essence of Goethe's being and put its mark on his conception of "life-worthy." I recall the strange impression of paradox and commanding boldness that I got when as a young man, having received from Schopenhauer the great licence to pessimism, I came for the first time, with understanding, in the "Epilogue to the Bell," on this word "life-worthy." "The life-worthy shall death make his prey" — this combination which so far as I know had not existed till then, and which Goethe invented. Life taken as the highest criterion; to be worthy of it spoken of as the loftiest nobility, which, if things were as they should be, should protect from destruction: that was confusing to my youthful notion of aristocracy, which quite definitely amounted to a sublime incapacity and lack of vocation for ordinary life; and indeed the striking combination is full of a defiantly positive attitude to life, affirmation of it above and beyond all pessimism, which in my eyes constitutes a very high and very general manifestation of bourgeois character: the bourgeois attitude towards life (*Lebensbürgerlichkeit*) means being solidly planted in life, the aristocratic bearing of nature's privileged ones, who, not very far distant from the brutish, look with contempt on "yearning hunger after the unattainable." I said this sort of aristocracy is not far from the brutish; for there is something brutish about the reliance on the life-force: it speaks in those words of the eighty-one-year-old Goethe about those weaklings who make their exit early from life — for instance poor Sömmering, who had just died at seventy-five. "On the other hand I'm proud of my friend Bentham, that highly radical ass; he stands up well, and is a few weeks older than I am." And here that priceless story is in place about the fun Goethe made of that same Bentham, the English economist and utilitarian, and of his radicalism. Somebody answered him that His Excellence himself, if he had been born in England, could scarcely have avoided radicalism and the role of a fighter against abuse.

"What do you take me for? You think I would be spying out abuses and tacking names onto them? I, who if I had been born in England would have been living on abuses? If I had been born in England I should have been a duke, or better still a bishop with revenues of thirty thousand pounds sterling."

"Very fine. But suppose Your Excellence had not drawn the big prize in the lottery; suppose you had drawn a blank?"

To which Goethe: "Not everybody, my dear friend, *is made for the big prize*. Do you think I should have played such a foolish trick (*sottise*) as to draw a blank?" That is the bourgeois sense of security, the psychology of the aristocratic consciousness, that one can never, under any circumstances, be other than privileged and favoured.

It may seem surprising that this favourite child of the powers above denied and rejected the idea advanced by the envious and the adoring of his happy lot in life. "Be quiet," he says, "I never was happy; if you added up all the good hours of my life they would not come to a single month all together. It was just everlastingly rolling the stone, which had to be lifted up again and again." And then come the touching, the all-explanatory words: "The claims on my activity, from without and within, were too many." Well, so not happy, and that on account of the very greatness of the tasks that his genius set for him, the completion of which the importunate world was always trying to prevent. And what then is the relation between this pride in vitality and health and illness? Genius, we well know, cannot be normal in the narrow-minded simple bourgeois acceptation of the word, nor is the man most blest by nature ever, in the philistine sense, natural, healthy, or regular. In the physical constitution there is much that is frail, irritable, prone to crisis and illness; and in the psyche much that puts off the average man: it affects one as uncanny; it is close to the psychopathic. Goethe himself is well aware of it; he makes a maxim of it to Eckermann: "The extraordinary performance of such men," he says – and he means "such men as myself" – "presupposes a very sensitive organization, in order that they may be capable of unusual perceptions and can hear the heavenly voices. Such an organization, then, is in conflict with the world, and its elements are easily disturbed and injured; he who does not combine a high degree of toughness with his great sensitivity is easily subject to a progressive tendency to illness." The peculiar vitality of the genius is once and for all defined in the words he applied to his friend Schiller: "With suffering, with death was he familiar"; but he himself, who stood on a much more friendly footing with life, was he not, after all, the same? The hæmorrhages he had in his youth indicate a tubercular tendency, and a hundred signs of extreme irritability, easy fatigue, profound moodiness, as well as several attacks of severe illness even up to an advanced age, suggest an instability, a threat constantly present, and they also prove what strength and will to survive, one might say what ethical vitality, held this nature as it were to its task and let it carry through a whole canonical human life to the unusual age of eighty-two years. And that was no joke, physically or mentally.

Wohl kamst du durch, so ging es allenfalls.
Mach's einer nach und breche nicht den Hals!

Well, you made shift, you managed to arrive –
Just let them do as much, and still survive!

"A man who wrote *Werther* at twenty," he cries, "how is he going to live at seventy?" And the bourgeois view becomes very much a question when in the late poem to the hero of his youthful novel he thus apostrophizes that much wept-over shade:

Zum Bleiben ich, zum Scheiden du erkoren,
Gingst du voran und hast nicht viel verloren.

It was your lot to go and mine to stay:
You went before and missed not much, I'd say.

He was afraid of this little book of disturbing sensitivity which once on a time had made the world mad with death-drunkenness; he confessed in his old age that he had read it only once since its first appearance and had taken care not to do it again. "Those are nothing but fireworks," he said, "they give me an uncanny feeling, I am afraid of slipping back into the pathological state that produced them!" The mature man insisted in theory that art should present all that was a healthy affirmation of life; and what he called the contemporary "lazaretto poetry" was a misapplication of art. He opposed to it the Tyrtæan, the poetry that not only sings battle songs but also arms man with courage to fight the battle of life. But did Goethe always practise what he preached? Not in *Werther;* and for a poet of harmony and Tyrtæan incitement to life it is an odd choice of subject, when he dresses up his most personal feelings in the life story of an actual colleague, which leads into the madhouse and the cloister. The bourgeois view would stand on strict morality and demand an unconditional affirmation of the moral view, reason and morality being the twin pillars of life. But Goethe, most unbourgeois-wise, defends what people call "the morbid and overstrained"; he insists that the overstrained and morbid are states of nature and that the "so-called healthiness" can only consist in a balance of oposed forces. He contradicts his "famulus" when the latter says there is no decisive gain for pure culture to be reaped from reading Byron: his morality is too questionable for that. "Why not indeed?" answers Goethe. "Byron's dash, his boldness and grandiosity, is not all that worth something? We must take care not always to seek the cultured in the explicitly pure and moral. Everything great is culturally formative, as soon as we are aware of it." I call that an utterance above and beyond the bourgeois. An even more extreme view, the most extreme in this field that ever came out of his mouth, was: "The French are pedants; that is to say, they cannot get away from the form." Let us make no mistake: in this strange contempt for form, expressed in the word "pedantic," there lies the acceptance of the chaotic, the sympathy with death, with which precisely the French have often reproached the Germans. Georges Clemenceau, whose political enmity against the Germans was intellectual as well, and who possessed all the psychological subtlety of his race, once said: "The Germans love death: read their literature: at bottom it is only death they love." Goethe's words quoted above are very German words; at the same time they go far beyond the bourgeois point of view.

Apparently, after all, a man need only be an artist, a creator, as Goethe was, in order to hold life sacred and be loyal to it. His open-armed welcome to life is best shown in the fact that despite all rejection of the political, all the conservatism bound up with the rejection, there is no smallest trace of reactionary spirit. The variety, the endless dilettantism of his nature made it possible for him to be called as witness or even protagonist of the most divergent points of view. But one thing above all is not possible: to invoke him in the interest of intellectual reaction. He was no "*Fürst der Mitternacht*," no Metternich, doing violence to life out of bleak fear of the future. He loved order, but he explicitly put understanding in its service; understanding and light. He scorned stupidity and obscurity. "The human mob," he said in *Wilhelm Meister*, "fears nothing more than reason; it ought to fear stupidity if it understood what is really frightful; but the other is too uncomfortable, it must be brushed aside; whereas stupidity is merely fatal, and that will keep." We do not know, or we like to forget, that in 1794 when Freiherr von Gagen issued a summons wherein he challenged the German people, and in particular Goethe, to put their pens at the service of the "good" – in other words, the conservative – cause, actually that of a new Confederation of German Princes, with the aim of rescuing the country from anarchy, the so-called henchman, after thanking him courteously for the confidence reposed in him, said that he did not consider it feasible to unite princes and writers in a common task. Against reaction in art and darkening of counsel he stood his ground at all times, even to warding off a certain antiquarian fashion in painting. He is a fighter for freedom and strength in art, he admires Molière because he chastised mankind by drawing them as they really are; he would have liked to forbid young girls the theatre, in order to give the stage the freedom of picturing life regardless, for men and women who know life as it is.

Despite all the ill will he remained exposed to, the pettiness of which it is hard to imagine today, he spoke to the whole nation and was a national writer. In his latter years this formed of course the basis of his self-consciousness, a self-consciousness not natural to any human soul, but in which a poet must in time find himself, as in his fate. The bourgeois lad of once upon a time, who sat with his painting tools or his books at the table in the attic room in the Hirschgraben at Frankfurt, as a sixty-year-old man made the humanly touching confession that he "had, with difficulty, learned greatness": greatness to seek satisfaction for his influence in wide national spheres and epochs. He learned more than that. His appeal to the great world, explainable in an author whose literary career began with such far-reaching success as the *Werther*, grew stronger with the years. I mean the insight that poetry is a common property of mankind and that, particularly for us Germans, it behooves us to look outside the narrow circle of our own surroundings, in order not to fall, individually and nationally, into a pedantic self-conceit. "Instead of limiting oneself to oneself," is his doctrine, "the German must take the world into himself in order to influence the world. Thus I like to look round," he adds, "among strange nations, and advise everybody to do the same. National literature does not mean much now, the epoch of world literature is at hand, and everyone must now work to hasten it." He creates this term "world literature," he sets it up half as established fact, half as a challenge to the times. World literature: of course to him that is not the mere sum and content of all account of human intellectual life, set down in writing; rather it is that highest and choicest bloom of the written word, to which his own production long since belonged, and which, wherever it springs, is, by virtue of its own towering, universal rank, everywhere recognized and acknowledged as a possession of humanity, and along with it the realization that the time is come when only the universally valid is on the order of the day or comes into consideration; the day of the purely domestic product being now over. Truly everything that he himself wrote had long been known and accepted by common consent as world literature: by no means only what was influenced by the Mediterranean tradition and classic models minted by a humanistic spirit, but also what was exemplarily Nordic and German in his work, like the first part of *Faust* and the "novel of education" (*Bildungsroman*) *Wilhelm Meister*. The elderly man had the satisfaction of receiving from the Scottish Carlyle the English translation of this book, with a letter of ardent, childlike affection and devotion. He might turn the pages of a French edition of *Faust*, illustrated with drawings by Eugène Delacroix. On the just published Helena episode in the second part of *Faust* he read complimentary critiques in the reviews of Edinburgh, Paris, and Moscow; and it is perhaps in place here to speak of satisfaction, for this world-echo of his work must have repaid him for many a malicious or contemptuous slur at home. "No nation," he says, "has good judgment about what is done and written within her borders. The same may be said of all epochs." A witty Frenchman has comprehended the two pronouncements in one: *L'étranger, cette posterité contemporaine.*

Doubtless there was much anticipation in Goethe's statement about world-literature. The developments in the ten decades after his death, the vast improvement in communications, the wings thus given to commerce, the convergence of all Europe, yes, of the world, rather hastened than retarded by the Great War; all this was needed before the epoch could become real and actual, which Goethe felt was on the way – to the extent, indeed, that today the danger of confusing the world-possible and world-valid with what is only world-current (a less important international possession) lies very near, and is exploited by provincial spirits in order to discredit generally recognized achievements. Deliberately, in the same breath, they refer to genuine world-renown and its cheap imitation, thinking in this way to discredit the greater-than-national at the same time with the less-than-national and the between-national. This possibility was not present in Goethe's time, or was present in a much less degree. It was never possible to ascribe the foreign honours paid him to the un-German flatness of the plane he lived on.

What is interesting here is the bourgeois, supra-bourgeois character of Goethe's prepossession for the great and the world-wide, a characteristic that finds striking expression in certain names that he gives to this tendency to expansion. He speaks, that is, of a "free trade of conceptions and feelings"; which is a characteristic transference of liberal economic principles to the intellectual life. But not only in the spatial does this freedom and expansion hold good, but also in time: he has sought in "wide circles of epochs," says Goethe, satisfaction for his influence. He is a citizen of not only one century; I have sought above to indicate his native and kindred relation to earlier centuries. Here I am interested to assert his appeal to the present and future, the bearing his nature has upon us and beyond us; and symbolic for this influence is to me the meetings of the great friend of life with Arthur Schopenhauer. He who as a boy had seen Mozart as a grey old man, on entering an evening company turns neither right nor left but goes straight up to the young philosopher, whose doctor's thesis on the *Fourfold Root of the Principle of Sufficient Reason* he had just read, and congratulates him on the extraordinary performance. He takes the hand of the man who was working on *The World as Will and Idea*, the classic statement of European pessimism of the second half of the highly bourgeois nineteenth century, which so decisively influenced on the one hand Wagner, on the other Nietzsche. The scene has been preserved; it represents a wonderful moment in intellectual history. Goethe, Schopenhauer, Wagner, Nietzsche – there it all is, the firmament of our youth with its fixed stars; Germany and Europe at once, our origins, of which we are proud, for all origins, all sense of an intellectual origin, are aristocratic: "The artist must have an origin, must know whence he comes," Goethe says. It is the great world-home, whose children we are, the bourgeois intellectual world, which precisely as a world of the mind is an extra-bourgeois one and leads, through Nietzsche, Goethe's pupil, into new, post-bourgeois, still nameless future worlds. The bourgeois has a certain intellectual transcendence, in which it abrogates the position and gets transformed. Goethe's saying: "Whence comes our finest culture here, unless it from the burgher were," has a larger meaning than that curious word *Bildung* (culture), which sounds so old-fashioned today. I have asked and I ask again: Where did they come from, the great deeds of liberation of the great revolutionary spirits, "*und wenn sie nicht vom Bürger wären*"? The will and the vocation to the abrogation of the bourgeois, the highly dangerous adventure of the aspiring thought, that is the passport which intellect itself has offered to the man of the bourgeoisie. That son and grandson of Protestant clergymen, in whom the romanticism of the nineteenth century achieved the conquest of itself, whose martyr death on the cross of thought broke a path to unspeakably new beginnings, Friedrich Nietzsche: where did his roots lie, if not in the soil of bourgeois humanity? And just such a self-conquest of the bourgeois by the power of intellect we find in the novel of Goethe's old age, the *Wanderjahre*.

The subject-matter of this book is self-conquest of individual humanity and a bold, prophetic rejection of it in favour of human and cultural, educational fundamentals and principles, which belong only to our day and only today have taken a grip on the general consciousness. The work is shot through with flashes of thought which point us far away from all that one thinks of as bourgeois conceptions, far from the classical and bourgeois notions of culture, to shape and impress which Goethe stood in the first rank of workers. The ideal of individual human universality is dropped, and an age of one-sidedness proclaimed. The inadequacy of the individual is there that reigns today: only collectively do men consummate humanity; the single becomes function, the conception of the commonwealth comes out; and the jesuitical militaristic spirit of the Pedagogic Province, lighted as it is by gleams of art, leaves scarcely a survival of the individualistic and "liberal" bourgeois ideal.

This bold and dreamlike gaze of the old Goethe into a new post-bourgeois world was just as remarkable, just as magnificent, as the growing sympathy of the old man for utopian, world-technical matters, his enthusiasm for projects like the Panama Canal, about which he wrote with urgency and detail as though it were more important to him than all the poetry in the world — and so it was in fact. His pleasure in all technical progress and civilization and communications is not surprising in a poet who wrote the second part of *Faust;* wherein the protagonist of the drama experiences his greatest moment in the realization of a utilitarian dream, the draining of a swamp. What an affront to the one-sided philosophical and æsthetic trend of the period! And the old Goethe, amazing, inexhaustible, expends himself explaining the possibility of connecting the Gulf of Mexico with the Pacific Ocean, and the incalculable benefits such a work would confer upon civilized and uncivilized mankind. He counselled the United States to take the project in hand and romanced about the flourishing commercial cities that would of course gradually rise on the Pacific coast where nature had prepared the way with spacious harbours. He could scarcely wait for all this, this and the linking of the Danube with the Rhine, which would truly be an undertaking more vast than any hope; and a third thing, great too: the Suez Canal for the English. "To see all this," he cries, "it would be worth while to hold out another fifty years or so." He let his eyes rove all over the world, they did not stop at his own country; his joy in the future was comprehensive, it needed the space of the whole world and the heightening of life; the joys and sorrows of strange peoples came as close to him as his own. It was the benevolent imperialism of a very lofty mind, which understood freedom in the sense of greatness and whose prophesyings about "world-literature" came from the same source.

The bourgeois attitude passes over into that of a world community by virtue of technical and national utopianism; it passes over — if one takes the word broadly enough and is willing to understand it undogmatically — into the communistic. It is sober, this enthusiasm. But what is needed today is to convert to practical activities a world that is perishing of a suffocating soulfulness. Who was it said that the Germans should be forbidden to use the word "temperament" for a period of fifty years? The burgher is lost, and loses touch with the new or coming world, if he cannot bring himself to part from the life-destroying, easy-going ideologies that still condition him, and address himself stoutly to the future. The new, the social world, the organized, planned, and unified world in which humanity will be freed from such human, unnecessary burdens, injurious to self-respect and common sense; this world will come, and it will be the work of that great practical sense to which all effective minds, all those opposed to a decadent and provincial soulfulness, must today subscribe. It will come, for an outward and national order of things, adequate to the stage which human intelligence has now reached, must be created, or — in the worst case — be established by violent revolution, in order that the things of the soul may once more be justified. The great sons of the bourgeoisie, who grew out of that stage into the intellectual and super-bourgeois, are witnesses that boundless possibilities lie in the bourgeois stage, possibilities of unlimited self-release and self-conquest. The times challenge the middle class to remind itself of its native potentialities and to become equal to them both mentally and morally. The right to power is dependent upon the historic task to which one feels and may feel oneself called. If we deny it or are not adequate to it, we shall disappear; we shall simply yield the stage in favour of a human type free from the assumptions, the commitments, and the outworn prejudice which – one sometimes fears – may prevent the bourgeoisie of Europe from being adequate to the task of guiding state and economy into a new world. No doubt, the credit which the bourgeois republic still enjoys today, this possible but now short-term credit, rests in the last analysis upon the belief that democracy, whatever her power-hungry foes pretend to be able to do, *can do it too:* namely, lead forward into the new and the future. Not merely by solemn celebration of their own renown can the bourgeoisie show itself worthy of its great sons. The greatest of them, Goethe, issues the challenge:

Entzieht euch dem verstorbenen Zeug,
Lebend'ges lasst uns lieben!

Things that are dead let us shake off,
And love the living ones!

GOETHE AND TOLSTOY

1922

At the beginning of our century a man was still living in Weimar, Julius Stötzer by name and schoolmaster by calling, who, as a sixteen-year-old student, had dwelt under the same roof with Dr. Eckermann and only a few steps away from Goethe's door. Young Stötzer and a schoolmate and fellow lodger would now and again, with beating hearts, catch gleams and glimpses of the hallowed form as the old man sat by his window. But the lads were possessed by a desire to see him for once close at hand and get a good look at him. They applied to his famulus, their house-mate, and implored him by some means or other to procure them this boon. Eckermann was a kindly soul. One summer day he let the boys in by the back gate to the garden of the illustrious house; and there, hugely confused, they stood and waited for Goethe; who, to their consternation, did actually appear. He was strolling about the garden in a light-coloured house-coat – very probably the famous flannel dressing-gown we wot of – and catching sight of the lads went up to them. There he stood, wafting odours of eau-de-Cologne, with his hands, of course, on his back, and his abdomen to the fore; with that air of a city father beneath which, so we are told, he hid his self-consciousness – and asked the youths their names and what they wanted. Probably all in one breath; which indeed, if it thus happened, so added to the austere effect that they could scarcely get out an answer. However, they stammered something; whereupon the old man bade them be diligent in their tasks – which they were free to interpret as meaning that they would do better to be at them and not stand gaping here – and went his way.

So much for that – it happened in the year 1828. – Thirty-three years afterwards, one day about one o'clock Stötzer – now an experienced and devoted master in the secondary schools – was about to take the second class of the session when a seminary pupil stuck his head in at the door and announced that a stranger wanted to see Herr Stötzer. And without more ado the stranger entered at his heels: a man considerably younger than the schoolmaster, with a thinnish beard, prominent cheek-bones, and small grey eyes, with furrows between the heavy brows. He neglected to introduce or otherwise account for himself; but simply and straightway asked what lessons there were this afternoon, and on hearing that there was first history and then language, professed himself well pleased. He said that he had been visiting schools in southern Germany, France, and England; and sought an acquaintance with those of northern Germany as well. He spoke like a German. You would take him for a schoolmaster, from the comments he made, his well-informed, intelligent questions, and the way he kept putting things down in his notebook. He stopped for the whole of the lesson-hour. The children wrote a theme, an exercise on some subject in their copy-books; and the stranger said he was greatly interested in these compositions – might he take them away with him? "Dear me," Stötzer thought, "that *is* naïve." Who was to reimburse the children for their copy-books? After all, Weimar was a poor city. . . . He said as much, in politer phrases. But the stranger replied that that might be managed, and went out. Stötzer sent a message to the director, telling him of the unusual occurrence. And the adjective he used was the correct one – though it was only much later that he understood how correct it had been. For at the moment and on the spot it could not mean much to him, when the stranger came back, with a bundle of writing-paper under his arm, and gave his name to Stötzer and the director: Count Tolstoy, from Russia. But Schoolmaster Stötzer lived to a ripe old age, and consequently had plenty of time to hear about the gentleman whose acquaintance he had thus made.

This man, then, who lived in Weimar from 1812 to 1905, and whose life was otherwise no doubt uneventful enough, might boast of having enjoyed one extraordinary privilege: the personal acquaintance of both Goethe and Tolstoy, the two great men whose names form the subject of this essay. Yes, Tolstoy was in Weimar! When he was thirty-three years old – for he was born in the year that saw young Stötzer's interview with Goethe – Count Leo Nikolayevich came to Germany from Brussels (where he had in the first place met Proudhon and been convinced by him that *la propriété* is *le vol*, and in the second place had written the story called *Polikuchka*) and visited the city of Goethe. As a distinguished stranger and guest of the Russian Embassy he was admitted to the house on the Frauenplan, which was not then open to the public. We are told, however, that he was more interested in the

Fröbel kindergarten, conducted by one of Fröbel's own pupils, and studied its pedagogic system with the greatest zeal and curiosity.

You see, of course, why I have told you this little tale. It was in hope to render more palatable the "and" at the top of the page, which must have made you lift your eyebrows at first sight. Goethe and Tolstoy. What sort of arbitrary and unseemly combination is that? Nietzsche once reproached us Germans with a peculiar clumsiness in the use of the word "and." We said "Schopenhauer and Hartmann," he sneered; we said "Goethe and Schiller" too — he was very much afraid we even said "Schiller and Goethe"! Setting Schopenhauer and Hartmann aside; as far as Goethe and Schiller are concerned, Nietzsche's highly subjective dislike of moralists and theatre people should not have led him so far astray as to deny a relationship which is not less valid because of the inherent and typical contrast it displays. Its best spokesman, indeed, was its supposedly affronted half! It was hasty of Nietzsche, it was unjustifiably autocratic, thus to mock, and in his mockery to invoke, or assume, an order of merit which is, and must remain, highly controversial, the most controversial thing in the world. It is not on the whole the German way to be hasty in deciding precisely this question of all questions. We instinctively avoid putting ourselves on record, on one side or the other. We prefer a freehanded policy, and so, personally, do I; and I mean to stick to this policy, to support and glorify it, in all that follows. Precisely this policy, and no other, is the meaning of the conjunction when we say "Goethe *and* Schiller": where it converts the combination to an antithesis, and combines with the deliberate intention of contrast. No one who has ever come into contact with the sphere of German thought represented by that classic essay which comprehends all the others and makes them superfluous — I mean Schiller's *Naive und Sentimentalische Dichtung* — can fail to find this "and" deeply antithetic. Another precisely similar instance is the conjunction "Tolstoy *and* Dostoyevsky." On the other hand, if we deny the "and" its right to point a contrast, and confine its function to asserting essential affinity, essential similarity — what then? Would there not at once take place in our fancy a change of partners? On profound intellectual, nay, rather, on profoundly natural grounds, would not Schiller and Dostoyevsky move together, and on the other side — Goethe and Tolstoy?

You will be feeling far from satisfied. Obviously. You will say: there is something besides quality, there is position, there is rank. All honour, you will say, to antithesis, but things which differ so much in order of greatness really cannot be placed alongside like that. Granted that the one was a European humanist and thorough-paced pagan, while the other was an anarchist, and a primitive Oriental Christian to boot. But the German world-poet, whose name one names with the highest, with Dante, with Shakespeare, and the realistic novelist who in our own era and not so long ago ended his enigmatic life, and that truly in a most enigmatic manner; to speak of these two in the same breath – it simply will not do, it is an offence against the aristocratic instinct, it is in bad taste.

We put on one side the paganism of the one, the Christianity of the other. Let us leave them there – we may find time to come back to them later on. But as for this aristocratic instinct, if you like to call it that; let me say roundly that so far from offending against it with my parallel, I do it explicit honour. Are you certain you have no delusions – are you sure your perspective is not distorted in this matter of rank and relative greatness? Turgenyev, in his last letter to Tolstoy, written on his death-bed in Paris, in which he conjured his friend to return to literature and stop tormenting himself with theology, Turgenyev was the first to give Tolstoy the title of "the great writer of Russia," which he has had ever since, and which seems to mean that he holds in the eyes of his countrymen the same rank that the author of *Faust* and *Wilhelm Meister* does in ours. Tolstoy himself, as we were saying, was Christian through and through. Yet his humility was not so exaggerated as to prevent him from setting his name boldly beside the greatest, yes, beside the legendary great. He said of *War and Peace:* "Modesty aside, it is something like the Iliad." He was heard to say the same of his earliest work, *Childhood*, *Boyhood*, *Youth*. Was that megalomania? To me, frankly, it sounds like plain and simple fact. "*Nur die Lumpe*," says Goethe, "*sind bescheiden*." A heathen saying. But Tolstoy subscribed to it. He saw himself always of heroic grandeur; and as early as at thirty-seven, writing in his diary, he ranked his own works, the finished and the still to write, with the great literature of the world.

In the judgment, then, of those competent to render it, the great writer of Russia; by his own estimate, the Homer of his time – but that is not all. After Tolstoy's death Maxim Gorky published a little book of reminiscences, the best book, in my humble opinion, that he has written. It closes with the words: "And I, who do not believe in God, looked at him timidly, for some dark reason looked at him and thought: The man is godlike." Godlike. Extraordinary. Nobody ever said or thought that of Dostoyevsky, nobody ever could have thought or said it. He has been called a saint; and one might in all sincerity apply the word to Schiller, at least in the Christian sense which it must always connote, if without the specifically Byzantine flavour. But Goethe and Tolstoy, these two, have been found godlike. The epithet "Olympian" is a commonplace. It was not, however, only as a world-renowned old man of commanding intellect that Goethe had it applied to him; it was while he was still young, still the youth, of whose godlike, compelling gaze Wieland sang, that he had the attribute conferred upon him, a thousand times, by his own contemporaries. Riemer relates that at sixty the old man took occasion to make rather acridly merry over it. "The deuce take godlike," he cried. "What good does it do me to have people say: 'That is a godlike man,' when I go by? They behave just as they like, they impose on me just the same. People only call a man godlike when he lets them have their own way!" — As for Tolstoy, you could not say he was Olympian; he was not a humanistic god, of course. He was, Gorky says, more like some sort of Russian god, sitting on a maple throne under a golden lime tree; pagan, then, with a difference, compared with the Zeus of Weimar, but pagan none the less, because gods *are* pagan. Why? Because they are of the same essence as nature. One does not need to be a follower of Spinoza — as Goethe was, and had his own good reasons for it — to feel God and Nature as one, and the nobility that nature confers as godlike. "His superhumanly developed individuality is a monstrous phenomenon, almost forbidding, he has something in him of the fabled Sviatogor, whom the earth cannot hold." Thus Gorky, on Tolstoy. And I cite it in this matter of relative greatness. Gorky, for instance, goes on to say: "There is something about him which always makes me want to shout: 'Behold what a marvellous man lives upon this earth!' For he is, so to speak, in general and beyond everything else, a human human being, a man. That sounds like something we have heard before. It reminds us of — whom?

No, the question of rank, the aristocratic problem, is no problem at all, within the grouping I have chosen. It becomes one only when we change partners: when we take saintly humanity and couple it, by means of the antithetic conjunction, with the godlike; when we say "Goethe and Schiller," "Tolstoy and Dostoyevsky." Only then, I think, do we pose the question of aristocracy, the problem in ethics and æsthetics: Which is greater? Which is more aristocratic? I shall not answer either of these. I will let the reader come to his individual conclusion in this matter of value, according to his own taste. Or, less glibly put, according to the conception he has of humanity, which — I must add, *sotto voce* —

will have to be one-sided and incomplete to admit of his coming to any decision at all.

Is it not strangely moving to hear that one man had known them both, the creator of *Faust* and the "great writer of Russia"? For certainly they belonged to different centuries. Tolstoy's life covered the greater part of the nineteenth. He is absolutely its son. As an artist he exhibits all of its characteristics, and, indeed, those of its second half. As for Goethe, the eighteenth century brought him forth, and essential traits of his character and training belong to it — a statement it would be very easy to substantiate. Yet on the other hand one might say that just as much of the eighteenth, Goethe's century, survived in Tolstoy as there had already come to birth of Tolstoy's, of the nineteenth, in Goethe. Tolstoy's rationalizing Christianity has more in common with the deism of the eighteenth century than it has with Dostoyevsky's violent and mystical religiosity, which was entirely of the nineteenth. His system of practical religion — the essence of which was a destructive intellectual force that undermined all regulations, human and divine — had more affinity with the social criticism of the eighteenth century than with Dostoyevsky's moralization, although those were, on the one hand, far more profound, on the other far more religious. And Tolstoy's *penchant* for utopias, his hatred of civilization, his passion for rusticity, for a bucolic placidity of the soul — an aristocratic passion, the passion of a nobleman — to all that, the eighteenth century, and indeed the French eighteenth century, can lay claim. And, on the other hand, Goethe. What most astonishes us in that masterpiece of his old age, the sociological novel *Wilhelm Meisters Wanderjahre*, is the intuition, the keenness and breadth of vision — they seem positively occult, but are simply the expression of a finer organism, the fruit of the most sensitive penetration — which anticipate the whole social and economic development of the nineteenth century: the industrialization of the old cultural and agrarian countries, the triumph of the machine, the rise of the organized labouring classes, the class conflict, democracy, socialism, Americanism itself, with the intellectual and educational consequences of all these.

But when all is said, and whatever the chronological affinity of these two great men, they cannot be called contemporaries. Only four years did the two of them inhabit this mortal sphere together: from 1828, when Tolstoy was born, to 1832, when Goethe died. Which does not prevent them from having one cultural element of their intellectual and spiritual make-up in common, and that a very real and positive one – to say nothing of universally human elements like Homer and the Bible. I mean the element Rousseau.

"I have read the whole of Rousseau, the whole twenty volumes, including the lexicon of music. What I felt for him was more than enthusiasm; it was worship. At fifteen I wore round my neck, instead of the usual cross, a medallion with his picture. I am so familiar with some of the passages in his works that I feel as though I had written them myself." These are Tolstoy's words, taken from his *Confessions*. And certainly he was Rousseauian more intimately, more personally, more damagingly, so to speak, than was Goethe, who as a man had nothing in common with poor Jean Jacques's enigmatic and not always ingratiating complexities. Yet hear Goethe (I quote from an early review): "Religious conditions, and the social conditions so narrowly bound up with them; the pressure of the laws, the still greater pressure of society, to say nothing of a thousand other factors, leave the civilized man or the civilized nation no soul of his own. They stifle the promptings of nature, they obliterate every trait out of which a characteristic picture could be made." That is, from the literary point of view, *Sturm und Drang*. But from the intellectual and historical, it is Rousseauianism. It bears the impress of revolution, even of anarchy; though in the Russian seeker after God that impress is religious and early Christian, whereas in Goethe's words the humanistic trend can be felt, the irradiation of a cultural and self-developing individualism which Tolstoy would have banned as egoistic and unchristian. But unchristian, egoistic, it is not: it means work on man, on mankind, on humanity, and it issues, as the *Wanderjahre* shows, in the social world.

What two ideas does the very sound of Rousseau's name inevitably evoke – aside, that is, from the idea of nature, which is, of course, first and foremost? Why, naturally, the idea "education" and the idea "autobiography." Jean Jacques Rousseau was the author of *Émile* and of the *Confessions*. Now, both these elements, the pedagogic and the autobiographic, are present in full strength in Goethe as in Tolstoy; they cannot be dissociated from the work or the life of either. It is as an amateur pedagogue that Tolstoy has been introduced in this essay; and we know that for long years he was nothing else, that he forced into this channel the whole violence of the passion that was in him, and wrestled theoretically and practically to the very verge of exhaustion with the problem of the Russian primary school. As for Goethe, needless to say, his was a pedagogic nature in the fullest sense of the word. The two great monuments of his life, one in poetry and one in prose, the *Faust* and the *Wilhelm Meister*, are both creative treatments of the theme of education. And whereas in the *Lehrjahre* the idea is still that of the individual forming himself — "for to form myself, just as I am, was darkly, from my youth up, my purpose and my desire," says Wilhelm Meister — in the *Wanderjahre* the educational idea is objectivated, and issues in social, even in political concepts; while at the heart of the work is, as you know, the stern and beautiful Utopia of the *Pedagogic Province*.

The second association, the autobiographic, the confessional, is of course easy to attest in both authors. That all of Goethe's works represent "fragments of one great confession" we should know ourselves even if he did not tell us; and is not *Dichtung und Wahrheit*, next to the *Confessions* of Saint Augustine and Rousseau, the most famous autobiography in the world? Well, and Tolstoy too wrote confessions: I mean in the main a book with that title, laid down throughout on the line of the great self-revelations that runs from the African saint to Strindberg, the son of the servant. But Tolstoy is in the same case with Goethe: not by virtue of one book alone is he autobiographical. Beginning with the *Childhood, Boyhood, Youth*, throughout the whole body of his work, he is autobiographical to an extent that makes it possible for Merezhkovsky, the great Russian critic, to say: "The artistic work of Leo Tolstoy is at bottom nothing else than one tremendous diary, kept for fifty years, one endless, explicit confession." Yes, and this critic adds: "In the literatures of all times and peoples there will hardly be found a second example of an author who reveals his personal and private life, often in its most intimate aspects, with such open-hearted sincerity." Well — open-hearted. I may be allowed a comment upon the somewhat euphemistic epithet. One might, if one wanted to be invidious, use a different adjective to characterize this sincerity — an adjective that would suggest what Turgenyev had in mind when he once ironically referred to the shortcomings inevitable in a great writer: by which, obviously, he meant the lack of certain restraints, the absence of a customary reserve, discretion, decency, shame, or, on the positive side, the domination of a definite claim on the love of the world — an absolute claim, indeed, in that it is all one to the revealer whether he reveal virtues or vices. He craves to be known and loved, loved because known, or loved *although* known; that is what I mean by an absolute claim on love. And the remarkable thing is that the world acknowledges and honours the claim.

"A life that is romantic has always self-love at the bottom of it." I like this saying; and subjoin that self-love is also always at the bottom of all autobiography. For the impulse a man feels to "fixate" his life, to exhibit its development, to celebrate his own destiny in set literary form and passionately invoke the sympathy of his contemporaries and posterity, has for a premise the same uncommonly lively sense of his own ego which, according to that penetrating saying, is at the bottom of a life full of romantic happenings. Subjectively, for the man himself, but also objectively for the world at large. Of course, this love of self is something different, something stronger, deeper, more fruitful, than any mere self-complacency or self-love of the ordinary kind. In the finest instances it is what Goethe in the *Wanderjahre* calls "*Ehrfurcht vor sich selbst*," and celebrates as the highest form of awe. It is the grateful and reverent self-absorption of the darling of the gods, that rings with incomparable sincerity from the lines:

Alles geben die Götter, die unendlichen,
Ihren Lieblingen ganz:
Alle Freuden, die unendlichen,
Alle Schmerzen, die unendlichen, ganz.

It is a proud and naïve interest in the mystery of high preferment, tangible superiority, perilous privilege, whose standard-bearer the chosen one feels himself to be; it is a craving to bear witness, out of the deeps of experience, how a genius is shaped; a desire to link together, by some miracle of grace, joy, and service; it was this desire that brought forth *Dichtung und Wahrheit* and in the truest sense inspires all great autobiography.

"I felt the need," writes Tolstoy of his youthful period, "to be known and loved of all the world; to *name my name*, the sound of which would greatly impress everybody, so that they would troop round me and thank me for something. . . ." That was quite early, before he had conceived any of his creative works or envisaged the idea of founding a new, practical, earthly, dogmaless religion — though this idea, according to his journal, had occurred to him by the time he was twenty-seven years old. His name, he feels, his mere name, Leo Tolstoy, this formula for his darkly and mightily stirring ego, should, as it were, serve notice to the world; whereby, for some reason as yet unknown, the world should be greatly impressed, and feel impelled to surround him in grateful throngs. Long after that, in 1883 — at about the same date that Tolstoy posed for an artist friend, sitting at his table and writing — he reads aloud to another friend and admirer, the one-time officer Tchertkov, from the manuscript of his just-completed personal revelations *What Does My Faith Consist In?* He reads from this manuscript a categorical reprobation of military service, on the grounds of his Christianity; which so gratifies the ex-officer that he hears nothing else, ceases to listen, and only rouses out of his absorption when he hears, suddenly uttered, the reader's own name. Tolstoy, coming to the end of his manuscript, had, with particular distinctness, says Tchertkov, enunciated the name signed underneath the text: "Leo Tolstoy."

Goethe once played a little literary hoax with his own name, which I have always found singularly touching. You will recall that in the *Westöstliche Diwan* he selected for himself as the lover of Marianne-Zuleika the name of Hatem (the most richly giving and receiving one). The choice betrays a blissful self-preoccupation. Now, in one of the poems, a glorious one, he uses this name at the end of a line, where, however, it does not rhyme as according to the structure of the verse it should, and the name which would rhyme if it stood there is another, is Goethe's own; so that the reader involuntarily makes the substitution mentally as he reads. "Only this heart," says the already white-haired lover to the youthful beloved,

Nur dies Herz, es ist von Dauer,
Schwillt in jugendlichstem Flor;
Unter Schnee und Nebelschauer
Rast ein Ätna dir hervor.
Du beschämst wie Morgenröte
Jener Gipfel ernste Wand,
Und noch einmal fühlet Hatem
Frühlingshauch und Sommerbrand.

"And again, anew feels Goethe . . ." With what delightful playfulness the poet makes the reader eliminate the name Hatem, which does not give the rhythm his ear expects! The Eastern masquerade is abandoned for autobiography, the ear confutes the eye, and Goethe's own name, beloved of men and gods, emerges with peculiar clarity, rhymed to perfection and irradiated by the most beautiful thing the world of sense can show: the rosy dawn.

May one call that "self-satisfaction," that awestruck sense of plenitude, of copious abundance, which pervades the consciousness of the darling of the gods? Goethe all his life had set his face against the affectation that might condemn such a feeling. He let it be known that in his opinion self-condemnation was the business of those who had no ground for anything else. He even openly spoke a good word for ordinary vanity, and said that the suppression of it would mean social decay, adding that the vain man can never be entirely crude. Whereupon follows the question: Is love of self ever quite distinguishable from love of humanity?

Wie sie sich an mich verschwendet,
Bin ich mir ein wertes Ich;
Hätte sie sich weggewendet,
Augenblicks verlör' ich mich.

And is not young Tolstoy's dream of glory, his craving to be known and loved, evidence of his love to the great *Thou* of the world? Love of the ego and love of the world are psychologically not to be divorced; which makes the old question whether love is ever altruistic, and not utterly egotistic, the most idle question in the world. In love, the contradiction between egotism and altruism is abrogated quite.

From which it follows that the autobiographical impulse scarcely ever turns out to be a mere dilettante trifling. It seems to carry its own justification with it. Talent, generally speaking, is a ticklish, difficult conception; the point of which is really less whether a man *can do* something than whether a man *is* something. One might almost say that talent is nothing more or less than a high state of adequacy to one's lot in life. But whose life is it that possesses this dignity in the face of destiny? With brains and sensibility anything can be made out of any life, out of any life a romantic existence can be made. Differing in this from the pure poetic impulse, which so often rests upon sheer self-deception, the autobiographic, as it seems, always presupposes a degree of brains and sensibility which justifies it beforehand; so that it need only become productive to be certain of our sympathy. Hence the conclusion I drew: that if the world sanction the love of self, which is at the bottom of the impulse, it will as a rule respond to it as well.

"Behold, what a marvellous creature lives upon this earth!" Gorky, contemplating Tolstoy, utters this inward cry. And this cry it is to which all biography seeks to move the world. Any human life, given brains and sensibility, can be made interesting and sympathetic, even the most wretched. J. J. Rousseau was not precisely one's idea of a darling of the gods. The father of the French Revolution was an unhappy wretch, half or three-quarters mad, and probably a suicide. Certainly the blend of sensibility and catarrh of the bladder displayed in the *Confessions* is not, æsthetically speaking, to everybody's taste. Nevertheless, his self-exposure contains and constitutes a claim upon the love of the world, which has been so abundantly honoured, with so many tears, that really one might call poor Jean Jacques the well-beloved, *le bien-aimé*. And this world-wide emotional response he owes to his bond with nature — rather a one-sided bond, it must be owned, for certainly this fool of genius, this exhibitionistic world-shaker, was a stepchild of the All-Mother rather than one of her pets, an accident of birth instead of a god-given miracle of favour and preference. His relation to nature was sentimental in the fullest sense of the word, and the tale of his life swept over the world in a wave of sentiment, not to say sentimentality. Poor Jean Jacques!

No, not in this tone does one refer to the two whom men called godlike, divine; in whom, as we have seen, important traits of Rousseau's character are reproduced. For they were not sentimental, scarcely had they occasion to yearn for nature, they themselves were nature. Their bond with her was not one-sided, like Rousseau's — or if it was, then it was nature who loved them, her darlings, loved them and clung to them, while on their side they drew away, and strove to free themselves from her heavy and earth-bound domination; with indifferent success, it must be said, looking at them both singly and together. Goethe confesses: "So here I am, with all my thousand thoughts, sent back to be a child again, unacquainted with the moment, in darkness about myself." And to Schiller, the singer of the highest freedom, he writes: "How great an advantage your sympathy and interest will be to me you will soon see, when you discover in me a sort of sluggishness and gloom which is stronger than myself." And yet we may agree that Goethe's highly humanistic effort to "convert the cloudy natural product into a clear image of itself (i.e., of reason) and so discharge the duty and the claim of existence," as Riemer with extraordinary beauty expresses it, was crowned with a purer success than the attempt of Count Leo Nikolayevich Tolstoy to transform his life into the holy life of our blessed father the Boyar Lev, as Gorky says. This process of making a Christian and a saint of himself, on the part of a human being and artist so loved of nature that she had endowed him with godlikeness, was, as an effort at spiritual regeneration, most inept. Anglo-Saxondom hailed it with acclaim, but, after all, the spectacle is painful rather than gratifying, compared with Goethe's high endeavour. For there is no conflict between nature and culture; the second only ennobles the first, it does not repudiate it. But Tolstoy's method was not the ennoblement but the renunciation of self, and that can quite easily become the most mortifying kind of deception. It is true that Goethe, at a certain stage in his development, called *Götz* the work of an undisciplined boy; but never did he so childishly and miserably calumniate his own art as the aging Tolstoy did, when he regretted having written *Childhood*, *Boyhood*, *Youth*, the fruit of his fresh youthful vigour, condemning it as insincere, literary, sinful; or when he spoke at large of "the artistic twaddle" that filled the twelve volumes of his works, and to which "people today ascribe an unmerited significance." That is what I call false self-renunciation, a clumsy attempt at spiritualization. Yet renounce himself as he would in words, his very existence gave him the lie; and Gorky looked at him, the patriarch with the "sly" little smile and the artist hands with their swollen veins, and thought to himself: "The man is like God."

Weimar, and Yasnaya Polyana. There is no spot on earth today whence power streams out as once from these two, no shrine strong in grace, the resort of pilgrims, whither the longings and vague hopes of men, their need and craving to adore, turn as they did thitherward at the beginning of the nineteenth and the beginning of the twentieth century. We possess descriptions of the state Goethe kept in Weimar; when he, now no longer merely the creator of certain works, but a prince of life, the highest representative of European culture, civilization, and humanity, with his staff of secretaries, his higher aides and eager friends at his back, bore up, with that bestarred official dignity which the world enjoined upon him and behind which he hid the mysteries and abysses of his genius, against the onrushing tide of civilized humanity – princes, artists, youths, and rustics, to whom the consciousness of having been vouchsafed one glimpse of him might gild the rest of their lives; even though the great moment itself might and often did turn out to be a chilling disappointment. In much the same way, I say, the little Russian village became, about 1900, the centre and nodal point, the shrine whose virtue was such that it drew all the world. The host of pilgrims was even more colourful, more international, more heterogeneous; for during the century communications had increased, the world had broadened out. South Africans, Americans, Japanese, Australians, natives of the Malay Peninsula, Siberian refugees, and Indian Brahmins, representatives of all the European nations, scholars, poets, artists, statesmen, governors, senators, students, military personages, workmen, peasants,

French politicians, journalists of every stripe, from every country on the globe; and again youth, youth from all over the world. "Who does not go to him?" asks a Russian writer: "to greet him, to express sympathy with his ideas, to seek relief from tormenting problems." And his biographer Birukov says: "One and all they troop to this village and then go home to talk about the great words and great thoughts of the grey old seer who lives there."

"Great words and great thoughts." Of course. But it is quite likely the words and thoughts with which the prophet regaled them were not always so remarkable. Neither were Goethe's; out of sheer embarrassment he might fail to utter great things to those who waited on him. But it is a question whether people ever went to Weimar or to the village called "Bright Meadow" for the sake of the great words and thoughts they might perchance hear, or were led by a much more profound and elemental craving. I shall be accused of mysticism if I say that the attraction such shrines possess for all the world, so that men promise themselves salvation from a visit, is not at all intellectual in its nature but something else entirely. "Elemental" is the only word for it. For Goethe's case, I may quote Wilhelm von Humboldt, who declared, a few days after the master's death, that the strangest thing of all was the way this man had exercised so powerful an influence, without as it were meaning to at all, unconsciously, unintentionally, by the mere fact of his existence; this, he says, quite apart from his intellectual activity as a thinker and poet, and as an outgrowth of his great and unique personality. Well and good. But, after all, we use the word "personality" when we want to express an idea that at bottom escapes definition. Personality is not immediately a matter of mind or spirit—nor yet of culture. Our conception of it is one that takes us outside the domain of the rational, into the sphere of the mystic and elemental, into the *natural* sphere. "A great nature"—that is another phrase we use in our effort to find a formula and a symbol that shall express power streaming forth and drawing the world to itself. But nature is not spirit; in fact, this antithesis is, I should say, the greatest of all antitheses. Gorky not only disbelieved in Tolstoy's Christian, Buddhistic, Chinese gospel of wisdom; he did not even believe that Tolstoy believed in it. And yet he gazed at him, and thought, in amaze: "The man is like God." It was not spirit, but nature, moved him to this inward cry. And when the pilgrims trooped to Weimar and "Bright Meadow," the refreshment and quickening they dimly hoped for was not of the mind; it was the sight of and contact with great vital energy, with human nature richly endowed, with the lofty nobility of a beloved child of God. For one does not need to be a Spinozist, like Goethe, who had his own good reasons for being one, to hail the favourites of nature as the favourites of God.

Schiller, great sufferer though he was, was kinder, more human to his visitors. This we learn for instance from the actor Friederich, who says he left this glorious poet "more consoled," after having just previously taken a chill, to speak figuratively, at an audience on the Frauenplan. "Goethe's whole appearance," he goes on, "seemed measured and formal. I sought in vain a trait that betrayed the genial creator of *The Sorrows of Werther* or *Wilhelm Meisters Lehrjahre*. You can imagine how this frigid reception and unfriendly treatment put me off, it was so contrary to all my expectations. Dearly should I have liked to say to Goethe: 'What sort of graven image are you? It is impossible that you could have written the *Lehrjahre*.' But I choked it down." One is reminded of the Moscow worthy with whom Gorky drove away from Yasnaya Polyana: who for a long time could not get his breath at all, only kept ruefully smiling and ejaculating as in a daze: "Well, well, that was a cold douche! Gracious, but he's stiff! And I thought he was an anarchist!" Perhaps, even probably, if it had been Dostoyevsky he visited, he would have found him more anarchistic – in other words, less "stiff" – and would have parted from him "more consoled," as did the good Friederich from the glorious Schiller, who even let Friederich recite to him. On the other hand, neither Schiller's nor Dostoyevsky's genius would have turned any odd corner of the earth into a shrine for pilgrims. Anyhow, neither of them lived long enough for that. They died too young, they did not reach the patriarchal years of Goethe and Tolstoy, nature denied them the dignity and consecration of great age, she did not grant them to be characteristically fruitful throughout all the stages of the human scene, to live a whole and classic human life. True, it may be said that the dignity that comes with length of days has nothing to do with spirit. A greybeard may be stupid and ordinary; yet men do regard with religious awe his white hair and wrinkles; his is a natural nobility conferred by length of years – but natural nobility is probably a pleonasm. Nobility is always natural. People are not ennobled, that is rubbish; they are noble by birth, on the ground of their flesh and blood. Nobility then is physical: on the body and not on the mind all nobility has always laid the greatest stress. That may explain a certain strain of brutality which has always been peculiar to human nobility. And is there not something brutal too, in its way, heathenish, sagalike, in the arrogant way Goethe sometimes boasted of his vitality, his indestructibility? When he was eighty-one he said to Soret: "Well, so Sömmering is dead. He was barely a miserable five-and-seventy years old! What poor things men are, not to be brave enough to hold out longer than that! On that score I really must do justice to that frightfully radical ass my friend Bentham; he is quite well preserved, and he is a few weeks older than I am myself!"

So Schiller and Dostoyevsky, to get back to them, were not vouchsafed the ennoblement that comes with length of days. They died comparatively young. Why? Well, because they were sick men, as everybody knows, both of them; one consumptive, the other epileptic. But I raise two questions: First, do we not feel that their illness was deeply founded in the very being of the two of them, an essential and typical trait of the kind of men they were? And second, does it not seem that in their case it is the disease itself that engenders or brings out a nobility sharply distinguished from that love of self and the autobiographical pride of birth which is part of its consummate sense of its own ego? Schiller's nobility and Dostoyevsky's nobility mean a quite different sort of deepening and heightening of their humanity—yes, of their *humanity*, in view of which does not disease appear precisely as an aristocratic attribute of heightened humanity? It follows then that the phrase "natural nobility" is no pleonasm after all; that there does exist another kind of nobility besides that conferred by nature on her favoured sons. Clearly there are two ways of heightening and enhancing human values: one exalts them up to the godlike, and is a gift of nature's grace; the other exalts them up to the saintly, by grace of another power, which stands opposed to her and means emancipation from her, eternal revolt from her. That other power is the power of the spirit. But the question which of these two is higher, which kind of enhancement of human values is the nobler: this it is which I called the aristocratic problem.

Here, with all due reserve, a little philosophy of disease may not be out of place. Disease has two faces and a double relation to man and his human dignity. On the one hand it is hostile: by overstressing the physical, by throwing man back upon his body, it has a dehumanizing effect. On the other hand, it is possible to think and feel about illness as a highly dignified human phenomenon. It may be going too far to say that disease *is* spirit, or, which would sound very tendentious, that spirit is disease. Still, the two conceptions do have very much in common. For the spirit is pride; it is a wilful denial and contradiction of nature; it is detachment, withdrawal, estrangement from her. Spirit is that which distinguishes from all other forms of organic life this creature man, this being which is to such a high degree independent of her and hostile to her. And the question, the aristocratic problem, is this: is he not by just so much the more man, the more detached he is from nature – that is to say, the more diseased he is? For what can disease me, if not disjunction from nature? "*Tut der Finger dir weh,*" says Hebbel epigrammatically, "*schied er vom Leibe sich ab,*

Und die Säfte beginnen, im Gliede gesondert zu kreisen:
Aber so ist auch der Mensch, fürcht' ich, ein Schmerz nur in Gott."

Was it not Nietzsche who called man "*das kranke Tier*"? What did he mean, if not that man is more than beast only in the measure that he is ailing? In spirit, then, in disease, resides the dignity of man; and the genius of disease is more human than the genius of health.

You will deny that; you will not agree to have it so. But, in the first place, disease, as a philosophical term, is by no means a negation and a condemnation. It is merely a statement, which need be no less acceptable than the term "health," there being a nobility of disease as there is a nobility of health. And, in the second place, may I remind you that Goethe identified the Schillerian conception of the "sentimental" with that of disease? After, that is, he had previously identified the antithesis of "simple and sentimental" with that of classic and romantic. "The conception of classic and romantic poetry," he said one day to Eckermann, "that is abroad today, and making so much strife and schism, came originally from Schiller and me. My poetical maxim has been objectivity of treatment, and I wanted it to prevail. But Schiller, whose method is entirely subjective, thought his way was right, and wrote the essay on simple and sentimental poetry in defence of his conception." Again: "I have thought of a new phrase which states not too badly the relation between the classic and the romantic. The classic I call the healthy, the romantic the diseased. If we distinguish classic and romantic on this basis, we shall soon clarify the situation."

Here, then, we have an order of things according to which, on the one hand, the simple, the objective, the sound, and the classic are identical; and, on the other hand, the "sentimental," the subjective, the pathological, the romantic. Thus one might call man the romantic being, in that he, a spiritual entity, stands outside of and beyond nature, and in this his emotional separation from her, in this his double essence of nature and spirit, finds both his own importance and his own misery. Nature is happy, or she seems so to him. For he, involved in tragical paradox, is a romantically miserable being. Does not all our love of our kind rest on a brotherly, sympathetic recognition of the human being's well-nigh hopelessly difficult situation? Yes, there is a patriotism of humanity, and it rests on this: we love human beings because they have such a hard time — and because we are one of them ourself!

Tolstoy, in his *Confessions*, remarks that as a small child he knew nothing of nature, he had not even noticed her existence. "It is not possible," he says, "that I was given neither flowers nor leaves to play with, that I did not see the grass or the sunlight. And yet up to my fifth or sixth year I have no memory of what we call nature. Probably we have to get free from her in order to see her, and I myself was nature." From which can be deduced that even the mere seeing of nature, and our so-called enjoyment of her, are not only a specifically human condition, but one full of yearning emotion, in other words pathological, implying as it does our separation from her. Tolstoy's recollection is that he felt the pain of this separation for the first time when his childhood under the care of nurses came to an end and he moved over to his older brothers and the tutor Feodor Ivanovich in the lower storey. Never again, he assures us, did he feel so strongly what a sense of duty meant, and what, accordingly, moral and ethical obligation: "the feeling of the Cross, to carry which every one of us is called. It was hard for me to part from all I had known from everlasting. I was sad, sunk in poetical melancholy; less because I had to part from human beings, my nurse, my sisters, my aunt, than because I was leaving my little bed with its curtains and pillows. Moreover, I was apprehensive of the new life I was entering." The appearance of the word "Cross" in this connection is significant, not only with reference to Tolstoy, but also for the thing itself, the process of loosing oneself from nature. This process was felt by Tolstoy as painful and ethical: painful because ethical, and ethical because painful. He gives it a moral and an ascetic significance, as that which actually comprises all man's ethical obligation. To be humanized means, for him, to be denaturalized; and from that moment on, the struggle of his existence consists in this sort of humanizing process: in the divorce from nature, from everything that was natural and to him peculiarly so, for example from the family, the nation, the state, the church, from all the passions of the senses and the instincts, from love, the hunt, at bottom from all of physical life, and especially from art, which meant to him quite essentially the life of the body and the senses. It is quite wrong to think of this struggle as a crisis of conversion taking place suddenly in his later years; to make its inception roughly coincide with the beginning of old age. When the news came that the great Russian writer was as though stricken by a sort of mystical madness, the Frenchman Vogüé declared that he had long expected it. He was quite justified. The germ of Tolstoy's intellectual development had lain in *Childhood*, *Boyhood*, *Youth;* and the psychology of Levin in *Anna Karenina* plainly indicated what further course it would take. Besides, we have the evidence of Tolstoy's comrades-in-arms when he was an officer, the Sebastopol time. They give the clearest picture of the violence with which the struggle even then raged within him. But here we should note that his wrestling to break the strong bonds in which nature held him, regularly led up to disease, immediately assumed the form of illness. "Leochen is completely consumed by his writing now," so his wife, Countess Sophia Alexandrovna, puts it, about the year 1880, when he buried himself in theology and the philosophy of religion. It is a sight her love hates to see, and she constantly tries to call him back to creative work. "His eyes are strange and staring, he hardly speaks at all, he is like a being from another world, and is positively not capable of thinking of earthly things. . . ." "Leochen is quite sunk in his work. His head pains him all the time. He is very much changed, and become a rigid and practising Christian. But he has got grey, his health is weak, he is sadder and more silent all the time." – "Tomorrow we shall have been here a month," she writes in 1881 from Moscow, "and the first two weeks I wept every day without stopping, because Leochen was not only in a gloomy state, but fallen into a kind of despairing apathy. He ate nothing and did not sleep, sometimes literally wept – I honestly believe I shall lose my reason." And to her husband himself: "I am beginning to think that when a happy man suddenly begins to see only the horrible side of life, and has no eyes for anything good, he must be ill. You should do something for it, I say this in all seriousness. It seems so clear to me, I suffer so to see you. . . . Did you never know before that there were people in the world who were hungry, miserable, unhappy, and wicked? Open your eyes: there are also strong and healthy, happy and good ones. If God would only help you – what can I do? You must be ill," the poor woman wails – and is he not? He himself writes: "My health grows worse and worse, often I wish

I could die. Why I am so reduced I do not know myself. Perhaps it is age, perhaps illness. . . ."

Compare with this the descriptions of him when he had sought in the holy animalism of married life a refuge from the insoluble riddles that his intellect set him; and then, with that power which the critics delighted to call "bearlike" – Turgenyev sought in vain to convince him that it came from the source whence all things come – created his two epic novels *War and Peace* and *Anna Karenina*. "He was always light-hearted then," his sister-in-law relates, "in high spirits, as the English say, fresh, healthy, and jolly. On the days when he did not write he went hunting with me or his neighbour Ribikov. We hunted with greyhounds. . . . Evenings he played patience in Tantchen's room." What happy days! Who can blame poor Countess Sophia Alexandrovna for scarcely containing herself for joy when she hears that her hollow-eyed Christian is planning a new imaginative work? Her happiness is touching. "What gladness suddenly filled me, to read that you mean to write something creative again! What I have so long awaited and hoped for has come to you. That is salvation, that is happiness, in it we shall come together again, it will console you and irradiate our life. This is the work you were made for, and outside this sphere there is no joy for your soul. God give you strength to cling to this ray of light, in order that the divine spark may flare up in you again. The thought fills me with ecstasy. . . ."

Goethe's and Tolstoy's biographies show that these great writers both alike suppressed for years their gift of plastic creation – for which, as Countess Sophia Alexandrovna says, they were born – and both in the service of a directly social activity – that is to say, on highly moral grounds. Tolstoy suppressed the artist in him in favour of his activities as *mirovoi posrednik* (justice of the peace) and schoolmaster without pay. Goethe governed the dukedom of Saxe-Weimar, for ten years of his early manhood dedicated his powers to excise regulations, details of book manufacture, levies of recruits, construction of streets and water-conduits, workhouses, mines and quarries, finance, and other such matters – while Merck, in the style of Turgenyev, was constantly concerned to rescue him for literature, and he himself, with increasing resignation, steeling himself by inward exhortations to patience and fortitude, held himself to the heavy, hard, unrewarding, unnatural task. Added to all this, in Goethe's case, there was that somewhat seraphic affair with Frau von Stein. No doubt it was most beautifully instrumental in the process of civilizing the son of the Titans; but after all it did justice to but one of those famous two souls, which had, alas, their dwelling in his breast, and it let the other, the one with the "*klammernde Organen*," the "avid organs," go empty away. — Well, in both cases, Goethe's and Tolstoy's, the result is illness. "My office as justice of the peace," writes Tolstoy, "has ended in destroying my good relations with the landowners, quite aside from the fact that it injures my health." Teaching the village children had the same result. True, in his pedagogical journal he claims that the exercises the children wrote were more accomplished than the writings of Leo Tolstoy, Pushkin, and Goethe; yet he discerns something evil and even criminal in his intercourse with them, it seems to him that he abuses and corrupts their souls. "It seemed to go very well," he says in the *Confessions*, "but I felt that I was mentally not healthy enough and that it could not go on so for much longer. I was more ailing mentally than physically; I threw it all overboard and drove out to the Kalmucks of the steppes to drink mares' milk and lead an animal life." — This absconding to the steppes vividly recalls the secret flight to Italy which was Goethe's salvation, after he too had seen that it could not go on so for much longer. The thirty-four-year-old man had become silent, taciturn, in plain words melancholy. He thought it was probably natural that a man should become serious over serious things. His health was actually undermined; by the time he was six-and-thirty his face was the face of a victim of exhaustion. For the first time he thought of taking a cure. He began to be aware of the ruinous perversity of his existence; expressed his view in the shrewd understatement that he was meant for private life. And fled before destruction. The parallel continues to hold: for Leo Nikolayevich, returned from the steppes and the mares'-milk cure, marries his Sophia Alexandrovna, who from then on finds herself almost continuously in the family way, and with epic and primeval power creates his two great novels. While Goethe, back from Italy, takes Christiane Vulpius unto himself and, freed from the cares of office, gives his mind to his natural tasks. So much as a gloss upon a philosophy of disease.

Art is objective, creative contemplation, closely bound up with nature. Critique, on the other hand, is the moralizing, analysing attitude toward life and nature. In other words, critique is spirit; whereas creation is the preoccupation of the children of God and nature.

"In poetry my maxim was the objective principle," says Goethe. "I am a plastic artist (*ich bin ein Plastiker*)." Indeed, the contrast between Goethe's position and that of his great counterpart

(Schiller standing for idealism, moralization, rhetoric — in short, for critique) is too well known to need labouring. Goethe regarded his own inborn poetic gift "quite as nature." His tolerance, his attitude of live and let live, the complaisance of his character, are all consonant with this view. They are based on the Spinozan concept of the perfectitude and necessity of all being, on the idea of a world free from final ends and final causes, in which evil has its rights like good. "We struggle," he declares, "to perfect the work of art as an end in itself. They, the moralists, think of the ulterior effect, about which the true artist troubles himself as little as nature does when she makes a lion or a humming-bird." It is a primary maxim with him that art is as inimical to purpose as nature herself; and this is the point where the follower of Spinoza sympathizes with Kant, who conceives detached contemplation as the genuine æsthetic state, thus making a fundamental distinction between the æsthetic-creative principle and the ethical-critical one. "When," says Goethe, "philosophy confirms and enhances our original feeling of our oneness with nature, turning it into a profound and tranquil contemplation, then I welcome it." I could cite ten or twelve other places in his works where in the name of art he repudiates the moral sanction — which indeed is always social as well. "It is possible, I suppose, for a work of art to have a moral effect; but to demand from the artist a moral purpose and intention is to spoil his craft for him." — "I have, in my trade as a writer, never asked myself: How shall I be of service to the world at large? All I have ever done was with the view of making myself better and more full of insight, of increasing the content of my own personality; and then only of giving utterance to what I had recognized as the good and the true."

When we contrast the Christian-social ethics of Tolstoy as an old man with Goethe's pagan and cultural idealism, we must not forget that the Tolstoyan socialism had its origin in the most private and personal need, the profoundest concern with the salvation of one's own soul. A permanent dissatisfaction with self, a tortured seeking for the meaning of life, was the source of this socialism. The moralist began all his teachings and reforms with a self-discipline (the *Confessions*, that is) such as the true and proper social critic never demands of himself. Revolutionary in the real and political sense of the word he can by no means be called. "The significance of the Christian doctrine," he declares, "is not that in its name society shall forcibly be reformed. It is that one shall find a meaning to life." And it should be pointed out that Tolstoy's original conception of art corresponded precisely to Goethe's —

a fact that will surprise none but those who in all good faith accept him as a child of spirit, like Schiller and Dostoyevsky, on the ground of his naïve and clumsy efforts at spiritual regeneration, and fail to recognize in him a natural nobility akin to Goethe's own. Tolstoy's hatred of Shakespeare, which dates from much earlier than is generally realized, undoubtedly has its roots in antagonism against that universal and all-accepting nature: in the jealousy which a man enduring moral torment was bound to feel in face of the blithe irony of an absolutely creative genius. It was a reaction against nature, against the simple, against indifference to the moral point of view; and an impulse toward spirit — that is, toward an ethical and even social revaluation — a reaction so whole-souled, indeed, that it ended in his playing off against Shakespeare Mrs. Harriet Beecher Stowe, the creater of *Uncle Tom's Cabin* — an absurdity that only goes to show how very much the child of nature he was. Genuine sons of spirit and of the idea, like Schiller and Dostoyevsky, do not go aground on such fantastic coasts. Tolstoy's critical and moral faculty; in short his bias toward spirit, was but secondary, an act of will, and a feeble will at that. It always balked at organic union with his mighty creative gift; we have unequivocal declarations from him to the effect that, in his view, pure creative power stood higher than talent with a social coloration. As an old man he criticized Dostoyevsky for going in for politics, much as Goethe had criticized Uhland's activities in that line. At the age of thirty-one, in 1859, as a member of the Moscow society of the Friends of Russian Literature, he made a speech in which he so sharply accented the superiority of the purely artistic elements in literature over merits due to ulterior or ephemeral causes that the president of the society, Khomyakov, reminded him in a sharp rejoinder that a servant of pure art might very well, without knowing or wishing it, find himself indicting society.

An outburst of intellectual misgivings, of that humility of spirit to which the sons of nature are prone, occurs at the end of Tolstoy's novel *Lucerne*. Here is a splendid lament over the fate of man, who, with all his need of positive redemption, is flung into an ever billowing and shoreless ocean of good and evil. "If man," cries Tolstoy, "had only once learned not to judge and think so sharply and decisively, and not always to give answers to questions which are only put in order that they may remain forever questions! If he would only comprehend that every thought is at once false and true! . . . Men have divided up into sections this ever-rolling, boundless, eternally mingled chaos of good and bad;

they have drawn themselves imaginary boundary-lines in this sea, and they expect the sea to divide according to their lines. As if it were not possible to make millions of other divisions, from other points of view, and on different planes! . . . Civilization is good, barbarism evil; freedom is good, unfreedom evil. This imaginary knowledge destroys in human nature the *original blissful and instinctive striving towards good*." And asking himself whether in the souls of the poor there may not be more happiness and affirmation of life than in that of the callous rich man against whom, for his own part, his heart revolts, he bursts out with the words: "Endless is the goodness and wisdom of Him who has permitted and commanded all these contradictions. Only to you, poor worm, so presumptuously struggling to accomplish your schemes and devices, only to you do they seem contradictory. He looks mildly down from His radiant, immeasurable height and rejoices in the endless harmony wherein in endless opposition you all do move!"

Could one express oneself more "Goethically"? Even the "*Harmonie des Unendlichen*" is here. This is not mere philosophical or moral doubt; such words are too light, too thin, too intellectual to characterize the piety, the religious acceptance, the adoration of nature, that breathe from Tolstoy's page. This is not the voice of the prophet, schoolmaster, and reformer; here speaks the child of this world, the creative artist. Nature was his element, as she was the element, the beloved, kindly mother, of Goethe – and his constant tearing at the bond that held him fast to her, his desperate urging away from her in the direction of spirit and morality, from creation to critique, has much to command our respect and reverence, though at the same time there is about it something painful, tormenting, and humiliating, which is not present in the character of Goethe. Look at Tolstoy's attitude toward music, it is most instructive. When he met Berthold Auerbach in Dresden, that not too profound moralist told him that music is an irresponsible enjoyment, and added that irresponsible enjoyment is the first step toward immorality. Tolstoy, in his journal, made this clever and abominable phrase his own. His hatred and fear of music had the same moral and social basis as his hatred and fear of Shakespeare. We are told that at the sound of music he grew pale and his face became drawn with an expression very like horror. Notwithstanding, he was never able to live without music. In his earlier years he even founded a musical society. Before beginning work he habitually seated himself at the piano – that means a good deal. And in Moscow, when he sat beside Tchaikovsky and listened to the composer's Quartet in D major, he began to sob at the *andante*, before everybody. No, unmusical he was not. Music loved him, even though he, great moralizing infant that he was, felt that he ought not to return her love.

There is that legend of the giant Antæus, who was unconquerable because fresh strength streamed into him whenever he touched his mother earth. The lives of Goethe and Tolstoy irresistibly recall that myth. Both sons of mother earth, they differ only therein, that one of them was aware of the source of his nobility, the other not. There are places in Tolstoy's remorseful confessions where he touches the earth, and all at once his words, which, so long as they dealt in theory, were wooden and confused, are imbued with the most penetrating sensuousness, with an irresistible force and freshness of life. He recalls how once as a child he went nutting with his grandmother in the hazel wood. Lackeys instead of horses draw the grandmother's little carriage into the grove. They break through the undergrowth and bend the boughs, full of ripe, already dropping nuts, down into the old lady's lap and she gathers them into a bag. Little Leo marvels at the strength of the tutor, Feodor Ivanovich, who bends the heavy branches; when he lets go they spring up again and slowly mingle with the others. "I can feel how hot it was in the sun, how pleasantly cool in the shade, how we breathed the sharp scent of the foliage, while all round us the girls were cracking nuts between their teeth; we munched the full, fresh, white kernels without stopping." – The fresh, full, white kernels cracking between the girls' teeth: that is Antæus-Tolstoy, and the strength of his mother the earth streams through him, as it did when he wrote *War and Peace*, where his rather vague, fine-drawn, not very convincing philosophical digressions are followed by pages of which Turgenyev wrote: "They are glorious, they are the very best there is, everything original, everything descriptive, the hunt, the night boat-ride and all – nobody in Europe can touch him."

And Goethe: how the Antæus-consciousness governed his whole existence! How constantly it conditioned his seeking and shaping! Nature is to him "healing and comfort" after the visitations of passion; and while he well knows that to know her "one must have moulded all the manifestations of the human being into one definite and distinct entity," that true research is unthinkable without the gift of imagination, he is wary of the fantastic, avoids speculative natural philosophy, guards himself against losing touch with the earth, and calls the idea "the result of experience." The imagination that guides his research is intuitive, it is the inborn sympathy of the child of nature with the organic. It is Antæan, like the imaginative power which conditions his creative art, nor is that, either, capricious in its nature, but precise and based on the sense-perceptions. Such is the imagination of the creative artist. The sons of the thought, of the idea, of spirit, theirs is another kind. We will not say that the one creates more reality than the other. But the figures created by the plastic fancy possess the realism of sheer being; while those created by the "sentimental" artist evince their actuality by action. Schiller himself makes this distinction. Apart from the things they do, he himself confesses, they have something shadowy—"*etwas Schattenhaftes*" is his expression. Translate this from the sphere of German idealism into the Russian and revelational, and you get, as a sort of national pendant to Schiller's world of idea, rhetoric, and drama, the shadow-world of Dostoyevsky, over-life-size and exaggeratedly true. A catchword occurs to one from the philosophy of art, that is in everybody's mouth today, or at least was yesterday: the word "expressionism." Really, what we call expressionism is only a late form, strongly impregnated with the Russian and revelational, of romantic idealism. Its conflict with the epic attitude toward art, the conflict between contemplation and ecstatic vision, is neither new nor old, it is eternal. And it finds complete expression in on the one side Goethe and Tolstoy, on the other Schiller and Dostoyevsky. And to all eternity the truth, power, calm, and humility of nature will be in conflict with the disproportionate, fevered, and dogmatic presumption of spirit.

Very much, yes, precisely as Goethe's "profound and tranquil contemplation," his precise and sensuous fancy, the lifelikeness of his characters, stand in relation to the ideal visions of Schiller and the activism of his creations, so the mighty sense-appeal of Tolstoy's art stands to Dostoyevsky's sickly, distorted dream-and-soul world. Indeed, the contrast becomes even more pointed by reason of differences between nations and periods. Tolstoy, the realistic novelist, the prince-and-peasant scion of a race still young, displays in his art a sensuousness more powerful, more immediately fleshly in its appeal, than does the German humanist and classicist, bourgeois-born and patrician-bred, in his.

Compared with Eduard and Charlotte, the lovers in the *Wahlverwandtschaften*, Vronsky and Anna are like a fine strong stallion and a noble mare. The comparison is not mine; it has often been made. A certain school of Russian criticism, hostile, of course, and on a low plane, found most offensive Tolstoy's animalism, his unheard-of interest in the life of the body, his genius for bringing home to us man's physical being. These critics wrote, for instance, that *Anna Karenina* reeked with the classic odour of babies' diapers. They raved at the salaciousness of certain scenes, and ironically reproached Tolstoy for omitting to describe how Anna takes her bath and Vronsky washes himself. They were wrong even in the fact; for Tolstoy does tell us how Vronsky washes, we see him rubbing his red body. And in *War and Peace* we are vouchsafed a glimpse of Napoleon naked, in the scene where he has his fat back sprayed with eau-de-Cologne. A critic wrote in *Die Tat* about this book: "Its main theme is the satisfaction of any and every human being within the fold of wedded bliss, conceived in the grossest sense." And then the same critic, parodying Tolstoy's style, proposed to him that he write another novel treating of Levin's love for his cow Pania.

All this, of course, is on a lower plane than the criticism of Goethe which Caroline Herder wrote to Knebel: "Oh, if he would only give some soul to his characters! If only there were not so much philandering in everything that he writes, or, as he himself so likes to call it, so much 'good feeling.'" But unenlightened comment such as this may very well be illuminating none the less, even though unawares and as it were on false pretences; and these remarks, in their folly, do undoubtedly contain a grain of truth. Caroline's "philandering" is a mincing, sentimental word to characterize what Goethe wrote; yet it has a certain aptness, if the comparison is between his frank realism and the lofty insubstantiality of Schiller's world. It is not such a bad joke, either, to make Levin fall in love with his cow. It hits off the fleshliness of Tolstoy's art as contrasted with the holy soulfulness of Dostoyevsky's — especially when we remember Tolstoy's personal passion for one of the preoccupations of farm life — namely, the breeding of cattle and pigs. It is an interest quite proper, of course, to a landed proprietor; yet where so strongly marked as this surely not quite without deeper meaning.

I am still resolved not to pass judgment. I did, indeed, throw out the question of nobility, the matter of rank. But I am wary of hasty decisions, and even at the risk of being called vacillating, I hold to my policy of the free hand and my faith in its ultimate fruitfulness. Why should I not be a cautious judge of the swaying battle, when I know that what I called above the arrogance of spirit is one with that great and highly affecting principle which we call freedom?

Schiller's loftiest boast is the freedom of the singer. But Goethe's attitude toward the conception of freedom is at all times cautious, not only in the political field, but consistently, fundamentally, and in every connection. Of Schiller he says: "In his latter years, when he had had enough of freedom in a physical sense, he went over to it in the realm of the ideal, and I might almost say that it killed him; for it caused him to make demands on his physical powers that were altogether too much for them. I have great respect for the categorical imperative, I know how much good can come of it; but one must not carry it too far, for then this idea of the ideal freedom certainly leads to no good." — I confess that this habit of using Schiller's heroic life to point a warning against exaggerations in the use of the categorical imperative has always made me smile. To confront the moral with the natural is always humorous. But in other places where this child of God expresses himself about heroes and saints his words have quite a different ring and bear witness frankly and sincerely to the nobility of spirit. He declared one day that he passed for an aristocrat, but that Schiller was at bottom much more of a one than he. The remark bears directly upon the problem of aristocracy: certainly not in the political field, nor yet to the fact that Schiller had spoken of the "eternally blind," to whom one must not lend Heaven's torches of light; no, it has immediate reference to the aristocracy of spirit, which Goethe was at the moment comparing with his own, the aristocracy of nature, and finding it the more lofty of the two. "Nothing disturbed him," he says admiringly, "nothing constrained him, nothing distracted the flight of his thoughts. He was as great at the tea-table as he would have been in the council-chamber." This admiring wonder rises from the depths of Goethe's Antæus nature, which had no consciousness at all of a freedom like that, of such independence and unrestraint. Rather he knew himself to be constantly conditioned by a hundred circumstances; influenced, obligated, willingly indeed, with a certain pride in his earth-bound aristocracy, yet influenced and obligated none the less. Pantheistic necessity was the fundamental feeling of his existence. It is not enough to say he did not believe in the freedom of the will. He denied the conception, he denied that such a thing was even conceivable. "We belong to the laws of nature," he says, "even when we rebel against them; we are working with her, even when we work against her." That dæmonic determinism of his whole being was often felt by others. They said he was possessed, and not able to act voluntarily. His earth-bound state manifested itself, for instance, in such sensitiveness to weather that he called himself a regular barometer.

And we may not take it that he felt his dependence, which amounted to compulsion, as personally lowering, or that his will had ever rebelled against it. The will is the spirit: nature is by way of being mild and easy-going. Thus the aristocrat in bondage may feel a noble pride as he bends the knee to the dark power to which he belongs and which guides him so well; and yet be capable, as Goethe's case shows at least, of a gesture of elegant homage before the aristocracy of freedom. "*Denn hinter ihm,*" says Goethe in the Epilogue to *The Bell*, with reference to Schiller:

Denn hinter ihm in wesenlosem Scheine
Lag, was uns alle bändigt, das Gemeine.

Truly this is homage which breathes a spirit of the most profound abnegation. For what *is* "*das Gemeine*"? Nothing else than the natural, from the point of view of spirit and of freedom. For freedom is spirit; it is release from nature, rebellion against her; it is humanity conceived as emancipation from the natural and its bondage, this emancipation being the thing that is actually human and worthy of humanity. Here we see the question of aristocracy flowing together with that of human dignity. Which is finer, which worthier of humanity, freedom or bonds, self-will or submission, the moral or the natural? If I refuse to answer, it is in the conviction that this question can never be answered with finality.

But, on the other hand, the moral "sentimentalist" can be no "sentimentalist" at all if he does not on his side display an even livelier and profounder eagerness to pay homage to the aristocracy that is of nature. Unquestionably there is a certain charming humility in the attitude of spirit toward nature, a delicate readiness, often quite unrequited, to pay her respect, which is one of the greatest and most touching phenomena of the higher life. Dostoyevsky read Tolstoy's early work *Childhood, Boyhood, Youth* in Siberia, in the periodical called the *Contemporary*, and was so taken with it that he inquired on all sides after the anonymous author. "Calm, deep, clear, yet unfathomable as nature is unfathomable, that is the impression it leaves," he writes. "There it is, and everything, even the smallest detail, shows the beautiful unity of the temperament from which it flows."—No, these are not Dostoyevsky's words, though they might have been. It is Schiller who writes thus, about *Wilhelm Meister*, in that letter in which, for the first time, he apostrophizes Goethe as "Dearest Friend": an emotional form of address, in which, so far as I know, Goethe never explicitly acquiesced. Dostoyevsky wrote the profoundest and most loving of all existing critiques of *Anna Karenina;* a masterpiece of enthusiastic exposition, which Tolstoy, perhaps, never even read (he never did read criticisms of his works), to say nothing of his ever feeling impelled to write reviews of anything by Dostoyevsky. When Fyodor Mikhailovich died, Tolstoy is said to have said: "I loved that man very much." But his consciousness of the fact came a little late in the day; for while Dostoyevsky was alive Tolstoy never troubled his head about him; while afterwards, in a letter to Strakhov, Dostoyevsky's biographer, he compared him with a horse, who seemed a splendid creature and worth a thousand rubles, until suddenly he went lame, and then the fine strong animal was not worth a groschen. "The longer I live," he said, "the more I think of men who are not lame." But this horse-philosophy as applied to the author of *The Brothers Karamazov* does not seem quite happy, to put it mildly.

We know, and we rejoice to know, that in the case of Goethe and Schiller nature's attitude to spirit was altogether more brotherly and dignified, and on a higher plane. But if Goethe played here too the part of Hatem, the richly bestowing and receiving one, he did not after all take from the dear friend more than he gave him, to say nothing of all he gave by virtue of his mere existence, unconsciously, involuntarily. Was not Schiller's part in the relationship, after all, that of service? I think so, myself, simply because it lies in the nature of the thing, because Schiller did not in the least need, to keep him fruitful, the meed of praise, love, inspiration, which he bestowed upon Goethe. And I note that such a letter as his famous first one, which knit the bond between them, in which with kindly hand he "gave the sum" of Goethe's life, he never did get from Goethe in return.

One utterance of Schiller's to Goethe has always delighted me, it seems to characterize the relationship so wonderfully. I mean the passage in a letter where he warns Goethe against Kant, his own spiritual master and his idol. Goethe, he tells him, can only be a Spinozan; his beautiful simple nature would be at once vitiated by contact with a philosophy of freedom. It is no more and no less than the problem of irony that we catch sight of here: without exception the profoundest and most fascinating in the world. For we see here that nothing is more foreign to spirit than a desire to convert nature to itself. It warns nature against itself. To the moral "sentimentalist," all that is nature seems beautiful and highly worth preserving. Knowledge feels that life is beautiful; and this is the feeling of the moral for the simple, of the holy for the divine, of nature for spirit; and in this peculiarly absolute judgment of values resides the ironic god, resides Eros. Spirit accordingly enters into a relationship with nature which is in a sense erotic, in a sense determined by male-female sex-polarity. And by virtue of the relation it can venture to abase itself and dare the ultimate self-surrender, without thereby resigning any of its own nobility. Indeed, it will always retain the accent of a certain tender contempt. In Hölderlin's lines precisely this emotional irony is immortalized:

Wer das Tiefste gedacht, liebt das Lebendigste,
Hohe Tugend versteht, wer in die Welt geblickt,
Und es neigen die Weisen
Oft am Ende zu Schönem sich.

On the other hand, this simple nature too has an ironic mood, which is one with the objectivity of its character and precisely coincides with the conception of poetry, inasmuch as it lifts itself above its subject, above joy and grief, good and bad, death and life, to play freely with them. Goethe speaks of this mood in *Dichtung und Wahrheit*, with reference to Herder.

It is plain that what kept Goethe apart from Schiller so long was, more than anything else, the latter's prepossessions on the subject of freedom: his conception of human dignity, which was entirely based on the dictatorship of spirit — that is, was entirely revolutionary in character — which conceived in this emancipated sense all humanity, all nobility, all human nobility — and that, to a nature like Goethe's, must have seemed both odious and insulting to nature. It is, for instance, certain *a priori* that Goethe took the greatest umbrage at the famous essay *Über Anmut und Würde*. In it occur things like the following: "Movements which have as principle only animal sensuousness belong only, however voluntary we may suppose them to be, to physical nature, which never reaches of itself to grace. If it were possible to have grace in the manifestations of physical appetites and instincts, grace would no longer be either capable or worthy to serve as the expression of humanity." That one might describe as idealistic malice of spirit against nature, and so Goethe must have regarded it. For it is audacious to assert that grace cannot come out of the sensuous, nor nature reach to grace. Grace, then, is not a manifestation worthy of humanity; for that desire can express itself with charm, and instinct with grace, is a "charming" fact of experience. And when Schiller goes on to say: "Grace is a beauty not given by nature, but produced by the subject itself . . . it is the beauty of form under the influence of free will; it is the beauty of those particular phenomena which the person himself determines. Architectonic beauty does honour to its author; nature, charm, and grace do honour to him who possesses them. The one is a gift, the other a personal merit" – the moral distinction he draws between talent and personal merit becomes a consummate affront to Goethe's vital consciousness and his aristocratic feeling. "Fools never think," says Goethe, "how fortune and merit are linked together." What he means by "fortune" is what Schiller calls "nature" and "talent," and distinguishes from free human merit. While Goethe, half-maliciously, half-paradoxically going about to deprive the word "merit" of the moralistic flavour that clings to it, likes to talk about "inborn merit." Everybody is free to call this a logical contradiction. But there are cases where logic is confronted by a metaphysical certainty higher than itself; and Goethe, who on the whole was certainly no metaphysician, undoubtedly felt the problem of freedom to be a metaphysical one. That is to say, an undemonstrable intuition told him that freedom, and therewith merit and demerit, were not a matter of the empirical but of the intelligible world; that, to speak with Schopenhauer, freedom does not consist in *operari* but in *esse*. Herein lies the humbleness of his aristocracy, the aristocracy of his humility; both of them so categorically opposed to Schiller's idealistic evaluations, his personal and moral pride in his freedom. Goethe, when he wants to characterize the principle that composes his essential nature, speaks humbly and gratefully of a "gift of fortune." But the conception of a "gift," of "grace," is more aristocratic than one might think. What it means is the indissoluble union of fortune and merit, a synthesis of freedom and necessity; in short, "inborn merit"; and the gratitude, the humility, carry with them that metaphysical consciousness of being at all times and absolutely certain of the favour of destiny.

There is, in Goethe's case, an amazing bit of evidence on this point, which I cannot refrain from quoting. Speaking of Bentham, he says it is the height of madness for the man, at his age, to be so radical. He is answered that if His Excellence had been born in England he could hardly have escaped being a radical and reformer. Whereat Goethe, with Mephistophelian mien: "What do you take me for? You think I would be spying out abuses and tacking names on to them? I, who if I had been born in England would have been living on abuses? If I had been born in England I should have been a duke, or better still a bishop with revenues of thirty thousand pounds sterling." – "Very fine. But suppose Your

Excellence had not drawn the big prize in the lottery; suppose you had drawn a blank?" To which Goethe: Not everybody, my dear friend, is *made for the big prize.* Do you think I should have played such a foolish trick (*sottise*) as to draw a blank?"

All that, of course, is in jest. But is it only in jest? Does it not rather voice that deep metaphysical certainty that never and under no circumstances should he or could he be other than favoured and privileged, ever other than well-born? And in this certainty is there not after all something like a consciousness of freedom of the will, if only of freedom after the event? Really, it is priceless. To be born into the world a starving revolutionary, an idealistic "sentimentalist," that he calls a *sottise.* Is that the irony the children of God wreak on the children of spirit? If there be such a thing as inborn merit, then there is inborn demerit as well; and if it is a *sottise* to come into the world an average man, or poor, or sick, or stupid, then the criminal is indeed not only empirically but metaphysically culpable. For merit and reward, guilt and punishment, are conceptions that belong together. And one punishment at least, all those merit who have committed the *sottise* of drawing a blank in life's lottery: that of eternal destruction; whereas the chosen ones get eternal life too at the end. "*Wer keinen Namen sich erwarb, noch Edles will, gehört den Elementen an; so fahret hin!*" But as the possibility of nobly aspiring and achieving a name is not a matter of empirical freedom of the will, this "*so fahret hin*" is a piece of gross heartlessness. And if the conception of election by grace, to which that of metaphysical depravity corresponds, is a Christian conception, at any rate it shows Christianity turning its aristocratic side outwards.

I said awhile back that it seemed to me not accidental that Schiller and Dostoyevsky were sick men and did not, like Goethe and Tolstoy, arrive at a reverend length of days. Rather I was inclined to regard their poor health as fundamental to their characters. Quite as symbolic is the further external fact that the two great realists and creative artists were of upper station, born to a privileged social status, whereas the heroes and saints of the idea, Schiller and Dostoyevsky, one the son of a Swabian army surgeon and the other of a Moscow hospital physician, were the children of modest people and spent all their days in pinched and homely, one might almost say undignified circumstances. I call this biographical fact symbolic, because it testifies to the Christianity of the spirit, whose kingdom, as the Scriptures say, is not of this world – in personalities as little as in the realm of the ideal and the artistic. Wherein it opposes a perpetual contrast to the kingdom of nature and nature's favourites, whose rank and essence are quite and entirely "of this world," the physical, pagan world. Therein lies their "realism." And they were, both Tolstoy and Goethe, realists enough to feel a naïve enjoyment in their privileged status, yes, in a sort to lay stress upon it and show themselves imbued by a consciousness of it; which would impress one as curiously unenlightened were it not plain that they themselves regard it in a symbolic sense and even rather childishly assimilate it in their own minds to their consciousness of their higher, extra-social, human aristocracy. Goethe's patrician birth was so dear to him that his patent of nobility, when he had it in his hands, meant "nothing, simply nothing." "We Frankfurt patricians," he said, "always felt ourselves like nobility." But in the same conversation and connection, by way of refuting a slur upon himself as the obsequious servant of royalty, he puts it thus: "Yes, I felt so much at ease (*so wohl in meiner Haut*), and so very much the aristocrat, that if they had made me a prince it would not have surprised me." I may say in passing that it would have become him to be a prince. Had he taken up Napoleon's invitation to transfer his activity to Paris, had he written there the *Cæsar* Napoleon wanted him to write, in which he need only have given vent to the hatred he had felt as a youth for the "base, the contemptible murder," the Emperor would certainly have made him a prince, as by his own account he would have done for Corneille as well. My point is to show how, in Goethe's mind, the consciousness of his social position lay very close to that of his nobility as a human being, as a child of God. The two flow together in one and the same consciousness of nobility, or "inborn merit."

Count Leo Tolstoy came, as we know, from one of the oldest and finest of Russian families. When we read his books, *Childhood*, *Boyhood*, *Youth*, or *Anna Karenina*, that picture of high life in Moscow, we are impressed with the fact that the author is a man who was brought up with all the advantages. We get the same feeling when we read *Dichtung und Wahrheit* or *Die Wahlverwandtschaften.* And in Tolstoy too we find the same familiar and perhaps childish phenomenon we noticed in Goethe: his noble blood and the distinction conferred by his great gifts both belonged to him quite simply because they belonged to him, and his consciousness of them mingled in his joy in himself, of which, despite all his attacks of poverty of spirit, he possessed a very great deal. His fame as a writer, so he wrote to his father-in-law, delights him very much; he finds it most pleasant to be an author *and* a nobleman. An author and a nobleman – all his Christianity, all his anarchism, to the contrary and notwithstanding, he never ceased to be a striking combination of those two. When Turgenyev first made the acquaintance of the youthful Tolstoy he said: "Not a word, not a gesture of his is natural. He is constantly posing; it is a mystery to me how such a sensible man can take such childish pride in his silly title." This is the same Turgenyev who wrote to a French publisher: "I am not worthy to untie his shoe-laces"; so it is unlikely that the first-quoted remark misrepresents the facts. As for the aged Tolstoy, Gorky relates: "His comfortable, democratic manner took many people in; and I have often seen Russians, who judge people by their clothes, gush over him with their famous 'simplicity of manner,' which might better be called 'beastly familiarity.' And suddenly, from under his peasant beard, and his rumpled democratic blouse, the old Russian *barin*, the aristocrat of aristocrats, would peep forth; and in the chill that emanated from him the confiding visitor's nose would be frost-bitten. It was a joy to see this blue-blooded creature: the noble charm of his gestures, the haughty reticence of his speech, the murderous and fastidious sharpness of his tongue. He displayed just so much of the *barin* as these servile souls needed to see; when they roused the *barin* in Tolstoy it came easy and natural and overwhelmed them so that they shrivelled up and whined." – The blue noses call up memories of Weimar, chilling memories of receptions and formal calls – only that Goethe was never malicious enough to put on the democratic pose; and his most frigid manner concealed more love than Tolstoy ever felt – Tolstoy, whose last and most frightful secret Turgenyev's penetrating mind laid bare: it was that Tolstoy could love nobody but himself! But it was a "joy," in Gorky's sense of the word, to see Tolstoy for instance at the Petrov yearly fair, whither he drove from his estate in Samara in the seventies. His charm made him very popular in the merry whirl of peasants, Cossacks, Bashkirs, and Kirghiz. Even with drunken folk, we are told, he did not hesitate to strike up a conversation. And then came the following quiet and characteristic little episode. A drunken peasant, in his excess of feeling, wanted to embrace Tolstoy. But one stern and speaking look from Leo Nikolayevich's eyes met the man and sobered him in a twinkling. He dropped his hands of himself, and said: "No? Well, all right, then." What was there in that look to make it have such an arresting, quenching, sobering effect? Was it the consciousness of the *barin*? Or of the great author? In such a case it is quite impossible to distinguish between them – as little objectively as doubtless it was subjectively.

"When Leo Nikolayevich wanted to please," Gorky tells us, "he could do it better than a pretty and clever woman. Imagine a crowd of all sorts of people sitting in his room: the Grand Duke Nikolai Mikhailovich, the house-painter Ilya, a social-democrat from Yalta, a musician, a German, the poet Bulgakov, and so on; they all look at him with the same enamoured eyes, while he expounds to them the doctrine of Lao-tse. . . . I used to look at him just like the others. And now I long to look at him once more – and I shall never see him again." – One thing is obvious: it was *not* the doctrine of Lao-tse which brought that lovelorn look into all their eyes. The teaching would have roused very scant general interest but for the expounder. But that look in every eye is the very same that Karl August had in mind when he passed on to Goethe the greetings sent by Napoleon on the Emperor's way back from Russia: "You see," he added, "heaven and hell are both making eyes at you."

Yes, and the democratic mouzhik blouses were immaculate, made of soft fine material, highly comfortable and pleasant to wear, and the linen was scented. Of course, he did not scent it himself. The Countess attended to that, and he, who liked it very much, pretended not to notice, just as he pretended not to know that the vegetarian dishes he exclusively ate were all prepared with bouillon. "His face is that of a peasant," reports an eyewitness, "with a broad nose, a weather-beaten skin, and thick, beetling brows with small, piercing grey eyes beneath them. But, despite the peasant features, no one could fail to recognize at first glance the fine, cosmopolitan Russian gentleman, member of the very highest society." Conversing thus in English or French with a Grand Duke, he reminds one very much of Goethe, on whom princes waited, and who thought it no derogation of his nobility, human or divine, to season it with a little knack for polite nothings. When Tolstoy visited Alexander Herz in London, his daughter, young Natalia Alexandrovna, begged to be present in a dark corner, that she might behold in the flesh the author of *Childhood, Boyhood, Youth.* With beating heart she awaited Tolstoy's appearance. She was bitterly disappointed to see a man dressed in the latest fashion, with good manners and a flow of speech, the subject-matter of which was exclusively the cock-fights and boxing-matches he had seen in London. "Not a word that came from his heart, not a word that could have corresponded to my expectations, did I hear during the single interview at which I was present."

Nothing of the sort is reported of Dostoyevsky or Schiller. Never did these by their worldliness disappoint the expectations of their audience. The sons of spirit make personally a spiritual impression, as the hopeful average man expects those to do who are soul-shakers. That lofty, pallid, suffering-saint and criminal look of Dostoyevsky corresponded to the idea the Russians got of the phenomenon of his genius, just as Schiller's mild, intrepid, fanatical, and equally ailing psysiognomy, with open shirt-collar and flowing silk neckerchief, corresponded to the image which the German mind might have formed of its hero. Whereas on the other hand Goethe, if we accept Riemer's description of him as he moved among his guests in a blue coat, "the powerful, expressive face showing the effects of sun and fresh air, with the black side-locks floating about it, the hair bound in a queue, was more like a well-to-do, comfortable farmer, or a well-tried staff-officer in mufti, than like a shrinking and sensitive poet." And it is true, *a priori,* that neither of those other two ever estranged ardent admiration by displaying a banal enthusiasm for cock-fighting and boxing. Whereas the sense of sport, the taste for bodily exercise, physical training, and physical enjoyment, played an essential role in Tolstoy's life as in Goethe's. We call these tastes gentlemanly and thus indicate the physical basis of the well-born-ness which is of this world. "One must see him," wrote Riemer about Goethe; "how strong and firm he stands on his feet, with what bodily agility and sure step he moves. Early gymnastic training, dancing, fencing, skating, riding, even coursing and racing, had given him this mobility and suppleness; he could never make a false step on the worst path or be in danger of slipping or falling; easily and swiftly he passed over smooth ice, narrow foot-paths and bridges, and rocky steeps. As a youth he climbed among chasms and shingle with his princely friend, mounted towering rocks and Alpine crags with the boldness of a chamois; and so throughout his fifty years of geological exploration no mountain has been too high for him, no shaft too deep nor passage too low, no cave labyrinthine enough. . . ."

The great interest that Leo Tolstoy took in his body showed itself negatively as well as positively. Negatively, in his Christian and ascetic grumblings at his beastly physical body, in such utterances as that the body is a hindrance to the good man, and in such phrases as: "I am ashamed to speak of my disgusting body." Positively, in all the training and care he gave it. His interest in it begins at the moment — of which he speaks in the *Confessions* — when he sat as a little child in a wooden tub, enveloped in the smell of the bran-water in which he was being bathed, and for the first time noticed his little body with the ribs visible on the breast in front, and straightway feels drawn to it by a very strong inclination. Tolstoy's face was, humanly speaking, ugly, and he suffered greatly on account of it, convinced that there could be little joy in store for a creature with such a broad nose, such thick lips, and such small grey eyes. He confesses that he would have given anything he had for a handsome face. The youth who is tortured by the problem of death, and ponders all the high and ultimate questions with as much maturity as the "aged prophet," this youth is at the same time perpetually occupied with his own appearance, is obviously possessed by the desire to be elegant and *comme il faut;* sets the greatest store by physical development, gymnastic exercise; drills, rides, and hunts as though he had no higher ambition in his head nor thought of any. His passion for the hunt is so excessive that he confesses to his wife that of human beings he never forgot Sophia Alexandrovna, but out hunting he forgot everything but his double-barrelled shotgun. From more than one letter of those who knew him in his prime we see what a daring sportsman he was, how he sprang with astonishing agility over gullies and chasms and would spend whole days in the wild. We are told that a better companion could not be conceived of. The pacifism, Christian, Buddhistic, or Chinese, of his latter days forbade him of course to kill animals, although his indestructible physical strength and trained agility would still have allowed him to hunt and though he still cherished the greatest desire to. He bade it farewell. He submitted himself to a test and found he had fortitude enough to let the hares run. And in his case that meant a good deal, as we see from the following anecdote, related by Gorky. Tolstoy put on a heavy overcoat and thick boots and took Gorky for a walk in the birch woods. He leaped like a schoolboy over puddles and ditches, shook the raindrops from the boughs, lovingly stroked the moist, satiny trunks of the birch trees, and talked about Schopenhauer. . . . "Suddenly a hare got up under our feet. Leo Nikolayevich gave an excited start, his face lighted up, he let out a halloo like an old huntsman. Then he looked at me with a curious smile and began laughing, a hearty human laugh. At this moment he was irresistible." – Still finer is the story of the hawk which the old man saw circling above his chickens, about to swoop. Leo Nikolayevich stares up at the bird of prey, his hand over his eyes, and says in an "excited whisper": "The rascal! Now, now! He's coming . . . oh, he's afraid. . . . I'll call the stable-boy." He calls, the hawk disappears. But Tolstoy is taken with regrets. He sighs and says: "I shouldn't have called. Then he would have swooped." They are his chickens. But all the sympathy of the venerable prophet of pacifism is with the hawk.

Of his son Ilyusha he wrote in a letter: "Ilyusha is lazy, he is growing, and his soul is not yet overwhelmed by organic processes." What does he mean by that? Growing is itself an organic process, and if growing is innocent, so too will be the organic processes which growth brings about, and with which Tolstoy was only too well acquainted, since they made his life a burden to him all his days. The church's conception of woman as *instrumentum diaboli* was with him something more than a mood from the time of the *Kreuzer Sonata;* it dates from much earlier, from the journals of his boyish days; and he speaks of organic processes in the sense of that early Christian Pope who, in order to mortify the flesh, made a detailed list of all its disgusting and evil-smelling functions, the functions of this body which in the end has to submit to the final indignity of putrefaction. That kind of cross-grained speculation Tolstoy would be just the one to set about, and he did. Very sensual men well know such moods. Maupassant somewhere calls the action of coition filthy and ridiculous – "*ordurier et ridicule.*" Could objectivity further go? But such blithe and cynical objectivity was not Tolstoy's sort. His hatred of the organic has a shattering accent of subjective torment and rage. And yet he is so much the darling of the creative impulse of organic life that one must go back to Goethe to find a human being who was "*so wohl in seiner Haut*" as he. Yes, the parallel is even more exact. In both of them, and in just the same way, the most beatific organic well-being, amounting to organic rapture, mingled with a rooted melancholy and the profoundest intimacy with death. Goethe, when he was a riotous, dandiacal student in Leipzig, might any moment quit the society of men, the card-play and dance, and yield himself to solitude. We have plenty of witnesses to his brilliance, his childish, fantastic extravagances in the circle of his friends, with the Jacobis, Heinse, Stilling in Elberfeld. He cuts capers, dances round the table like a clown, in short cannot contain himself for a mysterious intoxication; the philistines sitting round think he has gone mad. And that is the same Goethe whose Werther drove more than one young man to self-destruction, and who practised himself in suicide by keeping a sharp dagger on his bed-table and trying every evening to drive it a little further into his body.

We have noted the same excess of animal spirits in Tolstoy; in whom, indeed, they persisted up to an old age lacking in the dignity, stateliness, and formal gravity of Goethe's latest period. Which need surprise nobody. For we cannot doubt that Goethe led a more earnest, laborious, exemplary life than the Slavic Junker; or that his cultural activities presupposed far more genuine self-abnegation, restraint, and discipline than Tolstoy's uttermost ineffectual efforts at spiritualization, sticking fast as these always did in a bog of fantastic absurdity. Tolstoy's aristocratic charm was, and Gorky so depicts it, that of a noble animal. He never managed to arrive at the dignity of man the civilized, man the triumpher over odds. It is lovely to hear of all the pranks he played with the children, his droll conceits, the gymnastic feats he performed for and with them; the endless croquet, lawn-tennis, and leap-frog parties in the garden at Yasnaya Polyana. He not only shared all the activities of youth, but he was the life and soul of them. The sixty-year-old man runs races with the boys, his bicycle trips extend, much to the Countess's anxiety, over thirty versts. "When there is some activity requiring agility, strength, and suppleness," comments a bystander, "he never takes his eyes off the players, he puts his whole soul into their success or failure. Often he cannot resist and joins in with a youthful fire and muscular suppleness which the onlooker could only envy." In the family circle he performed the sheerest absurdities. He had invented a game called "Numidian horsemen," which made the children weep with delight. Leo Nikolayevich would suddenly spring from his chair, lifting his hand, and run about the room flapping it in the air, whereupon everybody, grown-ups, children, and all, followed suit. That is, I repeat, charming, though a little bizarre. It becomes more so when we learn that all these high spirits occur in the years after his "conversion," in the period of his soul-crises, his ascetic eclipses and theological broodings. But what shall be said of the incident recorded by his father-in-law, Behrs? They were walking about the room together in light converse one evening, when suddenly the elderly prophet sprang upon Behrs's shoulder. He probably jumped down again at once; but for a second he actually perched up there, like a grey-bearded kobold – it gives one an uncanny feeling! I do not ask my readers to imagine Goethe, in his later period, leaping unexpectedly on a visitor's shoulder. There is a decided difference of temperament, that is clear. But the resemblance is no less so.

Looking more closely at the matter, I find that there is a complex of problems, a "problematic," peculiar to the sons of nature, the creative and objective artists, which is entirely foreign to the children of the idea, and, for all the brilliant sunshine of favour they move in, casts a strange dark cloud upon them which must considerably chill their consciousness of aristocratic well-being. My feeling is that it is pure error to think that conflict and complexity are things of the spirit, while nature's kingdom must be all brightness and harmony. It looks as though the contrary were the case. If what we call happiness consists in harmony, clarity, unity with oneself, in the consciousness of a positive, confident, decisive turn of mind, if, in short, it is peace resident in the soul, then obviously happiness is a state far easier for the sons of spirit to arrive at than for the children of nature. For the latter, though surely singleness of heart should be their lot, seem never to attain the joy and peace it might confer. Nature herself appears to weave in their very being a questionable strand, an element of contradiction, negation, and all-pervasive doubt, which, since it cannot conduce to goodness, cannot conduce to happiness either. Spirit is good. Nature is by no means good. One might say she is evil, if moral categories were admissible with reference to her. She is, then, neither good nor evil, she escapes definition, as she herself refuses to define and judge; she is, speaking objectively, indifferent, and as this indifference of hers appears subjectively and spiritually in her children, it becomes a complication that has more to do with torment and evil than with happiness and goodness, and which certainly seems come not to bring peace into the world, like the human and benevolent spirit, but rather doubt and dire confusion.

Obviously I am not speaking here of the comparatively harmless conflict between the Faustian "two souls," the battle between the impulses of a strong animal constitution and the yearnings after "*Gefilden hoher Ahnen*" — a battle, and a "problematic," of which Goethe speaks out of such deep experience, and which not only made Tolstoy's youth a period of such hardship, so torn with remorse, but persisted in him up to old age. I am speaking of something that seems at first blush to be much blither and simpler: a position something like that of Goethe between Lavater and Basedow, in which Goethe designates himself as "*das Weltkind in der Mitten.*" That sounds simple, and pleasant, and self-complacent, and was probably so meant. And yet in the word "*Weltkind*" and the associations that surround it there is something sinister, a difficulty and a "problematic," by contrast with which the "prophetic" existence is nothing less than sweetness and light and plain sailing. "Goethe's tendency to negation," writes Chancellor von Müller on some occasion or other, "and his incredible judicial-mindedness came out strong again." "There is something," Gorky writes about Tolstoy, "which presumably he will never reveal to a human being, which appears darkly in his conversation, and is hinted at in his journals. To me it seems like the apotheosis of negation, the deepest and most hideous nihilism, springing from a stratum of boundless and hopeless despair, from a solitude of which probably no one else in the world has ever been so frightfully aware." No one? It was not Tolstoy who created the so lyric figure of Mephistopheles — though indeed the Mephistophelian element was never lacking to any period of his life. The ceaseless, tormenting effort to shape that which he calls his conception of life, to arrive at truth and clarity and inward peace, found expression in his youth, partly in a gloomy irritability that led to duels and scenes with his friends, which he took in desperate earnest, as matters of life and death, killing and dying; but partly also in malicious negation in general, an inimical spirit of contradictiousness, which, as we are expressly assured, made a quite Mephistophelian impression. Though of course this was not a nihilistic but a moral attitude, and was not assumed save in opposition to things that were not true — only they were simply everything! In the young Tolstoy there was observable, "from the beginning, a sort of unconscious enmity toward all accepted laws in the kingdom of thought. No matter what the opinion expressed; and the greater the authority of the speaker, the more was Tolstoy at pains to take up and accentuate an inimical attitude. If you watched him as he listened, and saw the sarcastic curl of his lip, you could not avoid the impression that he was thinking, not so much of answering what was said, as of himself saying something that should surprise and confound the speaker." That is nihilism, that is malice. But it is not so much cold malice as it is a tortured spite against anybody who fancied he held the secret of clarity and truth. It is a disbelief in clarity and truth. This spite, and this incredulity, were especially directed against Turgenyev, the clear-eyed and human man with whom he never could get on. "Tolstoy," said Turgenyev, "early developed a trait which, lying as it does at the root of his gloomy conception of life, has caused him great suffering. He has never managed to believe in the sincerity of mankind. Every expression of feeling seemed to him false; and he had the habit, due to his extraordinarily penetrating gaze, of boring through with his eye the man he considered insincere." And when Turgenyev said this, he added the confession that never in his life had he encountered anything with such power to dishearten him as this same piercing gaze, which, accompanied by two or three biting remarks, could bring to the verge of madness anybody who did not possess particularly strong self-control. Now, Turgenyev's self-control was strong. He was at the height of his literary success; serene and untroubled, he could encounter the complexities of his younger colleague with the calmness of a man who lived on good terms with himself. But precisely this security was what troubled Tolstoy. He seems to have gone deliberately about with this tranquil good-natured man, working with such a clear conviction that what he did was right, to goad him past the bounds of self-control. Simply this conviction that he knew and did what was right was more than Tolstoy could bear; for certainly he himself did not in the least know what was right. Garschin says: "In his view, the people who passed for good were merely hypocrites, who paraded their goodness and pretended to the certainty that their work served a good end." Turgenyev too saw in Tolstoy this strange, sinister, malicious bent. He resolved to hold fast to what he considered "right" and not to lose his self-control; so he avoided Tolstoy, left St. Petersburg, where the latter was living, and went first to Moscow and then to his own estate. But—this is most significant of all, as evidence of Tolstoy's state of mind—Tolstoy pursued him. Pursued him step for step, "like a lovesick girl," to use Turgenyev's own phrase.

All which is pretty steep—and very telling, very extraordinary. Above all, it shows how completely the old Tolstoy, of whom Gorky writes, was foreshadowed in the young one. Did he really ever find out what was "right"—the real, the true, the incontrovertible? For others he did, he gave them conviction. But he himself never got free of the negation and neutrality of the elemental character. "Rousseau," he said, "lied and believed his lies." Did he believe his own lies? No, for he did not lie. He was elemental, nihilistic, malicious, and unfathomable. "Would you very much like to know?" he asks.—"Very much."—"Then I will not tell you." And he smiles and plays with his thumbs. This smile, this "sly little smile"—Gorky speaks of it again and again. There is something not only extra-moral but extra-mental, extra-human, about it; it bespeaks the mystery of the "natural," the elemental, which is not at all kindly disposed, but rather takes pleasure in confusion. According to Gorky, the old man loved to put insidious questions. "What do you think about yourself?" "Do you love your wife?" "How do you like mine?" "Do you like me, Alexei Maximovich?"—"Disingenuous!" Gorky cries. "The whole time, he is making an experiment, testing something out, as though he were going into battle. It is interesting, but not to my taste. He is the devil, and I am a babe in arms beside him. He ought to leave me alone."

One day Gorky sees the aged Tolstoy sitting alone by the sea. This scene is the crowning point of his reminiscences. "He sat, his head on his hands; the wind blew the silver hair of his beard through his fingers. He was looking far out across the sea, and the little green waves rolled docilely to his feet and caressed them, as though they wanted to tell the old wizard something about themselves. . . . He seemed like an ancient stone come alive, that knew and pondered the beginning and end of all things, and what and how would be the end of the stones and grasses of the earth, the waters of the sea, the whole universe from the sun to the grain of sand. And the sea is a part of his soul, and all about him comes from him and out of him. In the old man's musing quietude I felt something portentous, magic. I cannot express in words what I more felt than thought at that moment. In my heart were rejoicing and fear, then all melted together in one single blissful feeling: 'I am not bereft on this earth, so long as this old man is living on it.' " And Gorky steals away on his tiptoes that the sand may not crunch under his tread and disturb the old man's thoughts.

The mystical reverence that Gorky here depicts is not that which lays hold on us at sight of the heroes of the idea. Neither Dostoyevsky nor Schiller has inspired this sort of awe and shuddering, however saintly they seemed. So much is certain. Nor can the reverence felt for Goethe be of just this same nature — though akin to it. The Tolstoyan greatness and remoteness is wild and primeval and pagan in its nature, it is antecedent to culture. It lacks the human, the humanistic element. This ancient of days and of wisdom, musing there at the edge of the everlasting sea, wrapped up in the All, conning the beginning and end of things — the picture evokes a twilit, prehuman, uncanny world of feeling, a world of incantations and runes. What he is pondering, the Norns whisper thee by night. He was like, says the shaken beholder, an ancient stone come alive: note that, a stone, not anything that civilization has produced, not man made in the likeness of God, not a human being like Goethe. Goethe's humanistic divineness is clearly something quite different from the primeval, pagan formlessness of Tolstoy's, which makes Gorky say of him: "He is the devil." And still, at the very bottom, the common factor persists: in Goethe too there is the elemental, the sinister, the dark, neutral, negation- and confusion-loving devil.

There is a saying of his, arbitrary enough, yet with an accent of hidden suffering, that opens to us more of his inner self than many a clear and wise and ordered utterance. "If I am to listen to the opinion of others," he said (and only listen to it, observe, not accept it), "then it must be positively expressed. Problems I have enough in myself." That is a confession, put in the form of a demand. It has a proud, Olympian accent, but the voice that utters it quivers with impatience, with painful irritation at the inner complications, which makes it so imperative that the positive should come from without. . . . "Out of one of his eyes looks an angel," writes someone who made his acquaintance on a journey, "out of the other a devil; and his speech is deep irony on the score of all human affairs." Of all? That is great, but it is not generous – and, after all, is he not a man himself? One who often saw him says: "Today he was altogether in that mood of bitter humour and sophistical contradictiousness he is so prone to display." Again we have the negation, the spirit of contradiction and malice, of which gentle young Sulpice Boisserée has such a story to tell in his diary. "At eleven o'clock I am with Goethe again. The invective continues." He has a go at all sorts of things: politics, æsthetics, society, religion, Germany, France, philhellenism, parties, and so on, in such a style that poor young Boisserée feels – "*mit allen diesen moquanten Reden*" – as though he were "at a witches' sabbath." That is saying a good deal. It is either too strong, considering the word "*moquant*" which he uses, or else that word is a good deal too weak – which is more likely. Anyhow the entry, from the year 1826, shows the confusion to which the petulant old man could reduce simple and humble-minded people. An observer who must have been no fool wrote something about him which stirs a secret horror that is somehow paralysing. "He is tolerant, without being mild." Just consider what that means. Toleration, indulgence, is always, in our human experience, associated with mildness, with benevolent feeling toward man and the universe; so far as I know, it is a product of love. But tolerance *without* love, *harsh* tolerance – what would that be? It is more than human, it is icy neutrality, it is either something godlike or something devilish.

I shall be saying nothing new, but it may serve to bring order and clarity into our thoughts to keep the fact before us: all national character belongs to the natural sphere, and all tendency toward the cosmopolitan to the spiritual. The word "ethnic" brings together two conceptions which we do not ordinarily connect, paganism and nationalism; thus by implication, and conversely, every super-national and humane point of view is classified in our mind as Christian in spirit.

Goethe's alleged devotion to paganism (in the *Wanderjahre* he reckons Judaism among the ethnic and heathen folk-religions) would lead us accordingly to expect of him an outlook basically anti-humanistic and folk-national. That we should be entirely wrong in this expectation, as a basic constitution in him, as "nature," might be arguable. However, so far as he was himself aware, he was consciously a humanist and a citizen of the world. Despite all his nature Olympian and divine, he was in a high degree Christian in spirit. Nietzsche placed Goethe, historically and psychologically speaking, between Hellenism and pietism; and thus expressed the combination of creative and critical, simple and "sentimental," ancient and modern, in Goethe's character. For Goethe's "pietism" is of course nothing else than his modernity. Many centuries of Christian cultivation of the subjective – a whole century of pietistic, introspective, autobiographical dicipline – were needed to make possible a work like *Werther*. Which is as much as to say that in the impulse to autobiography Christian and democratic elements are mingled with that naïve, spoilt-darling claim on the world's affections of which we spoke above. They are the same as that democratic tendency out of which Tolstoy likes to consider his confessions as emanating, when, in true Rousseauian fashion, he resolves "to write a history of his life, utterly and entirely true to fact," in the belief that this "will be more useful to mankind" than those previous twelve volumes full of literary twaddle. He seems unaware that they are quite as autobiographical, quite as ethical in character, as anything could be, and disowns them as pagan and artistic, as self-indulgent and "irresponsible."

Goethe, with all his aversion to the "Cross," did often and expressly acknowledge his reverence for the Christian idea. It is as significant as it is surprising to come upon the idea of the sanctity of suffering in the Pedagogic Province; and if Goethe saw in the church "elements of weakness and instability" and in its precepts "*gar viel Dummes*," still he bore witness that "there is in the Gospels an effective resplendence and majesty, issuing from the person of Christ, of a character in which only the divine appear upon this earth." "The human spirit," he says, with sympathetic and openly acknowledged fellowship, "will never rise higher than the majesty and moral elevation of Christianity, as it radiates from the Gospels." But Goethe's Christianity manifests itself in the admirable attitude, as of a pupil to a master, which he had toward Spinoza, whom he called "*theissimus*" and of whom he said that nobody had spoken of the Divinity so like the Saviour as he. If, indeed, the dualistic separation of God and nature is the fundamental principle of Christianity, then Spinoza was a pagan, and Goethe was too. But God and nature are not all the world: there is the human, the humane, as well; and Spinoza's conception of humanity is Christian, in so far as he defines the phenomenon man as the becoming-*conscious* of the God-nature in the human being, as a bursting forth out of mere dull being and living; accordingly, as liberation from nature, and so as *spirit*. Again, there is absolutely nothing pagan about that famous *Mastery of the Passions by their Analysis;* and just as little in the Spinozan motif of renunciation ("*Entsagung*"), which becomes the general motif of Goethe's life and work, like the idea of freedom for Schiller and the idea of redemption for Wagner.

On the contrary, it was just this pathos of renunciation that cast such a Christian shade upon the pagan, aristocratic, child-of-nature well-being of Goethe's life and lent his spirited features an expressly Gothic trait of suffering not to be overlooked save by the gross popular belief in his aristocratic good fortune. How much resignation must have darkened the end of this apparently consummate and favoured existence! His life-work, though almost superhuman, remained entirely a fragment—it is putting it mildly to say that "not all the dreams of blossoms ripened"—Wagner's performance, for instance, or Ibsen's, is incomparably more a rounded and effective whole. One may put it that Goethe's spirit was far more powerful than his nature, greater than his power to give it form or than his organically allotted span; and it is easy to understand that vehement demand of his for immortality, which is one of the magnificent, dæmonic expressions of his personality: Nature, he cried, was bound to give him a new body when the one he had could no longer sustain his spirit.

Consider even his love-life, which likewise the popular mind tends to think of as sunlit and blissful, divinely favoured and without a cross. Certainly he was much loved and rich in love; certainly to him much enjoyment was given. In the realm of the erotic he had his spells of coarseness, when he behaved a little like a garden god: when, ingenuous and unsentimental as the antique world, he would enjoy without stint and indulge without a qualm. His marriage, a misalliance, socially and intellectually, was a result of this attitude of mind. But where he loved so that lofty poesy was the result, and not merely a Venetian epigram ticked out in hexameters on a maiden's back; where it was serious, the romance regularly ended in renunciation. He never actually possessed Lotte or Friederike, nor Lilli, nor the Herzlieb, nor Marianne, nor even

Ulrike — and not even Frau von Stein. He never loved unrequited — unless in the immensely painful, absurdly shattering affair with little Levetzow. Yet in all these cases resignation was the order of the day: either on moral grounds, or for the sake of his freedom. Mostly he bolted.

But the renunciation I mean was a deeper and higher thing. In his stature, his lineaments, his proportions as he stands today in the eyes of the nation, he is what he is as the work of renunciation. I am not speaking generally, I do not refer to the sense of sacrifice which is the meaning of all art; nor to the struggle with chaos, the surrender of freedom, the creative constraint which is its inner essence. Goethe's pathos of renunciation — or, since we are speaking of permanent forces dominating the whole of existence, his ethos of renunciation — is of a more personal kind. It is his destiny, it is the instinctive mandate of his especially national gift, which was essentially civilizing in its mission. Or, rather, might this destiny and mission, this bond, this conditioning limitation and pedagogic duty of renunciation, be after all something less personal to him than it just now appeared? Might it perhaps be the law of his destiny, innate and inviolable save at the expense of heavy spiritual penalties; the imperative which is the essence of the German spirit, destined always, as it is, somehow and in some degree, to feel itself called to a cultural task? — I spoke of the consciousness of a community of feeling, which Goethe must, at moments, have felt with Christianity. What did it consist in, and to what had it reference? Goethe pays homage to the "moral culture" of Christianity — that is, to its humanity, its civilizing, anti-barbarian influence. It was the same as his; and the occasional homage he paid it undoubtedly springs from his recognition that the mission of Christianity within the confines of the Germanic peoples bore a likeness to his own. And here, in the fact that he conceived his task, his duty to his nation, as essentially a civilizing mission, lies the deepest and the most German significance of his renunciation. Does anyone doubt that there were in Goethe possibilities of a greatness and growth wilder, ranker, more disruptive, more "natural," than those which his instinct for self-conquest allowed him to develop, and which today give our mental picture of him so highly pedagogic a cast? In his *Iphigenie* the idea of humanity, as opposed to barbarism, wears the impress of civilization — not in the polemical and even political sense in which we use the word today, but in the sense of moral culture. It was a Frenchman, Maurice Barrès, who pointed out that the *Iphigenie* is a "civilizing work," in that it "stands for the rights of society against the arrogance of intellect." The phrase fits almost better that other monument of self-discipline and self-correction, yes, almost of self-mortification, which has been a target for ridicule on account of its affected atmosphere of courts and culture: I mean the *Tasso*. Both are works of resignation, of German and schoolmasterish renunciation of all the advantages of barbarism. Wagner, on the other hand, the voluptuary, did not renounce them; he yielded to them all, with huge effectiveness; and his punishment is that the acclaim accorded to his riotously national art grows daily cruder and more popular.

My subject is still the aspiration of the children of nature toward spirit; which is just as sentimental in kind as is the converse striving of the sons of the spirit toward nature, and may function with varying degrees of aptitude or success, with more or less naïveté or subtlety. Compared with Goethe's majestic work of spiritualization, I cannot find that Tolstoy's struggles to throw off nature's yoke were crowned with great success. But I am whimsical enough to relish putting my finger on the mighty kernel of racial loyalty which dwelt at the heart of the Christianity of the one and the humanity of the other. And that kernel was, of course, in other words, their aristocratic integrity; for racial loyalty is aristocratic by nature, while Christianity, humanity, and civilization all represent the conflicting principle of the spirit of democracy, and the process of spiritualization is at the same time one of democratization. What Tolstoy aptly calls his "democratic trend" – aptly, because the word "trend" implies a will and a direction somewhither, indicating an effort and not mere being – finds emphatic expression now and again in Goethe as well. "One would have," he says, "to become *Catholic* at once, in order to have a share in the lives of humanity!" To mingle with humanity, on equal terms, to lead the life of the people, and in the market-place, seems at such moments happiness to him. "In these small sovereign states," he cries, "what wretched, isolated men we are!" And he praises Venice as a monument to the power, not of a single despot, but of a whole people. But such phrases, clearly, are meant more correctively than absolutely; they are self-critical comments, meant to redress the balance of his German and Protestant aristocratism – "tendencies," then, sentimental leanings, of the same kind as the radical and pacifistic bent of the Russian giant, in whose "holiness" a penetrating eye can see so much self-deception, childishness, and "let's pretend."

A close observer like Gorky, or a shrewd critic like Merezhkovsky, felt at once and keenly the patriarchal and sensual quality, the life-bound animalism, which lay beneath the sanctification. Tolstoy married at thirty-four the eighteen-year-old Sophia Alexandrovna Behrs, who from then on was scarcely ever anything but "expectant," and was confined thirteen times. Through long, creative years his marriage was an idyll of family life, full of healthy, God-fearing animal pleasure, against a lavish economic background of agriculture and cattle-breeding. The atmosphere was Judaic Old Testament rather than Christian. Tolstoy knows the same great simple love of existence, the everlasting childlike joy of life, that possessed Goethe's soul. When he "praises each day for its beauty," when he "marvels at the richness of God's kingdom" expressing itself therein, how "each day He sends some new thing to distinguish it," we are reminded of what may have lain at the bottom of Goethe's conception of "*Behagen.*" Waves of piercing sensuous enjoyment of nature break upon him even in the years of gloom, when he meditates suicide, plans the *Confession* — in short, conjures up that misunderstanding to which his sanctification falls prey, and dehumanizes and shrinks the majesty of the patriarch, Christianizes and conventionalizes it into the Anglo-Indian model.

Merezhkovsky called him the great seer of the body, in contrast to Dostoyevsky the visionary of the soul; and truly it is the body to which his love and deepest interest belong, to which his knowledge refers, by which his genius is conditioned. We see this so clearly in his reaction to old age. In 1894 he writes: "Age is approaching. That means the hair falls out, the teeth decay, the wrinkles come, the breath gets bad. Even before the end, everything turns frightful, disgusting; sweat, rouge, powder, all sorts of beastliness. Then what has become of that which I have served? Where has beauty gone? It is the essence of everything. Without it there is nothing, no life." — This description of dying while the body still lives may pass for Christian, by virtue of its insistence on misery and its characterization of the flesh, revolting and insulting on the spiritual side. But the physical apprehension of old age and death is through and through pagan and sensual.

Aksakov says of Tolstoy: "His gift is *bearlike* in kind and degree." And is it not this "bearlike" quality of his genius that made Tolstoy "the great writer of Russia," the author of *War and Peace*, the epic poet of the people's struggle against Rome, against Napoleon? I openly declare my deliberate intention to cast doubt on the pacifism which the prophet of humanity so didactically professed. Not, I hasten to add, from any anti-pacifistic sentiments on my own part; merely out of a sense of humour. That Tolstoy was in his youth a soldier and an officer we know. From his biography we learn that he was heart and soul a soldier; and we have evidence of his heroic and warlike enthusiasm in the Sebastopol days — that "splendid time," that "glorious time," that time of touching pride in the Russian army, when he was confessedly saturated with patriotic feeling and thrilled by his experience of comradery under arms, first felt when the serious moment is at hand. His attitude toward the Serbo-Turkish war of 1877 is still full of conviction. It is a *real* war, he says, and it moves him. The distinction between "real" and "unreal" doubtless indicates some progress in the direction of pacifism. But is pacifism "real" so long as it is conditional and must progress in order to exist?

In 1812, at least, there *was* a "real" war, and its history occupied Tolstoy long before he became the great writer of Russia by dint of it. He treated of it, quite in the patriotic key, in his school at Yasnaya Polyana. From all we hear, he dealt with it on a mythical rather than a historical basis; but he expressly declared that he presented his pupils with these legends of a warlike mythology in order to rouse their patriotic feeling. And then the root-and-branch Russianism, the fundamental folk-character of his peasant-patrician nature, comes out strong in his epos, whose theme is a defensive war waged against the invasion of Latin civilization. *War and Peace* had a huge popular success, though the critics and military men had some fault to find. *On the intellectual side it was weak*, they said; its philosophy of history was narrow and superficial; it was mysticism and sophistry to deny the influence of individuals on events. But the creative power, the "bearlike" strength of it, were unanimously declared to be beyond all discussion, as well as its enormous genuineness as a folk-epic. The liberal criticism of Russia admitted that it was "Russian to the core," that it "presented the soul of the Russian people, in its whole range and variety, in all its lofty simplicity, with a sheer creative power that had never been equalled." But the critics took in bad part Tolstoy's "wilful remoteness from all contemporary *currents of progress*" — a phenomenon and a reproach which were to recur with the appearance of *Anna Karenina*. "*Anna Karenina* I don't like," Turgenyev wrote, "though there are splendid things in it: the race, the mowing, the hunt. But the whole thing is soured; it *smells of Moscow*, and old maids and incense and Slavophils and high life and all that." In a word, Turgenyev, the *Sapadnik*, rejected with horror the Oriental element in the novel, and with him went the whole liberal-radical party; some ignored *Anna Karenina*, others sneered or called names, while the Slavophils and the aristocrats and court party rubbed their hands in glee. In fact Tolstoy, in an intellectual and political sense, had the reactionaries on his side; and they could have little appreciation of the artistic qualities of his work. The liberals were liberal enough to know how to value these, and they did so, albeit in that state of bewilderment into which people always fall at the sight of genius in the camp of reaction. Witness the bewilderment of Europe over Bismarck.

The paradox is worth a little attention. Our idealists would have us believe that genius, the creative power, must, as a living force, act only in the service of progress and human purpose, and be justly denied to the forces that side against life, show sympathy with death, and are inimical to freedom and progress and thus bad in the human sense. We would almost accept it as metaphysical evidence for the goodness of a thing if a capital piece of writing were done in its name. And really, it does seem that, as a rule, the reactionary camp suffers from lack of talent. But not invariably. The reactionary genius does occur, the brilliant and conquering ability does act as attorney for retrograde tendencies – and nothing dazes the world more than the sight of this paradoxical phenomenon. Sainte-Beuve said of Joseph de Maistre that he had "nothing of a writer but the gift" – a comment which perfectly expresses this bewilderment and precisely indicates the thing I mean.

Liberal and progressive Russia must have seen in Tolstoy just this – a case of a great gift in the service of reaction. But it is clear enough that this great gift is of one essence with his fundamental Russianism, his immense integration with the people, his pagan and natural aristocracy; and that the tendency toward democratic spiritualization was – just tendency, romantic in its nature and crowned, after all, by such strikingly indifferent success! His tremendous Orientalism found intellectual expression in this mockery at and denial of European progress; and this it was which must necessarily and profoundly alienate all the Westernizing and liberalizing, all the "Petrinic" elements in Russia. Actually, he quite frankly scouted the Western belief in progress, which, he said, had been accepted by the Russia of Peter the Great. They had, he said, observed the operation of the law of progress in the Duchy of Hohenzollern-Sigmaringen, with its three thousand inhabitants. But then came China, with its two hundred million inhabitants, and knocked the theory of progress into a cocked hat. Which did not for one moment prevent them from believing in progress as a general law of mankind; they took the field with cannons and guns to instruct the Chinese in their thesis. Yet ordinary human understanding tells us that if the history of the larger part of mankind, which we call the Orient, does not confirm the law of progress, then this law does not obtain for the whole of mankind, but forms at most an article of faith for a certain part of it. Tolstoy vows that he himself is unable to find a universal law in the life of mankind, and that history might be co-ordinated just as well in the light of any other idea or "historical whimsy" as in that of progress. And more than that, he does not see the slightest necessity of finding laws for history — quite apart from the impossibility of the thing. The universal, eternal law of perfection, he says, stands written in the soul of every human being; it is only an error to carry it over into the field of history. So long as it remains personal, this law is fruitful and accessible to all; applied to historical conceptions, it is idle talk. The general progress of mankind is an unproved thesis. It does not exist for any of the nations of the East; hence it is just as unfounded to assert that progress is a primary law of mankind as it would be to say that blondness is — all people being blond save those with dark hair.

It is remarkable to see how ideas from the sphere of an idealistic individualism, which is German, and places human perfection within the individual soul, are here found in the company of others which constitute the most decisive challenge to an arrogant Europe setting itself up as intellectual arbiter of the world. Tolstoy protests against what he considers the childishness of this attitude, which confuses western Europe with humanity as a whole; and the protest betrays that his gaze is directed eastward. It betrays, in a word, his Asiatic bias: anti-"Petrinic," primitive Russian, anti-civilization — in short, *bearlike*. What we hear is the voice of the Russian god on the maple throne under the golden lime tree.

The voice of our humanistic deity has a different ring. Goethe, beyond a doubt, hated and despised Asia. The element of Sarmatian wildness in which Tolstoy found himself so much at home, and which merely gets rationalized in his late prophetic period, would always remain remote and foreign to the spirit of the great German, with its exclusively cultural bias. A journey Goethe once made into Upper Silesian Poland was the occasion of what contact he had with the Slav. His impressions are "mostly remarkable negatively." He observes ignorance, lack of culture, low standards of living, stupidity. He feels himself "remote from cultured men." His attitude at the time of the War of Liberation, offensive as it was to patriotic feeling, the admiring and personally friendly respect he felt for the classic phenomenon of Napoleon ("the man is too big for you"), belong in this same category. "It is true," he says in 1813, "I no longer see French and Italians, but in their stead I see Cossacks, Bashkirs, Croats, Magyars, Kashubes, hussars, brown and otherwise." This enumeration of Eastern races has an extraordinarily contemptuous ring. That the Cossacks and Kashubes were in the country as allies and the French as enemies seems not to matter to him. He confesses, indeed, that he too is glad to be rid of the Gallic *soldatesca;* yet he is obviously not far from finding more humiliation in the alliance with Russia and the dependence of Germany upon the east than in her subjugation upon the west; and certain it is that the humanism of the writer who created the *Iphigenie* has more affiliation with the humanity of western Europe, which has given the mould to our civilization, than with the shapeless and savage human nature of Half-Asia.

Unpatriotically he declared that he could not hate the French – he owed them far too much of his culture. The words are only right and proper. But (just as in Tolstoy's case) the fun begins directly it is a question of his nature, of that pre-intellectual fundamental constitution we were talking about, which had its own ways of finding expression, and which is so extraordinarily un-French that it might well be described as pre-eminently German. It would be wrong to bring in evidence here his coldness towards "freedom." For in the first place the principle of order (*ordre*) is something just as French and classic and rationalist as the principle of freedom, which on party grounds is set over against it. And in the second, there is nothing un-German about freedom. We know with what éclat Goethe cited Guizot's dictum that Germany gave the idea of personal freedom to the world. But there is in Goethe something that rebels against the idea, against the doctrinaire and theoretic; a lack of faith that the particular, existing under definite conditions, could ever be improved by the method of abstraction; a realism, that is, and a scepticism, in matters political, which one may as well call un-French as particularly German – taking France as the country of revolution and Germany as the country of a certain national weakness for the living, historically conditioned, "organic." We must remember that he was a practical politician, he had governed Saxe-Weimar. But the practical sphere is not propitious to spirit; it is a training in cynicism, as many a politician has found out, even in France, where more than one radical has become a conservative and turned the guns on the people after he came to power. Perhaps Goethe might have been more generous-minded, politically speaking, if he had not lost his idealism in the practical sphere. But this too is unlikely, since from the very beginning he was insensitive to historical democracy, to history defined as the evolution of the idea in the masses; he was fundamentally unacquainted with enthusiasm for political ideas, and in general conceived of history as the biography of great men — an aristocratism which is as different from Schiller's high-flung democratic gesture as it is from the Christian-mouzhik disparagement of heroes in *War and Peace*.

It would be foolish to think of him as servile, despite the anecdote about Beethoven and the imperial company on the promenade at Karlsbad. His subservience to princes was purely mundane in its character, wherever no personal friendship came in play. When in 1794 Freiherr von Gagern published his challenge to the intelligence of Germany, and to Goethe in particular, to put its pen at the service of the "good," that is to say the conservative cause — no other than that of a new alliance of German princes for the purpose of saving the country from anarchy — Goethe, after thanking him politely for the confidence reposed in him, made the characteristic reply that he considered it impossible for princes and writers to unite upon a common task. Notwithstanding which, we need waste no words over his strictly negative attitude toward the French Revolution.

On the intellectual side, his view of humanity was a cynical one — that is to say, it was radically sceptical. But we know that this was on the intellectual side alone, from the fact that it did not prevent him from loving his fellow men. We have his confession that the mere sight of the human countenance could cure him of the blues. What he did not believe in was drawing up articles and holding love-feasts. We shall never know whether Hegel was mocking or spoke in honest enthusiasm when he said: "As long as the sun has stood in the firmament and the planets circled round it, it has never been seen that a human being stands on his head — i.e., on his understanding — and bases reality upon it." Whether jest or earnest, it was this that revolted Goethe. He judged it to be entirely against nature to try to insist that the whole of mankind find just one choice of means, just one route toward civic happiness. Upon which I may comment as follows: that, in the first place, one such utterance, by virtue of its strongly nationalist, individualist, aristocratic emphasis, outweighs the whole burden of his indifference toward the War of Liberation, and that surely he who uttered it was only prevented by his admiration for the genius of Napoleon — likewise aristocratic in its origin — from seeing in the *Imperator* the standard-bearer of precisely this democratic "insistency." But, in the second place, we must admit that he had a right to set up as an advocate of nature. To quote again:

Franztum drängt in unsern verworrenen Tagen, wie einstmals
Luthertum es getan, ruhige Bildung zurück.

(Driven by the spirit of France in our troublous days, as aforetime
By the spirit of Luther oppressed, quiet culture retreats.)

What a telling synthesis this, of France and Luther; how unprejudiced by national feeling! It is all one to him whether the unrest, the distraction, come from this side or that of the Rhine. No matter whence it comes, it is his enemy, the enemy of nature and culture, of the *ruhige Bildung* which is at the bottom of his idea of humanity. The distich shows clearly—shows it despite all *Lust am Protestieren*—where he would have stood, say, in the sixteenth century. In the name of that lofty conception of *Bildung*, in which nature and culture unite, he would have been for Rome against the Reformation—or else he would have taken up an ambiguous and irresponsible position, as Erasmus did, of whom Luther said that repose was dearer to him than the Cross. "The Cross"—a couple of centuries later, that was the Revolution. Revolution was the spirit—and to Goethe his *ruhige Bildung* was dearer.

Here, for a moment, Erasmus and Goethe meet, in an atmosphere of patrician quietism, humanistic love of peace. But the parallel does not long hold—there is too much difference in the scale, and, after all, men's character, the essence of their being, is greatly affected by their proportions. Tolstoy's "folkishness," for instance—is it not the expression and apanage of his bearlike bulk? Are they not one and the same thing? And may we not draw from Goethe's greatness the *a priori* conclusion that his humanistic cosmopolitanism must contain a good-sized racial core? Erasmus, the subtle, was not "folkish." It was Luther who was that. And truly, in scale, in essence, as an embodiment of Germanic greatness, Goethe belongs more with Luther than with the humanists—yes, more even with Bismarck, to whom he is much closer than a certain antithesis, he loved abroad, would seem to show.

Dangerous, perhaps, to say so—as giving aid and comfort to the cave-bears of nationalism the world over—but sometimes it is hard not to feel sceptical about the genuineness and validity of Goethe's humanism. A godlike man, like Tolstoy. But is it possible that the antique, humanistic, Jovelike attributes of his godhead were more a convention than we think; that they did not go very deep, and that he himself, all the time, like Tolstoy, the Russian god under the golden lime tree, was an ethnic divinity, an eruption of that Germanic and aristocratic paganism which claims both Luther and Bismarck as its sons, and which, on both sides, played a role in the ideology of the late war?

An open hostility, against Goethe as well as against Bismarck, is at work in certain literary, humane, and radical circles, a demand for his dethronement. It cannot be without all sense or justification. Goethe, as a follower of Spinoza, conceived of all natural final causes and purposes as anthropomorphic fictions; thus he was disinclined to an anthropocentric, emancipatory conception of humanity, which teleologically refers everything to itself and looks upon art as a servant of mankind. His synthesis of art and nature is not humanitarian. An approach by the route of the senses is natural to him: it makes him see the burning of a peasant house as real and appealing to his sympathies, whereas "the Fall of the Fatherland" he would find an empty phrase. All which, frankly and flippantly spoken, is never very far removed from the brute.

There is in him a feeling for power, for the struggle "until one proves stronger than the other"; in such sentiments the pacifism of spirit would find it impossible to rejoice. It "makes him sad to be friends with everybody." He "needs anger." Certainly, that is not Christian love of peace — though Lutheran it may be, and Bismarckian to boot. One might say much — and much has been said — in evidence of his love of strife, his fondness for "pitching in and punishing," his readiness to close the mouth of opposed opinions by a show of power and to "remove such people from society." But best of all I love — if here too only because it is so amusing — the tale of Kotzebue and the Schiller celebration which Kotzebue got up with the sole and single purpose of annoying Goethe and playing Schiller off against him. That low-minded Kotzebue! He *knows* that the plan will annoy the old man; he also knows that Goethe can forbid the celebration by virtue of his office. So he puts the choice squarely before him: he can forbid it, and thereby betray his jealousy and despotism; or, if he hesitates to go so far, he can pocket up the annoyance. With majestic simplicity Goethe chooses to exercise his power. He *forbids the celebration.* Bismarck would have done the same.

In the soul-economy of this breed of giants are certain parallel traits. There is violence and there is sentimentality: crude words both to describe what I mean, crude and naturalistically derogatory; yet it is my humour to use them; for even if I wanted to I could not ignore the hidden irony — quite objective, quite unsuspected irony, of course — involved in their gigantic loyalties, their aristocratic servitude. They were both "faithful German servants of their Lord" (oh, my God!): the "civilian Wallenstein" and the despot of *Kultur;* they were German "*Edelknechte*" both; and there was nothing hypocritical about it all, only their giant-sensibilities functioning at full height. The similarity of the character and situation is so strong as to bewilder one: Karl August and the simple old man whom Bismarck "served" blend into one single symbolic figure. In the year 1825 he of Saxe-Weimar celebrated the fiftieth jubilee of his reign, which was at the same time the fiftieth year of Goethe's residence in Weimar. On this day Goethe calls himself "his master's most enraptured servant." He is the first with his congratulations, at six o'clock at the Roman villa in the park. The emotion is great and genuine. "Together to our latest breath!" We set the venerable Wilhelm going to meet Bismarck on the landing with just such another embrace; while a fugitive red mounts in the cheeks of Roderich von Posa, who turns away with the words: "I cannot be a courtier!"

I confessed in the beginning my tendency to make a matter of intrinsic value out of the matter of size. The greatest German poet must also be the most German one — that is an association more immediate and inevitable than even the causal, it is temporal, it is simply the future tense. And it was sanctioned by a source that will be universally accepted as authoritative. It was Father Jahn, who, *motu proprio*, in the year 1810 declared that Goethe was the most German of poets — quite unperturbed by the fact that Goethe behaved at all times as distantly and unsympathetically toward *teutsche Bruderschaften* as Tolstoy toward Slavic. And then, in 1813, when he had very nearly succeeded in bringing himself into bad odour as a man without a country, Varnhagen von Ense cried out: "Goethe not a patriotic German? All the freedom of Germania early found a home in his breast, there to become, to our never-sufficiently-to-be-acknowledged advantage, the pattern, the example, and the root of our culture. In the shade of this tree we all live and move. Never did roots thrust firmer and deeper into the soul of our Fatherland, never did shoots more lustily suck strength from its breast. That our youth feel pride in their arms, loftiness in their spirits, hath more reference to him than to many another who may lay claim to great activity therein."

Good, fine, powerful words. They proceed from the truth that in national matters very little depends on what a man says or the opinions he holds; on what he does, on the other hand, everything.

When a man has written *Götz, Faust, Wilhelm Meister*, the *Sprüche in Reimen* and *Hermann und Dorothea* — a poem that Schlegel honoured with the epithet "*vaterländisch*" — he can indulge in a bit of cosmopolitan irresponsibility, just as the "great writer of Russia" could indulge in the rationalizing Christian pacifism of his latter period. The national is so much second nature that one may address oneself to the mind without running the risk of literary unrealism; and as nature Goethe always felt the national — we see it, among others, in the famous remark to Eckermann: "National hatred is a queer thing after all. You will always find it keenest and most violent *in the lowest stages of culture*. But there is a stage where it quite disappears, and one stands in a way above the nations and feels the well- or ill-being of a neighbouring people as though it were one's own. This stage was comformable to my nature, and I had confirmed myself in it long before I reached my sixtieth year."

Spiritual regeneration. This summons to achieve the spirit is the sentimental imperative of the favourites of nature; just as that of the sons of spirit is the summons to achieve the form. And they respond to it — with more or less of aptitude. Tolstoy's self-imposed task of shaking off the natural man was but spiritualizing the savage; yet a touching and honourable sight, even alongside of Goethe's majestic culture. The main thing is that nothing should come too easy. Effortless nature — that is crude. Effortless spirit is without root — or substance. A lofty encounter of nature and spirit as they mutually yearn toward each other — that is man.

Gorky says of Tolstoy a quite extraordinary and startling thing: he suggests the possibility that Tolstoy, despite the strength of his reason, sometimes hoped, or at least the thought occurred to him, that possibly nature would make an exception and grant him physical immortality. "The whole broad earth looks toward him: from China, from India, from America, from everywhere stretch hither living, vibrating threads, his soul is for all and for always. Why should not nature break her law and grant one man physical immortality — why not?" What madness! But even if it is not true, even if the sensible old man never came on such a monstrously presumptuous thought — even so, it is very telling that Gorky should have come on it for him. It shows what seemed to a competent observer to be Tolstoy's relation to nature and life. — And Goethe? Is it likely that the grey-haired lover of Fräulein von Levetzow never rebelled against the limitations of human life, as

Napoleon did at the limitations of human power, when he complained that men had become unbelievers, unwilling to acknowledge him a god, as they had his brother Alexander? Shall we imagine him utterly incapable of the thought which Gorky ascribes to the old Tolstoy: that nature might conceivably hesitate to destroy him, her darling son, as she did all ordinary humankind?

Yet die he did, unawares, at the age of eighty-three. Nature, as it were, tenderly got round him. He had been ailing; he settled down in his armchair for a rest and a nap, and he was gone. The passage in which Eckermann describes the appearance of the corpse is famous. "The body lay naked, folded in a white sheet; they had put large pieces of ice round, to keep it fresh as long as possible. Friedrich (the servant) unwrapped the sheet, and I was astounded at the godlike splendour of those limbs. The chest exceedingly powerful, broad and deep; the arms and thighs full and gently muscular; the feet slender and very chaste in form; and nowhere on the body a trace of fat or shrinking or decay. A perfect human being lay in great beauty there before me; and the delight I felt made me forget for a moment that the immortal spirit had forsaken such a frame."

Let there be no misunderstanding. Nobody asserts that Goethe and Tolstoy were, so to speak, four-square; that by contrast with the morbid geniuses Schiller and Dostoyevsky they were "normal" in the common acceptation of the word. Even the genius most endowed by nature is never natural in the philistine sense; that is to say, normal, healthy, and according to rule. In his physical there must always be something high-strung and irritable, prone to crises and disease, in his physical always something foreign to the average man, affecting him uncannily — something almost psychopathic; though the philistine must not be allowed to put it like that. . . . No; what I refer to here is that *sense-endowment* possessed by the noble race of Antæus and celebrated by Goethe's Faust in the words he addresses to the Earth-Spirit:

Erhabner Geist, du gabst mir, gabst mir alles,
Warum ich bat. Du hast mir nicht umsonst
Dein Angesicht im Feuer zugewendet.
Gabst mir die herrliche Natur zum Königreich,
Kraft, sie zu fühlen, zu geniessen. Nicht
Kalt staunenden Besuch erlaubst du nur,
Vergönnest mir, in ihre tiefe Brust,
Wie in den Busen eines Freunds, zu schauen.

"Power to feel and to enjoy nature." Tolstoy's sense-endowment, as an individual, must have been that of a noble, highly sensitive animal, most perfectly equipped by nature and strengthened and sublimated by the contemplative power and awareness of the human being. His eyes, the small, keen grey eyes under the bushy brows, were like a falcon's. They saw everything. They were capable of analysis so penetrating as sometimes to seem fantastic. A critic once wrote of him: "You are sometimes capable of saying 'such and such things about the constitution of a certain man indicated that he wanted to travel to India.'" His sense of smell, it seems, was especially penetrating. The fact plays no small part in the sensuous atmosphere of his writing, and appears to have conflicted at times with his own human feeling. "However much I dislike to speak of it," he says in his *Recollections*, "I can still remember the characteristic sharp odour that was personal to my aunt, probably in consequence of some carelessness in dress."

I have already spoken of Goethe's sensitiveness to weather conditions. It was due to his almost exaggerated sense-endowment; and became positively occult when that night in his chamber in Weimar he felt the earthquake of Messina. Animals have a nervous equipment that enables them to feel such events when they occur and even beforehand. The animal in us transcends; and all transcendence is animal. The highly irritable sense-equipment of a man who is nature's familiar goes beyond the bounds of the actual senses and issues in the suprasensual, in natural mysticism. With Goethe the divine animal is frankly and proudly justified of itself in all spheres of activity, even the sexual. His mood was sometimes priapic—a thing which of course does not happen with Tolstoy, in whose nature the element of antique culture was missing. In him the voice of sexual desire spoke in no classic accents; it revelled Russianly in its strength; yet at the same time it always had a moral cast, was at all times followed, probably even accompanied, by profound remorse. Tolstoy's comrades from his Sebastopol period bear witness to the fury with which even at that time the battle between sensual and spiritual impulses raged within him. According to them, young Count Tolstoy was a glorious comrade, the life and soul of his battery, overflowing with high spirits. When he was away, they were disconsolate. "We would hear nothing of him," says the narrator, "for a whole day, for two or three days. At last he would come back, the very picture of the prodigal son; gloomy, knocked up, out of sorts with himself. He would take me aside and begin to confess. He confessed everything, simply everything, his gambling, his carousing, where he had spent his days and nights – and, would you believe it, his remorse and suffering were as deep as though he had committed some great crime. His despair went so beyond all bounds that it was painful to behold. That was the sort of man he was. He was, in a word, very remarkable, and, to tell the truth, I never did quite understand him."

That we can well believe. The remorse and suffering to which the young officer was a witness sprang of course from that conflict within Tolstoy's own breast which afterwards gave him such unrivalled power to stir the conscience and prick man's fear of God awake. But the depth of his moral necessity is a precise measure of the violence of his instincts; and though his natural man bore heavier and heavier on his Christianity as time went on, so that he craved surcease from its stings, yet he never, up to the end, attained to peace. Tolstoy in sex matters held out as long as Goethe, who mocked himself thus:

Alter, hörst du noch nicht auf?
Immer, Mädchen!

But his state of mind toward woman, whom he had early learned to regard, after the manner of the Fathers, as *instrumentum diaboli*, had long since assumed such a form that an experience like that of Goethe with Ulrike was unthinkable. Stranger still – or no, in a man of his parts and magnificence it is only what we should expect – we find not a trace of cant or prudishness or even delicacy in all his recorded utterances on this subject. On the contrary, they are all of a pagan frankness that borders on the cynical. He goes walking by the sea with Gorky and Anton Chekov, and suddenly he levels at Chekov a question about the latter's youth, using a crude Biblical word with rather startling effect. Anton Pavlovich is confused; he pulls at his little beard and mutters something in reply. The old man lets him stammer awhile, then, looking out to sea, delivers himself, in four words, of a confession of his own, in good round terms, ending with a very low and vulgar peasant word. "When they come from his rugged lips," says Gorky, "words like that lose their barrack-room flavour and sound quite simple and natural."

Again, he says: "If Leo Nikolayevich were a natural scientist, he would certainly evolve the most ingenious hypotheses, and make the greatest discoveries." Gorky has not here in mind Tolstoy's remarkable sense-equipment; but I am inclined to associate the two ideas. Nor, it would appear, has he Goethe in mind when he ascribes to Tolstoy a latent genius for the natural sciences; but I have. To me it seems a pertinent fact that Goethe, in Venice — this was in 1790, at the time of those amorous adventures celebrated in the *Epigrams* — saw a broken sheep-skull on the Lido, and had that morphological insight into the development of all the bones of the skull out of the vertebræ which shed such important illumination upon the metamorphosis of the animal body. When Gorky says that Tolstoy, if he had gone in for it, would have made brilliant discoveries in the field of natural science, there can be no doubt of his meaning. He has in mind that initiated sympathy with organic life which those must possess who are her favoured sons — a sympathy not far from Eros, and in which Goethe's biologic intuitions have their source; for example, his incredibly sure-footed anticipation of the cell theory.

Does it not find expression, this sympathy, in the youthful Goethe's Ganymede-pathos? "*Mit tausendfacher Lieberwonne sich an mein Herz drängt deiner ewigen Wärme heilig Gefühl.*" "*Aufwärts an deinen Busen, all-liebender Vater!*" Does it not find expression in his pantheism, which is only the objectivation of his feeling, in such wise that his own utter surrender gives him to know the divine not as something from without, but as irradiating him through and through? In any case, this organic sympathy, this living interest, is entirely directed toward life, toward the "*ewige Wärme*"; whereas — and what could be more characteristic of the difference between these two, nature's great children? — Tolstoy's strongest, most tormenting, deepest, and most productive interest has to do with death. It is the thought of death that dominates his thoughts and writing, to such an extent that one may say no other great master of literature has felt and depicted death as he has — felt it with such frightful penetration, depicted it so insatiably often. Tolstoy's poetic genius for questioning death is the pendant to Goethe's intuition in the field of natural science; and sympathy with the organic is at the bottom of both. Death is a very sensual, very physical business; and it would be hard to say whether Tolstoy was so interested in death because he was so much and so sensually interested in the body, and in nature as the life of the body, or whether it was the other way about. In any case, in his fixation with death, *love* comes into play too: for the fear of death, this source of Tolstoy's poetry and his feeling for religion, is fear of the love of nature, it is the negative, naturalistic other side of Goethe's Ganymede-impulse.

"*Du führst,*" says Goethe-Faust to the Earth-Spirit:

Du führst die Reihe der Lebendigen
Vor mir vorbei und lehrst mich meine Brüder
Im stillen Busch, in Luft und Wasser kennen.

"My brothers." We know that it was Goethe who took in all seriousness the idea of "man's close relation to the beast," and that before science had got far enough on to do so; his possession by this thought, this profound and true intuition, shows us the child of nature in all his sympathy with the organic. Schiller's humanity, his conception of man, which was at bottom emancipatory, haughtily inimical to nature, would have found little pleasure in such a conception; and one does not discover ideas to which one is unsympathetic; that is to say, ideally unsympathetic. There is not such a thing as an assumptionless science. Scientific discoveries are always the result of an ideal assumption: the mediæval statement "*Credo ut intellegam*" is eternally right. Belief is the instrument of knowledge; and without the preconceived, previsioned idea of a unified plan on which is based the development of the higher vertebrate world, including man — in the plant world the conception of the "primitive plant" — Goethe never would have found the *os intermaxillare* in man. I may speak of the amusing contradiction between his discovery and the humanistic explanation he gave it. He says that the intermaxillary bone is variously shaped, in animals, according to circumstance and necessity; but that when it came to man, the highest in the scale, it hid itself for shame, "afraid of betraying an animal voracity." Ideal human pride might retort that it was truly inhuman to spy out the shamefaced hidden bone and bring it to the light.

Yet how remarkable and significant it is to see Goethe's medical and biological interest being seasoned from the start with the humanistic, with his concern with man and his beauty! And consequently with art too; since art with Goethe was a humanistic discipline, and all the disciplines and faculties of human endeavour, human wisdom, human power, were seen by him as variations and adumbrations of one and the same great compelling and enchanting interest and concern, which is man. To study humanity from the angle of medicine and the natural sciences did not lie in his family tradition, as it did in Schiller's and Dostoyevsky's, both of whom were sons of physicians, and neither of whom gave a thought to man's physical side. On the other hand, we know that ever since his Leipzig days Goethe had occupied himself with medicine, associated every day with medical men in Strassburg and, as seriously as though medicine, not art, the explicitly so-called *belles-lettres*, were his calling in life, worked in the dissecting-rooms and spent time in the obstetrical clinic and the clinic for internal diseases. The spirit in which he pursued these studies, the kind of interest he took in them, is clear from the fact that he himself later in life lectured to young artists in the academy on the bony structure of the body. The same thing comes out even plainer in the words he puts into the mouth of Wilhelm Meister in the *Wanderjahre*, when the hero takes his surgical training. His primary interest is in anatomy; and we get some very curious information on the point of previous preparation in a quite different field of activity.

"By a peculiar method, which no one would guess, I had already made good progress in knowledge of the human frame; and this was during my theatrical career. When you come down to it, the physical man, after all, plays the principal role there — a fine man, a fine woman! If the manager is lucky enough to have got hold of these, the writers of comedy and tragedy are assured. The free footing upon which such society lives makes their associates more familiar with the peculiar beauty of the uncovered limbs than any other relationship; different costumes often oblige them to make visible what otherwise is generally concealed. On this point I might have much to say, as also of physical defects which the sensible actor must recognize in himself or others, in order, if not to correct, at least to conceal them. In this way I was sufficiently prepared to give consistency to the anatomical course which taught me to know the outer parts more accurately, whilst the inner parts too were not strange to me, inasmuch as a certain perception of them had always been present to me."

This is, I repeat, a significant bit of information. We learn, not only that the acquaintance with the human form, which Wilhelm owed to the "free footing" of theatrical life, was a happy preparation for his anatomical studies; but also that both, his leaning to the theatre and his interest in medicine, were expressions of one and the same profound interest, his sympathy with the organic and its highest revelation, the human form — an interest, and a sympathy, nor far removed, as I said, from Eros. For instance, when Wilhelm Meister, one day in the dissecting-room, finds that his subject is "the most beautiful female arm that ever twined itself about a young man's neck" — and cannot bring himself to mutilate with his instruments this "glorious manifestation of nature." Out of this incident there comes about his acquaintance with that remarkable man the "plastic anatomist," a sculptor who prepares from wax or other material anatomical dissections possessing the fresh colour and appearance of the natural subjects, in the hope of employing his ingenuity and fertility of method to make the demonstrations more valuable to students and medical practitioners the world over. There follow the most pregnant conversations upon the association of plastic art and anatomical knowledge, and the two intertwine in the most wonderful way when the master "cast in a plastic mass the beautiful torso of a youth and now was skilfully trying to divest the ideal form of the epidermis, to change the beautiful living form into a veritable preparation of muscular tissue."

Here the prose work of Goethe's later period refers to his own youthful thoughts and experiences as a student. He had early discovered and stated that a knowledge of nature and a knowledge of art reciprocally heighten each other. "As I observe nature," he wrote from Rome, "so I now observe art, and win what I have so long striven after, a perfect conception of the highest that has been accomplished by man; and *my soul gets formed* more on this side and looks into a freer field." "Architecture and sculpture and painting are to me now like mineralogy, botany, and zoology," he says in a letter to Herder. And again: "We can finally rival nature by the use of art only when we have learned from her, at least to some extent, the way she proceeds in the formation of her works. . . . The human form cannot be comprehended merely by looking at the surface of it; one must lay bare its inwardness, disjoin its parts, observe the connection between them, note the dissimilarities, be instructed in the action and counteraction, print upon one's mind the hidden and dormant and basic features of a phenomenon, if one wants really to see and imitate it as it moves, a beautiful, indivisible whole, in living waves before our eyes." These are Goethe's words, and who could doubt their truth? Who would deny that it advantages the artist to have knowledge of something beneath the skin, so that he can paint what is not seen as well as what is: in other words, if he stand to nature in another relation besides the lyrical, if, for example, he is a physician on the side, a physiologist, an anatomist, and quietly knows what he knows about the *dessous* as well? The envelope of a human body consists not only of the mucous membrane and cornea of the epidermis, but underneath one has to imagine the corium with its oil and sweat glands, blood-vessels and tubercles, and under that again the adipose tissue, the upholstery that lends the form its charm. But what the artist knows and thinks tells too: it flows into his hand and has its effect; it is not there and yet somehow it is, and just this it is that gives perspicuousness. Art, I repeat, is only one humanistic discipline among others; all of them, philosophy, jurisprudence, medicine, theology, even the natural sciences and technology as well, are only variations and subspecies of one and the same high and interesting theme — toward which we can never take up a sufficiently varied and many-sided attitude, for it is man; and the *human form* is the summary of them all, it is, to speak with Goethe, "the *non plus ultra* of all human knowledge and activity, the alpha and omega of all things known unto us."

Autobiography, and education. The two conceptions meet again when we envisage this idea of the human form, this loftiest expression of our sympathy with the organic. Yes, in view of this idea, so genuinely creative, the two conceptions flow into one humane whole: the pedagogic element resides, consciously or unconsciously (and if unconsciously, so much the better), in the autobiographic; it follows from it, it grows out of it.

Goethe somewhere calls Wilhelm Meister his "beloved likeness (*sein geliebtes Ebenbild*)." In what sense? Does a man love his own likeness? Unless he suffer from hopeless self-complacency, should not the sight of it make him aware of his own shortcomings? Yes, of course, it should. And this very awareness of a need of improvement and completion, this consciousness of his own ego as a task, a moral, æsthetic, cultural obligation, becomes objective in the hero of the autobiographical novel, the epic of education. To this personage the creative ego acts as guide, philosopher, and friend — at once identical and superior — to an extent that makes Goethe once refer to his Wilhelm as "a poor dog." The phrase bespeaks a parental tenderness, not only toward the poor fellow in his *dunklen Drange* whom he created in his own image, but also toward himself. And thus, at the very heart of the autobiographic pathos there takes place the turn for the pedagogic. And this process of objectivation goes on in Wilhelm Meister through the introduction of the society of the Tower, which takes in hand his destiny and human development and leads him in mysterious ways. More and more plainly in the *Lehrjahre* does the original idea of a personally conducted adventure in self-improvement tend toward the pedagogic; until in the *Travels* it issues entirely in the social, yes, even in the political. At the end of the *Faust* there is an unmistakable flashing-up in poetry of the same vision of the union of self and society in the educational process. For the Enlightened, who on earth "*immer strebend sich bemüht*," is received on high by the youthful saved, who sing:

"Wir wurden früh entfernt
Von Lebechören;
Doch dieser hat gelernt,
Er wird uns lehren."

Nobody has ever loved his own ego, nobody was ever egocentric, in the sense of conceiving of his own ego as a cultural task and toiling early and late in pursuance of it, without reaping, almost as though by accident, educational influence in the outer world, and the joy and dignity of a leader and former of youth. The harvest never comes save at the height of life, and the moment of his realization of it is the sublime moment in the life of the productive human being. He never foresees, or even suspects, the moment beforehand. The autobiographical "poor dog," with his mind from his youth up wholly on the difficulties of ploughing his own furrow, or, in the religious phrase, on the saving and justification of his own soul, will not have imagined he can teach anything, to improve or to convert men. Yet the day comes when, still incredulous, still astonished, he realizes that he has been teaching while he learned – shaping, guiding, leading, training, putting his own stamp on youth, by the power of words, by that lofty instrument of culture which is Eros-filled and binds the hearts of men. And from the day of his realization this knowledge possesses his whole life with a certainty, a creative bliss which leaves far behind it all ordinary human joys of love and fatherhood – just as the life of the mind is wont to exceed all personal and sensual things in value, beauty, and splendour.

"I am reading Goethe. My mind teems," Tolstoy wrote in his journal at the beginning of the sixties. He was then a man of some thirty years and had not long returned to Russia and begun his work as a preaching and practising pedagogue. What was he reading? Was it contact with German idealism and humanism that made his mind so to "teem"? It was an alien sphere to him. For in Tolstoy (otherwise than in Goethe) the origin of the pedagogic impulse was immediately social and ethical. A man of parts and attainments, said he, must share with those who lack such blessings before he can derive pleasure from them himself. The motive seems a poor one to me; rationalizing and humanitarian, like all the conscious thought of the great artist just then, I find it deeply inferior to the beautiful humanity of Goethe, in whom the social ideal was an organic outgrowth of the cultural and educational. But what Tolstoy thought was usually smaller than what he was. And to come back to our starting-point: what was it made his mind "teem" when he read Goethe and at the same time set to work as single-handed schoolmaster and founder of a primary school to put into practice the pedagogic ideas that rumbled in his belly?

Or, rather, to experiment with them. For he had made up his mind to settle, by actual experiment, what it was that the people, and in particular youth, wanted to be taught; it had not been settled, and that it had to be settled was his primary pedagogical thesis. "The people," he said, "this most interested party in the whole situation, party and judge in one, listens quietly to our more or less ingenious exposition as to the best way of preparing and presenting its mental fodder. It is not disturbed; for it perfectly knows that in the great business of its mental development it will never take a false step, or accept anything that is false; and that all efforts to force it into paths unsuited to it, for instance German paths, will be like water on a duck's back." One must recognize, Tolstoy declares in writing and controversy, that the German type of school is a desirable one; that is a fact for which history vouches. But, even so, one may as a Russian hesitate to enter the lists in favour of a primary school which does not yet exist there. What historical argument can be brought for the assertion that Russian schools must be like those in the rest of Europe? The people, he says, need education, and every human being seeks it unconsciously. The more highly cultivated classes, society, and government officials, seek to extend the benefits of their knowledge and to educate the less educated masses. One would suppose that such a concurrence of the needs of both classes, the giving as well as the receiving, would suffice. But no. The masses steadily oppose all efforts made in their behalf to educate them, so that these are often entirely futile. Whose is the fault? Which is more justified: the opposition, or the system against which it is directed? Must the opposition be broken or the system altered? The latter, Tolstoy decides, is the case. "Shall we not," he asks, "confess honourably and openly that we do not, cannot, know what the needs of the coming generations will be; but that we feel none the less bound to investigate? That we will not charge the masses with ignorance because they will not accept our education; but rather accuse ourselves of both ignorance and arrogance if we go on trying to educate them on our own lines? Let us at last cease to see hostility in the resistance of the people to our system; and find in it the expression of the people's will, which alone should guide us. Let us at last accept the fact, so clearly evinced by the whole history of pedagogics, that if the educating class are to know what is good and what bad, the class to be educated must have full power to register dissatisfaction, and opportunity to reject a system which they instinctively find unsatisfying; that, in short, *freedom* is the sole criterion of educational methods."

"The sole criterion of education is freedom, the sole method experience, experimentation." This is Tolstoy's first and highest pedagogic maxim. According to him, the school should be at once a means of education and an experiment performed on the rising generation, an experiment productive of ever new results. It should, in other words, be an educational laboratory, where the experiment of pedagogic science seeks to create a firm basis for itself. To do this, it is necessary that it function under circumstances that ensure the value of its results — that is, in freedom. The school as it is, Tolstoy declares, enfeebles the children by distorting their mental faculties. During the most precious period of development it wrenches the child out of the family circle, robs him of the joy of freedom, and makes of him a jaded, suppressed creature, upon whose face rests an expression of weariness, fear, and boredom, while with his lips he repeats strange words in a language he does not know. But if we give the people freedom during their training, then we also give them the chance to speak out on the score of their necessities, and furthermore to choose among the kinds of knowledge offered. Philosophers from Plato to Kant have unanimously striven to free the school from the fetters of tradition. They have sought to discover wherein the intellectual needs of man consist, and to build up new schools on these more or less correctly envisaged needs. Luther demands that the masses shall study the Scripture from the original text, and not from the commentaries of the Fathers. Bacon advises the study of nature from nature herself and not from the works of Aristotle. Rousseau wants to teach life *from life*, as he conceives it, and not from outworn experience. All philosophy stands for freeing the school from the idea of instructing the younger generation in that which the older generation held to be science; and in favour of the idea of teaching them what they themselves need. And we can see by the history of pedagogic science that every step forwards consists in greater natural *rapport* between pupil and teacher, in less compulsion and greater facilitation of the process of learning.

Tolstoy, then, an anarchistic pedagogue, sets his face against discipline. "The school in which there is less compulsion," he says, "is better than the one in which there is more. The method which can be introduced without increased disciplinary strain is good; one which requires greater severity is surely wrong. Take a school like mine and try to carry on conversations about tables and corners of rooms or shove little dice to and fro. A frightful disorder will reign at once, and it will be absolutely necessary to restore order. But tell them an interesting story or set them an interesting task, or let someone write on the board and the others correct, and *let them all out of their benches*, and they will all be busy, and there will be no mischief, and no increased discipline will be necessary. We may safely say that this way is good."

"The children bring nothing with them," thus Tolstoy describes the procedure at Yasnaya Polyana, "neither primers nor copy-books. These are no tasks to take home. They need not remember anything – nothing of what they did the day before. They need carry nothing, either in their hands or in their heads. They bring nothing with them but their receptive natures and the conviction that school will be just as jolly today as it was yesterday; they only think of the instruction when it has begun. No one who comes late is ever scolded, and they never come late, except some of the older ones, whose fathers occasionally keep them to work. When that happens, they run as fast as they can to school and get there breathless."

Lucky village children of Yasnaya Polyana! But it is comprehensible that Tolstoy tries to make the school at least pleasant for his pupils; his faith in its educational value is weak, and he makes in the end no secret of his conviction – which he declares he derived from personal observation in the schools of Paris, Marseille, and other cities of western Europe – that the greater part of popular education is gained, not from school, but from life; and that free public instruction, by means of lectures, clubs, books, exhibitions, and so on, remains far superior to any teaching in schools. But be that as it may; what interests us here is not the rightness or wrongness of Tolstoy's ideas, but rather what is characteristic in them; and characteristic they certainly are, in the highest degree, and from every point of view, not only in a personal sense, but also as a sign, even as an augury of his time.

What strikes one first of all, then, is a note that sounds in clearest contradiction to certain other of his doctrines: to the pacifistic and antinational ones, to the thesis of democratic equality he preached in his latter days. It is the national note. He emphasizes the right of the Russian people to an education suited to their genius, independently of the foreign spirit. His root-and-branch Russianism, at this time still quite unregenerate, denies the right of the upper and official classes, with their west-European liberal education, to force upon the masses an education not suited to their actual needs. Here he is turning against Peter the Great, who created these official classes and gave them their orientation toward liberalism and the west. Tolstoy's educational ideas are all extreme anti-"Petrinic," anti-western, anti-progressive. He openly declares that the educated class is not capable of giving the masses their proper training, conceiving, as it does, that the well-being of the people lies in the direction of civilization and progress. What speaks out of Tolstoy's mouth, what rules his thinking, is Moscow. It is that leaning toward Asia which so alarmed Turgenyev and others like him in Tolstoy's writings and which here is elevated to a pedagogic principle. His anarchism, his faith in the anarchistic principle as the single reasonable basis of communal human life; his doctrine that absolute freedom makes all discipline superfluous — all these are part of it, and it and they are expressed in Tolstoy's prescription to "let all the children out of the benches" and free them from every oppressive sense of duty.

This "*letting all the children out of the benches*" — a picturesque and stimulating formula — is a perfect symbol for Tolstoy's social and political (or, rather, his anarchistic, antipolitical) views. His famous letter to Czar Alexander III develops these most concisely. The new Czar's father had been murdered on the 13th of March 1881; and Tolstoy wrote begging him to exercise clemency toward the murderers. He here sets down for the Emperor, in words so compelling that one almost wonders at their not prevailing, the two *political* expedients that had been applied up to date against increasing political disorder: first, force and terror; and second, liberalism, constitution, parliament. Both these have finally shown themselves impotent. There remains, however, a third expedient, which is not of a political nature and which has at least the advantage of having never yet been tried. It consists in the fulfilment of the divine will regardless of consequences, without any cautious reservations of policy; quite simply in love, forgiveness, the requital of evil with good; in mildness, in non-resistance against evil, in freedom. . . . In a word, Tolstoy advises the Czar to "let all the children out of the benches"; he counsels anarchy — I am not using the word in a derogatory sense, but quite objectively, to specify a definite social and political gospel of salvation.

The Asiatic bias of this great Russian genius has already been shown to be a mixture of various psychical elements: Oriental passivity, religious quietism, and an unmistakable tendency to

Sarmatian wildness. Here, in this anarchistic theory, it lies down with quite different company: with the revolutionary ideals of western Europe, with the educational and political conceptions of Rousseau and his pupil Pestalozzi, in both of whom there is present the element of wildness, the return to nature – in short, the anarchistic element in another form and under other colours. Here, then, we are arrived at the common factor in the education of our two protagonists – but with a difference. On the educational side, Goethe fell away from his allegiance to Rousseau. Pedagogic Rousseauianism, as preached and practised by its founder, revolted him. Furiously, even desperately, he rejected it, and the anarchical individualism of the revolutionary education.

Boisserée tells how Goethe expressed to him his distress on the score of Pestalozzi and his system. For its original purpose and in its original setting, where Pestalozzi had only the children of the people in mind, the poor who lived in their isolated huts in Switzerland and could not send their children to school, it might be a capital idea. But it became the most destructive one in the world so soon as it ceased to confine itself to elementary teaching and went on to language, art, the general field of knowledge and power, which of course presupposed a *previous tradition*. . . . And then the insubordination this cursed kind of education aroused: look at the impudence of the little school-urchins, who feel no awe of any stranger, but rather put him in a fright instead. All respect gone, everything done away with that makes human beings human beings in their relations with each other. "What should I have been," cried Goethe, "if I had not always been obliged to show respect for others? And these men, in their madness and frenzy, to reduce everything to terms of the single individual and be simply gods of self-sufficiency! They think to educate a nation which shall stand against the barbaric hordes, just as soon as the latter shall have mastered the elementary tools of understanding, which Pestalozzi has made it so very easy for them to do."

Tradition, reverence – which "makes human beings human beings in their relations with each other" – conformity of the ego within a noble and estimable community; do you not feel the nearness of the Pedagogic Province? Let me recall a moment that dream so wise and splendid, at once austere and blithe, in which can be traced much of the humanism of the eighteenth century, much of the spirit of the *Zauberflöte*, of Sarastro and the "moving toward good with one's hand in a friend's"; and which at the same time contains so much that is new and bold and, humanly speaking, advanced that it cannot be called less revolutionary than Tolstoy's educational ideas. Only, of course, the anarchistic flavour is utterly lacking; while its conception of humanity and human dignity, culture and civilization, is so consonant with solemn regulation and gradation, with such a pronounced sense of reverence, of traditions, symbols, mysteries, and rhythm, with such a symmetrical, almost choreographic restraint in its freedom, that I may be permitted to call it statesmanlike in the best and finest sense, by way of pointing the contrast to Tolstoy's letting the children out of the benches." However, the boys and youths of Goethe's dream-province do not sit glued to their benches either; at least we do not see them thus. The basis of their education is quite in the Pestalozzian style: it is husbandry. And their training goes forward in the open air, work and play constantly accompanied by singing. We are told, quite explicitly, what its essence is: "Wise men lead the boys to find out themselves what is fitted for them; and shorten the by-ways into which man will often too readily turn aside." Every well-marked bent to a pursuit is fostered and cultivated, for "to know and practice one thing rightly gives higher culture than half-way performance of a hundred things." But if the education is thus adapted to the individual, it is not thereby in the very least individualistic – so little, in fact, that respect for convention is insisted upon, and regarded as a conspicuous characteristic of genius; for genius understands that art is called art just because it is not nature; and easily accommodates itself to paying respect to the conventions, in the view that they represent "an agreement arrived at by the superior elements of society, whereby the essential and indispensable is regarded as the best." That is hostility toward the voluntary, with a vengeance; and the Head is at pains to define and interpret it by a musical parallel. "Would a musician," he asks, "let a pupil make a wild attack on the keyboard or invent intervals to please himself? No, the striking thing is that nothing is left to the choice of the learner. The element in which he is to work is fixed, the tool he must use put into his hand, even the way he shall use it is prescribed – I mean the change of fingers, in order that one get out of the other's way and make the path plain for its successor; until by dint of this regulated co-operation and thus alone the impossible at last becomes the possible." – It is not by chance, I insist, that the Heads of the Province draw their parallel from the field of music: is she not truly the most spirited symbol for that regulated co-operation of manifold elements toward an end and goal which is culturally noble and worthy of humanity? In the Pedagogic Province song presides over all the activities, everything else is linked with it and communicated by it. "The simplest pleasures as well as the simplest tasks are animated and impressed by song; yes, even our instruction in morals and religion is communicated in this wise." Even the elements of knowledge, reading, writing, reckoning, are derived from song, note-writing, and putting text beneath, and from observing the basic measures and notation — in short, as agriculture is the natural, so music is the spiritual element of education, "for from it level paths run out in all directions."

Another great German and shaper of German destiny comes to mind here: Luther's view of music as an instrument of education was very like Goethe's. "*Musicam*," he says, "I have always loved. One should accustom youth to this art, for it makes fine, capable people. A schoolmaster who cannot sing I will not look at." And in the schools under his influence there was almost as much singing as in the Pedagogic Province — whereas no one would know whether they sang in Tolstoy's school or not. To the wanderer through the Pedagogic Province it seems as though none of its inhabitants did anything of his own power, but as though a mysterious spirit animated them through and through, leading them on toward one single great goal. This spirit is the spirit of music, of culture, of "regulated co-operation," whereby alone at length "the impossible" — that is to say, the state as work of art — becomes possible; it is a spirit remote from and hostile to all barbarism; one would like to be allowed to call it a German spirit.

The salutation in three degrees, whose meaning, the threefold reverence, is kept secret from the boys themselves, because mystery and respect for the mysterious is a moral and civilizing influence; the insistence upon modesty and decorum; the lining up and standing at attention of the young human being in face of the world, and his honourable comradeship with his kind; the enhancing of his own honour through the honours he renders; all this militarism so highly imbued with the spirit and with art — how far it is from the rational radicalism of Tolstoy's Christianity, with its heart of wildness! Is it anyway credible that, in essentials, a remarkable likeness subsists between the educational conceptions of our two geniuses?

Tolstoy in all pious simplicity once declared that the world can find salvation simply by no longer doing anything which does not seem inherently reasonable: that is to say, anything which our whole European world is doing today; for example, teaching the grammar of dead languages. What finds utterance, what bursts forth, in this polemic against the study of ancient tongues is the revolt of the Russian people against humanistic civilization itself. Tolstoy's unclassic paganism stands revealed, his ethnic godhead, which, according to Gorky, was not Olympian, but more like that of a Russian god, "sitting on a maple throne, under a golden lime tree." Tolstoy's pedagogic writing betrays an extremely anti-humanistic, anti-literary, anti-rhetorical conception of the relative importance of different branches of study. He has anything but the traditional European view of the importance of the discipline of reading and writing; entertaining not the faintest humanistic fear of "analphabetism," but rather openly defending what to our way of thinking would almost amount to a state of barbarism. "We see people," he says, "who are equipped with all the knowledge necessary for farming; who perfectly comprehend all its bearings, though they can neither read nor write; or capital military leaders, tradespeople, foremen, machine-overseers, labourers, all people who got their training from life, not books, and stored up large resources of information and reflection, but who, again, can neither read nor write. On the other hand we see people who can both read and write, but who have not profited by this advantage to learn any new thing." When he dwells upon the conflict between the needs of the people and the learning forced upon them by the ruling classes, he has in mind the fact that the elementary schools are an outgrowth of the higher ones. First the church school, then the higher education, then after that the primary school – a false hierarchy, for it is false that the primary school, instead of conforming to its own needs, should conform – only on a smaller scale – to the demands of the higher education. His meaning is clear. He finds the folk-school too literary, too much subordinated to the classical ideal of education, not practical or vital enough, not guided by the principle of training for a calling in life. But we shall be mistaken in expecting from him any greater kindness for either the system or the spirit of the higher institutions of learning. He accuses them of being "entirely divorced from actual life." He compares the true education derived from life itself with that offered to the academic student, and finds that the former produces men capable in their calling, the latter merely "so-called people with a university education – advanced, that is to say irritable, sickly liberals." He gives "Latin and rhetoric" another hundred years of life, not more, and so much only for the reason that "when the medicine has once been bought, one must take it." The phrase betrays plainly enough his attitude toward classical education, toward the traditional European culture, toward humanism. It betrays at the same time his attitude toward the west and civilization, his folk-hatred of all that is not of the people, that is foreign, that comes from abroad, that has merely a cultural value – in short, the anger of primitive Russia against Peter the Great.

It is time we looked round in the Pedagogic Province for the place where youth busies itself with the ancient tongues. And, after all, it is rather a shock not to find it. Goethe is not such a barbarian as to despise the study of language or languages, as a cultural instrument. He calls it enthusiastically the most sensitive in the world, and emphasizes its value as a civilizing agent, by having his imaginary pupils take it in connection with the rude tasks of stable-work; so that, caring for and training animals, they do not become like animals themselves. But the languages here are modern languages. The tongues of various nations are studied in turn – but Latin and Greek, it will be noted, are not in the curriculum.

Well, there are other things which are not expressly mentioned either. But that precisely these subjects should be absent is after all rather striking. Was Goethe a humanist, or was he not? In the first place, his humanism was always of another and a broader kind than merely the philological. And in the second place, the impress of a certain high austerity lies upon all the regulations of the Pedagogic Province, despite the Parnassian blitheness that reigned there. There is no doubt that Goethe, in his consciously pedagogic period, felt toward the humanistic, Winkelmannian ideal of education much as Tolstoy and Auerbach did about music: a moral severity against the sybaritic, dilettante, the roving and ranging, sipping and changing, which he considered the danger of the "universally human" ideal as applied to pedagogy. He considered this danger more threatening than the peril of specialization and its consequent narrowness and impoverishment – the horrors of which we later comers, to be sure, have learned to know. He espouses the cause of vocational against verbal training, out of the same anti-literary tendency which we observed in Tolstoy; sharing with him the conviction that human culture makes sounder progress by the method of limitation; he is radical enough to use the *Wanderjahre* as a mouthpiece through which to shout "*Narrenpossen* (Stuff and nonsense)!" at the "universally human" educational ideal and "all its works." That is severe. But today, when nobody any longer can live on his income, does it not sound like an uncommonly clear-sighted prophecy when he declares: "Whoever from now on does not take to either an art or a trade will have a hard time of it"?

I have made no secret of my tendency to interpret the paganism of the children of nature in a primarily ethical sense. And I am greatly strengthened by this astonishingly radical and decisive rejection, on Goethe's part, of a humane and literary education. Almost I might have dared interpret that gruff "*Narrenpossen!*" as the revolt of Germanic folkishness against the humanistic culture itself. I have every warrant for asserting that Goethe would have fought like Tolstoy the folly of offering watered scholarship to the people for education – a folly by which one waters the people's sense and spirit, debases and insults, instead of, as one fondly imagines, elevating them! Goethe, who in the *Wahlverwandtschaften* advances – surreptitiously, "*weil die Menge gleich verhöhnet*" – the reactionary and esoteric doctrine: "Bring up the boys to be servants and the girls to be mothers, then all will be well": was he the man to advocate the breeding of "advanced, that is to say irritable and sickly liberals"? And was there not perhaps prophetic vision at work in the severity and the limitations of his educational principles? Did his sense of time, like the Russian's, give "Latin and rhetoric" a limit of some hundred years of life? Strange events in our Europe today incline one to regard his maxims in a prophetic light.

The great Revolution in Russia brought to the light of day – that light which is so good at illuminating the *surface* of things – the western Marxism which had put its impress upon Tolstoy's country. But it must not blind us to the spectacle of the Bolshevist Revolution as the end of an epoch: the epoch of Peter the Great, the western, liberalizing, European epoch in the history of Russia, which now, with this Revolution, faces eastward once more. It was to no European idea of progress that the last Czar fell victim. In him Peter the Great was murdered, and his fall opened to his people not the path toward Europe, but the way home to Asia. But is there not also in western Europe, precisely since the time of this crisis – whose prophet Leo Tolstoy was, although Moscow sees it not – is there not also in western Europe a feeling alive that not only for Russia, but for it, for us, for all the world there is at hand the ending of an epoch: the bourgeois, humanistic, liberal epoch, which was born at the Renaissance and came to power with the French Revolution, and whose last convulsive twitchings and manifestations of life we are now beholding? The question is put today whether this Mediterranean, classic, humanistic tradition is commensurate with humanity and thus coeval with it, or whether it is only the intellectual expression and apanage of the bourgeois liberal epoch and destined to perish with its passing.

Europe seems to have answered the question already. The anti-liberal rebound is more than plain, it is palpable. It finds political expression in a disgusted turning away from democracy and parliamentary government, in a beetle-browed about-face toward dictatorship and terror. Italian fascism is the precise pendant to Russian bolshevism; all its archaistic gesturings and mummery cannot disguise its essential hostility to the humane. And on the Iberian Peninsula, where the destruction of the liberal system was still more obvious than in Italy, things have taken the same course, even more decisively; military dictatorship has been well established there for some time. But, indeed, all over Europe – as a consequence of the war and a sign of an anti-liberal temper – the waters of nationalism are mightily swollen. The individual peoples of Europe display a turkey-cock self-assertiveness, a furious self-deification, in striking contrast to the poverty and prostration of the continent as a whole.

The spiritual destinies of France are remarkable indeed, and of immediate importance to us Germans. In the first years after the war no country seemed more confirmed in the bourgeois-classical tradition. France seemed the one truly conservative country in all Europe. Far from thinking of war as a new revolution, it was bent instead, after the victory and on the basis of the victory, on seeing in it nothing but the confirmation and the consummation of the old, the bourgeois order of 1789. To such questions as the one I have raised above, France made answer with tranquil irony. If Germany, she said, wanted to dream apocalyptic dreams, let her do so by all means; for herself, she felt very comfortable in her classical tradition. Once on the occasion of an international exchange of ideas I had sought to get some of these matters expressed; and I remember how a contributor to the French official newspaper organ answered me that France had always been and would always remain *solidement rationaliste et classique*.

But that was the voice of official, bourgeois, conservative France, not the other France, loftier, young, intellectual, secretly astir. Certainly, this new France is beginning to "dream apocalyptically"; there is of late a good deal of reason to doubt that she feels as much at home as she used to in her tradition. What M. Poincaré, who has no better name for it, knows and hates as "communism" is nothing but the process that is going on there of undermining his bourgeois, classical, old-revolutionary France; the disintegration of the Latin conception of civilization by the action of spiritual ferments which have filtered in from the outside and are doing their work in the blood of the youth – a new, anti-bourgeois, spiritual, and proletarian revolution; and we in Germany think we have ground for hope that, if there are to be atmospheric changes, we too may get a little more air to breathe. For in France the interests of nationalism and of the humanistic culture coincide, in so far as both are based upon the conviction of the absolute supremacy of the Latin civilization and its mission of world-domination as an abiding concern of humanity. Whereas a spirit of European solidarity, and a certain readiness, however conditional, to come to terms with Germany, are more likely to be found on the side of the "communistic" new-revolutionary France, which is no longer quite so sound on the score of its cultural Latinity.

Germany's position, with reference to these phenomena to the west of her, is a difficult and complicated one. For us Germans ourselves, and for the world at large, it is highly important that she see it clearly and recognize it for what it is. For in Germany too there exist the two camps, a humanistic and a "communistic" – with this difference only, that here the national fixation exists, not, as in France, in the humanistic camp, but in the "communistic"; from which it follows that two peoples may behave the same, culturally speaking, and reach quite different results, and that there are circumstances under which the pursuance of the same spiritual tendency may be the worst possible method of arriving at political *rapprochement*.

I do not propose to dwell upon German fascism, nor upon the circumstances, the quite comprehensible circumstances, of its origin. It is enough to say that it is a racial religion, with antipathy not only for international Judaism, but also, quite expressly, for Christianity, as a humane influence; nor do its priests behave more friendly toward the humanism of our classical literature. It is a pagan folk-religion, a Wotan cult: it is, to be invidious – and I mean to be invidious – romantic barbarism. It is only consistent in the cultural and educational sphere, where it seeks to check the stream of classical education, to the advantage of the primitive German heritage. And it does not or it will not see what an unhappy pendant it thus furnishes to the anti-Latinism of modern-minded France, and how very much it plays into the hands of M. Poincaré, the Communist-hater. To profess paganism in Germany today, to worship Odin and hold feasts of the solstice, to conduct oneself like a folk-barbarian, is to prove those French patriots in the right who would like to erect on the Rhine the breastwork of Occidental civilization; it is asininely to compromise the position of those Frenchmen who do not make such fine distinctions between Latinity and barbarism, and who are interested in peace, understanding, compromise, and a "gentleman's agreement" with Germany.

This is what I meant when I said that to pursue the same spiritual tendency may be the most wrong-headed of all possible ways for two nations to arrive at a *rapprochement*. Now is not the moment for Germany to make anti-humanistic gestures; to pattern itself upon Tolstoy's pedagogic bolshevism; to characterize as ethnical savagery the rebuke that Goethe administered to the hedonism of the general humanistic ideal in education. No, on the contrary, it is the time for us to lay all possible stress upon our great humane inheritance and to cultivate it with all the means at our command – not only for its own sake, but in order to put visibly in the wrong the claims of Latin civilization. And, in particular, our socialism, which has all too long allowed its spiritual life to languish in the shallows of a crude economic materialism, has no greater need than to find access to that loftier Germany which has always sought with its spirit the land of the Greeks. It is today, politically speaking, our really national party; but it will not truly rise to the height of its national task until – if I may be allowed the extravagance – Karl Marx has read Friedrich Hölderlin: a consummation which, by the way, seems in a fair way to be achieved.

Beautiful is resolution. But the really fruitful, the productive, and hence the artistic principle is that which we call reserve. In the sphere of music we love it as the painful pleasure of the prolonged note, the teasing melancholy of the not-yet, the inward hesitation of the soul, which bears within itself fulfilment, resolution, and harmony, but denies it for a space, withholds and delays, scruples exquisitely yet a little longer to make the final surrender. In the intellectual sphere we love it as irony: that irony which glances at both sides, which plays slyly and irresponsibly – yet not without benevolence – among opposites, and is in no great haste to take sides and come to decisions; guided as it is by the surmise that in great matters, in matters of humanity, every decision may prove premature; that the real goal to reach is not decision, but harmony, accord. And harmony, in a matter of eternal contraries, may lie in infinity; yet that playful reserve called irony carries it within itself, as the sustained note carries the resolution. In the foregoing pages I have tried it, this "infinite" irony; and my readers may judge upon which extreme it more enjoyed playing, at which side of the eternal contradiction it took keener aim – and draw their conclusions accordingly; only not too far-reaching ones!

Irony is the pathos of the middle . . . its moral too, its ethos. I said that it is not, in general, the German way to be hasty in deciding the aristocratic problem – if I may, in this phrase, sum up the whole complex of contrasted values dealt with in the present essay. We are a people of the middle, of the world-bourgeoisie; there is a fittingness in our geographical position and in our *mores.* I have been told that in Hebrew the words for knowing and insight have the same stem as the word for between.

That German writer who has most urgently pondered upon the problem of aristocracy was, philologically speaking, greatly daring when he invented a derivation for the name of the German people: from *Tiusche-Volk;* that is, *Täusche-Volk.* But, for all that, the idea is full of esprit. A people settled in the bourgeois world-middle must needs be the *täuschende*, protean folk: a race that practises sly and ironic reserve toward both sides, that moves between extremes, easily, with non-committal benevolence; with the morality, no, the piety of that elusive "betweenness" of theirs, their faith in knowledge and insight, in cosmopolitan culture.

Fruitful dilemma of the middle, thou art freedom and reserve in one! Let them tell us, as they have told us, that this free-handed policy of ours has brought us, in actual practice, to grief. Practice is doubtful, this disaster even more so. More than probably it came upon us for our own best good; more than probably we were striving to bring it about in a deeper sense than any in which man ever strives to encompass his happiness. Again, devotion in the face of failure is no more noble than humility in the face of success; and nothing but defeatism could shake our faith in the rightness and sanctity of a spiritual attitude whose craving for freedom and ironic reserve is justified, not as an end and aim, but as a final synthesis and harmony, the pure idea of man himself.

That mutual character of the sentimental longing – of the sons of spirit for nature, of the sons of nature for spirit (for, as we found, it is not spirit alone that is sentimental) – argues a higher unity as humanity's goal; which she, in very truth the standard-bearer of all aspiration, endows with her own name, with *humanitas.* That instinct of self-preservation, full of reserve as it is, felt by the German people in their central position as a world-bourgeoisie, is genuine nationalism. For that is the name we give to a people's craving for freedom, to the pains they take with themselves, to their effort after self-knowledge and self-fulfilment. So too the artist is loyally and devotedly convinced that his only thought is to wrest his own work and his very own dream out of the block of stone; and yet, in some solemn and moving hour, may learn that the spirit which possessed him had a purer source, that from the stone he carved there is emerging a loftier image than he knew.

Folk, and humanity. It was a seer out of the east, one of those who, like Goethe, Nietzsche, and Whitman, have looked long into the slowly mounting dawn of a new religious sense – it was Dmitri Merezhkovsky who has said that the animal contains the beast-man and the beast-god. The essence of the beast-god is as yet scarcely comprehended by man, yet it is only the union of the beast-god with the god-man that will some day bring about the redemption of the race of mankind. This "some day," this idea of a redemption, which is no longer Christian and yet not pagan either, carries in itself the solution of the problem of aristocracy, as well as justifying, yes, sanctifying, all ironic reserve on the subject of ultimate values.

We have dealt with confidence with great natures, great creative artists, children of God, in whom the beast-god was strong, as also their sense of self, their feeling for repose, for woman, for the people; we have revelled in the intellectual power of those world-spirits who tempered and humanized their confessed egotism with a strain of the didactic impulse. More hesitantly we have trenched upon the god-man sphere of those others, their emotional opposites, the men of deeds, the sons of spirit, the saintly and sickly. The true saying of that Russian that the essence of the beast-god is as yet scarcely apprehended by man might strengthen our faith in the ironic doctrine that there is more of grace among those who at bottom "can love nobody but themselves." But well we know that there is no deciding the question which of these two lofty types is called to contribute more and better to the highly cherished idea of a perfected humanity.

ANNA KARENINA

1939

TODAY high tide is at ten. The waters rush up the narrowing strand, carrying foam-bubbles and jelly-fish – primitive children of an unnatural mother, who will abandon them on the sands to death by evaporation. The waves run up, almost to the foot of my beach-chair; sometimes I must lift away my plaid-wrapped legs as the waters encroach and threaten to cover them. My heart responds blithely, though also with utter respect, to these sportive little tricks the mighty ocean plays me; my sympathy, a deep and tender, primitive, soul-extending stirring, is far indeed from any annoyance.

No bathers yet. They await the midday warmth to wade out into the ebbing tide, little flutters and shrieks escaping them as they begin their pert yet fearful toying with the vast. Coast-guards in cork jackets, lynx-eyed, tooting their horns, watch over all this amateurish frivolity. My "workshop" here surpasses any I know. It is lonely; but even were it livelier, the tumultuous surf so shuts me in, and the sides of my admirable beach-chair, seat and cabin in one, familiar from my youth up, is so peculiarly protective that there can be no distraction. Beloved, incomparably soothing and suitable situation – it recurs in my life again and again, as by a law. Beneath a sky where gently shifting continents of cloud link the blue depths, rolls the sea, a darkening green against the clear horizon, oncoming in seven or eight foaming white rows of surf that reach out of sight in both directions. There is superb activity farther out, where the advancing waves hurl themselves first and highest against the bar. The bottle-green wall gleams metallic as it mounts and halts and curls over, then shatters with a roar and an explosion of foam down, down, in ever recurrent crash, whose dull thunder forms the deep ground-bass to the higher key of the boiling and hissing waves as they break nearer in. Never does the eye tire of this sight nor the ear of this music.

A more fitting spot could not be for my purpose: which is to recall and to reflect upon the great book whose title stands at the head of my paper. And here by the sea there comes to mind inevitably an old, I might almost say an innate association of ideas: the spiritual identity of two elementary experiences, one of which is a parable of the other. I mean the ocean and the epic. The epic, with its rolling breadth, its breath of the beginnings and the roots of life, its broad and sweeping rhythm, its all-consuming monotony—how like it is to the sea, how like to it is the sea! It is the Homeric element I mean, the story going on and on, art and nature at once, naïve, magnificent, material, objective, immortally healthy, immortally realistic! All this was strong in Tolstoy, stronger than in any other modern creator of epic art; it distinguishes his genius, if not in rank, yet in essence, from the morbid manifestation, the ecstatic and highly distorted phenomenon, that was Dostoyevsky. Tolstoy himself said of his early work *Childhood* and *Boyhood:* "Without false modesty, it is something like the Iliad." That is the merest statement of fact; only on exterior grounds does it fit still better the giant work of his maturity, *War and Peace*. It fits everything he wrote. The pure narrative power of his work is unequalled. Every contact with it, even when he wished no longer to be an artist, when he scorned and reviled art and only employed it as a means of communicating moral lessons; every contact with it, I say, rewards the talent that knows how to receive (for there is no other) with rich streams of power and refreshment, of creative primeval lustiness and health. Seldom did art work so much like nature; its immediate, natural power is only another manifestation of nature itself; and to read him again, to be played upon by the animal keenness of this eye, the sheer power of this creative attack, the entirely clear and true greatness, unclouded by any mysticism, of this epic, is to find one's way home, safe from every danger of affectation and morbid trifling; home to originality and health, to everything within us that is fundamental and sane.

Turgenyev once said: "We have all come out from under Gogol's *Mantle*"—a fiendishly clever pun which puts in a phrase the extraordinary uniformity and unity, the thick traditionalism of Russian literature as a whole. Actually, they are all there simultaneously, its masters and geniuses, they can put out their hands to each other, their life-spans in great part overlap. Nikolai Gogol read aloud some of *Dead Souls* to the great Pushkin, and the author of *Yevgeny Onyegin* shook with laughter—and then suddenly grew sad. Lermontov was the contemporary of both. Turgenyev, as one may easily forget, for his frame, like Dostoyevsky's, Lieskov's, and Tolstoy's, belongs to the second half of the nineteenth century, came only four years later than Lermontov into the world and ten before Tolstoy, whom he adjured in a touching letter expressing his faith in humanistic art, "to go back to literature." What I mean by thick traditionalism is illustrated by an anecdote that most significantly connects Tolstoy's artistically finest work, *Anna Karenina*, with Pushkin.

One evening in the spring of 1873, Count Leo Nikolayevich entered the room of his eldest son, who was reading aloud to his old aunt Pushkin's *Stories of Byelkin;* the father took the book and read: "The guests assembled in the country house." "That's the way to begin," he said; went into his study and wrote: "In the Oblonsky house great confusion reigned." That was the original first sentence from *Anna Karenina.* The present beginning, the *aperçu* about happy and unhappy families, was introduced later. That is a marvellously pretty little anecdote. He had already begun much and brought much to triumphant conclusion. He was the fêted creator of the Russian national epos, in the form of a modern novel, the giant panorama *War and Peace.* And he was about to excel both formally and artistically this chef-d'œuvre of his thirty-five years in the work he had now in hand, which one may with an easy mind pronounce the greatest society novel of world literature. And here he was, restlessly prowling about the house, searching, searching, not knowing how to begin. Pushkin taught him, tradition taught him, Pushkin the classic master, from whose world his own was so remote, both personally and generaly speaking. Pushkin rescued him, as he hesitated on the brink; showed him how one sets to, takes a firm grip, and plumps the reader *in medias res.* Unity is achieved, the continuity of that astonishing family of intellects which one calls Russian literature is preserved in this little piece of historical evidence.

Merezhkovsky points out that historically and pre-modernly only Pushkin among these writers really possesses charm. He inhabits a sphere by himself, a sensuously radiant, naïve, and blithely poetic one. But with Gogol there begins what Merezhkovsky calls critique: "the transition from unconscious creation to creative consciousness"; for him that means the end of poetry in the Pushkin sense, but at the same time the beginning of something new. The remark is true and perceptive. Thus did Heine speak of the age of Goethe, an æsthetic age, an epoch of art, an objective-ironic point of view. Its representative and dominant figure had been the Olympian; it died with his death. What then began was a time of taking sides, of conflicting opinions, of social consolidation, yes, of politics and, in short, of morals — a morality that branded as frivolous every purely æsthetic and universal point of view.

In Heine's comments, as in Merezhkovsky's, there is feeling for temporal change, together with feeling for its opposite, the timeless and perpetual. Schiller, in his immortal essay, reduced it to the formula of the sentimental and the naïve. What Merezhkovsky calls "critique" or "creative consciousness," what seems to him like contrast with the unconscious creation of Pushkin, as the more modern element, the future on the way, is precisely what Schiller means by the sentimental in contrast to the naïve. He too brings in the temporal, the evolutional, and – "*pro domo*," as we know – declares the sentimental, the creativeness of conscious critique, in short the moralistic, to be the newer, more modern stage of development.

There are now two things to say: first, Tolstoy's original convictions were definitely on the side of the æsthetic, of pure art, the objectively shaping, anti-moralistic principle; and second, in him took place that very cultural and historical change which Merezhkovsky speaks of, that move away from Pushkin's simplicity towards critical responsibility and morality. Within his own being it took such a radical and tragic form that he went through the severest crises and much anguish and even so could not utterly repudiate his own mighty creativeness. What he finally arrived at was a rejection and negation of art itself as an idle, voluptuous, and immoral luxury, admissible only in order to make moral teachings acceptable to men, even though dressed in the mantle of art.

But to return to the first position: we have his own unequivocal declarations to the effect that a purely artistic gift stands higher than one with social significance. In 1859, when he was thirty-one years old, he gave, as a member of the Moscow society of Friends of Russian Literature, an address in which he so sharply emphasized the advantages of the purely art element in literature over all the fashions of the day that the president of the society, Khomyakov, felt constrained to rejoin that a servant of pure art might quite easily become a social reformer even without knowing or willing it. Contemporary criticism saw in the author of *Anna Karenina* the protagonist of the art for art's sake position, the representative of free creativeness apart from all tendentiousness or doctrine. Indeed, it considered this naturalism the characteristically new thing; the public must in time grow up to it, though at present they had got used, in the works of others, to the presentation of political and social ideas in the form of art. In point of fact, all this was only one side of the business. As an artist and son of his time, the nineteenth century, Tolstoy was a naturalist, and in this connection he represented – in the sense of a trend – the new. But as an intellectual he was beyond (or rather, he struggled amid torments to arrive beyond) the new, to something further still, on the other side of his, the naturalistic century. He was reaching after conceptions of art which approached much nearer to "mind" (*Geist*), to knowledge, to "critique" than to nature. The commentators of 1875, impressed by the first chapters of *Anna Karenina* as they appeared in a Russian magazine, the *Messenger*, seeking benevolently to prepare the way with the public for the naturalism of the work, did not dream that the author was in full flight towards an anti-art position, which was already hampering his work on his masterpiece and even endangering its completion.

This development was to go very far, the vehemence of its consistency shrank from nothing: neither from the anti-cultural nor even from the absurd. Before long, he was to regret in public having written *Childhood* and *Youth*, the work of his freshest youthful hours—so poor, so insincere, so literary, so sinful was this book. He was to condemn root and branch the "artist twaddle" with which the twelve volumes of his works were filled, to which "the people of our day ascribe an undeserved significance." It was the same undeserved significance that they ascribed to art itself—for instance, to Shakespeare's plays. He went so far—one must set it down with respect and a sober face, or at least with the smallest, most non-committal smile—as to put Mrs. Harriet Beecher Stowe, the author of *Uncle Tom's Cabin*, far above Shakespeare.

We must be at pains to understand this. Tolstoy's hatred for Shakespeare dated from much earlier than is usually supposed. It signified rebellion against nature, the universal, the all-affirming. It was jealousy of the morally tormented for the irony of the absolute creator, it meant the straining away from nature, naïveté, moral indifference, towards "*Geist*" in the moralistically critical sense of the word; towards moral valuations and edifying doctrine. Tolstoy hated himself in Shakespeare, hated his own vital bearish strength, which was originally like Shakespeare's, natural and creatively a-moral; though his struggles for the good, the true and right, the meaning of life, the doctrine of salvation, were after all only the same thing in another and self-denying form. The immensity of his writings sometimes resulted in a gigantic clumsiness which forces a respectful smile. And yet it is precisely the paradoxically ascetic application of a titantic helplessness arising from a primeval force that, viewed as art, gives his work that huge moral *élan*, that Atlas-like moral muscle-tensing and flexing which reminds one of the agonized figures of Michelangelo's sculpture.

I said that Tolstoy's hatred of Shakespeare belongs to an earlier period than is generally thought. But all that which later made his friends and admirers like Turgenyev weep, his denial of art and culture, his radical moralism, his highly questionable pose of prophet and confessor in his last period — all that begins much further back, it is quite wrong to imagine this process as something suddenly occurring in a crisis of conversion in later life, coincident with Tolstoy's old age. The same kind of mistake occurs in the popular opinion that Richard Wagner suddenly got religion — whereas the matter was one of a development vastly and fatally consistent and inevitable, the direction of which is clearly and unmistakably traceable in *The Flying Dutchman* and in *Tannhäuser*. The judgment of the Frenchman, Vogüé, was entirely correct when, on the news that the great Russian writer was now "as though paralysed by a sort of mystic madness," Vogüé declared that he had long ago seen it coming. The course of Tolstoy's intellectual development had been present in the seed in *Childhood* and *Boyhood* and the psychology of Levin in *Anna Karenina* had marked out the path it would take.

So much is true, that Levin is Tolstoy, the real hero of the mighty novel, which is a glorious, indestructible signpost on the woeful Way of the Cross the poet was taking; a monument of an elemental and creative bear-strength, which was first heightened and then destroyed by the inner ferment of his subtilizing conscience and his fear of God. Yes, Levin is Tolstoy — almost altogether Tolstoy, this side Tolstoy the artist. To this character Tolstoy transferred not only the important facts and dates of his own life: his experiences as a farmer, his romance and betrothal (which are completely autobiographic), the sacred, beautiful, and awe-full experiences of the birth of his first child, and the death of his brother — which forms a pendant of equal and boundless significance — not only there but in his whole inner life, his crises of conscience, his groping after the whole duty of man and the meaning of life, his painful wrestling over the good life, which so decisively estranged him from the doings of urban society; his gnawing doubts about culture itself or that which his society called culture, doubts of all this brought him close to the anchorite and nihilist type. What Levin lacks of Tolstoy is only just that he is not a great artist besides. But to estimate *Anna Karenina* not only artistically but also humanly, the reader must saturate himself with the thesis that Constantin Levin himself wrote the novel. Instead of being the man with the pointer, indicating the incomparable beauty of the painting as a whole, I shall do better to speak of the conditions of difficulty and stress under which the work came to birth.

That is the right word: it came to birth; but there did not lack much for it not to be born. A work of this kind, so all of one piece and that piece so absorbing, so complete in the large and in the small, makes us suppose that its creator gave himself utterly to it with entire and devoted heart and, like one driven to self-expression, committed it, so to speak, in one gush to paper. That is a misapprehension; although, even so, the origin of *Anna Karenina* does in fact lie in the happiest, most harmonious period of Tolstoy's life. The years in which he worked on it belong to the first decade and a half of his marriage with the woman whose literary image is Kitty Shtcherbatsky and who later suffered so much from her Lievotshka—until at last just before his death the old man broke away and ran. It is she who, in addition to her constant pregnancies, and her abundant activities as mistress of the farm, as mother and housewife, copies *War and Peace* seven times with her own hand—that first colossal intellectual harvest of the period that brought the doubting, brooding man relative peace in the patriarchal animalism of marriage and family life in the country. It was the period at which the poor Countess looked so yearningly back when Leochen had become "the prophet of Yasnaya Polyana" and succeeded under self-torture, and even so up to the end never quite succeeded, in brooding to death all his sensual and instinctive passions: family, nation, state, church, club, and chase, at bottom the whole life of the body, but most particularly art, which for him quite essentially meant sensuality and the body's life.

Well, those fifteen years were a good, happy time, though from a later, higher point of view, good only in a low and animal sense. *War and Peace* had made Tolstoy the "great writer of Russia," and as such he went to work to write a new historical and national epos. He had in mind a novel about Peter the Great and his times. And for months he carried on conscientious and comprehensive studies for it in the libraries and archives of Moscow. "Lievotshka reads and reads," it says in the Countess's letters. Did he read too much? Did he take in too much, did he spoil his appetite? Oddly enough, it turned out that the Czar reformer, the imperial compeller of civilization, was at bottom an unsympathetic figure to Tolstoy. To hold the position he had achieved as the national epic-writer, he had wanted to repeat his performance in *War and Peace*. It would not come off; the material unexpectedly resisted him. After endless preparatory labour he flung the whole thing away, sacrificed his whole investment of time and study, and turned to something quite different: the passion and stumbling of *Anna*

Karenina, the modern novel of St. Petersburg and Moscow high society.

The first onset, by dint of Pushkin's help, was fresh and blithe. But before long Tolstoy got stuck, though the reader in his untrammelled enjoyment would never guess it. For weeks and months the work only dragged on or did not go at all. What was the trouble? Household cares, children's illnesses, fluctuations in his own health – oh, no, these were all nothing compared with a piece of work like *Anna Karenina* – or they ought to be. What is really disturbing is doubt of the importance and personal urgency of what we are doing. Might we not do better to learn Greek, to get some fundamental knowledge of the New Testament? Then the schools for the children of peasants we have founded. Should they not claim more of our time and thought? Is not the whole of belles-lettres folly? And is it not our duty or even much more consistent with our deepest need to bury ourselves in theological and philosophical studies in order to find at last the meaning of life? That contact with the mystery of death which he had had when his older brother died had made a strong impression on Tolstoy's own vitality, powerful to the point of mysticism, which demanded spiritual wrestling, not in a literary way but in something confessional on the pattern of Saint Augustine and Rousseau. Such a book, sincere as far as human power could make it, weighed on his mind and gave him increasing distaste for writing novels. Actually, he would never have finished *Anna Karenina* if it had not begun appearing in the *Rusky Vyestnik* (*Russian Messenger*) of Katkov. The fact made him responsible to the publisher and the reading public. In January 1875 and the following three months successive numbers of the novel appeared in the magazine. Then they left off, because the author had no more to deliver. The first months of the next year produced a few fragments, then seven months' pause. Then in December one more number. What we find simply enchanting, what we cannot imagine as originating in anything except a state of prolonged inspiration – Tolstoy groaned over. "My tiresome, horrible *Anna Karenina*," he wrote from Samara, where he was drinking mares' milk. *Sic!* Literally. "At last," he wrote in March 1876, "I was driven to finish my novel, of which I am sick to death." Of course in the process the enthusiasm and eagerness came back by fits and starts. But it was just at such times that the writing was prone to go more slowly – owing to fastidious artistry that caused endless filing and remodelling and improving out of a stylistic perfectionism which still shows through the most inadequate translation. This amazing saint took his art the more seriously the less he believed in it.

The publication dragged on, with constant interruptions, as far as the eighth book. Then it stopped, for now the thing had become political and the national epic-writer of Russia had in the latest number expressed himself so heretically about Slavophilism, the current enthusiasm for the Bulgarian, Serbian, Bosnian brothers in their fight for freedom against the Turks, the much ado over the volunteers and the patriotic nonsense uttered by Russian society, that Katkov dared not print it. He demanded cuts and changes, which the author in high dudgeon refused to make. Tolstoy had the final numbers printed separately with a note on the disagreement.

What I have boldly called the greatest society novel in all literature is an anti-society novel. The Bible text: "Vengeance is mine, I will repay, saith the Lord," stands at its head. The moral momentum of the work was certainly the desire to lash society for the cold, cruel rebuff inflicted by it on a woman who goes astray through passion but is fundamentally proud and high-minded, instead of leaving to God the punishment for her sins. Indeed, society might well do just that, for after all it is society and its irrevocable laws that God too avails Himself of to exact the payment. It shows the fatal and inevitable character of Anna's doom that it proceeds inscrutably, step by step, up to the frightful end out of her affront to the moral law. So there is a certain contradiction in the author's original moral motive, in the complaint he lodges against society. One asks oneself in what way would God punish if society did not behave as it does? Custom and morality, how far are they distinguishable, how far are they—in effect—one and the same, how far do they coincide in the heart of the socially circumscribed human being? The question hovers unanswered over the whole novel. But such a work is not compelled to answer questions. Its task is to bring them out, to enrich the emotions, to give them the highest and most painful degree of questionableness. Thus it will have performed its task, and in this case the story-teller's love for his creature leaves no doubt at all, no matter how much suffering he painfully and relentlessly visits on her.

Tolstoy loves Anna very much, one feels that. The book bears her name; it could bear no other. But its hero is not Anna's lover, the strong, decent, chivalrous, and somewhat limited officer of the Guards, Count Vronsky. Nor is it Alexander Alexandrovich,

Anna's husband, with whatever profound skill Tolstoy has modelled this incomparable, at once repellent and superior, comic and touching cuckold. No, the hero is another person altogether, who has as good as nothing to do with Anna's lot, and whose introduction in a way twists the theme of the novel and almost pushes its first motive into second place. It is Constantin Levin, the introspective man, the author's image – he, no other, with his brooding and scrutinizing, with the peculiar force and obstinate resistance of his critical conscience, that makes the great society novel into an anti-society novel.

What an extraordinary fellow he is, this surrogate of the author! What in the French *pièce à thèse* is called the *raisonneur* – Levin is that in Tolstoy's society world. Yet how un-French! To amount to something as a critic of society, one must, I suppose, be in society oneself; but precisely that he is not in the least, this tortured, radically remote *raisonneur*, despite his native right to move in the highest circles. Strong and shy, defiant and dubious, with an intelligence of great anti-logical, natural, even helpless abundance, Levin is at bottom convinced that decency, uprightness, seriousness, and sincerity are possible only in singleness, in dumb isolation, each for himself; and that all social life turns him into a chatterer, a liar, and a fool. Observe him in the salons of Moscow, or on cultural occasions when he has to make conversation, play a social part, express "views." Such a coming-together of people seems to him banal, he sees himself a blushing fool, a prattler, a parrot. This Rousseauian quite sincerely considers all urban civilization, with the intellectual and cultural goings-on bound up in it, a sink of iniquity. Only life in the country is worthy of a man – though not the country life that the city man in sentimental relaxation finds "charming." Levin's learned brother, for instance, even boasts in a way that he enjoyed such an unintellectual occupation as fishing. No, what Levin means is the real, serious life on the land, where you have to work hard, where the human being dwells truly and perforce at the heart of that nature whose "beauty" the guest from civilization sentimentally admires from outside.

Levin's morality and conscientiousness are strongly physical, having reference to the body and bound up with it. "I need physical exercise," he says to himself, "otherwise my character suffers." He resolves to help the peasants with the mowing and it gives him the highest moral and physical pleasure (a splendid and Tolstoyan chapter). His scorn of the "intellectual" or, better, his disbelief in it, estranging him as a product of civilization, involving him in contradictions, is radical. It leads him, when he has to come right down to it, into paradoxes, into opinions hard to express among civilized beings. Take for instance popular education – or, worse still, any education at all. Levin's position towards it is the same as his position towards nature: "The same people whom you say you love." – "I never said that," thought Constantin Levin. – "Why should I bother my head about schools where I shall never send my own children and where the peasants will never send theirs either? And on top of that, I am not even convinced that it is necessary to send them!" – "You can make better use of a peasant and labourer who can read and write than of one who cannot." – "No, ask anybody you like," countered Constantin Levin decisively; "a worker with some schooling is distinctly worse." – "Do you admit that education is a blessing for the people?" – "Yes, that I admit," responded Levin thoughtlessly, and saw at once that what he had said was not really just what he thought. – Very bad! A difficult, dangerous case! He recognizes the blessings of "education," because what he "really" thinks about it, in the nineteenth century, cannot be put into words and for that reason may even be unthinkable.

Of course he moves in the thought-channels of his century, and they in a certain way are scientific. He "observes humanity, not as something standing outside of zoological law but as something dependent on its environment, and he proceeds from this dependence in order to discover the laws lying at the base of its development." So at least the scholar understands him; and it is no other than Taine to whom he there makes acknowledgment, good, great nineteenth century. But there is something in him that either goes back behind the scientific spirit of his epoch or goes on beyond it, something desperately bold, inadmissible, impossible in conversation. He lies on his back and looks up at the high and cloudless sky. "Do I not know that that is infinite space and not a round vault? But however I screw up my eyes and strain my sight I cannot see it not round and not bounded; and in spite of my knowledge about infinite space I am incontestably right when I see a solid blue dome, and more right than when I strain my eyes to see beyond it. . . . Can this be faith?"

But whether faith or the new realism, it is no longer the scientific spirit of the nineteenth century. In a sort of way it recalls Goethe. And Levin-Tolstoy's sceptical, realistic, rebellious attitude towards patriotism, towards the Slavic brethren and the war volunteers, does the same. He declines to share in the enthusiasm, he is solitary in the midst of it, precisely as Goethe was at the time of the Freiheitskrieg – although in both cases something new, the democratic, joined the national movement and for the first time the popular will conditioned the conduct of the government. That too is nineteenth-century; and Levin, or Lievotshka, as the poor Countess called him, could simply not do with the truths of his time. He called them comfortless. He is a step further on; I cannot help calling it a very dangerous step, which, if not safeguarded by the profoundest love of truth and human sympathy, can quite easily lead to black reaction and barbarism. Today it takes no forlorn, single-handed courage to throw overboard the scientific discipline of the nineteenth century and surrender to the "mythus," the "faith" – in other words, to a paltry and culture-destroying vulgarity. Masses of people do it today; but it is not a step forward, it is a hundred miles backwards. Such a step will be in a forward direction only when it is taken for humanity's sake, only if another step follows it straightway, moving from the new realism of the solid blue vault to the neither old nor new but humanly eternal idealism of truth, freedom, and knowledge. Today there are some desperately stupid ideas about reaction in the air.

A digression – but a necessary one. Levin, then, cannot do with the ideals of his epoch, he cannot live with them. What I call his physical morality and conscientiousness is shaken to the depths by the experience of the physically transcendent and transparent mysteries of birth and death; and all that the times teach him about organisms and their destruction, about the indestructibility of matter and the laws of conservation of energy, about evolution, and so forth, all that looks to him not only like utter ignorance of the whole problem of the meaning of life but also like a kind of thinking that makes it impossible for him to get the knowledge he needs. That in infinite time, infinite space, infinite matter, and organism, a cell frees itself; that it persists for a while and then bursts and that this bubble is he himself, Levin; that seems to him like the malicious mockery of some demon. It cannot indeed be refuted; it must be overcome some other way, that one may not be driven to shoot oneself.

What to his profounder necessities looks like a mortal lie and a kind of thinking which is no sort of instrument for the apprehension of truth – that actually is the naturalistic materialism of the nineteenth century, whose inspiration is honest love of truth, despite the comfortless pessimism that is its necessary aura. The honesty must be preserved; but a little illumination is required in order to do justice to life and its deeper concerns. So there is real humour in the fact that in *Anna Karenina* a simple little peasant shows the brooding man the way out of his despair. This little peasant teaches him, or recalls to his mind, something he has always known: true, he says, living for our physical well-being and in order to fill our bellies is natural and inborn and laid upon us all. But even so, it is not righteous or even important. What we have to do is to live for the "truth," "for our souls," "as God wills," for "the Good." How wonderful that this necessity is laid upon us just as naturally inborn and imposed as the need to fill our bellies! Wonderful indeed; for the sure conviction common to all men that it is shameful to live only for the belly, and that one must rather live for God, for the true and the good, has nothing to do with reason, but quite the contrary. It is reason that makes us care for the body and in its interest to exploit our neighbours all we can. Knowledge of the good, asserts Levin, does not lie in the realm of reason; the good stands outside the scientific chain of cause and effect. The good is a miracle, because it is contrary to reason and yet everyone understands it.

There is something outside of and beyond the melancholy science of the nineteenth century, which resigned all attempt to give meaning to life. There is a spiritual factor, a spiritual need. And Levin is enchanted and soothed by this absurdly simple statement of the human being's supra-reasonable obligation to be good. In his joy he forgets that also that melancholy materialistic naturalistic science of the nineteenth century had, after all, as motive power, human striving for the good. He forgot that it was stern and bitter love of truth that made it deny meaning to life. It too, denying God, lived for God. That, too, is possible, and Levin forgets it. Art he does not need even to forget; he knows, it seems, nothing about it, obviously thinking of it only as the society prattle of the "cultured" about painting, the Luccas, Wagner, and so on. Here is the difference between him and Leo Tolstoy. Tolstoy knew art; he has suffered frightfully from and for it, achieved mightier things in it than the rest of us can hope to achieve. Perhaps it was just the violence of his artist personality that made him fail to see that knowledge of the good is just the opposite of a reason to deny art. Art is the most beautiful, austerest, blithest, most sacred symbol of all supra-reasonable human striving for good above and beyond reason, for truth and fullness. The breath of the rolling sea of epic would not so expand our lungs with living air if it did not bring with it the astringent quickening spice of the spiritual and the divine.

LESSING

1929

[A speech delivered on the two hundredth birthday of Lessing, January 22, 1929, in the Prussian Academy of Art, Berlin]

AT times, my friends, the word "classic" has for me a significance that I might almost call mythical; when its accepted meaning — shall we say standard, or exemplary? — seems dry and thin, abstract and bloodless, a diaphanous humanistic conception, to which, even while I accept it, I long to give body and content. For the classic, as I prefer to conceive it, is the prototype in the etymological sense of that word: it is the original, the first living individual embodiment of a form of spirit; the first impression, as it were, of a primitive type, upon which later manifestations, perceiving, will base themselves and walk in its steps. A mythus, then, for the type is mythical, and the essence of the myth is recurrence, timelessness, a perpetual present. In this sense only is the classic a prototype, not in the empty sense of exemplar. Classic times, those were patriarchal times, times of the first foundation of the national life.

I say national; for I must attach to the national this conception of a beginning, in order not to embark upon a perfectly shoreless sea, but with some hope of reaching ground firm enough for the mind to pause and rest upon. For whither should we arrive if we divest the word "beginning" of all its relative character? There *are* only conditioned beginnings. The world of events is nothing but a stage setting whose shifting scenes lure us from beginnings backward to earlier beginnings and so into the infinite; the beginning of beginnings lying, I suspect, not in time at all, being transcendent. The history of peoples too has many beginnings — as, for example, the history of the German people. But at the beginning of the path we tread today, the path of civilization and action, to follow to whose distant goal is a duty laid upon us, our children and grandchildren, stands the myth, one out of whose calendar of feasts we are celebrating today. For first on the route which leads to national unification, for which its intellectual labours broke the ground, laid the foundations, made the path, is our national literature.

The clear-eyed champion whose memory we celebrate today was born two hundred years ago in Kamenz, Saxony, and led the life of a free-lance writer. It was Lessing's mission, in virtue of his penetrating understanding, to make divisions and distinctions; yet his genius was unifying. "Before him," so runs a contemporary letter with reference to *Minna von Barnhelm*, "no German author succeeded in inspiring with the same enthusiasm nobility and people, learned and laity alike, or in pleasing them so universally." Goethe praised the "completely north-German national content of the same work, admiring what has since so often been admired, the way in which a specifically north-German product succeeded in delighting the whole of Germany, uniting all Germans in conscious sympathy. While *Nathan der Weise*, our great critic's last word as a poet – uttered in accents of the profoundest wisdom, which evoked from its greatest admirer (Goethe once more) the cry: "May the divine sentiments of patience and tolerance there expressed ever remain precious and sacred in the nation's eyes!" a poetic composition that is the last word in benevolence – *Nathan der Weise* stands for unification of a still higher sort: its conscious pedagogic goal is the peace of mutual understanding, the peace of mankind. This same brave spirit, so national in character and achievement, who as a poet led Germany towards unification, while as dramatic critic he rent asunder the authority of the French canon – he it was who called patriotism a "heroic weakness," and declared that nothing was further from his desire than to be praised as a patriot, a man who would forget that he should be a citizen of the world. The Hamburg dramaturge makes merry over the provincialism of certain comedies of manners, whose author would like to "take the pathetic little traditions of the corner where he was born for the customs of the common fatherland," whereas the truth was that nobody cared a jot "how many times in the year, or where, or when, green cabbage is eaten." Thus he sets against the provincial point of view the intellectual conception of a common fatherland – the national, this is, against, or at least above, the sectional. But he is also aware of a point of view wherein the national in its turn appears as the sectional; he expresses it in the wish that "there might be in every state men who are above popular prejudice and know precisely when patriotism ceases to be a virtue." Those are his words – the words of a free man and a genuine. They imply that the intellectual and the humane are only a heightening and extension of the natural and national, and they make plain that the trend to further unification lies inherent in the national idea itself, though all unrecognized by those tribal-minded exclusionists who, in amazing miscomprehension, inscribe the latter on their banner and see in it nothing but the slogan of segregation and animosity.

Lessing's national mission was one of clarification by criticism. His was a penetrating and inspired understanding. Nathan's phrase: "we must distinguish," might be set as a motto above his great analytical contributions, the *Laokoon*, the *Hamburger Dramaturgie*, and the theological controversies. Definition, limitation, lucid statement were his peculiar joy and gift; they were, to employ once more that singularly pregnant word, his mission. For singularly pregnant it is, that in the conception, with its implication of task, function, and tool, there is an interplay of the personal and the supra-personal imperative. When a young nation girds itself up to a heightening and burgeoning of its culture, certain duties lie upon it: to put its intellectual house in order, to stabilize theory and law, to lay down national principles, to distinguish and clarify. And these become gift and mission, passion and mastery, in a man who may, at moments, think of himself as a teacher, but with all his shrewdness certainly never draws a line between the impulse that urges him on and the tasks that grow to him out of the depth of the general.

Lessing was from the first the founder of a mythical type – mythical because it constantly reappears in the flesh. He is the classical creative intelligence, the patriarch of the writing tribe. Most personally and vividly he represents the ideal productive type, the kind of intellectual whose performance is viewed in some quarters with a jaundiced eye, as mere profane writing, sharply and contemptuously distinguished from the sacred sphere of the afflatus. We all know how popular this distinction is, particularly in Germany, and particularly now. Our current critique simply lives on it. And at bottom, I feel, it partakes of that same stuffiness, that provincial, "green-cabbage" point of view of which Lessing spoke. It is self-righteous and spiteful; nor is its position tenable, since the line between creative authorship and mere "writing" runs, of course, not outwardly, between the products, but inwardly, within the personality itself; and because it is possible to imagine, combined in one person, the trained writer endowed with initiative and the conscious, clear-eyed creative artist who could say:

Ich bin nicht kalt. Ich sehe wahrlich
Nicht minder gern, was ich in Ruhe sehe.

Lessing' s own classic personality is a proof that the combination exists. The enthusiasts of simplification underestimate the awkwardness of a distinction that is constantly being blurred and obliterated through the critical factor of language itself. An art whose medium is language will always show a high degree of critical creativeness, for speech is itself a critique of life: it names, it characterizes, it passes judgment, in that it creates. There is, of course, such a thing as detachment, objectivity—the "reverent neutrality" of which a certain hymnist speaks. But it must have followed the intoxication, on that being felt as something which needed checking. Detachment, indeed, is not productive, but it is possible to conceive of creation and craftsmanship as different stages in the development of a work, united by an act of cool objectivation. We need waste no praise on this last—but then, neither need we deny it relationship with the will to mortality. Again, the enthusiasts of simplification forget, or do not observe, how the conscious and the unconscious dovetail into each other in the productive; or how much of the naïve, the unconscious—of the dæmonic, to use their own sinister and darling word—enters into and determines all conscious action.

The type that we are analysing possesses a self-critical acumen, a modesty and candour which unfortunately play all too easily into the hands of those who would deny its claims to membership in the charmed circle of creative artists. Such a man typically runs to meet adverse criticism, not to forestall it, but because he has an objective eye on his own performance. He it is who always says the best things about himself—not complimentary things, but conveying the truth as he sees it, however black and forbidding. Then the others parrot it after him, seldom to his credit, and rather to be able to use his own words against him: "He said so himself, you know." Lessing's love of truth is essentially radical; he has an ungovernable gift for "hunting out the truth in the very last hole," as he puts it; there would of course be a peculiar zest in the game when self-knowledge was the prize. Some pleasing instances of the thing I mean are to be found in his own creative work; as when Minna says to Tellheim that there is a certain hard, casual way of referring to one's own misfortunes, and Tellheim hastens to answer: "Which at bottom is only boasting and complaining too." Or in *Emilia Galotti*, when Conti the painter speaks of his dissatisfaction with himself as an artist, adding: "And yet I am sometimes quite satisfied with my own lack of self-satisfaction." Lessing, paying homage to the critical spirit, and disowning the complaint that it acts as a wet blanket to genius, asserts that to it alone he owes all that is tolerable in his work, and that he flatters himself to have won from it something akin to genius. "I am neither actor nor poet," he says. "I do not feel in myself the living spring that rises by its own power and shoots upward in such streams of richness, freshness, and purity. With me everything must come out through pressure and pipes." How they have been quoted against him, the pressure and pipes! But if he was right, not so were the others who quoted him. In Lessing's world, truth is very relative – one gets used to that. It becomes humanized, as it were, the criteria lying less in the matter under dispute than in its defender. Goethe never concurred in these judgments of Lessing about himself. The influence he wielded, Goethe says, in the long run gave the lie to his detractors. Goethe was all for letting the end try the man. But if one cannot wait for the judgment of time, then surely one may cite the pre-eminent qualities of personality, originality, boldness. Genius, one may say, betrays itself in the unexpected, in the sudden coming-to-be of something undreamed-of beforehand. It manifests itself in the possibility of something new of its kind, which could be triumphantly valid only by the power of personality. Genius in art, then, would be the surprise, the wonder and enchantment, the something dared that seemed quite impossible until it was done. In the light of this definition the old question as to Lessing's rank as an author becomes demonstrably idle. For creations like Minna and Nathan bear precisely this imprint of the new and the surprising, of something risked that became possible only by dint of being done, valid and triumphant only by virtue of the mingled characteristics of shrewdness and naïveté. They may, because they can – and only so. Less vital than they are they could not maintain themselves. And in face of this objective artistry, this disarming intelligence, this cordial good sense rising to the highest pitch of amenity, it would be callous and pedantic to challenge its claim to the title of creative art.

Such was Otto Ludwig's view: he said of *Minna von Barnhelm* that the old indictment must fall, in view of an art that could so swell out a single seed-corn of matter as to make of it a play of inexhaustible interest. And yet it is just this art of "swelling out," of irresistibly, inexplicably enlarging upon, that constitutes another trait of the classic type which I describe. Invention is not its strong point; but it can invest the detail, and the uttermost detail, with rich and unfailing charm. It has small concern with plot and, lacking talent therein, dispenses with all but the minimum required to give backbone to the composition. Its strength lies in the power to give that little effectiveness and beauty: digging it in, building it out, exploiting it, sharpening its lines, accenting its facets, illuminating the obscurest corner of its theme, until what would in another's hand be boresome becomes genuinely entertaining. All this, I repeat, is no less characteristic of the type than is its self-critical candour. But in the first place, there is something Dürerish, something of the German *Meister* about this careful, busy, ingenious activity, this lively reverence for detail, which cannot be condemned as lacking all communion with the Muses. And in the second place, this bareness out of which a virtue grows may be conceived as the truest badge of creative authorship – at least Schopenhauer says that the greatest works succeed with the minimum of contrivance.

The case is the same with the third trait of the type, the characteristic which we might call its masculinity, or its preoccupation with the masculine. The male suits incomparably better than the female its talent for characterization. Its men are drawn with more depth, power, certainty. Minna is admittedly far outranked by the melancholy and meticulous Tellheim. To begin with, he is much more masculine than she is feminine – a fact for which old Mendelssohn accounted by saying that Lessing was most successful with those characters which were nearest his own – as, for instance, with Tellheim, Odoardo, and the Templar. The last has always been considered the freshest and most vivid characterization of youth upon the German stage, or any stage. It was Friedrich Schlegel who remarked upon how thoroughly Lessing's characters are Lessingized. It is a mark of the type – we might well call it lyrical subjectivity, and thus derive it from the explicitly and peculiarly poetic!

Again, there is a certain proud economy of output, the opposite to unintelligent productivity. Lessing presents a comedy – *the* comedy – as if to say: "See, this is the way to do it! His pride and his critical dignity forbid him to follow it with ten poorer ones; he passes on to another form. Such shrewdness, such self-awareness are surely to be appraised higher than dull, haphazard, uneven performance – surely they rank as artistic gift, and if so, then poetic.

But poetic the medium of our type is not. His language is not poetic. Not in the Orphic sense, not high, not a mystery. There is much justice in the accusation that it is dry, that it wants feeling and acme. It does not mount as high as the sources, the fount and well-spring of our idiom. It is simply cultured, pithy and shrewd. It demands of itself merely clarity, neatness, precision: *d'être clair et précis,*" as Lessing himself puts it. That it does not lack vigour is rather remarkable. On the contrary, it aims at and attains that quality in considerable degree, for it has the gift of appositeness, and of a phrasing that makes it at once discursive and dramatic. If our type set itself one day to compose verse, it will be prosaic, like Nathan's, spoken, not sung; very pleasant to hear, not lacking in rhythm, but without *melos,* having no meltingness; such uninspired verse, indeed, that Friedrich Schlegel could speak of its "disillusioned note." And yet verse of such golden-hearted good sense that unless you have steeled your heart beforehand, you yield to it none the less. Marvellous, the power wielded by such dry good sense! Goethe was "quite bowled over" ("*ordentlich prosterniert*"). He is said never to have tired of praising *Nathan* as the loftiest masterpiece of human skill. To quote Schlegel once more, Lessing was "the Prometheus of German art." In the beautiful funeral oration pronounced by Herder over his grave, Lessing's prose was declared to be the most original since Luther. Truly, if this German was not poetic, it was so much else that it can afford to renounce the vague title to honour which the adjective conveys.

We might go on to cite other weak points in Lessing's armour; they would be just so many traits of the type of which he is the classic example. His sensuous equipment was slight, his demands in this respect amounting almost to indifference — for instance, in the *Laokoon,* in his treatment of antique sculpture, his senses never absolve him from the duty of analysis. And yet this in many ways superannuated investigation into the line of demarcation between painting and poetry contains here and there an *aperçu* that is certainly creatively felt. Take that painful perception of the law that language can only praise, not reproduce beauty; that challenge to the poet to give up description and instead paint for us the satisfaction, the sympathy, the love, the delight that beauty confers — "for thereby," says he, "you have painted beauty herself." Possible that this anti-descriptive flight into the lyrical constitutes Lessing's approach to the dramatic. Otherwise there lies no little irony in the fact that this prosaic, half-acknowledged poet, with his limited powers of imagination, should have chosen as a medium of self-expression precisely that creative art-form which since Aristotle has passed for the highest in every school of æsthetics. And not only chosen it, but vivified it in a way that may faintly be called epoch-making.

Or was it the quality of logic in the drama that attracted Lessing, was it the dialectician in him that made him a dramatist? Here we come upon another and most striking trait of our mythical type — the one that above all others makes the man of temperament misdoubt its right to poetic rank. The tendency to polemic — what he himself called the spitfire irascibility (*Spitzbübin Iraszibilität*), the love of controversy for its own sake — runs through all his works. He puts in the pepper and salt, sometimes slyly, sometimes with reckless hand; the passion for seasoning grows upon him apace, until it seems that he finds the merely creative and dramatic very flat by contrast. Now, the view that the poet must not be a controversialist is deep-rooted in the German mind. He is supposed to accept all phenomena as they come, with calm and lofty simplicity, and then transmute them. He is degraded and dishonoured if he display any feeling about the times or the world he lives in, any sensitiveness towards its bad, or base, or stupid manifestations. He is descending into the market-place, he is "mixing in trade." World and reality are obviously so well aware of their own innate commonness as perforce to despise whoever makes himself common with them. The right sort of poet, they feel, is a creature who sees nothing, marks nothing, suspects nothing, and whose "pure" foolishness is as wax in the hands of baser interests. If he does see anything, if he runs the gauntlet against shams and injustices and the besotting of the people, against the lying confusion between, shall we say, high-flown patriotism and big business, then he is no poet, but a "writer," and an unpatriotic one to boot.

So that if anything could bring Lessing's good name as a poet into disrepute with his countrymen it would be his zeal in polemic. Heine has put it most wittily: Lessing, the giant, he says, in his rage let fly a few random rocks at certain nonentities — to whom then these rocks served as gravestones to keep them from being forgotten. Lessing himself was not insensible to the superfluity of honour which he showed to some of his opponents. "I should not like," he wrote of one of his controversies, "to have the value of this inquiry measured by its occasion. That is so despicable that only the way in which I have used it can excuse me for wanting to use it at all." To which he appends a little apologia for polemic which even today is entirely pertinent. "Not, indeed," he says, "that I did not regard our modern public as a bit too squeamish with regard to controversy or anything suggesting controversy. It seems to want to forget that it owes to sheer contradiction its enlightenment on many subjects of first importance, and that if human beings had never yet quarrelled over anything in this world neither would they be of one mind over anything to this day.

Scepticism, denial, the tendency to these, not merely form a trait of the classic type which Lessing founded; doubt is its native heath, its religion, the soil in which it lives and flourishes. Doubt as belief, scepticism as a positive passion — such is quite genuinely the paradox exhibited by Lessing. It is a paradox of the heart and not of the understanding; and one with it is a conception of truth and feeling for truth that scarcely occurs in such flower a second time in the history of the human intellect. We have already seen how Lessing makes truth relative to the human element. Man, he asserts, proves his worth not in the possession or the supposed possession of truth, but in the sheer pains he has taken to come at it. That is to subjectivate the value of truth and almost truth itself. It implies a profound philosophic doubt of the objective, together with a passion for research, as which alone he envisages human morality. For how false it would be to confuse this philosophic doubt with nihilism, with intentional malice! He once said of his *Nathan der Weise:* "It is not at all a satirical piece, such as ends with a burst of mocking laughter. It is an affecting piece, such as I have always written." Instead of satirical he would have said nihilistic, had the word been current in his time. His scepticism is as far from flippancy as is his wit, which is a scorching wit, but not supercilious — a genuine expression of his way of reacting to life. He is witty even in the letter where he describes the birth and death of his little Traugott, written while his wife lay dying. Wittiest of all he is when some display of sanctimonious orthodoxy rouses his wrath and dips his restless pen in gall. He it was who spoke the immortal words: "If God held all the truth in His closed right hand and in His left the single ever living urge towards truth, though with the proviso that I must forever err, and said to me: 'Choose!' I should bow down humbly before His left hand and say: 'Father, give me this. Pure truth is for Thee alone!' " Note the fervour of the utterance. These are not the accents of irreligion, but of a religious doubt that approaches a worship of the infinite and a perpetual striving towards it.

But what orthodoxy saw therein was a stiff-necked rejection of revelation. This great Protestant had angered literal Lutheranism to the core; it sought — but in vain — to provoke him in the struggle to a compromising admission of his actual beliefs. It looked as though Lessing fought, not so much on behalf of some truth, or of truth in general, as out of a passion for administering small dagger-thrusts that should rouse his opponents out of their comfortable intellectual and spiritual landlordism. And yet the theological controversy with Hauptpastor Goeze is very far from being a satirical or nihilistic performance. There is no "burst of mocking laughter" about it; it is "touching and kindly, such as I have always written." In its fine-tempered ductability, its calm in the face of provocation, in the brilliance of its sallies, in its high seriousness, it is very probably his best work; I would even say his best creative work. It is easier to see this today, now that its theology has ceased to be anything but background and *point d'appui* for ethical and intellectual generalizations.

"The letter is not the spirit" – this is Lessing's position and his theme. It is a position that out-Luthers Luther, carrying him on beyond the text and the letter; by it he probably meant to suggest the saving of religion and the spirit, since the letter was no longer to be saved. For was it not short-sighted of Lutheranism to base religion on the Bible alone, since that must one day fall a sacrifice to the critics? But this discrimination between the spirit and the letter would mean the saving of the Bible too from the crude enthusiasm of those who would have it that the spirit is naught without the letter. True, in Lessing's glorious controversial writings there come into play so much irony, so much veiled allusion, so much dialectical virtuosity, so much tactical dissembling, that after all some confusion is inevitable. Even the virtuosity is confusing, as being the product not of callousness, vanity, or satiric bent, but of a deep seriousness, passionate and "touching." Was Lessing really seeking to save Christianity, by saying that it had been there before the Scripture and would be when the Scripture was no more? Yet he wrote a twelfth *Anti-Goeze*, the *Nathan;* and of it he said that he would be content if it taught one out of a thousand readers to doubt the evidence and the universality of his religion. And if this religion were Christianity – what then? Lessing was more radical than he dared to express; but it was precisely in his ambiguity that he was radical. In order to be a thorn in the side of bigoted Lutheranism he chimed in with the Catholics; on the other hand, he was offensive to rationalists and the Enlightenment, and had more sympathy with downright orthodoxy than with the half-way kind watered down with liberalism. Was that perfidy and bad faith? The nation in general never found it so; Lessing has always been considered a pattern of courage and manliness. Only this manliness, this trustworthiness, was not of a simple kind, but such as an artist can possess, varied and played upon by his art, not only in the matter of form but likewise in that ultimate passion which is the organic secret of all creation. Precisely when Lessing seemed to stand right, he was standing farther left than anything his age could conceive.

And so when this greatest Protestant between Luther and Nietzsche takes the field against a literal interpretation of the Scriptures and the proselytizing romanticism of the Catholic Church seizes on his sallies and turns them to the advantage of the Roman tradition and authority, it is hard to conceive anything more disingenuous. But at least the fact is evidence — the only piece of its kind in Germany — that brains can fight on the side of reaction. Even so, Catholic romanticism should have too much pride to wish to yoke to her chariot a spirit so diametrically opposed to hers. But how much worse still is the only too common sight, that of plain and simple un- and anti-intelligence counterfeiting and dressing itself out in the gifts of the spirit! How many times today has the new truth had occasion to cry out to those who think that everything is grist to their mill: "That was not what we meant!"

No, it was not meant as Clemens Brentano would have it mean. For it was the spirit of Luther and no other that Lessing invoked against Lutheranism. "Great, misunderstood man! Thou hast freed us from the yoke of tradition; but who is to free us from the intolerable yoke of the letter? Who will give us at last a Christianity *such as thou wouldst teach it now,* as Christ Himself would teach it?" "*Wie Du es itzt lehren würdest!*" That is perfect Lessing. It is the formula for all the spiritual, living present, that the letter, that history, would slay. And misunderstood is every great genius whom the yesterday-men will not see as *historically* great, conditioned and limited by the century that bore him; taking him literally instead, invoking his authority precisely against that which he, or his like, would teach now. Their error is great when they yearn for the great man of yesterday back again, thinking he would be on their side. If he came, they would not know him. A French writer has finely said that a masterpiece must not look like a masterpiece. There may be exceptions: the masterpiece of the day may appear in the half-burlesque mask of the historic, uniting the appeal of the familiar and prized with that of the new and daring, when your genuine conservative will scent the parody and brand it as profane. But though this may happen now and again, yet the French writer's dictum applies not only in the realm of art but for all life, all being and becoming in time. A man in whom the conservatives, the people with their heads fixed on backwards, think to recognize a reincarnation of a past genius is in all probability not the great man of today. That full-blooded, mighty and pugnacious man Hauptpastor Goeze, as he stood with his fist on the Bible and his rockfast faith in the revealed Word, must have looked to the short-sighted far more like the historic Luther than did the volatile Lessing, dissembler and sceptic, and altogether less Lutheran than Fritzian to the view. But Pastor Goeze was not the "new Luther," merely a Luther stuck fast in the toils of time; whereas the really new, the Luther "*von itzt*," was Lessing.

He himself, once so living and present, is now a historically conditioned figure; his one-sided – and once so salutary – tendency to rationalism, his doctrine of an abstract virtue, put into the mouth of Nathan, which all too humanly sweeps away the conception of *religio* and will hear nothing of any inborn and positive faith-content, is today no longer quite viable. The Enlightenment, whose true son and faithful knight Lessing always, despite all temperamental irregularities, remained, is today intellectually out of date; it has made way for a fuller-blooded, deeper, more tragic conception of life. All this is undeniable. Yet the modern Lessing would still, I think, be minded to enter the field against the further swing of the pendulum. We are so far gone in the irrational – to the joy of all baser enemies of light, all priests of the dynamistic orgasm – that it now looks like an evil and dangerous rebound, and a rebound against the rebound will by degrees become inevitable. The chthonic crew has already had too much water to its mill; it must be frightened back into the darkness whither it belongs by mother-right. The spirit of the historic Lessing has a task today; its importance must not be underestimated, despite all modern, anti-rational hostility to mind, all that anti-idealism which forms one side – but only one – of Nietzsche's mind-drunken prophecy, and which, in both morals and politics, is highly susceptible of abuse. In Lessing's name and spirit let it be ours to aim beyond every type of fascism at a union of blood and reason, which alone merits the name of complete humanity.

This great controversialist of ours did not become nihilistic, did not "leave the field with a burst of mocking laughter." He was kindly. And this his nation, and all the nations, should count his highest claim to praise. He pondered long and deeply. That he then made play with the conclusions to which he came was not done for the sake of the play. His was a spirit as full of faith, love, and hope as any that has lived and taken thought for the lot of man. He, manliest of spirits, had faith in the coming age of humanity. Let me end on those words in which he bore witness to his faith, words full of an inward emotion that lifts his usual lively clarity of style to a level but seldom – and then how movingly – attained by him: "Wise Providence, move onward, at thine own unnoted pace. But let me never, because I mark not, despair of thee, even when thy step seems to tend backwards. It is not true that the shortest line is always the straight one."

KLEIST'S *AMPHITRYON*

1926

What is loyalty? It is loving without seeing; it is triumph over a hated forgetfulness. We meet a face we love, and after some looking at it during which our feeling is confirmed, we are parted from it. Forgetting is certain, all pain of parting is only pain at certain forgetting. Our senses have little imagination, our capacity to remember is weaker than we like to think. Let us no longer see, and we cease to love. What we have left is only the certainty that each new meeting of our nature with this living manifestation will certainly renew our feeling, make us love it again, or, more properly, love it still. This awareness of a natural law, this holding fast to it, is loyalty: love that had to forget why. It is faith in a love which may speak while it is living, because it is sure of reliving in conformity with the law so soon as it sees.

It is after this fashion I have loved Kleist's *Amphitryon;* forgotten it, yet treasured it, even during a forgetting due to lack of time and opportunity to see it again. The present anniversary has made both time and opportunity; I read it again and the response of my nature to this work is true to its old form. I am delighted, I glow with pleasure. It is the wittiest, charmingest, the most intellectual, the profoundest and most beautiful theatre piece in the world. I knew that I loved it—now, praise God, again I know why.

I mean to talk about it as though it were new, as though I were the only person who had ever read it or talked about it. I will take care neither to read what other people have written about it, nor to admit to myself that I could possibly have read what they said. Out of spite I will do this, as well as out of fear of the disheartenment and shrinking we are prey to when we hear other people talk with cool professional judgment about the object of our ardent partiality. Our judgments are more passionate, more jealous, the more inspirational they are, the freer from critical dexterity. Just fresh from the impact of the special intonation and reminiscent style of Jupiter's announcement: "Unto you shall be born a son, of the name of Hercules"; with the shivers of uncanny responsiveness still running down my back, it is frightful, it is offensive to read the bald and jejune statement in the critique that of course this is an introduction of a Christian motif and a reference to the overshadowing by the Holy Ghost.

No, I have not read any of this thick-skinned stuff; so far as I am concerned *Amphitryon* has never been dealt with by any literary historian up to now. I have sometimes had visions of a volume of essays that ought to be written: a critique of those dear and precious great old books, the ones towards which one has special personal relations of love and insight. The treatment should be fresh and immediate, untrammelled as though the works themselves had just appeared in print. If I were certain of living to a hundred, I would make a start on this series.

Furthermore, I am discounting any knowledge of Kleist's forerunners in the field: Molière, Rotrou, Plautus. I know naught of them. Kleist's *Amphitryon* is an original creation; so it is if by creation we understand not making something out of nothing but rather the kindling of spirit in matter. So far as Kleist's *Amphitryon* goes, Plautus and the French comedies are simply material; Adam Müller, the first publisher of the play (its author was lying at the time in a French prison), earns the gratitude of every sensible person when he says in his shrewd yet enthusiastic preface: "For whether nature or the work of some previous master immediately inspires a poet does not matter much. Poetry flourishes most gloriously when she knows only one hand which puts in hers the material and the tools; if she knows how to take from Molière just as easily, simply, and characteristically as from nature or sheer fantasy." The further development of Müller's thought is just as fine. They certainly knew how to write in Germany in those days! And they kept the same level up till the middle of the century: the level of an æsthetic culture in which the best intellectual powers of the nation were applied to problems like the one under discussion. For a long time now they have been applied to others – it would certainly be feeble and anachronistic to bewail the fact. The days of that literary barbarism which followed the decline of the romantic movement are numbered if not sped. Here too the name of Nietzsche means the dawn of a new epoch; much has happened since his time to link the newest world with the world of our forefathers across decades of bourgeois stultification; a renewed idealism triumphs in the sciences; today German writing is no worse than writing yonder across the Rhine; we get a view of a lighter, more resilient, lean and athletic form of life, in which neither muscle nor brain is being atrophied, spirit and form avail themselves in common of an easy, natural, organic power, utility, and technique. Such a view is no longer inadmissible. A conservatism of the future, cheerfully remote from all crudely emotional reactionism, may, with its eye fixed on the new, play with old forms of expression in order to save them from oblivion. Such an attitude may turn out to prove the most serviceable for further development.

To come back to Kleist's immediate forerunner: I know that the point of Molière's version is the courtly witticism: "*un partage avec Jupiter n'a rien qui déshonore.*" And Kleist shows the childlike facility that makes an artist take over elements either from reality or from a naïve model (one sees it in Shakespeare too). He has adopted the sense of the passage. "Zeus," he makes his Thunderer say in the last scene, "Zeus has pleasured himself in thy house" – and Alcmene's earthly spouse regards the fact not only as honourable but even as highly flattering. Goethe found this a "shabby" conclusion, whereas he was far enough from objecting to it in his French favourite. Justice was not Goethe's strong point. Only good-for-nothings (*Lumpe*), it seems, are just. And yet his majesty might have graciously pleased to glance at the concluding lines of the god's godlike, unabashed declaration, which elevates, transmutes, and palliates the French bowing and scraping and makes it metaphysically acceptable to the spirit of his composition as a whole. I mean the almost impossibly dialectical lines:

Was du, in mir, dir selbst getan, wird dir
Bei mir, dem, was ich ewig bin, nicht schaden.

What you, in me, to you have done, will you
With me, where I eternal am, not injure.

That is Kleist's way of deifying or demonizing the preposterous.

The way Mercury as Sosias talks to poor Charis, the bewildering worldly scepticism with which the god shatters the virtuous bourgeois standards of the honest, straightforward shrew, making the sin seem easy and pleasant – it might have reminded Goethe of Mephisto, and the element of social satire, of witty generalization, has been by no means lost in the German challenger; it comes out provocatively when Charis holds up the tenderness of Jupiter-Amphitryon for Alcmene as a pattern for her sham husband, telling him he should be ashamed as an ordinary little man to be outdone in wedded love by a lord of the great world. Or when Sosias, with peasant slyness, answers Amphitryon's command to tell him the truth with the preliminary question: does he want him to be truthful as an honest chap is, or truthful the way they are at court. These are survivals from the earlier version: amusing social comments that smile their way into a poetry full of mystical intellectuality and extraordinary sensitiveness – for that is what Kleist's translation has made of the material. For a translation it is, in the very strongest sense of the word: the actual and incredible transference, kidnapping, and captivation of a work of art out of its own sphere into another one originally quite foreign to it; from one century into another, one nationality into another. It is a radical Germanization and romanticization of a masterpiece of French art.

Well, now the play has begun: it is night, Sosias enters with his lantern; and if this actor is a comedian and mimic of pith and parts his introductory monologue has put the audience already in a mood to laugh and enjoy. He is a droll dog, Sosias, as well as a cowardly one. His job is to set out the general situation; but he does not do it *ad spectatores*, not as a declamation. He soliloquizes, he makes a scene of his office as messenger, using his lantern as the other party. He calls it Alcmene, Mistress, Excellence, and makes it whisper its replies. He revels in his own mother wit, is not even faintly interested in enlightening us, his audience; but we do manage to be brought up to date about Amphitryon, the Theban fieldmarshal, and the battle at Pharissa. This first opening to show the poet's skill in the use of iambics could not be given to a mere beginner. Not for nothing does the little yokel clap his hands at the courtly eloquence his mission inspires him to utter. When then is he coming? he makes the mistress ask, and answers:

Gewiss nicht später, als sein Amt verstattet,
Wenn gleich vielleicht so früh nicht, als er wünscht.

Surely not later than his task permits,
Though not so soon perhaps as he would choose.

Very slick. As pendant to so much slickness I might mention, out of its context, the panic in metres, the clustered iambics with which Sosias greets a certain apparition.

Ach bei den Göttern der Nacht! Ich bin verloren.

Ah, by the gods of night! Now I am lost!

For a second figure, emerging in the dimness and speaking in a crisp soliloquy, completes the exposition and expresses itself as concerned for the bliss "which in Alcmene's arms today to savour, Zeus the Olympian has come down to earth, hiding his godhead in Amphitryon's guise." A second figure? No, the same! But distinct from the first. Sosias again, Sosias himself, his second self, perhaps his first, perhaps the right Sosias, and in any case to that extent Sosias as well as the first one, that, while the shadow is murmuring those classic names, a favourite situation of the romantic spirit, the meeting of doubles, has been effected.

We begin to realize the charms such material had for the poet, charms which determined him to make it his own, to put his mark on it, to work it over. They were not classic charms, not social or poetic, not actually, either, the lively fascinations of a satiric love-intrigue. They were stranger than that and – one may say – worse. They issue in anguish punctuated by jests. In comparison with the elegant high spirits of the model they make a Flemish-Dutch impression. They work profound bewilderment, in which of course the audience, knowing it all beforehand, does not share. Yet the author's incomparable power of suggestion compels them to endure and suffer too. The audience, I repeat, is kept informed. For the second Sosias, indistinguishable from the first, and so quite possibly the real one, presents himself, by means of a dramatic twist, as that which, beneath his peasant mask, he really is. The first Sosias says that he will now take himself home and discharge his task; upon which the second one comments:

Du überwindest den Merkur, Freund, oder
Dich werd' ich davon abzuhalten wissen.

You'll get the better, friend, of Mercury
Or else I shall know how to hold you back.

Mercury, then! With this name the introduction ends; the drama, the distraction of hearts and minds, can begin. And it now duly sets to, with the scene in which a good and faithful ordinary little man is beaten, is thrashed, until his consciousness of self, his sense of his own identity, that natural and unarguable feeling, dissolves under the blows.

You may consider it a harsh sort of practical joke if you like, and it may be so played. Funny it is, and witty, lightened and heightened by the language and the skilful realistic side-splitting verse: "His ser – ?" "His servant." "You?" "I, yes, Amphitryon's servant." "Your name is — ?" "Sosias." "So — ?" "Sosias." And so on. Shatteringly funny; but at bottom, we confess, no joke at all, certainly not a good-natured one, but rather a subtle, comic and tragic psychological experiment of the most biting kind, a visitation upon the head of a simple soul to whom it is utterly incomprehensible. Poor Sosias, what all he has to bear, from that first pert, childlike, first-person answer to his double! As for us spectators, we can bear it and find it amusing: we know it is all just a play, and will all come out right in the end. But if we actually had to go through with it we might end with our reason considerably impaired. Certainly, in a later scene, where he has to give the news to his master, Sosias is mentally upset to any eye; to put it clinically, has developed a bad case of schizophrenia. What Jupiter's glib servant does to a human soul in furtherance of his master's lust is cruel, because Mercury is not satisfied with forcing his victim to an outward pretence of giving up his identity in favour of his opponent, on pain of more beatings. No, for the god, by virtue of his omniscience, his dazzling power of penetrating the bounds of individual human consciousness, convinces Sosias actually and inwardly; and the stations on the way of his passion are so heart-rending to the listener just because the poet gives us to feel them by words and outcries fetched up from the very depths of the poor soul's being.

The scene is brilliantly managed. At first Sosias is touchingly sure of himself. Not that he is particularly set on his own identity or his personal ego. It is no such overpowering piece of good luck, no great privilege to be born Sosias, the little peasant slave. But he learns the compelling force of self, the necessity and divine sanction of one's own identity; learns that in him the will to live has taken on the special stamp of willing to be Sosias and that is inalienable.

"You dare," cries Hermes, "to tell me, shameless, to my face that you Sosias are?" And the other answers:

Ja, allerdings.
Und das aus dem gerechten Grunde, weil es
Die grossen Götter wollen; weil es nicht
In meiner Macht steht, gegen sie zu kämpfen,
Ein andrer sein zu wollen als ich bin;
Weil ich muss Ich, Amphitryons Diener sein,
Wenn ich auch zehenmal Amphitryon,
Sein Vetter lieber oder Schwager wäre.

Why, yes, of course.
And that upon the best of grounds, because
The great gods will it so; because it not
Stands in my power to fight against them,
To want to be another than I am;
Since I must I, Amphitryon's servant, be
Though ten times rather I'd Amphitryon be,
His cousin or brother, rather far than me.

Further on, he says:

Ach, lass mich gehn,
Dein Stock kann machen, dass ich nicht mehr bin,
Doch nicht, dass ich nicht Ich bin, weil ich bin.
Der einz'ge Unterschied ist, dass ich mich
Sosias jetzo, der geschlagne, fühle.

Oh, let me go,
Your stick can fix it that I no more am,
But not that I'm not I, because I am.
The only difference that I can see
Is that Sosias, I, in short, feel beaten.

An admission that is nowhere near enough for his tormentor. By threats of more belabourings he who up to now has called himself Sosias is reduced to admit that he has obviously made a mistake, and he says as much, only to learn that this other man, this brutal shadow, is verily that which he had supposed himself to be. Ye eternal gods! So he must renounce himself and let his name be stolen by an impostor? As yet he sees nothing but cheating and violence; he thinks, unhappy wretch, it is only a matter of the name, and urges the other honestly, as from man to man, to give him understanding of how one gets the idea of such an impractical piece of thievery.

Wär' es mein Mantel, wär's mein Abendessen;
Jedoch ein Nam'!

Were it my coat, were it my evening meal;
But just a name!

However, the frightful being will not be reasoned with, and Sosias breaks out:

Fahr' in die Höll'! Ich kann mich nicht vernichten,
Verwandeln nicht, aus meiner Haut nicht fahren,
Und meine Haut dir um die Schultern hängen.
Ward, seit die Welt steht, so etwas erlebt? . . .
Bin ich mir meiner völlig nicht bewusst?
Hat nicht Amphitryon mich hergeschickt?

Then go to hell! I just cannot destroy me,
Transform myself, jump outside my own skin,
To hang it as you want it, round your shoulders.
Was, since the world was made, a suchlike thing? . . .
Am I not fully of myself aware,
Has not Amphitryon me hither sent?

And so on. Only a god could be pitiless in face of such primitive and fully justified revolt. The tortured ego summons itself to the clearest consciousness, it repeats to itself the circumstances of its own life — and has to hear, has to learn to believe, that all of that belongs to the other man, nothing is his own, nothing is Sosias' save the beating. And now the enemy speaks of him as of himself, tells him his secretest thoughts and feelings, not in the second person, which would be uncanny enough, but in the first, and proves to him with blinding irresistibility that in very truth he alone represents the Sosias ego. It is frightful. The real, inward shattering begins, it draws near. "He is right there!" thinks the poor soul:

Und ohne dass man selbst
Sosias ist, kann man von dem, was er
Zu wissen scheint, nicht unterrichtet sein.
Man muss, mein Seel', ein bisschen an ihn glauben.

And so unless oneself
Sosias is, one can, of all he seems
So well to know, surely not be informed.
I must, my soul, a little him believe.

And now he notices what we have already seen, that the other is of the same height and build and has the same sly peasant ways. And he tests "himself" further, asks "himself" the most out-of-the-way details, and finds that his self-awareness is no guide either outside him or in.

Er weiss um alles. – Alle Teufel jetzt!
Ich fang' im Ernst an mir zu zweifeln an. . . .
Zwar wenn ich mich betaste, wollt' ich schwören,
Dass dieser Leib Sosias ist.
– Wie find' ich nun aus diesem Labyrinth?

He knows it all. In all the devils' names!
I am beginning now to doubt myself. . . .
Though when I pinch myself, I'd surely swear
This body is Sosias.
How find I now out of this labyrinth?

He does not. And a last striking utterance of the true Sosias is enough to make him cease the struggle.

Nun ist es gut. Nun wär's gleichviel, wenn mich
Die Erde gleich von diesem Platz verschlänge. . . .
Ich sehe, alter Freund, nunmehr, dass du
Die ganze Portion Sosias bist,
Die man auf dieser Erde brauchen kann.
Ein Mehreres scheint überflüssig mir.
Fern sei mir, den Zudringlichen zu spielen,
Und gern tret' ich vor dir zurück.

Well, then, all right. Now were it all the same
If the earth were to swallow me where I stand. . . .
I see, old friend, by now that you
As large a dose of this Sosias are
As anyone has need of on the earth.
And more to me doth seem superfluous.
Far be it from me to play the importunate,
And gladly do I yield my place to you.

That is the abdication. What follows is something essential and moving: the cry, clothed in drolly polite commonplace, of this stripped soul, this life robbed of its content. He begs for a new identity to replace the old.

Nur habe die
Gefälligkeit für mich, und sage mir,
Da ich Sosias nicht bin, wer *ich bin?*
Denn etwas, *gibst du zu, muss ich doch sein.*

Only one thing:
Do me a single little favour: say
Since I am not Sosias, then who am I?
For something, you'll admit, I surely must be.

The god's consolation is feeble. Mercury replies:

Wenn ich nicht mehr Sosias werde sein,
Sei du's, es ist mir recht, ich will'ge drein.

When I Sosias longer shall not be,
Then be you he, for my part I don't care.

That will have to do. Sosias decamps, his wits a-glimmering. The monologue in which the god and "stand-in" excuses his conduct to himself and us, refers only to the outward act, the beating, which, he says, the cowardly rascal deserves, even if not just at that moment, and which he would have to take on account. What has been done to Sosias' mind, and whether the little peasant deserved that, too, troubles the ambrosial one not at all.

Are we angry with him? Are we put out? No, strange to say. The game was cruel, but we took it as a game; it kept the bluff, humorous note, not really offensive, it combined a convincingness of power with a godlike, poetic, insensitive light-headedness, in a way that is the secret of a poet who has devices to make not only possible, not only tolerable, but fascinating, a subject beyond a doubt chosen for the sake of its highly morbid charm.

Bustle, torches. Enter the fair Alcmene. Enter her husband, the proud figure of the Theban field-marshal. We know, having listened so far, that this in fact is not Amphitryon, but the king of all the gods, in love beneath his station, and come down to earth to steal the embraces of a daughter of earth in the guise of a mortal man to whom she belongs and pertains. What follows is in the accents of Shakespearianly voluptuous love-comedy:

Lass, meine teuerste Alkmene, dort
Die Fackeln sich entfernen. Zwar sie leuchten
Dem schönsten Reiz –

Dearest Alcmene, do, I beg you, bid
The torches move away. True, they illume
The fairest charm –

So he shuns the light, this early-rising hero of a night so memorable for Alcmene. Easy he scarcely is. A certain fidgetiness is unmistakable. He has been blessed and, since he mixes the superterrestrial in his doings, he has also blessed, to the highest, most grateful degree. But the deception, the moral and amatory questionableness of the enterprise, prevents him from perfect joy, perfect pride, perfect calm. He bills and coos, he caresses—yet almost against his will there escape him signs of a scruple which betrays him. Or rather, not him, not his deceit, but the conflict between his love and his conscience. He speaks of marriage, of its lawful rights and duties. He would like, he says, to owe these hours of bliss, not to the wedded complaisance of the consort, not to convention, but to her heart alone. In other, plainer words, which he himself may not use: he wants to have given and received his bliss as himself and not as the husband and earthly spouse with whom, so far as Alcmene has any idea, he is identical; who will be entitled to reckon to his own credit in his score of blisses the treasures and sweet evidences of gratitude the past night has harvested, unless he, Zeus, succeeds in calling up in Alcmene's mind some distinction, be it ever so casuistic, in her thoughts and feelings between him and the other, between Amphitryon and Amphitryon; unless he manages to make the beloved see Amphitryon in double guise, as spouse and as lover, who indeed are one in the person of the human Amphitryon, but for this one night were two, though not in the consciousness of the innocent adulteress; so that the lover can speak the more confidently of joy, the more room the consort grants in her consciousness to this purely theoretic distinction, of which after all she is perfectly unaware. Well, it is hard to get her to do it. "Beloved and spouse!" her chaste tones answer to all questions as to which one she had received the past night. Far from drawing out the thorn, she presses it deeper in, by asking whether it is not alone this holy relation that justifies her in receiving him. Recklessly he exposes himself in the effort to convince her of the distinction. In his quality as Amphitryon the lover he expresses "himself" with such jealous vehemence about Amphitryon the husband that the poor man seems to have an existence outside him; he shows such animosity that the two egos seem quite distinct, even to the point of betraying the truth. He does not hesitate to speak of a disgraceful substitution, calls "himself" (the husband) a "puppy," a "conceited Theban field-marshal," and declares that he would willingly leave Alcmene's virtue to that parading coxcomb if he but might "himself" keep her love. One more step and he is unmasked. And at bottom would he not be glad? But Alcmene thinks this odd and morbid talk is a jest, though she does admit in face of his insistence that this night has shown her how sometimes the lover can distinguish himself from the husband. The god swims in bliss. At once he presses her further. He demands that Alcmene must never again confuse the unique bliss they have had together with the everyday life of her married state; she might – he dares to say – think of him when Amphitryon comes back! That is pretty strong! His craving to shove aside the husband whom Alcmene has embraced in him and who keeps coming between him and the beloved is as torturing as it is paramount in his mind – it makes him throw caution to the winds. Even Alcmene's careless "Yes, yes!" has put him beside himself. At the last minute he steals still one more little confirmation: Alcmene is pressing him to spend with her at least the remnant of the too swiftly speeding night; and at once he greedily asks:

> *Schien diese Nacht dir kürzer als die andern?*

> Seemed to thee this night shorter than the rest?

At Alcmene's shamefaced "Ah"! he exclaims in utter ravishment: "Sweet child!" And now completely beside himself, quite outside his role, he reveals to her that the kindly goddess of the rosy dawn has been conniving to lengthen out the darkness. And now he goes, with the final arrogant, bewildering lines:

> *Leb' wohl. Ich sorge, dass die anderen*
> *Nicht länger dauern, als die Erde braucht.*

> Farewell! And care I'll take the others
> Linger no longer than the earth hath need.

Such words the son of Cronus speaks, but not Amphitryon. What did the beloved little human head make of them? Ah, she thinks he is drunk with love – and he is that too.

Mercury, as easy victor in the fight for Sosias' identity, presents the satyr-play. He makes his Mephistophelian entrance with Charis, Alcmene's maid, "his" wife. And by now it is day.

The next stage is a hopelessly involved explanatory scene between the real Amphitryon and the mentally unbalanced Sosias. May we not account it to his distracted state that Sosias speaks bad verse? "The order that I gave you – ?" questions the general, and Sosias answers:

Ging ich
Durch eine Höllenfinsternis, als wäre
Der Tag zehntausend Klafter tief versunken,
Euch allen Teufeln und den Auftrag gebend,
Den eg nach Theben und die Königsburg.

Through hell's own darkness, even as though
The day were sunk ten thousand fathoms deep,
You to all devils and your errand giving,
I took the way to Thebes and the Citadel.

"*Euch allen Teufeln und den Auftrag gebend*"—that is bad, and not even easy to understand, though the construction is legitimately Kleistian. Sosias means that in his fright he wished his master and his errand at the devil; and it is amusing to hear him take the permission to speak out for licence to speak disrespectfully. Poetic inversions like "and your errand" shoved in after "to all devils" are often stylistically most effective. But this one is faulty, because *gebend* (giving) needs a *zu* (to) not manageable in the verse; and also, the word "devils" and the word "errand" are too close together not to cause confusion. And in the last line the word *nach* (to), which in place of "towards" or "in the direction of" might govern both Thebes and the Citadel, but in fact it cannot properly govern the latter. Well, it is a completely discountenanced little peasant who speaks the lines. Anyhow, his confusion about his own identity, besides bringing his master to the verge of desperation, imparts to the scene a side-splittingness, a farcical wit from which the rascal extracts the last drop of effect. His madness consists in speaking in the first person not only of his former self, but also of his mirrored image now inhabited by the god. That he thereby disconcerts and humiliates his haughty lord's sense of logic is a sort of part payment for his own sufferings:

Ich hielt mich für besessen, als ich mich
Hier aufgepflanzt fand lärmend auf dem Platze,
Und einen Gauner schalt ich lange mich. . . .
Ins Haus! was! ihr seid gut! auf welche Weise?
Litt ich's? hört' ich Vernunft an? untersagt' ich
Nicht eigensinnig stets die Pforte mir?

I thought myself possessed, to find me here
Weeping my tears upon this very spot,
And me, a swindler soundly swinged for it. . . .

Into the house! What! You are good! Forsooth,
How shall I? Did I not bate, heard I not reason,
And obstinately barred the gate to me?

What can a still mentally sound Amphitryon make of that? And when finally he hears that Sosias himself gave himself a beating, he finds it beneath his dignity to go on with a parley so lacking in human reason. He breaks off disgusted and orders Sosias to open the house door. The latter behind his back utters the classic comment: "'Twas ever thus!"

Weil es aus meinem Munde kommt,
Ist's albern Zeug, nicht wert, dass man es höre;
Doch hätte sich ein Grosser selbst zerwalkt,
So würde man Mirakel schrein.

Being my mouth it issues from,
It's silly stuff, not worth a body's hearing;
But if a nobleman had thrashed himself
People would shout: "A miracle!"

Considering certain intellectual turns the poet gives his theme, certain associations and side-lights he knows how to invest it with, the word "miracle" used at this point, and coming from Sosias' mouth, has a ring of self-mockery; to my mind it is not unlikely that it was so intended. But now Alcmene appears, and the unenviable warrior is staggered by fresh misunderstandings and humiliations.

He has surprised his wife, that he knows. How much he has surprised her he has no idea. He is aware by now, without comprehending why, that the message announcing his arrival was never delivered. But of course he is utterly ignorant of the fact that Alcmene has already "received" him in the higher person of the god. In the ensuing scene this fact, this "miraculous" fact, makes impossible any understanding between them, though the audience is delightfully and shatteringly conscious of the situation and poor Amphitryon is driven to the obvious conclusion, peculiarly bitter to the warrior fresh from his triumphs, that he is most certainly a cuckold: French comedy against a metaphysical background. An audience is always roused to a pitch of impatient suspense by scenes like this, where the actors and victims seem obstinately to persist in their incomprehension. Why do they? After all, this world is one in which, yes, miracles do come to pass, so they must be possible; and yet nothing happens, nobody gets the idea. Even their extremest anguish is not enough to make them light on the thought of such a possibility. There they are, blind and helpless, struggling in a net which, if only the perfectly obvious thought were to flash through their heads, they would brush away like a spider-web. Take that almost unbearable "spear and swear" scene in the second act of *Götterdämmerung*, where a purely extraneous complication created by the legendary property of the potion is exploited in a tragical piece of theatre that must strike any listener today to whom the tragic dénouement is something to be avoided at any price, as illegitimate and unfair. A golden lad like Siegfried; a setting and story in which magic potions and caps of invisibility are quite the regular thing; yet to nobody at all, certainly not to Brünnhilde, the one-time goddess, whose hen-mindedness on this occasion is maddening enough, does the idea occur: "The man must have drunk something!" Is not the scene in *Amphitryon* rather like? It is, though Kleist gets his effects more conscientiously. "We have drunk a devil's brew and now our brains are washed away," Sosias says at one point; that is only a metaphor, still it sheds something like a ray of light. Amphitryon himself in his extremity remarks:

Ich habe sonst von Wundern schon gehört,
Von unnatürlichen Erscheinungen, die sich
Aus einer andern Welt hieher verlieren.

I have heard speak of wonders before now,
Unnatural manifestations,
Wandering here lost out of another world.

He says that about the diadem which he thought to send to Alcmene by Sosias and which she has already received from the hands of Jupiter. He says it about the empty casket with unbroken seals. But there had been a Callisto in Hellas, and a Europa; so he must have heard of more than just wonders and unnatural manifestations in general. Alcmene tries to recall to "him" how "he," in transports, "with strangely thrilling oath" swore to her that never had Hera Zeus so filled with bliss; she repeats to him:

Du sagtest scherzend,
Das du von meiner Liebe Nektar lebtest,
Du seist ein Gott, und was die Lust dir sonst,
Die ausgelass'ne in den Mund mir legte!

AMPHITRYON

Die ausgelass'ne in den Mund mir legte!

Thou saidst in jest
Thou from my loving bosom nectar sippdst,
Thou wast a god – and other suchlike vows
Which the extreme abandonment of lust
Put in thy mouth.

AMPHITRYON

Abandonment of lust put in my mouth!

– Certainly all this is pretty glaring. It is hard to see how they can be so naïve. But all he sees is:

Doch heute knüpft der Faden sich von jenseits
An meine Ehre und erdrosselt sie.

But now today the thread comes from beyond,
Winds round my honour, choking it to death.

That is the whole point with him: he feels like a French soldier, and a married one at that; his honour is at stake; and he is in no state to use his intelligence or bring his wits to bear on the situation. His nature is direct, courageous, primitively male. He sees that he is betrayed, Alcmene's words leave no room for doubt; but he also sees that there is something not quite canny about the whole thing. He does not say: let us be calm, let us be cautious, let us suspend our judgment. Man, god, or devil, he will have at the foe, the thief of his honour, he will resist to the uttermost. He will tear the web, hack the knots, call up his wife's brother, the generals, the whole army to witness the truth and the deception.

Dann werd' ich auf des Rätsels Grund gelangen,
Und wehe! ruf' ich, wer mich hintergangen!

This riddle's answer then I shall espy,
And woe to the betrayer is my cry!

That is the rhymed ending of strong feeling; Alcmene also avails herself of it when with bleeding heart she renounces a husband who is obviously planning to play a contemptible trick, denying that he has been with her this night, in order to recover his freedom. The pair part in hopeless discord. Sosias and his wife take their place. The poor fellow has to pay for all the moral bewilderment that the diabolical Hermes has sown in Charis' poor soul. Meanwhile Alcmene has taken another step on the path of disillusionment. She has discovered the signature on the diadem. She comes, she flies with Amphitryon's present to her maid, and it is truly touching to see her in her terror try to make Charis agree with her that she has made a stupid mistake; she will rather lose her mind than her honour and desperately demands that Charis shall read with her fingers and say that the engraved letter is an A. The simple woman trusts her own eyes and says it is a J.

This is the hardest blow of all to the pure-minded woman. She begins, as Sosias has already done, as Amphitryon will do, to doubt herself. Until now she was sure of herself; she could even — humiliating, shocking, and painful as it was — believe that her husband was playing her a trick. But now she must begin, how much against her will, to convince herself of his uprightness and learn to mistrust her own senses. Mistrust them far worse than if it had been proved to her that she could not read. We must put ourselves in her place; we do so in all sympathy, by virtue of the poet's mighty power of suggestion. She has embraced Amphitryon, the beloved spouse. It was he, and it was she, and if it was not he, then it was not she, for her feeling for him is bound up with her own identity, and if that be lost, then all is lost.

O Charis! — Eh' will ich irren in mir selbst!
Eh' will ich dieses innerste Gefühl,
Das ich am Mutterbusen eingesogen
Und das mir sagt, dass ich Alkmene bin,
Für einen Parther oder Perser halten.

O Charis! Sooner will I mistake myself!
Sooner will I this innermost sense
That I drew in at the maternal breast
That says to me that I Alcmene am
Take for a Parthian or a Persian.

It is one of those Kleistian conflicts which so put Goethe off. It is the "confusion of feeling" to which, as he says, this author is prone, and which he condemns as morbid. Shall I say that I have never been able to understand the cruel coldness of his beloved majesty against Kleist and Kleist's tendency to pathological subject-matter; to agree with it or even to find it consistent? Morbid, capricious, exaggerated — how shall I take reproaches like these from the lips of a psychologist like Goethe, who had the liveliest pleasure as a writer in the mastery of novel and intimate psychological material; who made his Achilles utterly forget, in his love for Polyxena, the early doom hanging over him "in the mad folly of his nature"; Goethe, who wrote to Schiller that "without pathological interest one would scarcely win the applause of the time"? Where psychology is, there is also the pathological; the line between the two is fluid. Tasso, I suppose, is healthy? To call Werther extreme would be a mistake? A figure like Mignon is not in the least calculated to cause any mental bewilderment? Had he, in his stern and stately greatness, forgotten everything? Did he, pedagogue and humanist, choose to dissemble and disavow everything that "went too far," everything dangerously human in his own poetic past? They should have spoken more openly to him. But to speak openly to a great man is probably not the German way.

Alcmene calls it a mad assertion, that another man "appeared unto" her; and this "appeared" is the word used from now on. Its syllables hang over the rest of the action and transfer it into the mystical. She recalls the obvious distress of her husband, whom she knows to be as incapable of guile as herself; she recalls the singular abuse Amphitryon the lover heaped upon Amphitryon the husband; all that goes through her like a lightning-flash. The distinction between the two, upon which he who "appeared unto" her insisted with such suspicious obstinacy, only now really shakes her to the depths; and ungently pressed by Charis, who asks whether she is sure, she sees herself driven to a most touching, most intimate confession. Sure?

Wie meiner reinen Seele! meiner Unschuld!
Du müsstest denn die Regung mir missdeuten,
Dass ich ihn schöner niemals fand als heut.
Ich hätte für sein Bild ihn halten können,
Für sein Gemälde, sieh, von Künstlerhand,
Dem Leben treu, ins Göttliche verzeichnet.
Er stand, ich weiss nicht, vor mir wie im Traum
Und ein unsägliches Gefühl ergriff
Mich meines Glücks –

As of my innocence and my own pure soul!
Else you would need to misconstrue the feeling
That never more splendid was he than today.
I could indeed have taken him for his image,

For his portrait painted by an artist hand.
Though true to life, yet drawn as one divine.
He stood, I know not, before me as in a dream,
And the feeling unspeakable seized upon me
Of my great happiness.

The glorious woman! And asks, moreover, not to have her "feeling" misinterpreted! He whom she received was Amphitryon. But since it was the god, he was an Amphitryon ampler, stronger, richer than himself, and so, after all the unspeakable joy of the night, had it not borne some trace of guilt? Then had she, when she had thought to be smiling at the jest, in truth betrayed the husband with the lover, Amphitryon the human being with his ideal image? Yes, but only him with himself. What scruple could be more morbid than this, if it were not for the one objective fact, the frightful sign, the J on the diadem instead of an A. When her husband returns she throws herself, jewel, signature, and all, at his feet to find the answer, whether life or death. It is the god. And now between her and him there unfolds the "*scène à faire*," the brilliant, the masterly, the admired heart of the play; by virtue of which it towers so incomparably above every other treatment of the subject-matter.

Impossible to analyse in words the charm and depth of the situation, the intellectual heights and anguished emotional stresses of this lofty dialogue. Three times is beauty, girded like diamond in her innocence, stirred to the bottom of her tender childlike soul, forced to mount through stages of the harshest self-examination; to realize and distinguish among her own emotions, cruelly urged on by a tenderly reverent yet yearning god who towards the end curses the madness that lured him "hither" and, conquered, at last learns to console himself with the prestige and the triumph of his divinity. The whole scene is shot through with illusions daring and reverent at once, which play upon it an unearthly transcendent light.

Alcmene, holding the ominous symbol in her hand, laments the shocking self-assurance that she had displayed towards her consort, who in accents of utter sincerity declared himself betrayed and outraged. She humbles herself, she is full of distrust of her own nature, she is ready to believe that another "appeared unto" her if he, Amphitryon, persists in denying that it was he. She manages to utter with her lips what still her heart must fail to understand — so potent is the irrefutable symbol she holds in her hand. She suffers in the high style, just as Sosias' pangs were in the low and farcical vein. But the god's reply, tender and shamefaced at once, now involves them in the mystery. "My glorious one!" he says.

Wie könnte dir ein anderer erscheinen?
Wer nahet dir, o du, vor deren Seele
Nur stets des Ein- und Ein'gen Züge stehn?

How could it be another appeared unto you?
To you, oh wonder, on whose soul are printed
The lineaments of one and one alone?

And to her fervent question whether it was he, whether it was not he, he answers majestically: "It was I." This "I" is ambiguous. Who says it? Amphitryon, but also the god, the one speaking for the other; and this intellectually intriguing ambiguity continues throughout to characterize what he says, though sometimes he lets slip some unmistakable evidence of his higher essence, half involuntarily but half in the overmastering wish to make himself and his passion known, to let the creature learn once and for all who it is who loves her:

Ich war's. Sei's wer es wolle. Sei – sei ruhig.
Was du gesehn, gefühlt, gedacht, empfunden,
War ich: wer wäre ausser mir, Geliebte?
Wer deine Schwelle auch betreten hat,
Mich immer hast du, Teuerste, empfangen,
Und für jedwede Gunst, die du ihm schenktest
Bin ich dein Schuldner, und ich danke dir.

It was I. Be who it will. But yet – be calm.
What you have seen, felt, thought, experienced,
Was I; who could it be but me, beloved?
Whoever he who hath thy threshold crossed,
Me always hast thou, dearest one, received;
For each and every joy thou gavest him
Am I thy debtor, and I thank thee now.

She hears that from her husband's lips. In it she hears goodness and tender indulgence towards her shame – but even so, she hears her shame. "Who would it be but me?" He says that, in whom the all is comprehended and who has taken on himself an identity over which he has command, as over every other he chooses. He says it through the lips of this I, this Amphitryon, so that it takes on the meaning: only I, your husband, have you to thank for tokens of love which, whomever you also embraced, you knew you had from no one but from me, since all that approaches unto you is Amphitryon. With double tongue, godlike and manlike, he assures her of her inviolable purity; but it is just the equivocal, stilted sublimity of his style that fails to console the honest, upright little heart. "It was I": that was what she wanted and needed to hear—but without trimmings; and he adds a subtle interpretation which goes far to destroy the clarity of his first words, turning the blessed "I" into the destructive and accursed "him." She says she has received her sentence:

Auf diesen Fall war ich gefasst.
. . . Leb wohl!

Upon this case I was resolved.
. . . Farewell!

The god Jupiter is in straits. She will hear nothing, she will not live, if her once pure soul is now no longer immaculate. "I, the shamefully deceived one!" she cries, in honest childlike simplification of the actual state of things; a misconception, in fact, just that, and the bewildered lover feels it bitterly. He takes occasion to confess his bitterness, confesses in words that may serve the beloved as consolation, for they express the incurable pain of the third party in the human cry that he, Amphitryon, has no ground for envying the other. "He" (I), he cries, "my idol, was the one deceived." What unutterable emotion lies in the mad word he applies to her: this god and creator calls the tender creature his idol! He speaks of the "evil art" of that other which has deceived himself but not her, not her unerring feeling. He speaks of the thorn "he" wears in his heart, which no art of the gods can tear out, and through the lips of Amphitryon (Amphitryon, who may laugh at jealousy since every kiss she gave "the other" only binds her closer to the spouse) he indulges himself in confession of his own divine envy. If, he says, he could undo this mysterious happening, he would not—not for the joys of Olympus, not to save Zeus' immortal life! What abasement! What denial of his higher essence! Even as the madness of love, inexcusable. And truly it should serve to soothe and tranquillize the creature. Yet the aim is at least half pretence, an excuse to lay his unbridled longing at her feet.

But in vain. Alcmene will go away, she will die. At least, she would sooner die than ever lay her spotted bosom down in her consort's bed. She swears it; with all the passion of her woman's honour she calls the immortal avengers of the broken oath to witness, and the embarrassed deity has to hasten to protect an upright soldier from the consequences of such an oath. He pulls himself together; though he still speaks of himself in the third person, what he really says is nothing less than an unmasking. "Thy oath," he says:

> *kraft angeborner Macht, zerbrech' ich,*
> *Und seine Stücken werf' ich in die Lüfte.*

> By virtue of my inborn might I break
> And fling the shattered pieces to the air.

He tells her the truth. Not in a voice of thunder now, presumably; not as a crushing revelation, no; he is subdued, quiet, almost short, almost sad. His veiled and sober countenance turned away, he speaks in the hushed silence which follows his surprising outburst of supreme power:

> *Es war kein Sterblicher, der dir erschienen,*
> *Zeus selbst, der Donnergott, hat dich besucht.*

> It was no mortal that to you appeared,
> But Zeus the Thunderer, he came unto you.

Even so, it is the thunder-clap, the climax of the scene. What follows, in swift alternation, is the raging storm and the paralysis of death, now in whispers, now in furious key. Alcmene thinks him mad. Before she can believe her ears he must thrice repeat the monstrous statement; and when she is convinced that she has heard aright she calls him impious, thus to accuse the high Olympians of wanton offence. She is quite right, beyond any doubt; and when Jupiter forbids the rash creature ever to let such a word cross her lips, he is displaying his dignity in the wrong place. For according to human, non-metaphysical standards, what happened was certainly a wanton offence; and never, to speak frankly, has a god put himself in so ridiculous and awkward a plight. He gets angry – which does not speak for a clear conscience. "Silence, I say; I command you!" That is all he finds to say; and therewith sound common sense and virtue must hold its tongue. Yet not quite so completely that she is not able to utter a horrified "Unhappy wretch!" And then follows a pause while the appointed guardian of the divine order, driven into a corner, tries to see where he stands.

He does it best as Amphitryon, and as Amphitryon he reproaches her for ingratitude in face of an elevation such as has fallen to the lot of but few of her sex. Through her husband's lips he pays homage to the god lover and to those on whom his eye has rested. If she, he says, feels no envy of their skyey lot, at all events he, her husband, envies the husbands of those elect, and wishes he might have sons like those of Tyndareus. But she – truly, how could she rise to such heights, she who, bitterly enough, knows no height more lofty than to see a mortal, himself, at her feet!

At that her modesty revolts. What blasphemy! If she rejects such a visitation as absurd, she does so not out of pettiness of soul but out of humility. If it had been he, should she now be living, would she not be consumed as once Semele, by that glowing ardour? She, so all-unworthy of such favour, she the sinner?

He smiles. And this smile prefigures the wonderful answer he makes her. A poetic passage fuller and more feelingful than almost any other in the whole composition, an answer combined of the erotic and the theological:

> *Ob du der Gnade* wert, *ob nicht, kommt nicht*
> *Zu prüfen* dir *zu.* Du wirst über dich,
> Wie er dich würdiget, ergehen lassen.

> That thou art *worthy* or unworth the favour
> Concerns *thee* not to prove. *Thou sufferest merely*
> *The exaltation he confers upon thee.*

The shimmering play of intellect and spirit, the intrinsic double essence of the piece, at once social comedy and metaphysical exercise – it is all expressed in this smile, where the unsearchable heights meet the unsearchable depths of the heart. The idea gleams through of election, of godlike arbitrary favour and the elevation of the unworthy. And at the same time it expresses the whole painful and prejudiced irony of absolute, unquestioning, uncritical love. Love, being the force that confers value, does not ask for worthiness. It *is;* and this *is* is sovereign. We err, when we think we love because of some virtue. God erred, when He thought He loved us for our virtues.

> *Du wirst über dich,*
> *Wie er dich würdiget, ergehen lassen.*

> Thou sufferest merely
> The exaltation he confers upon thee.

That is the tenderly imperious order of consciously superior love for the living creature that knows not how it is with it; Alcmene for a moment submits, yet only to return to her first idea that this is all a kindly manœuvre to distract her mind; she returns to her despair, her abnegation. He has to point out to her the diadem with the letter J instead of A, in order that she may begin to believe. When he has brought her far enough to think of the monstrous as a possibility, he seeks to remind her, in the guise of human speculation, of her guilt and the meaning of such a "visitation." It must have been thus: she aroused the god, she wronged him by the earthly concentration and expectancy of her thoughts and actions, which one would be obliged to call idol-worship. She has — and he gives her puzzling psychological instances that make her shudder — quite forgotten the love of god in her human love, prayed to the image instead of to the creator; she has not perceived the one in the other, but always meant the image when she fell on her knees before the creator. If Jupiter visited her, it was to take revenge for this forgetfulness, to force her to think of him.

She might well smile. If he really did come, the most high god, for this purpose, then he chose a bad method. For he had to come as Amphitryon, to procure satisfaction that could scarcely be sweet to him, since it was always just Amphitryon who was "in mind," and not himself. It had to be so: Alcmene "needs features" to imagine the deity, and the features are those of her husband; but it is the god's aim to make her make distinctions: as before between husband and lover, so now between the image and the god. He, the image, the husband, obtains promises from the contrite one for the god; only him will she have in mind at his altar — "and not me." She will be mindful of the past night, the sacred night of love, when she looks at the miraculous sign on the diadem; and in that distinctive memory — the husband receives her assurance — she will not be distracted by the husband. These were achievements — had not the god's efforts to complete her religious education had more than a little of the lover about them; had he not used the religious argument to usurp the husband's place, and for that very reason turned out to be shatteringly unsuccessful.

He leaves no stone unturned. Let the god just once reveal, he says, his immortal visage — how poor and cold would her love for "him" (Amphitryon) appear, compared with that glowing immortal love! But the tactless creature — tactless out of sheer innocence — reassures him. "My dearest!" she says. Could she go back a day in time and bolt her door against all the gods and heroes, she would do it, he can rest assured — here he would interrupt, but she finishes her sentence, poor innocent, beaming with self-satisfaction:

So willigt' ich von ganzem Herzen ein!

With all my heart, how gladly would I do it!

Then it is, the god curses the folly that lured him to this mortal creature. She cannot understand his trouble, since, after all, what she said was agreeable to hear; she asks him wherein she has displeased him, and the god launches into that highly sentimental plea, vibrating with feeling, magnificent and tender in equal degree, which is the poetic climax of the play, its lyric heart:

Du wolltest ihm, mein frommes Kind,
Sein ungeheures Dasein nicht versüssen? –

And would you not, my dear and pious child,
Sweeten his lot of awful majesty? –

"Child," he says. He called her "beloved" before, and "heavenly creature"; called her "my idol." But here he says "child," and it is the right and sensitive word. He woos her, through the mouth of a mortal, for the deity, the sovereign ruler of the world, the lonely artist-spirit out of whom the whole teeming work of creation proceeded; here perceived and painted in chaste classicistic, æsthetic fullness, in marvellous composition of sunset and nightingales, mountain and waterfall – and he too – he would wish to be loved.

So viele Freude schüttet
Er zwischen Erd' und Himmel endlos aus;
Wärst du vom Schicksal nun bestimmt,
So vieler Millionen Wesen Dank,
Ihm seine ganze Ford'rung an die Schöpfung
In einem einz'gen Lächeln auszuzahlen,
Würd'st du dich ihm wohl – ach!

So much fullness of joy
Endlessly over heaven and earth he pours;
And wert thou now by destiny elected
So many millions beings' debt of thanks,
Sum of his claim against the whole creation
In one, one only single smile to pay him,
Wouldst thou not then thyself – but ah!

It is the "ah!" that always ends such a wooing, such a question; for that smile he asks in payment, that smile is not intended for the petitioner. All created things exchange it with each other, while he must play tricks and steal the features of a victorious soldier in order to delude himself into believing that the smile is really meant for him. He is in the wrong. He would like to sicken Alcmene of the "image" and press the eternal upon her, but he himself languishes after the image, the kiss, in the voluptuous enjoyment of which the gratitude that he as creator feels, the gratitude of creation, is summed up.

Alcmene, a cultivated woman, even so calls it a "sacred duty" to gratify such a wish. But, she says, while the infatuated god listens in suspense, if she were left the choice she would like to distinguish between reverence and love, and knows perfectly well how she would apportion them. Then he takes the last step. He shows her the possibility that the god to whom she is ready to pay reverence, that he is Amphitryon, whom she loves. How happily the iambics express the accents of her now utterly distracted question:

> *Ich weiss nicht, soll ich vor dir niederfallen,*
> *Soll ich es nicht? Bist du's mir?* Bist *du's mir?*

> I cannot tell, shall I fall down before thee?
> Or shall I not? Art thou – *art thou* – to me?

But since he is Amphitryon, he cannot, she must, decide. How would she behave if he whom she embraces were the god descending from Olympus out of love for her?

Her little brain is hard at work. Touchingly she keeps repeating his questions. She struggles, for love of this extraordinary husband, she does her best. If he were the god to her – but wait, where then would Amphitryon be? In that case she would follow him whom she holds and to whom she must hold – and even down to Orcus. Good, good, and so it would be, so long as she did not know where Amphitryon was. But if he were to show himself at this moment?

She says: "You torture me!" It is the sigh, the "Ah – h!" of good modest humanity strained past its powers, visited, by a trick of fate, with a great passion. She does not understand how her Amphitryon would show himself to her, since she is holding Amphitryon in her arms.

But he is inexorable in his tender cruelty. He tells her her own conviction that she holds Amphitryon in her arms is no actual proof that he might not perhaps be the god; and what he above all wants to hear is how she thinks, in advance, her heart would decide and declare if now, while she is embracing him, Amphitryon were to appear. She repeats, she labours. And then, to get herself out of the fix, she prattles like a small child, yes, really in a way baby-talk, with pouting lips:

Ja — dann so traurig würd' ich sein, und wünschen.
Dass er der Gott mir wäre, und dass du
Amphitryon mir bliebst, wie du es bist.

Yes, so unhappy would I be, and wish
That he would be the god to me, and you
Would stay Amphitryon, just as you are.

"As you are!" That is all he gets, but he drinks it like nectar. He has the present advantage, since he has made use of the fact that virtually, among other things, he is, along with everything else, also Amphitryon, and thus she has told him what, were Amphitryon here, she would have said to him. But the creator, now grown more modest, is blissful. "My sweetest creature, most adored!" he cries. And once more sheltering her head on his breast, he orates, pompously, fatuously, without any proper regard to the rest of creation; finally falling out of his role — more or less to the effect that nothing such as she had come from his hand for æons. He appears to rant; she tells him he talks like God the Lord. But he retreats before her, half transfigured, grandly gesturing:

Sei ruhig, ruhig, ruhig!
Es wird sich alles dir zum Siege lösen.

Be calm, be tranquil!
He will resolve the whole for thee in triumph.

And he hastens off, presently to make a triumphant renunciatory heavenly re-entry.

But first comes the parody, the slapstick: a lively translation into the vulgar and farcical of all the high sobriety and lofty feeling that have gone before. It is the creative impulse mocking itself, it is in so coarse a key that one asks oneself: what kind of people are these poets, what is their fire, their frosty flame, in what sort of vicious, half-human relation do they stand to life and feeling, that they seek to intensify, heighten, illume, that they cram with brilliance, with all their arts and all their passionate pains — and then, as though they were utterly callous, as though they possessed not a jot of all this that they had just taken pains to show with such triumphant passion that they really had at heart; to make a long satyr nose at it and at us and at all their high-flown inspirations?

It is Sosias and Charis who are left on the stage, and Charis has heard rumours. What, the gods have been here? There have been illusions and metamorphoses? The master is sometimes not who he seems and so one has to be on one's guard? She reckons with the possibility that if she sees her own lawful spouse, poor Sosias, before her, perhaps someone else entirely, for instance far-darting Apollo, might be hiding behind those comical features? The joke lies in the reversed situation. For while Alcmene refused to think that the lord of heaven had inclined himself unto her, the ambitious and stupid Charis urges the role of divinity on her cudgelled little peasant, who resists with hands and feet and utters comparisons of the coarsest disapproval about the associations of gods and men. As for Charis, his once quarrelsome better half, she humbles herself in the most absurd way before the agreeable spectacle of his anger. There are witty, human touches within the boorish misunderstanding; as when the woman, at the thought that immortals are nigh at hand, says in the sentimental and immediate need of little people to get things cleared up:

Gewiss, wir hätten manche gute Seite,
Die unachtsam zu innerst blieb, mehr hin
Nach aussen wenden können, als geschehn ist.

Of course, we both had many a better side,
And kept it hid, though really we might
Have turned it outward oftener than we did.

And when Sosias replies that he certainly could have done with it, and altogether makes shrewd use of her unwanted meekness, exploiting the situation to show himself the master and ordering her to get him some sausage and cabbage at once, the parody extends even to the accents of the iambics:

Was zaudr' ich noch! Ist er's nicht? Ist er's nicht?

Why do I still delay – is he, or is he not?

But Sosias is not. He is, as he makes known to the indignant and disillusioned one, neither a dog nor a god but just "the old familiar ass"; and therewith a jolly human end to the act. We may draw breath in a prosaic air for a few minutes in order to be strong for the unnerving events that the poet intends us to assist at in great detail.

The old Hebrews had a word: *killel,* which means "curse"; but actually something more like "make air of," "destroy," take away somebody's life – the opposite of that blessing of recognition which was vouchsafed to Jacob after the wrestling with his strange antagonist. It is the terrors of being cursed that Amphitryon the Theban general must learn, according to the irrevocable decree of the immortals. He is "made light of"; that is almost entirely the content of the dramatic finale. He is undone. He uses the word himself time after time, and his suffering gives us a new and frightful conception of its meaning. It is the psychology of defeat that we become acquainted with through him, and if in the end he is restored, made "weighty" again, weightier even than before, yet, though the proverb says "All's well that ends well," which may be dramatically right even here, what the poor sword-eater has gone through he has gone through and will never forget – let us hope to his advantage – for as long as he lives. Certainly we shall not, at least not if – as has not yet been the case – we have seen the play adequately produced and performed.

Was für ein Schlag fällt dir, Unglücklicher!
Vernichtend ist er, es ist aus mit mir.
Begraben bin ich schon, und meine Witwe
Schon einem andern Eh'gemahl verbunden.

Unhappy man, what blow is fallen on thee?
It crushes me, and I am quite undone –
I am already buried and my widow
Already to another consort wedded.

Amphitryon so expresses himself, out of the depths of his uttermost debasement – or even not quite the uttermost. For in the previous scene, which forced the words from him, the scene with Jupiter's sharp-witted aide, Mercury, who out of sheer boredom is persuaded to play the cruellest sort of practical joke; Mercury who as Sosias does not recognize his master, does not "acknowledge" this man who dares to give himself out as master of the house; Mercury treats him as an impostor, a fool, a drunken vagabond, drives him from all self-control, and finally reveals to him that "he," Amphitryon, is in the palace with Alcmene, and anyone who disturbs the lovers' blissful slumbers will get what he deserves from him, Sosias. Even this comic and disgraceful scene is exceeded by the horrible experience the poor man has yet to undergo, the confrontation with his own image, that I who has taken his place and is crowding him out of "his" existence, "his" weight, his own identity.

It is a repetition of the pitiable experience that befell Sosias in the beginning, but in even more frightful and pathetic form. For this time it is a lord, a great gentleman, a feared and envied prince of this world; and his "disgrace," to which he constantly refers, is the deeper, the higher he is used to carry his head, the more imperious the self-respect which is here called in question, shaken, shattered, "undone." "Eternal and just gods!" he cries when his own friends, the generals, very doubtful whether he has true Amphitryonic right on his side, prevent him from bathing his sword in the blood of the "lying hell-hound" who tried to drive him from Thebes, from Alcmene's heart, from the world's knowledge, and if possible out of the "very fastness of the consciousness" – "can so sunk a wretch be sunk still further?" And truly all that is no joke, it goes beyond a joke, it borders on being flayed alive, and Amphitryon might well ask the high gods, who grant that all this undeserved punishment fully pays for the questionable love-affair of one of themselves, whether they really think they are just.

And yet the piece as a whole is not distressing, it preserves a high degree of gaiety and tolerableness; it is, by its intellectual appeal, saved from the charge of lightness; and the æsthetic demand for justice, for a sense of sympathy and fellow-feeling, is nowhere seriously infringed on. The poet has a care for this requirement from the first, taking thought for it both in the pathetic and in the vulgar. Before he lets the alter ego of the hungry Sosias destroy for him the finest symbol of his right to exist, his sausage and cabbage, he makes him forfeit our sympathy to some extent, when the little peasant boasts overbearingly at table of his martial deeds, though in fact he had shrewdly got out of the way. His ego wants to exalt itself and now it is for the moment cruelly extinguished. And as for Amphitryon, the great, the vain field-marshal of the Thebans, in his discomfiture, too, every moment perceptible, lies a moral lesson. Has he not, this wealthy and luxurious man, adored by his wife, by everyone flattered, not at all chary of blows when his servants blunder; has he not dwelt all too defiantly in the strong fortress of his own individuality, presumed too far on the fact that he happens to be the master? "Before me in the dust," says Zeus, in his very form, "shall he bow his face!"

Mein soll er Thebens reiche Felder alle,
Mein alle Herden, die die Triften decken,
Mein auch dies Haus, mein die Gebieterin,
Die still in seinen Räumen waltet, nennen.

All the rich fields of Thebes he mine shall name,
Mine all the herds that all the meadows cover,
Mine too this house and mine the mistress of it
Who silent in its halls still reigns – all mine.

Amphitryon is to learn that all that says I, whether high or low, belongs to the world-spirit, out of which it comes and into which it goes; that we shall do well not to stress too "aristocratically" our sense of our own person, our own distinctiveness from the general, if it happened to wear a happy lot in life; not to take ourselves too "heavily" in order not to be made "light of," light as air, some fine day, by a whim of the gods.

When Amphitryon, at the awful sight of his double, declares that now the riddle is solved, he means the riddle of his pure wife's infidelity. By whom and how deeply his "honour," his individuality, is attacked he does not yet understand; he still dwells much too securely in the fortress of his proud consciousness to consider that possible which does in fact happen: namely, that everybody, first Sosias, then his people and his friends, and at last – that is the final blow, and it shatters his self-possession – his own wife "forsake him," deny, reject, leave him literally undone, and recognize that terrible other one as himself. When he would make short work of it and use his sword on this apparition, this sham opponent and ego-enemy, his generals prevent him, saying they cannot tolerate this quarrel between Amphitryon and Amphitryon, and with regard to him display a scepticism that puts him beside himself not less because every honour they think to show his antagonist, every loyalty they pay him, is meant for Amphitryon – that is to say, for himself.

He does not despair so soon, he fights for his honour. "Truth" must finally triumph and deceit be vanquished away. He still has other faithful souls, and he brings them up, the doughty "chiefs" – while on the opposite side the citizenry of Thebes streams up, summoned by "him" – that is, by that other man who has robbed him of his "weight." Amphitryon calls the people "my friends" – did he usually do that? Ah, he well knows why he does it; he must play the demagogue a bit, he needs the people, needs their voice, needs for dear life that they shall bear witness to him, know him, "acknowledge" him, not in the other man, but in himself. So now he charges them to bear witness:

All diese Blicke werft in einen Spiegel,
Und kehrt den ganzen vollen Strahl auf mich,
Von Kopt zu Fuss ihn auf und nieder führend,
Und sagt mir an, und sprecht, und steht mir Rede:
Wer bin ich?

All of your eyes now turn upon a glass,
And bend the whole full beam upon me,
From head to foot carry it up and down
And tell me – speak, and answer to my question:
Who am I?

And in saying that, he means not only to force them to vouch for and guarantee his "honour," his identity; he also wants to hear, hear from others, that he and no other is Amphitryon. And when he has heard it he draws a deep breath: "Well, then! Amphitryon. The thing is this": and begins to fortify them for the superhuman test to which their memory, faith, and reason will be subjected by the expected appearance of another, whom to call Not-Amphitryon is impossible, and to consider Also-Amphitryon would be madness, and who therefore can only be an unthinkable and lying evil shadow of Amphitryon's honour.

How sure they all are of themselves and him! They find it absurd that he thinks he might bend the plume in his helmet in order to strengthen their loyalty and distinguish himself as Amphitryon. In particular the chieftain Argatiphontidas is very much annoyed; he is a boaster and bully introduced to lighten the painfulness of the scene with a little comic human nature. Obviously these are aristocratic and military touches brought in to round out the conception of this bumptious satyr-figure: reminders of the out-of-date type of chivalry, unhampered in his dashing self-assurance by any faintest notion of the difficulty of things. With a flow of bombast, he stands ready to cut through every knot with his good sword. Choleric confidence in his own good sense, stupidity amounting to a rush of blood to the head, expresses itself thus:

Wenn eure Feldherrn hier gezaudert haben,
Als jener Aff' erschien, so folgt ein gleiches
Noch nicht für den Argatiphontidas.
Braucht uns ein Freund in einer Ehrensache,

So soll ins Auge man den Helm sich drücken
Und auf den Leib dem Widersacher gehn.
Den Gegner lange schwadronieren hören,
Steht alten Weibern gut; ich, für mein Teil,
Bin für die kürzesten Prozesse stets;
In solchen Fällen fängt man damit an,
Dem Wildersacher ohne Federlesens
Den Degen querhin durch den Leib zu jagen.
Argatiphontidas, mit einem Worte,
Wird heute Haare auf den Zähnen zeigen. . . .

If here your generals have shilly-shallied
When the other ape turned up, so is not he,
Argatiphontidas. If ever a man
Has need of a friend in an affair of honour,
Then let him set his helmet on his brow
And have at the foe forthwith. To await
Long windy speeches from the enemy
Is for old wives. But I, for my part,
Have always been and am for the shortest way.
And that, in all such cases, is to thrust
Your dagger cleanly without more ado
Right through and out the body of your man.
Argatiphontidas, in other words,
Today will show what sort of stuff he's made of.

The "man of honour" type could not be better portrayed. Even the typical reference to himself in the third person and by name is here, and amusingly stressed:

Sorgt nicht. Hier steht Argatiphontidas.

Fear not. Here stands Argatiphontidas.

He will come a cropper, he will not be left a leg to stand on, like the rest of them, even Sosias, who has prepared himself to back precisely this Amphitryon because he had got nothing to eat from the other. For now, in order to resolve the riddle in a metamorphosis in which not only he but the other sufferers are involved, the other Amphitryon appears; he comes from table, with Alcmene, his own Sosias, Charis, and the generals who have adhered to him; and the air resounds with the cries in which the crowd greet the illusion:

Ihr ew'gen Götter! was erblicken wir!

Eternal gods! what do our eyes perceive?

It seems that Alcmene's lover has taken back his declaration that Jupiter has visited her. For she begins:

Entsetzlicher! ein Sterblicher, sagst du,
Und schmachvoll willst du seinem Blick mich zeigen?

Oh, frightful man! A mortal, so you say,
And you, oh shame, will show his face to me?

But he explains:

Die ganze Welt, Geliebte, muss erfahren,
Dass niemand *deiner Seele nahte,*
Als nur dein Gatte, als Amphitryon –

For the whole world, beloved, has to learn
That no one ever hath thy soul approached
Save only him, thy spouse, Amphitryon –

words which, so long as they are still wrapped in a metaphysical veil, must sound to the husband like the most mocking of insults. He thinks the moment has come for his revenge upon the murderous villain, he believes the people and the chiefs are behind him. But the fact that had ensured Alcmene's bliss the previous night is now patent: the almighty one is more fully, more essentially, ideally Amphitryon than is Amphitryon himself, he exceeds him in selfhood, he thrusts him out, the true Amphitryon, not the real one. The latter's way is barred: "Halt, you!" The phrase must be noted; to any sympathetic person it is the last straw to be addressed as "You, there," not even by name; he has no name, no honour more, for over there Amphitryon stands. He summons them, his supposed adherents, imploring, invoking, shrieking: "Argatiphontidas!" They fail him. Then again he utters that word, of whose meaning he is now fully aware, the word "Undone!" and falls, choked with suppressed fury, into Sosias' arms.

They are a little cheap, a little too godlike, Jupiter's words to him: "Fool that thou art!" Amphitryon is no fool, when he falls senseless from his sufferings. They have exceeded his human powers, they are more than he has deserved, one must admit; and in the god's "Hark to a word or so," there is a half-pitying recognition of the facts, while Sosias' dry comment: "My soul, he cannot listen, he is dead," is a human reaction which we feel inclined to echo. Amphitryon does not come to himself at his god-ego's half-pitying summons, only at the words:

Der ist's, den seine eigne Frau erkennt.

He it is, whom his own wife doth recognize.

When, that is, poor Alcmene, shattered, anguished, is summoned to decide. Then he says:

—Wenn sie als Gatten ihn erkennen kann,
So frag' ich nichts danach mehr, wer ich bin:
So will ich ihn Amphitryon begrüssen.

If she can know and claim him as her spouse,
Then never more will I ask who I am:
But recognize him as Amphitryon.

It has gone that far with him—but not yet far enough, Jupiter thinks. For since he never would be able to greet the other as Amphitryon, he speaks in the firm belief that she *can* acknowledge no one but himself; speaks in order to pledge himself as one might say "or I'm a Dutchman," though at the same time he thinks he would better support the waverer with the most touching appeals and intimate memories:

Alkmene! meine Braut, erkläre dich:
Schenk' mir noch einmal deiner Augen Licht!

Alcmene, my bride, oh give your voice, Alcmene!
Grant me once more the radiance of your gaze!

It would soften a stone; and not without some emotion does Jupiter also address her:

Gib, gib der Wahrheit *deine Stimme, Kind.*

Give to the truth thy voice, my child!

She does so. The stronger, the *truer* husband is once more triumphant.

"This man, my friends, here, is Amphitryon," she pronounces, taking his hand—and now Amphitryon has reached the lowest level of the dishonouring that comes before the reinstatement.

"That man Amphitryon—almighty gods!" One cannot help

sympathizing with him. He stares across at the other with eyes that are indeed his, but no longer Amphitryon's, their gaze directed upon Amphitryon—with the eyes of madness. "Alcmene! Beloved!" he groans, *de profundis*, in very truth. But now, judgment upon him having been pronounced, he is to be driven forth, and Alcmene, once decided, is now sure of her decision, and defends it with all the anger and scorn of her supposedly betrayed and disgraced soul.

Nichtswürd'ger! Schändlicher!
Mit diesem Namen wagst du mich zu nennen?
Nicht vor *des Gatten scheugebietendem . . .*

Unworthy! Shameless!
How dare you call me by that name? Not even
Before my husband's mild imperious face—

(I would call particular attention to the emphasis: it is upon "mild" more than on "imperious.")

—Antlitz bin ich vor deiner Wut gesichert?
Du Ungeheuer! mir scheusslicher,
Als es geschwollen in Morästen nistet!

Am I secure from your presumption,
O monster! more to me abhorrent
Than the marsh-brood!

The sweeter has been the passion she tasted, as she thinks, with him in the night just past, the less can she now satisfy her desire to express her loathing.

Der Sonne heller Lichtglanz war mir nötig,
Solch einen feilen Bau gemeiner Knechte
Vom Prachtwuchs dieser königlichen Glieder,
Den Farren von dem Hirsch zu unterscheiden?

And needed I the sun's bright glance to show
The difference between the stag and ox,
Those common limbs and structure of a knave
From this all-regal glory to distinguish?

And she curses her senses, which could be so grossly betrayed, and her heart—"not worthy even to know its own beloved." "Unhappy one!" cries he. "*Am I then he* who came unto you in the night just passed?" It is madness, the frightful things she says to him, because it was not he; and if it had been, it would have been even madder. What a coil! But Alcmene is no less desperate than he. She would fly to the desert, since the breast of a loving woman knows no guard, to protect herself from the shame and bespotting of such a failure. For the moment the god consoles her, only her, with a promise of unimaginable justification. Then he put the question again to Amphitryon whether he now recognizes him as Amphitryon. The other answers only with an angry groan. But when the men urge upon him whether he will still give this woman the lie, broken as he is, he rouses to utter a *credo*, a faith no longer in himself, but in the incorruptible purity and truth of his beloved's heart. It is the beginning of his restoration and elevation. "Not in the oracle," he cries,

> *würd' ich so vertraun,*
> *Als was ihr unverfälschter Mund gesagt.*
> *Jetzt einen Eid selbst auf den Altar schwör' ich,*
> *Und sterbe siebenfachen Todes gleich,*
> Des unerschütterlich erfassten Glaubens,
> *Dass er Amphitryon ihr ist.*

> would I so confide
> As in her lips' inviolable truth.
> Now I myself upon the altar swear,
> Upon immediate pain of sevenfold death,
> My steadfast and unshakable belief
> That he Amphitryon is, and hers.

He is at the goal, and with him the god. The miracle could not be merely outward, it must occur within his own soul, must become faith, "steadfast and unshakable." For now Zeus speaks:

> *Wohlan! Du bist Amphitryon.*

> Good, then! Thou art Amphitryon.

The second person, I think, must not be too much emphasized; rather the verb, or the name. For now at once, on the question who he is, this fearsome spirit – so they conceive him now – answers Jupiter, as though it were a matter of course: "Amphitryon!" They implore him to make himself comprehensible to mortals, and he replies in words great with mystical pantheism. Amphitryon's cry: "To me, my friends, come gather round me!" heralds a fundamental change of scene. They are no longer his foes, denying and threatening him. Something is going on that unites these human beings at odds over a verbal misunderstanding against the stranger and god. For it is plain that even while he uttered his last words, that other Amphitryon had been growing stranger and stranger, more and more retreating into a light that is not theirs, nor of this earth. "Think you it was Amphitryon appeared?" his voice sounds to the quaking Alcmene, and she, divining, perceiving, begs to be allowed to dwell longer in an error which was not hers but which she needs, if "thy light" is not forever to benight her soul. Strange, sweet immortal words he breathes to her in farewell. And when Amphitryon, now once more his own man, once more ready for anything, challenges him to reveal himself, then the god's tremendous "Then thou wouldst know?" drowns the little human voice. Clouds roll up, there are flashings and crashings, the eagle hovers, the bolt in its claws, they all fling themselves in the dust – all but one: the man, the beloved and husband, who holds her he never lost in his strong human arms and now receives the heroic announcement.

"Hermes!" It is the curt, haughty summons as the god vanishes, his adventure played out to the end, his desire quenched, once more himself, with no glance, no farewell, for those who now know what it was that happened to them. He summons the easy servant of his wishes and is lost in the upper spheres. One name, from the depths of a liberated breast, rings out: the name of him whom she holds in her arms, to whom she clings: "Amphitryon!" And while the generals all hasten to assure him of their overwhelmed submission, Alcmene breathes her final "Ah!" and the sweet confusion of a female heart mingles with that of a poetic dream.

Such is the piece. My love for it, my loyalty through the years, reaped the joyful reward of once more knowing why, as I reread its subtle lines. The blitheness of its mysticism, the warmth of its humour, are incomparable. Played as it deserves to be played, it would be a diversion in which atmosphere and intellect would both be celebrated in their equal due. But performances of *Amphitryon* have little in common with celebrations save their rarity; they are infrequent, and everyday theatre usage is against them. A young producer with brains and feeling, wit and art, might animate and refurbish, think and feel the piece through again from the beginning, get time and money to produce it as it deserves, with actors who combine a high degree of physical charm and talent with a flexible receptivity for the detailed directions his own enthusiasm would impart to them. The producer must certainly let me know when such a performance is in prospect. I would travel a long way to see it.

CHAMISSO

1911

AMONG our schoolbooks was one that stood out from all the rest. On the outside it looked dry and forbidding, like any textbook. But within it gave of its contents with lovely human charm. Actually, strange as it may seem, it was an amusing book, full from cover to cover of delightful things which got our interest straightway, with no dry bits in between. We read it without being told, for sheer enjoyment; we read on ahead of the class, and felt none of the usual pangs when the lesson hour came and the books lay open on the desks. It was almost like a game and the exercises they set us out of it were easy and amusing. We answered every question like a flash, in eager, excited voices. And if there was one of us who took no interest, let him be as redoubtable as he might in any other field, we put him down for a dull fellow.

This book must have been added to the school curriculum by some exceptionally kindly hand. It was called, quite simply, *The German Reader*. It was given us solely to the end that we should look at the language, our mother tongue—or rather that we should listen to it—as it smiled to see itself in verse. *The German Reader* contained a gay and varied collection of good stories, both rhymed and unrhymed, in prose and verse. If I were to come across it again, I wager that I could turn straightway to my old favourites.

There was the comic ballad about the fellow who was so upset because his pigtail hung down behind—he wanted it before. There was the humorous-serious anecdote about the Szekler Assembly—and it is my belief that its easy, unimpeachable structure of triplets with the single line so happily rounding out everything at the end gave me my earliest instance of masterly performance in that kind. There was the fine ode to an old washerwoman; what an enchantment that was, how it made my heart beat every time I came to the closing strophe:

Und ich, an meinem Abend, wollte . . .

I too at evening of my day. . . .

There was the tale of an evil deed, long hidden and unknown; I always fancied that the "flickering sunbeams" played on these pages to bring the crime to the light of day. We read the long-drawn-out tale of Abdullah and the eighty camels. The dervish appeared to him (the more unearthly in our eyes because we did not know exactly what a dervish was), and Abdullah became very wealthy and then a blind beggar all in one day, because of his own greed. Then there was the fearsome and fantastic story of the "right barber." The child giantess spread out her little cloth and scooped peasant and plough into it with her hands. The brave wives of Winsperg carried their husbands pick-a-back out of the gate. And lastly in a succession of rhymed chapters was unfolded the magic dream-poem of Cousin Anselmo and his ingratitude.

At the end of all these pieces was signed their author's name, a foreign-sounding one: Chamisso. The same name was on a richly bound volume I found in the glass bookcase in the smoking-room at home. This second book contained things such as our good little textbook could not boast; some of them frightful, like the story of the sunken castle, for a long time my greatest favourite, particularly on account of the "brazen minion" who was so brazen as to walk in her shoes over fine white bread. She seemed just that much more bedevilled because in fact I had no clear idea what a minion was. These earliest impressions are no doubt amazingly distorted by my childishly undeveloped powers of imagination. Did I not promptly, whenever my stomach was upset, dream the frightful dream of the men in the Zoptenberg? It was I myself and not the godly Johannes Beer from Schweidnitz who saw the three gaunt sinners sitting in the black-hung hall at the round table by the dim lamp. It was I who saw the curtain gape, behind it the horrid heap of ribs and skulls, the remnant of their crimes. I understood just enough Latin to give me goose-flesh when the three miscreants stammered their gloomy "*Hic nulla, nulla pax!*" Looking at the verses today I am struck afresh by the capital performance. How crisp and lively is the indirect discourse that is fitted into the verse! With what deftness and economy are chosen and applied those tools of the language calculated to arouse the most fear and horror! The cold and shuddering breath of the unwholesome place, the staring, shaking anguish of the accursèd ones, their stammering, teeth-chattering, pointing, starting, mowing, mouthing – how capital all that was! . . . And when evening came, we sat quietly at our ease and listened to our mother at the piano, singing the serene and lovely song-cycle of *Frauenliebe und Leben.*

This poet, whose name was so early familiar to us, this German author who was set before us lads as our first and best model, was a stranger, a foreigner. French songs were his lullabies. The air, the water, the nourishment of France shaped his body, the rhythm of the French tongue was the medium of all his thoughts and feelings till he was half-grown. Only then, at fourteen, did he come over to us. He never managed to converse with fluency in German. He reckoned in French. Tradition says that up to the last when he composed he first recited aloud in French and only after that poured his inspirations into a metrical mould — but after all, the result was masterly German.

It is amazing, it is even unheard-of. True, there have been cases of gifted men who were so drawn to the genius of a stranger folk that they changed their nationality, immersed themselves utterly in the ideas and problems of the people with whom they felt this affinity, and learned to use their pens adequately, even elegantly, in a tongue their fathers did not speak. But what is correctness, what even elegance, compared to the deep intimacy the artist must have! The knowledge of the ultimate mysteries and refinements, the uttermost control of his craft in tone and movement, in the reflex workings of words on one another, of their sensuous appeal, their dynamic, their special stylistic, ironic, pathetic value; that mastery — to put in a word what, after all, is unanalysable — of the delicate and powerful mechanism of language, which produces the literary artist and is indispensable to poet and writer. He who is born and called one day to enrich the literature of his land will quite early find himself peculiarly concerned with his mother tongue. The Word: there it is, it belongs to everybody, yet it seems to belong to him more in particular, in a more inward and gratifying sense than to anyone else. It is his earliest wonder, his first delight, his childish pride, the field of his private and unpraised efforts, the source of his strange and undefined superiority. At fourteen years, if the individual sustain this unusual relation to the Word, there may already have been some private beginnings. And then, at this age, to be set amongst strangers speaking strange thoughts in a strange tongue! Even though some latent, unexplained sympathy were already present; even though there was some unconscious adjustment to the German tempo and German laws of thought; still, and even so, how much conscious labour, how much wooing for the favour of our tongue was needed to make a German poet out of a French child!

And he hesitates long. Long considers it presumptuous to regard himself seriously as belonging to the German Parnassus. He is forty-one years old when he writes to a French friend: "When we were boys I wanted to be a poet; you too made German verses, though probably such flights have ceased ere now. With me not quite. I still sing, when song comes to my mind; I even collect these fugitive blossoms into a herbarium for myself and my loved ones for future times. But they remain in the family circle, as they should." Five years later, to Varnhagen's sister: "That I was and am no poet is abundantly clear; but the taste for it is still there." And only in the following year (1828) when he was attracting increasing notice from the public: "I almost think I am a German poet." One hears in his voice the pride, the still questioning joy with which he feels the garland on his head, his awe at the dignity which the nation bestowed by popular applause. A German poet: in those days that was something to be in the world. The word on the lips of a people of poets and thinkers was at the height of its significance. The romantic movement had put its seal on the European conception of poetry. Poetry – that was romanticism. But the romantic – that was German. In the letter I quoted, the easy equation of "to be a poet" with "to make German verses" is worth remark. Never was an epithet more intimately fused with its noun than in the phrase "*der deutsche Dichter*." To be a German, that almost meant to be a poet. To be a poet, that almost meant to be German. This may help us to understand the astonishing fact that the poetic talent of a foreigner could so happily strike root into the soil of the German language.

The fine poem *Boncourt Castle* is a metrical treatment of Chamisso's biography. It moved a warm-hearted monarch to tears. It describes the old feudal seat in Champagne, whose castle court sheltered the poet's childhood. Today the plough turns the soil on which it stood. Sadly but without rancour, the poet invokes a blessing on the dear earth now summoned to bring forth fruit; on the ploughman who tills it; and at the end the exiled grandson of the lords of Chamisso at Boncourt, with that melancholy resignation which suits so well the romantic poets, girds himself to travel the far spaces of the earth, a wandering singer, lute in hand.

The boy was born in 1781 and christened with the names Louis Charles Adelaide. The family were driven out in 1790 by the political tempest of the Revolution. They wandered for years in great privation through the Low Countries, Holland, Germany, and at last into Prussia. Here in Berlin, in 1796, they succeeded in getting for young Adelaide or Adalbert the position of page to the Queen Consort of Friedrich Wilhelm II. Two years later he begins his military career as ensign in a Berlin regiment of foot. In 1801 he is made lieutenant. When the First Consul permitted the lad's parents to return to France, Adalbert remained where he was. His literary production seems to have begun by then. He writes French verse, then German verse. Friendships grow up with like-minded youths, Varnhagen and Hitzig; and the fruit of these alliances is an *Almanac of the Muses*, which came out from 1804 to 1806, and, unripe as its contents were, won for young Chamisso the fatherly kindness of Fichte. Private studies in Greek, Latin, and incidentally in the living languages of Europe went on at the same time. Then years of war interrupted the service of the muse. Chamisso took part in the Weser campaign, was imprisoned in Hamelin, quit the service, and went back to Berlin. Meanwhile he had been orphaned. And now in Berlin, without hope for the future, he spent lonely, unfruitful years. A summons to the land of his fathers, to Napoléonville, as professor at the *lycée* released him from an intolerable situation. He hastened to France, whither in the days of his Berlin exile his heart may have fondly turned — or perhaps only thought it ought to turn. Nothing came of the professorship. The young *homme de lettres* was drawn into the orbit of Madame de Staël, that "magnificent, amazing woman," whom he admired not least as a power not subservient to the Emperor. He followed the proscribed heroine to Geneva and Coppet. And from there he writes to Fouqué, scion of the Normans: "Here I live, love, pursue my quiet German course; nowhere have I been more blockheadedly German than in Paris." Then, in 1812, he returned of his own free will to Berlin and continued at the university the scientific studies that he had embarked on in Paris. The events of the years 1813 to 1815, in which he could not take an active part, tear him asunder time after time, as he says in a *curriculum vitæ* composed by himself. "What my nearest friends shrieked at me when I left, I now say to myself: the times held no sword for me; yet it is maddening to be an idle spectator at such a popular movement of happy warriors." Shamefacedly, self-conflicted, he withdrew into solitude. It was a repetition, even harder to bear, of the restless period after his resignation from the army. Whither should he turn? He might be no German, yet felt a stranger to his French homeland. A newspaper came into his hands with a notice about a forthcoming Russian voyage of discovery "to the North Pole," under Otto von Kotzebue. He pricked up his ears, friends came forward to help, even the Privy Councillor August von Kotzebue, in Königsberg, was appealed to, and an earlier wish-dream of Chamisso's came unexpectedly true. In June 1815 he was appointed scientist on the forthcoming voyage of discovery to the South Seas and round the world. Hamburg, Copenhagen, Plymouth, Tenerife, Brazil, Chile, Kamchatka, California, the Sandwich Islands, Manila, the Cape of Good Hope, London, St. Petersburg – it was three years of luxurious gratification of his romantic wanderlust and love of the exotic; beyond doubt the richest, most rewarding years of his life, which filled the storehouse of his mind with an inexhaustible treasure of pictures and material and endowed him with food for contemplation for his whole productive life. The immediate literary fruit of these years was the attractive book *Travels round the World*, in its scientific aspect a volume of "Comments and Opinions on a Voyage of Discovery under Kotzebue." Actually, the most important result of the experience was of a personal and human kind. In those wild and distant scenes through which he passed, Chamisso's feeling for home, which had vacillated so long, became once for all fixed – and fixed upon Germany. Wanderlust and love of home are certainly not mutually exclusive. They may be friendly allies, and precisely in romantic souls may kindle and enhance the one the other. Chamisso's gentle heart, with its craving for companionship, had suffered from the conflict of double nationality and the indecision of not knowing in which soil he wanted to strike root. His travels taught him that when he turned his thoughts and feelings "homeward" it was to Germany they went. He found that all his hopes and humours, his love of language, science, and friendship bound him to her. By the dispensation of fate he had now in fact and in truth become at heart a German. Today we believe less in heart and more in blood and race; perhaps we even exaggerate this belief into a superstition. Thus we may have our doubts and in fact, under the pressure of a general devotion to the binding force of blood, may find that the case of Chamisso would be subjectively hardly possible. But in his time it was, and that must do us; the inward experience, like all powerful personal convictions, could and did preserve and demonstrate itself objectively through his German work. He landed in Swinemünde in October 1818, and greeted his German home in verse, begging her, in exchange "for so much love," for just one thing, that on her soil he might find a stone whereon one day to pillow his head and fall asleep. The verses belong to the loveliest, most moving, and most moved that he ever wrote. Thirteen years later, a fifty-year-old man, in like fervent syllables, he sang his thanks to "his dear German home" for all the friendliness she had shown to the "*gebeugten Gast*." That was not little; for it seems that along with the inner peace happiness and well-being accrued from without. Friedrich Wilhelm of Prussia, long an admirer of his art, took Chamisso under his protection, and made him assistant at the Botanical Gardens and Director of the Royal Herbaria, with pay sufficient. The homeless one founded a home, he married, there would be a little house, "and the modest little space is large enough to hold a new-awakened, gay and ample life." Peace and the esteem of his fellows spur him on, his reputation increases, in dignity and discipline his talent unfolds to mastery. Heine, his greater contemporary, admiringly says "with every year he grows younger and fuller of bloom." The next generation, to whom he had ever been a kindly counsellor and inspiration, held him in honour. Since 1832 he had, with Schwab and Gaudy, been publishing the German *Almanac of the Muses*, and in 1835 he was invited to become a member of the Academy of Science. But premonitions of death now began to be voiced in his verse. "Dream and Waking," written in 1837, is the retrospect, sad and glad, of one who feels himself at his journey's end. His lungs were attacked, and in the summer of 1838, at the height of his fame, he fell asleep. Fifty years later, Berlin, which might well regard him as her son, erected a monument to him in Monbijou Place.

He was a tall, mild man with long, straight hair and noble, almost beautiful features. Capable of friendship with children and savages, he loved to remember the Radak Islanders whose guest he had once been and whose beauty and nearness to nature he praises in the style of Rousseau. The Ulea-Indian Kadú, who served him in the South Seas, he considered "one of the finest characters" he had met in his life and one of the human beings he "loved the most." His scientific works, for instance the *Conspectus of Useful and Harmful Plants That Grow Wild or Cultivated in Northern Germany*, to mention one of them, are considered "valuable." But it is as poet that his name survives.

Chamisso's collected poems, which he first brought himself to publish in 1831, are only in small part in lyric. The immediately lyrical is infrequent, and not always happy; the hymnic, dithyrambic, ecstatic is wholly lacking. The somewhat unexciting epic, the well-wrought objective work, make up by far the larger part of his product; preambles and preludes such as:

Ich bin schon alt, es mahnt der Zeiten Lauf
Mich oft an längst geschehene Geschichten,
Und die erzähl' ich, horcht auch niemand auf.
So weiss ich aus der Chronik und Gedichten,

Wie bei der Pest es in Ferrara war,
Und will davon nur einen Zug berichten –

Now I am old, the passage of the years
Minds me of things that in past time befell,
And I relate them, though nobody hears;
From chronicle and verse I know full well
How in Ferrara in the plague it was,
And of them all one only I will tell.

That sort of thing indicates his attitude as a poet; even the flowery and lyrical, like *Frauenliebe und Leben* and *Lebens-Lieder und Bilder* come within the epic-dramatic compositions, unities of strophe and antistrophe, monologue and rejoinder. What strikes one is the abrupt, almost pathological contradiction between the ethereal delicacy of Chamisso's production in this kind and his indisputable fondness for strong, even horrible subjects. Public opinion did not criticize him from the first angle, of course; but it probably did from the second, and his partisans have cited in his behalf the friendship that bound him to the criminalist Hitzig. It was Hitzig, they said, who provided the poet in search of material with such exotic, not to say horrid subjects. The apology is as untenable as the reproach – which has also been levelled against Heinrich von Kleist. One might with more justice suppose that a friendship with the editor of criminalist periodicals was itself the consequence of Chamisso's requirement of objective material from the field of the abnormal and horrible. For the over-delicate and the brutal are complementary cravings of the romantic temperament. It is precisely this contrast that places Chamisso's works with all their Latin clarity and definition in the category of the romantic in literature.

Poems showing such a tendency to horrible subject-matter are, for instance, "Don Juanito Marques Verdugo de los Leganes," a story also used by Balzac, about a young Spanish grandee who on heroic grounds brings himself to execute the French blood-judgment on his own family; "Retribution," the excruciating anecdote of the executioner who in his sleep marks with his branding-iron the frightful betrayer of his daughter; the famous *terza rima* composition "Salas y Gomez," which, first appearing in the Wendish *Musenalmanac* of 1829, made a real sensation in the world of belles-lettres and permanently established the literary standing of the author. Today we do not quite follow the admiration which greeted this terrifying Robinsonade. Is not its poetic value rather problematic? What made the poet illuminate with his art the lamentable tale of the young business man cast away on an island, peopled only by water-birds, who gets to be a hundred years old and scratches his misery on three slate tablets? On his voyage round the world Chamisso had seen the bare cliffs of Salas y Gomez and, shuddering, said to himself that a man cast away there could probably sustain life all too long on birds' eggs. That might be ground enough to make him fill more than three hundred lines of verse with those shudderings; but not quite ground enough for us to find the thing particularly interesting. What we do admire without reservation is the form of the poem, the wrought bronze of the language. Certainly, Platen wrote the most perfect German sonnets; but with equal certainty Chamisso deserves the title of most masterly wielder of the *terza rima.*

However, Chamisso was no formalist, and as a conscientious artist scarcely at all dealt in the explicitly artificial. The ghazal, for instance, used with dazzling effect by Rückert and Platen, does not appear in his work. Other classic forms — the sonnet, the Sapphic ode, the Nibelung strophe — are not prominent either. And most lovable of all, as is lyric poetry in general, are two or three apparently artless things, quite simple in form, light and brief as dreams are, but quivering with feeling and extraordinarily forthright in their simplicity, like all confessions:

*Was Soll Ich Sagen?**

Mein Aug' ist trüb, mein Mund ist stumm,
Du heissest mich reden, es sei darum.

Dein Aug' ist klar, dein Mund ist rot,
Und was du nur wünschest, das ist ein Gebot.

Mein Haar ist grau, mein Herz ist wund,
Du bist so jung, und bist so gesund.

Du heissest mich reden, und machst mir's so schwer,
Ich seh' dich an, und zittre so sehr.

"The Old Washerwoman" is probably Chamisso's most popular poem; "Salas y Gomez" won him the applause of connoisseurs. But a European name, yes, a world reputation he achieved in a narra-

* See page 465 for literal translation.

tive prose work. Today, almost a hundred years after it was written, this little book will, I am convinced, have the same immediate and profound appeal.

The Marvellous Tale of Peter Schlemihl was, to begin with its literary history, written in the year 1813. At that time the poet, in a state of desperation, both personally and politically speaking, was botanizing on the estate of his friends the Itzenplitz family. He himself said he undertook the work to distract his mind and amuse the children of a friend (Eduard Hitzig). There are a few scraps of information about some small incidents that helped to shape the fable. Chamisso says in a letter: "I had lost on a journey my hat, portmanteau, gloves, handkerchief, my whole movable property. Fouqué asked me whether I had not also lost my shadow, and we began imagining such a mishap. Another time, turning the pages of La Fontaine, I read about a very obliging man in a company who turned all sorts of things out of his pockets as they were asked for. If one were to encourage the fellow, I thought, he might even take out a coach and four as well. With that the Schlemihl was born. And when once in the country I had leisure and was bored, I began to write." Wilhelm Rauschenbusch, the publisher of the two-volume Grote edition of Chamisso, a personal acquaintance of the author, adds that an essential factor in the development of the fable was a walk Chamisso once took with Fouqué at Nennhausen, the Fouqué estate. "The sun threw long shadows, so that little Fouqué, to judge from his, looked almost as tall as tall Chamisso. 'Look, Fouqué,' says Chamisso, 'what if I just rolled up your shadow and you had to walk along beside me without one!' Fouqué found the idea frightful, and Chamisso teasingly went on to exploit the subject." Need of distraction, then, playing uncle to some children, a travelling mishap, a chance remark about a book, a jest among friends, idleness and boredom – these are certainly modest motives and occasions for the origin of a composition which may justly be called immortal. Certainly that is the way stories arise. But the story that here arose received in the hands of a poet qualities calculated to charm the world. French and English, Dutch and Spanish translated it, America pirated it from England, and in Germany it was reprinted with the drawings of Cruickshank, the illustrator of Dickens. Hoffmann, when it was read aloud to him, is said to have hung on the reader's lips, beside himself with pleasure and suspense. One can readily believe it.

Is it in order to set down a few recollections, a few advance pointers about the charm of the tale? First: Peter Schlemihl has been called a fairy-tale; or even, because of the poet's idle assertion that he wrote it for the children of a friend, it has been called a fairy-tale for the young. That it is not. However indefinite its terrain, it is too much the novel; with all its whimsical vein, it is too modern, feverish, too much in earnest to come within the rubric of the fairy-tale. For the same reasons, in my opinion and experience, it is not particularly suitable for children. The story begins in a quite realistic, commonplace vein, and the real artistry of the writer lies in his knowing how to keep up the realistic bourgeois atmosphere to the end, all the while relating in the greatest detail the most fabulous and impossible circumstances. This in such a way that Schlemihl's adventures impress the reader as "strange" in the sense of a destiny seldom or never before visited upon an erring human being by the will of God; but never actually "strange" in the sense of an unnatural or irresponsible or "fairy" story. The autobiographical, confessional form, as contrasted with that of the typical fairy-tale, contributes to emphasize its truthfulness and reality. So, if I were challenged to classify Peter Schlemihl, I think I should call it a fantastic novelette or long story.

The theme derived from La Fontaine is happily employed on the very first page with the altogether discreet introduction of the grey man, that "silent, lean, tall, and gaunt elderly person" who at Lord John's garden party in all modesty and helpfulness produces, to the horror of the narrator, not only a dispatch-case and telescope, but a Turkish rug, a sizable marquee, and three bridled riding-horses out of his "tight-fitting" coat-tail pocket. It is the Devil; and he is capitally drawn, especially in the scene between him and Schlemihl on the lawn. No cloven hoof, no demonry, no diabolic glitter. An over-courteous, embarrassed man, who blushes (a pricelessly convincing touch) when he introduces the crucial conversation about the shadow. Schlemihl, hovering between horror and respect, treats him with aghast politeness. What this extraordinary amateur offers him in exchange for his shadow are good old familiar things: the genuine magic root, the mandrake; magic pennies; thieves' thalers; the napkin of Roland's squire; a gallows-mannikin; Fortunatus's wishing-cap, "newly refurbished." The story here refers to familiar and taken-for-granted paraphernalia of saga and fairy-tale, and this sustains its atmosphere of the legitimate and reliable. The befooled Schlemihl chooses the lucky purse; and then follows that priceless moment when the grey man kneels down and with admirable deftness loosens Schlemihl's shadow from the grass, lifts it from head to foot, rolls it up, folds it, and puts it in his pocket.

But now, of course, everybody – man, woman, and street Arab – straightway perceives that Schlemihl has no shadow and overwhelms him with scorn, pity, or horror. On this point I am not quite so sure as I was in the matter of the lucky purse. If a man meets me when the sun is shining and he casts no shadow, would I notice its absence? And if I did, would I not simply conclude that there was some peculiar optical factor unknown to me that made him seem to lack one? Well, no matter. Precisely the impossibility of checking up on and deciding this question is the real point of the book; granting the premise, everything follows with shattering consistency.

For what comes next is the portrayal of an apparently advantaged and enviable but actually romantically miserable existence, dwelling solitary in its own mind with a sinister secret – and certainly no poet has ever before succeeded in bringing home to the reader the emotions of such a man or depicting them with such convincing simplicity, realism, and sympathy.

The deciding factor is that the author managed from the start to convince us of the value and importance of a good healthy shadow for the respectability of a human being. So that we find such expressions as "sinister secret" and the like at worst only a bit exaggerated; we are prepared to see a man without a shadow as the most afflicted and repulsive human being under the sun. We see the wealthy Schlemihl leave his house by night and moonlight, wrapped in a voluminous cloak, with his hat drawn over his brows, driven by the tormenting desire to test the general opinion and read his doom out of the mouths of passers-by. We see him cringe beneath the pity of the women, the mockery of the young, the scorn of grown men, especially the portly ones, "who themselves cast a good broad shadow." We see him staggering heartbroken home when a sweet innocent child chances to cast her eye upon him from close at hand and at sight of his shadowless state veils her lovely face and passes on with averted gaze. His sense of guilt at this incident is boundless. And the narrative rises again to one of its most extraordinary heights in the episode with the painter, whom Schlemihl approaches in a roundabout way and asks whether he could paint a man an artificial shadow. The artist makes the chilling reply that whoever has no shadow should not walk in the sun, that is the safest and most reasonable way – and quits him with a "piercing" look.

The story goes on to tell with great fidelity to detail how Schlemihl tries to adjust himself more or less to his affliction. To his valet, a sturdy fellow with a kind face, he has in a weak moment confided his shameful infirmity; and the good soul, although horrified, conquers his feelings and, defying all the world, remains loyal and helps Schlemihl all he can. He supports his master, walks everywhere in front of or with him, and, being taller and broader, he covers him at critical moments with his own imposing shadow. Thus Schlemihl is able to go among people and play his part in society. "I had indeed," says he, "to pretend to many oddities of conduct. But all such eccentricities become the man of means." Defeats and humiliations are not lacking and presently comes that touching episode which is an immortal theme of romantic poetry: the love of the marked man, hunted, infamous, accursed, for a pure and unsuspecting maiden, to whom he turns like any simple, bourgeois human being.

I mean the unhappy idyll with the forester's daughter; there we have all the typical elements of the theme: the simple, foolish, match-making mother; the decent, distrustful father who "does not look so high"; the wooer's pangs of conscience, the intuitions of the girl, her tender attempt to penetrate her lover's secret, and her woman's cry: "If you are wretched, bind me to your wretchedness, that I may help you bear it." The old tale is told with such freshness, such convincing gravity, such veracity and detail, one loses sight of the fact that the premises are fantastic, since the poet himself seems wholly to have forgotten it. Nowhere is the story so little a fairy-story as here, nowhere so entirely a romance, reality, serious life. Those lines of verse seem to preside over this prose, lines fearful, fervid, strangely bold in their simplicity, like all confessions:

Du heissest mich reden und machst mir's so schwer,
Ich seh' dich an und zittre so sehr.

One would like to tell the whole story over again, put one's finger on every paragraph; but here is the rest of it. Nothing happier than the last chapter, where the Evil One, "as though used to such treatment," silently bows his head and stoops his shoulders and lets himself be thrashed by the faithful Bendel. Nothing more amusing than the point of the jest: "Now the whole affair of course became clear to me: the man must have had the invisible bird's nest which makes invisible him who has it but not his shadow, and then he threw it away!" Yes, yes! And no finer conclusion imaginable than the one invented by the poet. It is a good and soothing end, though at the same time an austere one, remote from the childlike optimism of the fairy-tale, where everything ends in wedding bells and "if they are not dead they live there still."

Schlemihl, shut out by early sin from human society, never returns to it and never regains his shadow. He remains solitary, he goes on doing penance. But he finds in nature a substitute for bourgeois happiness. By a fortunate chance, he is drawn to contemplate her and spends his life in the service of natural science. The author accompanies with a wealth of accurate geographical detail the account of his hero's travels in the seven-league boots – here again employing the method of supporting fantasy with realistic detail. An illustration of his carefulness as well as of his unobtrusive way of making plausible the fantastic is the brilliant little inspiration of the "brake-shoe." Innocently, with all the simplicity in the world, the idea of the brake-shoe is transferred to the slippers which Schlemihl draws on over his boots when he wants to take ordinary and not seven-league strides. Thus the writer succeeds in giving the whole impossibility a character of bourgeois realism which in the legend it never possessed. Now, a grotesque figure, magnificently satisfied with his lot, Schlemihl covers the backbone of this earth, striding and studying. He establishes the geography of unexplored regions, he botanizes and zoologizes in the grand manner, and he will take care to have his manuscripts submitted before his death to the University of Berlin. "I have faithfully striven," he says, "with all that I had of silent, stern, unintermitted effort, to depict what came before my inward eye; and my self-satisfaction has depended on making what I described coincide with the original." Here the fantastic improvisation of the poet's imagination merges into a confession. And is it only here that the confession occurs?

Chamisso has made it easy for his contemporaries and posterity to see that his Schlemihl is himself. Repeatedly and with evident pleasure he has used external detail to play upon the identity between the poet and his fictional hero. Why must Schlemihl's faithful servant be called Bendel? The name recurs in a humorous poem telling how Chamisso as a young lieutenant went to sleep over his Homer and failed to report for duty:

Stiefletten, Bendel, schnell! ich seh erschrocken,
Dass sich bereits der Obrist eingefunden.

Quick, Bendel, quick! My boots! I see appalled
The colonel's come, already he's advancing.

So he actually had a servant of that name. There is a letter to Hitzig wherein he fancifully relates how the shadowless world-wanderer personally brought him the manuscript of his memoirs.

The description of this man, even down to the tight-fitting black coat, is Chamisso's own — why? His explicit denial fits almost better: "The shadow," he asserts in the introductory poem "To My Old Friend Peter Schlemihl":

Den Schatten hab' ich, der mir angeboren,
Ich habe meinen Schatten nie verloren.

The shadow I was born with, good or ill,
I never lost it, and I have it still.

He goes on to lament:

Mich traf, obgleich unschuldig wie das Kind,
Der Hohn, den sie für deine Blösse hatten. —
Ob wir einander denn so ähnlich sind?!
Sie schrien mir nach: Schlemihl, wo ist dein Schatten?

Guiltless as any babe I had to bear
Their scorn when they your follies would deride:
Whether or not we like each other are,
"Schlemihl, where is your shadow?" still they cried.

This seems to be literally true, for Hitzig relates to Fouqué that some Berlin lad had mocked Chamisso on the street and called after him: "Just wait, Peter Schlemihl!" But we need not assume that the popularity of his double grieved the poet. Poets who give themselves away want at bottom to be recognized; for with them it is not so much a matter of the fame of their work as the fame of their life and suffering. But then, what was the experience, what was the suffering this poet had in common with his hero? Wherein lies his inner solidarity with poor Peter Schlemihl? How far is the little book a confession? And what does it mean to have no shadow? People have racked their brains over the mystery ever since the book appeared, they have devoted theses to it and answered it all too clearly and precisely by saying that the man without a shadow is the man without a country. But that would be to narrow down too much the "deeper meaning" of a motif which in the first instance was only a grotesque fancy. Schlemihl is no allegory; Chamisso was not the man to whom an intellectual idea was ever the primary thing in his production. "Only life," he said, "can recapture life." But precisely because that is true, he would not have been able without some basis of experience to fill out a comic idea into something so full of life and novelistic veracity. Need of distraction, avuncular benevolence, could never by themselves have enabled him to write the tale if he had not known himself to be in a particular situation that gave him power to animate it with verisimilitude out of his own personal lot.

But again, what was this peculiar and personal lot? Chamisso wrote a charming foreword to the French edition of *Peter Schlemihl.* Towards the end of it he says that his tale has fallen into the hands of thinking people who, accustomed to reading in order to be edified, are troubled because they want to know what the shadow was. And then, with a straight face, he proceeds to quote in French from an old tome the definition of the shadow:

De l'ombre.

Un corps opaque ne peut jamais être éclairé qu'en partie par un corps lumineux, et l'espace privé de lumière qui est situé du côté de la partie non éclairée, est ce qu'on appelle ombre. Ainsi l'ombre, proprement dite, représente un solide dont la forme dépend à la fois de celle du corps lumineux, de celle du corps opaque, et de la position de celui-ci à l'égard du corps lumineux. L'ombre considéré sur un plan situé derrière le corps opaque qui la produit n'est autre chose que la section de ce plan dans le solide qui représente l'ombre.

(Hauy, *Traité élémentaire de physique. T. II. §§ 1002 et 1006.*)

"*C'est donc de ce solide,*" Chamisso comments, "*dont il est question dans la merveilleuse histoire de Pierre Schlémihl. La science de la finance nous instruit assez de l'importance de l'argent, celle de l'ombre est moins généralement reconnue. Mon imprudent ami a convoité l'argent dont il connaissait le prix et n'a pas songé au solide. La leçon qu'il a chèrement payé, il veut qu'elle nous profite et son expérience nous crie: songez au solide.*"

"*Songez au solide!*" Here, then, is the ironic moral of the book, whose author knew only too precisely what it means to lack solidity, human regularity, bourgeois stability. "Thus," he writes in the autobiographical sketch we have from him, "in the years when the boy is growing to manhood I stood alone. I made verses. . . . Doubtful of myself, without station or occupation, bowed down and crushed, I spent in Berlin a gloomy time." He knew the torments of youth, the problems of the young man who, without any normal future to look forward to, cannot test his powers.

Wounded in his ego, he sees mockery and scorn wherever he turns, especially from the stout and solid, "who themselves cast a good broad shadow." He had perhaps even stranger insights into the fluctuating unreality and precariousness of his existence. By birth a Frenchman, he had made Germany his home and could say to himself that if chance had so willed, he might just as well have made it anywhere else. Somewhere in his writings he expressly declares that he had discovered in himself the gift of feeling at home everywhere. His extraordinary talent for languages was no doubt part of this feeling – we know that he possessed not only German but all sorts of other tongues as well, even Hawaiian. What was he, who was he anyhow? Nothing, everything? A creature, not a person, uncircumscribable, everywhere and nowhere at home? There may have been days when he felt that out of sheer vagueness and unreality he himself cast no shadow.

The shadow has become, in *Peter Schlemihl*, a symbol of all bourgeois solidity and human belongingness. It is spoken of as money is spoken of, as something which one has to respect if one wants to live among men; which one can only get rid of if one is minded to live exclusively for himself and his better self. The ironic summons: "*Songez au solide!*" applies to the bourgeois, as we would say today, to the philistines, to use the word of the romantics. But irony almost always implies making a superiority out of a lack. The whole little book is nothing but a profoundly experienced description of the sufferings of the marked and solitary man. It tells us that young Chamisso knew with painful vividness how to esteem the value of a healthy shadow.

Well, he got one! The pretty verses by his friend Hitzig, sent to Fouqué, the third member of the group, to announce the news of Chamisso's betrothal, explain that Schlemihl need no longer go without a shadow, that in fact he has three: first, the shadow of the Prussian eagle, which graciously hovers over him with its wings; second, the shadows of the trees in the Botanical Gardens, whose well-paid head he is; and finally, most beautiful of all, the shadow which has vowed not to leave him more – "Antonie – do we need more words?" And Chamisso himself sent a picture of his bride to Fouqué with the lines:

Den Schlemihl genannt sie hatten,
Reich in seiner Schatten Zier,
Gönnet jetzt von seinem Schatten
Strafend einen Schatten dir.

He whom once they knew as Schlemihl,
Brave in shadow clothed anew,
Here a shadow of his shadow
En revanche now gives to you.

It is the old story. Werther shot himself, but Goethe remained alive. Schlemihl, shadowless, strides booted over hill and dale, a natural scientist, "living to himself alone." But Chamisso, after producing a book from his sufferings, hastened to outgrow his problem-child phase. He settles down, becomes the father of a family and an academician, master of his craft. Only the eternally bohemian finds that stupid. One cannot be interesting forever. Either you die of your interestingness, or you become a master. – But *Peter Schlemihl* is one of the most charming youthful works in German literature.

PLATEN

1930

PLATEN, the lyric poet, passes for a protagonist of the austere, of frigid symmetry and classic formalism. Certainly, he opposed the decline of form, castigated the times because they surrendered to a flabby romanticism. He set against all that he found bad, against such dissolution, the pure, æsthetic art-forms, immemorial and sacred. "I swore" he says, in the immortal "Morning Lament":

Ich schwöre den schönen Schwur, getreu stets zu sein
Dem hohen Gesetz, und will, in Andacht vertieft,
Voll Priestergefühl verwalten
*Dein gross Prophetenamt.**

How could he fail of this feeling? It held him up, it sustained him through the pangs and humiliations of his short life, which was at once noble and distressful, not to say wretched.

Ein Trost nur bleibt mir, dass ich jeder Bürde
Vielleicht ein Gleichgewicht vermag zu halten
Durch meiner Seele ganze Kraft und Würde.

The power and valour, by dint of which his soul should triumph over the afflictions and derogations of his life, found expression in form; he brought the feeling fully to utterance in a sonnet, in the peculiarly art-refined *parlando*, in the style of this kind of verse, of which he possessed a mastery like to no other's:

Wem Kraft und Fülle tief im Busen keimen,
Die Form beherrscht er mit gerechtem Stolze,
Bewegt sich leicht, wenn auch in schweren Reimen.
Er schneidet sich des Liedes flücht'ge Bolze
Gewandt und sicher, ohne je zu leimen,
Und was er fertigt, ist aus ganzem Holze.

* For literal translations of the verse quoted in this essay see pages 465–8.

But only lack of knowledge can confine this poet to the field of the rationally formal and rhetorical; only ignorance can assert that he lacks softness, soaringness, lyric enchantment, music, that magic breath and bloom, those accents of inspiration, which the German, of all people, praises as truly lyric. True, as time went on, song meant more and more to him the spoken word, uttered conformably to a lofty cult. But the simple and melodious, the mystical and inspirational, are also there, as I could prove if space permitted. Let me give you but one poem from this softer, if you like romantic sphere: you all know it, surely many of you by heart, as I have known it from my early years – its fame rests upon its endless riches of psychological reference. Platen wrote it at twenty-nine, when he had behind him the cadet school and the pages' academy; his abortive career as lieutenant, his student period in Würzburg and Erlangen, and his first journey to Italy, which had as its fruit the Venetian sonnets. He wrote it ten years before he died; and it says so much of him, expresses him so fully, that by this one poem – by it and its title – one might identify the writer:

Wer die Schönheit angeschaut mit Augen,
Ist dem Tode schon anheimgegeben,
Wird für keinen Dienst der Erde taugen,
Wer die Schönheit angeschaut mit Augen!
Und doch wird er vor dem Tode beben.

Ewig währt für ihn der Schmerz der Liebe,
Denn ein Tor nur kann auf Erden hoffen,
Zu genügen einem solchen Triebe:
Wen der Pfeil des Schönen je getroffen,
Ewig währt für ihn der Schmerz der Liebe!

Ach, er möchte wie ein Quell versiechen,
Jedem Hauch der Luft ein Gift entsaugen
Und den Tod aus jeder Blume riechen:
Wer die Schönheit angeschaut mit Augen,
Ach, er möchte wie ein Quell versiechen!

Ever lives for him the pain of loving. Upon the man that made this confession Goethe once commented that he had not love. The great man erred. He could look down with loftily paternal praise and blame on Platen – and on whom not? The Ansbach scion of the aristocracy was not blest with a vitality strong and enduring enough to create in the grand style. He goaded himself on by making announcements of all that he felt within him and burned to express — and thus laid himself open to the charge of empty boasting. But just that which the great and godlike one thought to deny him was precisely what he had: namely, love. It saturates that poem, it fills his whole work: melancholy, adoring love, ever and again rising to higher flights of ardour; endless, unquenchable love, which issues in death, which *is* death, because it finds no satisfaction on earth. He, an early and hopeless victim, calls it "Beauty's dart."

We all know the piquant, half-playful, half-macabre coupling of the two ideas, love and death, and how the romantic movement married them in verse. Heine too did, in his romanticizing little songs and tales. But in this poem by Platen the two ideas are linked in a way far beyond the externally and sentimentally romantic; penetrating into a soul-world the primary and fundamental formula for which is precisely these lines: "*Wer die Schönheit angeschaut mit Augen*" — "He who once his eye hath bent on Beauty." And it is a world in which the imperative to live, the laws of life, reason and morality are nothing; a world of drunken, hopeless libertinage, which is at the same time a world of the most conscious form, the most deathlike rigidity; which teaches its adept that the principle of beauty and form does not spring from the sphere of life; that its only relation to life is at most one of stern and melancholy critique: it is the relation of mind to life. It is not love and death, in the sense of their association in the mouths of wits and romantics: not that conditions the world I mean. It is the idea of beauty and death, the idea that the arrow of beauty is the arrow of death and eternal pain of yearning: only there does it find full expression. Death, beauty, love, eternity: these are language symbols for this at once platonic and intoxicatingly musical soul-miracle so full of fascination and seduction; the poem I have quoted, a ritornello like a spell, monotonously and hopelessly returning upon itself, seeks in murmured measures to descant upon this theme. And those who on earth wear the order and are the knights of beauty are knights of death.

"Tristan"! Platen wrote the word above the poem. How strange! It must have been in some peculiarly abstracted and sleepwalking state, involved in far associations, that his hand traced this title above the lines. "Significant, almost clairvoyant," a modern writer, Ernst Bertram, called it, actually in the Venetian chapter of his *Nietzsche*, where he has other good things to say of such Venetian associations and kindred matters. Did I say too much when I referred to the endless psychological riches of association in the poem? And when I expressed the view that one could identify the poet by it and its title?

Platen-Tristan: in this summation of a joyless crusader of an order devoted to death and love, one may in utter seriousness respect him. But we must give her due to Truth, Beauty's earthly sister, who, as a child of life, can see also the funny side of things, and knows how to present it in such a way that love and reverence not only are not wounded but are humanly perfected and heightened. Platen's knighthood has not only the sadness of Tristan; not in this sense alone is he a melancholy knight. He is that in a grotesque sense too, he is both touching and absurd at once, a Don Quixote, a knight of the rueful countenance.

Platen-Don-Quixote! An errant soul, driven and animated by sublime folly, by a thankless, unseasonable, impossible, embittered arrogance and pugnacity. Constantly beaten and disgraced, up to the very last minute it swears that Dulcinea del Toboso is the most beautiful damsel under the sun, though in fact she is a peasant wench – and in even more fact some ridiculous student or other, named Schmidt – or whatever. Shall we not see him thus, this poet in the most hopeless and high-minded sense, yet not ceasing to love and honour him, as we love and honour Cervantes's fantastical hero, although his creator constrains us to laugh at him?

"Count Platen," wrote Felix Mendelssohn, after meeting him in Naples, "is a little, wizened man in gold-rimmed glasses, thirty-five years old; he rather alarmed me. The Greeks looked different. He inveighed most frightfully against the Germans, but forgot that he was doing it in German." This solitary, unstable little old man, fallen out with the Fatherland, very proud and bitterly insulted, had cried out:

Anstimmen darf ich ungewohnte Töne,
Da nie dem Halben ich mein Herz ergeben:
Der Kunst gelobt' ich ganz ein ganzes Leben,
Und wenn ich sterbe, sterb' ich für das Schöne.

What should quixotry be, if not this: to be born and bred to die "for Beauty's sake"? For what is the beautiful? What does it mean to us of today, this alabaster image, this at once sweet and schoolmasterish conception of gilt-edged symmetry and regularity? What was it even then, in a time of mounting realism and the dawn of modern social ideas? The beautiful – is it that youthful knee on which, in the theatre, Pindar fell asleep to the gods? Yes, so thought Platen, thus it lay in his mind and thus did it intoxicate him: his idea of beauty was classicistic, plastic, erotic, and Platonic in its origins, the product of an absolute æsthetic thesis; as one of its priests he felt himself dedicated by fate; a naked idol of perfection with a Greek-Oriental eye-formation, before whom he knelt in abasement and agonizing longing. For his own poor, hypochondriac, and sickly physical being dissolved in shame before this heavenly image, and all that he could do was, by obstinate and feverish labour at his art, to form his soul in its image, to be worthy of it.

Du hattest mich zu dir emporgehoben,
In deinen Augen schwamm ein lichter Funken,
Der Farben schuf, den Pinsel dreinzutunken,
Den reine Dichterhände Gott geloben.

It was thus, with undistracted, Don Quixotic faith and alacrity, that he had all his life done his uttermost to be received by the god; with immense patience and devotion he had wrought out of the golden shield of language the most splendid and enduring things; he had – with little or no thanks – performed miracles of stylistic and intellectual perfection, single-handed, all in order to become worthy to fall asleep to the gods on the knee of the little Theoxenos.

We live in a twilit time of naturalist unbelief and a just dawning idealism; of recognition and new possibilities of reverence; in a time, that is, which, compared with the pre-analytic, displays a reverence more deeply graven, more full of content, for it has experienced knowledge. It is fortunate that the decisive progress which our knowledge of the human being has made in the last few decades permits us to talk with a frankness already taken for granted, about much to which an earlier deference preferred to shut its eyes. Thus, literary history, out of lack of knowledge, and with a reserve today out of date, has spoken with foolish circumlocution about the decisive fact in Platen's life, his exclusively homosexual constitution. His contemporaries, forced to admire, but repelled by the highly poetic expression of this constitution, if they did not understand it in the modern sense, at least did not fail to recognize it – least of all Heinrich Heine, who took advantage of it in a vindictive lampoon in defence of his dearest, his Christianity, to quote the *Baths of Lucca;* referring to it rather mechanically, in the sense of an aristocratic vice. Platen himself had realized this, his profoundest impulse, and then again not realized it. He suggests it, in the sense of a sacred subjection to the beautiful, as the purity and consecration of the poet to the highest he knows, in love as well; and this half-understanding, this false idea that his love was in some sense higher, instead of a love like anybody else's, only – at least in his time – with smaller prospects of happiness; this miscomprehension made him unjust and incurably bitter over the scorn and ill treatment that his glowing devotion received on almost every occasion – an embitterment which was the chief cause of his quarrel with Germany and everything German, and which drove him into self-imposed exile and lonely death.

Wo Hass und Undank edle Liebe lohnen,
Wie bin ich satt von meinem Vaterlande!

That is the perfectly clear formula of the love-and-hate he felt for his country – and very reminiscent it is of Nietzsche's emotional ambivalence towards things German. It did not prevent him, this hatred, from dedicating to the name of Germany the poetic renown of which he always so fervidly and high-heartedly dreamed.

Geschieht's, dass je den innern Schatz ich mehre,
So bleibt der Fund, wenn längst dahin der Finder,
Ein sichres Eigentum der deutschen Ehre.

I spoke of Platen's ignorance or half-ignorance of himself. But he was not insincere, he was straightforward in his work according to the measure of his knowledge, and all that Heine hints in that pamphlet about hypocrisy and mystification is wrong. To dissimulate, to conceal, for that he possessed too firm and æsthetic an acceptance of passion, of every passion; nothing is more indicative of his scorn of craven harmlessness, his fundamentally arrogant will to self-exposure, than his cry:

Stumpfsinnige, was wähnt ihr rein zu sein? Ich hörte,
Dass keine Schuld so sehr, als solch ein Sinn entweihe;
Ich fühlte, dass die Schuld, die uns aus Eden bannte,
Schwungfedern uns zum Flug nach höhern Himmeln leihe.
Noch bin ich nicht so bleich, dass ich der Schminke brauchte,
Es kenne mich die Welt, auf dass sie mir verzeihe!

His only disguise lay in his choice of the traditional forms in which he poured himself out; they gave a frame of tradition to his kind of passion. The Persian ghazal, the Renaissance sonnet, the Pindaric ode, all of them knew the youth-cult and gave it literary legitimacy. In taking them over – and with what unheard-of brilliance he shaped them anew! – the emotional content could be taken over as well, an archaizing convention with impersonal effect, and so become possible for circulation. I am convinced that his choice of the poetic forms in which he so wonderfully shone was conditioned by the source of all his ardours and anguishes. Yet not alone out of caution, not out of fearfulness as Heine thought, but above all because the strictly formal and form-plastic character of the verse forms had an æsthetic and psychological affinity with his Eros. "The degree and kind of a man's sexuality," says Nietzsche, "permeate the very loftiest heights of his intellect."

He sometimes romanticized in a way which, especially in his particular case, is not very laudable. For instance:

Doch diese Liebe möcht' ich nie besiegen,
Und weh dem Tag, an dem sie frostig endet!
Sie ward aus jenen Räumen uns gesendet,
Wo selig Engel sich an Engel schmiegen –

upon which Heine remarked that that did not mend matters – it made us think of the angels that came to Lot, and of what happened to them before his door. Well, Heine thought of them. But I like better to think of the obscure passages in the old tales of chivalry, which the man of La Mancha read and which drove the poor soul in the most literal sense to don his armour. "The profundity of the non-sensual which made prey of my senses so shook my good sense that I must make sensible moan over your beauty." Yes, a Don Quixote of love deluded in a way more grotesque than love commonly can delude, Platen, shaken by a sensuality from the depths of the non-sensual, made sensible moan over the beauty of a stable-girl, or rather the upstandingness of a quite ordinary and average youth or two – a lament which, pray remember, now and then achieved the loftiest and remotest snow-peaks of the poetic.

Ich bin wie Leib dem Geist, wie Geist dem Leibe dir!
Ich bin wie Weib dem Mann, wie Mann dem Weibe dir!
Wen darfst du lieben sonst, da von der Lippe weg
Mit ew'gen Küssen ich den Tod vertreibe dir?

What a spirit-whisper of nameless love! One must read certain letters he wrote and received, to be able to measure the fearful and pathetic comicality of the situations into which his love-quixotry plunged him. But he was too well aware of his own intellectual stature not to measure aright his anguished subjection to the nothing-but-beautiful and the humiliations he suffered every moment from it. He was aware that loving abnegation raises one above the beloved object; he knew the platonic irony of the truth that the god is in the loving, not the beloved.

Dies macht verklärt dein Auge, das meine sieht,
Wie deines Leibs Gliedmassen Unsterblichkeit
Ausdrücken –

Immortality. He perfectly knew how immensely he gave of his abundance to those poor children of men upon whom his dazzled eyes rested, whose poor lips the spirit kiss of his song sealed to immortality. But the real, the Don Quixote absurdity lies in the inevitable thanklessness that was his portion. He might ever so melodiously assure the creatures of their favoured lot and of a death more beautiful in that immortal poesy had praised them living. But there was not one among them who thought otherwise of the honour than Sancho Panza would have thought. Indeed, even though one day the world might read that the poet had chosen "him above all others," the chosen one certainly felt nothing but middle-class relief at having his name left out of the game.

I say "out of the game"; for it was a game, in just the same sense and degree as Don Quixote's fantastic exaltation. And this reckless, passionate quixotry runs through Platen's whole work, it conditions his attitude to the world and to himself. His relation to fame, to fame as a poet, for instance, which was closer to his heart than all else, and about which he boasted all the time in advance, was entirely conditioned by it. It rested upon a certain high-minded backwardness in the emotions and ideas that moved him: upon pathetic, out-of-date notions about laurel wreaths and being crowned on the Capitoline. The classic idea of the "games" plays an important role; for instance, Platen, in the truly vainglorious inscription which he wrote betimes for his own tomb, said that he had won "second prize for odes" – as though it would have occurred to anybody to offer a prize for the best ode! Was it not a Don-Quixotry of the most obstinate and ruthless kind when he forced on the German language – often with splendid effect – forms that elevated yet tortured it, such as the ghazal and the hieratic formality of the ode, which led to the use of forced accents, such as Deutsch*land*, Wahr*heit*, Nach*sicht*, and so on. It is a sad comment upon so much devotion that today nobody would take the trouble to check up on Platen's metrical perfections.

A lofty convention, like the laws of metrics, governs his idea of the poet's function, his high- and light-hearted role upon earth, as he depicts it, not without affectation, in his songs. He conceives himself as a poetic, extravagant figure, the very ideal and image of the character:

Einmal will ich, das versprech' ich, ohne Liebgekose leben,
Wann die Blumen hier im Garten nach den Tafeln Mose leben –

This arrogant pose scarcely suits with the austere melancholy of his nature. It is accepted and acted out, it seems, solely for the sake of the beautiful traditional; with all its usual accompaniments of intoxication, licence, frenzy, effeminacy, defiance of virtue, scorn of "moral judges" – together with his own "bad fame" and sensual outbursts gallantly effervescing.

Kredenzt mir Wein, auf dass berauscht wie Hafiz
Ich phantasiere wild von deiner Schönheit.

And yet all that is only the acceptably formal garment of deep and genuine passion, deep and genuine scorn for the petty, middle-class meannesses of life. It is the poetic formulation of licence, of a radical æstheticism, addressed to, and all-too-well founded on, his own nature.

Beauty, which he worshipped and has certainly every reason to worship, is indeed the anti-useful and thus the anti-moral principle, since the moral is nothing but what is useful to life. The poet-immortality with which it plays is in reality radical anti-morality, a deep bond with the beautiful, even contrary to the interests of nature; hence his forthright demand that even "the good" shall bow before the high altar of the beautiful; hence his scorn of the cowardly knave who "beautiful form has known and not replied with endless constancy of love." The mortal libertinage of his Eros unites all free and hyper-useless elements in a bond against the mean, ordinary, anxious ones of life. By this route it links up with mind and spirit; and so it comes about that the more his æstheticism lifts itself out of the sensual, the more masculine it becomes. The beautiful is now simply the humanly decent, in contrast to all mental obfuscation, all slavish pettiness and dishonour born of tyranny; it becomes the source of a humanism which, as it were circumventing nature, brings him into enthusiastic political contact with the idea of the human. It was pure demagogy that made Heine try to conventionalize the figure of his opponent into a combination of Junker and priest, only because Platen was a Count. Nothing of the sort comes out in his intellectual, artistic, or political attitude; indeed, he was entirely an ally of Heine the free-thinker. He was the same in his admirable attitude to Goethe, who exchanged knowledge for enthusiasm. "Not this suffices"!

Nicht kann ich harmlos mich in die Pflanzenwelt
Einspinnen, anschau'n kantigen Bergkristall
Sorgfältig, Freund! Zu tief ergreift mich
Menschlichen Wechselgeschicks Entfaltung.

He was a political poet after Heine's own heart. He proclaimed freedom, celebrated its martyrs, suffered like anybody else under the conditions of his time in Germany; cursed the despot who with the right hand made the sign of the Cross, whilst with the left he nailed the people to it; and declared that mob and tyranny are brothers, freedom lifts a purified people above the mob.

Wir haben Jahre zugebracht,
Im eignen Gram uns zu versenken;
Nun hat sich erst der Wunsch entfacht,
Mit klarem Geiste das zu denken,
Was dunkel nur die Zeit gedacht.

Did he perhaps hope that the socialization, the politicizing of the beautiful into the humanly worthy would raise him above himself; that his own love of freedom would end by freeing himself? In vain: the swimmer never got free of the insidious weeds that wound round and dragged him down into the depths. Others fought, anger and struggle exalted them. With him, they were dammed up, they kept stagnating in psychological embitterment, turning into a hatred of mankind, in which, with perfect clarity, he recognized the forerunner of death.

Sein Zeitalter und er scheiden sich feindlich ab,
Ihm missfällt, was erfreut Tausend, während er
Scharfschtige, finstere Blicke
In die Seele der Toren wirft.

To have death in the heart: can it be told, with more frightful or more elevated accuracy, what that means? Those wonderful psychological lines of Goethe, out of the *Harzreise*, seem to have been coined with Platen in mind: "Ah, who can heal the pangs of him whose balm turned to poison? Who out of love's fullness drank hatred of mankind? First scorned, then a scorner, he feeds secretly in unsatisfying egoism on his own virtue." This feeding on one's own virtue, this unsatisfying egoism – such precisely was Platen's tragic case. Thence came his feverish self-praise, his prickly, frosty wit, his obstinate non-acceptance of any productivity except his own, his unhappy urge to argumentation, which hampered him and smothered his great dreams. At thirty he was already showing serious organic symptoms of tension and exhaustion. After a further nine years' stress of emotions and their suppression, he died at Syracuse of a vague typhus attack which was nothing but a pretext for the death to which obviously he was devoted from the first.

Platen-Tristan, Platen-Don-Quixote. In this hour of remembrance let us pay our respects, on the soil that gave him birth, to a life of nobility and suffering, which will most certainly remain a shining mark so long as our language and our culture shall endure.

Ein jedes Band, das noch so leise
Die Geister aneinander reiht,
Wirkt fort auf seine stille Weise
Durch unberechenbare Zeit.

THEODOR STORM*

1930

It was in September 1865, four months after the death of his wife Constance – a blow to which we owe the most heart-rending poem of love and loss in the German language – that Theodor Storm visited Ivan Turgenyev in Baden-Baden, where the latter was living with his friend Madame Viardot-Garcia and had sent a cordial invitation to his German colleague. The author of *Immensee* stopped two weeks in the vicinity of the author of *First Love* and *Spring Floods;* and despite the almost unnerving melancholy the poem evinces, he displayed a remarkable receptivity for the natural and social charms of the resort. Later he kept in touch with the Russian, sending him his stories and receiving from the estate near Moscow the French version of *Smoke*. Though the correspondence is not to be compared with the Storm-Keller letters, which Keller likened to a colloquy between a cloistered Father and a neighbouring colleague on the subject of a bed of freckled pinks; still, the thought has always pleased me that they did meet, that they knew each other and had friendly intercourse, these two masters between whom the grateful eyes of a young beginning writer was never able to choose. For to him, though in such charactistically different spheres, they were linked not only by their century but by some kinship of spirit and form, in the art of evocation and painful appeal. They are, thanks to nationality, more diverse than are Storm and Keller, though even so the latter's priceless drollery is only another, more racy southern form of that German craftsmanship which Storm too represents. But if we extend the field of comparison into the human and typical, then Storm and Turgenyev assume a truly fraternal likeness; they are one and the same figure in two variations, like children of one father but born of two different mother-earths.

Very early in this century a young beginning author wrote a lyric tale whose subject was the strife within a single breast between the homeland, bourgeois, northern, sentimental and the

* For literal translations of the verse quoted in this essay see pages 469–72.

stern, reckless, icy-ecstatic world of art and intellect. The author described his hero's father as a tall gentleman, inclined to melancholy, with thoughtful blue eyes and always a wild flower in his buttonhole. In this description he departed considerably from autobiographical reality; yet it was hardly arbitrary fantasy. The figure that hovered before his eyes arose from the feeling and consciousness of the double cultural origin of the little work in which he placed it: a domestic German scene and a cosmopolitan one. The figures of the two spiritual fathers of his tale, Storm and Turgenyev, the *doux géant* as his Parisian friends called the Scythian, ran together into the "father-image" of the tall, dreamy greybeard with the wild flower in his buttonhole.

I have looked at their pictures again, the heads of these two, heavy with art and thought. In them the nineteenth-century short-story form reached its peak in definition and fulfilment. Yes, they are brother-heads, differentiated by the climate of their birth and their talent. Storm's is a sailor's refined and spiritualized; held slightly to one side, with tiny wrinkles at the corners of the dreamy, peering blue eyes. Round the mouth lies the bitterness of exacting, inevitable strain. Typical "*plattdeutsch*": one hears the rather thin, pleasantly deliberate accents of his "home," where timbre and modulation both seem to express a nervous and querulous resistance to everything that was not "home"—even to the district immediately adjacent to Husum and Hademarschen. Then Turgenyev: the Slav, the melancholic artist, not entirely without affectation. There is the drooping lock, the swimming eye, grey and deeply melting to its depths. But the medium is mundane, the suffering Chopinesque; you scent Paris, Baden-Baden, Bougival, the world; world-literature, the prose writing of Europe. Theodor Storm could not have described the betrayal of pure feeling by society sophistication, the ensnaring of Sanin by Maria Nikolayevna in *Spring Floods;* and the low comedy of the married Polosov would have been beyond him. From his pen could never come a European masterpiece like the society novel *Fathers and Sons,* with its portrayal of the type of intellectual and political nihilist. Here are precision, virtuosity, lucidity, bathed in an atmosphere of perfection. This is higher, clearer, ampler air than the grave, mist-wrapped, withdrawn atmosphere in which the Holsteiner moves, in an art kind to the mystical and uncanny, the pagan northern art of *The Rider on the White Horse*. On the other hand, it is precisely here, in that very tale, written when Storm, an old man of seventy, was already in the shadow of death, it is just here that something of primeval power is finally achieved, some combination of human tragedy with the wild mystery of nature, something dark and heavy with the greatness and unknownness of the sea – something that Turgenyev, with all his fine sensitivity to nature, could never have trusted himself to attempt. Who could deny that as psychologist and story-teller he had the more definite, light-handed literary skill, shot through with satire and critique? But the Prose Poems, with all their atmosphere, do not outweigh Storm's lyric work, those poems of love and parting and memories, every syllable saturated with intense feeling, softness held in check by a sensitiveness for truth which saves it from sentimentality and all in all bears witness to the essentially masculine character of art.

I must go a little further into the poems. For, together with *Immensee*, they condition the picture of the literary artist which I cherished when I was young, before there had come into my field of vision his stern and steady growth up to old age, the conquest of youthful softness and moodiness, his development into a writer of tragic tales in the grand manner. In this ten times sorted and sifted lyrical treasure, gem stands almost next to gem. There is a constant, thrilling, concentrated power of expression about life and the emotions, a skill at shaping in the simplest form, which in certain poems – however old you are, however often you read them – unfailingly bring the catch in the throat as you are seized by that sweet and ruthless and woeful sense of life – for the sake of all this it was that the youth of sixteen or seventeen so clung to these accents. A French writer once remarked that even the word "art" was by the very sound of it remote from good nature and gentleness; it was the shriek of a bird of prey as it pounced. It is probably true, and Storm's lyrics show it, that art, even in its mildest, most candid and placable phases, takes you by the throat.

However tempted, I will not give examples, I will not quote, for there is no space. It is enough if I say that never and nowhere has the human been expressed with more penetrating simplicity and purity than in poems like "*Einer Tote*" ("A Dead Woman") or "*Spruch des Alters*" ("Saying of Old Age"), "Thy Comrade in Duties," "My Youngest Child," or the one simply called "Lot," which forms a less witty and more humble pendant to Heine's "*Es war eine alte Geschichte.*" In the same way one may recognize, in the admirable twelve-line picture "A Stranger" the forerunner of George's sixteen-line "The Stranger," though the latter's forms are more austere, its feeling more dæmonic. In "*Verirrt*" ("Astray") there is a ring of Herr Walther ("*Ein Vöglein singt so süsse*"); but the artificially archaic folk-song pattern, heralded a few times in the titles, retires in favour of an entirely dominant modernness of language, a cultural, lyrical production with a personal and unforgettable accent, of which at least half a dozen pieces are worthy to stand beside the best and highest in feeling and language and possess the unmistakable traits of immortality.

Again, where is the sound, and how could its compacted magic ever fade away, of the four strophes of "*Abseits*" ("Out of the Way"), with their world-forgotten summer-noontide mood and scent of warm growing things? Or of "*Meerestrand*" ("The Beach"): the Haff, the air like white cotton-wool, the evening light, with islands dreamlike in the mist; the seething sound of the wet mud, the lonely bird-cry, all the monotonous, timeless "So it was always"; the romantic, mysterious final cadence. The finality, simplicity, aptness of the picture are beyond all praise — and next it is another little miracle like in kind, "In the Wood": the vision of the little wood-fairy, sitting spun round with summer magic beneath the drooping boughs:

Sie sitzt im Thymiane,
Sie sitzt in lauter Duft;
Die blauen Fliegen summen
Und blitzen durch die Luft.

Der Kuckuck lacht von ferne,
Es geht mir durch den Sinn:
Sie hat die goldnen Augen
Der Waldeskönigin.

That is not marble nor the gilded monument — it is the most gossamer weave possible — yet it stands there forever.

In the same rank belong: "Hyacinth," elegant, tender, rich like the notes of a cello with feeling, melancholy, love-weariness; with its endlessly symbolic refrain: "*Ich möchte schlafen, aber du musst tanzen*"; "Over the Heath," with its rhythmic pilgrim tread echoing dully out of the earth, the convincing accents of the shuddering, sighing "Nevermore!"

Wär' ich hier nur nicht gegangen im Mai!
Leben und Liebe — wie flog es vorbei!

And then a double strophe that I have always especially admired, incomparable instance of Storm's refinement of sensitivity; the lines about the white feminine hand, which cannot but confess what the lips will not:

Die Hand, an der mein Auge hängt,
Zeigt jenen feinen Zug der Schmerzen,
Und dass in schlummerloser Nacht
Sie lag auf einem kranken Herzen.

What distinction of delicacy and feeling! The "And that," which as well as the previous noun depends on "shows," has about it something French, peculiarly suiting the subtle, yes, over-subtle stamp of the whole.

Let us pay honour to truth and extenuate nothing. Storm's own accents have lingered rather miserably on in German poesy or what passes for it; it has, rather regrettably, one must confess, made a school. From him, from his "*Nun sei mir heimlich zart und lieb*," and so on, much worthless and puerile stuff has come, much middle-class, gilt-edged rapture, not in the least like the mountain springs whence he drew his song. But could not one accuse the *Buch der Lieder* of like consequences? "By their fruits ye shall know them" is a terrible saying, and not always valid. If we are bent on being ruthless, we must make the seductive responsible for the mischief it brought about without intending to. But it is very hard to pin it down, even so; and the more you compare, the less you succeed. What followed after Storm, what came from him, is not Storm: in power, pretensions, subtlety, precision, personality, sustained ability, his own departs from all the flabby bourgeois stuff that thought to "tack on to" him – and, in the same measure, merely by his artistic merit he stands apart from the late-romantic dilettantism with which his time pullulated; not only from that but also from the highly gifted decadence of the same period, from Geibel, even from Heyse. There have been stormy revolutions in our literature, which have caused a complete change of air, sweeping its "fruits" into oblivion. He is a master, he remains.

I mentioned his love of home, his prepossession for it, his – so to speak – homesickness. Fontane, by comparison an alert man of the world and cosmopolite, called it Storm's "*Husumerei*" (Husumania). To characterize it unsympathetically, there is indeed something wilfully complaining in it, the kind of poor-spirited cant at which Goethe's lines were levelled:

In die Welt hinaus!
Ausser dem Haus
Ist immer das beste Leben;

Wem's zu Hause gefällt,
Ist nicht für die Welt –
Mag er leben!

But the Gascon of the Brandenburg Mark, whose work – at least in *Effi Briest* – is reckoned as world-literature, took care, despite an occasional grimace, not to judge his slower, heavier colleague in the sense of Goethe's words. Well he knew what the art of poetry possessed in him: more, loftier, more authentic, in his own keen-sighted judgment, than in the more elegant Heyse, who as a matter of fact did not himself lack admiration for the man of Hademarschen. Storm's artistry, high in quality, deep with inner experience, has nothing to do with simpleness or provinciality, nothing with what we once for quite a while called "domestic art." The stylistic heights, the purity to which the somewhat thin vernacular of his native tongue attained, sharply distinguish him from the comfortable mediocrity of that sphere; it commands a positive and universal adequateness of creative composition; while his "temperament" still possesses full romantic intellectuality and intensity, remote from any lapse into the sentimental. His exaggerated feeling for home has about it something that is strange in a poet; a philistine might find it hysterical. In essence it is longing, nostalgia, unsatisfiable by any reality, for it is addressed altogether to the past, the lost and sunken backward of time. He himself observes:

Liegt eine Zeit zurück in meinem Leben,
Wie die verlorene Heimat schaut sie aus,
Nach der im Heimweh die Gedanken streben.

There it is: temperamental, sentimental if you like, in a somewhat morbid sense – that is if we may so characterize this equation of past and home. In any case, it is a phenomenon frequent in literature; for seldom do the present and the joy of youth result in a poem, whereas the memory, the yearning after it, often. In vain does one search in Storm's lyrical work for the immediate glorification of the youthful May day which the Novemberish "*Vorbei*" celebrates in retrospect:

Heitere Jahre,
Glückliche Tage –
Wie Frühlingsfluten
Seid ihr verrauscht!

That is in the old romantic key — in which Turgenyev's creative work is also pitched. But in Storm it is sometimes concentrated to the point of being unnerving; it ends by being the expression of an obstinate and lachrymose psychology which finds the present nothing but a chill estrangement. He says of *Immensee:*

Aus diesen Blättern steigt der Duft des Veilchens,
Das dort zu Haus auf unsren Heiden stand,
Jahraus und -ein, von welchem keiner wusste,
Und das ich später nirgends wieder fand.

The noble simplicity of those cadences captivates the senses, it intoxicates, disarms, by virtue of just that interweaving and mingling of the two emotional concepts, home and the past, into a wild-violet perfume of endless nostalgic sensitivity. It is human feeling, nothing else, when he tells how his heart clings to the "grey town by the sea," that poverty-stricken Husum, set in its harsh, monotonous, mist-wrapped landscape; explaining that even so "youth's charm forever and aye" rests smiling on her. But the simple human leaves off and the mystery begins, in a poem like "Lost," likewise a masterpiece in a technical sense, uttered in one marvellous breath from beginning to end:

Was Holdes liegt mir in dem Sinn,
Das ich vor Zeit einmal besessen;
Ich weiss nicht, wo es kommen hin,
Auch, was es war, ist mir vergessen. . . .

and ending:

In grünem Schatten lag der Ort —
Wenn nur der weite Raum nicht trennte,
Wenn ich nur dort hinüber könnte,
Wer weiss! — Vielleicht noch fänd' ich's dort.

"If I could just get back again!" That is perfect Husumania; it has almost nothing to do with the soil, it is "temperament" in the purest cult, the utmost sublimation; nostalgia as idea, home as "mystery."

I have dwelt upon Storm's sensitivity and mental subtlety, his excessive degree of "temperament," and even spoken of a slight morbidness, in order to forestall a charge of bourgeois commonplace or sentimentality, of intellectual philistinism. Fontane, indeed, spoke of provincial simplicity, but the phrase does not really cover the case. The element of recklessness, eccentricity, irregularity, hostility to the normal and successful, native to the constitution of the artist, is more perceptible in Storm than it is in the amiably correct Fontane. With Storm, really, nothing is correct, however temptingly the vision of correctness may have hovered before his eyes, however he may have struggled to change his nature and model his life upon such a wish-image.

For instance, there is the family, the hearth-stone, kernel and core of the home. Storm loved it, he set the greatest store by it; family life was, in his own words, "the holiest depths of his soul." In letters to literary friends, for instance Keller, he never tires of regaling his correspondent with pæans upon domesticity, with faithful descriptions of afternoon teas, birthdays, Christmases, New Year's Eves — unconscious of the risk he ran of boring the tippling old bachelor in Zürich. And how was it, in sober truth, with the domestic idyll? Undoubtedly, it was very nice. His cousin, Constance Esmarch, whom he had married as a young lawyer of twenty-nine, made him a capital wife, long-suffering above all things, for as a husband he was what he had been as wooer, a tremendous pedagogue and schoolmaster, bent on improving her Segeburg girls'-school education, that there might be perfect intellectual communion between them. She had to be forbearing and understanding, for there was much to bear and understand; certainly he was ungrateful and unjust when one day he wrote to her: "You teach me, slowly but thoroughly, that one should not let his heart cling to a human being." We may take it for granted that there had never been passionate love between them. After her death, which inspired some of his most moving poems, he wrote: "Our hands lay in each other more in a feeling of tranquil sympathy. That was all very good and beautiful; but the passion for the living broke over me when the deceased was still my wife." Who is this "living" one, who becomes his second wife a year after Constance's passing? Her name was Dorothea Jensen; during his honeymoon she came to his room with her sister Cecilie: a thirteen-year-old girl, a slender, delicate blonde. He was embarrassed to find that this child loved him, and that, for his part, she has for him "a certain peculiar charm."

This peculiar charm, not quite suitable for a newly married man, is a repetition of an erotic episode of his student years, when he fell in love with an even younger child, the ten-year-old Berta von Buchau, in Hamburg. He devoted years to a poetic cult of this young creature, who did not care much about him at best, and at fifteen rejected his "frightened to death" wooing. This love of the immature does not seem quite "correct" either. Youths more often fall in love with mature women than with ten-year-olds. But we are dealing with a poet, and "about that child"—in other words, the unfolding blossom Do, who after the marriage was often in the house—"there was that intoxicating atmosphere which I could not resist." Constance was aware of it. She was also aware of little Jensen's love for her husband, and she behaved admirably—much better than did he, who was not even faithful in his unfaithfulness. Settled comfortably down in the passionless idyll of his married life, he egotistically forgot the girl he actually loved. Lonely, remote, resigned, "often in depressing dependence," she pines and fades—and he has not a thought, scarcely even human sympathy, to spare for her. It is Constance who has. She tries to get her to come to the house; she encourages her to weep herself out; she, the wife, still in perfectly good health, actually designates Dorothea as the second wife of her susceptible but forgetful husband.

He was endlessly attached to Constance, and Dorothea endlessly to him. She really "of all human beings wanted only him alone" whose feeling for her had slumbered, but waked again, or thought it did, when he was free. Was not Dorothea in a way bequeathed to him by the dear departed? He "cannot bear it" that life goes on, heedless, forgetful, while the moonbeams send their shafts down into her grave and play upon her coffin. But to be for long a widower, that he cannot bear either. There is only an interval for decency's sake and after that he marries Dorothea Jensen and has from her an eighth child to add to the seven from his Segeburg wife.

Was this marriage as sunny and full of domestic bliss as the first? Well, it seems to have displayed the imperfections of all earthly things. The north-German afternoon-tea atmosphere, the birthdays and feast-days were all there; but if the shadow of slumbering passions had lain upon the first marriage, the second was darkened by a sense of guilt. There were, as the biography puts it, "torturing discords" as a consequence of the past; and Dorothea became almost melancholy because Theodor would not let the children call her Mother, she must be "Aunt Do" to them. And then the eldest son. . . .

Storm loved this Hans of his with his whole heart. "Still and deep like a forest pool," he calls the lad, a true poet-child. But certain "peculiarities" become apparent, sometimes "very serious"; there comes an evening when the father looks at the handsome sleeping boy and ponders gloomily whether there may not be a strain of madness there. The poet-child becomes a drunkard, a hopeless case, unfit for life. The father's blood curdles with horror as he realizes that here is a case that only death can cure. This is the tragedy on which he so often dwelt, of which he so often spoke. His conception of the tragic was modern, not philological-antique. He would hear naught of guilt or punishment, certainly not of the "hero's" own guilt. "We atone," he said, "much oftener in life for the general guilt of which we are a part, the guilt of humanity and the time, society's guilt . . . the guilt of inheritance and the inborn and for the frightful things that come of them, against which we can do nothing, for the unavoidable limitations and so on. He who falls in the struggle, he is the true tragic hero." — Well, in the case of poor Hans, there can be no talk of inheritance: his father was not a drunkard but a poet with an irresistible inclination for certain intoxicating charms; a poet who, in a tale of marvellously grave and inexorable beauty, *Carsten Curator*, left a touching memorial to the sad lot of the son and the bewildered father-conscience. Being a poet is the most viable form of the "incorrectness" we are discussing.

The details of Storm's life are in all the encyclopædias. I content myself with rounding out with some further traits the picture I have here given.

I have already said much about Storm's temperament. The other and accompanying side of it is his sensuality. But the two go together, they are essentially the same thing: "temperament" is, so to speak, sensuality with blue eyes that have a tendency to grow moist. "I am a strongly sensual, passionate nature," he says, with some pride; and there are two things to be mentioned in connection with the statement. The first is that he made it in a letter dictated by him to his niece Helene; the second, that he was then fifty-six years old. The sensuality expresses itself not only as an inward bond with nature, vegetative sympathy; it comes out in the love poems as well: sometimes clear and joyous, sometimes as an uneasy, sultry sweetness, which poetizes the sinful in proper bourgeois style:

Sie war doch sonst ein wildes Blut;
Nun geht sie tief in Sinnen,
Trägt in der Hand den Sommerhut
Und duldet still der Sonne Glut
Und weiss nicht, was beginnen.

That is a specimen of his peculiar skill at portraying the burgeoning of the senses; a picture issuing out of a profounder excitation than his native simplicity would betray. It is that which makes him find such thrillingly urgent words for the sacred shame of surrender:

Du fühlst, wir können nicht verzichten;
Warum zu geben, scheust du noch?
Du musst die ganze Schuld entrichten,
Du musst, gewiss, du musst es doch.

The gratitude of the aging man for a last, late visitation of joyous intoxication has never been put with simpler effectiveness than in "Once More," where the transcending symbol of the "red rose passion" appears. The deathly hopelessness and helplessness, the anxiety of love –

Warum duften die Levkoien so viel schöner bei der Nacht?
Warum brennen deine Lippen so viel röter bei der Nacht?

the hopeless remorse of feeling forbidden:

Du stehst am Herd in Flammen und Rauch,
Dass die feinen Hände dir sprangen;
Du hast es gewollt, ich weiss es wohl,
Weil mein Auge daran gehangen. . . .

It is all expressed in Storm's poems, with the purest, most unforgettable lyric power. And if the emotion is stamped as sinful and proscribed, as in "*Geschwisterblut*" ("Brother and Sister") with its

. . . dass wir beisammen sind,
Mein Bruder, will nicht taugen . . .

yet it too at bottom is in the service of a romantically deeper glorification of passion, the same affirmation, actually, which bursts, with completely unchristian, not at all romantic exultation from the lines:

Wer je gelebt in Liebesarmen,
Der kann im Leben nie verarmen,
Und müsst' er sterben fern, allein,
Er fühlte noch die sel'ge Stunde,
Wo er gelebt an ihrem Munde,
Und noch im Tode ist sie sein.

Storm, in fact, has a trace, or more than a trace, of north-German paganism; above and beyond his artist temperament, it explains his wholly unbourgeois, free and positive relation to the sensual. And both are connected closely with his native love of home. We must remember that he was born in a sphere late and shallowly Christianized, which knows religion only as tribal piety and cult of the dead ("For the dead have belonged to it too"): this Frisian Thule, lying in furthest and mistiest remoteness from the Mediterranean homeland of faith in Jesus Christ. With its lips, even with its consciousness, it may confess that belief; but its roots and its ways lie firmly and faithfully fixed in the primitive pagan. As a child, however strange it may seem, Storm heard little or nothing about Christianity at home. The man was never a believer; in the poem "Crucifixus" he displays an antipathy to the sign of the Cross which reminds one of Mephisto's

I realize it is a prejudice;
Anyhow, there it is: I do not like it.

And at forty-six, in lines of unmistakable meaning, he expresses his concern to have priests keep away from his funeral, it being unsuitable to have Protestants, when he lay in the bonds of silence, preach to that which he once was. Any belief in resurrection, however familiar it must have been to the nature-lover by its origins in the mysteries of vegetation, he steadfastly rejected, even in hours when the temptation to yield to it must have been strongest, as at the death of his wife:

Da diese Augen nun in Staub vergehen,
So weiss ich nicht, wo wir uns wiedersehen.

In this contempt for a consolation not worth believing in, there speaks also a temporal element, the stout-hearted pessimism of his time, the natural-science materialism of the nineteenth century. But that was mainly on the surface. Deeper down lay his native northern paganism — and that of course made him a bit of an anti-Semite too, not consciously or fundamentally, since his training and his humanity, the broad-mindedness of his century, and his personal experience were against it. Yet emotionally and instinctively, one might say, he was. It is a pertinent fact that the Holsteiner never got the smallest assent from the Allemannian Gottfried Keller. Storm had been annoyed at a slighting remark by Georg Ebers, eminent Egyptologist and bad poet, on the subject of the short story as an art form; and had written an irritated letter to Keller about Ebers, "raised to the throne by the crowd and his own kind, the Jews." Keller coolly retorted that he knew nothing about Ebers's Jewish origins; but it did not take a Jew to make stupid remarks, and for every loud and yelping Jew there were two Christians of the same kidney. I tell the story to point out the difference in the psychology of the two spheres. It is good to make clear the associations involved: the blond, anti-Semite northerner is consistent to the very end, even in a personal case of the highest artistic refinement, however much the man in Zürich may have wondered at it.

He found other things to wonder at in the character of his northern friend: for instance, a leaning towards superstition and spooks, another sign of his pre-Christian origins, which the clearer, crisper, more southern perceptions of Meister Gottfried found quite incomprehensible – indeed, he took occasion to chide his fellow artist on the point. A tale like "Renate" he did not really like – if you read it you can understand why – neither the witch nor the rats were to his taste; still less so from the point of view of reason and self-control was the attitude of the author of *Death on the White Horse*, that admirable tale. It was equivocal and irresponsible, Keller found, in its view of the supernatural; that ghostly hide-and-seek in the fog was not permissible, intellectually or artistically. But what did he want? That is the north, that is the kindness of the poet for pagan superstition – and certainly it looks contradictory enough in an enlightened and sceptical son of the nineteenth century. But post-Christian enlightenment is no protection against superstition, if one has skipped the Christian stage.

As an artist Storm's folk- and pagan sympathy with the supernatural and ghostly, to which he always concedes a certain reality, comes out plainly and powerfully in his short stories. I mentioned "Renate"; but "Neighbour on the Left," with the sombre and horrible figure of old Jensen, belongs in the same category; and he often drew the mood and matter of his tales from old pagan chronicles and claptrap. In his young days he had got printed a collection of ghost-stories; which, however, he did not include in his collected works. Yet the pleasure he had in telling such tales at the delectable tea-hour continued into his old age. In his verse there is a mildly uncanny flavour, a sort of refinement on the superstitious, and even approaching the spiritualistic. "Oh, to the Dead be Faithful" is such a poem, admirable for the fine suggestiveness with which it hearkens to the toneless babble of departed souls and arouses a tender, solemn pity for their anguished efforts to make a loving word cross over the "fallen bridge." "There Is a Whisper in the Night" also belongs to this highly sensitive sphere.

Ich fühl's, es will sich was verkünden
Und kann den Weg nicht zu mir finden.

This touching, uncannily simplifying "something" is very genuine.

Sind's Liebesworte, vertraut dem Wind,
Die unterwegs verwehet sind?
Oder ist's Unheil aus künftigen Tagen,
Das emsig drängt sich anzusagen?

How apt and good is the *emsig* (busily)! As good as the mixture of religious and organic mystery in the closing lines depicting the death of his wife:

Der Atem Gottes wehte durchs Gemach,
Dein Kind schrie auf, *und dann warst du hinüber.*

Keller wrote him that the concessions to the mystical in the *Schimmelreiter* threatened to becloud the clear picture of the consciously and responsibly acting characters. That is humanism; and Keller might be certain that his friend would not be inaccessible to such an appeal. Superstition is only one manifestation of unbelief, and not the most serious. At bottom Storm's lack of Christianity is humanistic; one finds in his work and his life all the ingredients of humanistic conviction and position: æsthetic pride, which honours and loves the good, not on account of any hope of an after life, or for the sake of reward and recompense, but out of human decency; the confiding sensuousness which animates with classic charm such a pleasing, free, and gay little work as the *Psyche;* and, finally, that scepticism which unites culture and virility in a way peculiar to humanism alone. "The doubt in fists of honest men," he said, "it bursts the gates of hell." Nothing could be more humanistic. And the virility of the decided scepticism which speaks in the lines:

Schlug erst die Stunde, wo auf Erden
Dein holdes Bildnis sich verlor,
Dann wirst du niemals wieder werden,
So wie du niemals warst zuvor . . .

is repeated in his whole career, a trait of honest stout-heartedness which is perhaps the finest and most edifying thing in his character.

Der Eine fragt: Was kommt danach?
Der Andre: Ist es recht?
Und also unterscheidet sich
Der Freie von dem Knecht.

This sublimating transference of an old-German social relation into ethical terms is perfect Storm. He was a free man; despite all his softness and sensibility a man of defiant brow, as he showed at the beginning of the fifties, when Husum became Danish and round about him everybody served the foreigner; but he, incapable of adapting himself, shook the dust from his feet and went to Prussia. We owe to this voluntary exile undertaken out of sheer love of home the admirable "Farewell," the closing stanzas of which, quivering with profound sincerity, are the purest and most compelling expression ever uttered by true German patriotism. In just this same vein of free and upright humanity he wrote some rhymes for his sons to memorize, the pedagogic effectiveness of which is extraordinary; I can bear witness to the way the sayings can get into a boy's blood:

Was du immer kannst, zu werden,
Arbeit scheue nicht und Wachen;
Aber hüte deine Seele
Vor dem Karriere-Machen.

There will always be youth who find this teaching the word of salvation and as such will take its measures to heart with filial gratitude.

That his virility was not of a thick-skinned type needs no telling. Death, whose religious palliations he rejected, which to him simply meant the end, *sans phrase*, the hanging sword, the tax we must pay for the birth which was thrust upon us, occupied and darkened his thoughts from early on, and without cease. One might even speak of hypochondria and morbidness. He said, indeed, in verse, that he awaited calmly what that dark hour would vouchsafe him, for annihilation must be "worth something too." But this tranquillity did not mean much; and from the abyss of nothingness a wave of horror would sweep over him, of which he was probably not unconscious one hour of his life. Few poets have given such uncannily delicate and exact expression as that in the three strophes of "Beginning of the End," to those earliest intimations of death, the first insight into the oncoming inevitable, the first awareness of that gentle yet resistless laying-on. Another poem, unrhymed, free, full of trepidation, written obviously in an actual attack of dread of annihilation, describes death as the exhaustion of life and hope, as a falling by the way — and old eternal night buries us, after all our wrestling, striving, fearing, hoping — "together with all our dreams and longings," with that wordless pity which is the most awe-inspiring of all, but yet the truth, for all the rest are life's dreams . . . "that in the end one drifts away lonely and is lost"; "dread of the night of being forgotten, from it can be no escape"; he feels and tastes it all, over and over, clothes it in words for his children, saying: "That I shall no longer know about you, can do nothing more for you, that is frightful!"

They are a poet's fears. True, death is always the same; yet it does not always mean the same, its metaphysical weight varies. The woman, ideally, dies more easily than the man, for she is more nature than he and less person. Art surely is the best means of realizing the ego. If it go hand in hand with pessimistic opinions, with humanistic, natural-science paganism, and if the ego is not a spirit lofty enough to elect, like Goethe, its own aristocratic immortality, then the thought of death is hard to bear. But of course it is only the thought; in the end the actual event affects us all pretty much the same: the uncomplicated ego as well as the one which has at times reached a high pitch of realization. The dread and horror pass, and in peaceful, half-dreamy bewilderment we mostly murmur: "Now I will go to sleep."

Storm lived almost to one-and-seventy. His ailment was the local affliction that plays a fateful part in one of his most powerful tales: "A Confession": cancer of the stomach. He rose grandly to the occason and demanded that the doctor be frank with him as man to man. But taken at his word, he collapsed and gave himself over to gloom. It was clear to those about him that he would not finish the *White Horse*, the finest and boldest thing he had ever ventured on. "Children, this won't do," they said, and put their heads together to deceive the aged poet, who as an artist stood in a Tacitean-Germanic *sera iuventus*, but as a man had overestimated his strength. His brother Emil, a physician, held a consultation with two colleagues; after which science pronounced that the verdict of cancer was all nonsense, the stomach ailment not malignant. Storm believed the tale at once. His spirits rebounded; he spent a capital summer, in the course of which he celebrated his seventieth birthday with the good Husumers in festive mirth. Also he brought

Death on the White Horse to a triumphant conclusion, thus elevating to a height never before reached his conception of the short story as the epic sister of the drama.

I was bent on giving this little account as a conclusion to my tale. The masterpiece with which Storm crowned his life-work was a product of merciful delusion. The capacity to let himself be deluded came to him out of the will to live and finish the extraordinary work of art.

THE OLD FONTANE

1910

A NEW volume of Theodor Fontane's letters has been published—something quite enchanting. We now possess two volumes of letters to his family and two volumes of letters to his friends. Are there any more? They should be published. I mean particularly the utterances of his later life, letters written when he was an old man; for, compared with them, the letters of his young and middle years are unimportant. Does it not seem as though he had to grow old, very old, in order to fulfil himself completely? Just as there are youths born to be youths only, fulfilling themselves in early life and not maturing, certainly not growing old; so it would seem that there are other temperaments whose only appropriate age is old; who are, so to speak, classic old men, ordained to show humanity the ideal qualities of that last stage of life: benignity, kindness, justice, humour, and shrewd wisdom—in short a recrudescence on a higher plane of childhood's artless unrestraint. Fontane's was such a temperament. And it seems that he had been aware of it, had been in haste to get old, so that he might be old for a long time. In 1856, at the age of thirty-seven, he writes to his wife: "By the fact that I am beginning to take pleasure in music, I see clearly that I am getting old. Music and the beautiful lines of a statue begin to gratify me—the senses grow more refined and the first prerequisite of pleasure is: no strain! It is quite different when one is young." Twenty-three years later he writes to Hertz, his publisher: "I am only at the beginning. There is nothing behind me, everything is ahead, which is both fortune and misfortune at the same time. Misfortune too. For it is not agreeable to be known at the age of fifty-nine as 'a very little doctor.'" Fourteen years later he produces his masterpiece.

Let us look at his portraits: the youthful one in the first volume of the letters to his friends, and the late profile in the posthumous volume. Compare the pale, sickly, sentimental, somewhat insipid countenance of long ago with the splendid, virile head of the old man, his kindly, merry, penetrating eye; on his toothless mouth under the bushy white beard a smile of understanding gaiety such as one may note on certain portraits of old gentlemen of the eighteenth century. No no can doubt when this man, this mind, reached its highest point, or at what age he arrived at the consummation of his individual powers.

The later portrait shows the Fontane of the collected works and the *Letters*, old Briest, old Stechlin, it shows us the immortal Fontane. The mortal Fontane was, from all one hears, not so consummate; he must sorely have disappointed people at times. He was seventy when he spoke to his daughter about the strength and resilience which he felt was even more essential to enjoyment than to work; he confessed that the question: "What is the good of it all?" threatened to engulf him entirely. But apparently he only imagined that he ever had this kind of resilience and he had presumably forgotten that the querulous quietism of the "famous question" had troubled him more or less at all times. "To amuse yourself here," the thirty-seven-year-old Fontane writes from Paris, "you should possess certain good and certain bad qualities, none of which are mine. First of all, you should know French; a great virtue, which I do not possess. Then one ought to be a roué, play games of chance, run after the girls, make assignations, smoke Turkish tobacco, know how to handle a billiard cue, and so on. The man who has and knows naught of all this, he is a lost soul; he would better pack his trunks after he has looked on at the merry-go-round and made his cultural pilgrimage to the Louvre and Versailles." This is a somewhat morose dictum coming from a man at the height of his powers, upon whom the charms of Paris are playing for the first time in his life. But it is the opinion of a man living under intellectual pressure, absorbed by the duty to produce, and driven to think of pleasure with ill nature and ill will. And it is, above all, the dictum of a constitution which, though wiry, and destined to produce masterpieces late in life, was tortured by nerves; on the whole, not suited to youth, but attaining harmonious development only in old age, when no "resilience" is required of a man, either by others or by himself—a time in which the question: "What is the good of it all?" had become natural, socially acceptable, and therefore a sympathetic attitude of mind.

Fontane's nervous constitution must have been rather like Wagner's; for the latter, notwithstanding the fact that he could be lively to the point of foolishness at times, seems to have had a feeling of well-being only as an exception, throughout his long and vastly productive life; Wagner, constipated, melancholy, and sleepless, tormented generally, at the age of thirty finds himself in a condition where he sits down to weep for fifteen minutes at a time; he is afraid he may die before he finishes *Tannhäuser*. At the age of thirty-five he considers himself too old to undertake the execution of his plan for the Nibelung saga; he is constantly exhausted, "finished" every other minute; at forty "thinks of death daily" – and at seventy will set to work to write *Parsifal*. The difference in temperaments is, however, considerable; in the case of Fontane, everything is more moderate. Yet his letters bear witness to his easy exhaustion, his inner feeling of harassment. Obviously he did not believe that he would ever reach old age. He feels himself aging at thirty-seven; at fifty-seven he thinks himself at the goal. He has attained "all earthly happiness"; he has loved, has married, has got children, received two decorations and been put in the encyclopædia. Only two things are lacking: to be named privy councillor and to die. "I am sure of the one, and the other I can do without." Two years later there is an annoying incident in the theatre: "at bottom only a trifle; and yet for about a quarter of an hour I felt as if I could not budge from the place. My heart beat violently, I had severe pain round my loins. . . . Nervous I have always been – but not like that. And then I tell myself: What do you want? Life is behind you; most other men of fifty-eight are played out even worse." He is used up, life is behind him, and all that he will still be able to give the world is a mere eighteen volumes, each one up to *Effi Briest* better than the one before.

In one of the letters dating from the seventies, during a marital disagreement, he tries to explain his nervous irritability and moroseness towards his wife: "When I cannot get ahead with my work," he writes, "or have the feeling something has miscarried, it affects my spirits; when I am oppressed like that I cannot be obliging, lively, adaptable, and charming." But he was probably one of those whose life task seems to grow to heroic proportions because it seems to themselves that they never get ahead; who attain perfection because they always feel they are unsuccessful. Charming though his letters are, I have not met anyone who knew him personally and found him lively, adaptable, or charming. People remember him as a "cranky" old gentleman who displayed very little joyous overwhelming desire to create. A lady who met him at a resort told me that in answer to her question how he had got on with his work that day, he replied: "Shocking badly. I sat in the arbour here and for an hour and a half not an idea occurred to me. And just when it was about to begin and dribble a little, the children came and made a noise; and that was the end of work for the day." The lady made a derogatory remark about this kind of creative gift. In a man supposedly talented, engaged in writing as a profession, such a confession was simply shameful. Probably the old man would have been inclined to agree; he was modest, he thought well enough of himself, but certainly did not consider himself great. And although he was by this time and by training a member of that heroic European generation to which Bismarck, Moltke, William I, Helmholtz, Wagner, Menzel, Zola, Ibsen, and Tolstoy belonged, he was without that pretence or exaggerated "selfness," that view of one's ego in the light of immortality, that megalomania which shattered the nerves of the sensitive geniuses of the 1870's.

The word "dribble" already appears in a letter dating from the fifties. "I surely have a poetic nature, more than thousands of others who worship themselves for possessing it; but I have not a great nor a pure poetic temperament. It only dribbles along." Here too, as everywhere, he refers to himself without unpleasant humility, indeed, but quietly, simply, almost with resignation. It is the key of the words he used in December 1885, when the old man, almost a shadow, standing supported on his stick on the steps at San Souci, pronounced on the standing and rank of the German poet.

"Und sein Metier?"
"Schriftsteller, Majestät. Ich mache Verse!"
Der König lächelte: "Nun hör' Er, Herr,
Ich will's Ihm glauben; keiner ist der Tor,
Sich dieses Zeichens ohne Not zu rühmen,
Dergleichen sagt nur, wer es sagen muss,
Der Spott ist sicher, zweifelhaft das andere.
Poète allemand! . . ."

"And what's your calling?"
"Writer, Your Majesty. I scribble verses."
The King could not forbear to smile. "Indeed,
I do believe you, sir! For only fools
Would boast of such a trade, or even speak of it
Unless they were obliged to. Ridicule
Will be your portion, not much else, I fear,
Poète allemand!"

The letters say the same thing in prose somewhere: "It is the same old story: a man who simply must be a writer will be one. He will finally feel that he is in the only proper place for him;

and in that feeling will find comfort and even happiness. But the others, not born to it, would better leave it alone." A dictum that ought to be set down in the commonplace book of all the young folk who come to ask whether they possess "talent"; for all those of the tribe of poor Wechsler, who was buried in July 1893, and of whom Fontane wrote to Rodenberg: "Such lives always make a tragic impression on me; but the feeling is not unmixed. Many others are mingled with it, such as: 'Why did the fool not stay behind his counter?' and so forth. It sounds harsh, particularly coming from a man who once stood behind a counter himself. And still, I am right." A man who can think so objectively as that must have been inwardly quite sure of himself, in spite of the "dribbling," when he left the counter of Rose's pharmacy. Or was he like so many of us who, daring greatly, not caring whether it be for good or ill, left long ago some counter or other to pledge ourselves to the spirit and the Word? Or as in early times young men went to follow the drums, out of idleness, light-headedness, or the impossibility of living in a bourgeois world? At any rate, Fontane knew that even when he was already somebody, indeed when (in one special field, the ballad) he marched at the head of the procession, many still spoke and thought of him as he did of poor Wechsler.

His life, his drab, distressful life, is sketched incidentally in the letters. "Without fortune, without family backing, without proper education and knowledge, without robust health, I entered life equipped only with a certain poetic talent and an ill-fitting pair of trousers, always baggy at the knees. And now picture to yourself how, out of a certain natural necessity, I had to fare. I might even add a certain Prussian necessity, which is much worse. Of course there were good times too, solacing, hopeful times, with the consciousness of one's own worth growing ever stronger. But on the whole I may say that I was always exposed to slights and doubts, to smiles and shoulder-shrugs. . . . That I bore all this with indifference, I cannot aver. I suffered from it, but on the other hand I can say that I did not suffer very greatly; which was and still is due to my having a very clear perception of the factual. I always took life as I found it and gave in to it. That is to say, outwardly, not in my inner spirit." And then he speaks of the established powers and actualities which existed in Prussia as everywhere else, to which he "gave in," even when, later on, almost at the end, they began to show him favour. He gets a doctorate *honoris causa*, he receives a decoration; and he finds that "decorations are for the other people. . . . If I were a socially prominent individual, an object of veneration, or even of respect, such a distinction would mean little to me. But in view of the fact that in Germany, particularly in Prussia, you are only somebody if you have received 'the commendation of the state,' such a decoration really has practical value: people look at you with more respect and treat you better. And therefore blessed be Gossler, who put me down for it." Goethe made similar observations to Eckermann about decorations and titles: "They save you many a knock." And this simple reasoning expresses a good deal of the German mentality, much Bismarckian realism, much Kantian distinction between pure and practical reason. In his own mind Fontane not only knew himself to be independent of the powers that be; he also considered it foolish to count in general on mankind, on praise, applause, honours, as though they meant anything at all. "We should," he said, "rather fill our minds with the conviction that such things are meaningless; we should find our satisfaction wholly and only in work, in our own activities." As for riches, his disdain of them as a means to happiness often went so far as to become actual pity. "Wherever there is much money, there is always a skeleton in the cupboard. The older I get, the more I feel – in other words, the more keenly I observe – the curse of gold. It seems almost a divine command that man should earn his daily bread, the statesman of course with a difference from the hired labourer, but always by labour, with a modest competence. Inherited millions are only a source of unhappiness; and even rich philanthropists are wretched because they see the abjectness and meanness of the human race, and it spoils their pleasure in what they can do." No matter: his attitude towards great riches was without either envy or scorn. For his own person, he might agree with that saying of Silvio Pellico, that a mean between poverty and riches, making it easy to understand both states, is the most appropriate for educating the spirit of man. But as a poet, he was prone to feel admiration for greatness, as did Heine in his attitude toward the Rothschilds; he derived æsthetic pleasure from the contemplation of splendid opulence. "Real wealth," he writes to his daughter, "impresses me, or at least gratifies me; all its manifestations please me in the highest degree, and I like to live among people who employ five thousand miners, build factory cities, and dispatch expeditions to colonize Africa. Large shipping princes, who man whole fleets, tunnel-builders, canal-makers who link up continents, lords of the press and railway barons can count on my respect. I want nothing from them, but to see them live and work makes me feel good; ever since I was young everything big has had a magic charm for me, I fall in with it without the least personal desire." What he really despised was what he called the penny-wise housekeeping of the middle classes which looked down its nose at poverty like his own. "A piece of bread," he said, "is never 'penny-wise'; a piece of bread is the best thing there is, it is life, it is poetry. But a fine dinner of roast goose with white Zeltinger wine and whipped-cream tart, with a beaming hostess flattering herself that she has rescued me from my humdrum existence for two hours; that is just 'penny-wise' and worse because of the state of mind it shows." Fontane has been called a philistine; he has even been known to call himself that. Yet the middle position, mediocrity, he felt in his soul to be petty and trivial; while in poverty he saw the favourable, though not the indispensable condition for the artist: freedom to observe and to develop. "When I look back," he writes in 1883 from Norderney, "I find my life here very like the one I led in London, thirty-one years ago. I walked from Hyde Park to Regent's Park, admiring at every step. I looked down entranced from Richmond Hill at the may tree in bloom; the air I breathed, the scenes of wealth and plenty, everything pleased me; but still I moved among them like a stranger, like one somehow not entitled to share fully and wholly in these splendours. I was always the other side of the hedge. And here it is the same. But fortunately life evens things up, and the blind see with their fingertips. To observe the world means more to me than to possess it; one gets one's share of happiness and pleasure, the same as those who are favoured by fortune."

And yet how out-of-date this apparently small middle-class life, with all its narrow loyalties, must seem to us "moderns." Times have changed, the forces of civilization, the so-called "destructive forces," have moved so triumphantly against the "established powers," the position of art and artists, the increased authority of the intellect have risen to such a height that humility like Fontane's seems to us almost pathetic. What are orders and titles to us? Who would want them, just to make people stare? The social status of the man of intellect is greatly improved, even though he may not have been "put down" for a decoration. That is clear. "Only fools would boast of such a trade unless they were obliged." But in Munich a swindler was recently caught in a first-class hotel. After his signature in the register he had added as his profession the word "writer." What more could we ask?

But Fontane's modesty had deeper roots than his social attitude; it was rather the result of that ultimate scepticism of the artist which is directed against the arts as a whole; and of it one may say that it is the very foundation of the artist's honesty. It is very amusing, though a bit affected, when Fontane lets people say, on his seventieth birthday: "Too bad about him, he did not even go to the university" – or when he refuses to go to Weimar for the inauguration of the Goethe-Schiller Archives, because he might run the risk of being addressed familiarly with a Latin "or even Greek" quotation, which always gives him the feeling: "Earth, open and swallow me!" But from the depth of his being comes this, written to a critic, at the age of seventy-nine: "I am especially grateful to you for pointing out that I take the field not only against others, but also against myself. And if I could have followed my inclination I would have marched against myself in quite a different fashion. For despite all the inevitable vanities one has, one comes to look on oneself as something pretty questionable. 'Thou comest in such a questionable shape.'" It was part of his civic virtue, his leaning towards discipline and order, and even more part of that honest rationalism with which the solemn artist-priests and artist-fakirs will have nothing to do – that he felt this questionable element in the type called "artist," that cross between Lucifer and Punch. Only one other had that feeling. Note the intolerance and vehemence in the following criticism of Spielhagen's characters in his novels: "Always the notion that a poet, a painter, or any other artist is something special, while the rest of the crowd is on the lowest level (and it was always that way), on such a low level that most of them need to be flogged. There are very few exceptions to this rule; Scott was one. But Byron, again, is dreadful. If the artists are real artists, one can just shut one's eyes a bit; but it is disgusting to adulate their arrogance, their nonsense, their disregard of morals. Just the phrase 'my art is sacred to me' (especially from the lips of actresses) is enough to kill me." – Magda Schwarze must have been still in the dramatic school at that time. – But do the words not sound like a quotation from *Fröhlichen Wissenschaft* (*Joyful Wisdom*)? It is the same sort of thing as the observations à la Rubek of the sixty-year-old Fontane about the contrast between art and life and the advantage, the superiority, of the everyday, ungifted kind of existence. "Ah, how lucky," he writes, "are the lieutenants, the six-foot Junkers, and all the rest of the Don Juan clan! I take back everything I said (while I could still dance) in favour of lyric poetry, and against all good-looking, laughing, well-washed youthful victors over girls' hearts. The bookworm, be he ever so decent and clever, is really only pleasing to himself and a small handful of others. The world passes him by and beckons to life and beauty. The exceptions are rare and often only seeming. Heyse's successes should be credited to his personality more than to his poetic talent." And when he is misunderstood he attempts to explain his point of view. "It is one of my favourite occupations when I talk to my family to point out the relative unimportance of art, knowledge, and erudition, especially of lyric and epic poetry (making fun of myself), and to praise (perhaps to exaggerate) the qualities and advantages of gay and handsome creatures to whom the hearts of their fellow men continue to turn. When I was young myself, I thought otherwise: looks were nothing, talent, genius, everything."

That is as it should be. The right to be ironic about things of the intellect and "literature" (a modern affectation used offensively by those not competent to do so) is one which must be paid for by great accomplishments. The artist scepticism for art and artists is permissible only where it is combined with that artistic devotion, that industry which Fontane, a real northerner in this respect, almost indentified with genius. A distich addressed to the painter Adolf Menzel runs as follows:

Gaben, wer hätte sie nicht, – Talente, Spielzeug für Kinder!
Nur der Ernst macht den Mann, nur der Fleiss das Genie.

Gifts, who is he that's without them? Talents, playthings for children!
Seriousness alone marks the man, diligence only the genius.

To which corresponds a passage in the letters: "Nowadays there are no longer mere 'talents.' At least, they signify nothing, nothing at all. Whoever really practices an art today and wants to accomplish something in his chosen field must have talent, of course, but along with it education, insight, good taste, and rigid industry. However, there is more to this kind of industry than mere mass production. Storm took more time to write a little lyric than Brachvogel did to write a three-volume novel. He may have gone walking more than did Brachvogel; but he had a hundred times more diligence as an artist. An ordinary man writes down masses of stuff as it goes through his head. The artist, the true poet, often searches for the right word for a fortnight."

Education, insight, good taste, and diligence. This northerner, who had more of the Prussian Mark in him than the French Gascogne, was not for the Dionysiac, but rather for enlightenment, knowledge of the ideal, which, by the way, is characteristic of the great epochs of poetic creation. He cites Goethe: "The performance of a good poet and writer is always in proportion to his enlightenment. It is possible to write something good, yes, perhaps something better than you can ever achieve again even with enlightenment. Granted. But such things are a gift of the gods, and, being god-given, come but seldom. Once a year, perhaps, and the year has three hundred and sixty-five days. For the remaining three hundred and sixty-four the important thing is the critical faculty, the measure of enlightenment. In the field of poetry I had this enlightenment thirty years before I got it in prose writing. Therefore I read my poetry with pleasure, or at least without chagrin; whereas my prose writings of that period embarrass me continually, they make me blush." "All I have produced," he confesses elsewhere, "is 'psychography' and criticism, creation in the dark, put to rights in the light. It happened that I wrote this short story with half or a quarter of my powers; but in the end no one will notice it." Such remarks and confessions about his own creation abound throughout the letters. They are stimulating to read because of their naturalness, their immediacy of feeling; they afford a glimpse into the workshop of a keen and passionate artist.

For example, he speaks of the little aids to creation which help to delude the artist and assist him over the fact that in reality everything must be taken from the void and from his own inner life. "You need to be conscious of a certain modicum of factual information at hand; in this awareness you create. How often have I heard people say: 'But you did not use it.' That is wrong. I have indeed used it. It spooks about behind the scenes." Or with reference to the unburnt letters which betray Effi, he discusses the trivial and the forced, and emphatically declares that the trivial is in his estimation decidedly the lesser evil. Or he rejects, vehemently and dogmatically, the stylistic corrections that an editor had deemed necessary in the manuscript of *Ellernklipp*. "I am ready," he writes, "to sacrifice for you my stops; but the 'ands,' where they occur in great number, you must leave me. For I flatter myself, just between us two, that I am a stylist; not one of those insufferably glib writers who have one key and one form for everything, but a true stylist. In other words, I am a writer who does not force his old-fashioned Marlitt and Gartenlaube style on his prose, but rather one who takes his manner and style from the subjects he treats. And that is how it is that I write sentences fourteen lines long and then others which scarcely contain fourteen syllables, sometimes not even fourteen letters. And that is the way it is with my 'ands.' If I adjusted everything to the 'and' style, I should deserve to be shut up. However, I write *with-and* short stories and *without-and* short stories, always considering the content and adapting myself to it. Where it is modern, it is without 'and.' The simpler, the more naïve, the more *sancta simplicitas*, there the more 'ands.' 'And' is Biblical and patriarchal, and everywhere where my purpose is to achieve such effect, 'and' cannot be omitted." The easy impressiveness of this preachment, "taking the manner and style from the subject," is delightful. Taking the style from the subject, letting the content speak; this was one of Fontane's pet ideas, and in his excellent criticism of Keller he returns to the theme at more length. Keller, he says, is in reality a teller of fairy-tales. He does not tell stories of a definite century, nor of a definite country or specified communities with specific customs and languages. Instead, he has for his purpose a kind of fairy-tale language, always the same, and in this language the old and the new, the high and the low, participate equally. The historical element has no chance at all, even in stories like *Dietegen*, which are not fairy-tales at all, but pretend to represent historical and cultural conditions. And what is the reason? It is the fact that the Swiss poet, notwithstanding his talents, his humour, and his artistic nature, does not possess the gift of style. Indeed, what is style? "If," says Fontane, "one understands by style the so-called characteristic way of writing epitomized in Buffon's *'le style c'est l'homme,'* then Keller has not only got style, but more style than anyone else. But this is an old-fashioned sense of the word, its place has been taken by a definition that in my opinion is much more correct: 'A work possesses style in proportion to its objectivity; in other words, the more the theme speaks for itself, the freer it is from fortuitous qualities and personal mannerisms counter to the idea to be expressed. If this is right, and I think it is, then we must regard Keller's work as lacking, rather than possessing, style. He gives to all and sundry a very definite, very personal note, which sometimes fits it and sometimes not, just as it happens. If it fits, then, let me repeat, you get the best effects of all; if not, you get dissonances, which sometimes cry to heaven. Keller knows no *suum cuique,* he constantly offends against the prescript: 'Give unto Cæsar.' Ruthlessly he gives over the things that are God's into the hands of Keller."

Strange! This is Fontane himself speaking; but if we read over these last five Fontane sentences, noting their tone and rhythm aside from the content, we may well ask ourselves if we might not easily come upon them in the dialogue of one of his novels. Might they not be part of a conversation between Rex and Czako with their friend Stechlin—aside from the question whether Prussian lieutenants would ever be able to converse with such intellect and charm! To tell the truth, the objection that Fontane raises against Keller – if it be an objection – applies as well, or nearly as well, to himself as it does to Keller. He too gives over the things that are God's into the hands of Fontane, but who would want it otherwise? The objection is no objection, and Fontane's theory of style, influenced by naturalistic trends, is not what he practised at his best. True, every theme has its own style, and the man of mannerisms is worth as little as the glib writer. But that kind of stylistic mimicry which enables a writer to permeate every turn of his subject with the atmosphere of the world that he aims to present by no means excludes his own stylistic peculiarities and the unity of his product. Richard Wagner, resembling in this respect every artist who deserves the name, never used the same thing twice, and is stylistically different in every one of his works. Which does not prevent us from realizing that even in a single line, in a single measure from any one of them, he is recognizable as himself, and utterly himself. The gist of the whole matter is that the artist does not speak himself, he makes things speak for him, but makes them speak in his own peculiar idiom. And again: who would wish that Fontane had done otherwise?

There is something positively enchanting in his style, especially in his old age, as we observe it in his letters of the eighties and nineties. If I may be permitted the personal confession: no writer of past or present stirs in me that kind of sympathy and gratitude, that immediate, instinctive delight, that reflex gaiety, warmth, and satisfaction, which I feel reading any of his verse, any line of his letters, any scrap of dialogue. This expansive prose, easy-going, lucid, with something of the ballad about it; easy to speak, elliptical – despite its apparent artlessness and lack of effort it has a certain elevation, a roundness and fullness, a kind of inner determination which is evidently possible only after long practice with poetic forms. It is in fact much nearer poetry than its unostentatious simplicity would lead you to believe, for it has poetic conscience, the essentials of poetry, it is written with poetry in view. The verses of his old age, concentrated and perfect as they are, so that one knows them by heart at once, are stylistically more and more like his prose; in just the same way his prose becomes refined in the same measure in which (I beg his pardon for the phrase) it goes downhill. He has often been called a *causeur;* he has even called himself so. The truth, however, is that he was a singer, even when he seemed merely to prattle; and his gift as *causeur*, which, after *Effi Briest*, got the upper hand in a way rather questionable for a poet, consists in a kind of subtilization, to such an advanced degree that finally there is nothing left but a very deft play of wit and atmosphere. Was that a decline? He seems to have thought so. "This book," he writes about *Poggenpuhls*, "is not a novel and has no subject-matter. The 'how' must take the place of the 'what'; nothing pleasanter can be said to me about it than that. Of course a literature cannot be based simply and solely on the taste of a very, very old gentleman; but as a side-issue it will do." A view that is fitting for him, but would not be for us others. If our story-telling literature had been influenced more by this taste of a very, very old gentleman, we should now have more art and less philistinism in the German novel. And the most remarkable thing is that this stage of senility and decadence is the very time when he is making plans for the *Likedeeler*.

"I want to write a new novel," he writes on March 16, 1895; "whether it gets finished or not makes little difference. A perfectly grand novel, unlike everything that I have ever written, different from anything ever done before, although some people will be inclined to classify it with *Ekehardt* or *The Ancestors*. But it is quite different really: being meant to amalgamate my oldest and most romantic ballad style with my most modern and realistic novels. Such a mixture would approach most nearly 'The Trousers of Herr von Bredow,' with this difference, that the 'Trousers' have something funny about them, as they should; whereas my novel is conceived as a fantastic and grotesque tragedy. Its name is *The Likedeelers*. The Like-dealers (equal dealers) lived about 1400. They were a group of communistic pirates, something like Karl Moor and his band in Schiller's *Robbers*, who fought under Klaus Störtebeker and were executed *en masse* on the Grasbrook in Hamburg in 1402. I have it all clearly in mind, only a trifle is missing: the information. I see it all in my mind's eye, like a phantasmagoria; and like a phantasmagoria it will be in the end. But before that, it must have had definite form and shape in my head for some time. . . ." And then he asks for books, for source material, and avows that he has the courage to attack even archives.

If *The Likedeelers* had been written, we should now have a historical novel of the highest poetic calibre, such as France has in *Salammbô* and Belgium in *Ulenspiegel*. It was not to be. Was the time not ripe? Several times, even up to July, there is talk about the plan and the studies for it. Then silence.

This soundless shipwreck of a new and ambitious plan, so clearly envisaged; this eclipse of an idea so enthusiastically hailed, promising immortality; it gives us food for thought. Fatigue alone cannot be the reason for it. He was indifferent whether he would finish it or not. Was he afraid that such an undertaking would lead to his transgressing the limitations which, according to him, human nature (including himself) required, in order to achieve the full measure of its power?

"We need a small circle in order to be great"; "He who overestimates himself is small." "I could never manage the big jump." Looked at calmly, with true Fontane scepticism, the idea of *The Likedeelers* was prompted by ambition; and when recognized for what it was, discarded. Fontane had long been great by limiting himself; in the bourgeois, sublime; as a novelist he had been privately a poet. Late in life, for a few months, he dreamed of seeming what he had always been. Then, probably, he blushed for his presumption, found it ridiculous to gather up his old bones for so big a jump, and without more ado abandoned a work which proved less novel and untried than he had thought. The case is more typical than it seems. The circumstances and necessities of a superior nature, who for a long time dealt with and elevated mediocre and bourgeois themes, raising them, for the initiated, far above their original level, might now apply his parts to a subject worthy of them, thus revealing their nobility even to the most stupid. But in this case the charm of contrast is lacking, the familiar magic of the homely. A book that was to have been an achievement of consequence was not written; it proved, in a higher sense, to be superfluous.

Perhaps irritation was at the root of this project of the fantastic prose-ballad of the Likedeelers: irritation at the crude misconceptions to which up to the end he was exposed. "I went to bed with Maria Stuart, and arose with Archibald Douglas. The fantastic and romantic charmed me from my youth up and is in fact my most personal southern-France nature. And now Hart comes along and tells me that I am a good fellow, quite a decent chap, but an inveterate philistine with a Prussian ramrod up my back. Ye gods!" Was Fontane a romantic? His visit to Bayreuth in 1889 is a complete failure. Merely for physical reasons; towards the end of the overture he feels a bit bad and gets out. But it is likely that he would not have felt ill if *Parsifal* had appealed to him, and his amusing account of the fag it all was betrays that sacred art and religious theatre were not in his line. Was he a romantic? Surely not in the German sense of the word. His romanticism is of Romance origin, a Cyrano de Bergerac romanticism, fighting and versifying. Themes of horror, the prison, and the block appear, as retribution for passion and sin. But at bottom this romanticism is rationalism, a gay spirit and liberal sensuality; it altogether lacks the ominous musical note, the perfervid metaphysical quality, the cloudy profundities. And despite all the delight in historical subjects, there is no trace of a reactionary trend, of hatred against "the age." A courageous modern point of view is characteristic of Fontane, as it is today of the poet Richard Dehmel.

Among the contradictions of this untrammelled spirit not pledged to any one creed, who saw at least two sides of everything in his life, is the circumstance that one fine day he comes out with surprising definiteness against Prussian Germany, and declares that Oberammergau, Bayreuth, Munich, and Weimar are places where one could enjoy life. Surely that other passage is more characteristic in which he speaks of the Berlin public, the public of the metropolis and royal residence, and says it is worth more, and he likes it better than the public of Saxony and Thuringia, brought up on Marlitt, eternally gossiping and knitting. There is still another passage, dealing with morals, where, like Nietzsche with his "Wartburg" and "boarding-school" morality, Fontane makes fun of Saxon Thuringia and its pretty small-town conventions.

At that time he was seventy, and growing younger all the time. The literary "revolution" finds him in his best form; he composes lively verses about the old fellows who weep over the delusion that they are indispensable – he cannot understand it – and the young men, who hold the stage, whose day it now is. Around the year '80, there are, as it is fitting, remarks hostile to the classic writers. "For our attitude towards them is highly involved, even if only because we too want to make something out of the boring and the mediocre and practise literary idol-worship just as we do political." Even against Schiller, who until that time was "Number One," he is seen for a moment to take an aggressive position. The half-foreign Fontane sees in the genius of Schiller something half foreign, compared with the national and popular spirit of Bürger. The classic-worship, in fact "all that was written between the thirties and 1870," "is dead as a doornail." "The high-flown style will not come back." And though the noisy little people, crying aloud, irritated him, the seventy-five-year-old Fontane welcomed Hauptmann's *Weavers* as "excellent," "epoch-making," "a splendid specimen of German literature."

Among his comments on important modern writers, those on Strindberg are truly and wonderfully Fontane. More than one instinctive feeling – his discretion, his tact, his fairness, his sense of decency, must have revolted against this unpleasant genius, as they did against the unhappy Stauffer, of whom he said: "Such a genius should never exist; and if being a genius means to be this, then I'd rather be a weaver." Strindberg's *Confession of a Fool* provokes this comment: "Who writes a book of this kind writes it out of revenge, is of course a rapscallion." Yet he immediately adds: "On the other hand, it is true that we always, or nearly always, have to thank the most questionable characters for the most important revelations, disclosures, events – revolutions are usually started by the rabble, by gamblers or madmen, and what should we do without revolutions?" Are these the words of a philistine, a stiff-necked adherent of law and order? He asks, rhetorically, what should we do without revolutions? Nor is this a mere mood. The Likedeelers theme appeals to him because of its "social-democratic modernity." The author of the history of the Prussian Mark writes to his English friend James Morris: "Only the fourth estate is interesting. The bourgeois is frightful, the nobility and church are behind the times, they never change. The new and better world begins only at the fourth estate. One would have to say this even if there were only very small signs of it. But such is not the case. What the workers think, write, speak, has far outstripped the thinking, writing, and speaking of the traditionally ruling classes. Everything is more genuine, truer, more living. They, the workers, take hold of things in a new way, they have not only new goals, but new roads leading to them." This was written in 1896. Eighteen years earlier he had written to his wife: "The masses have only been held in check by fear or religion, by church or secular rule, and the attempt to accomplish it without these great world provosts may be regarded as a failure. Then it was thought that education would be a substitute, and 'compulsory education' and compulsory military service were glorified. Now we have a fine mess. With both of these the state, yes, more, society, has given itself a stick for its own back: compulsory education has taught everybody to read, and the conceit of the half-educated has destroyed the last vestige of authority. Military training has taught everyone to shoot and thereby the unorganized mass has been organized into workers' battalions." This view, today become a commonplace, was new and startling in the seventies; the passage, like many others, reminds one of Nietzsche, who asks derisively: "In a word, who do you want? If you want slaves, you are a fool to bring up masters." Between this state of mind and the unqualified enthusiasm of the old Fontane for the "fourth estate" there certainly took place much development, much consciousness of his own modernity, his amazing growth into youth and the future. But it is equally certain that he was the kind of man in whom both opinions, the conservative and the revolutionary, could exist side by side. His political awareness was complicated by his temperament as an artist; it was, in a very elevated sense, not reliable; and at bottom he could scarcely have been surprised when, on his seventy-fifth birthday, it was not the Stechows, the Bredows, and the Rochows who came to pay their respects, but the other morally questionable aristocracy, the "almost prehistoric" nobility.

It was this complicated temperament rather than "a defective sense of formality" (though the two may perhaps be the same) that was responsible for the fact that Fontane "did not get on": that the creator of old Derfflinger, old Dessau, old Zieten, and the ode in celebration of the Berlin Entry could not get himself officially enrolled in the Order of the Eagle and admitted to court, like the painter Adolf Menzel. Indisputably, in the plastic artist, the great craftsman, the intellectual and ambiguous aspect of his work coincides with its technical aspect more intimately than in the writer. In his case the ruling powers may well take the matter for the spirit; and nothing prevents him, the intellectually inarticulate, harmless, irresponsible creator, from wearing with a good grace the decorations, titles, and ceremonial robes they bestow on him. A great painter may become official, a great writer never. For everything that constitutes the rank, the charm, and the value of his personality, the subtle intellectual distinctions, the problem-posing, the wilful undiscipline, must make him seem in the eyes of the ruling classes both disloyal and suspect. Official Prussia could scarcely be asked to take seriously the merits of the patriotic poet who one day declared that "Borussianism" was the lowest of all the forms of culture that ever existed.

Wilful undiscipline: perhaps Fontane would have been willing to admit this description of his political connections. In 1887 he was to register his vote. "At the eleventh hour they tried to get me to the polling-place by dispatching a man to round me up. But I steadfastly refused to go. In my case, things are so complicated that I cannot decently and honourably give my vote." In 1890 he is more flippant: "And now I must go out to put my ballot into the box, for the first time in many years. Why should it be? Finally I was reduced to counting my buttons. Only he who knows nothing knows without any doubts."

An unreliable bird! Was it not Fontane who as a dramatic critic once confessed that he might just as easily have said the opposite of what he did say? He liked the aristocracy "as people and in novels," but politically he found it went "too much against the grain." And he had to get used to seeing his "underground predilection for the nobility treated with suspicion," because he sang the tune in his own way and not according to the notes in front of him. He likes Jews, "really prefers them to the Wendish Germans," and in spite of his dearly beloved aristocracy, had to acknowledge "that all liberality and culture, at least here in Berlin, comes to us through well-to-do Jewry." But he does not want to be governed by the Jews, is altogether not liberal, and from his patriarchal, idyllic home in Neubrandenburg expresses himself disparagingly concerning "laws for freedom." People consider the *Traveller* a glorifier of the Prussian Mark, do they? He declines the honour. "I wanted to say, and I really did say it: 'Children, it is not so bad as you make out'; and so far I was right. But it is foolish to try to read into my books that I had a passion for the Mark and its inhabitants. So silly as that I am not." Certainly, after that, there is nothing more to be said, despite Gossler and "getting put on the list." But, after all, this is only the reserved mood of a moment, a withdrawal of the fastidious personality from an unattractive theme. What the *Travels* really signify is set down in another passage, in plain words: "Critically," so it runs, "it should be emphasized that from the book you can not only learn to know the Mark and its inhabitants, but equally, despite all unattractiveness and impossibility of these heavy-handed slaves of duty and blunderbusses of bureaucracy, how this least of Germany's people was called to be its first." Here we have the willing surrender of the beauty-lover to the necessity of accepting the fact that in political life not sensibility, not the graces and the muses, but efficiency and rude discipline are the bearers of historical missions.

He glorified Bismarck several times in verse, he speaks of him in the letters. And I do not know whether verse or prose reveals more, both about Bismarck and about Fontane. The figure of the German Chancellor is viewed here with a psychological reserve, yes, even spitefulness, as very great and very suspect. But the old man does not permit the young folk the right to question. On Bismarck's birthday in 1895 he writes: "The students must be enthusiastic, that is their confounded duty. For us oldsters things are different, or at least more complicated. This mixture of superman and slyboots, this founder of nations and evader of the stud-tax, this bulldog, this cry-baby who has never muddied the smallest stream – he gives me a mixed feeling, I feel no burst of warm and single-minded admiration. . . ." He was too loyal to take sides with the political genius as against the claims of legitimacy. "In the whole thing, I am from the very beginning on the Kaiser's side. Bismarck has been the greatest disregarder of principles that ever lived, and a 'principle' has finally undone him, defeated him; the very same principle he had inscribed on his banner and according to which he never acted. The power of the Hohenzollerns — a well-earned power — was stronger than his genius and his guile. He is very much like Schiller's Wallenstein (the real Wallenstein was different). A genius, a saviour of the state, in feeling an arch-traitor. I this and I that — and when things cannot go on that way, then complaints of ingratitude and tears of north-German sentimentality. Where I see Bismarck as the instrument of Divine Providence, I take off my hat; where he is himself, Junker, climber, dike-inspector, I don't like him at all." Nor was Fontane enough of a cynic and pessimist (making, with Montaigne, a distinction between them) to be able to acclaim unconditionally the Machiavellianism of the founder of the Prussian state; since, in his heart, he put the "honourable" before the practical. "He is the most interesting figure imaginable, I know none more so; but this constant tendency to deceit, this perfection of underhandedness, is intrinsically offensive to me; when I look to be elevated, then I must indeed direct my gaze to other heroes." At which other heroes? Myth and psychology are two different things: where they dwell together in one bosom, where singer and writer are united in one person, there contradictions emerge. The tribute of admiration that the psychological writer pays to greatness is not "pure and ardent," like the feelings of the students; he does not view the hero in order to be elevated. The hero is to him "the most interesting figure imaginable"; but from "interest" — that reaction peculiar to writers and psychologists — is no great step to all realism, all the ironies and spites which knowledge is prone to. In the quoted passages the sceptical psychologist is speaking of a living hero. Bismarck's death allowed Fontane to go back to the mythical, respectful, elevated contemplation of this last manifestation of German greatness, the attitude which, only three short years before, he had thought right and proper only for the young.

Widukind lädt ihn zu sich ein:
Im Sachsenwald soll er begraben sein.

Widukind bids him to come in:
In Saxon forest shall he lie down.

As guardian of the myth, the poet is conservative. But psychology, on the other hand, is a most effective mine-laying tool of democratic enlightenment. In the letters Fontane wrote in his later life – in the letters, that is, aside from his works – this glorifier of the war-loving Prussian aristocracy demonstrates the revolutionary and democratic stamp of his ideas; there are pacifist, anti-militaristic utterances which should be taken not merely as a well-meaning and flexible adaptation to the revolution in literary values current in the eighties; but as a product of his own personality, of that part of him which was rationalistic-humanitarian eighteenth-century (and twentieth-century?). They considerably justify that "suspicion" which his "basic, still-existing preference for the aristocracy" encountered. Men of his sort must always be complicated and unreliable in their political behaviour; for the contradictions into which they are pushed by contemporary events can be resolved and reconciled only in the future.

This spectacle of the old Fontane has hardly a counterpart in the history of the intellect. It is a phenomenon of old age returning artistically, intellectually, and morally to youth, a second and true youth and maturity, in advanced years. "As the years progress, I have grown younger," the twenty-eight-year-old youth wrote to a friend, "and the joy of life, which is actually a heritage of youth, seems to increase in me the longer the thread of years is spun out." That is an early recognition of his peculiar vitality. He was born to become "the old Fontane," who is destined to live; the first six decades of his life were almost consciously only a preparation for the last two, spent detached and benign in the deepening shadow of the final riddle. His life seems to show that only maturity for death is real maturity for life. Ever freer, ever wiser, this rare and amiable temperament ripens toward the acceptance of the ultimate answer. Among his papers, after his death, these fine lines were found:

Leben; wohl dem, dem es spendet
Freude, Kinder, täglich Brot,
Doch das Beste, was es sendet,
Ist das Wissen, das es sendet,
Ist der Ausgang, ist der Tod.

Life; how good, to whom it proffers
Children, joys, and daily bread,
But the best of all it offers
Is the knowledge that it offers,
Is the parting hour, is death.

SUFFERINGS AND GREATNESS OF RICHARD WAGNER

1933

[*Written on the occasion of the fiftieth anniversary of Wagner's death, and delivered at the University of Munich, February 10, 1933*]

◇◇◇◇◇◇◇◇◇◇

Il y a là mes blâmes, mes éloges et tout ce que j'ai dit.
MAURICE BARRÈS

SUFFERING and great as that nineteenth century whose complete expression he is, the mental image of Richard Wagner stands before my eyes. Scored through and through with all his century's unmistakable traits, surcharged with all its driving forces, so I see his image; and scarcely can I distinguish between my two loves: love of his work, as magnificently equivocal, suspect and compelling a phenomenon as any in the world of art, and love of the century during most of which he lived his restless, harassed, tormented, possessed, miscomprehended life, and in which, in a blaze of glory, he died. We of today, absorbed as we are in tasks which – for novelty and difficulty at least – never saw their like, we have no time and little wish to give its due to the epoch – we call it the bourgeois – now dropping away behind us. Our attitude toward the nineteenth century is that of sons toward a father: critical, as is only fair. We shrug our shoulders alike over its belief – which was a belief in ideas – and over its unbelief – that is to say, its melancholy relativism. Its attachment to liberal ideas of reason and progress seems to us laughable, its materialism all too crass, its monistic solution of the riddle of the universe full of shallow complacency. And yet its scientific self-sufficiency is atoned for, yes, outweighed, by the pessimism, the musical bond with night and death, which will very likely one day seem its strongest trait. Though another, not unconnected with it, is its wilful love of mere largeness, its taste for the monumental and standard, the copious and grandiose – this again, strange to say, coupled with an infatuation for the very small and the circumstantial, for the minutiæ of psychological processes. Yes, greatness, of a turbid, suffering kind; disillusioned, yet bitterly, fanatically aware of truth; conscious too of the brief, incredulous bliss to be snatched from beauty as she flies—such greatness as this was the meaning and mark of the nineteenth century. Plastically represented, it would resemble a Michelangelo statue, an Atlas of the moral world, stretching and relaxing his muscles. Giant burdens were borne in that day—epic burdens, in the full sense of that strong word: one thinks not only of Balzac and Tolstoy, one thinks of Wagner as well. When the latter, in 1851, sent his friend Liszt a letter with the formal plan of the *Ring*, Liszt answered from Weimar: "Go on with it, and work on regardless! You ought to take for your motto the one the Chapter of the Cathedral of Seville gave to the architect who built it: 'Build us,' they said, 'such a temple that future generations will say the Chapter was mad to undertake anything so extraordinary.' And yet—there stands the Cathedral." That is genuine nineteenth-century.

The enchanted garden of French impressionistic painting, the English, French, and Russian novel, German science, German music—no, it was not such a bad age; in fact, it was a perfect forest of giants. And only now, looking back from a distance, are we able to see the family likeness among them all, the stamp which, in all their manifold greatness, their age set upon them. Zola and Wagner, the *Rougon-Macquarts* and the *Ring of the Nibelungs*—fifty years ago who would have thought of putting them together? Yet they belong together. The kinship of spirit, aims, and methods is most striking. It is not only the love of size, the propensity to the grandiose and the lavish; not only, in the sphere of technique, the Homeric leitmotiv that they have in common. More than anything else it is a naturalism that amounts to the symbolic and the mythical. Who can fail to see in Zola's epic the tendency to symbol and myth that gives his characters their over-life-size air? That Second Empire Astarte, Nana, is she not symbol and myth? Where does she get her name? It sounds like the babbling of primitive man. Nana was a cognomen of the Babylonian Ishtar: did Zola know that? So much the more remarkable and significant if he did not.

Tolstoy, too, has the same naturalistic magnificence of scale, the same democratic amplitude. He too has the leitmotiv, the self-quotation, the standing phrases to describe his characters. He has often been criticized for his relentless carrying through, his refusal to indulge his reader, his deliberate and splendid longwindedness. And of Wagner Nietzsche says that he is surely the impolitest of all geniuses: he takes his hearer, as it were, and keeps on saying a thing until in desperation one believes it. Here they are alike; but more profoundly alike still in their common possession of social and ethical elements. True, Wagner saw in art a sacred arcanum, a means of salvation for a corrupted society, whereas Tolstoy, toward the end of his life, repudiated it altogether, as trivial and self-indulgent; but his disparity is not important. For as self-indulgence Wagner too repudiated art. He wanted it saved and purified for the sake of a corrupted society. He was all for catharsis and purification, he dreamed of an æsthetic consecration that should cleanse society of luxury, the greed of gold and all unloveliness; hence his social ethics were closely akin to those of the Russian epic writer. And there is a likeness in their destinies too; for critics have seen in the character of both a temperamental split, causing something like a moral collapse, whereas the truth is that both lives display throughout their course the strictest unity and consistency. It has seemed to people that Tolstoy, in his old age, fell into a kind of religious madness. They do not see that the Tolstoy of the last period lay implicit in characters like Pierre Besuchov in *War and Peace* and Levin in *Anna Karenina*. Similarly, Nietzsche would have it that Wagner toward the end was a broken man, prostrate at the foot of the Cross; he overlooks or wishes others to overlook the fact that the emotional atmosphere of *Tannhäuser* anticipates that of *Parsifal*, and that the latter is the final, splendidly logical summing up of a life-work at bottom romantic and Christian in its spirit. Wagner's last work is also his most theatrical – and it would be hard to find an artist career more consistent than his. An art essentially sensuous, based on symbolic formulas (for the leitmotiv is a formula – nay, it is a monstrance; it claims an almost religious authority) must be leading back to the church celebration; and indeed I do believe that the secret longing and ultimate ambition of all theatre is to return to the bosom of the ritual out of which – in both the pagan and the Christian world – it sprang. The art of the theatre is already baroque, it is Catholicism, it is the church; and an artist like Wagner, used to dealing with symbols and elevating monstrances, must have ended by feeling like a brother of priests, like a priest himself.

I have often thought about the likeness between Wagner and Ibsen, and found it hard to decide how much of it is due to their contemporaneity and how much to personal traits. For I could not but recognize, in the dialogue of Ibsen's bourgeois drama, means and effects, fascinations and wiles already known to me from the sound-world of the other artist; could not but be convinced of a kinship which in part of course lay in their common possession of greatness, but how very much too in their way of being great! How much they are alike in their tremendous self-sufficiency, in the three-dimensional rotundity and consummateness of the life-work of both; social-revolutionary in youth, in age paling into the ritual and mythical! *When We Dead Awaken*, the awesome whispered confession of the production-man bemoaning his late, too late declaration of love of life – and *Parsifal*, that oratorio of redemption: how prone I am to think of the two together, to feel them as one, these two farewell mystery plays, last words before the eternal silence! Both of them apocalyptic climaxes, majestic in their sclerotic languor, in the mechanical rigour of their technique, their general tone of reviewing life and casting up accounts, their self-quotation, their flavour of dissolution.

What we used to call *fin-de-siècle*, what was it but the miserable satyr-play of a smaller time, compared with the true and awe-inspiring end of the epoch whose swan-song was the last work of these two great wizards? For northern wizards were they both, crafty old weavers of spells, profoundly versed in all the arts of insinuation and fascination wielded by a devil's artistry as sensuous as consummate; great in the organization of effects, in the cult of detail, in all sorts of shifting meanings and symbolic senses, in the exploitation of fancy, the poetizing of the intellectual; and musicians they were to boot, as men of the north should be. Not only the one who consciously acquired his music because he thought it might be useful in his career of conquest; but also the other, though only privately, through the intellect and as a second string to the word.

But what makes them even to confusion alike is the way each subjected to an undreamed-of process of sublimation a form of art which, in both cases, stood at the time at rather a low ebb. In Wagner's case the form was opera, in Ibsen's the social drama. Goethe says: "Everything perfect of its kind must go beyond its kind, it must be something else, incomparable. In some notes the nightingale is still bird; then it surmounts its species, seeming to want to show to every other feathered fowl what singing really is." In just this sense Wagner and Ibsen made the opera and the social drama consummate; they made something else, incomparable, out of them. The other half of the comparison also rings true: sometimes, and sometimes even in *Parsifal*, Wagner is still opera; sometimes in Ibsen you can hear the creaking of the Dumas technique. But both are creative, in that sense of perfection and consummation; they have it in common that they took the accepted and made out of it something new, something undreamed-of.

What is it that raises the works of Wagner to a plane so high, intellectually speaking, above all older musical drama? Two forces contribute, forces and gifts of genius, which one thinks of in general as opposed; indeed, the present day takes pleasure in asserting their essential incompatibility. I mean psychology and the myth. Indeed, psychology does seem too much a matter of reason to admit of our seeing in it no obstacle at all on the path into the land of myth. And it passes as the antithesis of the mythical as of the musical – yet precisely this complex, of psychology, myth, and music, is what confronts us, an organic reality, in two great cases, Nietzsche and Wagner. A book might be written on Wagner the psychologist, on the psychology of his art as musician not less than as poet – in so far as the two are to be separated in him.

The technique of using the motif as an aid to memory had already been employed on occasion in the old opera; it was now gradually built up, by the profoundest virtuosity, into a system that made music more than ever the instrument of psychological allusion, association, emphasis. Wagner's treatment of the love-potion theme, originally the simple epic idea of a magic draught, is the creation of a great psychologist. For actually it might as well be pure water that the lovers drink, and it is only their belief that they have drunk death that frees their souls from the moral compulsion of their day. From the beginning Wagner's poetry goes beyond the bounds of suitability for his libretto – though not so much in the language as precisely in the psychology displayed. "The sombre glow," sings the Dutchman in the fine duet with Senta in the second act:

> The sombre glow I feel within me burning –
> Shall I, O wretch, confess it for love's yearning?
> Ah, no, it is salvation that I crave –
> Might such an angel come my soul to save!

The lines are singable; but never before had such a complex thought, such involved emotions, been sung or been written for singing. The devoted man loves this maid at first sight, but tells himself that his emotion has nothing to do with her; rather it has to do with his redemption and release. Again, seeing her as the embodiment of his hopes for salvation, he neither can nor will distinguish between the two longings he feels. For his hope has taken on her shape and he can no longer wish it to have another. In plain words, he sees and loves redemption in this maiden — what interweaving of alternatives is here, what a glimpse into the painful abysses of emotion! This is analysis — and the word comes up in an even bolder and more modern sense when we think of the youthful Siegfried and observe the way Wagner, in his verse and against the significant background of the music, gives life to the springlike germination, the budding and shooting up of that young life and love. It is a pregnant complex, gleaming up from the unconscious, of mother-fixation, sexual desire, and fear — the fairy-story fear, I mean, that Siegfried wanted so to feel: a complex that displays Wagner the psychologist in remarkable intuitive agreement with another typical son of the nineteenth century, the psychoanalyst Sigmund Freud. When Siegfried dreams under the linden tree and the mother-idea flows into the erotic; when Mime teaches his pupil the nature of fear, while the orchestra down below darkly and afar off introduces the fire motif: all that is Freud, that is analysis, nothing else — and we recall that Freud, whose profound investigation into the roots and depths of mind has been, in its broadest lines, anticipated by Nietzsche, shows an interest in the mythical, precultural, and primeval which is narrowly associated with the psychological.

"Love in fullest reality," says Wagner, "is only possible within sex; only as man and woman can human beings love most genuinely, all other love is derivative, having reference to this or artificially modelled upon it. It is false to think of this love (the sexual) as only one manifestation of love in general, other and perhaps higher manifestations being presumed beside it." This reduction of all love to the sexual has an unmistakably psychoanalytical character. It shows the same psychological naturalism as Schopenhauer's metaphysical formula of the "focus of the will" and Freud's cultural theories and his theory of sublimation. It is genuine nineteenth-century.

The erotic mother-complex appears again in *Parsifal*, in the seduction scene in the second act — and here we come to Kundry, the boldest, most powerful creation among Wagner's figures — he himself probably felt how extraordinary she was. Not Kundry but the emotions proper to Good Friday were Wagner's original point of departure; but gradually his ideas more and more took shape about her, and the decisive conception of the dual personality, the thought of making the wild *Gralsbotin* (messenger of the Grail) one and the same being with the beguiling temptress, supplied the final inspiration — and betrays the secret depths of the fascination that drew him to so strange an enterprise.

"Since this occurred to me," he writes, "almost everything about the material has become clear." And again: "In particular I see more and more vividly and compellingly a strange creation, a wonderful world-demonic female (the *Gralsbotin*). If I manage to finish this piece of work it will be something highly original." Original — that is a touchingly subdued and modest word for the result he actually produced. Wagner's heroines are in general marked by a trait of lofty hysteria; they have something sleep-walking, ecstatic, and prophetic which imparts an odd, uncanny modernity to their romantic heroics. But Kundry herself, the Rose of Hell, is definitely a piece of mythical pathology; her tortured and distracted duality, now as *instrumentum diaboli*, now as salvation-seeking penitent, is portrayed with clinical ruthlessness and realism, with a naturalistic boldness of perception and depiction in the field of morbid psychology that has always seemed to me the uttermost limit of knowledge and mastery. And Kundry is not the only character in *Parsifal* with this extravagant type of mentality. The draft of this last work of Wagner says of Klingsor that he is the demon of the hidden sin, he is impotence raging against evil — and here we are transported into a Christian world that takes cognizance of recondite and infernal soul-states — in short, into the world of Dostoyevsky.

Our second phenomenon is Wagner as mythologist, as discoverer of the myth for purposes of the opera, as saviour of the opera through the myth. And truly he has not his like for soul-affinity with this world of thought and image, nor his equal in the power of invoking and reanimating the myth. When he forsook the historical opera for the myth he found himself; and listening to him one is fain to believe that music was made for nothing else, nor could have any other mission but to serve mythology. Whether as messenger from a purer sphere, sent to the aid of innocence and then, alas, since faith proves inconstant, withdrawing thither whence it came; or as lore, spoken and sung, of the world's beginning and end, a sort of cosmogonic fairy-tale philosophy — in all this the spirit of the myth, its essence and its key, are struck with a certainty, an elective intuition; its very language is spoken with a native-bornness that has not its like in all art. It is the language of "once upon a time" in the double sense of "as it always was" and "as it always shall be"; the density of the mythological atmosphere — as in the scene with the Norns at the beginning of the *Götterdämmerung*, where the three daughters of Erda indulge in a solemn-faced gossip about the state of the world, or in the appearances of Erda herself in the *Rheingold* and *Siegfried* — is unsurpassable. The overpowering accents of the music that bears away Siegfried's corpse no longer refer to the woodland youth who set forth in order to learn fear; they instruct our feeling in what is really passing there behind falling veils of mist. The sun-hero himself lies on his bier, struck down by blind darkness, and the word comes to the aid of our emotions: "the fury of a wild boar," it says, and "he is the accursed boar," says Gunther, pointing to Hagen, "who mangled the flesh of this noble youth." A perspective opens out into the first and furthest of our human picture-dreamings. Tammuz, Adonis whom the boar slew, Osiris, Dionysius, the dismembered ones, who are to return as the Crucified whose side a Roman spear must pierce that men may know him – all that was and ever is, the whole world of slain and martyred loveliness this mystic gaze encompasses; and so let no one say that he who created Siegfried was in Parsifal untrue to himself.

My passion for the Wagnerian enchantment began with me so soon as I knew of it, and began to make it my own and penetrate it with my understanding. All that I owe to him, of enjoyment and instruction, I can never forget: the hours of deep and single bliss in the midst of the theatre crowds, hours of nervous and intellectual transport and rapture, of insights of great and moving import such as only this art vouchsafes. My zeal is never weary, I am never satiated, with watching, listening, admiring – not, I confess, without misgivings; but the doubts and objections do my zeal as little wrong as did Nietzsche's immortal critique, which has always seemed to me like a panegyric with the wrong label, like another kind of glorification. It was love-in-hate, it was self-flagellation. Wagner's art was the great passion of Nietzsche's life. He loved it as did Baudelaire, the poet of the *Fleurs du mal*, of whom it is told that in the agony, the paralysis, and the clouded mind of his last days he smiled with pleasure when he heard Wagner's name: "*il a souri d'allégresse*." Thus Nietzsche, in his paralytic night, used to listen to the sound of that name and say: "I loved him very much." He hated him very much too, on intellectual, cultural, ethical grounds – which shall not be gone into here and now. But it would be strange indeed if I stood alone in the feeling that Nietzsche's polemic against Wagner pricks on enthusiasm for the composer rather than lames it.

What I did take exception to, always – or rather, what left me cold – was Wagner's theory. It is hard for me to believe that anyone ever took it seriously. This combination of music, speech, painting, gesture, that gave itself out to be the only true art and the fulfilment of all artistic yearning – what had I to do with this? A theory of art that would make *Tasso* give way to *Siegfried*? I found it hard to swallow, this derivation of the single arts from the distintegration of an original theatrical unity, to which they should all happily find their way back. Art is entire and complete in each of its forms and manifestations; we do not need to add up the different kinds to make a whole. To think that is *bad* nineteenth-century, a bad, mechanistic mode of thought; and Wagner's triumphant performance does not justify his theory but only itself. It lives, and it will live, but art will outlive it in the arts, and move mankind through them, as it always has. We should be children and barbarians to suppose that the influence of art upon us is profounder or loftier by reason of the heaped-up volume of its assault upon our senses.

Wagner, as an impassioned man of the theatre – one might call him a theatromaniac – inclined to such a belief, in so far as the first desideratum of art appeared to him to be the most immediate and complete communication to the senses of everything that was to be said. And strange enough it is to see, in the case of his principal work, *The Ring of the Nibelungs*, what was the effect of this ruthless demand of his upon the drama, which after all was the crux of all his striving, and of which the fundamental law seemed to him to be precisely this utter, all-inclusive sense-appeal. We know the story of how this work was written. Wagner was working on his dramatic sketch of Siegfried's death; he himself tells us that he found it intolerable to have so much of the story lying before the beginning of the play, which had then to be woven in afterwards as it proceeded. He felt an overpowering need to bring that previous history within the sphere of his sense-appeal, and so he began to write backwards: first *Young Siegfried*, then the *Valkyrie*, then the *Rheingold*. He rested not until he had reduced the past to the present and brought it all upon the stage – in four evenings, everything from the primitive cell, the primeval beginnings, the first E-flat major of the bass bassoon at the commencement of the overture to the *Rheingold*, with which then he solemnly and almost soundlessly set to. Something glorious was the result, and we can understand the enthusiasm of its creator in view of the success of a scheme so colossal, so rich in new and profound possibilities of effectiveness. But what was it, really, this result? Æsthetics has been known to repudiate the composite drama as an art form. Gillparzer, for instance, did so. He considered that the relation of one part to another resulted in imparting an epic character to the whole – whereby, indeed, it gained in sublimity. But precisely this is what conditions the effectiveness of the *Ring* and the nature of its greatness: Wagner's masterpiece owes its sublimity to the epic spirit, and the epic is the sphere from which its material is drawn. The *Ring* is a scenic epic; its source is the dislike of the antecedent doings that haunt the stage behind the scenes – a dislike not shared, as we know, by the classic nor by the French drama. Ibsen is much closer to the classic stage, with his analytical technique and his skill at developing the backgrounds. It is amusing to think that precisely Wagner's theory of dramatic sense-appeal was what so wonderfully betrayed him into the epic vein.

His relation to the single arts out of which he created his "composite art-work" is worth dwelling upon. It has something peculiarly dilettantish about it. In the still loyal fourth *Thoughts out of Season* (*Unzeitgemässe Betrachtungen*) upon Wagner's childhood and youth, Nietzsche says: "His youth is that of a many-sided dilettante, of whom nothing very much will come. He had no strict, inherited family tradition to make a frame for him. Painting, poetry, acting, music, came as naturally to him as an academic career; the superficial observer might think him a born dilettante." In fact, not only the superficial but the admiring and impassioned observer might well say, at risk of being misunderstood, that Wagner's art *is* dilettantism, monumentalized and lifted into the sphere of genius by his intelligence and his enormous will-power. There is something dilettante in the very idea of a union of the arts; it could never have got beyond the dilettante had they not one and all been ruthlessly subordinated to his vast genius for expression. There is something suspect in his relation to the arts – something unæsthetic, however nonsensical that may sound. Italy, the plastic and graphic arts, leave him cold. He writes to Frau Wesendonk in Rome: "See everything for me too – I need to have somebody do it for me. . . . I have my own way of responding to these things, as I have discovered again and again, and finally quite conclusively when I was in Italy. For a while I am vividly impressed by some significant visual experience; but – it does not last. It seems that my eyes are not enough for me to use to take in the world."

Perfectly understandable. For he is an ear-man, a musician and poet; but still it is odd that he can write from Paris to the same correspondent: "Well, well, how the child is revelling in Raphael and painting! All very lovely, sweet, and soothing; only it never touches me. I am still the Vandal who, in a whole year spent in Paris, never got round to visit the Louvre. That tells the whole story." Not the whole; but after all something, and that something is significant. Painting is a great art — as great as the composite art-work. It existed before the composite art-work and it continues to do so — but it moves him not. He would have to be smaller than he is for one not to be wounded to the heart for the art of painting! For neither as past nor as living present has it anything to say to him. The greatness that grew up, as it were, beside him, the French impressionistic school — he hardly saw it; it had nothing to do with him. His relations with it were confined to the fact that Renoir painted his portrait; not a very flattering portrait — we are told that he did not much care for it. But his attitude toward poetry was clearly different. Throughout his life it gave him infinite riches — especially Shakespeare; though he speaks almost with pity of "literature-writers" in defence of the theory by which he glorifies his own powers. But no matter for that; he has made mighty contribution to poetry, she is much the richer for his work — always bearing in mind that it must not be read, that it is not really written verse but, as it were, exhalations from the music, needing to be complemented by gesture, music, and picture and existing as poetry only when all these work together. Purely as composition it is often bombastic, baroque, even childish; it has something majestically and sovereignly inept — side by side with such passages of absolute genius, power, compression, primeval beauty, as disarm all doubt; though they never quite make us forget that what we have here are images that stand not within the cultural structure of our great European literature and poetry, but apart from it, more in the nature of directions for a theatrical performance, which among other things needs a text. Among such gems of language interspersed among the boldly dilettante, I think in particular of the *Ring* and of *Lohengrin* — the latter, purely as writing, is perhaps the noblest, purest, and finest of Wagner's achievements.

His genius lies in a dramatic synthesis of the arts, which only as a whole, precisely as a synthesis, answers to our conception of a genuine and legitimate work of art. The component parts — even to the music, in itself, not considered as part of a whole — breathe something rank and lawless, that only disappears when they blend into the noble whole. Wagner's relation to his language is not that of our great poets and writers, it wants the austerity and fastidiousness displayed by those who find in words the best possession and the most trusted tool of art. That is proved by his occasional poems; the sugared and romantic adulations of Ludwig II of Bavaria, the banal and jolly jingles addressed to helpers and friends. One single careless little rhyme of Goethe is pure gold — and pure literature — compared with these versified platitudes and hearty masculine jests, at which our reverence for Wagner can only make us smile rather ruefully. Let us keep to Wagner's prose, to the manifestos and self-expositions on æsthetic and cultural matters. They are essays of astonishing mental virility and shrewdness, but they are not to be compared, as literary and intellectual achievements, with Schiller's works on the philosophy of art — for instance, that immortal essay on *Naïve and Sentimental Poetry*. They are hard to read, their style is both stiff and confused, again there is something about them that is overgrown, extraneous, dilettante: they do not belong to the sphere of great German and European prose; they are not the work of a born writer, but the casual product of some necessity. With Wagner every separate achievement was like that, always the product of necessity. Happy, devoted, complete, legitimate, and great he is, only in the mass.

Then was his musicianship too only the product of the demands made upon him by the whole overpowering product, only the result of strength of will? Nietzsche says somewhere that the so-called "gift" cannot be the essential thing about genius. "For instance," he cries, "what very little gift Richard Wagner had! Was ever a musician so poor as he still was in his twenty-eighth year?" And it is true that Wagner's musical beginnings were all timid, poor, and derivative, and lie much later in his life than is usually the case with great musicians. He himself says: "I still remember, round my thirtieth year, asking myself whether I possessed the capacity to develop an artistic individuality of high rank; I could still trace in my work a tendency to imitation, and looked forward only with great anxiety to my development as an independent original creator." That is a retrospect, he wrote it as a master, in 1862. But only three years earlier, when he was forty-six, in Lucerne, he had days when he simply could not get forward with the *Tristan;* he writes to Liszt: "How pathetic I seem to myself as a musician I cannot find words strong enough to tell you. At the bottom of my heart, I feel an absolute tyro. You should see me sitting here, thinking 'It simply *must* go'; then I go to the piano and dig out some wretched trash, to give it up again, like a fool. Imagine my feelings, my inward conviction of my utter musical incapacity. And now you come, oozing it out of all your pores, streams and springs and waterfalls of it, and I have to listen to what you say of me! Not to believe that it is sheer irony is very hard. My dear chap, this is all very odd, and believe me, I am no great shakes." That is pure depression, inapplicable in every word, and doubly absurd in the address to which it went. Liszt answers it as it should be answered. He reproaches him with "frantic injustice toward himself." Every artist knows this sudden shame, felt on confronting some masterly performance. For the practice of an art always, in every case, means a fresh and very careful adaptation of the personal and individual to the art in general; thus a man, even after he has received recognition for happy performances of his own, can suddenly compare them with the work of others and ask himself: "Is it possible to mention my own adaptation in the same breath with these things?" Even so, such a degree of depressive self-depreciation, such pangs of conscience in the presence of music, in a man who is in the middle of the third act of *Tristan* — there is something strange about it, something psychologically remarkable. Truly he had paid with a deal of poor-spirited self-abasement for the dictatorial self-sufficiency of his later days, when he published in the Bayreuth papers so much scorn and condemnation of the beautiful in Mendelssohn, Schumann, Brahms, to the greater glory of his own art! What was the source of these attacks of faint-heartedness? They could only come from the error he made at such moments: of isolating his musicianship and thus bringing it into comparison with the best, whereas it should only be regarded *sub specie* of his whole creative production — and vice versa; to this error is due all the embittered opposition that his music had to overcome. We, who owe to this wonder-world of sound, to this intellectual wizardry, so much bliss and ravishment, so much amazement at sight of this giant capacity, self-created — we find it hard to understand the opposition and the repulsion. The expressions that were used, descriptions like "cold," "algebraic," "formless," seem to us shockingly uncomprehending and lacking in insight; with a want of receptivity, a thick-skinned poverty of understanding that inclines us to think they could only have come from philistine spheres, forsaken alike of God and music. But no. Many of those who so judged, who were impelled so to judge, were no philistines, they were artistic spirits, musicians and lovers of music, who had her interest at heart and could with justice claim that they were able to distinguish between the musical and the unmusical. And they found that this music was no music. Their opinion has been completely counted out, it has suffered a mass defeat. But even if it was false, was it also inexcusable? Wagner's music is not music to the same extent that the dramatic basis (which unites with it to form a creative art) is not literature. It is psychology, symbolism, mythology, emphasis, everything — only not music in the pure and consummate sense intended by those bewildered critics. The texts round which it twines, filling out their dramatic content, are not literature — but the music is! Like a geyser it seems to shoot forth out of the myth's precultural depths — and not only seems, for it actually does it — and in very truth it is conceived, deliberately, calculatedly, with high intelligence, with an extreme of shrewdness, in a spirit as literary as the spirit of the texts is musical. Music, resolved into its primeval elements, must serve to force philosophic conclusions into high relief. The ever-craving chromatics of the *Liebestod* are a literary idea. The Rhine's immemorial flow, the seven primitive chords — like blocks to build up Valhalla — are no less so. I walked home one night with a famous conductor who had just finished conducting *Tristan;* he said to me: "That is not even music any more." He voiced the sense of our common emotion. But what we say today with acceptance, with admiration, could not but have sounded in the beginning like a furious denial. Such music as Siegfried's Rhine Journey, or the Funeral March, of unspeakable glory for our ears, for our spirits, they were never listened to, they were unheard-of in the worst sense of the phrase. This stringing together of symbolic musical quotations, till they lie like boulders in the stream of musical development — it was too much to ask that they be considered music as Bach, Beethoven, and Mozart are music. Too much to ask that the E-flat major triad at the beginning of the *Rheingold* be called music. It was not. It was an acoustic idea: the idea of the beginning of all things. It was the self-willed dilettante's exploitation of music to express a mythological idea. Psychoanalysis claims to know that love is composed and put together out of elements of sheer perversity; yet, and therefore, she remains love, the most divine phenomenon this world has to show. Well, now, the genius of Richard Wagner is put together out of streams of dilettantism.

But what streams! He is a musician who can persuade even the unmusical to be musical. That may be a drawback in the eyes of *illuminati* and aristocrats of the art. But when among the unmusical we find men and artists like Baudelaire — ? For him, contact with the world of music was simply contact with Wagner. He wrote to Wagner that he had no understanding of music, and knew none except a few fine things by Weber and Beethoven. And now he felt an ecstasy that made him want to make music with words alone, to vie with Wagner in language — all of which had far-reaching consequences for French poetry. A pseudo-music, a music for laymen, can do with converts and proselytes such as this; even the austerest music might be envious of them — and not of them alone. For there are things in this popular music so splendid, so full of genius, as to make such distinctions ridiculous. The swan motif in *Lohengrin* and *Parsifal*, the summer full-moon music at the end of the second act of the *Meistersinger* and the quintet in the third act; the A-flat major harmony in the second act of *Tristan*, and Tristan's visions of the lovers striding across the sea; the Good Friday music in *Parsifal* and the mighty transformation music in the third act; the glorious duet between Siegfried and Brünnhilde at the beginning of the *Götterdämmerung*, with the folk-song cadence; "*Willst Du mir Minne schenken*" and the ravishing "*Heil Dir Brünnhilde, prangender Stern*"; certain parts from the Venusberg revision of the *Tristan* time — these are inspirations that might make absolute music grow red with delight or pale with envy. I have selected them at random. There are many others that I might have cited to display Wagner's astonishing skill in modifying, modulating, and reinterpreting a motif already introduced: for instance, in the prelude to the third act of the *Meistersinger*, where Hans Sachs's Shoemaker's Song, already known to us from the humorous second act as a lusty workman's song, is lifted to unexpected heights of poetry. Or take the recasting — of rhythm and timbre — and the restatement that the so-called faith motif undergoes; we hear it first in the overture and many times throughout the *Parsifal*, beginning with Gurnemanz's great recitative. It is hard to refer to these things with only words at one's disposition to wake them. Why, as I think of Wagner's music, does some small detail, a mere flourish, wake in my ear, like the horn-figure, technically quite easy to describe, and yet quite indescribable, which in the lament for Siegfried's death harmonically foreshadows the love motif of his parents? At such moments one scarcely knows whether it is Wagner's own peculiar and personal art, or music itself, that one so loves, that so charms one. In a word, it is heavenly — though only music could make one take the gushing adjective in one's mouth without shame.

The general tone, psychologically speaking, of Wagner's music is heavy, pessimistic, laden with sluggish yearning, broken in rhythm; it seems to be wrestling up out of darkness and confusion to redemption in the beautiful; it is the music of a burdened soul, it has no dancing appeal to the muscles, it struggles, urges, and drives most labouredly, most unsoutherly — Lenbach's quick wit characterized it aptly when he said to Wagner one day: "Your music — dear me, it is a sort of luggage van to the kingdom of heaven." But it is not that alone. Its soul-heaviness must not make one forget that it can also produce the sprightly, the blithe, and the stately — as in the themes of the knights, the motifs of Lohengrin, Stolzing, and Parsifal, the natural mischievousness and loveliness of the terzetto of the Rhine maidens, the burlesque humour and learned arrogance of the overture to the *Meistersinger*, the jolly folk-music of the dance in the second act. Wagner can do anything. In the art of characterization he is incomparable; to understand his music as a method of characterization is to admire it without stint. It is picturesque, it is even grotesque; it is all based upon the perspective required by the theatre. But it has a richness of inventiveness even in small matters, a flexible capacity of entering into character, speech, and gesture such as was never seen in so marked a degree. In the single roles it is triumphant: take the figure of the Flying Dutchman, musically and poetically encompassed by doom and destruction, wrapped round by the wild raging of the lonely seas. Or Loki with his elemental incalculableness and malicious charm, or Siegfried's dwarf foster-father, knock-kneed and blinking; or Beckmesser's silly spite. It is the Dionysiac play-actor and his art — his arts, if you like — revealing themselves in this omnipotent, ubiquitous power of depiction and transformation. He changes not only his human mask; he enters into nature and speaks in the tempest and the thunderbolt, in the rustling leaf and the sparkling wave, in the rainbow and the dancing flame. Alberic's tarn-cap is the comprehensive symbol of this genius for disguise, this imitative all-pervasiveness: that can enter as well into the spongy hopping and crawling of the lowly toad as into the care-free, cloud-swinging existence of the old Norse gods. It is this characteristic versatility that could encompass works of such absolute heterogeneity as the *Meistersinger*, sturdy and German as Luther himself, and *Tristan's* death-drunken, death-yearning world. It marks off each of the operas from the others, develops each out of one fundamental note that distinguishes it from all the rest; so that — within the entire product, which after all is a personal cosmos — each single work forms a closed and starry cosmos of its own. Among them are musical contacts and relations that indicate the organic nature of the whole. Accents of the *Meistersinger* are heard in *Parsifal;* in the *Flying Dutchman* we get anticipations of *Lohengrin*, and in its text hints of the religious raptures of *Parsifal*, as in the words: "*Ein heil'ger Balsam meinen Wunden*," "*Der Schwur, dem hohen Wort entfliesst.*" And in the Christian *Lohengrin* there is a pagan residuum, personified by Ortrud, that suggests the *Ring*. But on the whole each work is stylistically set off against the rest, in a way that makes one see and almost feel the secret of style as the very kernel of art, well-nigh as art itself: the secret of the union of the personal with the objective. In every one of his works Wagner is quite himself, not a beat therein could be by anybody else, each bears his unmistakable formula and signature. And yet each is at the same time stylistically a world of its own, the product of an objective intuition that holds the balance with the personal will-power and entirely resolves it in itself. Perhaps the greatest marvel in this respect is the work of the seventy-year-old man, the *Parsifal:* here the uttermost is achieved in exploring and expressing remote and awful and holy worlds – yes, *Tristan* nothwithstanding, this is the uttermost point reached by Wagner, it witnesses to a power of blending style and emotion even beyond his usual capacity; to these sounds one surrenders with ever new interest, unrest, and bewitchment.

"A bad business, this," writes Wagner from Lucerne in 1859, in the midst of his absorbing labours on the third act of *Tristan*, which have renewed his interest in the long-since envisaged and already sketched figure of Amfortas. "A bad business! Think of it, for God's sake: it has suddenly become frightfully plain to me that Amfortas is my Tristan of the third act, at his unthinkable culmination." This process of "culmination" is the involuntary law of the life and growth of Wagner's productions, and it is the result of self-indulgence. All his life long he was labouring to utter Amfortas, in accents broken by torment and sin. He was already there in Tannhäuser's "Ah, how the weight of sin oppresses me!" In *Tristan* they seemed to have reached their uttermost and shattering expression; but in *Parsifal*, as he recognizes himself, with horror, they must undergo another "unthinkable culmination." It is a matter of screwing up his language to the highest pitch and then unconsciously seeking ever stronger and intenser situations to go with them. The material, the single works, are stages and successive transformations of a unity possessed by the self-contained and consummate life-work – which "develops" but to a certain extent was present from the beginning. This is the explanation of the telescoping, the dovetailing of conceptions; from which it results, in an artist of this kind and calibre, that what he is working on is never merely the task in hand; for everything else is weighing upon him and burdening the productive moment. Something apparently (and only half apparently) planned, planned for a lifetime, comes out when we know that Wagner in 1862 wrote quite definitely to von Bülow from Bieberich that *Parsifal* would be his last work. This was a round twenty years before it was actually performed. The *Siegfried* will have been sandwiched in between *Tristan* and the *Meistersinger*, and the whole *Ring* worked up, in order to fill in the holes in the scheme. During the whole of

Tristan he had to carry on at the *Ring*, and in *Tristan*, from the beginning, there are hints of *Parsifal*. The latter was present even during the sound and healthy, Luther-spirited *Meistersinger;* it had been waiting since 1845, the year of the first performance of *Tannhäuser*, in Dresden. In 1848 comes the prose draft which condenses the Nibelung myth into a drama: the putting on paper of *Siegfried's Death*, which was to end in the *Götterdämmerung*. But meantime, between 1846 and 1847, the *Lohengrin* is composed, and the action of the *Meistersinger* drafted, as a satyr-play and humorous pendant to *Tannhäuser*. This fourth decade of the century, in the middle of which he will be thirty-two years old, rounds out the working plan of the whole of his life, which will be carried out in the following four decades up to 1881, all the plays being dovetailed in together by simultaneous working on them all. His work, strictly speaking, has no chronology. It originates, of course, in time; but it is there all at once, and has been there from the beginning. The last achievement, foreseen as such from the beginning, and completed with his sixty-ninth year, is then in so far release that it means the fulfilment, the end and the exitus, and nothing more comes after it; the old man's work on it, the work of an artist who has entirely lived out his powers, is nothing more than just work on it. The giant task is finished, is complete; the heart, which has held out the storms of seventy years, may, in a last spasm, cease to beat.

This creative burden, then, rested on shoulders which were far from being as broad as Saint Christopher's; on a constitution so weakly, to judge by appearances and by subjective evidence, that no one would have expected it to hold out to carry such a burden to its goal. This nature felt itself every minute on the verge of exhaustion; only by exception did it experience the sensations of well-being. Constipated, melancholy, sleepless, generally tormented, this man is at thirty in such a state that he will often sit down and weep for a quarter of an hour on end. He cannot believe that he will live to see the *Tannhäuser* finished. To undertake at thirty-six to bring the *Ring* to completion seems to him presumption; when he is forty, he "thinks daily of death" – he who will be writing *Parsifal* at almost sixty-nine.

His martyrdom is a nervous complaint, one of those organically intangible illnesses which victimize a man years on end and make his life a burden, without being actually dangerous. It is hard for the victim to believe that they are not; more than one place in Wagner's letters shows that he regards himself as devoted to death. "My nerves," he writes at thirty-nine to his sister, "are by now in complete decline; it is possible that some change in my outward situation will stave off death for some years yet; but cannot stop the process." And in the same year: "I am nervously very ill, and after several efforts at a radical treatment of the disease have come to the conclusion that there is no hope of recovery. My work is all that keeps me up; but the nerves of my brain are already so ruined that I cannot work more than two hours in the day and then only if I lie down for two hours afterwards and perhaps can fall asleep a little." Two hours daily. By such small stages, then, at least at times, this whole gigantic life-work is erected; struggling all the time against rapidly supervening exhaustion, complement to a tough elasticity which can in no long time restore the easily exhausted energies. And the moral name of this process is patience. "True patience displays great elasticity," Novalis notes; and Schopenhauer praises it as the genuine courage. It is this moral and physical combination of courage, patience, and elasticity that enables this man to carry out his mission; Wagner's history, as scarcely that of any other artist, gives us an insight into the peculiar vital structure of genius: this mixture of sensibility and strength, delicacy and endurance, which is compact of labour against odds and all-unexpected rewards, and out of which great works come. It is not surprising that in time it displays a sense of being kept on through the self-will of the task itself. It is hard not to believe in a metaphysical wilfulness of the work that is struggling towards realization, whose tool and willing-unwilling victim the author is. "In fact I do very wretchedly indeed, but I do" – that is a despairing, self-mocking cry out of one of Wagner's letters. And he does not fail to set up a causal nexus between his sufferings and his art; he recognizes art and illness to be one and the same affliction – with the result that he tries to escape from them, naïvely, by the help of a water-cure. "A year ago," he writes, "I found myself in a hydropathic establishment, where I hoped and wanted to become an entirely healthy man by the healing of my senses. I was wishing for the kind of health that would make it possible for me to get rid of art, the martyrdom of my life; it was a last desperate struggle for happiness, for real, respectable joy in life, such as only consciously healthy people can have."

How touching is this confused and childish utterance! He looks to have cold water cure him of art; that is, from the constitution that makes him an artist. His relation to art, to his destiny, is complex almost beyond hope of unravelling, highly contradictory, involved – sometimes he fairly seems to be quivering in the meshes of a logical net. "So I am to do this too?" cries the forty-six-year-old man, after going at length and with animation into the symbolic and intellectual content of the *Parsifal* plan. "And music for it too! Thanks very much. Whoever wants to may do it, I'll fight it off as long as I can." The words have an accent of feminine coquetry; they are full of trembling eagerness for the work, awareness of the inward voice "Thou must," and the voluptuous pleasure of resistance. The dream of getting free, of living instead of creating, of being happy, continues to recur in the letters; the words "happiness," "disinterested happiness," "noble enjoyment of life," are everywhere expressed as the opposite to the artist existence; as also the conception of art as substitute for all direct forms of enjoyment. At thirty-nine he writes to Liszt: "I decline more and more surely from day to day. I lead *an indescribably worthless life*. Of real enjoyment of life I know nothing; for me enjoyment, *love* [he underlines the word] are imaginary, not experienced. My heart had to be absorbed in my brain, my life had to become artificial; now I can only live as 'artist,' all the human being is absorbed in that." We must admit that never before has art been characterized in stronger words, in more desperate frankness, as drug, intoxicant, *paradis artificiel.* And he has attacks of violent revolt against this artificial existence, as on his fortieth birthday, when he writes to Liszt: "I want to be baptized anew; will you be godfather? I'd like for us both to get clean away, out into the world! Come out with me into the wide world – even if we just went gaily to smash there, and sank into some abyss!" One thinks of Tannhäuser, clinging to Wolfram to drag him away to the Venusberg; for certainly the world and "life" are, as in a fever-dream of renunciation, conceived as the Venusberg, as a state of thoroughgoing bohemian *je m'en fichisme* and the self-destruction of mad dissipation – in short, as all that for which art offers him a "worthless" substitute.

On the other hand, or rather in strange alternation with this, art appears to him in a quite different light: as a means of release, as sedative, as a condition of pure contemplation and surrender of the will; for thus philosophy taught him to regard it, and with the docility and goodwill common to children and artists he was anxious to obey. Oh, he is idealist! Life has its meaning not in itself but in the higher things, the task, the creative activity, and thus "to be forever struggling to produce what is needed" as he is, "to be often for long periods of time unable to think of aught but how I must act in order to get outward peace for even a little while and get hold of what is necessary for existence, and to that end to have to depart so utterly out of my own character, to have to appear to people from whom I need things to be so entirely different from what I am – that is really maddening. . . . All these cares are so fit and natural to the man to whom life is an end in itself, who gets all the joy he finds in things out of the trouble he has to take to bring them about, and who can simply never understand why that is so absolutely disgusting to the likes of us, since it is the common lot of mankind! That anybody should look on life as not an end in itself, but as an indispensable means to a higher goal – who really does understand that at the bottom of his soul?" (Letter to Mathilde Wesendonk, Venice, 1858.) In truth, it is a shameful and degrading thing to be obliged to fight for life like that, to go on one's knees for it, when life itself is not at all what one wants, but one's higher goal lying above and outside life: art, creation, for whose sake one must fight for rest and peace, and which themselves appear in the light of rest and peace. And even when one has finally by dint of struggling achieved the conditions for work – which are not so easily satisfied – then only begins the actual and higher voluntary drudgery, the productive struggle involved in art. For what he fancied, in his deluded philosophizing while he struggled for the baser ends of existence, to be pure "idea" and redeeming wisdom, proves to be the real wheel of Ixion, the last and uttermost convulsion of the labouring will.

Purity and peace – a deep craving for these two lies in his breast, complementary to his thirst for life. And when the craving reacts against his attempt to seize upon immediate pleasure, then art – it is a fresh complication in his relations to her – appears to him in the light of a hindrance to his healing. What we have here is a variation of the Tolstoyan repudiation of art, the cruel denial of one's own natural endowment, for the sake of the "spirit." Ah, art! How right was Buddha when he called it the broadest path that leads away from salvation! There is a long and tempestuous letter written from Venice to Frau Wesendonk, in 1858, in which he sets this forth to his friend, in discussing his idea of a Buddhistic drama, *The Victors*. "Buddhistic drama" – there was precisely the difficulty. It is a contradiction in terms – as had become clear to him when he tried to utilize dramatically, and in particular musically, the idea of a being utterly free, lifted above all passions, such as the Buddha was. The pure and holy one, through knowledge tranquillized, is, artistically speaking, dead – that was quite clear. It was a piece of good luck that, according to the sources, Sha-kya Muni Buddha had a last problem to face, was involved in a final conflict: he had to come to the decision, despite his former principles, to receive the Dragon's Daughter into the company of the elect. And thus, thank God, he became a possible subject for artistic treatment. Wagner rejoices; but at the same moment the life-bound nature of all art, the knowledge of her temptress power, falls heavily upon his conscience. Has he not already caught himself in the act of preferring the play and not the spirit? Without art he might be a saint, with her he never will. If the highest knowledge and the deepest insight were vouchsafed him, it could only make him what he was, a poet, an artist; they would stand there before him, soulfully evident, an enchanting picture, and he would not be able to resist giving it created being. Worse yet, he would even take pleasure in the devilish antinomy! It is horrible – but fascinatingly interesting – one might make a romantic psychological opera out of it – and that, more or less, is what Wagner has done, in the letter to Frau Wesendonk, which is a sort of first draft. Goethe asserts: " One cannot withdraw from the world more securely than through art, one cannot knit oneself more securely to it than through her." That tranquil and grateful statement – see what becomes of it in the head of a romantic!

But whatever guise art adopts, and whether she is a betrayal of the joys alike of sense and of salvation, in any case the work goes on, thanks to that elastic power of recovery which he himself must admire in secret; the scores pile up, and that is the main thing. This man knows as little as do any of us the right way of living. He *is lived*, life squeezes from him what it wants – that is to say, his works – regardless of the mazes his thought wanders in. "My child, this *Tristan* is getting *frightful!* This last act! I am afraid the opera will be forbidden – if the whole thing is not to become a burlesque through bad production. Only mediocre production can save me. Too good would make people crazy. I cannot imagine it otherwise. I have been driven as far as this! Alas! I was just in full train – adieu!" A note to Frau Wesendonk. A quite un-Buddhistic note, full of excited, half-terrified laughter at the madness and badness of what he is doing. This infirm and melancholic man – what a fund of good temper, what indestructible resiliency he must have possessed! His disease, after all, consists in being a variation of the bourgeois variety of health. He gave out a vital magic that made Nietzsche call association with him the one great joyful experience of his life. And he had, before everything else, the inestimable power of throwing emotion on one side and giving free rein to the commonplace. Among his artists in Bayreuth, after a day of strenuous labour, he would announce the advent of rest and relaxation, crying out: "Now not another serious word!" He understood them perfectly, these little theatrical people whom he needed for the realization of his ideas; despite the great intellectual disparity, he was himself theatre-blood through and through, a comrade of the Thespian car. His simple-minded friend Heckel from Mannheim, the first stockholder of Bayreuth, tells priceless things on this subject. "Very often," he writes, "the relations between Wagner and his artists were extremely jolly and free-and-easy. At the last rehearsal in the salon of the Hôtel Sommer he actually, out of sheer high spirits, stood on his head." Again one thinks of Tolstoy: I mean the time when the grey-bearded prophet and melancholic Christian felt such a superabundance of vitality that he actually jumped up on his father-in-law's shoulder. One is no less artist than are the tenors and soubrettes that call one master: a human creature inclined — at bottom — to being and making merry, an instigator to all kinds of festivities and diversions — in profound and most healthful contrast to the wise and knowledgeable and commanding intelligence, the perfectly serious human being, like Nietzsche. It is well to understand that the artist, even he inhabiting the most austere regions of art, is *not* an absolutely serious man; that effects and enjoyment are his stock-in-trade, and that tragedy and farce can spring from one and the same root. A turn of the lighting changes one into the other; the farce is a hidden tragedy, the tragedy — in the last analysis — a sublime practical joke. The seriousness of the artist — a subject to ponder. And perhaps to shudder at — if what we mean is the intellectual veracity of the artist being, for his artistic veracity, the famous "serious playing" — that purest, loftiest, and most moving manifestation of the human mind — does not come in here. But the other, what is to be said for it: and in particular for the seriousness of that seeker after truth, that thinker and believer Richard Wagner? The ascetic and Christian ideals of his later period, the sacramental philosophy of salvation won by abstinence from fleshly lusts of every kind; the convictions and opinions of which *Parsifal* is the expression; even *Parsifal* itself — all these incontestably deny, revoke, cancel the sensualism and the revolutionary spirit of Wagner's young days, which pervade the whole atmosphere and content of the *Siegfried*. It did not, it might not exist any longer. If the artist was intellectually sincere in these new, later, and probably definitive views, then the works of the earlier epochs, recognized as erroneous, sinful, and pernicious, must have been denounced and extirpated, burned by their creator's very hand, so as not to be any longer a stumbling-block to humanity. But he does not think of it – actually the idea does not even occur to him. Who could destroy such beautiful compositions? So they continue to exist, side by side, and they continue to be played; for the artist has reverence for his biography. He yields himself to the varying psychological moods of life as it passes, and portrays them in works which to the eye of reason may contradict each other, but are individually all beautiful, and all worth keeping. To the artist, new experiences of "truth" are new incentives to the game, new possibilities of expression, no more. He believes in them, he takes them seriously, just so far as he needs to in order to give them the fullest and profoundest expression. In all that he is very serious, serious even to tears – but yet *not quite* – and by consequence, not at all. His artistic seriousness is of an absolute nature, it is "dead-earnest playing." But his intellectual seriousness is not absolute, it is only serious for the purposes of the game. Among comrades the artist is so ready to mock at his own seriousness that Wagner could actually send the *Parsifal* text to Nietzsche with the signature: "R. Wagner, Member of the Consistory." But Nietzsche was no comrade. Such good-natured winking could not appease the sour and deadly, the absolute seriousness of his feeling against the Popish Christianity of a production – of which, however, he does say that it is the highest sort of challenge to music. When Wagner, in a childish fury, threw a Brahms score down from the piano, the spectacle of such jealous desire for single domination made Nietzsche sad; he said: "At that moment Wagner was not great." If Wagner by way of relaxation talked nonsense and told Saxon jokes, Nietzsche blushed for him. I can understand Nietzsche's embarrassment at this alacrity in moving from one plane to another; but something in me – perhaps fellow-feeling with Wagner as an artist – warns me not to understand it too well.

His acquaintance with the philosophy of Arthur Schopenhauer was the great event in Wagner's life. No earlier intellectual contact, such as that with Feuerbach, approaches it in personal and historical significance. It meant to him the deepest consolation, the highest self-confirmation; it meant release of mind and spirit, it was utterly and entirely the right thing. There is no doubt that it freed his music from bondage and gave it courage to be itself. Wagner had little faith in the reality of friendship. In his eyes, and according to his experience, the barriers of personality separating one soul from another make solitude inevitable, and full understanding an impossibility. Here he felt himself understood, and he understood completely. "My friend Schopenhauer"; "A gift from heaven to my loneliness." "But one friend I have," he writes, "whom I love ever to win anew. That is my old Schopenhauer, who seems so grumpy and is always so deeply loving." "When I have urged my feelings to their utmost, what a joy and refreshment to open that book and suddenly find myself again, to see myself so well understood and clearly expressed, only in quite a different language, which suffering quickly makes me understand . . . that is a wonderful and gratifying reciprocal effect, and ever new because ever stronger. . . . How beautiful, that the old man knows nothing of what he is to me, and *what I am to myself through him!*"

A piece of good luck like this, among artists, is only possible where they speak different languages; otherwise catastrophe and deadly rivalry ensue. But where the medium of one is thought, of the other form, all jealously engendered by the similarity or proximity of mental states is obviated. The *pereant qui ante nos nostra dixerunt* has no bearing, nor has Goethe's question: "Does one live, then, when others live?" On the contrary, the very fact of the other's existence means help at need, it means unexpected and blessed clarifying and strengthening of one's own being. Never probably in the history of the mind has there been so wonderful an example of the artist, the dark and driven human being, finding spiritual support, self-justification, and enlightenment in another's thought, as in this case of Wagner and Schopenhauer.

The World as Will and Idea: what memories of one's own young intoxications of the spirit, one's own joys of conception, compact of melancholy and gratitude, come up at the thought of the bond between Wagner's work and this great book! This comprehensive critique and guide, this poesy of knowledge, this metaphysics of impulse and spirit, will and idea as conceived by the artist, this marvellous thought-structure of ethical, pessimistical, and musical elements — what profound, epoch-making, human affinities it displays with the score of the *Tristan*! The old words come back in which the stripling described the Schopenhauer experience of his bourgeois hero: "He was filled with a great, surpassing satisfaction. It soothed him to see how a master mind could lay hold on this strong, cruel, mocking thing called life and enforce it and condemn it. His was the gratification of the sufferer who has always had a bad conscience about his sufferings and concealed them from the gaze of a harsh, unsympathetic world, until suddenly, from the hand of an authority, he receives, as it were, justification and licence for his suffering – justification before the world, this best of all possible worlds which the master mind scornfully demonstrates to be the worst of all possible ones." They come back, these old phrases of gratitude and homage that still express so well the tremulous rapture of the past – and of the present: that rousing out of brief and heavy sleep, that sudden and exquisitely startling awakening, to find in one's own heart the seed of a metaphysic which proves the ego to be illusion, death a release from that ego's insufficiency; the world a product of the will, and his own eternal possession, so long as he does not deny himself in knowledge, but finds his way from error to peace. That is the conclusion, the doctrine of wisdom and salvation subjoined to a philosophy of the will which has little to do with the wisdom of peace and rest, being a conception that could only have its source in a nature tormented by will and impulse; in which, indeed, the impulse to clarification, spiritualization, and knowledge was just as strong as the other sinister urgency; the conception of a universal Eros which expressly considers sex to be the focus of the will, and the æsthetic point of view, as that of pure and disinterested contemplation, the only and primary possibility of release from the torture of instinct. Out of the will, out of desire contrary to better knowledge, this philosophy, which is the will's intellectual denial, is born; and thus it was that Wagner, whose nature was profoundly akin to the philosopher's own, felt it and seized upon it with the greatest gratitude, as something essentially his own and answering to his needs. For his nature too was combined of urgent and tormenting desires for power and pleasure, together with longings for moral enlightenment and release; it was a conflict of passion and desire for peace. And thus a system of thought which is an extraordinary mixture of quietism and heroics, which calls "happiness" a chimera and gives out that the highest and best we can attain to is a life of heroic struggle, must have rejoiced a nature like Wagner's, must have seemed made to fit him and created for him.

The official works on Wagner assert in all seriousness that *Tristan* was not influenced by the Schopenhauerian philosophy. That seems to me a curious lack of insight. The arch-romantic worship of the night embodied in this sublimely morbid, consuming, enchanting work, deep-dyed in all the worst and highest mysteries of the romantic essence, has about it nothing specifically Schopenhauerian. The sensuous, supersensuous intuitions in the *Tristan* come from a remoter source: from the perfervid and hectic Novalis, who writes: "Union joined not only for life but for death is a marriage that gives us a companion for the night. Love is sweetest in death; for the living death is a bridal night, a sweet mysterious secret." And in the *Hymns to Night* he complains: "Must morning always come? Does the domain of the earthly never cease? Will it never be that love's sweet sacrifice shall burn forever on the altar?" Tristan and Isolde call themselves the "Night-consecrate" – the phrase actually occurs in Novalis: "Consecrated to the night." And still more striking from the point of view of literary history, still more significant for the sources of *Tristan*, for its emotional and intellectual bases, are its associations with a little book of evil repute, I mean Friedrich von Schlegel's *Lucinde*. I quote a passage from this work: "We are immortal as love. I can no longer say my love or thy love, both being so utterly one, love as much given as returned. It is marriage, eternal union and bond between our spirits, not alone for what we call this world, but for a true, indivisible, nameless, infinite world, for our whole, everlasting life and being." Here is the mental image of the love- and death-potion: "Thus I too, if the time seemed come, would drain a cup of laurel-water with thee, freely and gladly, as the last glass of champagne we drank together, with the words: 'Let us drink out the rest of our lives!' " And here is the thought of the *Liebestod:* "I know you too would not outlive me, you would follow to the grave your impatient spouse, from love and longing you would descend into the flaming abyss whither the Indian woman is driven by a desperate law which by harsh and deliberate enforcement violates and destroys the most delicate sanctuaries of the free will." And there is a reference to the "exaltation of voluptuousness," surely a very Wagnerian formula. Here indeed is an erotic, mystical prose poem, in praise and adoration of sleep, the paradise of rest, the holy silence of passivity, which in *Tristan* becomes the lulling motif of the horns and the divided violins. And it was nothing less than a literary discovery that I made, when as a young man I underlined the ecstatic passage between Julian and Lucinde: "Oh, eternal yearning! For the fruitless desire and vain brilliance of the day die down and expire, and a great night of love knows eternal repose," and wrote in the margin: "*Tristan.*" To this day I do not know whether anyone has ever remarked this case of unconscious verbal memory and imitation, as little as I know whether scholars are aware that Nietzsche took from *Lucinde* his title for the book he calls *Fröhliche Wissenschaft* (*Joyous Wisdom*).

Its cult of the night, its execration of the day, are what stamps the *Tristan* as romantic, as fundamentally affiliated with all the romantic aspects of emotion and thought — and as such not needing the Schopenhaurian sponsorship. Night is the kingdom and home of all romanticism, her own discovery, always she has played it off against the empty vanities of the day, as the kingdom of sensibility against reason. I shall never forget the impression made upon me by Linderhof, the castle of the ailing and beauty-consumed King Ludwig; for I saw there the preponderance of the night expressed in the very proportions of the rooms. This little pleasure palace situated in the wonderful mountain solitudes has rather small and insignificant living-rooms, and only one room of relative magnificence of size and decoration: the sleeping-chamber. It is full of the heavy splendour of gilding and silk, its state bed lies under a canopy and is flanked by gold candelabra. Here is the true state apartment of the royal chalet, and it is dedicated to the night. This deliberate stress upon the night, the lovelier half of the day, is arch-romantic; and its romanticism is bound up with the whole mother- and moon-cult which since the dawn of human time and human sun-worship has stood opposed to the male and father-religion of the light. Wagner's *Tristan* belongs, generally speaking, to this world.

But when the Wagner authorities say that *Tristan* is a love-drama, as such contains the strongest affirmation of the will to live, and in consequence has nothing to do with Schopenhauer; when they insist that the night therein celebrated is the night of love "*wo Liebeswonne uns lacht,*" and that if this drama has a philosophy at all, then it is the exact opposite of the doctrine which would deny the will, and that precisely on that ground it is independent of the Schopenhaurian metaphysics — it seems to me that all this betrays a strange psychological insensitiveness. The denial of the will is the moral and intellectual content of Schopenhauer's philosophy, of secondary significance and not the crucial point. His philosophic system is fundamentally erotic in its nature, and in so far as it is that the *Tristan* is saturated with it. The quenching of the torch in the second act of the mystery play is emphasized in the orchestra by the death motif, the lovers' cry of transport: "*Selbst dann bin ich die Welt,*" with the longing motif out of the depths of the psychological and mythical accompanying music — is that not Schopenhauer? Wagner is mythological poet not less in *Tristan* than in the *Ring;* even the love-drama deals with a myth of the origin of the world. "Often," so he writes from Paris in 1860 to Mathilde Wesendonk, "I look with yearning toward the land of Nirvana. But Nirvana soon becomes *Tristan* again. You know the story of the Buddhistic theory of the origin of the world? A breath troubles the clearness of the heavens" – he writes the four chromatic ascending notes with which his *opus metaphysicum* begins and ends, the *g*-sharp, *a*, *a*-sharp, *b*-natural – "it swells and condenses, and there before me is the whole vast solid mass of the world." It is the symbolic tone-thought which we know as the "*Sehnsuchts* motif," and which in the cosmogony of the *Tristan* signifies the beginning of all things, like the E-flat major of the Rhine motif in the *Ring*. It is Schopenhauer's "will," represented by what Schopenhauer called the "focus of the will," the yearning for love. And this mythical equating of sexual desire with the sweet and fatal world-creating principle that first troubled the clear heaven of the inane – that is so Schopenhauerian that the refusal of the experts to see it looks like obstinacy.

"How could we die," asks Tristan in the early, not yet versified draft; "what would there be of us to kill that would not be love? Are we not utterly and only love? Can our love ever end? Could I ever will to love, love no more? Were I now to die would love die too, since we *are* naught but love?" The quotation shows the unhesitating equation of love and will on the part of the poet. The latter stands simply for the love of life, which cannot end in death, though it is freed from the fetters of individuality. Most interesting it is too to see the love-mythus sustained as a conception of the drama and preserved from any historical or religious clouding or distortion. Phrases like "Whether bound for hell or heaven," surviving in the draft, are omitted from the production. We have here doubtless a conscious weakening of the historical element, but it is limited to the intellectual and philosophical and only happens in the interest of these. And it suits admirably with a most intensive technique of coloration, applied to the landscape settings, the cultural elements, the racial characteristics of the protagonists. It is stylistic specialization of incredible ability and certainty of touch. Nowhere does Wagner's skill at mimicry triumph more magically than in the style of the *Tristan* – this not as a matter of language merely, by phraseology in the spirit of the court epic; for with intuitive genius he is able to saturate his word- and tone-painting in an Anglo-Norman-French atmosphere, with a discernment that shows how completely the Wagner soul is at home in the pre-national sphere of European life. The divorce from history, the free humanization, takes place only in the field of speculative thought, and then in the service of the erotic myth. For its sake heaven and hell are cut out. Christianity too, since it would amount to historical atmosphere. There is no God, no one knows Him or calls upon Him. There is nothing but erotic philosophy, atheistic metaphysics: the cosmogonic myth in which the *Sehnsuchts* motif evokes the world.

Wagner's good normal way of being ill, his rather morbid way of being heroic, are simply indications of the contradictions and cross-currents in his nature, its duality and manifoldness, as manifested in such apparently contradictory elements as the psychological and mythological bents to which I have already referred. To call him romantic is still probably the most apt characterization of his nature; but the concept romantic is itself so complex and changeable that it seems to be less a category than the abandonment of categories.

Only in the romantic can popular appeal unite with the extreme of subtlety, with an over-stimulated, "heinous" indulgence (to use a favourite word of E. T. A. Hoffmann), in means and effects – and it alone can make possible that "double optic" of which Nietzsche speaks with reference to Wagner: that knows how to cater to the coarsest and the finest – unconsciously, of course, for it would be stupid to introduce the element of calculation – whose *Lohengrin* can enrapture spirits like the author of the *Fleurs du mal* and at the same time serve to elevate the masses; that leads a Kundryish double life as a Sunday afternoon opera and as the idol of initiate and suffering and supersensitive souls. The romantic – in league, of course, with music, toward which it continually aspires, without which it can have no fulfilment – knows no exclusiveness, no "pathos of distance"; it says to nobody: "This is not for you"; one side of its nature stands with the least and lowest, and let nobody say that is the case with all great art. Great art may elsewhere too have succeeded in uniting the childlike and the elevated; but the combination of the extremely *raffiné* with fairy-story simplicity, the power to materialize – and popularize – the highly intellectual under the guise of an orgy of the senses; the ability to make the essentially grotesque put on the garment of consecration, the Last Supper, the bell, the elevation of the Host . . . to couple sex and religion in an opera of greatly daring sex-appeal, and to set up that sort of holy-unholy artistic establishment in the middle of Europe as a kind of Lourdes theatre and miraculous grotto for the voracious credulity of a decadent world – all that is nothing but romantic. In the classic and humanistic, the really high sphere of art, it is quite unthinkable. Take the list of characters in *Parsifal:* what a set! One advanced and offensive degenerate after another: a self-castrated magician; a desperate double personality, composed of a Circe and a repentant Magdalene, with cataleptic transition stages; a lovesick high-priest, awaiting the redemption that is to come to him in the person of a chaste youth; the youth himself, "pure" fool and redeemer, quite a different figure from Brünnhilde's lively awakener and in his way also an extremely rare specimen – they remind one of the aggregation of scarecrows in A. von Arnim's famous coach: the enigmatic gypsy witch; the good-for-nothing, who is a corpse; the golem in female form; and the Field-Marshal Cornelius Nepos, who is a slip of mandrake grown beneath the gallows. The comparison sounds blasphemous; and yet the solemn personages in *Parsifal* have the same flavour of romantic extravaganza, they spring from the same school of taste as do von Arnim's disreputable crew, though the fact would be more obvious if the literary form were fiction instead of drama. As it is, the music, with its sanctifying, mythologizing power, shrouds it from view; it is music's power over the emotions that makes the ensemble appear not like a half-burlesque, half-uncanny impropriety of the romantic school, but as a miracle play of the highest religious significance.

Youth is typically susceptible to this elusive problem of art and the essence of the artist, it has a melancholy understanding of the ironic interplay of essence and effect; in this field I recall many an utterance of my own young days, characteristic of the Wagner passion that has gone through the fire of the Nietzschean critique, dictated by that "disgust of knowledge" – which is the foremost and peculiar lesson youth learns therefrom. Nietzsche said he would not touch the *Tristan* score with the tongs. "Who will dare," he cries, "to utter the word, the right word, for the *ardeurs* of the *Tristan* music?" I am more open to the rather comic old-maidishness of this question than I was when I was twenty-five years old. For what is there so venturesome about it? Sensuality, enormous sensuality, mounting into the mythical, spiritualized, depicted with the extreme of naturalism, sensuality unquenchable by any amount of gratification – that is the "word." And one asks whence comes the violent bitterness against sex that expresses itself in such a psychological denunciation in the question of Nietzsche, the "free, very free spirit." Is not this Nietzsche the arch-moralist and clergyman's son? And what has become of his role as defender of life against morality? He applies to the *Tristan* the mystic's formula: voluptuous pleasure of hell ("*Wollust der Hölle*"). Good. And one need only compare the mysticism of the *Tristan* with that of Goethe's "blessed longing" and its "higher mating" to feel how little we are in the Goethe sphere. But Nietzsche himself is after all no poorer instance than Wagner of the fact that the soul-state of the Western world in the nineteenth century has deteriorated by comparison with Goethe's epoch. And the sort of lashing to fury or drugging to calm which are among Wagner's effects – the ocean too can show the same, and nobody thinks of dragging its psychology to the light of day. What is allowed to great nature should be allowed to great art; when Baudelaire, in naïve artistic rapture, and quite without moral prejudice, speaks of the "ecstasy of bliss and understanding" which the *Lohengrin* overture put him in, and raves of the "opium intoxication," of the "desire that in high places circles," he shows much more courage and intellectual freedom than Nietzsche with his suspicious caution. Though, after all, the phrase in which Nietzsche characterizes the Wagner craze as "a slight unconscious epidemic of sensuality" still has its justification, and it is precisely the word "unconscious" that, in view of Wagner's romantic popularity, may irritate such as feel the need of clear thinking; may be a ground for "preferring not to be there."

Wagner's power of concentrating the intellectual and the popular in a single dramatic figure is nowhere better displayed than in the hero of his revolutionary phase – in Siegfried. The "breathless delight" with which the future director of the Bayreuth Theatre one day witnessed a puppet show – he tells about it in his essay on Actors and Singers – bore practical fruit in the setting of the *Ring*, which is an ideal popular diversion with just the right kind of go-ahead hero. Who can fail to recognize in him the little whip-cracker of the county fair? But at the same time he is a northern sun-myth and god of light – which does not prevent him from being something modern too, out of the nineteenth century, the free man, the breaker of tablets and renovator of a fallen society: Bakunin, in short, as Bernard Shaw, with cheerful rationalism, quite simply calls him. Yes, he is a clown, a sun-god, and an anarchistic social-revolutionary, all rolled into one, what more can the theatre demand? And this art of combination is simply an expression of Wagner's own mingled and manifold nature. He is not musician and not poet, but a third category, in which the other two are blended in a way unknown before; he is a theatre-Dionysius, who knows how to take unprecedented methods of expression and give them a poetic basis, to a certain extent to rationalize them. But in so far as he *is* poet, it is not in a modern, literary, and cultivated spirit, not out of his mind and consciously, but in a much deeper and devouter way. It is the folk-soul that speaks out of him and through him; he is only its tool and mouthpiece, only "God's ventriloquist," to repeat Nietzsche's good joke. At least, this is the correct and accepted theory of his artistic position, and it is supported by a kind of unwieldy awkwardness that his work betrays when considered as literature. And yet he can write: "We should not underestimate the power of reflection; the unconsciously produced work of art belongs to periods remote from ours, and the art product of the most highly cultivated period cannot be produced otherwise than in full consciousness." That is a blow between the eyes for the theory which would ascribe an entirely mythical origin to his works; and indeed, though these indubitably bear in part the marks of inspiration, of blind and blissful ecstasy, yet there is so much else, so much cleverness, wittiness, allusiveness, calculated effect; so much dwarfish diligence accompanies the labours of gods and giants, that it is impossible to believe in trance and mystery. The extraordinary understanding displayed in his abstract writings does not indeed act in the service of spirit, truth, abstract knowledge; but to the advantage of his work, which it labours to explain and justify, whose pathway it would smooth, both within and without. But it is none the less a fact. And there would remain the possibility that in the act of creation he was entirely shoved aside to make room for the promptings of the folk-soul. But my feeling of the improbability of this is strengthened by various more or less well-authenticated statements from those who knew him, to the effect that by his own account some of his best things were produced by dint of sheer hard thinking. "Ah, how I have tried and tried," he is reported as saying, "thought and thought, until at last I get hold of what I wanted!"

In short, his author- and creatorship has contact with both spheres: the one that lies "remote from ours" as well as the one where the brain long ago developed into the modern intellectual tool we know. And hence the indissoluble mingling of the dæmonic and the bourgeois which is the essence of him. Much the same is true of Schopenhauer, who is accordingly Wagner's next of kin, both in time and in temperament. The unbourgeois extravagance of his nature, which he himself laid at the door of music ("it makes a purely exclamatory man of me," says he; "the exclamation point is the only satisfying punctuation to me so soon as I leave my notes"), this extravagance finds expression in the exaggerated character of all his moods, particularly the depressive. It comes out in the strange destinies of his outer life – destiny being nothing more than the unfolding of character – his wry relations with the world, his hunted, outlawed, broken and battered existence; he puts it in the mouth of his *Wehwalt* Siegmund:

Drew I to men or to women,
Many I met, where I them found,
If I for friend, for woman wooed,
Ever still was I despisèd,
Curses lay upon me.
What right ever I wrought
Still to them seemèd it wrong;
What to me evil appear'd
Others reckoned it right.
Fell I on feud, whither I went;
Where I me found, scorn met me.
Long'd I for bliss, waked I but woe.

Every word comes from experience; not one but is coined out of his own life; in these fine lines there is no more than he wrote in prose to Mathilde Wesendonk: "Since the world, in all seriousness, does not want me" – or to her husband: "I am so hard to accommodate in this world, that a thousand misunderstandings are always likely to take place. This is my great trouble . . . the world and I knock our heads together and the thinnest skull gets cracked – no wonder I have my nervous headaches." The desperate humour of this is quite in character. Once, round his forty-eighth birthday, he speaks of the "crazy mood" he was in, in Weimar; it delighted everybody, but originated solely in the circumstance that he did not dare be serious, simply did not dare any more, for fear of going to pieces. "This is a fault of my temperament, and it gets worse and worse. I fight against it, for sometimes it seems to me I shall weep myself away." What a luxury of debility! What *Kapellmeister Kreisler* eccentricity! All this passionate up and down, this frenzied and tragic emotionalism, reduced to its starkest elements, accursed, yet pining for rest and peace, he has concentrated in the figure of the Flying Dutchman; it lives and glows with the colours of his own anguish; the great intervals in which the score of this role swings to and fro are most calculated to create this impression of wild agitation.

No, this is no bourgeois – at least not in any sense of being adaptable or conformable to rule. And yet he has the atmosphere of the bourgeoisie, the atmosphere of his century, about him, as has Schopenhauer the capitalist philosopher: the moral pessimism, the mood of decline set to music — that is genuine nineteenth-century, and goes with its tendency to the monumental, its penchant for size — as though size were a property of morality. He has, I say, the atmosphere of the bourgeois, and not only in this general sense but in one much more personal. I will not insist that he was a revolutionary of the '48, a fighter for the middle class and thus a political citizen. For he was that only in his own peculiar way, as an artist and in the interest of his art, which was revolutionary and might hope for imagined advantages, better conditions, and more effectiveness from an upset of the existing order. But there are more intimate traits of character — despite its genius and its inspiration — which distinctly suggest the bourgeois attitude. As when he moved into that asylum on the green hill near Zürich and in the enjoyment of his sense of well-being wrote to Liszt: "Everything is arranged for permanence and convenience, and precisely as one would wish; everything is just in the right place. My study has the same fastidious air of comfort and elegance that is familiar to you; the desk stands by the big window. . . ." The fastidious order and also the bourgeois elegance he requires of his surroundings correspond to the element of shrewd and calculated industry which accompanies the dæmonic in his work, and supplies the bourgeois flavour of it. His later self-dramatization as *Deutscher Meister* with the black velvet cap had its good inward and natural justification; despite all volcanic manifestations it would be a mistake to overlook the old-German element, the loyal-eyed, industrious, and ingenious artisan, which is just as essential to it. He writes to Otto Wesendonk: "Let me tell you briefly the state of my work. When I began it I abandoned hope of being able to bring it to a conclusion in short order. . . . Partly because I was so full of cares and troubles of all sorts that I was often incapable of production. But partly also because I soon discovered my peculiar relation to my present work (which now I simply cannot do in a hurry, but can find pleasure therein only because I owe to good ideas that come to me even the smallest detail in it and work it out accordingly). I see this so clearly and unchangeably that I am obliged to give up any hasty or incomplete work which alone would enable me to finish in good time." That is the "uprightness and good faith" which Schopenhauer inherited from his merchant forebears and which he claimed to have carried over into realms of the mind. It means solid, painstaking, accurate work, and it shows itself in the scores: they are clean, careful work, nothing slovenly about them — even that product of transport, the *Tristan*, is a model of clear, painstaking calligraphy.

But it cannot be denied that Wagner's taste for bourgeois elegance has its degenerate side; it betrays the tendency to put on a character that is quite remote from the sixteenth-century German *Meister* in the Dürer cap; it is bad nineteenth-century, it *is* bourgeois. The smack of the modern middle class (as distinct from the old civic spirit) is there, unmistakably in his human and artistic personality: all this luxury and extravagance, this silk and satin and "*Gründerzeit*" grandeur; it is of course a trait of his private life, but the roots of it go deep down. It is the time and the taste of the Makart bouquet with the peacock feathers which used to adorn the gilt and upholstered salons of the bourgeoisie; the fact is known that Wagner had the idea of engaging Makart to paint his scenery. He writes to Frau Ritter: "I've been having for some time now another craze for luxury (*ein Narr an Luxus*); whoever knew what it has to take the place of for me would consider me very modest indeed. Every morning I sit down and work in the midst of it; it is absolute necessity to me, for a day without work is torture." It would be hard to say which is more bourgeois, the love of luxury, or the torture felt at a day without work. But it is at this point that we discover the bourgeois striking back again into the disordered and unsavoury realms of art, and taking on a character which, morbid as it is, has something dignified and even touching about it; something to which the word "bourgeois" is quite inapplicable. Here we enter a different field altogether, the fantastic domain of *stimulation* – Wagner treats of it, with restraint and circumlocution, in a letter to Liszt: "It is actually only with the most genuine despair that I take up my art again. If this must happen, if I must once more resign reality and plunge into that sea of fantasy, then at least my imagination must get help and support from somewhere. I cannot live like a dog, I cannot sleep on straw and drink bad brandy. I must be soothed and flattered in my soul if I am to succeed at this gruelling job of creating a world out of nothing. In order to take up the plan of the *Ring* again and envisage its actual performance, there had to be all sorts of contributing factors to give me the necessary atmosphere of art and luxury. I *had* to be able to live better than I have done in the past!" His "*Narr an Luxus*" is well known, the technique that had to come to the help of his fancy: the wadded silk dressing-gowns, the lace-trimmed satin bed-covers embroidered with garlands of roses, these are the palpable expressions of an extravagance of taste which ran up debts in thousands. Arrayed in them he sits down mornings to the gruelling job, by dint of them he achieves the "atmosphere of luxury and art" necessary to the creation of primitive Nordic heroes and exalted natural symbolism, to the conception of his sun-blond youthful hero striking sparks from the anvil as he forges his victorious sword – all which goes to swell the breast of German youth with lofty feelings of manly glory.

In reality the contradiction is without significance. Who thinks of Schiller's rotten apples – the smell of which used to make Goethe nearly faint – as an argument against the lofty sincerity of his works? Wagner's working-conditions happen to come higher than Schiller's – and it would not be hard to think of costumes (for instance, dressing up as a soldier or a monk) more suitable than satin dressing-gowns to the stern service of art. But in both cases we are dealing with an artist pathology, harmless even though a bit weird; only philistines would be misled by it. Yet after all there is some difference between the two. In all Schiller's work there is no trace of the odour of decay which stimulated his brain; but who would deny that there is a suggestion of satin dressing-gowns in Wagner's art? True it is that Schiller's purposeful idealism realizes itself much more purely and unequivocally in the influence his works exert than Wagner's ethical attitude does in his. He was zealous for reform in a cultural sense, he was against art as a luxury, against luxury in art; he wanted the purification and spiritualization of the operatic theatre – which he conceived of as synonymous with art. He referred with contempt to Rossini as "Italia's voluptuous son, smiling away in luxury's most luxurious lap"; he spoke of the Italian opera as a "daughter of joy," of the French as a "cold-smiling coquette." But his ethical attitude as artist, the hatred and hostility these phrases suggest, does not find very happy expression in either the meaning or the method of his own art, which brought the bourgeois society of all Europe to bow beneath its spell. What was it drove these thousands into the arms of his art – what but the blissfully sensuous, searing, sense-consuming, intoxicating, hypnotically caressing, heavily upholstered – in a word, the luxurious quality of his music? Eichendorff's song of the bold young bachelors, one of whom wastes his life in evil dissipations, characterizes temptation as "the wantoning waves," as "the billows' bright maw." Wonderful. None but a romantic could so suggestively characterize sin – and Wagner, in *Tannhäuser* and *Parsifal*, has done as much. And Wagner's orchestra, is it not just such a "bright maw" out of which, like Eichendorff's young Fant, one wakens "weary and old"?

If we must, in part, answer in the affirmative such questions as these, we are bound at the same time to recognize that we are dealing with what one calls a tragic antinomy, with one of the involved contradictions and incongruities in Wagner's nature. There are many of these, and a good part of them have to do with the relation between intention and effect in art; therefore it is highly important to emphasize here the complete and honourable purity and idealism of Wagner's position as artist, in order to obviate all possible misunderstandings on the score of the mass success his art achieved. All criticism, even Nietzsche's, tends to attribute the effectiveness of art to a conscious and deliberate intention of the artist, and to suggest calculation. Quite falsely and mistakenly: as though every artist does not do just what he *is*, what seems good and beautiful to *him;* as though there could be a kind of artist to whom his own effectiveness was a sham, instead of being, as it always is, an effect first of all upon him, the artist himself! Innocent may be the last adjective to apply to art; but the artist, he is innocent. An enormous success, such as that which Wagner's theatre of music "aimed at," was never before vouchsafed to great art. It is fifty years since the master's death; and every evening this music envelops the globe. This art of the theatre, this art of shaking the masses, owns such elements — imperialistic, world-subduing, despotic, powerfully *agaçante*, inflammable, demagogic elements — as to make one deduce a monstrous ambition, a Cæsar's will to power as the force that set them in motion. The truth looks different. "So much I tell you," Wagner writes from Paris to his beloved. "Only the conviction of my own purity gives me this power. I feel myself pure; I know in my deepest soul that I always worked for others, never for myself; and my constant sufferings are a proof to me." If that is not true, it is at least so sincere that scepticism is silenced. He knows naught of ambition. "Of greatness, fame, conquest of the masses," he assures Liszt, "I think nothing." Not even conquest of the masses? Perhaps, in the mild form of mastership and popularity, as ideal, wish-dream, as the romantic, democratic conception of art and artists, which the *Meistersinger* so sturdily and splendidly embodies. Yes, the popularity of Hans Sachs, against whom the "whole school" labours in vain seeing the people hold him dear — that is a wish-dream. In the *Meistersinger* there is a coquetting with the folk as final arbiter of art, which is the opposite of the aristocratic position and highly indicative of Wagner's democratic revolutionarism in art, his conception of it as a free appeal to the feeling of the people. What a contrast to the classic, courtly, and elegant notion of art obtaining in that time when Voltaire wrote: "*Quand la populace se mêle de raisonner, tout est perdu*"*!* And still, when this artist reads Plutarch, he feels, unlike Karl Moor, dislike of the "great men," and would not be like them for anything. "Hateful, violent, greedy little natures—because they have nothing in themselves and must always be sucking it in from outside. Away with your great men! I agree with Schopenhauer: not he who conquers, but he who overcomes the world, is worthy of admiration. God save me from these Napoleons!" Was he a world-conqueror, or a world-overcomer? And his "*Selbst dann bin ich die Welt*," with its world-erotic theme and accent—of which of the two is that the formula?

In any case, the charge of ambition in the ordinary worldly sense is not tenable; because he worked at first without hope of immediate results, without any prospect of them under the actually existing circumstances and conditions. Worked in the void of fancy, as it were, for an imaginary ideal stage, the realization of which, for the time, was not to be thought of. Certainly there is no talk of shrewd calculation and ambitious exploitation of possibilities in the letter he writes to Otto Wesendonk: "For this I see: I am only wholly what I am when I create. The performance of my works belongs to a purer time—a time which I must first prepare for by my sufferings. My closest friends have only astonishment for my new labours: no one who has relations with our official art-life feels strength to hope. And they are right. Nothing shows me better how far ahead I am of everything round me." The loneliness of genius, its remoteness from actuality, has never been more arrestingly expressed than in these words. But we—we of the last decade of the nineteenth century and the first third of the twentieth, of the World War and the slow decline of capitalism; we in whose day Wagner's art bestrides the theatres of the civilized world and triumphs everywhere in unabridged performances—we are those "purer times" which he had to prepare through his sufferings? Is the humanity of from 1880 to 1933 the one to prove the height and goodness of an art by the giant success we have vouchsafed it?

Let us not ask. We see how his genius proves itself by the fact that it seeks to come near the world, to adapt itself to the world—and cannot. A comic operetta, a satyr-play to the *Tannhäuser*, a diversion for him and his audience; the best of wills to create something light and enjoyable—it turns out to be the *Meistersinger*. Well, then, something Italian, something tuneful, lyrical, and singable, with a small cast, easy to produce, quite simple: and the result is — *Tristan.* One cannot make oneself smaller than one is: one does what one is, and art is truth — the truth about the artist.

Yes, the vast universal effectiveness of this art had, originally and personally speaking, very pure and spiritual sources. This was first of all due to its own lofty plane, where no deeper scorn is known than that for effect, for "effect without cause." And next because all the imperial, demagogic, and mass-effective elements must be conceived in a quite ultra-practical and ideal sense as having reference to all too revolutionary conditions yet to be achieved. In particular the innocence of the artist comes in play, where the will to rouse enthusiasm expresses itself, powerfully instrumented, in a national appeal, celebrating and glorifying the German spirit, as happens quite directly in *Lohengrin*, in King Henry's "German Sword," and in the *Meistersinger* on the honest lips of good Hans Sachs. It is thoroughly inadmissible to ascribe to Wagner's nationalistic attitudes and speeches the meaning they would have today. That would be to falsify and misuse them, to besmirch their romantic purity.

The national idea, when Wagner introduced it as a familiar and workable theme into his works — that is to say, before it was realized — was in its heroic, historically legitimate epoch. It had its good, living and genuine period; it was poetry and intellect, a future value. But when the basses thunder out at the stalls the verse from the "German Sword," or that kernel and finale of the *Meistersinger:*

> Though Holy Roman Empire sink to dust
> There still survives our sacred German art,

in order to arouse an ulterior patriotic emotion — that is demagogy. It is precisely these lines — they already appeared at the end of the first sketch, dated Marienbad, 1845 — that attest the intellectuality of Wagner's nationalism and its remoteness from the political sphere; they betray a complete anarchistic indifference to the state, so long as the spiritually German, the "*Deutsche Kunst,*" survives. Even so he was not thinking of German art, but rather of his music-theatre, which is far from being solely German, having taken unto itself not only Weber, Marschner, and Lortzing, but also Spontini and Grand Opera — but that is another matter. At bottom perhaps he thought, like that greatest unpatriot of them all, Goethe: "What do the Germans want? Have they not me?"

All his life long, Richard Wagner dreamed of an ideal public for his art, in the sense of a classless society, founded on love, freed from luxury and the curse of gold; thus as a politician he was much more of a Socialist, a believer in a cultural utopia, than he was a patriot in the sense of the all-powerful state. His heart was for the poor against the rich. His participation in the '48 cost him twelve years of torment and exile; later, repenting of his "reckless" optimism, in face of the *fait accompli* of Bismarck's empire, he minimized his share in it and identified it as best he could with the realization of his dream. He went the way of the German bourgeoisie: from the Revolution to disillusionment, to pessimism and a sheltered and contemplative resignation. And yet we find in his writings the opinion – in a certain sense the very un-German opinion: "Whoever tries to get away from the political befools himself!" So living and radical a spirit was of course aware of the unity of the problem for humanity, of the inseparability of mind and politics; he did not cling to the delusion of the German citizen, that one may be a man of culture yet not of politics – this madness to which Germany owes her misery. His attitude toward the Fatherland, from the founding of the empire to his settling down in Bayreuth, was always that of the solitary; misunderstood, repulsed, full of scorn and criticism. "Oh, how full of enthusiasm I am for the German league of the Germanic nation!" he writes from Lucerne in 1859. "God forbid that that reprobate of a Louis Napoleon should lay his hands on my dear German league: I should feel too upset if anything were to alter there!" In exile he was consumed with longing for Germany; but the return brought him nothing but bitter disappointment. "It is a miserable country," he cries, "and it is a just judgment that says the German is mean-spirited." But observe: these unfavourable comments refer solely to the German unreadiness to accept his work; their animus is quite childish and personal. Germany is good or bad according as it has faith in him or denies it to him. Even in 1875 he replies to a flattering remark that the German public has surrendered to him to a most unexampled extent, with the bitter comment: "Oh, yes, the Sultan and the Khedive have taken patrons' tickets."

It is an honour to his artist heart that at the same time he could envisage the fulfilment of his German desires in the foundation of the empire by Bismarck, the new empire for which Nietzsche could not find enough words of passionate execration; that he was ready and able to see in it the right soil for his cultural labours. The – little German – resurrection of the German Empire, a phenomenon of overpowering historical success, strengthened in

Wagner, his friend Heckel says, a belief in the development of a German culture and art – in other words, the possibility that his artistic contribution, the sublimated opera, might be realized. It was this hope that gave rise to the *Kaisermarsch;* to the poem to the German army before Paris, which only shows that without music Wagner is no poet; to the incredibly bad taste of the *Capitulation,* a satire on Paris in her agony, in 1871, which is in every sense a betrayal of Wagner's higher self. But above all it gave rise to his manifesto "On the Production of the Festival Play: *The Ring of the Nibelungs,*" to which he received one single reply – from friend Heckel, the piano-dealer in Mannheim. The opposition to Wagner's plans and pretensions, the fear of siding with him, remained very great; but the foundation of the empire coincided with the foundation of the first Wagner Society and the issue of patrons' cards for the festival plays. The organization, full of compromises, as always, the realization, was beginning. Wagner was a good enough politician to link his affairs with the Bismarck empire; he saw in it an incomparably successful feat, and he attached his own fortunes to its chariot. The European hegemony of his art has become the cultural equivalent to the political hegemony of Bismarck. The great statesman to whose labours he thus married his own understood it not at all; he never troubled about it, he considered Wagner a crazy chap. But the old Kaiser – who understood no better – went to Bayreuth and said: "I never thought that you would bring it off!" The works of Wagner were installed as a national concern, as an official apanage of the empire; and they have remained more or less bound up with the red, white, and black – however little they have to do in their deeper essence and the quality of their Germanness with all or any empires based on power and war.

When we discuss the involutions and inconsistencies of Wagner's contradictory nature, we should not leave out of account the grandiose combination and interweaving of Germanness and cosmopolitanism: it is part of his being, characterizing it in the most absolutely unprecedented and thought-provoking way. There always has been, and there is today, a German art of high rank – I am thinking especially of the literary field – which belongs so entirely to the quiet and domestic Germany, is so peculiarly and intimately German, that it is able – albeit in a very high sense – to command influence and honour only within our borders, resigning entirely all claims upon a European audience. That is a destiny like another, it has nothing to do with values. Much more insignificant stuff, the universal commonplace of the day, easily crosses the frontiers and by its very nature is everywhere understood. But other works, equal in rank and value to the exclusively domestic product, may prove to be anointed with the drop of European and democratic unction that opens the world to them and assures them international currency.

Wagner's works are of this kind – though with him one cannot speak of a drop of oil, for they fairly drip with it! Their Germanness is deep, powerful, unquestionable. The birth of drama from music, as it is consummated, purely and enchantingly, at least once, at the height of Wagner's creative powers, in the *Tristan*, could only spring out of German life; and as German in the highest sense of the word we may also characterize its tremendous sense-appeal, its mythological and metaphysical tendencies; above all, its profoundly serious consciousness as art, the high and solemn conception of the art of the theatre, with which it is filled and which it communicates. But in and with all that, it has a universal rightness and enjoyability above all German art of this high rank; and I shall remain within the frame of its creator's chosen circle of thought if I reason back from the practical manifestation to the informing will. *Richard Wagner as a Cultural Phenomenon*, a book by a non-German, the Swedish Wilhelm Peterson-Berger, is very shrewd and good on this point. The writer speaks of Wagner's nationalism, of his art as a national art, and remarks that German folk-music is the only field not comprehended in the Wagnerian synthesis. In the *Meistersinger*, and in *Siegfried*, he may, for purposes of characterization, strike the folk-key; but it is not the fundamental note or the point of departure of his tone-poesy, from which it gushes spontaneously, as is the case with Schubert, Schumann, and Brahms. It is necessary to distinguish between folk-art and national art: the first has a domestic, the second a foreign goal. Wagner's music is more national than of the people. It has many traits indeed which *foreigners in particular* find German; but it has, according to this author, an unmistakably cosmopolitan cachet.

It seems to me that this analysis of Wagner's Germanness is very finely felt and expressed. Yes, Wagner is German, he is national, in the most exemplary, perhaps too exemplary, way. For besides being an eruptive revelation of the German nature, his work is likewise a dramatic depiction of the same; a depiction the intellectualism and the poster-like effectiveness of which is positively grotesque, positively burlesque; it seems calculated to move an eager and palpitating world-public to the cry: "*Ah, c'est bien allemand, par exemple!*" Well, then, this Germanness, true and mighty as it is, is very modern — it is broken down and disintegrating, it is decorative, analytical, intellectual; and hence its fascination, its inborn capacity for cosmopolitan, for world-wide effectiveness. Wagner's art is the most sensational self-portrayal and self-critique of the German nature that it is possible to conceive; it is calculated to make Germany interesting to a foreigner even of the meanest intelligence; and passionate preoccupation with it is at the same time passionate preoccupation with the German nature which it so decoratively criticizes and glorifies. In this its nationalism consists; but it is a nationalism so soaked in the currents of European art as to defy all effort to simplify or belittle it.

"You will serve the cause of one whom the future will hail as greatest among the great." Charles Baudelaire wrote this sentence in 1849 to a young German Wagner enthusiast and musical critic. The prophecy, astonishing in its assurance, springs from passionate love, from elective passion; and the critical acumen of Friedrich Nietzsche is displayed in the fact that he recognized this affinity without being aware of the expression of it. "Baudelaire," he says in the studies to the *Fall Wagner*, "was once the first prophet and advocate of Delacroix; perhaps today he may be the first Wagnerian in Paris." Only years later did he see the letter in which Wagner thanked the French poet for his homage — and he exulted. Yes, Baudelaire, the first admirer of Delacroix, that Wagner of the realm of painting, was actually the first Wagnerian in Paris and one of the earliest of true and passionate and artistically understanding Wagnerians. His article on *Tannhäuser*, written in 1851, was the decisive and pioneer utterance upon Wagner; it has remained historically the most important. The joy that Wagner's music gave him, the joy of finding oneself anew in the artistic conceptions of another, he had discovered in but one other case, his literary acquaintance with Edgar Allan Poe. These two, Wagner and Poe, are Baudelaire's gods — a singular juxtaposition to the German ear! It puts Wagner's art all at once in a new light; it suggests associations with which our patriotic commentators have not familiarized us. It opens up a whole world of colour and fancy, lovesick for death and beauty, the Western world of high and late romanticism; a pessimistic world, adept in strange intoxicants and refinements of the senses, fanatically addicted to all sorts of æsthetical speculations and combinations; in Hoffmannian, Kreislerian dreams of the correspondence and inner relation between colours, sounds, and odours, of the mystical transformations of the mingled sense. . . . In this world we are to see Richard Wagner: as the most glorious brother and comrade of all these sufferers from life, given to pity, seeking for transport, these art-mingling symbolists, worshippers of "*l'art suggestif*," whose need it is "*d'aller au delà, plus outre que l'humanité*," to quote Maurice Barrès, the latest convert of the cult, lover of Venice, the *Tristan* city, the poet of blood, desire, and death, nationalist at the end, and Wagnerian from beginning to end.

Sind es Wellen/sanfter Lüfte?
Sind es Wogen/wonniger Düfte?
Wie sie schwellen, /mich umrauschen,
soll ich atmen, /soll ich lauschen?
Soll ich schlürfen, /untertauchen,
süss in Duften/mich verhauchen?
In des Wonnenmeeres/wogenden Schwall,
in der Duftwellen/tönenden Schall,
in des Weltatmens/wehendem All –
ertrinken – /versinken –
unbewusst – /höchste Lust! *

That is the last and highest word of the world I mean, its crown and triumph, stored and saturated with its spirit; and it was Wagner and the early Nietzsche who conventionalized its European, mystic-sensual art into something not too impossible for German culture, and related it to the landmarks of tragedy – Euripides, Shakespeare, Beethoven. Afterwards Nietzsche regretted his act, being irritated by a certain German lack of clarity in psychological matters; he over-emphasized Wagner's European traits and poured scorn upon his German mastership. Wrongly. For Wagner's Germanness was strong and genuine. And that the romantic should reach its climax and achieve its universal success in German and in the guise of the German *Meister* was determined for it beforehand, by its very nature.

A last word upon Wagner's relation to the past and to the future. For here too there reigns a duality, an interweaving of apparent contradictions, similar to the antithesis of Germanness and Europeanism which I have just analysed. There are reactionary traits in Wagner, traces of reversion and cult of the dark past; we might interpret in this sense his love of the mystical and mythological; the Protestant nationalism in the *Meistersinger* as well as the Catholic spirit in *Parsifal;* his general fondness for the Middle

* See page 472 for literal translation.

Ages, for the life of knights and princes, for miracles and perfervid faith. And yet my feeling for the true nature of this artist phenomenon, conditioned through and through as it was by renewal, change, and liberation, strictly forbids me to take literally his language and manner of expression, instead of seeing it for what it is, an art-idiom of a very figurative sort, with which something quite different, something entirely revolutionary, keeps pace. This stormily progressive creative spirit, so charged with life despite all its soul-heaviness, its bond with death; this man who gloried in a world-destroyer born of free love; this bold musical pioneer, who in *Tristan* stands with one foot already upon a-tonal ground – today he would probably be called a cultural Bolshevist! – this man of the people, who all his life long and with all his heart repudiated power and money, violence and war; whose dream of a theatre – whatever the times may have made of it – was one set up to a classless community; such a man no retrograde spirit can claim for its own; he belongs to that will which is directed toward the future.

But it is idle to conjure great men out of eternity into our now and here – to the end of asking them their views upon questions that were put differently in their day and thus are foreign to their spirit. How would Richard Wagner stand toward our problems, our needs and the tasks before us? That "would" has a hollow sound, the position is unthinkable. Views are of secondary importance, even in their own present; how much more so when that has become past! What is left is the man, and his work, the product of his efforts. Let us be content to reverence Wagner's work as a mighty and manifold phenomenon of German and Western culture, which will always act as the profoundest stimulus to art and knowledge.

RICHARD WAGNER AND THE *RING*

1937

IN a lecture on Richard Wagner, given in the University of Munich in 1932, I took leave, all unconscious, of my native Germany. And in that lecture I used these words: "My passion for the Wagnerian enchantment has accompanied my life ever since I was first conscious of it and began to make it my own and penetrate it with my understanding. All that I owe to him, of enjoyment and instruction, I can never forget: the hours of deep and single bliss in the midst of the theatre throngs, hours of nervous and intellectual transport and rapture, perceptions of great and moving import, such as only this art vouchsafes."

The words express an admiration which has never been diminished, no, not even come near to being or ever could be, by any scepticism or any unfriendly usage to which the great object of it may offer a handle. How good that this is so! For admiration is the best thing we have; yes, if I were asked what emotion, what reaction to the phenomena of this world, to life and art, I considered the finest, happiest, most constructive, most indispensable, I should answer unhesitatingly: admiration. What other answer can there be? What would man be, above all what would an artist be, without admiration, enthusiasm, absorption, devotion to something not himself, something much too large to be himself, yet something to which he feels most intimately allied, most powerfully congenial – to approach which more nearly, to "penetrate with the understanding," to make utterly his own, his nature passionately demands? Admiration is the source of love, it is love itself – which would be no deep love, no passion, and, above all, without soul, if it were incapable of doubt, if it could not suffer for its object. Admiration is humble and proud at once, proud of itself; it knows jealousy, the youthful challenge: what do you know about it? It is the purest and fruitfullest, the vision and the stimulus to competition, it makes the highest demand, it is the strongest and sternest discipline, the incentive to one's own contribution; it is the root of all talent. Where it is not, where it withers, nothing more sprouts, all is arid and impoverished.

In this outspoken belief in the productive power of admiration I am but a pupil of the mighty artist whom I celebrate today. In the famous *Communication to My Friends*, Wagner attributes artistic capacity directly to the gift of admiration – or, as he puts it, "the power of capacity to receive." "The earliest will of the artist," he says, "is nothing but the satisfaction of the involuntary urge to imitate what most engages us." A statement in the first place altogether characteristic of its author and his own genius, which is fundamentally imitative, the actor-type. But in the second place it is a statement containing much objective truth. This one thing, he says, conditions the character of the artist: that he, in contradiction to the political man, who refers the outer world only to himself and his own advantage but never the reverse – the artist gives himself unreservedly to impressions which his receptive nature finds sympathetic; impressions of life and, above all, of art; for what first of all conditions the artist as such is the definitely and purely artistic impressions he gets. But the degree of them is accurately measured according to his power to receive, which must be in ecstatic abundance, full to running over, in order that they may result in the urge to communicate. The artist power lies in the fullness of this abundance, conditioning the enthusiasm; it is nothing other than the need to give out again the excess he has received. Power, power of love and of life, power to take what it needs, what it knows to be akin: that is the essence of genius. In other words, it is receptivity, which, at the fullest height, must become necessary to production.

I repeat: the objective truth of this confession is indisputable. It is an assertion as fine and spirited as it is apt, that the gift of admiration, the capacity to love and learn, the power of assimilation, adaptation, transmutation, continual personal development, is the basis of every great talent. And we ourselves, who are celebrating our admiration of a great work, do well to begin with this explicit tribute to the power of admiration itself.

He was a great admirer, the master of the *Ring*. Not only in youth, the time proper to enthusiasm, but, commensurate with his great vitality, up to his old age, up to his death. We are told that during his last period, in the Vendramin Palace in Venice – and also earlier in Bayreuth – he used to entertain the family and friends in the evenings by reading aloud all sorts of compositions literary and musical: Shakespeare, Calderón, Lope, Indian and Norse legends, Bach, Mozart, Beethoven – with a running commentary of admiring explanation and trenchant, enthusiastic criticism. It is touching to hear him speak of Mozart's "tender genius of light and love"; whom surely he had always deeply admired, but perhaps only now, in his contemplative age, when his own much less celestial, so much more ponderous, heavy-laden harvest had been gathered in, was able to pay him pure, untrammelled homage. Yes, it seems that admiration for the beauties of others, far from being the prerogative of the active and combative years, perhaps only in age – the day's work done, the ego no longer needing to insist, to mirror itself, to compare – perhaps only then is admiration truly free to revel in pure impartiality. Kant says: "What pleases without interest is beautiful." Well, to him who had it laid upon him mightily to bring forth the beautiful, other beauties can please only "without interest." The praise he lavishes no longer needs to flatter himself, to reassure or defend him. The old master admires Felix Mendelssohn, he calls him "an example of a sunny, measured, fine artistic sense": praise which is not especially relevant to himself. Beethoven was always the highest and greatest; Wagner as an old man still said of him: "One cannot talk about him without falling into the ecstatic key." After the performance of the "*Hammerklavier*" Sonata, ravished by these "pure spectra of being," he bursts out in the extraordinary words: "But such a thing is only conceivable for piano, pure folly to play it before the public." That from the great theatre-man and mass hypnotizer – who always, on a high plane, appealed to the masses and had to have them for the success of his mission. What he says about the piano sonata – is it not a free, self-forgotten acknowledgment of an inwardness and seclusion of the soul which was not his line at all: the loving, yes, jealous protection of a rank against which he did not measure himself? Is it not quite disinterested admiration?

Next to Beethoven he can put only Shakespeare: next the highest idealistic the highest realistic, the frightful mirror of life. He reads to his family the chronicle plays; reads *Hamlet*, *Macbeth*. Sometimes the creator of *Tristan* has to pause to wipe the tears of pure artist rapture from his old eyes. "What did not the man see?" he cries. "*What* did he see? He remains the incomparable! Just a miracle – that is the only way to take him!" What, the "word-drama," "literary composition," as he had been used contemptuously to call it, all at once it produces the incomparable, the miracle? Then what about that doctrine of salvation, the art of all the arts, which should first realize art, and to which the future should belong? Well, that was the dialectic of the fray, passionate, indispensable propaganda for himself. It can stand as written, in the book, where it belongs. But in spoken words, having quite fulfilled himself, he can freely be filled by another; he pays homage to the heights and peaks of human creation, seeing them certainly as high above himself as Goethe in his lifetime declared that he saw them.

And Goethe himself? Him too we encounter in the Venetian evenings, he too enjoys the admiration of the old master, and in a highly characteristic field. It is the "classical Walpurgisnacht" out of the second part of *Faust* that the great myth-lover likes to read in his little circle and then expend himself in expressions of agreement and amazed admiration. "This," he would say, "is probably the most original and artistically perfect thing Goethe ever wrote. Such a unique reanimation of antiquity, with such freedom of form, such masterly humour, so full of genius in its lively perceptions, in a style of the finest artistry." He would repeat over and over that it was an incomparable phenomenon. – It is good to see Wagner's genius bowing, here in the private circle, before Goethe's; for in his writings nothing like it occurs that I know of. It is a most remarkable event. It touches and tranquillizes one, this contact between two figures otherwise such poles apart, from such remote and opposed spheres: these two mighty and contradictory manifestations of the spacious German spirit, the northern musical and the Mediterranean plastic; the cloudy, moralistic sky and the azure serene; the Germany of folklore and saga and the European Germany; Germany as emotional nature and Germany as intellect and perfected civilization. Indeed, we are both these, Goethe and Wagner, for both are Germany. They are the highest names we have for the two souls in our breast, always straining away from each other, always having to learn anew to find fruition in the struggle which is the living fount of inward richness. The more elevated the nature, the more certainly does this doubleness and schism run through its very heart; yet here, with the profoundest gratification, we see it bridged over for a moment by Wagner's selfless admiration, in his old age, for Goethe's Greek phantasmagoria.

Of course it is not mere chance that it is just the myth that makes the bridge. Our old myth-smith and interpreter, who after he wrote *The Flying Dutchman* declared that from then on he wanted to tell only fairy-tales, is enchanted to meet his very urbane opposite number in this primeval field, his own peculiar terrain. He cannot enough rejoice and wonder at the easy, confident, blithe, and brilliant charm with which he moves within it. What a difference, indeed, between the Wagnerian and the Goethian way of dealing with the myth! Even aside from the different spheres, in that Goethe peoples his immaterial theatre not with dragons, giants, and dwarfs, but with sphinxes, griffins, nymphs, sirens, "psyllæ and marsæ" – in other words, not with primitive German but primitive European shapes, to Wagner's eyes certainly not representative enough of the German soul to be suitable for musical treatment. But even aside from that, what antagonism between the two artists, in attitude and feeling! Greatness, indisputable greatness in both. "*Gestalten gross, gross die Erinnerungen.*" But the splendour of the Goethian vision is undimmed by accents of tragedy or pathos. He does not celebrate the myth, he jests with it, treats it with affectionate, teasing familiarity; he controls it down to the smallest and remotest detail and makes it visible in blithe and witty words, with a niceness which has in it more of the comic, yes, of gentle parody, than of the sublime. It is a myth-diversion, quite suitable to the world-revue character of the Faust composition. Nothing could be more un-Wagnerian than Goethe's ironic way of conjuring the myth; and certainly the classical Walpurgisnacht would have had little or nothing to say to the younger Wagner when he was wrapped up in his own work. Only when his artist comprehension was set free for pure, objective contemplation could he have admired it.

Wagner's personal approach to the myth – that is to say, his development away from a practitioner of the traditional opera form to a revolutionary in art and inventor of a new species of drama born of myth and music, calculated vastly to heighten the intellectual status, the artistic value of the operatic stage, and to lend it a truly German seriousness – this approach, this development, is always worth fresh consideration, it will always remain highly remarkable and in the history of art and the theatre well worth thinking about. And the human interest is great as well. For with its æsthetic and artistic impulses are united moral and social ones, which alone give it its full emotional value. What we have here is a catharsis, a process of purifying, cleansing, intellectualizing, which is to be valued humanly so much the higher because this was the most passionate conceivable nature, ravaged by violent and obscure compulsions to powerful effects and enjoyments, under which he laboured, in which he fulfilled himself.

We know how the pressure of this artist nature, versatile to the point of danger, first concentrated upon the great historic opera, and in the traditional form familiar to the public achieved a triumph with *Rienzi*, which would have decided any other man to continue on this well-trodden path. What prevented Wagner was the soundness of his intellectual conscience, his capacity for disgust, his instinctive, still unformulated repugnance to the insipid role of luxurious entertainment played by the musical theatre in the prevailing bourgeois society about him. It was, in particular, his own relation to music, too reverent, too German, in an old and high sense of the word, not to feel its true essence betrayed by "grand opera." He found it simply a shame that it should serve as a sounding flourish, an aural ornamentation to a pompous middle-class spectacle; in him music yearned for purer, more appropriate dramatic associations. His fruitful burrowings into the romantic field of the saga are equivalent to the conquest of that purely human element which he considered, by contrast with the historical and political, to be the true and native sphere of music. But at the same time it meant for him the rejection of a bourgeois world of cultural decadence, false education, money rule, sterile scholarship, and mindless tedium, in favour of a folkishness, a folk-reality, which, as he came more and more to feel, was the social and artistic, the redeeming and purifying future state.

Wagner experienced modern culture, the culture of bourgeois society, through the medium and in the image of the opera-theatre activity of his time. The position of art, or of that which as an artist was his concern, became to him in this modern world a criterion for the value of bourgeois culture as a whole. Is it surprising, then, that he learned to hate and scorn it? He saw art debased to a means of luxurious enjoyment, the artist become a slave to wealth. He saw shallowness and jog-trot apathy where he wanted to see serious devotion and consecration. He saw, with rage and chagrin, the waste of enormous resources — not to lofty ends, but for what he as an artist most despised, for effect. And finding nobody who minded all that as he did, he deduced the worthlessness of the political and social conditions that produced it and were linked up with it. He deduced the need of revolutionary change.

So Wagner became a revolutionary. He became one as an artist, because he promised himself that from the alteration of all things happier conditions for art, for his art, the mythical-musical folk-play, would flow. He had always denied that he was a political-minded man, and never concealed his dislike of the activities of political parties. When he accepted the Revolution of 1848 and took part in it, he did so out of revolutionary sympathy in general, scarcely at all on account of its concrete goals, for his actual dreams and hopes went far beyond them — went, indeed, *beyond the bourgeois epoch itself*. We must be clear on this point: a work like the *Ring*, which Wagner conceived after *Lohengrin*, was composed as a challenge to the whole of bourgeois culture and civilization as it had been in the ascendant since the Renaissance; its mingling of primevalness and futureness addresses itself to a classless folk-world that did not exist. The resistance it met, the indignation it aroused, was not so much directed at what was revolutionary in its form, the fact that it broke with the rules of a form of art (opera) and publicly came out against them. No, the hostility had another and quite different source. The German "Goethe-man," who knew his *Faust* by heart, raised angry and contemptuous protest, a highly respectable protest, whose source was the still existent bond with the cultural world of German classicism and humanism, from which this work declared itself free. The cultivated German laughed at all this Wagalaweia, all these alliterations, as a barbaric innovation; if the word had existed at that time he would have called Wagner a "*Kultur*-Bolshevist" – and not without all reason. The enormous, one may say planetary success which, notwithstanding, the bourgeois world vouchsafed to this art, thanks to its appeals to nerves, senses, and brain, is a tragicomic paradox; it must not make us forget that it was conceived for quite a different public and has social and moral aims reaching far beyond the capitalistic and bourgeois order into a brotherly humanity founded in love and justice and freed from the madness of power and gold.

The myth, for Wagner, is the language of the still creative folk – hence he loves it, and as artist gives himself utterly to it. The myth: for him that is simplicity, anti-culture, nobility, purity – in short, what he calls the purely human – and what, at the same time, is the uniquely musical. Myth and music, that is drama, that is art itself; for only the purely human seems to him the proper field for art. How unavailable for art – or for what he understands by the word, all the formally historical and derivative, by contrast with the purely human, pure as a spring is pure – he only rightly understands when he finds himself faced with the choice between two sources of material, which have been possessing his consciousness even during the composition of *Lohengrin:* Friedrich Barbarossa and Siegfried's death. There is a long struggle and much delving into theory over the decision between these two themes. How the saga of the primitive hero triumphed over the imperial story, Wagner himself relates in the great *Communication to My Friends*, written later, in Switzerland, altogether the most revealing contribution of all that we owe to our great artist's love of confession. In it he explains how just because of its historical and political character he could only have dealt with the Barbarossa material (which had attracted him as a theme out of Germany's past) in the form of spoken drama and would have had to relinquish the music, which after all he needed as a rounding out and fulfilment of his creative nature. When he wrote *Rienzi*, when he was still a composer of opera, he might have been able to think of a Friedrich drama set to music. But he was no longer a composer of opera and could feel no desire to return to that stage — the less so because he always naïvely equated his own personal success with that of art itself, being convinced that opera, like spoken drama, after he had overcome it, would simply disappear forever; that the novel thing he was contributing — namely, the myth-music theatre — was the art form of the future. But for his purposes, only the unhistorical, the "purely human," freed from all convention, would serve his turn. Then how happy was he that as he penetrated deeper and deeper into his material, the Siegfried saga, he found that he could dredge out more and more historical dross, free the subject from successive layers of disguises, and take it back to where it issued newborn, a purely human manifestation of the poetic folk-soul. This extraordinary revolutionary was just as radical about the past as about the future. The saga was not enough for him; it must be the saga in its most primitive form. The mediæval *Nibelungenlied* was already modern, distorted, dressed up; it was history, far from being early and folkish enough to serve the art he had in mind. He must penetrate back to the original sources, back to the pre-German, Scandinavian, early Germanic Edda-roots: these alone were the sacred depths of the past, corresponding to his sense of the future. He did not yet know that even within his work he would not be able to bring himself to stop at any beginning already somehow weighed down by history, and to start from that point, as it were *in medias res;* that here too he would be by a magnificent compulsion forced back to the beginning and arch-beginning of all things, the primeval cell, the first contra E-flat of the prelude to the prelude; that it would be laid upon him to erect a musical cosmogony, yes, a myth-cosmos, himself, and endow it with profound organic *bios*, the singing spectacle-poem of the beginning and end of the world. But so much he did already know, that in his insatiable burrowings into the ultimate depths and dawns he had found the man and hero whom he, like Brünnhilde, loved before he was born, *his* Siegfried, a figure that enchanted and gratified as well his passion for the past as his avidity for the future, for it was timeless: the human being — they are his own words — "in the most natural, blithest richness of his sense-endowed manifestation; the masculine embodiment of the spirit of unique, eternal, procreative instinctiveness; veritable doer of deeds; in the fullness of the highest, most immediate power and most unquestioned loveliness." This unconditioned, untrammelled figure of light, then, this unsafeguarded, independent, self-responsible being, relying upon his own strength alone, radiant with freedom, fearless, guiltless doer and fulfiller of destiny, who by the noble and natural event of his death brought about the twilight of old, worn-out world-powers, redeemed the world by lifting it to a new level of knowledge and morality – him Wagner makes the hero of the drama conceived as belonging to the music, which, no longer in modern verse, but in the alliterative accents of his Old Norse sources, he sketched and called *Siegfried's Death*.

He was not to produce it at home. Involved in the Dresden uprising of 1849, Wagner became from one day to the next a political refugee and, as we say, "*im Elend, im Ausland*" (wretched, that is, abroad). But it was not Switzerland, the foreign land, that was his misery and heart-break – it was Germany, it was his own country. In Switzerland he soon found friends such as he had not found at home; under their protection his whole further work as far as *Parsifal* saw the light. He suffered under the failure of the Revolution, as he did later when Prussia triumphed over Austria and Prussian hegemony was established in Germany. The whole German political development up to 1870 – and who knows whether only till then – went counter to his wishes, which accordingly were the wrong wishes. But the worship of facts is not a very high-minded attitude toward history, and history is nothing so grand that one need feel particularly sorry for the little peoples who play small or no part in it; or that desires cherished by superior men but not honoured by history should therefore be without any honour at all. Perhaps, who knows, Germany and Europe might be better off if German history had gone as Wagner wanted it – that is, in the direction of freedom – his wishes being shared by many superior Germans, and the failure of them having driven the author of *Siegfried's Death* into exile in Switzerland.

We need waste no regret on that. Nowhere, not even at home, could his life-work have developed more wonderfully than in Switzerland, and we have plenty of documentary proof that he was grateful. "Let me now work myself out in peace," he writes in the autumn of 1859 to Otto Wesendonk. "Let me create the works I there conceived, in this tranquil, glorious Switzerland, with my eyes on the towering, gold-crowned mountains. They are marvels, and nowhere else could I have conceived them."

Marvels, *Wunderwerke:* it is beautiful to see how openly he says that, in his tragic, dearly paid happiness – says it because it is the simple truth. No description better fits these amazing manifestations of art, and to nothing else in the whole history of artistic production are they more applicable, certain of the greatest achievements of architecture, a few Gothic cathedrals, alone excepted. And, after all, the words do not imply absolute supremacy. I should not be so very much tempted to describe as *Wunderwerke* other dear and indispensable possessions of our culture and our hearts: *Hamlet*, let us say, *Iphigenia*, the Ninth Symphony. But the score of *Tristan* – and particularly when we consider it in its psychologically puzzling, almost mystifying proximity to the *Meistersinger;* both of them mere recreation after the conquest of the minutiæ that went to the gigantic thought-structure of the *Ring* – that is *Wunderwerk*. It is the work of a perfectly unique eruption of talent and genius; the achievement at once deeply serious and completely ravishing of a magician as possessed by emotion as he was drunk with his own cleverness.

To have sheltered this extraordinary being so long, and had him as guest, must be very memorable to Switzerland; and a performance of the entire *Ring* such as the State Theatre of Zürich now proposes is a lively summons to recall the connection of the work with the city of Zürich, a connection such as no other city can boast. If that is due to chance, it is none the less a pregnant and praiseworthy chance. Yes, it is right and fitting that this triumph of the German mind and soul, which was destined to make conquest of the world, should have come to birth in the free and favouring atmosphere of Zürich, a metropolis not in size but in situation and mission; always friendly to all European avant-garde ventures – as we hope it will continue to be. Here Wagner lived, in the fifties of the last century. They saw the maturing and a large part of the musical composition of the work; here, in the "lower room of the dependence of Hotel de Baur," on four successive evenings from the 16th to the 19th of February 1853, there took place the first readings of the work, by the composer himself, before an invited audience. From Zürich are dated hosts of letters about the progress and the delays, the rapt absorption: sanguine and definite statements like this of March 1854 to his niece Clara Brockhaus: "Since November the *Rheingold* has been begun and finished; I am just doing the instrumentation. In the summer I shall compose the *Walküre*, spring of next year we get to *Siegfried;* so that in the summer of year after next I expect to be done with Siegfried's Death too." That was an error. Where and when the *Götter-*

dämmerung was finished is only told in the tablet on the house at Triebschen. The master of the *Ring* was an exceedingly critical and fastidious artist, who, as he puts it in another letter, could find pleasure in his work only so far as he could thank the smallest detail of it (and the mammoth work is full of the "smallest detail") only to good ideas (*guten Einfällen*). That does not happen so fast. But now that Zürich is revisualizing the whole *Ring*, in all its greatness and completeness, it may say, with Goethe's Count in *Tasso:* "And call it in a certain sense my own."

From Zürich too, or more precisely from Albisbrunn, whither he went on an excursion, he sent off the great letter of November 20, 1851 to Liszt. Here for the first time he develops and justifies to his Weimar friends and patrons the plan of his mammoth work. "Learn herewith," he solemnly begins, "in its strictest truth the history of the creative project with which I have been for a long time occupied, and the direction it must necessarily take." And then he tells the extraordinary tale, thrilled and amazed himself as he sets it down, which we relive with him to learn how little the artist knows of his own work; how little, in the first instance, about the self-will of the task he is letting himself in for; not dreaming what the work really *wants* to become, what it, precisely as his work, must become, and before which the artist often enough stands with the feeling: "That I didn't want, but now I must, God help me!" Ambition, the ego's pallid face, does not preside at the beginning of great works, it is not the spring that moves them. The ambition does not belong to the artist but to the work, which means to be much bigger than the artist thought he dared to hope or feared he would be driven to; it lays its will upon him. Wagner had not fixed his mind on making a scenario of a world-epic which should fill four evenings and stagger the world. That he had to do just that he discovered, fearfully and pridefully, instructed by the work itself. He had done *Lohengrin*, now he wanted to do Siegfried's Death. He had already written or half-written it in words, now he wanted to carry it out in music, but that did not work — not yet. One could not just put the work on the stage like that, and before the audience of his dream; one had the duty of preparing it. How? By means of another one. This one was too full of prehistory; it was really only the last chapter of a whole myth, which lay before him and had either to be known beforehand or else woven into it as information. The second was awkward, artistically speaking; the first made demands upon the knowledge of the audience. Wagner was not the man to make such demands. Where he went to work, there the world began from the beginning, and nobody need know anything to understand it. Perhaps he already divined that just here and just now the world would really have to begin quite from the beginning, but he did not admit it to himself. What he did see at once was that all too many premises, too many demands on his audience's powers of association, contradicted the character of mythical primitive simplicity in which the work hovered before his eyes. He admitted that he would first have to write a *Young Siegfried* in which the prehistory would, as far as possible, receive a treatment directly appealing to the senses.

He wrote the forest scene and found it charming. He straightway went to work to set it to music and the composition flowed easily from his hand. But suddenly it seemed to him that he must first do something about his health, and he betook himself to a cold-water cure. That was the *Flucht in die Krankheit*, the retreat into illness, the flight from his work. He felt the greatest eagerness for it — and yet not a proper eagerness — not yet. Something was not in order, and this something was not his health; for however precarious that was, he would not, under other circumstances, have given it a second thought. No, it was his conscience. A fresh self-examination was due: the *Young Siegfried* would not be enough, he could not begin with him either. Far too many necessary references, everything that gave the plot and character of the two present works their striking, far-reaching significance, must even now remain unpresented and left in the realm of ideas. That was not the work's own notion of itself, however much it might be the notion of the artist, a fearful soul, ever prone at bottom to wish that the cup might pass from him. But this was a cup which insisted on being drunk to the dregs. The idea of a non-present once-upon-a-time was good, it would even be highly striking and significant — he would see to that. But the once-upon-a-time must some time have been the present, one must really remember it because one had been there and only needed to be reminded of it by the music. All the business of Siegmund and Sieglinde and Wotan's difficulty and Brünnhilde's defiance of him in acting according to his real will — all that had to appear on the stage on a first evening, however much of an affliction the task was and however many years of his life it would cost him. The *Valkyrie* had to be written. And when he knew this he already knew that three evenings would of course not be enough; that to be consistent there must be a fourth, a first play, wherein everything to the uttermost had to be spread before the people's simple minds, straight back to the first and earliest, the primeval event, the theft of the gold, Alberich's curse, the curse of love and the cursing of the gold, the very first flash of the sword-thought in Wotan's mind. In the beginning was the Rhine.

So then the afflicted one wrote to Liszt and begged him not to think that the whole mad plan had originated in calculation or superficial whim. Rather it had impressed itself upon him as the inevitable consequence of the nature and content of the material that now filled him and compelled him to a complete production. "You will understand," he writes, "that not just mere thinking, but even more enthusiasm inspired me with my new plan." Nothing easier to believe, when one thinks what was achieved in the course of the next two decades: a *non plus ultra* of almost unfathomable ingenuity and overwhelming wealth of meaning. The enthusiasm it engenders, the feeling of splendour that so often thrills us, which can be compared only with sensations roused by nature in her greatest moods – high mountain peaks at sunset, the sea in storm – permits us to guess at the rapture of the inspiration. What part "thinking" played and plays here, that of the creator and that of the listener as well; whether at this point thought and inspiration, reflection and emotion, can be sharply differentiated, these are questions the answers to which, I believe, cannot be entirely based on Wagner's statement that to him feeling is everything, reason nothing, his art turns only to the first, the second may not enter in. Artists do misunderstand themselves, and Wagner may have been nearer his own understanding when he wrote: "Do not let us underestimate the power of thought. The work of art produced unconsciously belongs to periods which lie far remote from ours; the work of art of the highest period of culture cannot be produced save consciously." These are his words. And certainly in his whole work – and particularly in the *Ring* – alongside of things that bear the stamp of inspiration, of blind and blissful transport, there is so much witty and ingenious thinking, so allusive and so sensibly woven, so much diligent dwarfery next that of gods and giants, that it is impossible to believe in trance and mystery. Indeed, Wagner's unique fascination rests on the fact that his genius is an entirely unexampled mixture of the greatest modernity and intellectuality with elements of a mythic, primitive folkishness. That in his effects a sharp division and conflict exist between reflection and inspiration is contradicted above all by his relation to music, which was of the mind, pre-eminently intellectual, and decisively conditioned the development of the *Nibelung* plan from a drama to a tetralogical mythus.

None of this comes in question in the great letter to Liszt. And yet it seems certain that not the drama but the music was "to blame" in what happened to Wagner with his material. Why was it he could not begin with the plot of *Siegfried's Death* but was carried back to the beginning of things? Because the drama would not take in the prehistory? But drama in itself has nothing against prehistories. On the contrary it often takes pleasure in developing them, a method that is known as the analytic. Classic and French drama both practised this method, and Ibsen too, who in this respect stood near the classic. If Wagner's medium had been only poetic composition, he could have practised it as they did. But he was not only a poet but a musician, and on top of that not one alongside of and outside of the other, but both at once in primitive unity; he was musician as poet and poet as musician, his relation to poesy was that of the musician, so that his language was forced back by music into a primitive state, while his dramas without music were only half-compositions. And his relation to music was not purely musical, but poetic to the extent that the intellectual side, the symbolism of music, its attraction and significance, its value in the memory, its associative magic, decisively influenced this connection. It had been his musical artistry that had led him to the gradual dropping of the traditional opera forms and inspired him with his new technique of theme and motif weaving—new in so far as it had never before been applied to the whole drama to this extent. It had begun with *The Flying Dutchman*, the musical kernel and seed had been Senta's ballad in the second act, the compacted image of the whole drama, which then as a complete fabric spread itself out over the whole work. In *Tannhäuser* and *Lohengrin* the musical-poet treatment was further developed and refined, elevated out of simple reminiscence by an ever more evolved art of remodelling the thematic material, of which earlier composers had already availed themselves (for instance, the touching repetition in the last scene of Gounod's *Faust* of the waltz from the fair). And now here, in the case of the Nibelung myth, this idea-and-senses technique promised effects and enjoyments of a scope and authority never before seen; under conditions that drove Wagner to his vacillations and introspections, because when he wanted to embark straightway on the composition of *Siegfried's Death*, he found that they were still unsatisfied. Upon the drama he could embark, and partly suggest its backward far-reaching epic previous history, partly assume it to be familiar. But he could not embark upon the music, for it too had to have its previous history, one just as profound as the drama. And this could not be communicated, the drama could not feed from it intellectually, not live musically on its memories; it could not arrive at the climax, the greatest and most thrilling triumph of the new dramatic technique of weaving and association, unless this primeval music somehow and somewhere came to hearing in actual combination with the dramatic moment. Of course one could write earth-shaking music for the death of the world's sublimest hero (*hehrsten Held der Welt*), and for his funeral train, born out of the tragic moment and self-sustained without reference to anything else. But would that not be like the old writers of opera, who wrote "numbers," whose invention always had to do with one scene, without reference to the whole or to its poetic intent? What if he spread out his method, his theme-fabric, not only over one scene but over the whole drama; what if he vastly broadened it, applied it not to one drama alone but to a whole epic sequence of them, in which everything was brought in, from the very beginning on? That would be a very feast of association, a whole world of profound and brilliant allusion, a moving magnificence of musical thinking such as would at times force tears of rapture from everybody's eyes — the rapture which he himself experienced at the mere thought, and about which he wrote to Liszt. Then the dirge for Siegfried, the so-called funeral march, would be something different from any sumptuous operatic funeral pomp. For it would be an overwhelming celebration of memory and mind. The longing questions of the boy about his mother; the hero motif of his clan, begot by an unfree god to godlessly free deed; the love motif of the brother-sister parents, wonderfully led up to; the sword mightily leaping from the scabbard; the great fanfare formula of his own nature, announced of yore, first from the mouths of the Valkyrie; the sound of the horn, prolonged in mighty rhythms; the beautiful music of his love to the once-awakened; the old lament of the Rhine daughters over the stolen gold and the gloomy tone-painting of Alberic's curse: all these splendid, reminiscent phrases, weighted with fate and feeling, should pass by amid earth-shakings and thunderings, with the body borne high on its bier — and that was only one instance of all the significant solemnity and mythical exaltation promised by this drama turned scenic epos. Back to the beginning, the beginning of all things, and its music! For the Rhine depths with the glittering hoard, round which the Rhine daughters sported and played — all that was the innocent, primitive state, still untouched by greed and curse; and one with it was the *beginning of music*. Not only mythical music. He, the poet and composer, would produce the mythus of music itself, a myth-philosophy, a poem of music-creation, its erection into a world of symbols splendidly linked together, all out of the E-flat major three-tone chord of the flowing depths of the Rhine.

Thus was the gigantic work conceived, a work without compare, one may say with no exaggeration or disloyalty to other art-creations, from other, perhaps purer spheres. For it is *sui generis*, a work apparently departing from the modern, and yet in the subtlety, the awareness and developed lateness of its resources extremely modern, primitive in its emotion and its romantic, revolutionary intent; a world-poem overgrown with music and soothsaying nature, where the primeval elements of being are the actors; Night and Day hold speech together; mythical, primitive types of humanity, the blond, golden-haired children of joy, meet together with the brood of hatred, affliction, and revolt, in the depths and windings of the fairy-tale plot. The pendant to Siegfried is Hagen, a figure that for sinister power towers over all earlier or contemporary conceptions, from the Hagen of the *Nibelungenlied* down to Hebbel's. Wagner's creative and theatrical power of character-drawing triumphs as perhaps nowhere else in the figure of the half-gnome; and the words of the text contribute mightily to its success. As when Hagen, in answer to the question why he did not share in the brother-oath, mockingly characterizes himself:

Mein Blut verdärb' euch den Trank!
Nicht fliesst mir's echt
und edel wie euch;
störrisch und kalt
stockt's in mir;
nicht will's die Wange mir röten.
Drum bleib' ich fern
vom feurigen Bund.

My blood would curdle your drink!
Not flows it in me
True and noble like yours;
Sullen and cold
It thickens in me,
Will no redden my cheek.
So I stand off
From the fiery bond.

That is a picture, a mythical character-mask for the stage, compressed into words. Hagen talking in his sleep, in the night conversation with Alberic; Hagen keeping the hall alone, while the free sons and joyous comrades must fetch him the ring of world-dominion; above all, Hagen as the wild and grotesque herald to Gunther's unblest marriage – the theatre knows nothing nearer to the dæmonic than these scenes.

To have doubts of Wagner's gift as a poet has always seemed absurd to me. What could be more fine and profound, poetically speaking, than Wotan's relation to Siegfried: the paternally superior bantering of the god, his weakness for his destroyer, the surrender of the old power for love of the eternally young? The wonderful music which the composer has found to express all this, he owes to the poet. But again, what all does the poet not owe to the musician? How he seems often only to understand himself when he calls to his aid his other supplementary and explanatory language, which in simple truth is for him the kingdom of subliminal knowledge, unknown to the Word up there! Mime's attempt to teach Siegfried to fear, his malicious description of the shivering and shaking, is painted over a cellarage of the darkly distorted fire-music and the equally discoloured and distorted motif of the sleeping Brünnhilde. Accompanying the dwarf's description of fear is the sound of that which in the *Ring* is the symbol of all frightful things, that which is fear and terror itself, *par excellence;* that which guards the rocks: fire, which Siegfried will not fear, for he will break through without learning it. But at the same time, down in the darkness, the music haunts and hints at the thing which is really to teach him fear: the memory of the sleep-banned one, of whom he knows naught, but whose awakener he is fated to be. The audience, gazing and listening, will be brought back to the end of the evening before: it will understand that in the depths of Siegfried's soul, so hard of understanding in the matter of fear, there stirs a feeling, a guess at the actual source of fear: love, which the stupid youth has not yet learned either but is to learn along with fear, for the two are musically and emotionally the same. – Earlier, under the linden tree, he had dreamed of how his mother looked: his mother, a human being and a woman. The motif of love of woman, the theme of "*Weibes Wonne und Wert*" from Loki's narrative in the second scene of the *Rheingold*, rises from the orchestra. Again it is the same complex of mother-image and women's love that breaks out in words when Siegfried frees the Walküre from the cuirass and discovers "That is no man!" "Fiery fear fixes my eyes, my senses swing and sway! Whom call I to aid, who shall help me—Mother, be mindful of me!"

Nothing can be more Wagnerian than this mixture of mythical primitiveness and psychological, yes, psychoanalytical modernity. It is the naturalism of the nineteenth century, consecrated through the myth. Yes, Wagner is not only an incomparable painter of external nature, of tempest and storm, rustling leaves and dazzle of waves, rainbows and dancing flames. He is also a great seer of animate nature, the eternal human heart: about the rocks of virginity he sets the ring of fiery fear, to be broken through by the primitive male, driven by his awakening creative mission; who then at sight of all he longs for and fears breaks out in his cry for help addressed to the sacred feminine principle from which he sprang, the mother. In Wagner's work and world the great and only thing is emotional primitive poesy, the first and simplest, the pre-conventional, pre-social; only this seems to him at all suitable for art. His work is the German contribution to the monumental art of the nineteenth century, which in other countries appears principally in the form of the great social novel-writers: Dickens, Thackeray, Tolstoy, Dostoyevsky, Balzac, Zola. Their works, towering up in the same moral loftiness, are *European* nineteenth-century, literary and social critique, social world. The German contribution, the German manifestation of this greatness, knows and wants to know nothing of the sociological; for it is not musical, and above all certainly no subject-matter for art. The only true material is the mythical, the purely human, the unhistorical, timeless primeval poesy of nature and the heart; it is truly the flight from the social and the antidote for all its corruption; from its depth the German spirit creates what is perhaps the loftiest, most compelling art the century has to offer. The unsocial, primevally poetic is its own mythus, the typical and fundamentally conditioned national character, which distinguishes it from other national mentalities and types. There is some temporal kinship, for instance, between Zola and Wagner, between the symbolic naturalism of the Rougon-Macquart novels and Wagner's art. I am not thinking of the leitmotiv alone. But the essentially typical and national difference is the social temper of the French work and the mythic, primitive poetry of the German. The old, involved question: What is German? finds perhaps its most convincing answer in this difference. The German spirit is, socially and politically, essentially uninterested. In its depths—for the work of art springs from those depths and one may recognize the fact as decisive—this sphere is foreign to it. We may appraise this statement not only negatively; if you like you may speak of a positive vacuum, a lack and a deficiency. And it is probably true that in times when social problems occupy the forefront of the field; when the idea of a social and economic equilibrium, a more just economic order, is recognized as paramount by every alert conscience and its realization as the most pressing moral task – that under such circumstances this deficiency – fruitful in other times and under other conditions – seems not the happiest thing in the world and appears to lead to disharmony with the will of the world-spirit. In view of our world-problems it leads to attempts at solutions which are in fact only evasions, and which wear the mark of mythical substitutes for a true social ideal. It is not hard to recognize such a substitute in today's state and social experiment. Translated out of the political into the psychological, it means today: I do not want the social, I want the fairy-tale. Only that in the field of politics the fairy-story becomes a lie.

I spoke further back of the misuse made of the great phenomenon that is Richard Wagner. I knew that I must return to the subject. I find it impossible to speak of Wagner today and omit to guard myself against such misuse. Wagner as the artist prophet of a political present supposed to be mirrored in him – well, more than one prophet has turned away in horror from the realization of his prophecy and preferred to seek his grave in a foreign land rather than even be buried in the place where it came to pass. But it would offend against the best in us, our admiration, to concede that there can be any talk here of realization, even in a distorted form. Folk and sword and myth and Nordic heroics: these, on certain lips, are but unworthy plunderings from the Wagnerian vocabulary. The creator of the *Ring*, with his past- and future-drunken art, was not sprung from the epoch of bourgeois culture, only to exchange it for a soul-destroying state totalitarianism. German Spirit was everything to Wagner, German State nothing; as he already makes clear in the words which are the mainspring of the *Meistersinger:* "Let Holy Roman Empire sink to dust, There still remains our Holy German Art." In the great work we are about to see, he taught that the curse of gold and the thirst of power leads to inward confusion, until it can love only its free destroyer. Wagner's real prophecy is not goods nor gold nor lordly pomp, nor sad compacts of lying bonds – it is the heavenly melody which at the end of the *Götterdämmerung* rises from the burning citadel of earthly power and restates in music the same theme as that of the closing lines of the other German poem of life and world: *Das Ewig-weibliche zieht uns hinan.*

SCHOPENHAUER

1938

THE PLEASURE we take in a metaphysical system, the gratification purveyed by the intellectual organization of the world into a closely reasoned, complete, and balanced structure of thought, is always of a pre-eminently æsthetic kind. It flows from the same source as the joy, the high and ever happy satisfaction we get from art, with its power to shape and order its material, to sort out life's manifold confusions so as to give us a clear and general view.

Truth and beauty must always be referred the one to the other. Each by itself, without the support given by the other, remains a very fluctuating value. Beauty that has not truth on its side and cannot have reference to it, does not live in it and through it, would be an empty chimera—and "What is truth?" Our conceptions, created out of the phenomenal world, out of a highly conditioned point of view, are, as a critical and discriminating philosophy admits, applicable in an immanent, not in a transcendent sense. The subject-matter of our thinking, and indeed the judgments we build up on it, are inadequate as a means of grasping the essence of things in themselves, the true essence of the world and of life. Even the most convinced and convincing, the most deeply experienced definition of that which underlies the manifestation, does not avail to get at the root of things and draw it to the light. What alone encourages the spirit of man in his persistent effort to do this is the necessary assumption that our own very being, the deepest thing in us, has the same universal basis, that it must of necessity root therein; and that accordingly we may be able to draw from it some data wherewith to clarify the relation of the world of phenomena with the true essence of things.

That sounds modest. It is not far removed from the Faustian "and see that we can nothing know!" And all the bumptiousness of philosophy with its "intellectual point of view" and "absolute thought" sounds like *hubris* and silly bounce beside it. In fact, if its origins in the critical and national school are united with a choleric and polemic temper, it may come about that the grim and contemptuous word "wind-baggery" will be levelled against such arrogance, against a philosophy of "absolute knowledge." And yet the school of thought thus assailed has some right to return the compliment. For with the devaluation of all objective knowledge, with the statement that it offers us nothing but phenomena; with doubts about the intellect as an adequate, trustworthy instrument of knowledge; even with the justification of all philosophizings, only on the ground that our most intimate self – something quite different and much earlier in time than the intellect – must have at its very root a connection with universal foundations; with all these considerations there enters a subjective factor into our conception of the knowledge of truth, an element of the intuitive, of equation with the emotional, or even an imbalance on the side of passion and pathos, which from the point of view of pure mind might merit the epithet "wind-baggery." At least, in so far as an *artist's* conception of the world, including not only the head but the whole man with heart and senses, body and soul, merits the same severe epithet. The world of emotions and passions, that is the same as the world of beauty, in accordance with the mysterious law which binds feeling and form, makes feeling ever crave form, yes, makes them in origin one: a conception of the world born in passion lived and suffered with the whole human being, will always bear the stamp of the beautiful. It will know nothing of the sense-destroying dryness and boredom of pure intellectual speculation; it will emerge as a soul-novel, as a symphony of ideas, wonderfully composed, developed from one single thought kernel, existing everywhere – in a word, as a work of art, working by virtue of all art's magic. And just as the anguished yearning for favour and grace, for a deep affinity between suffering and beauty is resolved in form, just so it is beauty that vouches for its truth.

The philosophy of Arthur Schopenhauer has always been regarded as pre-eminently creative, as an artist-philosophy *par excellence*. Not because it is so markedly or so extensively a philosophy of art – actually its æsthetics occupies somewhat more than a quarter of the whole work. Nor yet because its style is so perfectly, consistently clear, so rounded, its presentation and language so powerful, so elegant, so unerringly apposite, so passionately brilliant, so classically pure, so magnificently and blithely severe – like never any other in the history of German philosophy. All this is only "phenomenal"; it is merely the inevitable and inborn beauty of form expressed in the essence, the inner nature of this kind of thinking, an emotional, breath-taking nature, playing between violent contrasts, between instinct and mind, passion and redemption—in short, a dynamic artist-nature, which cannot reveal itself in any other way than as the personal creation of truth, convincing by virtue of its having been lived and suffered.

That is why this philosophy has found among artists and the initiated in art its most enthusiastic admirers and fanatical converts. Tolstoy called Schopenhauer "the genius *par excellence* among men." For Richard Wagner, who was introduced to him by the poet Georg Herwegh, the teaching of Schopenhauer was "a gift from heaven," the greatest boon, the most illuminating, productive, stimulating, intellectual experience he ever had, nothing more and nothing less than a revelation. Nietzsche, whose mission it was to bring art and knowledge, science and passion, even nearer to each other, to make truth and beauty mingle together, even more tragically and thrillingly than Schopenhauer before him; Nietzsche saw in this man his great teacher and master. Still young, he had dedicated to him one of the *Thoughts out of Season:* "Schopenhauer as Teacher." And especially at the time of his adulation of Wagner, when he wrote *The Birth of Tragedy*, he moved entirely in Schopenhauerian trains of thought. Even after this great self-conqueror had renounced both Wagner and Schopenhauer, in itself a decisive event in the history of the human intellect, he never ceased to love where he had ceased to believe, and in the late work *Ecce Homo*, that almost frighteningly *spirituelle* last phosphorescence of his over-stimulated and solitary career, there is a page on *Tristan* that reveals no estrangement but, on the contrary, much passion. Indeed, this spirit, as noble as it was unsparing towards itself, offered up to the end the most explicit homage to the great figure of the philosophic shaper of his youth. One may say that his thinking and teaching after he had "got over" Schopenhauer were a continuation and interpretation of his teacher's world-picture instead of an actual departure from it.

The history of Schopenhauerian thought goes back to the sources of the life of thought in our Western world, whence issue European science and European art, and in which the two are still one. It goes back to Plato. The Greek philosopher taught that the things of this world have no real existence; they are always becoming, they never *are*. They are of no avail as objects of actual knowledge, for that can subsist only in what is in and of itself and always in the same way; whereas they, in their multiplicity and their purely relative, borrowed existence, which might as well be called non-existence, are never anything but the subject of an opinion based on sense-experience. They are shadows. The only things that have real existence, that always are and never pass away, are the actual originals of those shadows, the eternal *ideas*, the primeval forms of all things. These are not multiple, being by their very nature each unique, each the archetype, the shadows or imitations of which are merely like-named, ephemeral, individual things of the same kind. Ideas do not, like these, come up and die away; they are timeless and truly existent, not becoming and passing like their perishable imitations. Of them alone, then, can there be actual knowledge, as of that which always and in every respect *is*. Concretely: *the* lion, that is the idea; *a* lion, that is pure seeming, and it follows that it cannot be the object of pure knowledge. The banal objection may be raised that only the phenomenal image of the single "empirical" lion affords us the possibility of getting any knowledge not only of the lion as such, but certainly of the lion as idea. But precisely the immediate intellectual subordination of the experience got from the phenomenal image of the single lion, to the "*leonitas*," the *idea* lion, the pure and general thought-image of the animal; the subsumption of every special and temporal perception in the general and intellectual, thus an achievement in abstraction, the penetration of every conditioned and transitory actuality, the deepening and clarifying of mere *seeing* till it becomes the contemplation of the absolute, unclouded and abiding truth, which is behind and above the manifold single manifestations and to whose name these answer — that is the philosophical challenge which Plato made to the humanity of his time.

We see that this thinker knew how to derive a far-reaching significance from the distinction between the definite and the indefinite article; he made of it a learned paradox. For paradoxical it certainly is, to say that knowledge can only refer to the invisible, the thought-about, perceived in the mind; it is paradoxical to explain the visible world as a phenomenon, which, in itself worthless, has a reality and meaning only through that of which it is an expression. The reality of the actual — only a loan from the mind! That was nothing — or only a bewilderment — to an ordinary human understanding! But in this "*épater le bourgeois*" always lay the mission and the satisfaction, the lofty martyrdom of knowledge in this earth; always she found her pain and pleasure in disobliging the ordinary common sense of men, in standing the popular truth on its head, in making the earth go round the sun, whereas any normal senses can see it does the reverse; in perplexing mankind, in beguiling and bedevilling them, by telling them truths that run contrary to what their senses tell them. But this happens when someone aims to teach the mind of man, to lead it to higher things, making it capable of new achievements. What

Plato, with his far-reaching exposition of the difference between the definite and the indefinite article, introduced into the early Occidental world, was the scientific spirit.

Obviously, it is the scientific spirit and training that teach us to subordinate to the idea the multiplicity of phenomena; that attribute truth and genuine reality to it alone and adhere to the contemplative abstraction and spiritualization of knowledge. Because of this discriminating distinction between the phenomenon and the idea, between the empiric and the intellectual, between the world of truth and the world of appearance, between the temporal and the eternal, the life of Plato was a very great event in the history of the human spirit; and first of all it was a scientific and a moral event. Everyone feels that something profoundly moral attaches to this elevation of the ideal as the only actual, above the ephemeralness and multiplicity of the phenomenal, this *devaluation* of the senses to the advantage of the spirit, of the temporal to the advantage of the eternal – quite in the spirit of the Christianity that came after it. For in a way the transitory phenomenon, and the sensual attaching to it, are put thereby into a state of sin: he alone finds truth and salvation who turns his face to the eternal. From this point of view Plato's philosophy exhibits the connection between science and ascetic morality.

But it exhibits another relationship: that with the world of art. According to such a philosophy, time itself is merely the partial and piecemeal view which an individual holds of ideas – the latter, being outside time, are thus eternal. "Time" – so runs a beautiful phrase of Plato – "is the moving image of eternity." And so this pre-Christian, already Christian doctrine, with all its ascetic wisdom, possesses on the other hand extraordinary charm of a sensuous and creative kind; for a conception of the world as a colourful and moving phantasmagoria of pictures, which are transparencies for the ideal and the spiritual, eminently savours of the world of art, and through it the artist as it were first comes into his own. He it is who may owe his bond to the world of images and appearances – be sensually, voluptuously, sinfully bound to them, yet be aware at the same time that he belongs no less to the world of the idea and the spirit, as the magician who makes the appearance transparent that the idea and spirit may shine through. Here is exhibited the artist's mediating task, his hermetic and magical role as broker between the upper and the lower world, between idea and phenomenon, spirit and sense. Here, in fact, we have what I may call the cosmic position of art; her unique mission in the world, the high dignity – which flings dignity away – of her functioning, can be defined or explained in no other way. The moon-symbol, the cosmic parable of all mediation, is art's own. To the old world, to primitive humanity, the planet was strange and sacred in its double meaning, in its median and mediating position between the solar and the earthly, the spiritual and the material world. Femininely receptive in relation to the sun but masculinely begetting in relation to the earth, the moon was to them the impurest of the heavenly, the purest of the earthly bodies. It did belong to the material world, but assumed therein the highest, most spiritual position, passing over into the solar, so hovering on the borders of two worlds, at once parting and uniting them, guarding the unity of the All, interpreter between mortal and immortal. Just this is the position of art between spirit and life. Androgynous like the moon, female in its relation to spirit, but masculine and begetting in life, the materially impurest manifestation of the heavenly, transitorily the purest and incorruptibly most spiritual of the earthly sphere, in its nature it is that of a moon-enchanted mediator between the two spheres. This mediating position is the source of its irony.

Plato as artist. I hold that a philosophy is effective not only — sometimes least of all — by reason of its ethical teaching, by the doctrine which it links to its interpretation of the world and its experience of it; but also and especially through this very experience itself. This indeed — not the spiritual and ethical concomitant of its doctrine of truth and salvation — is the essential, primary, and personal part of a philosophy. If one divorce from a philosopher his philosophy, there is much left; and it would be a pity if there were not. Nietzsche, the intellectually apostate pupil of Schopenhauer, wrote of his master:

> What he *taught* is put aside;
> What he *lived*, that will abide —
> Behold a man!
> Subject he was to none.

If the philosophy of Schopenhauer, which I am about to discuss, its validity and dynamic power, will never be quite abandoned, yet it proved as liable to abuse as the ascetic, scientific, and creatively fruitful message of Plato. I refer here to the exploitation that Schopenhauer suffered at the hands of a colossally gifted artist, Richard Wagner — of this perhaps more at another time. But whosesoever the blame, it certainly does not lie at the door of Schopenhauer's other teacher and inspirer, who contributed to the structure of his system. I mean, of course, Kant. Kant's bent was exclusively and positively on the side of mind – very much aloof from art, but by so much the closer to critique.

Immanuel Kant, the critic of pure knowledge, rescued philosophy from the speculation into which it had retreated and brought it back into the realm of the human intellect; made this his field and delimited the reason. At Königsberg in Prussia, in the second half of the eighteenth century, he was teaching something very like the premises laid down two thousand years before by the Athenian thinker. Our whole experience of the world, he declared, is subject to three laws and conditions, the inviolable forms in which all our knowledge is effectuated. These are time, space, and causality. But they are not definitions of the world as it may be in and for itself, of *das Ding an sich*, independently of our apperception of it; rather they belong only to its appearance, in that they are nothing but the forms of our knowledge. All variation, all becoming and passing away, is only possible through these three. Thus they depend only on appearance and we can know nothing through them of the "thing in itself," to which they are in no way applicable. This fact applies even to our own ego: we apprehend it only as manifestation, not as anything that it may be in itself. In other words, time, space, and causality are mechanisms of the intellect, and we call immanent the conception of things which is vouchsafed to us in their image and conditioned by them; while that is transcendent which we might gain by applying reason upon itself, by critique of the reason, and by dint of seeing through these three devices as mere forms of knowledge.

This is Kant's fundamental concept; and as we can see, it is closely related to Plato's. Both explain the visible world as phenomenal; in other words, as idle-seeming, which gains significance and some measure of reality only by virtue of that which shines through it. For both Plato and Kant the true reality lies above, behind, in short "beyond" the phenomenon. Whether it was called "idea" or "*das Ding an sich*" is relatively unimportant.

Both these concepts penetrated deeply into Schopenhauer's thought. He early elected the exhaustive study of Plato and Kant (Göttingen, 1809–11) and placed above all others these two philosophers so widely separated in time and space. The almost identical results they arrived at seemed best calculated to support and justify, to help construct the image of the world which he bore within himself. No wonder, then, that he called them the two greatest Occidental philosophers. He took from them what he could use, and it gratified his craving for the traditional that he could so well use it; although owing to his entirely different constitution – so much more "modern," storm-tossed, and suffering – he made out of it something else altogether.

What he took was the "idea" and the "*Ding an sich.*" But with the latter he did something very bold, even scarcely permissible, though at the same time with deeply felt, almost compulsive conviction: he defined the *Ding an sich*, he called it by name, he asserted – though from Kant himself you would never have known – that he knew what it was. It was the will. The will was the ultimate, irreducible, primeval principle of being, the source of all phenomena, the begetter present and active in every single one of them, the impelling force producing the whole visible world and all life – for it was the will to live. It was this through and through; so that whoever said "will" was speaking of the will to live, and if you used the longer term you were guilty of a pleonasm. The will always willed one thing: life. And why? Because it found it priceless? Because it afforded the experience of any objective knowledge of life? Ah, no. All knowledge alike was foreign to the will; it was something independent of knowledge, it was entirely original and absolute, a blind urge, a fundamentally uncausated, utterly unmotivated force; so far from depending on any evaluation of life, the converse was the case, and all judgments were dependent upon the strength of the will to live.

The will, then, this "in-itself-ness" of things, existing outside of time, space, and causality, blind and causeless, greedily, wildly, ruthlessly demanded life, demanded objectivation; and this objectivation occurred in such a way that its original unity became a multiplicity – a process that received the appropriate name of the *principium individuationis* (the principle of individuality). The will, avid of life, to wreak its desire objectivated itself in accordance with the *principium*, thus dispersing itself into the myriad parts of the phenomenal world existing in time and space; but at the same time it remained in full strength in each single and smallest of those parts. The world, then, was the product and the expression of the will, the objectivation of the will in space and time. But it was at the same time something else besides: it was the *idea*, my idea and yours, the idea of each one and each one's idea about himself – by virtue, that is, of the discerning mind, which the will created to be a light to it in the higher stages of its objectivation. We must understand aright this matter of the "higher stages." Schopenhauer, that is, a mystic as well as an exceedingly modern mind, fed and nourished on natural science, interpolated into his cosmogony of the will and the endless multiplicity of its emanations the concept of evolution. He did it out of affection for that philosophical factor which he took over from Plato and the ideas. He assumed, or established in the multiplicity of objectivations of the will, an order of rank, a series of stages, and in this way he won or he preserved the ideas – for when you looked at these they were no other than a series of stages of objectivations of the will. Taken singly, they were not a quite adequate objectivity of the will, because they were clouded by the forms of our knowledge. In fact we should not recognize any "exemplars," any occurrences, any change, any multiplicity, but only the existing, the pure and immediate objectivations of the will in its various stages, and the world, to speak with the schoolmen, would accordingly be a "*nunc stans,*" an abiding now of unclouded and everlasting ideas. Thus in the upper stages of its individuation, even in animals and especially in the human being, the highest and most complicated of all, the will, to give itself aid, comfort, enlightenment, and security, kindled the light of the intellect which should make an idea or representation of the world. Note that it was not the intellect that brought forth the will; the converse was the case, the will brought forth the intellect. It was not intellect, mind, knowledge, that was the primary and dominant factor; it was the will, and the intellect served it. And how could it have been otherwise, since, after all, enough knowledge even for the objectivation of will belonged to a later stage and without will simply had no chance to appear? In a world entirely the work of will, of absolute, unmotivated, causeless, and unvaluated life-urge, intellect had of course only second place. Sensibility, nerves, brain, were – just like the other parts of the organism and quite specifically like the sex organs, the opposite pole of the discerning brain – an expression of the will at a given phase of its objectivation. And the idea, coming into being through the will, was just as much intended to serve it and just as little an end in itself as were those other parts. This relation between will and mind, this premise of Schopenhauer that the first is only the tool of the second, has about it much that is humiliating and deplorable, much that is even comic. It puts in a nutshell the whole tendency and capacity of mankind to delude itself and imagine that its will receives its direction and content from its mind, whereas our philosopher asserts the direct opposite, and relegates the intellect – aside from its duty of shedding a little light on the immediate surroundings of the will and aiding it to achieve the higher stages of its struggle for life – to a position as mere mouthpiece of the will: to justify it, to provide it with "moral" motivations, and, in short, to rationalize our instincts.

Thus the Christian philosophers of the Middle Ages, whom the Devil had carried off when they retreated from the position that the reason existed for the sole purpose of making an apologia for faith. Kant ought to have heard that. And still Schopenhauer, who had taken from Kant the "*Ding an sich*" and from Plato the "ideas," was convinced that he was Kantian and Platonist in such an evaluation of the reason.

It was a remarkably pessimistic valuation. Indeed, all the textbooks tell us that Schopenhauer is first the philosopher of the will and second the philosopher of pessimism. But actually there is no first and second, for they are one and the same, and he was the second because and by virtue of his being the first; he was necessarily pessimist because he was the philosopher and psychologist of the will. Will, as the opposite pole of passive satisfaction, is naturally a fundamental unhappiness, it is unrest, a striving for *something* – it is want, craving, avidity, demand, suffering; and a world of will can be nothing else but a world of suffering. The will, objectivating itself in all existing things, quite literally wreaks on the physical its metaphysical craving; satisfies that craving in the most frightful way in the world and through the world which it has brought forth, and which, born of greed and compulsion, turns out to be a thing to shudder at. In other words, will becoming world according to the *principium individuationis*, and being dispersed into a multiplicity of parts, forgets its original unity and, although in all its divisions it remains essentially one, it becomes will a million times divided against itself. Thus it strives against itself, seeking its own well-being in each of the millions of its manifestations, its place in the sun at the expense of another, yes, at the expense of all others, and so constantly sets its teeth in its own flesh, like that dweller in Tartarus who avidly devoured his own members. This is meant in a literal sense. Plato's "ideas" have in Schopenhauer become incurably gluttonous. As stages of the objectivation of the will, space, time, and matter fall upon each other. The plant world has to serve as nourishment for the animal, each animal for another as prey and food, and thus the will to live gnaws forever at itself. And lastly man sees the whole created for his use but in his turn makes frightfully explicit the abomination of the struggle of all against all, the division of the will against itself. We express all this in the phrase *homo homini lupus*.

Everywhere that Schopenhauer takes occasion to talk of the anguish of the world and the rage for life of the will's multiple incarnations (and he talks much and explicitly about them), his extraordinary native eloquence, his genius as a writer, reach their utmost height of icy brilliance. He speaks with a cutting vehemence, in accents of experience and all-embracing knowledge that horrify and bewitch us by their power and veracity. Certain pages display a fierce and caustic mockery of life, uttered as it were with flashing eyes and compressed lips, and in showers of Greek and Latin quotations: a pitiful-pitiless coruscation of statement, citation, and proof of the utter misery of the world. All this is far from being so depressing as one would expect from the pitch of acuity and sinister eloquence it arrives at. Actually it fills the reader with strange, deep satisfaction, whose source is the spiritual rebellion speaking in the words, the human indignation betrayed in what seems like a suppressed quiver of the voice. Everyone feels this satisfaction; everyone realizes that when this great writer and commanding spirit speaks of the suffering of the world, he speaks of yours and mine; all of us feel what amounts almost to triumph at being thus avenged by the heroic Word.

Poverty, need, concern for the mere preservation of life — these come first. Then, when they are painfully allayed, come sexual urge, the sufferings of love, jealousy, envy, hatred, fear, ambition, avarice, illness — and so on and on, without end. All the evils whose source is the inner conflict of the will come out of Pandora's box. And what is left at the bottom? Hope? Ah, no. Satiety, tedium. For between pain and satiety every human being is tossed to and fro. The pain is positive, the pleasure merely the absence of pain — a negative, passing over at once into boredom, just as the tonic to which the melodic labyrinth leads back, just as the harmony in which disharmony issues, would bore us intolerably if they went on and on. Are there real satisfactions? They exist. But compared with the long torture of our desires, the endlessness of our requirements, they are short and scant, and to one gratified desire there are at least ten that remain unstilled. Moreover, the appeasement itself is only apparent, for the fulfilled desire soon makes a new vacancy — the first is now a known error, the second still unknown. No achieved object of desire can give lasting satisfaction. It is like alms thrown to a beggar, which merely linger out from day to day his miserable life. Happiness? It would be in repose. But precisely this is impossible for him who feels desire. To flee, to pursue, to fear disaster, to covet pleasure — it is all one: preoccupation with the will's incessant demands fills and animates the consciousness without cease, and thus the subject of the willing lies ever on Ixion's turning wheel, takes up water in the sieve of the Danaides, and plays the ever toiling Tantalus.

Scenes of torture and Tartarus, such as the case of Thyestes, who, raging with hunger, devoured his own members. Then is life a hell? Not quite; only approaching it, a foretaste. Hellish, certainly; since it is fixed, to start with, that every expression of the will to live has always something of the infernal about it, being itself a metaphysical stupidity, a frightful error, a sin, *the* sin. Do we feel the Christian, the Platonic note? Plato's already slightly ascetic and pessimistic devaluation of the senses by the soul, wherein alone reside all salvation and truth — here it is most grimly reasserted and reinforced; in two thousand years it has received an imprint of suffering and complaint foreign to the early Occidental: the actual world is the product of an arch-sinful, arch-stupid act of will, which never should have taken place; and if it has never become completely and formally a hell, that is because the will's will to live has not been vehement enough. If it were a little stronger still, had been a little more will to live, the hell would have been perfect. That sounds like a modification of the pessimism, but it is just a new jab, a biting rebellion against life and the accursed will — akin to that jest which Schopenhauer once permitted himself when he said life everywhere precariously balances on the edge of the still barely possible; this world is the worst of all conceivable worlds; for if it were even a little worse it could not be at all. He reminds one often of Voltaire. Sometimes because of the lucid and perfect form and triumphant wit. But he is superior to the Frenchman in a certain rich reconditeness in the depth and power of his intellectual life. Witness the doctrine of redemption which he has built into, which emerges from, his philosophy of the will; witness the longing for redemption. But yet: there *is* release from miseries and mistakes, from the errors and penalties of this life. This gift is laid in the hand of the human being, the highest and most developed objectivation of the will and accordingly the most richly capable of suffering. Would you think the gift might be death? Not at all. Death belongs utterly and entirely to the sphere of the phenomenal, the empirical, the sphere of change. It has no contact with transcendent and true actuality. What is mortal in us is merely the individuation; the core of our being, the will, which is the will to live, remains entirely unassailed, and can, *if it continue to affirm itself*, find out fresh avenues of approach to life. Herein, may I say in passing, resides the folly and immorality of suicide: in its futility. For the individual denies and destroys only his individuation, not the original error, the will to live, which in suicide is only seeking a route to more complete realization. So, then, not death. Redemption bears quite another name and has quite a different conditioning. One does not suspect the mediator who is to be thanked for this blessing when it comes. It is the intellect.

But the intellect – is it not the creature of the will, its instrument, its light in the darkness, destined only for its service? It is, and so remains. And yet – not always, not in all cases. Under peculiar, happy – ah, verily, under blissful – conditions; in exceptional circumstances, then, the servant and poor tool may become the master of his master and creator, may get the better of him, emancipate himself, achieve his own independence, and, at least at times, assert his single sovereignty, his mild, serene, and all-embracing rule. Then the will, put aside and shorn of power, falls into a bland and peaceful decline. There is a state where the miracle comes to pass, that knowledge wrenches itself free from will, the subject ceases to be merely individual and becomes the pure, will-less subject of knowledge. We may call it the æsthetic state. This is one of the greatest and profoundest of Schopenhauer's perceptions. And however frightful the accents he commands in describing the tortures of the will and the domination of the will, in equal degree his prose discovers seraphic tones, his gratitude speaks with surpassing exuberance, when abundantly and exhaustively he discourses of the blessings of art. The intellectual formulation and interpretation of this, perhaps Schopenhauer's most personal experience, he owes to his teachers, Plato and Kant. "Beautiful," Kant had declared, "is what happens without *interest*." Without interest. That, for Schopenhauer, and rightly, meant without reference to the will. The æsthetic gratification was pure, disinterested, free from will, it was "idea" in the most intensive, most hopeful sense of the word; it was clear, unclouded, profoundly satisfied contemplation. And why was it that? Here Plato came in, with the latent æstheticism of his philosophy of ideas. Ideas. They it was for which, in the æsthetic state, phenomena, the mere images of eternity, became transparent. The eyes opened upon ideas; and here was the great, pure, sunny, objective contemplation by which alone the genius, and even he only in his creative hours and moments, and with him his audience, was justified of his æsthetic achievement.

Well, and so it is the intellect that opens the way to such contemplation. Yes, the intellect, wrenched free from the will, became pure and disinterested knowledge. Needless to say, in art the word "intellect" does not apply in the narrow sense of the word; not thought, abstraction, understanding brought about the blessed state. Art could not be taught, it was a free gift of intuition. Intellect was therein only so far in play as it was intellect that made the world *idea*. One needed to know nothing about the metaphysical bearings of things, nothing of appearance and idea, of Kant or Plato, to be a part of art. It was philosophy's business to expound the nature of æsthetics and make it accessible to abstract thought – though it would have to be a philosophy with more understanding and actual *experience* of art than any we have had in the past or present. It knew and taught that the eye of art was that of creative objectivity – and if we recall here what was said earlier about the mediating services of art being the source of irony, we perceive that irony and objectivity belong together and are one.

Apollo, god of the Muses, "he who shoots his arrows from afar," is a god of distance, of space, not of pathos and pathology or involvement, a god not of suffering but of freedom. He is an objective god, the god of irony. In irony, then, as Schopenhauer saw it, in creative objectivity, knowledge was freed from its bondage to will, and the attention was no longer blurred by any motive. We reached a state of selfless resignation, where reference was had to things as sheer ideas, no longer as purposes; and a peace heretofore unknown was all at once vouchsafed us. "It is," says our author, "wholly well with us. It is the painless state praised by Epicurus as the highest good and the state of the gods; we are, for that moment, released from the base urge of the will, we celebrate the sabbath of our toil in the prison-house of will, the wheel of Ixion stands still."

Famous, oft-quoted words, lured from this bitter and tormented soul by the vision of the beautiful and the peace it purveyed. Are they true? But what is truth? An experience that finds such words to describe itself must be true, must be justified by the power of its feeling. Or should we believe that these words of sheer and boundless gratitude were coined to describe a relative, at bottom a merely negative, happiness? For happiness anyhow is negative, it is the surcease of torment; and even in all our glad objective contemplation of æsthetic ideas it cannot be other than the same. Schopenhauer, in the choice of the images he is inspired to use, unequivocally reveals the fact. This happiness too is temporal, transitory. The creative state, so he found, the sojourn among images irradiated by the idea – these would not bring the final redemption. The æsthetic state was but the prior stage to a perfected one, in which the will, not permanently satisfied in the æsthetic, would be once for all outshone by knowledge, would void the field and be annihilated. The consummation of the artist would be the saint.

Alongside of his æsthetics Schopenhauer places his system of ethics. He elevates ethics and thrones it above the other; for ethics was the doctrine of the conversion of the will in man, the highest stage of its objectivation; the theory of the will's self-abnegation by virtue of the insight into the frightful fallibility and worthlessness of the suffering world which was its effect and mirror, its objectivation — thus by virtue of the fact that the will to life came to understand itself as something to be definitely and absolutely rejected. How was that possible? How could a denial of the will come out of life, which was after all through and through a will to life? It became possible because the world was the result of an act of will and such an act could be nullified and cancelled by another act of will in the opposite direction. This was what knowledge did, tearing itself loose from will, renouncing its subservience, freed from its as it were cosmic slavery; and this act was the final activity, the inmost content of the ethics which made the transition.

What, after all, is ethics? It is the philosophy of the actions of human beings, the teaching of good and evil. The teaching? Then was the will, blind, causeless, and senseless as it was, teachable? Certainly not. Certainly virtue was not a thing to be taught; any more than was art. Just as a man could not become an artist by having explained to him the essence of the creative state, so he could not shun evil and ensue good by instruction in the nature of the one and the other, which Schopenhauer, as a philosopher, was ready to do. At all events, abstraction might be useful; and was, in the form of this or that dogma of various religions, the exoteric garb of esoteric wisdom, the garment of truth, truth, so to speak, for the people. The rational motive of a good deed did not so much matter, if the good deed was done. But it was done out of feeling, out of an intuitive recognition of truth, based upon penetration, on "seeing through," precisely as did the æsthetic state, on which subject Schopenhauer would presently give more detailed explanations. Just now he laid stress on making it clear that ethics could not be a codex of moral teachings, consisting of prescriptions for the will. No prescriptions could be issued to the will. It was free, absolute, all-powerful. Freedom, indeed, dwelt in the will alone, thus it existed wholly in transcendence, never in the empiric world, which was the objectivation of the world subsisting in time, space, and causality. Here everything was strictly causal, bound and determined by cause and effect. Freedom, like the will, was beyond and on the other side of the phenomenal, but there it was present and dominant, and therein lay the freedom of the will. As so often, the situation respecting freedom was just contrary to that conceived by ordinary common sense. It lay not in doing but in being, not in *operari* but in *esse*. In *doing*, indeed, then, inevitable necessity and determinacy reigned; while *being* was originally and metaphysically free. The human being who performed a culpable action had indeed so *acted* of necessity, as a being existing in the realm of the empiric, and under the influence of definite motives. But he could have *been* different; and his fear, his pangs of conscience, also had reference to his being, not his doing.

A bold, deeply felt, and at the same time a harsh thought. It is one of the most remarkable and, to a considered judgment, most compelling intuitions in Schopenhauer's construction of truth. What it rescued from empiricism for transcendence and timelessness and there in mysterious security preserved was a pair of moral and aristocratic concepts, to which Schopenhauer undoubtedly clung, and which he would unwillingly have seen go down in absolute determinism: they are guilt and merit. But their persistence depended upon the freedom of the will – and how many struggles there had already been on this point! However, it was always temporal freedom that was meant, freedom of the will within the phenomenon and with reference to the empirical character of man, as man himself experienced it in his own destiny and represented it to others as pleasant or unpleasant. So soon as the will had objectivated itself, become phenomenon, and entered into the individuation, then there was no trace of freedom left and accordingly neither praise nor blame. The human being behaved as being the individual he was, he had to behave under the influence of definite motives; but his doing and faring, the course his life took, his destiny, these were only the experience which he – along with others of his essence, his "intelligible" character, existing outside of and behind the manifestation – went through; and this character was like the whole world the product of a free act of will. In everything the will appeared precisely as it decided in itself and outside of time. The world was only the mirror of this will, and everything in it belonged to the expression of that which it willed, and was so just because it so willed. Accordingly, every being led his life with the strictest justice, and not only life, but the life peculiar to him, his individuality; and in all that befell him, yes, in all that could befall him, everything happened exactly right.

A harsh, cruel thought – arrogant, offensive, ruthless. To accept it runs contrary to our feelings – and yet it is precisely our feelings that are challenged by its mysticism. For it has at the bottom of it a mystic truth, by virtue of which the twin conceptions of merit and demerit, far from being invalidated, become even more profound and awe-inspiring. They are, of course, divorced thereby from the moral sphere as such. But aristocratic intellects, not much concerned with considerations of "justice," have always been inclined to favour this divorce. Goethe liked to talk of "inborn merits," an absurd phrase from any logical or ethical point of view. For "merit" is entirely and by definition an ethical concept; whereas what is inborn — be it beauty, talent, wit, refinement, or, in the sphere of outward destiny, good fortune — can thus not logically be merits. In order to speak of merit in this sense it must be the issue of choice, the expression of a will antecedent to the phenomenon. And this is just what Schopenhauer asserts when he harshly and haughtily declares that each of us, blest or unblest, gets exactly what he deserves.

But this aristocratic complaisance at injustice and the varied lot of mortals is soon enough resolved in the most peremptory and democratic equality; simply because the variations — and even the differentiation itself — are shown to be an illusion. Schopenhauer calls this illusion by a name drawn from Hindu metaphysics, which he greatly admires because of its pessimistic harmony with his own account of the world: he calls it the "veil of Maya." But much earlier he had, as Occidental scholars do, clothed it in Latin, thus: he says that the great illusion of inequality and injustice in the character, situation, and fate of individuals rests on the *principium individuationis.* Variation, inequality, are only attributes of multiplicity in time and space. That is to say, they are mere appearance, the notion which we, as individuals, thanks to the organization of the intellect, have of a world which in reality is the objectivation of the will to live, in the general and in the particular, in you and in me. But the individual, with his strong sense of being separate and set apart from the universe, does not recognize this — how could he, when the conditioning of his knowledge, the "veil of Maya," enfolding his vision and the outlying world, prevents him from getting sight of the truth? The individual does not see the essence of the truth. The individual does not see the essence of things, which is one, but its manifestations, which he beholds as separate and differing, yes, even opposed: pleasure and pain, the tormentor and the tormented, the joyous life of one and the other's wretched lot. You affirm, that is, for yourself, the one, and deny with special reference to yourself, the other. The will, which is your origin and essence, makes you demand good fortune and the enjoyment of existence. You stretch out your hands for them, you press them to you, and it escapes your notice that when you thus affirm these as goods, you affirm at the same time all the evils, all the torments in the world and press them no less to your heart. The evil that you do thereby, the evil that you inflict; on the other hand, your indignation at the world's injustice, your envy, yearning, and desire, your cosmic craving – all these come from the delusion of multiplicity, the false belief that you are not the world and the world is not you. All this comes from the illusion of Maya, from the illusory distinction between the I and the you.

Thence, likewise, comes your fear of death. Death is only the setting right of an error, a confusion – for every individual is a confusion. Death is nothing but the disappearance of an imaginary partition-wall shutting off the I you are enclosed in from the rest of the world. You believe that when you die this rest of the world will go on existing, while you, horrible to say, will be no more. But I say to you, this world, which is your idea, will no longer be; whereas you, precisely that in you which, because it is the will to live, fears death and rejects it, *you* will remain, will live. For the will, out of which you have your being, will always know how to find the gate of life. To it all eternity belongs; and together with life, which it recognizes as time, though actually it is perpetual present, time too will be vouchsafed you again. Your will, so long as it wills, is always sure of life, with all its torments and blisses. Better it were for you if it were not.

Meanwhile you live, as he who you are. You see and love, you look and long, you covet the unknown image of your desire – ah, so strange and different from yourself! – you suffer for it, you long to draw it to your heart, to draw it into you, to *be* it. But to be a thing is something quite different, and incomparably more grievous and onerous than to see it. The longing set up by the idea is all a delusion. You yourself are given to yourself, your body is given to you, as idea, as all the rest of the world is. But at the same time it is given to you as will – the only thing in the world that is given you at the same time as will. Everything else is for you only idea. The universe is, so to speak, a play, a ballet; all your natural, instinctive convictions tell you that it has nothing like the same reality as you, the spectator, have; that it is not to be taken with anything like the same seriousness as you yourself are. Trapped in the *principium individuationis*, shrouded in the veil of Maya, the ego sees all other forms of life as masks and phantoms, and is simply incapable of ascribing anything like the same importance or seriousness to them as to itself. Are not you the only actually existent thing, are you not all that matters? You are the navel of the world; if it be well with you, if the afflictions of this life be kept as far from you as possible, its blisses as near, that is the one vital thing. What happens to others is nothing by comparison. It does you neither good nor harm.

Such is the conviction of native, unbroken, and quite unenlightened egoism: absolute prepossession with the *principium individuationis.* To see through this principle, to divine its illusory, truth-shrouding character; to begin to perceive that the I and the you are indistinguishable the one from the other; to have the emotional intuition that the will is the same in the one and the all: such is the beginning and the essence of ethics. In other words, it deals with this knowledge, this emotional intuition, and describes its beneficent results, but it does not and cannot teach it, for just as little as æsthetics in the abstract ever made an artist, just so little can virtue be learned or taught. Man experiences it, as that Indian novice did before whose eyes a great spirit brought all the creations in the world, living and lifeless, and at each one said: *tat twam asi* — this is you. In this word, this insight, a gift of the intuition, lies all virtue, righteousness, all goodness and nobility — and in its ignorance, like a madness, the opposite of all that: namely, *evil.* Evil is that man who, so soon as no other outer power prevents him, inflicts evil. I mean a man who, not content with affirming the will to life as manifested in his own body, also denies the will manifest in other individuals and seeks to destroy their existence as soon as it is in the way of his own efforts. A wild, untamed will, one not content with the affirmation of his own body, speaks in the bad character. But there is above all so profound a prejudice in favour of the manifestation and the *principium individuationis* that it clings with iron grip to the distinctions fixed by the *principium* between its own person and all others. And accordingly it considers the existence of others wholly foreign to its own, severed from it by a deep abyss. It regards them as empty shells, and cherishes a profound conviction that reality is an attribute of itself alone. And thus we arrive at the definition of the *good* man; particularly when we contemplate the transitional type between it and the bad man: the *just* man. Justice is already a penetration of the *principium individuationis,* but to a lesser degree, more negative than positive, the rejection of wrong. The just man, in the assertion of his own will, does not go so far as the denial of the will represented in other individuals. He refrains from inflicting suffering on others in order to increase his own well-being. The principle of individuation is not to him as it is to the wicked man, an absolute dividing wall; rather in what he does and leaves undone he shows that he recognizes his own being, the will to life, as a thing apart, likewise in other beings, manifestations given him only as idea, and finds himself in them at least in so far as to make him guard himself from injuring them. That is a great deal; and it is always at once a great deal more: real goodness is already bound up with it. Let no one consider it weak! The good man is by no means an originally weaker manifestation of the will than is a bad one — unless he is merely good-natured, which does not come to much. No, it is knowledge that in him triumphs over the will. What knowledge? But it is clear; it is that the difference between him and others rests on an illusion which tempts to evil, is a deceiving manifestation, that the *in itselfness* of his own manifestation is also that of the unknown: namely, the will to life, which embodies itself in everything, animals as well and all nature, wherefore he will not even misuse a beast.

But here one must not stop at negatives or speak in them: goodness is positive. It performs the service of love. Its motive is profoundly emotional: were it not to do so, it would seem to itself like a man who starves today in order tomorrow to have more than he can eat. Just so it would seem to the good man to let others famish while he lived in abundance. For such a one the veil of Maya has become transparent; he has lost the great illusion whereby will, in its multiple manifestations, here starves and suffers, there enjoys, because it is after all the same will, and the same torture, which he thus both invokes and suffers. Love and goodness are *sympathy* — in recognition of the "*Tat twam asi*" (the "This thou art"), when the veil of Maya is lifted. Spinoza said: "*Benevolentia nihil aliud est, quam cupiditas ex commiseratione orta*" ("Goodness is nothing else than love born of sympathy"). But from this it is clear that as justice can rise to heights of goodness, so goodness in its turn can rise to greater heights: not only to most disinterested love and most magnanimous self-sacrifice, but verily to saintliness. For a man with such knowledge of love will regard the suffering of everything living as his own suffering, and make his own the pain of all the world. He sees the whole: sees life as an internal conflict; and continual pain, suffering humanity, suffering animal world, and the knowledge of the essence of things in themselves combine to lay a quieting hand upon his will. In him will turns away from life. Obliged, in his sympathetic understanding, to deny life, how then can he affirm even in himself the will to live, life being but the work, mirror, and expression of will? Thus to recognize, thus to resolve, means renunciation, means the ultimate quietism. And so it comes about that virtue passes over into *ascesis;* and this is a paradox, truly a high and great one: an individuation of the will here rejects the essence manifesting and expressing itself in its very own body. Its acts give the lie to its manifestation, they openly controvert it. That temporary, releasing subdual of the will, on which rests the happiness of the æsthetic state – it is completed in the renouncing, the ascetic, the saint. In him knowledge has forever made itself mistress over the will, entirely eclipses and cancels it. He bears the sins of the world, he atones for them, he is priest and sacrifice at once. As the body expresses altogether the will, so the sex organs express the assertion of the will above and beyond the individual life. The ascetic rejects the satisfactions of sex. His chastity is the sign that with the life of the body likewise the life of the will abrogates itself. What is the mark of the saint? That he does nothing of all that he would like to do, and does all that he does not like to do. We know some amazing spiritual examples of this attitude: we have seen it practised by born ascetics and priestly self-tormentors, who amid dithyrambic glorification of the power-drunken will celebrated the passion of their lives by doing nothing they would gladly have done and everything by which they injured themselves – pupils every one of the philosopher Schopenhauer and that properly only when they no longer willed to be. . . . If ascetic chastity were to become a general practice, it would bring about the end of the human race. And since all manifestations of the will are one, with man, the highest of these, would also fall away his feebler reflection, the animal kingdom. All knowledge would fail, and since without subject there is no object, all the rest of the visible world would dissolve and melt away. Man is the potential redeemer of nature. The mystic Angelus Silesius says:

> O man, all living love thee; there is much press about thee,
> All run to thee that they may reach their god.

Here, in rough outline, is the content of Arthur Schopenhauer's chief work, to which he gave the title *The World as Will and Idea* – a highly objective title, which yet in three words completely expresses not only the content of the book but also the man who created it, in his mighty darkness and just as mighty light, his profound sensuality and pure, austere intellectuality, his passion and his urge for redemption. It is a marvel of a book, whose thought, reduced to the shortest formula in the title and present in every line, is only one, and in the four sections or, better put, symphonic movements of which it is built up, reaches complete and all-sided development—a book based on itself, penetrated with itself, corroborating in itself in that it is and does what it says and teaches: everywhere you open it, it is all there, but to realize itself in time and space needs the whole manifoldness of its appearance unfolded in more than thirteeen hundred printed pages in twenty-five thousand lines of print, whereas actually it is *a nunc stans*, the abiding presence of his thought, so that the verses from the *Divan* apply to it as to nothing else:

Dein Lied ist drehend wie das Sterngewölbe,
Anfang und Ende immerfort dasselbe,
Und, was die Mitte bringt, ist offenbar
Das, was am Ende bleibt und Anfangs war.

Thy song rolls round as doth the starry sphere,
End and beginning one for evermore,
And when the turning middle doth appear,
'Tis still what end and what beginning are.

It is a work of such cosmic completeness and inclusive power of thought that one has a strange experience: if you have been occupied with it a long time, then everything else, everything, read in between or immediately afterwards seems strange, unenlightened, wrong, arbitrary, undisciplined by truth. . . . Truth? Is it then so true? Yes, in the sense of the highest and most compelling sincerity. But the adjective implies a modification. Does it contain and convey truth? Schopenhauer has not asserted that so clearly and incisively, not with the almost blasphemous pretension with which Hegel did it when he told his pupils: "Gentlemen, I can say: I not only speak the truth, I am the truth!" The corresponding summing up of Schopenhauer runs: "Mankind has learned from me something it will never forget." I find that better bred, more modest, as well as more acceptable. And when we are speaking about truth, it is a matter of acceptableness. Truth, it seems to me, is not bound to words, does not coincide with a definite wording; perhaps that may even be its chief criterion. That one never forgets what Schopenhauer says may be due to the fact that it is not just dependent on the words he uses for it, that one might use other words—and still a kernel of feeling would remain, an experience of truth so acceptable, so immune to attack, so right, as never before found in philosophy. One can live and die by it—particularly die: I would venture to assert that Schopenhauerian truth, its acceptableness, is fit to stand alone in the last hour, without effort, without strain of thought, even without words. Not for nothing does he say: "Death is the real inspiring genius or *musagetes* of philosophy. . . ." Indeed, without death, there would scarcely be any philosophizing. He is a great seer and sayer of death — the famous chapter in the second volume of *The World as Will and Idea,* "On Death and Its Relation to the Indestructibility of Our Being in Itself," belongs to the finest, one might say the profoundest (though he is always so profound) things he has written. And this expression goes together with his ethical pessimism, which is more than a doctrine, which is a character, a creative state of mind, a prevailing atmosphere, for which the still youthful Nietzsche confesses his love when he says: "I found pleasurable in Wagner what I do in Schopenhauer: the ethical air, the Faustian flavour, Cross, Death, and Grave." It is the prevailing intellectual atmosphere of the second half of the nineteenth century — the air of youth and home for those of us past sixty. In some ways we may have got out from under it; but that we preserve a grateful loyalty this little essay bears witness. Music too belongs to this ethical-pessimistic atmosphere: Schopenhauer was very musical, I have often called his great work a symphony in four movements; and in the third, devoted to the "object of art," he celebrates music as no other thinker has ever done, ascribing to her a quite special place, not beside but above the other arts, because she is not like them, the image of the phenomenon, but immediately the image of the will itself, and thus to all the physical of the world she depicts the metaphysical, to all appearance the thing itself. This philosophy leads one to the speculation that here too the intellect serves the will, and that Schopenhauer did not love music because he subscribed such a metaphysical significance to her, but rather because he loved her. But this love, so much is certain, has immediate spiritual relationship with his expertise in the things of death, and he might well have said that "without death there would scarcely have been any making of music."

Whoever is interested in life, I said in *The Magic Mountain,* is particularly interested in death. That is the trail of Schopenhauer, deeply imprinted, valid throughout life. It would also have been Schopenhauerian if I had added: "Whoever is interested in death seeks life in it"; and I did say it, if less epigrammatically, as a very young German, when it was a matter of bringing Thomas Buddenbrook, the hero of my early novel, down to his death; and I granted him to read that great chapter On Death who myself as a young writer, twenty-three or twenty-four years old, was just fresh from its impact. It was a great joy and I have taken occasion in my recollections to speak of it, and tell how I needed not to keep an experience like this to myself; that a beautiful opportunity at once came, to bear witness, to return thanks; that there was straightway a place to use it creatively. To him, the suffering hero of my novel of bourgeois life, which was the task, the burden, the virtue, the home and blessing of my young years, I gave the dear experience, the high adventure; I poured it into his life, just close to the end, I wove it into the narrative and made him find life in death, liberation from the bonds of his wearied individuality, freedom from a role in life which he had regarded symbolically and presented with courage and capacity, but which had never satisfied his spirit or his hopes and had been a hindrance to him in achieving something other and better. Schopenhauer is certainly something for the young, on the ground that his philosophy is the conception of a young man. When *The World as Will and Idea* appeared in 1818 – the first volume, which contained his system – he was a man of thirty; but it had taken four years to work it out, and the intellectual experiences which therein crystallized undoubtedly lie still further back; he was, when his book took shape in him, scarcely older than I when I read it. He grew to be an old man – developing and perfecting it, collecting the commentary, obstinately and tirelessly confirming and testing what was a gift of his youth, so that he affords the singular spectacle of an old man who in uncanny loyalty concerns himself up to his last moment with the work of his youth. But this it remained, in its very essence; and not for nothing does Nietzsche draw attention to this early conception when he says that a man has the philosophy proper to his years, and that Schopenhauer's world-poem has the stamp of the time of life when the erotic predominates. And the feeling for death, may one add; for young folk are much more familiar with death, and know much more about it, than the old, because they know more about love. The erotic of death, as a musical, logical system of thought, born of an enormous tension of mind and senses – a tension whose issue and leaping spark is precisely eroticism: such is the parallel experience of youth in its encounter with this philosophy, which it understands not morally but vitally, personally – not because of its doctrine, I mean its preachment, but because of its essence – and with which they are well agreed.

"Where shall I be when I am dead?" asks Thomas Buddenbrook. "Ah, it is so brilliantly clear, so overwhelmingly simple! I shall be in all those who have ever said, do ever or ever shall say 'I' –

especially, however, in all those who say it most fully, potently, and gladly!"

"Somewhere in the world a child is growing up, strong, well-grown, adequate, able to develop its powers, gifted, untroubled, pure, joyous, relentless, one of those beings whose glance heightens the joy of the joyous and drives the unhappy to despair. *He* is my son. He is I, myself, soon, soon; as soon as Death frees me from the wretched delusion that I am not he as well as myself.

"Have I ever hated life – pure, strong, relentless life? Folly and misconception! I have but hated myself, because I could not bear it. I love you. I love you all, you blessed, and soon, soon, I shall cease to be cut off from you all by the narrow bonds of myself; soon will that in me which loves you be free and be in and with you – in and with you all."

I shall be forgiven, I hope, for citing again this youth-lyric of mine, inspired by the intoxication of the twenty-year-old young man after drinking that metaphysical magic potion. I can testify that the organic shock it meant can only be compared with the one which the first contact with love and sex produces in the young mind – and the comparison is not fortuitous. But the passage is quoted to show that one can think in the *sense* of a philosopher without in the least thinking according to his sense; I mean that one can avail oneself of his thoughts – and thus can think as he would by no means have thought. Here, indeed, one thought who had read Nietzsche as well as Schopenhauer and carried the one experience over into the other, setting up the most extraordinary mixture with them. But my point is the naïve misuse of a philosophy which precisely artists are "guilty" of, and which I had in mind when I said that a philosophy is often influential less through its morality or its theory of knowledge, the intellectual bloom of its vitality, than by this vitality itself, its essential and personal character – more, in short, through its passion than its wisdom. In this way artists often become "betrayers" of a philosophy, and thus was Schopenhauer "understood" by Wagner, when he put his erotic mystery play as it were under the protection of Schopenhauer's metaphysics. The thing in Schopenhauer that worked on Wagner, in which the latter recognized himself, was the explanation of the world in terms of "will," the instinct, the erotic conception of the world (sex as "focus of the will") by which the *Tristan* music and its cosmogony of yearning are conditioned. It has been denied that *Tristan* was influenced by the philosophy of Schopenhauer – correctly in so far as the "denial of the will" comes in question: for it deals of course with a love-poem; and in love, in sex, the will asserts itself the most strongly. But precisely as a love-mystery the work is to the last degree Schopenhauerian in its coloration. In it, as it were, the erotic honey, the intoxicating essence, is sucked out of Schopenhauer's philosophy, but the wisdom left behind.

So artists go about to deal with a philosophy—they "understand" it in their way, an emotional way: for art needs to come only to emotional, to passionate experiences, not to moral ones, whereto philosophy, as a schoolmistress, felt herself at all times obligated. Even though no state-endowed "university philosophy," even though "subject to none," yet it was desirable for her moral conclusions to agree with the reigning morality—in the Occident, of course, Christianity; as a product of wisdom she did well to correspond to the religious result and confirm it. One might oneself be an atheist—and Schopenhauer was; if one is only a metaphysician it is always possible to arrive at results from another angle, which strengthen desirably the claims of religious morality. Schopenhauer had the good fortune, he discovered the possibility of arriving at highly moral results from highly sensual and passionate experiential premises; to a doctrine of compassion and redemption in agreement with Christianity—deducing it from the illusory nature of life, the delusion of the *principium individuationis:* compassion, Christlike love, the abrogation of egoism as the result of knowledge, which sees through the deception of the I and the you, the veil of Maya. Such a harmony cannot surprise the philosopher if he, like Schopenhauer, institutes a parallelism between religion and philosophy and sees in that "metaphysics for the people," which, as it is calculated for the great masses of humanity, can offer truth only in allegorical form, whereas philosophy offers it neat. He himself says: "The moral result of Christianity, up to the most exalted asceticism, one finds in my work rationally based and in association; whereas in Christianity they are based on sheer fables. Faith in these disappears more and more; thus people will be forced to turn to my philosophy." But the notion that in religion and philosophy there is only a matter of exoteric and esoteric truth, of which the one has become inacceptable so that the other must substitute for it—this notion does not prevent even for the philosopher's conscience the conclusion that it is not the religious morality that needs confirmation by philosophy, but the other way round; and for me there exists no doubt that a philosopher finds himself reassured by the agreement of the moral issues of his world-theory with the teachings of religion; and that Schopenhauer too feels himself legitimated as a philosopher thereby. "Subject he was to none." But for instance his train of thought led him to an ethical condemnation of suicide, because in it the will to life asserts itself, instead of refusing; and for that he was grateful to his train of thought: "the priest says just about as much only in a little different words."

At bottom he was lucky. He came into conflict with religion as little as with the state, and that thanks to the disdain with which it treated him; and which made him see in the Hegelian state-worship the greatest of all philistinism. For his part he judged the state as a necessary evil, and assured of his uncritical and forbearing disinterestedness those "who have the heavy task of governing men – that is, of upholding law and order, peace and quiet among many millions of one species, in the great majority boundlessly egotistic, unfair, dishonest, envious, malicious, and very limited and wrong-headed to boot; and of protecting the few who have any possessions against the innumerable numbers of those who own nothing but their physical strength." That sounds both grim and exhilarating – we feel a certain amount of agreement. But does not this conception of the state as an institution for the protection of property approach as nearly to "philistinism," though from another side, as Hegel's apotheosis of the state as the apex of all human striving and as "absolutely perfected ethical organism"? We know the inhuman horrors of a doctrine by which it would be the destiny of a man to be consumed in the state; know it from its consequences, for fascism as well as communism come from Hegel, and Schopenhauer himself had lived to see the theoretic prolongation of Hegelian state absolutism into communism. But however greatly we sympathize with the indignation which he felt at state totalitarianism, by which, as he said, "the lofty goal of our existence is quite ravished from our sight," the totality of the human, of which the political and social is a part, seems not to be better served by the philosopher-small-capitalist's renunciation of any interference with this sphere, the intellect's renunciation of all political passion, in the words of the jingle: "*Ich danke Gott an jedem Morgen, dass ich nicht brauch fürs heil'ge röm'sche Reich zu sorgen*" ("Each day I thank what Gods there be I need not care about the H R E") – lines which might well be applied to true philistinism and shirking of responsibility; they make us marvel how an intellectual fighter like Schopenhauer could make them his own.

It does not of course suffice as an explanation of a "disinterested contemplation" of the state, very close to the utterest political conservatism, to speak of Schopenhauer's deeply concerned interest in the preservation of the small but for a young bachelor philosopher adequate property inherited from his father, a Danzig merchant. It was a justifiable and at bottom highly intellectual interest; for this bourgeois property, to whose caretaker in naïve loyalty he degraded the state, was his one and all, his prop and support in this contemptible world; it gave him social freedom, the independence and solitude that he needed for his work; and the more incapable he felt of earning his bread himself in some official capacity, the more grateful he was all his life to the departed Heinrich Floris Schopenhauer for the priceless inheritance he bequeathed. But his unpolitical, anti-political – that is to say, conservative – position has of course a deeper root; it springs from his philosophy, for which an improvement and leading upward of the world as the manifestation of a principle evil and reprehensible in itself, the will, is utterly out of question, and which aims at redemption, not at liberation. How should a philosophy know much about how to deal with the idea of political freedom, to which freedom lies beyond the manifestation? But, above all, the political indifference of this philosophy is explained by its objectivism, by the value for salvation which it ascribes to objective contemplation and to it alone. For Schopenhauer's genius is nothing more nor less than objectivity – that is, the power of sustaining itself purely in a contemplative attitude, only as recognizing subject, as "clear world-eye." Here he makes contact with Goethe, whom he boundlessly admired, and to whose decisive influence the a-political character of German culture goes back. Philosophy, declares Schopenhauer, asks not the whither, the whence, the wherefore, but only the what of the world; it has for object the nature of the world, manifesting itself in all relations, but itself never subject to them, always itself; and the ideas of the same. From such knowledge proceeds, like art, also all philosophy – from it finally also issues that mental constitution which leads to holiness and to the redemption of the world. Art and philosophy, then, are quietist (for pure objectivism is quietism). They will on no account alter anything, they will only look at it. So that Schopenhauer has not a good word for "progress," and even less for the political activity of the people, the revolution. His behaviour in the '48 was grimly, comically petty – one cannot put other words to it. His heart was not at all with those who fanatically enough hoped at that time to give a direction to German public life which might have meant a happier turn to the whole of European history down to our day, and which was to the interest of every intellectual man

— the democratic direction. He called "the people" simply the "*souveraine canaille*," and ostentatiously lent his "goggles" to the officer who from Schopenhauer's house was reconnoitring the men on the barricades, that he might better direct the fire. Yes, in his will he appointed as his universal legatee "the fund established in Berlin for the support of the invalided Prussian soldiers and their families, survivors of those who fell to uphold and restore law and order in Germany in the struggles of the insurrection and revolt of 1848–49."

Again, his anti-revolutionary position is based on his conception of the world; not only logically and theoretically, but also as a matter of temperament. It is fundamental, it belongs to his system of morals, his ethical pessimism, to that atmosphere of "Death, Cross, and Grave" which out of psychological necessity is averse to rhetoric, to the freedom-pathos and to the cult of humanity. It is anti-revolutionary out of pessimistic ethic, out of hatred for the indecent optimism of the present-day demagogy of progress; and, all in all, there is about it the atmosphere of a certain only too familiar, only too reminiscently indigenous German intellectual middle-classness — German precisely because it is intellectual, and because its inwardness, its conservative radicalism, its absolute remoteness from all democratic pragmatism, its "pure genius," its foolhardy unfreedom, its profound lack of policy, is a specifically and legitimately German possibility. In this world Arthur Schopenhauer belongs, a middle-class citizen with the stigmata of genius, which lift his figure into the eccentric, but bourgeois indisputably, in the most intellectual and personal sense. One need only look at his life, his Hanseatic merchant origin. The settled life of the elderly man, in Frankfurt am Main, dressed always with old-fashioned elegance, his angular, pedantic, immutable, and punctilious daily course; his care for his health on the basis of sound physical knowledge — "Not pleasure but absence of pain does the reasonable man seek" — his exactness as a capitalist (he wrote down every penny, and in the course of his life doubled his patrimony by shrewd husbandry); the calm tenacity, sparingness and evenness of his methods of work (he produced for print exclusively during the first two hours of his morning and wrote to Goethe that loyalty and uprightness were the qualities he carried over from the practical into the theoretic and intellectual sphere, which made up the essence of his achievements and successes); all that testifies as strongly for the bourgeois nature of his human side as it was the expression of his bourgeois intellectualism that he so decisively rejected the romantic Middle Ages, priestly humbug, and knight-errant mummery, and considered that he based himself entirely on classical humanism; although –

But here we have a whole host of althoughs, which bring into question Schopenhauer's humanism and classicism, and seem rather to indicate that he should be called a romantic, or in any case to make one distinguish among the elements of his complex nature. In the narrower learned sense, as expert and scholar of ancient languages and literature, Schopenhauer was certainly a pre-eminent humanist; when as a young man destined by his father for trade, he had felt a compelling urge for learning, he had been bought off by an extended educational tour of Europe, and then after the death of his father changed over to study after all. He had lived in Weimar with his mother, the Frau Councillor and novelist Johanna Schopenhauer, a good friend of Goethe, and under the guidance of a young high-school teacher had zealously studied Greek and Latin and amazed his master with his torrential progress. He wrote fluent Latin, and the innumerable quotations in his writings from the ancient authors display a classical reading and knowledge as intimate as it is extended. When he quotes from the Greek he appends a flawless Latin translation. But his literary culture was by no means solely humanistic; it extended over the product of all Europe in all centuries, for his proficiency in modern languages dated from earlier than the classic, and his books are seasoned with quotations from English, French, Italian, and Spanish writers, as well as from German, especially from Goethe and from the mystics, almost more than from the classics. That gives him something cosmopolitan, superprofessional, learned, world-literary; and correspondingly his philological and humanistic equipment is rounded out by a real and objective knowledge of natural science, for which he had laid the foundation as a young student at Göttingen, and in the perfecting of which he busied himself all his life, as he needed it to support and empirically confirm his metaphysics.

Above all, Schopenhauer is a classical humanist on the æsthetic side, in his theory of the beautiful: his hypothesis that genius is conditioned as the highest objectivity is altogether Apolline and Goethian; he invokes Goethe, he thinks he stands on his side; he feels himself a "*Classiker*" and is, very extensively, in his thinking and judgments, particularly in the German-bourgeois humanistic sense I spoke of, which makes him despise feudal honorific claptrap as well as the pietistic reactionary tendencies, the neo-Catholicism of his own time. He respects the Christian allegory as a pessimistic religion of redemption, but of the various "*Landesreligi-*

onen" (established religions) he speaks altogether with philosophic superiority; and his religious "gift," in such a strongly metaphysical mind, must be called weak on the whole; one has only to read what he has to say here and there about faith and the service of God or the gods – it is not less rationalistic than, let us say, Freud's remarks on the religious "illusion."

In all this Schopenhauer is the humanist, altogether addressed to the classical and rational. I will go further and state that most importantly of all – all his misanthropy notwithstanding and all that he says about the corrupt condition of life in general and the distortions of the spirit of man in particular; notwithstanding his despair over the wretched social state one is born into as a human being – Schopenhauer is humanly full of pride and reverence as he contemplates the "crown of creation." To him the words mean, just as they did to the author of Genesis, man, the highest and most developed objectivation of the will. This most significant form of Schopenhauer's humanism perfectly – if by implication – accords with his political scepticism, his anti-revolutionarism. Man, according to him, is to be reverenced because he is the *knowing* creature. All knowing, of course, is fundamentally subject to the will out of which it sprang just as the head springs from the trunk. In the animal kingdom, indeed, this subjection of the intellect is never overcome. But look at the difference between man and beast in this relation between head and trunk. In the lower animal kingdom they are completely grown together, and in all animals the head is inclined to the earth, where lie the objects of the will; yes, even in the higher animals head and trunk are much more one than in man, whose head (Schopenhauer here uses the German word *Haupt*, to make the distinction clear) appears to be independently set on the shoulders, and uses the body to carry it, instead of being subject to it. This human advantage is shown pre-eminently in the Apollo Belvedere. The god of the Muses carries his mobile, wide-eyed head so easily on his shoulders that it seems to have escaped from the body and to need to take no further interest in it.

What association of ideas could be more humanistic than this? Not for nothing does Schopenhauer choose the statue of the god of the Muses as the image of human dignity. Art, knowledge, and the dignity of human suffering are here envisaged as one – a profound and significant perception of our pessimistic humanist. And since humanism in general is prone to rhetoric and the wearing of rose-tinted spectacles, we have here something quite new, and, I venture to assert, something in the realm of ideas considerably in advance of its time. In the human being, the highest objectivation of the will, the latter is most brightly irradiated by knowledge. But in equal measure as knowledge arrives at clarity, the consciousness is heightened, the suffering increases, and thus in man it reaches its highest point. Even in individuals it varies in degree. "The degree of suffering," says Nietzsche, "is determined by the position in the hierarchy." Here Nietzsche betrays his ultimate dependence upon Schopenhauer's aristocratic theory of man's noble vocation to suffer. And in particular the highest type of man, the genius. It is this vocation that gives rise to the two great possibilities that Schopenhauer's humanism envisages for man. They are: art, and consecration. Only the human being possesses the possibility of the æsthetic state, as "disinterested" contemplation of the idea; to humanity alone is it given to achieve the final redemption, the renunciation of the will to live, as the artist mounts to the still loftier stage of ascetic saintliness. To man is vouchsafed the opportunity to right the wrong, to reverse the great error and mistake of being; to get the supreme insight that teaches him to make the suffering of the whole world his own and can lead him to renunciation and the conversion of the will. And so man is the secret hope of the world and of all creatures; towards whom as it were all creation trustfully turns as to its hoped-for redeemer and saviour.

This is a conception of great mystical beauty. It expresses a humane reverence for the mission of man, such as outweighs all misanthropy and supplies the corrective to all Schopenhauer's loathing of humanity. To me the importance of it lies in this union of pessimism and humanism, revealed to us by the philosopher: the intellectual experience he affords us that the one in no wise excludes the other, and that in order to be a humanist one does not need to be a rhetorical flatterer of humanity. I am not much disturbed by the question of the *truth* of Schopenhauer's interpretations, in particular his exposition, taken over from Kant, of the beautiful and the æsthetic state, the famous "disinterestedness" over which Nietzsche, so much more advanced in psychological subtlety, not unjustly made merry. Nietzsche, the Dionysiast, turned against the moralization of art and the artist life, whose heightening and perfecting was to produce the ascetic and saint; against the alleged negativism of the productive and receptive æsthetic zeal as the liberation from the torment of the will; against the negation of pleasure altogether, thus against pessimism itself, which for him lay in the confrontation of a "true world" and a "world of appearance" of which even in Kant he had already scented and pointed out. He noted without comment (the commentary is still wanting) that Kant declared: "These statements of Count Nerri [an eighteenth-century Italian philosopher] I subscribe to with full conviction: *il solo principio motore dell' uomo è il dolore. Il dolore precede ogni piacere non è un essere positivo.*" Was that so contrary to the meaning of the writer wherein one reads: "Desire is a form of pain"? In any case it was against his anti-Christian conviction, which simply will not, for the sake of earth and life, agree to any "real world" at all. Which does not alter the fact that, precisely in æsthetics, he never denies his descent from Schopenhauer, even in the time of his apostasy. For when it says, in *The World as Will and Idea*, "that the essence of life itself, the will, existence itself, is a constant suffering, partly pathetic, partly terrible; on the other hand, the same as idea alone, simply looked at, or repeated through art, free from torment, makes a *significant spectacle* (*bedeutsames Schauspiel*)," Nietzsche is dealing with the justification of life entirely as an *æsthetic spectacle* and manifestation of beauty, not otherwise than Schopenhauer deals with "disinterestedness"; in that he only gives Schopenhauer's thought the intellectual turn into the anti-moral, drunken and affirmative, into a dionysism of justification of life, wherein truly Schopenhauer's moral, life-denying pessimism can be recognized only with difficulty, but yet which survived, in another coloration, with other labels and altered demeanour. Indisputably, a man can become the opponent of a thinker and yet remain intellectually his pupil. For instance, does a man cease to be Marxist by standing the Marxian doctrine on its head and deriving certain economic principles from the ideological and religious instead of the reverse? In the same way, Nietzsche remained a Schopenhauerian. He is protected from the dubious title of optimist by the conception of the hero implicit in his dionysism, which springs from pessimism. One hesitates to speak of optimism, where what we are dealing with is really a bacchantic pessimism, a form of assent to life which is not primary and naïve but rather a conquest, a notwithstanding, won from suffering. But we find the heroic in Schopenhauer too: "Happiness is impossible; the highest attainable is a heroic life."

But we should be careful not to take too literally or seriously Schopenhauer's humanistic attitude or his classical, Apolline pronouncements. In his case, as in many others, we must distinguish between the person and the opinion, the human being and his judgments. What warns us is Schopenhauer's extremist position, a grotesque and dualistic antithesis in his nature, a *romanticism* (in the most colourful sense of the word) which removed him further from the Goethian sphere than he would ever have let himself even dream of. I said that Schopenhauer adhered to the Kantian when he defined the æsthetic state as the tearing itself free of knowledge from will, whereby the subject ceases to be a mere individual and becomes a pure will-less subject of knowledge. But Kant, with his unemotional nature, would never have hit upon describing "*das Ding an sich*" as will, instinct, sinister passion, from which the artist state gained temporary deliverance; and his æsthetics of "without interest" is not the moral issue of a romantic and emotional dualism of will and idea, a world-conception of the contrast between sensuality and asceticism with all the terrors and dæmonic tortures of one side and all the satisfactions of the other; but, by comparison, the coolest intellectuality. Ascetism means killing off. But with Kant there was not much to kill, he would never have found, to describe the æsthetic state, the vehement images of extravagant gratitude that flocked into Schopenhauer's mind. Asceticism belongs to a world of romantic contrasts and has as premise frightful experiences of the will, instinct and passion, and deep suffering therefrom. The saint as consummation of the artist is the discovery of Schopenhauer, philosopher of the instincts and the emotion—not the thought-world of Kant, which, while certainly ruthless, was far more moderate-tempered; the fearfully, brilliantly intellectual tensions of Schopenhauer's world of contrast, with its two poles of brain and genitals, were entirely foreign to it.

Seldom has a book had a more expressive, more exhaustive title than Schopenhauer's chief work, his only work, in truth, developing his own original train of thought. All else that he wrote in a lifetime of seventy-two years only forms an assiduously collected accompaniment and reinforcement to it. *The World as Will and Idea.* That is not only the theme, in its most compendious formulation: it is the man, the human being, his personality, his life, his suffering. The compulsive force of this man, and in particular his sexual urge, must have been enormous—cruel and tortuous as are the mythological figures he employs to describe the bondage to the will. It must have opposed with such equal power the compulsive force of his urge for knowledge, his lucid and mighty intellectuality, as to produce a frightfully radical duality and conflict, with a correspondingly profound craving for release; and to issue in intellectual denial of life itself, the impeachment of his own essence as evil, erroneous, and culpable. Rightly, if in an elevated sense, one may call this tortuous and grotesque. Sex is to Schopenhauer the focal point of the will; in its physical objectivation the opposite pole of the brain, which represented knowledge. Obviously, his capacity in both spheres went far beyond the average; though that in itself would only speak for the intensity and range of his nature. What makes him a pessimist, a *denier* of the world, is just the contradictory and hostile, exclusive and anguishing relation of the two spheres to each other. We need not, though it would be easy to do so, fail to understand his pessimism as the intellectual product of that very richness and power. Here is a bipolar nature, full of contrasts and conflicts, tortured and violent; after its own pattern it must experience the world: as instinct and spirit, passion and knowledge, "will" and "idea." But suppose he had learned to reconcile them in his genius, in his creative life. Suppose he had understood that genius does not at all consist in sensuality put out of action and will unhinged, that art is not mere objectivation of spirit, but the fruitful union and interpenetration of both spheres, immensely heightening to life and more fascinating than either can be by itself! That the essence of the creative artist is nothing else—and in Schopenhauer himself was nothing else—than sensuality spiritualized, than spirit informed and made creative by sex! Goethe's interpretation and experience differed from the pessimist's; it was happier, healthier, more blithely "classic," less pathologic (I use the word in an intellectual, unclinical sense)—less romantic, shall I say? For Goethe, sex and spirit (mind) were the highest, most provocative charms in life. He wrote: "*Denn das Leben ist die Liebe, und des Lebens Leben—Geist*" ("For life is love, and spirit the life of life"). But in Schopenhauer genius intensified both spheres until they took refuge in the ascetic. To him, sex is of the Devil, a diabolic distraction from pure contemplation; knowledge is that denial of sex which says: "If thine eye offend thee, pluck it out." Knowledge as "peace of the soul," art as a sedative and liberating condition of pure contemplation unmarred by will; the artist as a half-way stage to sainthood, divorced from the will to live: that is Schopenhauer. And again, in so far as this conception of mind and art is objective, it approaches Goethe's, it has a classic cast. But being exaggerated and ascetic, it is definitely romantic, in one sense of the word, which would not have appealed to Goethe at all—as witness his attitude to Heinrich von Kleist. And accordingly with similar feelings he may have read *The World as Will and Idea;* agreeing in some places, but in the main rejecting, affected hypochondriacally—and have laid it by, shaking his head; as a matter of fact, we know that after a beginning of sympathetic curiosity he did not finish it.

The distance between one great man and another, which is the result of inevitable egotism, must not mislead us. Goethe too united, in his happier way, the classic and the romantic in himself – that, indeed, is one of the formulas to which one may reduce his greatness. It is no different with Schopenhauer: the combination of the two intellectual strains is rather to be reckoned to the advantage than the detriment of his greatness – in so far, that is, as greatness is reconciling, comprehensive, summing up an epoch. Schopenhauer combines much, his theory contains many elements: idealistic, scientific, yes, pantheistic; and that his personality is strong enough to bind these elements together, such as the classic and romantic, to blend them together into something new and unique so that there is no occasion to speak of eclecticism, that is the decisive thing.

But, after all, terms and antitheses like "classic" and "romantic" do not apply to Schopenhauer. Neither the one nor the other is adequate to describe a mentality later in time than those for whom those terms once played their role. He stands nearer to us than do the minds who in their day were occupied with such distinctions and ranged themselves accordingly. Schopenhauer's mental life, the dualistic, overstrained irritability and fever of his genius, is less romantic than it is modern. I should like to enlarge upon this distinction, but content myself with making it refer in general to a state of mind the increasing strain of which became only too marked in our Western world in the century between Goethe and Nietzsche. In this respect Schopenhauer stands between the two, he makes a bridge between them: more "modern," more suffering and difficult than Goethe, but much more "classic," robust, and healthy than Nietzsche. From which it is clear that optimism and pessimism, the affirmation or denial of life, have nothing to do with health and illness. Illness and health, accordingly, have to be used with great caution as criteria or valuations. They are biological conceptions, whereas the nature of man is not exhausted in the biological. But it would be hard to assert that Nietzsche's Dionysiac, anti-Christian enthusiasm was personally something healthier and more robust than Schopenhauer's resentment against life – or that, objectively or intellectually, he brought more health into the world. Much too much, in the way of confusion, did Nietzsche labour with this biological contrast; he summoned up a false idea of healthiness which tramples on the spiritual factor that might today heal Europe. But he himself indicates a step further in suffering, in subtlety and modernity—particularly in the quality in which, more explicitly than any other, he is the pupil of Schopenhauer—I mean as a psychologist.

Schopenhauer, as psychologist of the will, is the father of all modern psychology. From him the line runs, by way of the psychological radicalism of Nietzsche, straight to Freud and the men who built up his psychology of the unconscious and applied it to the mental sciences. Nietzsche's anti-Socratism and hostility to mind are nothing but the philosophic affirmation and glorification of Schopenhauer's discovery of the primacy of the will, his pessimistic insight into the secondary and subservient relation of mind to will. This insight, certainly not humane in the classical sense, that the intellect is there to do the pleasure of the will, to justify it, to provide it with motivations, which are often very shallow and self-deluding—in fine, to rationalize the instincts—conceals a sceptical and pessimistic psychology, an analysis of relentless penetration. And it not only prepared the way for what we call psychoanalysis, it was already just that. At bottom all psychology is the unmasking, the acute, ironic, naturalistic perception of the riddling relation that obtains between the reason and the instincts. A little dialogue in the *Wahlverwandtschaften* well illustrates this underhand game our natures play. Edouard, already in love after his first meeting with Ottilie, is made by Goethe to say: "She is an entertaining person." To which his wife replies: "Entertaining? She never opened her mouth." Schopenhauer must certainly have enjoyed this passage. It is a pleasant, blithely classic illustration of his own thesis, that one does not want a thing because it is good, but finds it good because one wants it.

He himself says, for instance: "Still, it must be remarked that in order to deceive himself, a man will prepare for himself apparently inadvertent errors, which are in fact secretly deliberate acts. For we deceive and flatter nobody with such ingeniousness as ourselves." In this casual remark are whole chapters, yes, volumes of analytic unmasking of psychology *in nuce*—as later so often, in Nietzsche's aphoristic writings, Freudian revelations are anticipated as by a flash of lightning. In an address in Vienna I pointed out that Schopenhauer's sinister domain of the will is entirely identical with what Freud calls the unconscious, the "id"—as, on the other hand, Schopenhauer's intellect entirely corresponds to the Freudian ego, that part of the soul which is turned outwards to the world.

This essay is an attempt to evoke today a figure little known to the present generation; and to reconsider and recapitulate his concepts. Its object is to reassert the idea of the connection between pessimism and humanism. I should like to hand on to a world where human feeling is today finding itself in sore straits the knowledge of this combined melancholy and pride in the human race which make up Schopenhauer's philosophy. His pessimism — that is his humanity. His interpretation of the world by the concept of the will, his insight into the overweening power of instinct and the derogation of the one-time godlike reason, mind, and intellect to a mere tool with which to achieve security — all this is anti-classic and in its essence inhumane. But it is precisely in the pessimistic hue of his philosophy that his humanity and spirituality lie; in the fact that this great artist, practised in suffering and wielding the prose of a great humane cultural epoch in our history, lifts man out of the biological sphere of nature, makes his own feeling and understanding soul the theatre where the will meets its reverse, and sees in the human being the saviour of all creation. Therein lie both his humanity and his intellectuality.

The twentieth century has in its first third taken up a position of reaction against classic rationalism and intellectualism. It has surrendered to admiration of the unconscious, to a glorification of instinct, which it thinks is overdue to life. And the bad instincts have accordingly been enjoying a heyday. We have seen instead of pessimistic conviction deliberate malice. Intellectual recognition of bitter truth turns into hatred and contempt for mind itself. Man has greedily flung himself on the side of "life" — that is, on the side of the stronger — for there is no disputing the fact that life has nothing to fear from mind, that not life but knowledge, or rather mind, is the weaker part and one more needing protection on this earth. Yet the anti-humanity of our day is a humane experiment too in its way. It is a one-sided answer to the eternal question as to the nature and destiny of man. We palpably need a corrective to restore the balance, and I think the philosophy I here evoke can do good service. I spoke of Schopenhauer as modern. I might have called him futurist. The chiaroscuro harmonies of his human traits, the mixture in him of Voltaire and Jakob Böhme, the paradox of his classic, pellucid prose, employed to lighten the darkest and lowest purlieus of being; his proud misanthropy, which never belies his reverence for the idea of the human being; in short, what I called his pessimistic humanity seems to me to herald the temper of a future time. Once he was fashionable and famous, then half-forgotten. But his philosophy may still exert a ripe and humanizing influence upon our age. His intellectual sensitivity, his teaching, which was life, that knowledge, thought, and philosophy are not matters of the head alone but of the whole man, heart and sense, body and soul; in other words, his existence as an artist may help to bring to birth a new humanity of which we stand in need, and to which it is akin: a humanity above dry reason on the one hand and idolatry of instinct on the other. For art, accompanying man on his painful journey to self-realization, has always been before him at the goal.

FREUD AND THE FUTURE

1936

[*A speech delivered in Vienna, May 9, 1936, on Freud's eightieth birthday*]

WE are gathered here to do honour to a great scientist. And the question may very properly be raised: what justifies a man of letters in assuming the role of spokesman on such an occasion? Or, passing on the responsibility to the members of the learned society which chose him, why should they not have selected one of their own kind, a man of science, rather than an author, to celebrate in words the birthday of their master? For an author, my friends, is a man essentially not bent upon science, upon knowing, distinguishing, and analysing; he stands for simple creation, for doing and making, and thus may be the object of useful cognition, without, by his very nature, having any competence in it as subject. But is it, perhaps, that the author in his character as artist, and artist in the field of the intellect, is especially called to the celebration of feasts of the mind; that he is by nature more a man of feast-days than the scientist and man of knowledge? It is not for me to dispute such a view. It is true, the poet has understanding of the feasts of life, understanding even of life as a feast – and here I am just touching, very lightly for the moment, upon a theme that may become a main motif in the chorus of homage which we are to perform this evening. But it is more likely that the sponsors of this evening had something else in mind in their choice: that is to say, the solemn and novel confrontation of object and subject, the object of knowledge with the knower – a saturnalia, as it were, in which the knower and seer of dreams himself becomes, by our act of homage, the object of dreamlike penetration. And to such a position I could not object, either; particularly because it strikes a chord capable in the future of great symphonic development. It will recur, more clearly accented and fully instrumented. For, unless I am greatly mistaken, it is just this confrontation of object and subject, their mingling and identification, the resultant insight into the mysterious unity of ego and actuality, destiny and character, doing and happening, and thus into the mystery of reality as an operation of the psyche — it is just this confrontation that is the alpha and omega of all psychoanalytical knowledge.

Be that as it may, the choice of an artist as the encomiast of a great scientist is a comment upon both. In the first place, one deduces from it a connection between the man of genius we now honour and the world of creative literature; in the second place, it displays the peculiar relations between the writer and the field of science whose declared and acknowledged master and creator the other is. Now, the unique and remarkable thing about this mutual close relation is that it remained for so long unconscious — that is, in that region of the soul which we have learned to call the unconscious, a realm whose discovery and investigation, whose conquest for humanity, are precisely the task and mission of the wise genius whose fame we celebrate. The close relation between literature and psychoanalysis has been known for a long time to both sides. But the solemn significance of this hour lies, at least in my eyes and as a matter of personal feeling, in that on this evening there is taking place the first official meeting between the two spheres, in the acknowledgment and demonstration of their relationship.

I repeat that the profound sympathy between the two spheres had existed for a long time unperceived. Actually we know that Sigmund Freud, that mighty spirit in whose honour we are gathered together, founder of psychoanalysis as a general method of research and as a therapeutic technique, trod the steep path alone and independently, as physician and natural scientist, without knowing that reinforcement and encouragement lay to his hand in literature. He did not know Nietzsche, scattered throughout whose pages one finds premonitory flashes of truly Freudian insight; he did not know Novalis, whose romantic-biologic fantasies so often approach astonishingly close to analytic conceptions; he did not know Kierkegaard, whom he must have found profoundly sympathetic and encouraging for the Christian zeal which urged him on to psychological extremes; and, finally, he did not know Schopenhauer, the melancholy symphonist of a philosophy of the instinct, groping for change and redemption. Probably it must be so. By his unaided effort, without knowledge of any previous intuitive achievement, he had methodically to follow out the line of his own researches; the driving force of his activity was probably increased by this very freedom from special advantage. And we think of him as solitary — the attitude is inseparable from our earliest picture of the man. Solitary in the sense of the word used by Nietzsche in that ravishing essay "What is the Meaning of Ascetic Ideals?" when he characterizes Schopenhauer as "a genuine philosopher, a self-poised mind, a man and gallant knight, stern-eyed, with the courage of his own strength, who knows how to stand alone and not wait on the beck and nod of superior officers." In this guise of man and gallant knight, a knight between Death and the Devil, I have been used to picture to myself our psychologist of the unconscious, ever since his figure first swam into my mental ken.

That happened late — much later than one might have expected, considering the connection between this science and the poetic and creative impulse in general and mine in particular. The connection, the bond between them, is twofold: it consists first in a love of truth, in a sense of truth, a sensitiveness and receptivity for truth's sweet and bitter, which largely expresses itself in a psychological excitation, a clarity of vision, to such an extent that the conception of truth actually almost coincides with that of psychological perception and recognition. And secondly it consists in an understanding of disease, a certain affinity with it, outweighed by fundamental health, and an understanding of its productive significance.

As for the love of truth: the suffering, morally conditioned love of truth *as psychology* — that has its origin in Nietzsche's lofty school, where in fact the coincidence of "truth" and "psychological truth," of the knower with the psychologist, is striking indeed. His proud truthfulness, his very conception of intellectual honesty, his conscious and melancholy fearlessness in its service, his self-knowledge, self-crucifixion — all this has psychological intention and bearing. Never shall I forget the deepening, strengthening, formative effect upon my own powers produced by my acquaintance with Nietzsche's psychological agony. In *Tonio Kröger* the artist speaks of being "sick of knowledge." That is true Nietzsche language; and the youth's melancholy has reference to the Hamlet-like in Nietzsche's nature, in which his own mirrored itself: a nature called to knowledge without being genuinely born to it. These are the pangs and anguishes of youth, destined to be lightened and tranquillized as years flowed by and brought ripeness with them. But there has remained with me the desire for a psychological interpretation of knowledge and truth; I still equate them with psychology and feel the psychological will to truth as a desire for truth in general; still interpret psychology as truth in the most actual and courageous sense of the word. One would call the tendency a naturalistic one, I suppose, and ascribe it to a training in literary naturalism; it forms a precondition of receptivity for the natural science of the psyche – in other words, for what is known as psychoanalysis.

I spoke of a second bond between that science and the creative impulse: the understanding of disease, or, more precisely, of disease as an instrument of knowledge. That, too, one may derive from Nietzsche. He well knew what he owed to his morbid state, and on every page he seems to instruct us that there is no deeper knowledge without experience of disease, and that all heightened healthiness must be achieved by the route of illness. This attitude too may be referred to his experience; but it is bound up with the nature of the intellectual man in general, of the creative artist in particular, yes, with the nature of humanity and the human being, of which last of course the creative artist is an extreme expression. "*L'humanité*," says Victor Hugo, "*s'affirme par l'infirmité*." A saying which frankly and proudly admits the delicate constitution of all higher humanity and culture and their connoisseurship in the realm of disease. Man has been called "*das kranke Tier*" because of the burden of strain and explicit difficulties laid upon him by his position between nature and spirit, between angel and brute. What wonder, then, that by the approach through abnormality we have succeeded in penetrating most deeply into the darkness of human nature; that the study of disease – that is to say, neurosis – has revealed itself as a first-class technique of anthropological research?

The literary artist should be the last person to be surprised at the fact. Sooner might he be surprised that he, considering his strong general and individual tendency, should have so late become aware of the close sympathetic relations which connected his own existence with psychoanalytic research and the life-work of Sigmund Freud. I realized this connection only at a time when his achievement was no longer thought of as merely a therapeutic method, whether recognized or disputed; when it had long since outgrown his purely medical implications and become a world movement which penetrated into every field of science and every domain of the intellect: literature, the history of art, religion and prehistory; mythology, folklore, pedagogy, and what not – thanks to the practical and constructive zeal of experts who erected a structure of more general investigation round the psychiatric and medical core. Indeed, it would be too much to say that I came to psychoanalysis. It came to me. Through the friendly interest that some younger workers in the field had shown in my work, from *Little Herr Friedemann* to *Death in Venice*, *The Magic Mountain*, and the *Joseph* novels, it gave me to understand that in my way I "belonged"; it made me aware, as probably behoved it, of my own latent, preconscious sympathies; and when I began to occupy myself with the literature of psychoanalysis I recognized, arrayed in the ideas and the language of scientific exactitude, much that had long been familiar to me through my youthful mental experiences.

Perhaps you will kindly permit me to continue for a while in this autobiographical strain, and not take it amiss if instead of speaking of Freud I speak of myself. And indeed I scarcely trust myself to speak *about* him. What new thing could I hope to say? But I shall also, quite explicitly, be speaking in his honour in speaking of myself, in telling you how profoundly and peculiarly certain experiences decisive for my development prepared me for the Freudian experience. More than once, and in many places, I have confessed to the profound, even shattering impression made upon me as a young man by contact with the philosophy of Arthur Schopenhauer, to which then a monument was erected in the pages of *Buddenbrooks*. Here first, in the pessimism of a metaphysics already very strongly equipped on the natural-science side, I encountered the dauntless zeal for truth that stands for the moral aspect of the psychology of the unconscious. This metaphysics, in obscure revolt against centuries-old beliefs, preached the primacy of the instinct over mind and reason; it recognized the will as the core and the essential foundation of the world, in man as in all other created beings; and the intellect as secondary and accidental, servant of the will and its pale illuminant. This it preached not in malice, not in the anti-human spirit of the mind-hostile doctrines of today, but in the stern love of truth characteristic of the century which combated idealism out of love for the ideal. It was so sincere, that nineteenth century, that—through the mouth of Ibsen—it pronounced the lie, the lies of life, to be indispensable. Clearly there is a vast difference whether one assents to a lie out of sheer hatred of truth and the spirit or for the sake of that spirit, in bitter irony and anguished pessimism! Yet the distinction is not clear to everybody today.

Now, Freud, the psychologist of the unconscious, is a true son of the century of Schopenhauer and Ibsen—he was born in the middle of it. How closely related is his revolution to Schopenhauer's, not only in its content, but also in its moral attitude! His discovery of the great role played by the unconscious, the id, in the soul-life of man challenged and challenges classical psychology, to which the consciousness and the psyche are one and the same, as offensively as once Schopenhauer's doctrine of the will challenged philosophical belief in reason and the intellect. Certainly the early devotee of *The World as Will and Idea* is at home in the admirable essay that is included in Freud's *New Introductory Essays in Psychoanalysis* under the title "The Anatomy of the Mental Personality." It describes the soul-world of the unconscious, the id, in language as strong, and at the same time in as coolly intellectual, objective, and professional a tone, as Schopenhauer might have used to describe his sinister kingdom of the will. "The domain of the id," he says, "is the dark, inaccessible part of our personality; the little that we know of it we have learned through the study of dreams and of the formation of neurotic symptoms." He depicts it as a chaos, a melting-pot of seething excitations. The id, he thinks, is, so to speak, open towards the somatic, and receives thence into itself compulsions which there find psychic expression—in what substratum is unknown. From these impulses it receives its energy; but it is not organized, produces no collective will, merely the striving to achieve satisfaction for the impulsive needs operating under the pleasure principle. In it no laws of thought are valid, and certainly not the law of opposites. "Contradictory stimuli exist alongside each other without cancelling each other out or even detracting from each other; at most they unite in compromise forms under the compulsion of the controlling economy for the release of energy." You perceive that this is a situation which, in the historical experience of our own day, can take the upper hand with the ego, with a whole mass-ego, thanks to a moral devastation which is produced by worship of the unconscious, the glorification of its dynamic as the only life-promoting force, the systematic glorification of the primitive and irrational. For the unconscious, the id, is primitive and irrational, is pure dynamic. It knows no values, no good or evil, no morality. It even knows no time, no temporal flow, nor any effect of time upon its psychic process. "Wish stimuli," says Freud, "which have never overpassed the id, and impressions which have been repressed into its depths, are virtually indestructible, they survive decade after decade as though they had just happened. They can only be recognized as belonging to the past, devalued and robbed of their charge of energy, by becoming conscious through the analytic procedure." And he adds that therein lies pre-eminently the healing effect of analytic treatment. We perceive accordingly how antipathetic deep analysis must be to an ego that is intoxicated by a worship of the unconscious to the point of being in a condition of subterranean dynamic. It is only too clear and understandable that such an ego is deaf to analysis and that the name of Freud must not be mentioned in its hearing.

As for the ego itself, its situation is pathetic, well-nigh alarming. It is an alert, prominent, and enlightened little part of the id—much as Europe is a small and lively province of the greater Asia. The ego is that part of the id which became modified by contact with the outer world; equipped for the reception and preservation of stimuli; comparable to the integument with which any piece of living matter surrounds itself. A very perspicuous biological picture. Freud writes indeed a very perspicuous prose, he is an artist of thought, like Schopenhauer, and like him a writer of European rank. The relation with the outer world is, he says, decisive for the ego, it is the ego's task to represent the world to the id—for its good! For without regard for the superior power of the outer world the id, in its blind striving towards the satisfaction of its instincts, would not escape destruction. The ego takes cognizance of the outer world, it is mindful, it honourably tries to distinguish the objectively real from whatever is an accretion from its inward sources of stimulation. It is entrusted by the id with the lever of action; but between the impulse and the action it has interposed the delay of the thought-process, during which it summons experience to its aid and thus possesses a certain regulative superiority over the pleasure principle which rules supreme in the unconscious, correcting it by means of the principle of reality. But even so, how feeble it is! Hemmed in between the unconscious, the outer world, and what Freud calls the super-ego, it leads a pretty nervous and anguished existence. Its own dynamic is rather weak. It derives its energy from the id and in general has to carry out the latter's behests. It is fain to regard itself as the rider and the unconscious as the horse. But many a time it is ridden by the unconscious; and I take leave to add what Freud's rational morality prevents him from saying, that under some circumstances it makes more progress by this illegitimate means.

But Freud's description of the id and the ego—is it not to a hair Schopenhauer's description of the Will and the Intellect, a translation of the latter's metaphysics into psychology? So he who had been initiated into the metaphysics of Schopenhauer and in Nietzsche tasted the painful pleasure of psychology—he must needs have been filled with a sense of recognition and familiarity when first, encouraged thereto by its denizens, he entered the realms of psychoanalysis and looked about him.

He found too that his new knowledge had a strange and strong retroactive effect upon the old. After a sojourn in the world of Freud, how differently, in the light of one's new knowledge, does one reread the reflections of Schopenhauer, for instance his great essay "Transcendent Speculations on Apparent Design in the Fate of the Individual"! And here I am about to touch upon the most profound and mysterious point of contact between Freud's natural-scientific world and Schopenhauer's philosophic one. For the essay I have named, a marvel of profundity and penetration, constitutes this point of contact. The pregnant and mysterious idea there developed by Schopenhauer is briefly this: that precisely as in a dream it is our own will that unconsciously appears as inexorable objective destiny, everything in it proceeding out of ourselves and each of us being the secret theatre-manager of our own dreams, so also in reality the great dream that a single essence, the will itself, dreams with us all, our fate, may be the product of our inmost selves, of our wills, and we are actually ourselves bringing about what seems to be happening to us. I have only briefly indicated here the content of the essay, for these representations are winged with the strongest and most sweeping powers of suggestion. But not only does the dream psychology which Schopenhauer calls to his aid bear an explicitly psychoanalytic character, even to the presence of the sexual argument and paradigm; but the whole complexus of thought is a philosophical anticipation of analytical conceptions, to a quite astonishing extent. For, to repeat what I said in the beginning, I see in the mystery of the unity of the ego and the world, of being and happening, in the perception of the apparently objective and accidental as a matter of the soul's own contriving, the innermost core of psychoanalytic theory.

And here there occurs to me a phrase from the pen of C. J. Jung, an able but somewhat ungrateful scion of the Freudian school, in his significant introduction to the Tibetan *Book of the Dead*. "It is so much more direct, striking, impressive, and thus convincing," he says, "to see how it happens to me than to see how I do it." A bold, even an extravagant statement, plainly betraying the calmness with which in a certain school of psychology certain things are regarded which even Schopenhauer considered prodigiously daring speculation. Would this unmasking of the "happening" as in reality "doing" be conceivable without Freud? Never! It owes him everything. It is weighted down with assumptions, it could not be understood, it could never have been written, without all that analysis has brought to light about slips of tongue and pen, the whole field of human error, the retreat into illness, the psychology of accidents, the self-punishment compulsion—in short, all the wizardry of the unconscious. Just as little, moreover, would that close-packed sentence of Jung's, including its psychological premises, have been possible without Schopenhauer's adventurous pioneering speculation. Perhaps this is the moment, my friends, to indulge on this festive occasion in a little polemic against Freud himself. He does not esteem philosophy very highly. His scientific exactitude does not permit him to regard it as a science. He reproaches it with imagining that it can present a continuous and consistent picture of the world; with overestimating the objective value of logical operations; with believing in intuitions as a source of knowledge and with indulging in positively animistic tendencies, in that it believes in the magic of words and the influence of thought upon reality. But would philosophy really be thinking too highly of itself on these assumptions? Has the world ever been changed by anything save by thought and its magic vehicle the Word? I believe that in actual fact philosophy ranks before and above the natural sciences and that all method and exactness serve its intuitions and its intellectual and historical will. In the last analysis it is always a matter of the *quod erat demonstrandum.* Scientific freedom from assumptions is or should be a moral fact. But intellectually it is, as Freud points out, probably an illusion. One might strain the point and say that science has never made a discovery without being authorized and encouraged thereto by philosophy.

All this by the way. But it is in line with my general intention to pause a little longer at the sentence that I quoted from Jung. In this essay and also as a general method which he uses by preference, Jung applies analytical evidence to form a bridge between Occidental thought and Oriental esoteric. Nobody has focused so sharply as he the Schopenhauer-Freud perception that "the giver of all given conditions resides in ourselves—a truth which despite all evidence in the greatest as well as in the smallest things *never* becomes conscious, though it is only too often necessary, even indispensable, that it should be." A great and costly change, he thinks, is needed before we understand how the world is "given" by the nature of the soul; for man's animal nature strives against seeing himself as the maker of his own conditions. It is true that the East has always shown itself stronger than the West in the conquest of our animal nature, and we need not be surprised to hear that in its wisdom it conceives even the gods among the "given conditions" originating from the soul and one with her, light and reflection of the human soul. This knowledge, which, according to the *Book of the Dead*, one gives to the deceased to accompany him on his way, is a paradox to the Occidental mind, conflicting with its sense of logic, which distinguishes between subject and object and refuses to have them coincide or make one proceed from the other. True, European mysticism has been aware of such attitudes, and Angelus Silesius said:

> I know that without me God cannot live a moment;
> If I am destroyed He must give up the ghost.

But on the whole a psychological conception of God, an idea of the godhead which is not pure condition, absolute reality, but one with the soul and bound up with it, must be intolerable to Occidental religious sense—it would be equivalent to abandoning the idea of God.

Yet religion—perhaps even etymologically—essentially implies a bond. In Genesis we have talk of the bond (covenant) between God and man, the psychological basis of which I have attempted to give in the mythological novel *Joseph and His Brothers*. Perhaps my hearers will be indulgent if I speak a little about my own work; there may be some justification for introducing it here in this hour of formal encounter between creative literature and the psychoanalytic. It is strange—and perhaps strange not only to me—that in this work there obtains precisely that psychological theology which the scholar ascribes to Oriental esoteric. This Abram is in a sense the father of God. He perceived and brought Him forth; His mighty qualities, ascribed to Him by Abram, were probably His original possession, Abram was not their inventor, yet in a sense he was, by virtue of his recognizing them and therewith, by taking thought, making them real. God's mighty qualities—and thus God Himself—are indeed something objective, exterior to Abram; but at the same time they are in him and of him as well; the power of his own soul is at moments scarcely to be distinguished from them, it consciously interpenetrates and fuses with them—and such is the origin of the bond which then the Lord strikes with Abram, as the explicit confirmation of an inward fact. The bond, it is stated, is made in the interest of both, to the end of their common sanctification. Need human and need divine here entwine until it is hard to say whether it was the human or the divine that took the initiative. In any case the arrangement shows that the holiness of man and the holiness of God constituted a twofold process, one part being most intimately bound up with the other. Wherefore else, one asks, should there be a bond at all?

The soul as "giver of the given" – yes, my friends, I am well aware that in the novel this conception reaches an ironic pitch which is not authorized either in Oriental wisdom or in psychological perception. But there is something thrilling about the unconscious and only later discovered harmony. Shall I call it the power of suggestion? But sympathy would be a better word: a kind of intellectual affinity, of which naturally psychoanalysis was earlier aware than was I, and which proceeded out of those literary appreciations which I owed to it at an earlier stage. The latest of these was an offprint of an article that appeared in *Imago*, written by a Viennese scholar of the Freudian school, under the title "On the Psychology of the Older School of Biography." The rather dry title gives no indication of the remarkable contents. The writer shows how the older and simpler type of biography and in particular the written lives of artists, nourished and conditioned by popular legend and tradition, assimilate, as it were, the life of the subject to the conventionalized stock-in-trade of biography in general, thus imparting a sort of sanction to their own performance and establishing its genuineness; making it authentic in the sense of "as it always was" and "as it has been written." For man sets store by recognition, he likes to find the old in the new, the typical in the individual. From that recognition he draws a sense of the familiar in life, whereas if it painted itself as entirely new, singular in time and space, without any possibility of resting upon the known, it could only bewilder and alarm. The question, then, which is raised by the essay, is this: can any line be sharply and unequivocally drawn between the formal stock-in-trade of legendary biography and the characteristics of the single personality – in other words, between the typical and the individual? A question negatived by its very statement. For the truth is that life is a mingling of the individual elements and the formal stock-in-trade; a mingling in which the individual, as it were, only lifts his head above the formal and impersonal elements. Much that is extra-personal, much unconscious identification, much that is conventional and schematic, is none the less decisive for the experience not only of the artist but of the human being in general. "Many of us," says the writer of the article, " 'live' today a biographical type, the destiny of a class or rank or calling. The freedom in the shaping of the human being's life is obviously connected with that bond which we term 'lived *vita*.' " And then, to my delight, but scarcely to my surprise, he begins to cite from *Joseph*, the fundamental motif of which he says is precisely this idea of the "lived life," life as succession, as a moving in others' steps, as identification — such as Joseph's teacher, Eliezer, practises with droll solemnity. For in him time is cancelled and all the Eliezers of the past gather to shape the Eliezer of the present, so that he speaks in the first person of that Eliezer who was Abram's servant, though he was far from being the same man.

I must admit that I find the train of thought extraordinarily convincing. The essay indicates the precise point at which the psychological interest passes over into the mythical. It makes it clear that the typical is actually the mythical, and that one may as well say "lived myth" as "lived life." But the mythus as lived is the epic idea embodied in my novel; and it is plain to me that when as a novelist I took the step in my subject-matter from the bourgeois and individual to the mythical and typical my personal connection with the analytic field passed into its acute stage. The mythical interest is as native to psychoanalysis as the psychological interest is to all creative writing. Its penetration into the childhood of the individual soul is at the same time a penetration into the childhood of mankind, into the primitive and mythical. Freud has told us that for him all natural science, medicine, and psychotherapy were a lifelong journey round and back to the early passion of his youth for the history of mankind, for the origins of religion and morality — an interest which at the height of his career broke out to such magnificent effect in *Totem and Taboo*. The word *Tiefenpsychologie* ("deep" psychology) has a temporal significance; the primitive foundations of the human soul are likewise primitive time, they are those profound time-sources where the myth has its home and shapes the primeval norms and forms of life. For the myth is the foundation of life; it is the timeless schema, the pious formula into which life flows when it reproduces its traits out of the unconscious. Certainly when a writer has acquired the habit of regarding life as mythical and typical there comes a curious heightening of his artist temper, a new refreshment to his perceiving and shaping powers, which otherwise occurs much later in life; for while in the life of the human race the mythical is an early and primitive stage, in the life of the individual it is a late and mature one. What is gained is an insight into the higher truth depicted in the actual; a smiling knowledge of the eternal, the ever-being and authentic; a knowledge of the schema in which and according to which the supposed individual lives, unaware, in his naïve belief in himself as unique in space and time, of the extent to which his life is but formula and repetition and his path marked out for him by those who trod it before him. His character is a mythical role which the actor just emerged from the depths to the light plays in the illusion that it is his own and unique, that he, as it were, has invented it all himself, with a dignity and security of which his supposed unique individuality in time and space is not the source, but rather which he creates out of his deeper consciousness in order that something which was once founded and legitimized shall again be represented and once more for good or ill, whether nobly or basely, in any case after its own kind conduct itself according to pattern. Actually, if his existence consisted merely in the unique and the present, he would not know how to conduct himself at all; he would be confused, helpless, unstable in his own self-regard, would not know which foot to put foremost or what sort of face to put on. His dignity and security lie all unconsciously in the fact that with him something timeless has once more emerged into the light and become present; it is a mythical value added to the otherwise poor and valueless single character; it is native worth, because its origin lies in the unconscious.

Such is the gaze which the mythically oriented artist bends upon the phenomena about him—an ironic and superior gaze, as you can see, for the mythical knowledge resides in the gazer and not in that at which he gazes. But let us suppose that the mythical point of view could become subjective; that it could pass over into the active ego and become conscious there, proudly and darkly yet joyously, of its recurrence and its typicality, could celebrate its role and realize its own value exclusively in the knowledge that it was a fresh incarnation of the traditional upon earth. One might say that such a phenomenon alone could be the "lived myth"; nor should we think that it is anything novel or unknown. The life in the myth, life as a sacred repetition, is a historical form of life, for the man of ancient times lived thus. An instance is the figure of the Egyptian Cleopatra, which is Ishtar, Astarte, Aphrodite in person. Bachofen, in his description of the cult of Bacchus, the Dionysiac religion, regards the Egyptian queen as the consummate picture of a Dionysiac *stimula;* and according to Plutarch it was far more her erotic intellectual culture than her physical charms that entitled her to represent the female as developed into the earthly embodiment of Aphrodite. But her Aphrodite nature, her role of Hathor-Isis, is not only objective, not only a treatment of her by Plutarch or Bachofen; it was the content of her subjective existence as well, she lived the part. This we can see by the manner of her death: she is supposed to have killed herself by laying an asp upon her bosom. But the snake was the familiar of Ishtar, the Egyptian Isis, who is represented clad in a garment of scales; also there exists a statuette of Ishtar holding a snake to her bosom. So that if Cleopatra's death was as the legend represents, the manner of it was a manifestation of her mythical ego. Moreover, did she not adopt the falcon hood of the goddess Isis and adorn herself with the insignia of Hathor, the cow's horns with the crescent moon between? And name her two children by Mark Antony Helios and Selene? No doubt she was a very significant figure indeed – significant in the antique sense, that she was well aware who she was and in whose footsteps she trod!

The ego of antiquity and its consciousness of itself were different from our own, less exclusive, less sharply defined. It was, as it were, open behind; it received much from the past and by repeating it gave it presentness again. The Spanish scholar Ortega y Gasset puts it that the man of antiquity, before he did anything, took a step backwards, like the bull-fighter who leaps back to deliver the mortal thrust. He searched the past for a pattern into which he might slip as into a diving-bell, and being thus at once disguised and protected might rush upon his present problem. Thus his life was in a sense a reanimation, an archaizing attitude. But it is just this life as reanimation that is the life as myth. Alexander walked in the footsteps of Miltiades; the ancient biographers of Cæsar were convinced, rightly or wrongly, that he took Alexander as his prototype. But such "imitation" meant far more than we mean by the word today. It was a mythical identification, peculiarly familiar to antiquity; but it is operative far into modern times, and at all times is psychically possible. How often have we not been told that the figure of Napoleon was cast in the antique mould! He regretted that the mentality of the time forbade him to give himself out for the son of Jupiter Ammon, in imitation of Alexander. But we need not doubt that – at least at the period of his Eastern exploits – he mythically confounded himself with Alexander; while after he turned his face westwards he is said to have declared: "I am Charlemagne." Note that: not "I am like Charlemagne" or "My situation is like Charlemagne's," but quite simply: "I am he." That is the formulation of the myth. Life, then – at any rate, significant life – was in ancient times the reconstitution of the myth in flesh and blood; it referred to and appealed to the myth; only through it, through reference to the past, could it approve itself as genuine and significant. The myth is the legitimization of life; only through and in it does life find self-awareness, sanction, consecration. Cleopatra fulfilled her Aphrodite character even unto death – and can one live and die more significantly or worthily than in the celebration of the myth? We have only to think of Jesus and His life, which was lived in order that that which was written might be fulfilled. It is not easy to distinguish between His own consciousness and the conventionalizations of the Evangelists. But His word on the Cross, about the ninth hour, that "*Eli, Eli, lama sabachthani?*" was evidently not in the least an outburst of despair and disillusionment; but on the contrary a lofty messianic sense of self. For the phrase is not original, not a spontaneous outcry. It stands at the beginning of the Twenty-second Psalm, which from one end to the other is an announcement of the Messiah. Jesus was quoting, and the quotation meant: "Yes, it is I!" Precisely thus did Cleopatra quote when she took the asp to her breast to die; and again the quotation meant: "Yes, it is I!"

Let us consider for a moment the word "celebration" which I used in this connection. It is a pardonable, even a proper usage. For life in the myth, life, so to speak, in quotation, is a kind of celebration, in that it is a making present of the past, it becomes a religious act, the performance by a celebrant of a prescribed procedure; it becomes a feast. For a feast is an anniversary, a renewal of the past in the present. Every Christmas the world-saving Babe is born again on earth, to suffer, to die, and to arise. The feast is the abrogation of time, an event, a solemn narrative being played out conformably to an immemorial pattern; the events in it take place not for the first time, but ceremonially according to the prototype. It achieves presentness as feasts do, recurring in time with their phases and hours following on each other in time as they did in the original occurrence. In antiquity each feast was essentially a dramatic performance, a mask; it was the scenic reproduction, with priests as actors, of stories about the gods – as for instance the life and sufferings of Osiris. The Christian Middle Ages had their mystery play, with heaven, earth, and the torments of hell – just as we have it later in Goethe's *Faust;* they had their carnival farce, their folk-mime. The artist eye has a mythical slant upon life, which makes it look like a farce, like a theatrical performance of a prescribed feast, like a Punch and Judy epic, wherein mythical character puppets reel off a plot abiding from past time and now again present in a jest. It only lacks that this mythical slant pass over and become subjective in the performers themselves, become a festival and mythical consciousness of part and play, for an epic to be produced such as that in the first volume of the *Joseph and His Brothers* series, particularly in the chapter "The Great Hoaxing." There a mythical recurrent farce is tragicomically played by personages all of whom well know in whose steps they tread: Isaac, Esau, and Jacob; and who act out the cruel and grotesque tale of how Esau the Red is led by the nose and cheated of his birthright to the huge delight of all the bystanders. Joseph too is another such celebrant of life; with charming mythological hocus-pocus he enacts in his own person the Tammuz-Osiris myth, "bringing to pass" anew the story of the mangled, buried, and arisen god, playing his festival game with that which mysteriously and secretly shapes life out of its own depths — the unconscious. The mystery of the metaphysician and psychologist, that the soul is the giver of all given conditions, becomes in Joseph easy, playful, blithe — like a consummately artistic performance by a fencer or juggler. It reveals his *infantile* nature — and the word I have used betrays how closely, though seeming to wander so far afield, we have kept to the subject of our evening's homage.

Infantilism — in other words, regression to childhood — what a role this genuinely psychoanalytic element plays in all our lives! What a large share it has in shaping the life of a human being; operating, indeed, in just the way I have described: as mythical identification, as survival, as a treading in footprints already made! The bond with the father, the imitation of the father, the game of being the father, and the transference to father-substitute picures of a higher and more developed type — how these infantile traits work upon the life of the individual to mark and shape it! I use the word "shape," for to me in all seriousness the happiest, most pleasurable element of what we call education (*Bildung*), the shaping of the human being, is just this powerful influence of admiration and love, this childish identification with a father-image elected out of profound affinity. The artist in particular, a passionately childlike and play-possessed being, can tell us of the mysterious yet after all obvious effect of such infantile imitation upon his own life, his productive conduct of a career which after all is often nothing but a reanimation of the hero under very different temporal and personal conditions and with very different, shall we say childish means. The *imitatio* Goethe, with its Werther and Wilhelm Meister stages, its old-age period of *Faust* and *Diwan*, can still shape and mythically mould the life of an artist — rising out of his unconscious, yet playing over — as is the artist way — into a smiling, childlike, and profound awareness.

The Joseph of the novel is an artist, playing with his *imitatio dei* upon the unconscious string; and I know not how to express the feelings which possess me — something like a joyful sense of divination of the future — when I indulge in this encouragement of the unconscious to play, to make itself fruitful in a serious product, in a narrational meeting of psychology and myth, which is at the same time a celebration of the meeting between poetry and analysis.

And now this word "future": I have used it in the title of my address, because it is this idea, the idea of the future, that I involuntarily like best to connect with the name of Freud. But even as I have been speaking I have been asking myself whether I have not been guilty of a cause of confusion; whether—from what I have said up to now—a better title might not have been something like "Freud and the Myth." And yet I rather cling to the combination of name and word and I should like to justify and make clear its relation to what I have so far said. I make bold to believe that in that novel so kin to the Freudian world, making as it does the light of psychology play upon the myth, there lie hidden seeds and elements of a new and coming sense of our humanity. And no less firmly do I hold that we shall one day recognize in Freud's life-work the cornerstone for the building of a new anthropology and therewith of a new structure, to which many stones are being brought up today, which shall be the future dwelling of a wiser and freer humanity. This physicianly psychologist will, I make no doubt at all, be honoured as the path-finder towards a humanism of the future, which we dimly divine and which will have experienced much that the earlier humanism knew not of. It will be a humanism standing in a different relation to the powers of the lower world, the unconscious, the id: a relation bolder, freer, blither, productive of a riper art than any possible in our neurotic, fear-ridden, hate-ridden world. Freud is of the opinion that the significance of psychoanalysis as a science of the unconscious will in the future far outrank its value as a therapeutic method. But even as a science of the unconscious it is a therapeutic method, in the grand style, a method overarching the individual case. Call this, if you choose, a poet's utopia; but the thought is after all not unthinkable that the resolution of our great fear and our great hate, their conversion into a different relation to the unconscious which shall be more the artist's, more ironic and yet not necessarily irreverent, may one day be due to the healing effect of this very science.

The analytic revelation is a revolutionary force. With it a blithe scepticism has come into the world, a mistrust that unmasks all the schemes and subterfuges of our own souls. Once roused and on the alert, it cannot be put to sleep again. It infiltrates life, undermines its raw naïveté, takes from it the strain of its own ignorance, de-emotionalizes it, as it were, inculcates the taste for understatement, as the English call it—for the deflated rather than for the inflated word, for the cult which exerts its influence by moderation, by modesty. Modesty—what a beautiful word! In the German (*Bescheidenheit*) it originally had to do with knowing and only later got its present meaning; while the Latin word from which the English comes means a way of doing—in short, both together give us almost the sense of the French *savoir faire*—to know how to do. May we hope that this may be the fundamental temper of that more blithely objective and peaceful world which the science of the unconscious may be called to usher in?

Its mingling of the pioneer with the physicianly spirit justifies such a hope. Freud once called his theory of dreams "a bit of scientific new-found land won from superstition and mysticism." The word "won" expresses the colonizing spirit and significance of his work. "Where id was, shall be ego," he epigrammatically says. And he calls analysis a cultural labour comparable to the draining of the Zuider Zee. Almost in the end the traits of the venerable man merge into the lineaments of the grey-haired Faust, whose spirit urges him

> to shut the imperious sea from the shore away,
> Set narrower bounds to the broad water's waste.
>
> Then open I to many millions space
> Where they may live, not safe-secure, but free
> And active. And such a busy swarming I would see
> Standing amid free folk on a free soil.

The free folk are the people of a future freed from fear and hate, and ripe for peace.

VOYAGE WITH DON QUIXOTE

1934

May nineteenth, 1934. It seemed a good idea to begin it by drinking a vermouth in the bar; accordingly we did so, while quietly awaiting the moment when the ship should start. I had taken out of my travelling-bag this notebook and one of the four little orange linen volumes of *Don Quixote*, the chosen companions of my trip. More unpacking was uncalled for at the moment. We had nine or ten days before us until we should land on the other side of the world. Another Saturday would come round, another Monday and Tuesday, before this well-conducted adventure of ours should reach its goal. The easy-going Dutch boat whose gangplank we had just mounted does not do it faster – why should she? The speed corresponding to her comfortable medium size is certainly saner and more natural than the shattering, record-breaking pace of those colossi which in six or even four days madly overlap the vast spaces that lie before us. *Piano, piano!* Richard Wagner thought that *andante* was the true German tempo. Well, there is something very arbitrary about all these half-way answers to the question "What is German?" And in the end it remains unsettled, leaving a negative impression because they appear to condemn as un-German all sorts of things that are not so at all – as, for instance, the *allegretto*, the *scherzo, and the spirituoso*! This remark of Wagner's would have been happier if he had left out all reference to the national – a sentimentalizing idea anyhow – and confined himself to the objective value that I ascribe to the quality of slowness. All good things take time; so do all great things. In other words, space will have its time. It is a familiar feeling with me that there is a sort of *hubris*, and a great superficiality, in those who would take away from space or stint it of the time naturally bound up with it. Goethe, who was certainly a friend of man, yet did not like to use artificial aids to his powers of perception, such as the microscope and telescope, would probably have agreed with this scruple. Of course, the question arises where the line is to be drawn and whether ten days are not just as bad as six or four. To be strictly orthodox, one would have to give the ocean as many weeks instead, and travel by the wind, which is a force of nature, just as steam is. As a matter of fact, we are using oil fuel. But these speculations approach the fantastic.

And yet my flights of fancy are explainable enough: their source is my own inward excitement. I have, quite simply, stage fright. And what wonder? My maiden voyage across the Atlantic, my first encounter with the mighty ocean, my first knowledge of it—and there, on the other side of the curvature of the earth, above which the great waters heave, New Amsterdam the metropolis awaits us! There are only four or five such in the world, only four or five of this unique and monstrous breed of cities, extravagant in size and kind, standing out even among what we call capital cities, just as in the natural kingdom, among the features of the landscape, the mountain, the desert, and the ocean belong in a category by themselves. I grew up on the Baltic, a provincial body of water. And the traditions of my blood are those of the small and old-established city, civilized and gentled, whose inhabitants are endowed with sensitive imaginations and capable of feeling for the elemental both a sense of awe and a sort of ironic distaste. Ivan Goncharov was once on the high seas during a violent storm. The captain had him fetched from his cabin to behold it: Goncharov was a writer, he said, the storm was magnificent, he ought not to miss it. The author of *Oblomov* came on deck, looked about him, and said: "Yes, it's a nuisance, isn't it?" And went below again.

It is soothing to realize that we are to confront the welter under the ægis of civilization and with all the protection it can afford. This stout ship, of whose white and shining stateroom doors, promenade decks, lounges, and carpeted flights of stairs we have just had a hasty view, she will carry us through, she and the officers and crew whose one mission in life it is to command the elements. She reminded me of that white train *de luxe* with the blue window-panes in which the traveller to Khartoum is borne through the grey waste, among the glowing hot, death-breathing hills of the Libyan and Arabian deserts. . . . Exposure: one has but to think the word, to realize all it means to live in the shelter of our human civilization. I have small respect for the man who, confronting elemental nature, has nothing to express but a pæan of admiration and feels her insensate hostility not at all.

And then, the season itself sets bounds to that hostility and greatly mitigates the perils of our adventure. Spring is far advanced; we need not anticipate any very extravagant misbehaviour on the part of the ocean. We hope that our sea-legs will stand the strain of the moderate demands that may be put upon them. And besides, have we not certain tablets tucked away in our hand-bags as a last resort for human frailty? In the winter-time it would be far otherwise. Friends of mine, artists on concert tour, have told me of the mingled terrors and absurdities of such a voyage. These we are not likely to be called upon to endure. The waves are mountains. They are Everests. No one may go on deck. The fretful Goncharov would not be dragged from his cabin and, anyhow, one can see the ocean better through the thick glass bull's-eye of the port-hole. You lie barricaded in your bed, you get up and fall down again – it is like nothing so much as the racking torments that pass for amusements at fun-fairs, for instance the switchback railway, destructive alike to nerves and digestion. From a giddy height you see your wash-stand swoop down upon you, while on the sloping, shifting floor your cannoning trunks perform a clumsy dance. There is a frightful, an infernal din, caused partly by the elements raging without and partly by the struggles of the labouring ship, trembling and throbbing all over as she pushes on. This may last three days and three nights. Imagine that you have two such behind you and are enduring the third. So far you have taken no food; the moment comes when you remember that one must eat. Since you have not died, though for hours together you have been quite resigned to go, the time comes when you are hungry. You summon the steward, for the bell still rings and the whole first-class hotel service of the ship still functions amid the general dissolution, disciplined to the very end. Such is the refined and admirable heroism of civilized human beings. The man comes, white-jacketed, table-napkined. He does not fall into the stateroom but stands erect in the doorway. He grasps your faint commands through the roaring of the gale. He goes and comes again, preserving by the swaying, yielding motion of his arms the sore-threatened equilibrium of his covered dishes. He must await a certain moment when the state of things in the universe will abet his depositing your tray, in a curve which he does not control but uses to serve his turn, upon your bed. He sees his moment, seizes it, behaves with resolution and discretion. He seems to be succeeding. But in that moment the outer universe changes its mind and the curve described by your tray deposits its contents upside down on your wife's bed. It is really impossible. . . .

Such are the tales I have heard, they come into my head while we drink our farewell vermouth and I scribble these lines. And why not? Though certainly I do not need them to heighten the respect I feel in the face of our undertaking, for I am respectful by nature; I wear, so to speak, my eyebrows permanently lifted. This is not the attitude of the cosmopolite, but of the provincial with a talent for fantasy inborn. With this gift a man can never be a cosmopolite, since up to old age it saves him, if I may use the flattering word, from any sense of superiority. To have the art of fantasy does not mean that one is able to think something out to a conclusion. It means to *make* something out of things—which, of course, is not cosmopolitan.—We are most surprisingly in act to repeat the voyage of Columbus. For days and nights we shall hover in cosmic space between two continents—even though with first-class service all the time—and I scarcely believe that our fellow passengers are having any thoughts on the subject; certainly not this thought. And anyhow, where are they? We are alone in the bar, whose spaciousness, decked with stamped leather, yawns invitingly at us. And I suddenly recollect that even on the tender which brought us across the bay from Boulogne-sur-Mer, we were as good as alone. The bar steward says that only four passengers including ourselves embarked at Boulogne; some dozen more came on at Rotterdam, while another four would turn up at Southampton. That was all. What did we think of that? We answered that the line must lose a pretty penny on such a voyage. Yes, it was bad; of course, it was "the depression." But on the eastbound trip, we agreed, things would look up. The European season for Americans began in June: Salzburg, Bayreuth, Oberammergau beckoned, there would be plenty—he did not say of what, but implied tips. He looked a good deal disturbed, but professed himself satisfied that the harvest would not be too bad. We for our part ventured the remark that it would be very pleasant to travel on a nearly empty ship. It would belong to us almost altogether; life would be like that on a private yacht. And the thought of all that undisturbed tranquillity brought me back to the reading I meant to do on the voyage, to the little orange-coloured volume lying beside me, the first of the row below-stairs.

Shipboard reading—it falls into a category generally despised. The usual view is that reading for a journey must be of the lightest and shallowest, mere foolery to pass the time. I cannot understand it. In the first place, this so-called light reading is the dullest stuff in the world; but even aside from that I cannot see why, especially upon a serious occasion like this voyage, one should decline below the level of one's intellectual habits and go in for the silly and jejune. Perhaps the conditions of life on shipboard, at once removed from the everyday and full of excitement, produce a mental and nervous condition in which silliness disgusts us less than usual. I was just now talking about respect. Since I have respect for this enterprise of ours, it is right and proper that I also take heed to the reading that accompanies it. *Don Quixote* is universal; just the right reading for a trip to the end of the world. It was no small adventure to write it; the passive adventure of reading it will worthily correspond. Strangely enough, I have never gone through the masterpiece systematically, from beginning to end. I will do so on board and in ten days come to the rim of this ocean of a book, at the same time as we come to the other rim of the Atlantic.

The windlass was making a din as I wrote down this resolve. We went on deck, to look back and forward.

May twentieth. I ought not to do what I am doing: sitting bent over to write. It is not conducive to well-being, for the sea is, as our American table-mates say, "a little rough," and though I agree that our ship moves quietly and steadily, yet her motions are more felt up here on this deck where the writing-room is than they are below. Nor is looking through the window advisable, for the rising and falling of the horizon attacks the head in a way well known from an earlier experience but forgotten until now. Also it is not very healthy to gaze down upon paper and script. Curiously, obstinately persevering is the old habit of settling to composition so soon as breakfast and the morning stroll are over. It persists under the most contrary circumstances.

Last night we stopped awhile outside Southampton and took on a few passengers — our last stop, for now the great unbroken journey lies before us. We have covered considerable distance in the night. The south coast of England is still faintly visible in the dim air; soon it will disappear and we shall have before us only the foam-laced vacant grey margin of the sea, beneath a sky equally vacant and grey. I already knew that the sea, in all its extent, seen from shipboard, makes upon me nothing like the impression I get from the beach. I feel none of the thrill of which I am sensible when I stand on solid ground and hear its long-loved roll. It is a disenchantment, and the reason is not far to seek. We have reduced the element to the status of highroad and railway, deprived it of its character of scenery, dream, idea, imaginary peep into eternity — in short, we have made a setting of it. A setting does not have æsthetic character — that belongs to the picture itself. Schopenhauer says: "Certainly it is beautiful to see things, but not beautiful at all to be things." It is quite possible that the truth of this remark, directed as it is against all longing of every sort, had a connection with my experience of the sea. It is not favourable to any illusion to become intimate with its object. Especially when you do it amid all the disgraceful comfort of first class.

Even so, some demands are still made upon you. There is the unavoidable nervous shock of those first hours after you have lost the solid ground under your feet in exchange for an unstable footing. For days you cannot credit the reality of walking down a staircase that has a wavy motion and lightly rises and falls beneath you. You hold your whirling and protesting head and would like to take the thing as a bad joke. – An absurd walk this morning on deck: a series of paralysed clingings and clutchings, interspersed with drunken plungings which, curiously enough, you accompany by deprecating head-shakes as though you really were in that undignified condition – just as one is prone to feel one's feet heavy when mounting a hill. Yet I rejoiced to be convinced that whatever discomfort it gave me, whatever hyperacidity or nervous upset, yet nothing can affect my love of the salt sea, which has endured since my childhood and is in my blood. Seasickness has nothing to do with it, since it leaves the mind intact and often the appetite as well! So I do not take the sea amiss, and would still be loyal to her, I think, even were my sufferings vastly more acute.

O thou wild friend of my youth,
We find each other once more!

– I recalled this morning the lines that Tonio Kröger could not finish, for his throbbing heart.

With symptoms of seasickness must also be reckoned the sleepiness, the utter craving to slumber, which one feels in the first days of a sea voyage. The high atmospheric pressure may be accountable, but surely even more the rocking motion of the boat, which lulls and confuses the brain – an ancient invention of nurses and nursemaids, old as the hills and, like the gifts of the poppy, not of a very innocent kind.

Yesterday afternoon, and last night in the blue salon, to the accompaniment of the music, I read *Don Quixote*. I will now continue to read, sitting in my deck-chair, a transmogrification of Hans Castorp's excellent reclining-chair. What a unique monument is this book! More conditioned in taste by its time than the deliberate satire against that taste would indicate; the whole spirit of the work utterly sycophantic in its protestations of loyalty; yet how its creative genius, critical, free, and human, soars above its age! Tieck's translation, the spirited medium of the classic romantic period, enchants me more than I can say. It is a beautiful instrument wherewith to render the spacious humour of this style—which is almost impressive enough to make me wonder whether humour after all is not the great essential element of the epic. Or even to make me consider them one and the same, though the statement could probably not be objectively sustained. A style that mingles the humorous and the romantic is surely well calculated to make the whole "great and remarkable historie" pass as a translation and commentary of an Arabic manuscript composed by a Moor, Cid Hamete Benengeli. Upon this manuscript the translator is supposed to base his tale. Indeed, the story often employs the indirect form; as, for instance, he will say: "The story goes on to tell" or " 'Allah be praised!' cried out Benengeli three times at the beginning of this chapter, after which he continued," and so forth. Immensely funny are the summary chapter-heads: "Of the wise and pleasant discourse which passed between Sancho Panza and his wife Teresa Panza, as well as other matters worthy of record"; or, with burlesque humour: "Of things which Benengeli says, he will learn who reads them, if he reads with attention." Humorous, finally, in the highest sense, is the portrayal of the two principals, so human and lively is the author's perception of character in all its many-sidedness and depth. He himself is proudly aware of this excellence, when he dwells on the despised and worthless sequel to his first part. This sequel was the work of an impudent bungler, who was tempted by the world-wide fame of Cervantes's novel to seek success with a continuation of it. The plagiary drove Cervantes to compose a second part himself, books seven to twelve in the completed work—though, as Goethe remarks, the theme was really exhausted in the first part. The author of the first sequel saw in Don Quixote naught by a gaby whom only the lash could cure of his delusions, in Sancho Panza merely a glutton. In more than one place in the second part of the true sequel Cervantes protests with jealous scorn against such a simplification. Likewise he embarks upon controversy, which is a model of dignity and moderation, though only in form. It needs the aid of rhetoric to incite a reader to take up the cudgels, while at the same time to preserve a dignity worthy of the man from La Mancha himself. "You would like it well, were I to attack him [the author of the false second part] with adjectives like 'silly,' 'impudent,' 'limited.' But it does not occur to me. His sin be on his own head; he has to answer to himself for what he has done, and that is the end of the matter." Very Christlike and very scrupulous. What really galls Cervantes is simply that "this gentleman" calls him an old cripple

— as though it were in the power of genius to hold back time that it should not go over his head; or as though he had got his mutilated hand in a tavern brawl and not in the glorious day of battle (referring to the naval battle of Lepanto). "And besides," he says with spirit, "we assume that a man composes not with his grey hairs but with his understanding, the which commonly improves with the years." That is delightful. But all the mildness and enlightenment of his grey hairs do not prevent him from setting forth the coarsest and most offensive tales to the reader as "the gentleman's" work, and as evidence that it is "one of the most devilish of the Devil's wiles to put it into a man's head that he too can write a book and get it printed and gain money and fame by it." Certainly they betray anger, furious hatred, and a spirit of revenge, these tales; they betray the half-unconscious pain of the artist when he sees confusion in men's minds between that which has success although it is good and that which has success because it is bad.

For it befell Cervantes that a plagiarism that gave itself out as a sequel to his book "went all over the world" and was as eagerly read as the original. It imitated the grosser and more popular qualities of the genuine work, seizing upon the folly of the hero and its inevitable nemesis, as well as upon the gluttony of Sancho Panza. But that was all. It could not attain to the deep human feeling, the melancholy, or the great art — nor, frightful to say, were these much missed. The public, it seems, saw no difference between the two versions. That is depressing for an author. When Cervantes talks about the disgust, the bad taste in his mouth, felt by the reader of the pseudo-*Quixote,* he is speaking for himself and not for his public. He had to write the second part to drive away the bad taste, not from his readers' mouths, but from his own; and it came there not alone from the badness of the performance but also on account of the success of his own first part. The reader must remember that the second part, "written down by the same artist and from the same matter" as the first, was composed in order to rehabilitate the success of the earlier one, to rescue its endangered honour. The second part has no longer the happy freshness and carelessness of the first, which shows how, *par hasard et par génie*, a blithe and vigorous satire grew into the book of a whole people and of all humanity. It would be less weighted down with humanism, cultural elements, and a certain literary frigidity if the ambition to achieve distinction had not played a part in its composition. But in especial the author labours in the second volume to bring out more clearly and consciously that depth and diversity in his delineation of the main characters of which I have already spoken. In this above all he would bear witness to "the same artist and the same matter" as in the first volume. Don Quixote is of course a simpleton; that is clear from his mania of knight-errantry. But his obsolete whimsy is also the source of such true nobility, such purity of life, such an aristocratic bearing, such winning and respect-compelling traits, physical and mental, that our laughter over his grotesque and doleful countenance is always mingled with amazed respect. No one can know him and not feel drawn to the high-minded and pathetic man, mad in one single point but in all others a blameless knight. It is pure spirit, disguised as fantasy, that sustains and ennobles him, that carries his moral dignity unscathed out of each and every humiliation. I find it exquisite that Sancho Panza the pot-bellied, with his proverbs, his mother wit, his shrewd peasant judgment of human nature, who has no use for the "idea" that results in beatings, but rather for the skin of liquor – Sancho Panza has feeling for this spirit. He loves his good albeit ridiculous master despite all the hardship that loyalty to him incurs; does not leave him nor stir from his side, but serves him with honest and admiring fealty – even though sometimes he may lie to him at need. All that makes even Sancho Panza worthy of our affection; it rounds out his figure with humanity and lifts it out of the sphere of the merely comic into that of genuine humour.

Certainly Sancho Panza is national in that he represents the attitude of the Spanish people towards the noble madness of chivalry. This is for good or ill his function. Since yesterday I have been pondering the fact. Here is a nation presented with a travesty of tragedy, a *reductio ad absurdum* of its national qualities, which it turns into its most prized classic masterpiece. Gravely, calmly, proudly, it looks as into a mirror at its own *grandezza*, its idealism, its lofty impracticality, its unmarketable high-mindedness – is this not strange? The historical greatness of Spain lies in bygone centuries. In ours it has to struggle with problems of adaptation. But as for me, what interests me is precisely the difference between what we pompously call history and our own inward, human history. Freedom, light-hearted self-criticism, probably do not ensure a people a prominent role in history. But they give it charm; and, after all, in the end even charm and its opposite play their roles in history. Whatever pessimistic historians may say, human beings have a conscience, even if only an æsthetic one, a feeling for good taste. They bow, of course, before success, before the *fait accompli* of brute force, even of successful crime. But at bottom they do not lose sight of the humanly beautiful, the violently wrong and brutalizing, which has happened in their midst; and in the end without their sympathy might and brute force can reap no lasting success. History is ordinary reality, to which one is born, to which one must be adequate. Upon it Don Quixote's inept loftiness of soul suffers shipwreck. That is winning, and ridiculous. But what would a Don Quixote at the other extreme be like? Anti-idealistic, sinister, a pessimistic believer in force—and yet a Don Quixote? A brutalized Don Quixote? Even Cervantes, with all his melancholic humour, had not gone so far as to conceive that.

May twenty-first. Chair on the promenade deck, plaid and mantle. The fog-horn has been going almost all the time since yesterday evening and most of the night too, I should say; now, this morning, its warning note sounds afresh. It is raining a little, the horizon, our daily infinity, is shrouded in grey, our speed has slowed down. It is windy too. But the sea is smooth as ever, and so we must not speak of bad weather.

Posted on the blackboard is a notice in English to the effect that passengers should assemble with their tickets at eleven o'clock at the numbered boat stations to receive instruction from the appointed emergency officers. I did not see whether others obeyed the order; but we, at least, after the bouillon, which is handed round at this hour by white-jacketed stewards, betook ourselves to the rendezvous. Despite all the thick coating of luxury, which makes one tend to forget the seriousness of things, this idea of an emergency appealed to me. As we went, not quite certain of our goal, we encountered the head steward, well known to us in the dining-room, and learned that he and no other was the captain of our life-boat, our instructor and deliverer. He is a jovial Dutchman, who speaks English and German with the same whimsical turn and glib inadequacy, very much of a good fellow on the surface, but with a calculating eye. He is clean-shaven, with glasses on a slightly hooked nose such as we are used to among the Swabians, in our country. He wears a coat with gold braid, in the evening it is short and cut like a dinner jacket. He led us to the emergency rendezvous, a spot on the open promenade deck, and in his pleasant, droll, guttural, and at the same time rather harsh Hollands German—quite offhand and easy he was—he explained to us the procedure of taking to the boats. Nothing more calculated to inspire confidence. The motor-boat comes down from the upper deck, very nice, only somewhat small for a high sea. It hangs there close to the railings, we get in, they lower it down to the water. Our officer says: "So, now I will take you home."

Home. Curious way to put it, as though riding there upon the waves we were to tell him our address and he would convey us thither in the motor-boat. And home: what does that mean, anyhow? Does it mean Kussnacht near Zürich, where I have lived for a year and am more of a guest than at home, so that I cannot regard it as a proper goal for a life-boat? Does it mean further back, my house in Herzogpark, Munich, where I thought to end my days and which has now revealed itself as nothing but a temporary refuge and *pied-à-terre*? Home — that must mean even further back, to my childhood home, the parental house at *Lübeck*, which still stands at present and yet is so deep-sunken into the past? What a strange captain you are, with your glasses and your golden triangle on your sleeve and your vague assurance about taking us "home"!

Well, at least we are now instructed; we chatted a little while with our guardian angel, for I wanted to know, in particular, whether he had already experienced the emergency and taken to the boats. "Three times," said he. Three times in his professional career had he done it — for a person who went to sea as much as he did it was scarcely avoidable. But how? How had it happened? "You run into something," he said, with mock surprise. You run into something, how else? — that was always happening when one went to sea. We could not imagine it, nor understand how the accredited arts of navigation, in which we blindly confide, should so easily and often miss fire, so that at any moment you might "run into something." But we could get nothing more definite from him. His meagre and glibly employed vocabulary prevented him. Perhaps it was just empty nothings he was telling us, like the fantastic and dreamlike phrase about taking us "home."

In the dining-room this head steward of ours is by preference at the service of those who are well provided with the world's goods. The American family constantly order outside the menu card, regaling themselves on lobster, champagne, omelets, and so on. The head steward moves from table to table, his hands behind his back, smiling with a shallow professional smile behind his glasses, bestowing a little of his joviality upon each. But at the American table he stops a long time, supervises the extra orders, or even lends a helping hand. We can contemplate all this prosperity with the greater detachment in that nobody suffers from it. The entire service is luxurious to the *n*th degree. It is not confined to a fixed menu; the whole crowded card, fresh every day, is at your disposal and you can put together your meal as you like. If you wanted to you could eat the whole thing from top to bottom every day, from hors d'œuvres to ice-creams. But how soon does man reach his limits! The management is well aware of the fact, and no doubt its principle of choice has proved itself economical, especially in the winter-time.

We sit at the round middle table with two officers: the young and attractive ship's doctor, an American, and the purser, a Dutchman of classic phlegm, and such an appetite that he always gets double portions. Then there is a good-natured little business man from Philadelphia who likes champagne, and in bearing and mentality seems to resemble our merchant type at home. Finally there is an elderly spinster dressed with bourgeois care and laughing a great deal out of pure friendliness. She has been visiting relatives in Holland and is on the way homewards. After landing she must cross a whole continent to get there, for she lives in the state of Washington, on the Pacific coast.

What journeys – many of them so senseless! My wife is beside herself over some twins from Rotterdam, whom we often meet on deck in their carriage. They are being taken on a visit to their grandmother in South Carolina. The old lady wants to see her grandchildren. Well and good. But it is frightfully egotistic, for South Carolina lies farther south than Sicily, in June the climate is insupportable, and if the Rotterdam babies get summer complaint, what will their self-willed grandmother say then? It is no affair of ours; but when one shares the same horizon with such proceedings, one has one's thoughts.

The babies' nurse is Jewish and reads modern books. Their mother eats with the elder brothers and sisters near us, in a corner of the room. All the occupants of the saloon are long since familiar to us. They are few, always the same. Nobody gets in or out – though despite the whimsicality of the thought I catch myself expecting a new face. There is a table of young Dutchmen, obviously on pleasure bent. They burst out in frequent guffaws. At the captain's table, in company with him, sits a distinguished American couple of advanced years. At tea-time this couple sit up very straight in a corner of the music room and read. They complete the list of passengers save for the Jonah of the boat, a raw-boned Yankee whose lips stick out in the Anglo-Saxon fish mouth, under which and not under the chin the English policemen wear their chin straps. He is a man in the middle of the thirties, who has a table all to himself and reads a book while he eats. He has no contact with anyone in the first class. But we see him in "tourist" playing shuffleboard with the Jewish exiles. His aloofness is offensive, he is not liked. Repeatedly I see him making notes in a notebook, in his desk-chair as well as at table. Everybody feels there is something wrong about it all. Who shuts himself off like this and then goes for entertainment to "tourist"? He must be a writer, aloof from the regular order of society and critical of it – but then his evening dress is quite correct. I a little envy him his singleness of purpose about the table and am rather jealous of the Jewish refugees whom he considers worthy of his society. My pride says to me that I am probably capable as they of following the trains of thought he confides to his notebook – though I admit that my interest in him is at present less social than æsthetic and psychological.

I have diverted myself the whole day with the epic wit of Cervantes, in making the adventures of the second part, or at least some of them, grow out of Don Quixote's literary fame, out of the popularity that he and Sancho enjoy, thanks to the earlier part, "their novel," the great history wherein they were first portrayed. They would never have got so far as the ducal court if the distinguished persons there had not known the extraordinary pair so well from reading about them and been enchanted to see them in the flesh and amuse themselves by giving them entertainment. That is new, and unique. I know nowhere else in literature where the hero of a novel lives on his own frame, as it were upon the reputation of his reputation. The simple reappearance of well-known characters in novel sequences, as in Balzac, is after all something quite different. Their existence is confirmed, their personalities achieve greater depth by virtue of our old acquaintance with them and the fact that they were there before and have come back. But they do not change their level; the order of illusion to which they belong remains the same. In Cervantes it is more than this: a sort of romantic illusion, a trick with an ironic undertone. Don Quixote and his squire, in this second part, quit the sphere of reality where they belonged, the novel where they first had their being, to move in person, as more lively realities, through a world which paid them joyous homage. And that world, in its turn, represents a higher stage of reality, although even it is a depicted world, the illusional evocation of a fictive past. Sancho Panza, in the presence of the Duchess, permits himself to jest: "That squire of his, who is, or ought to be, in the same history, called Sancho Panza, that am I, unless I was changed in the cradle, I mean in the press." Yes, Cervantes even evokes a figure out of the detested false sequel, and makes it convict itself out of its own mouth and show that the Don Quixote created by the same author cannot possibly be the right and true one. These are devices after the heart of E. T. A. Hoffmann himself. Indeed, they may be a clue to the source of much in the writers of the romantic school. It cannot be said that they were the greatest artists. But they have thought the most fruitfully about the weird depths, the trick mirrors and false bottoms of artistic illusion; and it is precisely because they were artists in and beyond art that they came so dangerously near to the ironic dissolution of form. It is well to be constantly aware that this is the intimate pitfall of every technique that seeks to combine the humorous with the realistic. From the comic touch of certain epic means of producing reality to the word-plays and artifices of downright buffoonery, faithful to form and yet amorphous, it is only a step. I do indeed give my reader an unexpected opportunity of seeing with his own eyes Joseph, son of Jacob, sitting by the well in the moonlight, and of comparing his bodily presence, fascinating if also humanly incomplete as it is, with the ideal renown that centuries have woven about his figure. But I hope that the humour of this method of seizing the occasion to evoke reality may still deserve the honourable name of art.

May twenty-second. So there goes on, with unresting engines, day by day our steady forward push across the great spaces of the ocean. In my bath in the morning, in the warm, sticky, faintly rotten-smelling sea-water, which impregnates my skin with salt and which I dearly love, I remind myself pleasantly that while we slept we have unrolled another large instalment of the endless perspective. The weather is trying to clear up; there is blue sky in sight, beautifying the water with gleams of southern colour. But soon the warmer light has faded again.

We like to stand towards evening on the boat deck with our faces to the wind, watching our course westwards across the ocean's curve. Always we go toward the setting sun, and our path diverges only the slightest; yesterday we steered straight into the sun, today we are deflected somewhat southwards. The course of a ship like ours through the reaches of water is proud and beautiful; as movement certainly more dignified than the roaring of a train round a curve. The absolute void before us is very striking – on a "stretch" followed by the ships of all seagoing countries. We are now in our fourth day, and so far we have not seen the smoke of a single steamer. The explanation is simple: there is too much room. The spaciousness has something cosmic; no matter how many ships, they lose themselves in it like stars in the sky, and only occasionally does one meet another.

Daily the blackboard warns us to set back our watches, from half an hour to forty minutes – yesterday it was thirty-nine. Officially this happens at midnight, but we perform the significant little act soon after dinner, in order that the night may be not all too long, the evening longer. Thus during music and reading do we relive a space in time, which we have already once passed through. It gives us to think, this setting the minute-hand to traverse a segment of time-path for the third time in a day. Ten times thirty-nine minutes is six and a half hours, which we lose — no, gain — on this voyage. Are we then going back in time whilst we press forward in space? Certainly, since our journey is westwards, against the motion of the globe. The word "cosmic," which I used before, is the only one adequate to the situation. World-space and world-time conceptions are pertinent, forcing themselves upon the consciousness despite all this superficial comfort, which makes light of the elements and seeks to rob them of their life-and-death character. We are coming into strange days, into regions of the earth's surface that turn round the sun otherwise than those where we have yet dwelt; where it will still be night and we still sleeping when it is bright daylight at home. All this is common knowledge. Yet I debate it with myself afresh. If we were to keep on travelling westwards, so that we returned via the farthest East, we should gain time all the way to the extent of a whole day and a breach in the calendar, and then slowly lose it again till we were where we were before. The same is true in our present case, when we shall not go all the way round but only back to our own continent. And no harm done. For we do not gain a day of life with a day of time. If we should try to impose upon the cosmic order and, having arrived over there, went neither forwards nor back but brooded over our six hours, guarding them as Fafner his hoard, the portion of life organically assigned to us would not be by one second increased.

What naïve reflections! And, after all, has not the cosmological view of the universe, by comparison with its opposite, the psychological, something puerile about it? As I write I think of Albert Einstein's bright round eyes, like a child's. I cannot help it. Human knowledge, research into human life, has a riper, more mature character than speculations about the Milky Way — with the profoundest respect I say it. Goethe says: "The individual is free to busy himself with whatever attracts and pleasures him, whatever seems to him of worth; but the true study of mankind is man!"

As for *Don Quixote*, it is indeed a strange product: naïve, unique, arbitrary and sovereign in its contradictions. I cannot but shake my head over the single tales scattered through it, so extravagantly sentimental they are, so precisely in the style and taste of the very productions that the poet had set himself to mock. He crams his hosts of readers full to their hearts' content with the very diet from which he would wean them – a pleasant cure! In those idylls he resigns his earlier role, as though to say that if the age wanted that sort of thing he could give it them, yes, even be a master at it. But I am not so clear about the position with regard to those humanistic speeches which he sometimes puts in his hero's mouth; whether he does not thereby distort the character, overstep its limits, and inartistically speak for himself. They are excellent, these speeches; for instance, upon education, and upon the poesy of nature and of art, which the knight in the green mantle gets to hear. They are full of pure reason, justice, human benevolence, and nobility of form, so that he in the green mantle is justly astonished, "and indeed so much that he wavered in his earlier opinion that the man must be foolish." Quite rightly so, and the reader should waver too. Don Quixote is a bit cracked but not in the least stupid, though the fact was not so clear, even to the author himself, in the beginning. His respect for the creature of his own comic invention grows during the narrative. This process is perhaps the most fascinating thing in the whole novel; it is a novel in itself, waxing proportionately with his regard for his work, which at first he conceived modestly, as a pretty crude and downright satire, without a notion of the extent to which his hero was destined to grow in stature, symbolically and humanly. The change in the point of view permits and even causes a considerable identification of the author with his hero, an inclination to assimilate his intellectual attainments to the author's own, to make him the mouthpiece of Cervantes's convictions and to heighten by cultural and intellectual gifts the picturesque charm which, despite his doleful exterior, his own mad idea develops in Don Quixote. It is his master's elegance of thought and diction that is often the source of Sancho's boundless admiration – and he is not the only one to be fascinated by it.

May twenty-third. Less motion; the weather is warmer. The milder and moister airs of the Gulf Stream prevail.

I begin the day with a fifteen-minute game of medicine ball with a steward from Hamburg, up on the boat deck. He is a reader of mine, he says. After that I breakfast, starting with half a grapefruit, that refreshing large orange of which there is apparently an inexhaustible supply on board. For our greater ease and enjoyment the pulp is loosened from the skin in the kitchen with a special instrument. On the other hand I have not succeeded in making friends with the tomato cocktail which Americans drink down before every meal. It is too sweet.

Since one must get exercise and the everlasting round of the promenade deck becomes a bore, we have taken up deck games and beguile some hours with them both morning and evening. We play shuffleboard in company with a friendly young Dutchman. The red squares full of numbers are painted everywhere on the decks; it is a good and lively game. You have a shovel-shaped stick with which to shoot the round pieces of wood onto a field, or rather into the middle of each field so that they do not touch any of the bounding lines. You must avoid the minus field and try to reach the one marked ten plus; if a piece has got stuck you must improve its lie with your next shot; and finally you must cannon your opponent out of the good positions. All which is easier said than done, and not made less difficult by the shifting nature of the field, which sways to and fro with the motion of the vessel. The best aim helps but little, for the pieces move apparently at random, guided by incalculable powers. Your vexation reinforces your exercise to the point of making you presently deserve and require a hearty meal.

A more complex game than shuffleboard is deck golf, played on a miniature artificial turf, otherwise a flat, green-covered platform. You are supposed to propel the light balls with bats from a cluster of six close-lying openings through one narrow door into the hole at the other end of the course – naturally in the fewest possible strokes. Theoretically one would be able, at least from one of the centre positions, to get through the gate and into the hole at a single shot. But who succeeds in doing it? Three shots make an honourable, two a brilliant record. Usually there are the worst sort of miscarriages and ricochetings, and then you meekly write up a six or seven on the blackboard.

For the tea-hour and after dinner we mostly sit in the blue salon, called the social hall, and listen to the music. Sometimes, especially in the afternoon, we are the only audience. For our sake, although we could do without it, the musicians play; but somebody must be present or they do not play. Sometimes, looking through the windows from the outside, we see the "unemployed" lounging dully at their music-stands. But if a single guest enters the hall, they seize their instruments and begin. The orchestra consists of piano, two violins, viola, and cello. The first violin conducts. The programs, naturally, are very light. A potpourri from *Carmen*, a *Traviata* fantasy, these are the "high spots." Commonly – that is probably the right word – they are all sugary pieces for the tea-hour. The more ambitious ones are all after Puccini, which delights civilized normal man the world over. So they serve it up even here in the midst of space, that he may feel himself well wadded by the usual and getting his money's worth. On such a voyage everything depends upon unconsciousness, upon sustaining a forgetful attitude of mind. But while the hackneyed music is doing its best I sometimes out of sheer native rebelliousness gaze out at the window of the social hall and again through the window of the promenade deck outside at the grey-green, foam-tossed wilderness, at the horizon, which rises, hangs poised for a few seconds, and then sinks again.

We applaud the musicians and they thank us through the first violin, apparently surprised and pleased each time. But they have their independent joy in their work as well; exchange glances at this or that place, discuss the rendering, and laugh among themselves. I look at them and reflect that we should be careful not to judge these men too lightly. There they sit and fiddle away sweet nothings. It is their job. But we have proof and precedent that they can sit like that and play *Nearer, My God, to Thee* up to the very last minute. . . . One must think of them in this light too.

At odd times I read in my orange-coloured volumes and am appalled at Cervantes's intemperate cruelty. For despite that considerable assimilation of the hero to his creator, of which I wrote yesterday, despite the author's high respect for the work of his brain, his inventiveness runs riot in ridiculous and humiliating pitfalls, into which the high-minded hero then tumbles and most comically disgraces himself—as in the adventure with the cheeses, which the "low-minded" Sancho Panza put into Don Quixote's helmet and which began to melt at the moment of high pathos and send streams of curd over the knight's eyes and beard, so that he thinks his brains are softening or he is sweating some horrible sort of sweat—whereat he forfends the thought that it might be a sweat of fear. There is something sardonic and desperately funny in such inventions—as, for another instance, that about the wooden cage in which Don Quixote was "cooped up" and dragged about. Humiliation could not further go. He gets endless beatings, almost as many as Lucius in the story of the Ass. And yet his creator loves and honours him. Does not all this cruelty look like self-flagellation, self-revilement, castigation? Yes, it seems to me as though here the author abandons to scorn his oft-flouted belief in the idea, in the human being and his ennoblement; that this grim coming to terms with reality is actually the definition of humour.

Cervantes puts into Don Quixote's mouth an admirable critique of the nature of translation. It seems to him, he says, that a translation from one language into another is like a Flemish carpet looked at on the wrong side: "for though the figures come out, they are full of threads which mar them and show them not in full beauty and completeness as on the right side. But I will not say that on that account translation is not a praiseworthy work." The metaphor is striking. Only two Spanish translators are exempted, Figueroa and Xauregui. With them one can scarcely distinguish between translation and original. They must have been extraordinary, those two. But in the name of Cervantes I should like to except another name: that of Ludwig Tieck, who in the German *Don Quixote* has made another right side to the carpet.

May twenty-fourth. Yesterday *The Golden Ass* came into my head and ran off my pen — not quite by chance, since I came upon certain affinities between the late-classic novel and *Don Quixote;* though in my ignorance I do not know if others have not found them before. The scenes and episodes I mean become striking by their inherent oddness and lack of motivation, indicating a diffused origin. It is significant that they are in the second, intellectually more ambitious part of the book.

There is, in the first place, in the ninth book, the story of "The Wedding of Camacho, with Other Delightful Incidents." Delightful? Why, this wedding is a frightful affair; but the word as it stands in the chapter-head anticipates the *blague*, the delusion, the secret mockery and farce, the tragic practical joke, which await the reader and most of the characters as well. In the end everything gives place to bewildered laughter. The rustic betrothal feast of the beautiful Quiteria with the rich Camacho is described with florid extravagance. Comacho is the happy rival of the scorned but stout-hearted Basilio, who is only scorned by command, for he has loved his neighbour's daughter Quiteria since childhood and she loves him in turn, so that they really belong together before God and man. The union of the fair one with the rich Comacho happens only by the iron command of the bride's father. The festivities have got as far as the betrothal when amid great outcry the unhappy Basilio appears, "clad in a black jacket, all welted with crimson in flames," and in a trembling voice makes a speech. He says that he, the moral obstacle to the full and undisturbed happiness of the pair, will put himself out of the way. He cries: " 'Long live the rich Camacho with the ungrateful Quiteria! Many and happy ages may they live; and let poor Basilio die, whose poverty clipped the wings of his good fortune and laid him in his grave!' So saying, he laid hold of his truncheon, which was stuck in the ground; and drawing out a short tuck that was concealed in it and to which it served as a scabbard; and setting what may be called the hilt upon the ground, with a nimble spring and determined purpose he threw himself upon it and in an instant half the bloody point appears at his back, the poor wretch lying along the ground weltering in his blood and pierced through with his own weapon."

One cannot imagine a more horrid interruption to a gay and splendid feast. Everyone rushes up, Don Quixote himself dismounts from his Rosinante to assist the unhappy wretch, the priest takes charge of him and suffers no one to draw the dagger from the wound before Basilio has confessed, for the drawing out and the death of the victim would be one and the same thing. The devoted one comes a little to himself and in a faint voice expresses the wish that Quiteria might give him her hand as his bride in the last moments of his life, thus extenuating his sinful death. What can he mean? Shall the rich Camacho resign in favour of Death? The priest warns the dying man to think rather upon his own soul and to confess; but Basilio, rolling his eyes and obviously at his last gasp, swears that he will never confess until Quiteria gives him her hand. This, then, a Christian soul being in the balance, comes to pass, with the consent to boot of the pious Camacho. But scarcely has the benediction been pronounced when up springs Basilio most nimbly, draws out the dagger from his body, which had served it for a sheath, and to the bystanders, who are crying out: "A miracle, a miracle!" pertly responds: "No miracle, only a stratagem." In short, it turns out that the dagger had not gone through Basilio's ribs, but through a lead pipe filled with blood, all this having been a trick arranged between the lovers. Thanks to the good nature of Camacho and the wise and kindly words of Don Quixote the whole results in Basilio keeping his Quiteria and the resumption of the feasting in honour of the bridal pair.

Is this really fair? The suicide scene is painted with complete seriousness and tragic emphasis. The emotions of horror roused not only in the other actors but in the reader as well are quite unequivocal. Yet in the end the whole thing dissolves in laughter and betrays itself as a farce and travesty. It is not a little annoying. The question is: are such practical mystifications really suitable for art – for art as we understand it? I am instructed by Erwin Rohde and by the excellent book which the mythologist and historian of religion Karl Kerenyi wrote in Budapest on the Greco-Roman novel, that the fabulists of late antiquity had an extraordinary love of such scenes. The Alexandrian novel-writers Achilleus Tatius relates in his *History of Leucippe and Cleitophon* how the heroine is slain horribly by Egyptian swamp robbers. The deed is described in all its barbaric detail. It takes place before the eyes of her beloved, who stands separated from her by a wide ditch, and who then is about to slay himself in despair upon her grave. But now companions appear, whom likewise he had thought dead, draw his beloved safe and sound out of the grave, and relate to him that they too had been captured by the natives; that the sacrifice had devolved upon them and that with the help of a property dagger, with the blade on a spring, and a piece of gut filled with blood they had pretended to carry out the deed. Do I deceive myself, or do this blood-filled gut and the trick dagger in *Don Quixote* come from the same school?

The second case is reminiscent of Apuleius himself. I mean the highly remarkable adventure of the ass's bray, which is told in the eighth and tenth chapters of Cervantes's ninth book. Two country justices, the ass of one of whom has run away, go together to the mountains where they think the ass is hiding, and since they cannot find it, try to lure it by imitating its bray, an art in which they are marvellously proficient. One stands here, the other there, and they bray against each other; and always when one makes himself heard, the other runs to the spot convinced that the ass is there, because only he could bray so like life. They overwhelm each other with compliments on their remarkable gifts. But the reason why the ass does not come is that he lies in the bushes devoured by wolves. The magistrates find him at length and, hoarse and exhausted, wend their way homewards. The story of the braying contest spreads abroad, so that the people of the village become the mock of all the neighbouring ones. They are put beside themselves by braying from all sides; bitter quarrels, yes, even passages at arms ensue between village and village, and Don Quixote and Sancho Panza march in upon the sally to one of these. For in the usual way the ass-villagers have made of the jest an honour and a watchword: they issue forth with a white satin banner upon which a braying ass is painted, under which emblem they march towards the anti-asses with lances, crossbows, partisans, and halberds to deliver them a battle. But Don Quixote puts himself in the way. He makes a lofty speech, wherein he admonishes them in the name of reason to desist from their purpose and not let it come to bloodshed for such trifles. They seem willing to listen to him. But now Sancho mixes in to clinch the matter and says that not only would it be folly to be angered at sound of a bray, but that also he himself in his youth could bray with such infectious verisimilitude that all the asses in the village answered him. And in token that it is an art, which, like swimming, once learned is never forgotten, he holds his nose and brays till all the near-by valleys echo — to his own huge undoing. For the villagers, not being able to bear hearing it, thrash him soundly, and even Don Quixote, quite contrary to his practice, must flee from the threat of their crossbows and partisans. He makes himself scarce; and Sancho, whom, scarcely come to himself, they have "set on his ass" and suffered to follow his master, joins him in flight. Moreover the squadrons, after they have waited the night in vain for the enemy, who have not come out, "returned to their homes joyful and merry" and, adds the scholarly poet, "had they known the practice of the ancient Greeks, they would have erected a trophy in that place."

Extraordinary tale! There are in it associations and affiliations about which I can hardly believe myself mistaken. The ass plays a singular role in the Greco-Roman representational world. He is the animal of Typhon-Set, wicked brother of Osiris; he is the Red One. The mythical hatred of him reached so far into the Middle Ages that the rabbinical Biblical commentaries call him Esau, the name of Jacob's brother, the wild ass. The idea of beating is closely and sacramentally bound up with this phallic conception. The phrase "to beat the ass" has a cult-coloration. Whole herds of asses were ritually beaten as they were driven round the city walls. Also there was the pious custom of pushing the Typhon beast off a rock — just the manner of death which Lucius barely escaped after being turned into an ass in the novel of Apuleius: the robbers threaten him with "*katachremnzesthai.*" Moreover he is beaten for braying, just like Sancho Panza, and continues to be beaten all the time that he is an ass — there are fourteen instances. I may add that according to Plutarch the inhabitants of certain villages so hated the voice of the ass that they put trumpeting under a taboo because it sounded like braying. May not the villagers in *Don Quixote* be a reminiscence of these hypersensitive citizens of antiquity?

It is strange to uncover such a primitive mythical inheritance innocently disguised in the Spanish Renaissance poet. Did he get it from direct knowledge of classic Roman literature? Or did the theme come to him by way of Italy, via Boccaccio? Let scholars decide.

It cleared up in the course of the day and we have a blue sky. The sea is violet-hued – is it not Homer's word? Towards midday we saw wonderful banks of cloud, one behind another, hovering over the water lighted up by the sun – milky-white cushions for angels' feet to tread! A bright and dainty vision.

May twenty-fifth. The young doctor has his misgivings about the weather. He concedes that it is beautiful, but so long as we are under the influence of the Gulf Stream there is no trusting it. Meanwhile we enjoy the happy change, the growing warmth which tells us that we are reaching more southerly zones, the azure purity, the smoother gliding over a quieter sea. We spend almost the whole day on the open boat deck, moving between sun and shade. The sun is treacherous. The wind in our faces prevents us from feeling the heat and meanwhile it does its injurious work unperceived.

Last evening there was cinema in the social hall – we do not lack even this gift of civilization, the company sees to that. But under the prevailing circumstances it seemed strange enough. The white screen was stretched across one end of the room, at the other was set up the wonder-apparatus for sight and sound that progress has developed out of the magic lantern of our childhood. We sit in the slightly swaying elegance of the social hall, in our fauteuils, in dinner jackets, at gilded tables. We drink our tea, smoke our cigarettes, and as in any capital or Eldorado on solid ground gaze at the moving and speaking shadows before us. The actors were in no way inferior to the audience. They were quite as elegant and well groomed. In fact, every actor on the screen is always a pattern of well-dressed well-being. It is the first essential and mitigates the distress of the audience over the trials he must go through. Spacious and elegant perspectives, dining-tables laden with crystal services and fruit – the film loves to make a display of wealth and luxury, mirroring the flattered rich, consoling the poor with dreams. This was an American film. It told the story of a business executive with a weakness for art, music, beauty, and romantic passion. He leaves his wife to pursue in Paris his iridescent dream. His mistimed effort suffers a mild shipwreck: the female who embodies his longing becomes the property of a young musician whom he has helped with money and support; the last scene shows him at the telephone announcing his return to his patient wife – perhaps a melancholy but still a tolerable end, for we know that the spacious salons and crystal table-services of his home await him; that even if he has been disappointed, his experience has had a tranquillizing effect.

It was a pity that so few of us witnessed this pleasing and apposite little drama — ten or twelve persons instead of hundreds in the blue and gold social hall of our luxurious liner. The vacant chairs spoke of loss and change, of a social economy already cracking asunder. Not even all of our stout-hearted forty were there. I missed the fish-mouthed, note-taking American. Where was he? Again with the Jewish exiles in "tourist"? An unsettling man. Travels first-class and takes his meals with us in a dinner jacket; but offensively abjures our intellectual diversions and betakes himself to a foreign, a hostile sphere. People ought to know where they belong. People ought to keep together.

The adventure with the lion is certainly the climax of Don Quixote's "exploits" and in all seriousness the climax of the novel. It is a glorious tale, told with a comic pathos, a sympathetic humour, which betray the poet's genuine enthusiasm for his hero's folly. I read it twice over and was utterly absorbed in its peculiarly moving, magnificently ridiculous contents. The meeting with the pennanted car in which are the African animals, "which the general of Oran was sending to court as a present to His Majesty," is charming as a cultural record. It is evidence of his extraordinary art that after all we have already read of Don Quixote's blind, ill-directed intrepidity, the author can keep us in breathless suspense throughout this adventure. To the horror of his companions and deaf to any reasonable objections, the knight insists that the keeper should let one of the ferocious and hungry animals out of the cage to do battle with him. It is remarkable how Cervantes can sustain a single motive and keep it fresh and effective throughout. Don Quixote's foolhardiness is so astonishing just because he is by no means so mad as not to be aware of it. "Encountering the lions," he says later, "was my unavoidable task, though I knew it to be most extravagant rashness, for I was very well aware that fortitude is a virtue placed between the two vicious extremes of cowardice and foolhardiness. But it is better the valiant should rise to the high pitch of temerity than sink to the low point of cowardice. For as it is easier for the prodigal to become liberal than for the covetous, just so it is much easier for the rash to hit upon being truly valiant than for the coward to rise to true valour." What moral intelligence! The observation of the man in the green mantle is most pertinent: "What he said was coherent, elegant, and well said; what he did was extravagant, rash, and foolish." One almost gets the impression that the author put it forward as a natural and unavoidable antinomy of the higher life.

The classic scene, depicted a hundred times in pictures, where the lean hidalgo dismounts from his mare, fearful lest her courage may not equal his own, and with his trumpery shield and sword, ready for the absurdest duel ever imagined, stands before the open cage full of heroic impatience to get to grips with his enemy—this extraordinary scene lives actually before me in the words of Cervantes. So does the issue of it, which ever so mildly stultifies the knight's heroics. For the king of beasts will not let himself in for such tricks and gambols. He gives one glance, then simply turns his rear foremost and lies unfeelingly down on the floor of his cage. Once more heroics have prosaically missed fire. The whole burden of the theme, all the scorn and mockery of its intent, come down upon Don Quixote's head in the contemptuous, indifferent behaviour of the royal beast. The knight is beside himself. He demands of the quaking keeper that he should beat the lion to rouse him to combat. But the man refuses, and at length makes the knight comprehend that he has already displayed the greatness of his courage. No warrior, however doughty, is bound to do more than to challenge his opponent and await him in the open field. If the latter flinches, the blame falls upon him and upon no one else. Don Quixote is finally satisfied. In token of his victory he puts upon his spear the same handkerchief with which he has wiped off his cheesy sweat—whereupon Sancho, who had run away, seeing it from the distance, says: "May I be hanged if my master has not vanquished the wild beasts, for there he summons us." It is a marvel.

In no other place comes out so strongly as here the author's utter readiness to exalt and to abase his hero. But abasement and exaltation are a twin conception the essence of which is distinctly Christian. Their psychological union, their marriage in a comic medium, shows how very much Don Quixote is a product of Christian culture, Christian doctrine, and Christian humanity. It shows as well what Christianity everlastingly means for the world of the mind and of poesy and for the human essence itself and its bold expansion and liberation. I have in mind my Jacob, who whimpered in the dust before the boy Eliphaz, dishonoured to the uttermost, and then, in a dream, out of the very depth of his abased soul produced his great exaltation. Say what you will: Christianity, the flower of Judaism, remains one of the two pillars upon which Western culture rests, the other being Mediterranean antiquity. The denial of one of these fundamental premises of our civilization and education — how much more of both of them — by any group of our European community, would mean its break with that community and an inconceivable, impossible diminishment of its human stature, who knows to what extent? The hectic attack of Nietzsche, the admirer of Pascal, upon Christianity was an unnatural eccentricity; it has always puzzled me, like much else in the character of that tragic hero. Goethe, more happily balanced and physically less hampered, did not allow his supposed paganism to prevent him from paying homage to Christianity and speaking out for it as the civilizing force that it is. Agitated times like ours always tend to confound the merely epochal with the eternal — as for instance liberalism with freedom — and to throw out the baby with the bath. Thus each free and thoughtful person, each mind which does not flicker in the wind of time, is forced back upon the foundations; driven to become once more conscious of them and to base more solidly upon them. The critique of the twentieth century upon Christian ethic (not to speak of dogma and mythology); the changes that come about naturally with the flow of life; no matter how deep these go, or how transformingly they work, they are and will remain superficial effects. They can never touch the binding authority of the cultural Christianity of the Western world, which once achieved cannot be alienated.

May twenty-sixth. Our newspaper is a very silly sheet, I must confess. It appears daily except Sundays; we need not lack for fresh print any more than for fresh bread. They shove the papers through the slot in our door, where we find them and pick them up when we come down before luncheon. We read them on the spot, for who knows what Europe will do once our backs are turned? Most of the sheet — that is, the advertisements and pictures — is printed beforehand and so possesses no immediacy. But our boat is also provided with wireless: seemingly so alone and forsaken upon the waste of waters, we are in contact with the whole world, can send out messages to every quarter and receive them in turn. Thus what flashes to us from all the continents is printed in the "stop-press" of our news sheet. What did we read today? In the zoological garden of a Western state an ailing tiger was given whisky as a medicine. The ravening beast conceived such a taste for strong drink that he would not give it up when he was cured but now daily demands his dram. That and other such matter we read in our ship's paper. Certainly this particular item is gratifying to read. Not in vain have our news-purveyors reckoned upon our sympathy with the spirit-loving animal. But yet: is there not something like an abuse here? A technical miracle like radio-telegraphy used to transmit such a kind of news over land and sea – ah, humanity, your mental and spiritual development has not kept pace with your technical, it has stopped far behind. Herein lies your lack of faith that your future can be more happy than your past. The gap between your technical maturity and your other unripeness creates precisely the unsatisfied craving with which you clutch at every sheet of news. And so we read of the hilarious tiger. We may be glad that it is no worse. But, after all, the case is the same with our frivolous radio as with our ship's musicians. Under certain circumstances it can send out S O S too. In the name of and for the dignity of technique one might almost wish that it might come to that!

Last evening the wind came up and the ship tossed a good deal in the night. But today we have fine weather again and summery warmth as well. We saw a large fish, like a dolphin, leap high out of the water. There is a report, doubtless false, that we have run over a whale. People repeat it, as a fitting and natural fillip to the voyage. But the bar steward did show us a flight of gulls rocking on the water a little way from the ship, a sign that land is not far off.

And still the day and hour of our arrival remain uncertain. We hear that with a favouring sea and good weather we shall land day after tomorrow in the course of the afternoon. But on the other hand there is the view that we had too much fog at first, that we are behind time and it will be Tuesday before we arrive in the Hudson. This uncertainty constitutes another difference – advantage, I had almost said – from travel by train. Despite all its comfort the sea voyage preserves something primitive. We are given to the incalculable element, we are subject to the inaccuracies of chance – and we like it. But why? In plain terms, because we can thus assert our impatience with mechanical civilization, our craving to reject and deny it as deadly for our souls and our lives? Because we can thus seek and affirm a form of existence that would be nearer the primitive, elemental, uncertain, risky, improvised as in war-time? But am I here voicing the ever growing love of the irrational – that cult for which my critical sense should be ever on the alert, since it is dangerous to humanity and fraught with abuse? My European sympathy for order and reason has made me resist it – more for the sake of equilibrium than because the danger was not present within myself as well. As a teller of tales I have reached the stage of the myth: I would humanize it, would seek, in my unlimited contempt for the soulfully and wilfully barbaric, a rapprochement between humanity and the myth. For I find therein more hope for the future of humanity than in a one-sided struggle against the spirit, time-seeking and enslaved to time, zealously trampling upon reason and civilization. To be able to look into the future one must indeed be of the time. But not only in the sense of actual movement, in which every donkey partakes, bursting with pride and scorn against liberal reactionaries of a different stripe. One must have one's time in oneself entire: not only the revolutionary period, especially when the revolutionary slogan is "Back to the ichthyosaurus!"—but time itself, in all its complexity and contradictoriness; for not one single thing, but many and manifold prefigure the future.

Very arresting and significant is the episode of the Morisco Ricote, the former shopkeeper from Sancho's village, who has been banished from Spain by the Edicts and slips back in pilgrim's garb, urged by homesickness but also in hopes of digging up a buried treasure. The chapter is a shrewd mixture of professions of loyalty and of the author's strict adherence to the church, his blameless submission to the great Philip III—and the most lively human sympathy for the awful fate of the Moorish people, who, attacked by the Edicts of the King, are sacrificed to the supposed interests of the state and driven into misery without regard for individual agony. Through the one position the author purchases immunity for the other; but I suspect, and it has always been felt, that the first was the political means to the second and that the sincerity of the author begins only there. He puts into the mouth of the unhappy Morisco himself an acceptance of His Majesty's commands, an acknowledgment that they spring from indisputable right. Many, he says, had not wanted to believe that the order was seriously meant and considered it a mere threat. But he saw at once that it was an actual law and as such would be put into execution at the appointed time. And what confirmed him in the belief was that he knew of the mischievous extravagant designs "which were such that in my opinion it was a divine inspiration that moved His Majesty to put so brave a resolution into practice." The shameful plots that justify the royal inspiration are not mentioned by name, they remain shrouded in darkness. But not all were guilty. "Some of us," says Ricote, "were steady and true Christian, but these were so few . . . and it is not prudent to nourish a serpent in one's bosom or to keep one's enemies within one's own door." The objectivity and moderation which the author puts in the mouth of the sufferer are most admirable. But gradually and insensibly they are diverted into quite another channel. The Moor says that the punishment was just, a soft and mild one in the opinion of some, but in reality the most terrible that could be inflicted. "Wherever we are we weep for Spain, for in short here were we born and this is our native country. We nowhere find the reception which our misfortune requires. Even in Barbary, and in all other parts of Africa where we expected to be received, cherished, and made much of, there it is we are most neglected and misused." Thus the Spanish Moor continues to mourn, so bitterly that it goes to the heart. "We knew not," he says, "our happiness till we lost it; and so great is the desire almost all of us have to return to Spain that we forsake wife and children and come back again at risk of our lives, so mighty is the love we bear it. And it is now I know, and find by experience, the truth of that common saying: 'Sweet is the love of one's country.' "

Such words as these, the expression of ineradicable natural affinity, obviously give the lie to the phrases about the snake in the bosom, the enemy in the house, the inspired justice of the Edicts, and so forth. The artist's dilemma, expressed in Ricote's speech in the second part of *Don Quixote*, speaks a more convincing language than his careful, obsequious tongue. He sympathizes with the persecuted and banned. They are as good Spaniards as himself or anybody; Spain is their true mother-land; she will not be purer, only poorer, after they have gone, while, once torn from her soil, they are everywhere foreign. Everywhere the words "at home" will be on their lips: "at home in Spain it was thus and thus"—that is, better than where they are. Cervantes, a poor and dependent writer, had all too much need to prove his loyalty; but after he has denied his heart and its honest convictions for only a few moments, he cleanses it again, better than Spain, with all her edicts, can cleanse herself. He condemns the cruelty of the decree that he has just approved—not directly, but by stressing the love of the exiles for their homeland. He even takes it on himself to speak of the freedom of conscience; for Ricote tells how he went from Italy to Germany and there found a sort of peace. For Germany was a good, tolerant country, "its people not standing much upon niceties and everybody living as he pleased, for in most parts of it there is liberty of conscience." Here it was my turn to feel patriotic pride, let the words be old which awake it in me. It is always pleasant to hear praise of home out of a stranger's mouth.

May twenty-seventh. The weather changes quickly at the seashore, but still more quickly and capriciously at sea, where the meteorological variations join forces with our progress and change of sky. Yesterday's summery warmth passed by evening into an overcast sky and an unseasonable sultriness, heavier, damper, and stickier than I have ever experienced. It harassed the nerves like a portent of storm or of some catastrophe. My evening clothes were a burden, I sat bathed in sweat under my stiff shirt, and especially the tea made me burst out in moisture. I do not know how far into the night it held, but today there is a complete change. The forenoon was cool and rainy, a fog came up and the fog-horn went for hours. But suddenly all that disappeared again. The wind changed, the fog lifted, the sky cleared, but despite the sunshine it remained — at least by comparison with the tropic evening of yesterday — so cold that one needed an overcoat and a rug to sit on deck.

A certain excitement makes itself felt. Today is Sunday. In the night, between tomorrow and the day after, they say, we shall get in, lie to in the bay, and land on Tuesday morning at seven.

I must return to what I wrote yesterday and make clear to myself how Cervantes's allegiance as Christian and loyal subject enhances the spiritual value of his freedom, the worth of his criticism. What concerns me is the relativity of all freedom; the fact that it needs to be conditioned and checked, not only outwardly but inwardly as well, in order that it may attain to spiritual worth and be expressive of a higher form of life. It is hard for us to imagine the state of feudal dependence in which artists of former times lived, before that emancipation of the artist ego which has come in with the bourgeois age. One may say that only in very rare cases has this latter been beneficial to the artist as a type. Once the guild of artists modestly based itself on its sense of craftsmanship. It was the fundamental constitution even of the greatest, even of that accidental genius who from time to time got so far as to bow before sovereigns and flower into supernal worth. The whole conception was probably more conducive to the sanity of the artist than are the present ones. In our day we *begin* with emancipation, with the ego, liberty, self-government. Modest simplicity is no longer the nourishing soil of greatness. Once, a given painter or sculptor, thinking to dedicate himself to the calling of beautifying and adorning the world, went as apprentice to a good master; washed brushes, ground colours, rose from the ranks. He became a useful help, to whom the old man doubtless left some work to do, just as the head surgeon at the end of an operation says to his assistant: "You finish!" Finally he himself became, if all went well, a master in his calling—and that was the height of his desire. He was called "*artista*" and the word covered both conceptions, that of artist and craftsman. Even today in Italy every master of a trade is so called. The genius, the great ego, the lonely adventurer, was an exception produced out of the modest, solid, objectively skilled cult of the craft; he achieved royal rank, yet even so he remained a dutiful son of the church and received from her his orders and his material. Today, as I said, we begin with the genius, the ego, the solitary—which is probably morbid. Hugo von Hofmannsthal, who, thanks to his Italo-Austrian origins, had much intuitive sympathy with the eighteenth century, once talked to me amusingly and wittily about the pathetic changes that had taken place in the musician's contacts with life. He said that in former days if you visited a musician he talked something like this: "Do sit down, have a cup of coffee, shall I play to you?" Today, he said, they all sit there like ailing eagles. Precisely. Artists have become ailing eagles because art has become solemn. It elevates and dejects the average artist, with unhappy results; it has made art solitary, melancholy, isolated, misunderstood, turned it, in short, into an ailing eagle.

It is certainly true that the poet represents an art world different from the graphic, the plastic, or the musical. Poetic and literary creation have a special place among the arts since in them the mechanical plays a smaller, in any case a different, role, more immaterial, more mental. On the whole its relation to the mind is more immediate. The poet is not artist alone; or rather he is artist in another, more intellectual way, since his medium is the word, his tool of the mind. But even with him it were desirable that liberty and emancipation stood at the end and not at the beginning, so that as a human being the artist would emerge from modesty, limitation, restraint, independence. For, once more, freedom has worth, it confers rank, only when it is won from unfreedom, when it is the process of becoming free. How much more powerful and intellectually significant is Cervantes's human sympathy for the fate of Ricote the Moor, and his indirect criticism of the state's harsh attitude, *after* he has expressed the submission which with him is a matter not of hypocrisy but of actual intellectual conditioning! All the human freedom and dignity, the emancipation of the artist spirit; the quixotic audacity that mingles cruel humiliation and moving nobility of soul—all this, the genius, independence, and daring, rests upon reverence before the Holy Inquisition, formal devotion to the monarch, acceptance of the protection of great men and their "well-known generosity," for example Count Lenos and Don Bernardo de Sandoval y Roxas. It soars up from these loyal limitations as involuntarily and unexpectedly as the work itself grows out of an entertaining, jesting satire — as which it was conceived — and into a monument of universal literature and symbol of humanity. I take it for a rule that the greatest works were those of the most modest purpose. Ambition may not stand at the beginning; it must not come before the work but must grow with the work, which will itself be greater than the blithely astonished artist dreamed; it must be bound up with the work and not with the ego of the artist. There is nothing falser than abstract and premature ambition, the self-centred pride independent of the work, the pallid ambition of the ego. So possessed, the artist sits there "like an ailing eagle."

May twenty-eighth. Last day on board. Yesterday we met a ship — an experience, for it was the first since we set out. This was a Danish boat, of about our size, with the Dannebrog at her stern. I enjoyed watching the signalled greeting which we exchanged, the chivalrous honour that ships everywhere pay each other in passing. A flageolet shrilled from the bridge; and a sailor hastened to haul down our Dutch colours, whilst the Dannebrog sank on the other boat. Then, as we passed, at a second signal the flags went up again and thus seagoing punctilio was satisfied. How charming is this salute! Seafaring men all over are bound into an international comradery by their distinctive calling, which is everywhere alike and everywhere, despite all modern mechanization, possessed by the spirit of bold adventure. So when they meet upon the wide and wildly moody element to which they are equally sworn, they do each other honour and through them the nations do the same. For ships are national emissaries and outlying territory, and they behave as such — so long as their nations are not at war. But that Denmark and Netherlands will not be. They are small, reasonable countries, dispensed of heroic historicity, whilst the others have at bottom nothing else in their heads but war. Thus the flag salute of the great ones has an uncanny air of propriety which ironically conceals quite other possibilities.

The sky is bright and sunny, the sea lightly crisped; the ship moves quietly, with a long, slow leaning to left and right probably caused by the course we are steering. But the difference in temperature from that of the last evening's sultriness remains astonishing. The night was very cold, the morning rather more than fresh, and even now we sit in the sun with plaid and overcoat.

I am inclined to find the end of Don Quixote a little weak. Death here assumes the character of a fixation against all unwarranted literary exploiting, and thereby itself takes on a literary artificiality that is not very convincing. It is not the same whether a beloved creation dies to the author or whether he *makes* it die, brings about and advertises its death, in order that no one else can make it live again. A literary death born of jealousy. But indeed this very jealousy betrays once more the poet's inner and proudly defensive identification with the eternally distinguished creation of his brain. His feeling is deep; no less sincere in that it expresses itself in jesting literary precautions against extraneous attempts at galvanizing the corpse. The priest demands of the notary a certificate "that Alonzo Quixano the Good, commonly called Don Quixote de la Mancha, has departed this life and died a natural death; and he insisted upon this testimonial lest any other author save only Cid Hamet Benengeli falsely should raise him from the dead and write endless stories of his exploits." Cid Hamet himself, however, evaporates at this juncture and betrays himself as the whimsical pretext he always was. He it is indeed who hangs up his pen by a brass wire upon a spit-rack and charges it to cry out to the presumptuous or wicked historians who would take it down to profane it:

> Beware, ye poet thieves, beware!
> Nor steal a single line;
> For Fate has made this work its care,
> And guaranteed it mine.

Who speaks? Who says "mine"? The pen? No, it is another speaker who utters the last line. "For me alone was Don Quixote born and I for him; he understood how to act and I to write, we were destined for each other, maugre and in despite of that scribbling impostor of Tordesillas who has dared or shall dare with gross and ill-cut ostrich feather to describe the exploits of my valorous knight; a burden too weighty for his shoulders and an enterprise beyond his dull and frigid genius." Well the poet knows what noble and humanly heavy burden he has borne in this history which has lightened the heart of all the world. He did not know it at the beginning, but he knew it. And how strange! At the very end he does not know it either. He forgets it again.

He says: "For my only desire was to bring into public abhorrence the fabulous and absurd histories of knight-errantry which, compared with my true and genuine *Don Quixote*, begin already to totter and will doubtless fall, never to rise again. Farewell." That is a return to the modest satirical parody which was the original intention of a work that grew so much beyond it. The death-bed chapter itself expresses this reversion. For Don Quixote is changed before he dies. The dying man wins — oh, joy! — his sane reason back. He has a long sleep, six hours long, and when he wakes he is by God's mercy mentally healed. His mind is free of the fog that had invaded it by the much reading of those dreadful books of knight-errantry; he sees their senselessness and depravity and will be no longer Don Quixote de la Mancha, knight of the doleful countenance, knight of the lions, but Alonzo Quixano, a reasonable man, a man like other men. That should rejoice us. But it rejoices us strikingly little, it leaves us cold, and to some extent we regret it. We are sorry about Don Quixote — as indeed we were sorry for him when affliction at his defeat stretched him out on his bed of death. For that is actually the cause of his demise; the doctor declares "that melancholy and vexation brought about his death." It is the deep dejection of seeing shipwrecked his mission as knight-errant and light-bringer that killed him. And we, hearing still in our ear that weak and sickly voice speaking the words: "Dulcinea is the most beautiful damsel in the world and I the unhappiest knight, but it is not fitting that my weakness should deny this truth; lay on, knight, with thy lance!" — we share in his defeat, though we know that his mission could not turn out otherwise, being the whimsy and maggot that it was. Even so in the course of the story the whimsy becomes so endeared to us that we are prepared and even eager to let it stand for the spirit, to feel for it as though it were spirit itself — and that we finely owe to the poet.

The case is most difficult. A conflict is present. If the work had only remained true to its original purpose of bringing to scorn the books of knight-errantry, through the ridiculous undertakings and overthrowings of a witless knight, then everything would be simple enough. But since all unexpectedly it expanded so much beyond its fundamental idea, the possibility of a satisfactory ending was destroyed. To let Don Quixote fall and die in one of his senseless enterprises was unthinkable, it would have gone beyond a joke and jarred on Cervantes's audience. To make him live after his return to sanity would not do either; that would be to make the husk survive beyond the soul; would be a degradation of the character below its lofty height — quite aside from the fact that for reasons connected with literary patronage he had to die anyway. I can see that it would have been neither Christian nor edifying to let him die in his delusion, saved indeed from the lance of the knight of the silver moon, but in despair over his downfall. It was needful that his despair be dissipated in his dying hour by the knowledge that it was all madness. But after all is there not death in the revelation that Dulcinea was not an adorable princess but a peasant girl off a dung-hill, and that all his actions, griefs, and aspirations were moonshine? Should he not then curse God and die? Certainly it was imperative to save Don Quixote's soul to sanity before he died. But in order that this salvation might be after our hearts, the author should have made his unreason less lovable.

Thus we see that genius may become an embarrassment, and that it can spoil an author's conception. However, not too much is made of Don Quixote's death. It is the sympathetically imagined passing, dignified and Christlike, of a good man, after he has confessed, received ghostly consolation, and set his earthly affairs in order with the notary. "As all human things, especially the lives of men, are transitory, incessantly declining from their beginning until they arrive at their final period; and as that of Don Quixote had no particular privilege from Heaven, to exempt it from the common fate, his end and dissolution came when he least thought of it." The reader must take that not too seriously, as did the friends whom Don Quixote left behind, his housekeeper, his niece, and Sancho, his former squire. These indeed mourned him with all their heart; the reader sees again what a good master he has been; yes, there is the grotesque description of "the sluices of their swollen eyes when the news that he must die forced a torrent of tears from their eyes and a thousand groans from their hearts." It is easy to give a comic turn to the description of sincere sorrow. "Human nature is human nature," "life must go on," and so forth. . . . We are told that during the three days of Don Quixote's agony, though "the whole house was in confusion, yet the niece ate, the housekeeper drank, and Sancho Panza made much of himself; for this business of legacies effaces, or moderates, the grief that is naturally due to the deceased." A mocking tribute to realism, an unsentimental attitude which may once have caused offence. The stoutest and boldest conqueror in the realm of human nature was always well armed with a sense of humour.

Afternoon, six o'clock. We have packed—which was quite a job, kneeling on the floor beside our trunks. The sense of arrival is pervading the ship. One sees the crew getting ready to stand by the ropes. Our American companions visibly rejoice in the homecoming which to us is the opposite. It is evening. On our right as we move slowly up the bay stretch the lights of Long Island, whose beaches and country estates we have heard celebrated. We go early to bed, tomorrow we rise early. To be ready is all.

May twenty-ninth. The weather is still fine, fresh and slightly misty. Since we took leave at dawn of our beds, where we have rocked so many nights through, the ship, which lay to during the night, so that for the first time we were without the throb of her engines, has slowly got under way. We have breakfasted, given the last touches to our luggage, handed out the final tips. Ready for arrival, we await it on deck. Through the mist rises a familiar figure, the Goddess of Liberty with her crown, a naïve classicistic symbol grown right strange to us today.

I feel dreamy from the early rising and strange experience of this hour. And I dreamed in the night too, in the unfamiliar silence of the engines; now I try to recall the dream which assembled itself from my reading. I dreamed of Don Quixote, it was he himself, and I talked with him. How distinct is reality, when one encounters it, from one's fancy! He looked different from the pictures; he had a thick, bushy moustache, a high retreating forehead, and under the likewise bushy brows almost blind eyes. He called himself not the Knight of the Lions but Zarathustra. He was, now that I had him face to face, very tactful and courteous, so that I recalled with strong emotion the words that I had read about him yesterday: "for in truth, as has been said before, both while he was plain Alonzo Quixano and while he was Don Quixote de la Mancha, he was ever of an amiable disposition and affable behaviour, and was therefore beloved, not only by those of his own family, but by all that knew him."

Pain, love, pity, and boundless reverence filled me altogether as this prescription became real. Dreamily they hover about me in this hour of arrival.

But such thoughts are too European for my surroundings—they face in the wrong direction. Ahead out of the morning mist slowly emerge the skyscrapers of Manhattan, a fantastic landscape group, a towered city of giants.

APPENDIX

CHAMISSO

[page 249]

WAS SOLL ICH SAGEN?

WHAT SHALL I SAY?

My eye is clouded, my lips are mute,
You bid me speak, and be it so.

Your eye is clear, your lips are red,
And what you wish is my command.

My hair is grey, my heart is sore,
You are so young, so full of health.

You bid me speak, and make it so hard,
I look at you and tremble sore.

PLATEN

[page 259]

I swore the splendid oath, to be true alway
To the high law, and deep in devotion sunk,
Full of priestly love administer
Thy great prophetic task.

[page 259]

One only hope remains, that I may still
Of any burden hold the balance true
By the whole power and valour of my soul.

PLATEN

[page 259]

Who feels in fullness all his bosom swelling,
In power and pride secure of form he singeth
And lightly moves, his weighty measures telling,
His song's swift arrow cuts he and it wingeth
Unlimed, inerrant, through its skill indwelling,
And all he writes in one pure flood he bringeth.

[page 260]

He who once his eye hath bent on Beauty,
He to Death already is devoted,
Never more avails for earthly duty,
Who but once his eye hath bent on Beauty,
Yet on Death to look he sore must tremble.

Ever lives for him the pang of loving
Since he is a fool who idly hopeth
On this earth to satisfy such craving;
Whom the dart of Beauty once hath piercèd
Ever lives for him the pang of loving.

Ah, like any spring he'd fail and perish,
Suck from every breath of air a poison,
Death would scent in scent of every blossom:
Who but once his eye hath bent on Beauty,
Ah, like any spring he longs to perish.

[page 262]

My tones may well no common music make,
Since never half-way I my heart surrendered;
Wholly to art my praise and life I rendered,
And when I die, I die for Beauty's sake.

[page 263]

Thou hast uplifted me to thee,
In thine eyes there swam a bright spark,
Which made colours to dip the pencil in,
To pledge pure poet-hands to God.

PLATEN

[page 264]

Where thankless hate a noble love requites,
How I have sickened of my Fatherland!

[page 264]

If so it be my inner fund shall measure
Ever more great, it lives, though long since gone the finder,
Of German honour the abiding treasure.

[page 264]

Oh fools, who madly dream of purity! I learnèd
That never guilt so sore as such a sin defileth;
I felt the sin, that once out of our Eden banned us,
Us plumèd pinions lent for flight to higher heavens.
I am not yet so pale that I have need of rouging;
I would the world shall know me now that it may pardon!

[page 265]

And yet this love I would not ever conquer
And woe the day whereon it cools and dies!
For from those blissful regions it was sent us
Where blessed angels to each other nestle.

[page 265]

As body to soul, as soul to body: I to thee!
I am as wife to man, as man to wife, to thee!
Whom other dar'st thou love, when from thy lips away
With endless kisses I from Death's arms rifle thee?

[page 266]

This glorifies thine eye, that mine doth see
How immortality thy body's members all
Express –

PLATEN

[page 267]

Some day will I, that I promise, live my life without
caresses,
When the flowers here in the garden live and keep
the laws of Moses.

[page 267]

Proffer me wine, so that like Hafiz drunken
Wildly I fantasy upon thy beauty.

[page 268]

Into the vegetable kingdom harmless to spin myself
round,
Heedfully study and mark hexagonal quartzes –
These can I not, friend! far too deeply moves me
The changeful unfolding of human destiny.

[page 268]

Many a long year have we wrought
In our own griefs ourselves to sink;
Now only doth the wish unfold
With clear mind and heart to think
What darkly time alone hath thought.

[page 268]

His age and he by mutual hate are sundered,
What gladdens thousands he at heart mislikes,
While his keen gaze and sombre
Pierces the souls of fools.

[page 269]

And every volume that so quietly
Mind to mind doth range arow
Silently sends on its message
Through æons of uncounted time.

◇◇◇◇◇◇◇◇◇◇◇◇◇◇◇◇◇◇◇

STORM

[page 273]

She sits amid the sprigs of thyme,
She sits in odours rare;
The blue flies hum
And glitter through the air.

From afar laughs the cuckoo,
And through my mind it runs:
She has the golden eyes
Of the forest queen.

[page 273]

If only I had not walked here in May!
Life and love – how it flew by!

[page 274]

The hand my eye doth hang upon
Shows that fine trace of pain
And that in sleepless night
On a sick heart it hath lain.

[page 275]

Back in my life there lies a time,
Like my lost home it looks,
Toward which my thoughts in longing strain.

[page 275]

Happy years!
Blithe days –
Like floods of spring
How are you sped!

[page 276]

From these pages mounts the scent of the violet
That there at home upon our meadows grew
Year in year out, of which nobody knew
And that I later nowhere else did ever find.

STORM

[page 276]

A sacred something in my mind
Lies that in past time once I owned;
I know not where it went,
And what it was I have forgot.

[page 276]

In a green shadow lay the spot –
If only distance did not lie between,
If I could only get back thither,
Who knows – perhaps I still might find it there.

[page 279]

She had always before been a wild young thing;
Now she walks sunk in dreaming,
Swings in her hand her summer hat
And heeds the glaring sun no whit
Nor knows what she shall do.

[page 280]

Thou feelst, we cannot forgo;
To give, why dost thou still shrink?
Thou must discharge the whole debt,
Thou must indeed, indeed thou must.

[page 280]

Why do the wallflowers smell so much sweeter at night?
Why do thy lips burn so much redder at night?

[page 280]

You stand by the hearth, in flame and smoke,
Till your delicate hands are rough;
You would have it so, I know it well,
For my eyes were resting on them.

STORM

[page 280]

. . . that we together are,
My brother, is not right –

[page 280]

Whoever lived in arms of love,
In life can never be poor,
Though he must die afar, alone,
He still can feel the blessed hour
When he was living from her lips,
And even in death she is his.

[page 281]

Now that these eyes to dust shall come,
I know not when we shall meet again.

[page 283]

I feel that something would speak to me
And cannot find the way hither.

[page 283]

Are they love-words, confided to the wind
And on the way blown away?
Or is it sadness from days to come
That busily strives to make itself heard?

[page 283]

God's breath went wafting through the room,
Thy infant wailed,
And then thou hadst passed over.

[page 283]

When once the hour struck that on earth
Thy sweet image faded and was gone,
Then you will never be again,
Just as you never were before.

STORM

[page 284]

One asks: What comes after?
The other: Is it right?
And here lies the distinction
Between free man and slave.

[page 284]

To be what is in your power
Shrink not from work day and night;
But guard your soul
For striving for career.

SUFFERINGS AND GREATNESS OF RICHARD WAGNER

[page 351]

Are they waves/of gentle airs?
Are they surges/of blissful fragrance?
How they swell/and swirl about me,
Shall I breathe them,/shall I listen?
Shall I sip/or dive below,
Sweet in fragrance/breathe me out?
In the swelling surge/of the ocean bliss,
In the sounding swirl/of the waves of scent,
In the wafting/world-breathing all –
Drown – /sink –
Unconscious – /highest bliss!

The Principal Works of Thomas Mann

FIRST EDITIONS IN GERMAN

DER KLEINE HERR FRIEDEMANN
[*Little Herr Friedemann*]. *Tales* — Berlin, S. Fischer Verlag. 1898

BUDDENBROOKS
Two volumes. Novel — Berlin, S. Fischer Verlag. 1901

TRISTAN
Contains Tonio Kröger. *Tales* — Berlin, S. Fischer Verlag. 1903

FIORENZA
Drama — Berlin, S. Fischer Verlag. 1905

KÖNIGLICHE HOHEIT
[*Royal Highness*]. *Novel* — Berlin, S. Fischer Verlag. 1909

DER TOD IN VENEDIG
[*Death in Venice*]. *Short novel* — Berlin, S. Fischer Verlag. 1913

DAS WUNDERKIND
[*The Infant Prodigy*]. *Tales* — Berlin, S. Fischer Verlag. 1914

BETRACHTUNGEN EINES UNPOLITISCHEN
Autobiographical reflections — Berlin, S. Fischer Verlag. 1918

HERR UND HUND
[*A Man and His Dog*]. *Idyll*
Contains also Gesang vom Kindchen, *an idyll in verse*
Berlin, S. Fischer Verlag. 1919

WÄLSUNGENBLUT
München, Phantasus-Verlag. 1921

BEKENNTNISSE DES HOCHSTAPLERS FELIX KRULL
Stuttgart, Deutsche Verlags-Anst.

BEMÜHUNGEN
Essays — Berlin, S. Fischer Verlag. 1922

REDE UND ANTWORT
Essays — Berlin, S. Fischer Verlag. 1922

DER ZAUBERBERG
[*The Magic Mountain*]. *Two volumes. Novel*
Berlin, S. Fischer Verlag. 1924

UNORDNUNG UND FRÜHES LEID
[*Disorder and Early Sorrow*]. *Short novel*
Berlin, S. Fischer Verlag. 1926

KINO
[*Romanfragment*] Berlin, S. Fischer Verlag. 1926

PARISER RECHENSCHAFT
Berlin, S. Fischer Verlag. 1926

DEUTSCHE ANSPRACHE
Ein Appell an d. Vernunft Berlin, S. Fischer Verlag. 1930

DIE FORDERUNG DES TAGES
Berlin, S. Fischer Verlag. 1930

MARIO UND DER ZAUBERER
[*Mario and the Magician*]. *Short novel*
Berlin, S. Fischer Verlag. 1930

GOETHE ALS REPRÄSENTANT DES BÜRGERLICHEN ZEITALTERS
Berlin, S. Fischer Verlag. 1932

JOSEPH UND SEINE BRÜDER
[*Joseph and His Brothers*]. *I. Die Geschichten Jaakobs. 1933. II. Der junge Joseph. 1934. III. Joseph in Ägypten. 1936. IV. Joseph, der Ernährer. 1943. Novel*
I, II, Berlin, S. Fischer Verlag
III, Vienna, Bermann-Fischer Verlag
IV, Stockholm, Bermann-Fischer Verlag

LEIDEN UND GRÖSSE DER MEISTER
Essays Berlin, S. Fischer Verlag. 1935

FREUD UND DIE ZUKUNFT
Lecture Vienna, Bermann-Fischer Verlag. 1936

EIN BRIEFWECHSEL
[*An Exchange of Letters*]
Zürich, Dr. Oprecht & Helbling A.G. 1937

DAS PROBLEM DER FREIHEIT
Stockholm, Bermann-Fischer Verlag

SCHOPENHAUER
Stockholm, Bermann-Fischer Verlag

ACHTUNG, EUROPA!
Stockholm, Bermann-Fischer Verlag

DIE SCHÖNSTEN ERZÄHLUNGEN
Stockholm, Bermann-Fischer Verlag

LOTTE IN WEIMAR
[*The Beloved Returns*]
Stockholm, Bermann-Fischer Verlag. 1939

DIE VERTAUSCHTEN KÖPFE
Eine indische Legende [*The Transposed Heads*]
Stockholm, Bermann-Fischer Verlag. 1940

DEUTSCHE HÖRER
[*Listen, Germany!*] Stockholm, Bermann-Fischer Verlag. 1942

DER GESETZ
[*The Tables of the Law*]
Stockholm, Bermann-Fischer Verlag. 1944

AMERICAN EDITIONS IN TRANSLATION
ALFRED A. KNOPF, NEW YORK

ROYAL HIGHNESS: A NOVEL OF GERMAN COURT LIFE
Translated by A. Cecil Curtis. 1916 (out of print)

BUDDENBROOKS
Translated by H. T. Lowe-Porter. 1924

DEATH IN VENICE AND OTHER STORIES
Translated by Kenneth Burke. 1925. Contains translations of *Der Tod in Venedig, Tristan, and Tonio Kröger* (out of print) *

THE MAGIC MOUNTAIN
Translated by H. T. Lowe-Porter. 1927. Two volumes

CHILDREN AND FOOLS
Translated by Herman George Scheffauer. 1928. Nine stories, including translations of *Der kleine Herr Friedemann* and *Unordnung und frühes Leid* (out of print) *

THREE ESSAYS
Translated by H. T. Lowe-Porter. 1929. Contains translations of *Friedrich und die grosse Koalition* from *Rede und Antwort*, and of *Goethe und Tolstoi* and *Okkulte Erlebnisse* from *Bemühungen*

EARLY SORROW
Translated by Herman George Scheffauer. 1930 (out of print) *

A MAN AND HIS DOG
Translated by Herman George Scheffauer. 1930 (out of print) *

* Now included, in a translation by H. T. Lowe-Porter, in *Stories of Three Decades.*

DEATH IN VENICE
A new translation by H. T. Lowe-Porter, with an Introduction by Ludwig Lewisohn. 1930 *

MARIO AND THE MAGICIAN
Translated by H. T. Lowe-Porter. 1931 (out of print) *

PAST MASTERS AND OTHER PAPERS
Translated by H. T. Lowe-Porter. 1933. Thirteen essays (out of print)

JOSEPH AND HIS BROTHERS
I. Joseph and His Brothers. 1934. II. Young Joseph. 1935. III [*two volumes*]. *Joseph in Egypt. 1938. IV. Joseph the Provider. 1944.* Translated by H. T. Lowe-Porter

STORIES OF THREE DECADES
Translated by H. T. Lowe-Porter. 1936. Contains all of Thomas Mann's fiction except the long novels

AN EXCHANGE OF LETTERS
Translated by H. T. Lowe-Porter. 1937 †

FREUD, GOETHE, WAGNER
Translated by H. T. Lowe-Porter and Rita Matthias-Reil. 1937. Three essays

THE COMING VICTORY OF DEMOCRACY
Translated by Agnes E. Meyer. 1938 †

THIS PEACE
Translated by H. T. Lowe-Porter. 1938 †

THIS WAR
Translated by Eric Sutton. 1940 †

THE BELOVED RETURNS
LOTTE IN WEIMAR
Translated by H. T. Lowe-Porter. 1940

THE TRANSPOSED HEADS
Translated by H. T. Lowe-Porter. 1941

ORDER OF THE DAY
Political Essays and Speeches of Two Decades
Translated by H. T. Lowe-Porter, Agnes E. Meyer, and Eric Sutton. 1942

LISTEN, GERMANY!
Twenty-five Radio Messages to the German People over BBC. 1943

THE TABLES OF THE LAW
Translated by H. T. Lowe-Porter. 1945

* Now included, in a translation by H. T. Lowe-Porter, in *Stories of Three Decades.*

† Also included in *Order of the Day.*

This book was set on the linotype in Janson, a recutting made direct from the type cast from matrices (now in possession of the Stempel foundry, Frankfurt am Main) made by Anton Janson some time between 1660 and 1687.

Of Janson's origin nothing is known. He may have been a relative of Justus Janson, a printer of Danish birth who practised in Leipzig from 1614 to 1635. Some time between 1657 and 1668 Anton Janson, a punch-cutter and type-founder, bought from the Leipzig printer Johann Erich Hahn the type-foundry which had formerly been a part of the printing house of M. Friedrich Lankisch. Janson's types were first shown in a specimen sheet issued at Leipzig about 1675. Janson's successor, and perhaps his son-in-law, Johann Karl Edling, issued a specimen sheet of Janson types in 1689. His heirs sold the Janson matrices in Holland to Wolffgang Dietrich Erhardt, of Leipzig.

Composed by The Plimpton Press, Norwood, Mass.; printed and bound by Kingsport Press, Inc., Kingsport, Tennessee.

Typography and binding based on designs by W. A. Dwiggins.